The OFFICIAL GUIDE for
GMAT®
review

Prepared for the
Graduate Management Admission Council
by Educational Testing Service

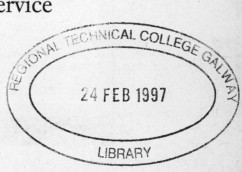

Inquiries concerning this publication should be directed to GMAT Program Direction Office,
Educational Testing Service, P.O. Box 6106, Princeton, NJ 08541-6106.

Graduate
Management
Admission
Council®

MBA Explorer

Visit our Web site at http://www.gmat.org
to register for the GMAT, order publications, search
for a school, or learn about opportunities
and resources available to prospective MBAs.

USA: 0-446-39612-5
CAN: 0-446-39613-3

39 HFL
061673

658·0076 GMA

Contents

Contents continued

Graduate Management Admission Council

The Graduate Management Admission Council (GMAC) is an organization of graduate business and management schools sharing a common interest in professional management education. The Council provides information to schools and prospective students to help both make reasoned choices in the admissions process. It also provides a forum for the exchange of information through research, educational programs, and other services among the broad constituency of individuals and institutions concerned with management education.

The Council has three basic service objectives:

1. to enhance the management education admission process by
   - developing and administering appropriate assessment instruments
   - developing other services and materials related to the selection process
   - informing schools and students about the appropriate use of such instruments and materials
   - providing opportunities for the exchange of information between students and schools

2. to broaden knowledge about management education by
   - conducting educational research
   - disseminating information about relevant research
   - encouraging the development and exchange of information by professionals in the field

3. to promote the highest standards of professional practice in the administration of management education programs and related activities by
   - developing appropriate standards of practice
   - offering educational programs and publications to provide essential knowledge, skills, and values
   - providing other opportunities for professional development

The Council currently contracts with Educational Testing Service (ETS) for development of GMAT test material, administration of the GMAT test, and preparation and distribution of GMAT score reports. The Council also determines policies and procedures for research and development of the GMAT; for publication of materials for students, guidance counselors, and admissions officers; and for nontesting services offered to management schools and applicants.

Member Schools

American Graduate School of International Management

The American University
Kogod College of Business Administration

Arizona State University
College of Business

Babson College
Babson Graduate School of Business

Baruch College
School of Business

Baylor University
Hankamer School of Business

Bentley College
Bentley Graduate School of Business

Boston College
The Wallace E. Carroll Graduate School of Management

Boston University
School of Management

Bowling Green State University
College of Business Administration

Brigham Young University
Marriott School of Management

California State University, Long Beach
College of Business Administration

Carnegie Mellon University
Graduate School of Industrial Administration

Case Western Reserve University
Weatherhead School of Management

Clark Atlanta University
School of Business Administration

College of William and Mary
Graduate School of Business

Columbia University
Columbia Business School

Cornell University
Johnson Graduate School of Management

Dartmouth College
The Tuck School

De Paul University
The Charles H. Kellstadt Graduate School of Business

Duke University
The Fuqua School of Business

East Carolina University
School of Business

Emory University
Goizueta Business School

Florida State University
College of Business

Fordham University
Graduate School of Business Administration

George Mason University
School of Business Administration

The George Washington University
School of Business and Public Management

Georgetown University
School of Business

Georgia Institute of Technology
School of Management

Georgia Southern University
College of Business Administration

Georgia State University
College of Business Administration

Harvard University
Harvard Business School

Hofstra University
Frank G. Zarb School of Business

Howard University
School of Business

Indiana University (Bloomington)
Graduate School of Business

INSEAD
The European Institute of Business Administration

Kent State University
Graduate School of Management

Lehigh University
College of Business and Economics

London Business School

Louisiana Tech University
College of Administration and Business

Marquette University
College of Business Administration

Massachusetts Institute of Technology
Sloan School of Management

Michigan State University
Eli Broad Graduate School of Management

New York University
Stern School of Business

Northeastern University
Graduate School of Business Administration

Northwestern University
Kellogg Graduate School of Management

The Ohio State University
Fisher College of Business

Old Dominion University
Graduate School of Business and Public Administration

Pennsylvania State University
The Smeal College of Business Administration

Purdue University (West Lafayette)
Krannert Graduate School of Management

Rensselaer Polytechnic Institute
School of Management

Rollins College
Crummer Graduate School of Business

Rutgers, The State University of New Jersey
Graduate School of Management

San Francisco State University
School of Business

Seton Hall University
W. Paul Stillman School of Business

Southern Methodist University
Edwin L. Cox School of Business

Stanford University
Graduate School of Business

Suffolk University
School of Management

Syracuse University
School of Management

Temple University
School of Business and Management

Texas A&M University
Graduate School of Business

Texas Christian University
M. J. Neeley School of Business

Tulane University
A. B. Freeman School of Business

The University of Alabama
Manderson Graduate School of Business

University of Arizona
Karl Eller Graduate School of Management

University at Buffalo (State University of New York)
School of Management

University of California, Berkeley
Walter A. Haas School of Business

University of California, Irvine
Graduate School of Management

University of California, Los Angeles
John E. Anderson Graduate School of Management

University of Central Florida
College of Business Administration

University of Chicago
Graduate School of Business

University of Cincinnati
College of Business Administration

University of Colorado at Boulder
Graduate School of Business Administration

University of Connecticut (Storrs)
School of Business Administration

University of Delaware
College of Business and Economics

University of Denver
Graduate School of Business

University of Florida
Graduate School of Business

University of Georgia
Terry College of Business

University of Hawaii at Manoa
College of Business Administration

University of Houston
College of Business Administration

University of Illinois at Chicago
College of Business Administration

University of Illinois at Urbana-Champaign
College of Commerce and Business Administration

University of Iowa
School of Management

The University of Kansas
School of Business

University of Kentucky
College of Business and Economics

University of Maryland
College of Business and Management

University of Miami
School of Business Administration

The University of Michigan
The Michigan Business School

University of Minnesota
Carlson School of Management

University of Missouri—Columbia
College of Business and Public Administration

University of Missouri—St. Louis
School of Business Administration

University of North Carolina at Chapel Hill
Kenan-Flagler Business School

University of Notre Dame
College of Business Administration

University of Oklahoma
College of Business Administration

University of Oregon
Graduate School of Management

University of Pennsylvania
The Wharton School (Graduate Division)

University of Pittsburgh
Joseph M. Katz Graduate School of Business

University of Rhode Island
College of Business Administration

University of Richmond
Richard S. Reynolds Graduate School

University of Rochester
William E. Simon Graduate School of
    Business Administration

University of San Francisco
McLaren School of Business

University of South Carolina
College of Business Administration

University of South Florida
College of Business Administration

University of Southern California
Graduate School of Business Administration

The University of Tennessee, Knoxville
College of Business Administration

The University of Texas at Austin
Graduate School of Business

University of Toronto
Faculty of Management

The University of Tulsa
College of Business Administration

University of Utah
David Eccles School of Business

University of Virginia
Darden Graduate School of Business Administration

University of Washington
Graduate School of Business Administration

The University of Western Ontario
Western Business School

University of Wisconsin—Madison
Graduate School of Business

University of Wisconsin—Milwaukee
School of Business Administration

Vanderbilt University
Owen Graduate School of Management

Virginia Commonwealth University
School of Business

Virginia Polytechnic Institute and State University
The R. B. Pamplin College of Business

Wake Forest University
Babcock Graduate School of Management

Washington State University
College of Business and Economics

Washington University (St. Louis)
John M. Olin School of Business

Yale University
Yale School of Organization and Management

Introduction

The Official Guide for GMAT Review has been designed and written by the staff of Educational Testing Service, which prepares the Graduate Management Admission Test used by many graduate schools of business and management as one criterion in considering applications for admission to their graduate programs. This book is intended to be a general guide to the kinds of questions likely to appear in the GMAT. All questions used to illustrate the various types of verbal and mathematical multiple-choice questions are taken from actual editions of the GMAT administered between June 1990 and June 1995.

The GMAT is not a test of knowledge in specific subjects—for example, it does not test knowledge specifically or uniquely acquired in accounting or economics courses. Rather, it is a test of certain skills and abilities that have been found to contribute to success in graduate programs in business and management. For this reason, it is useful to familiarize yourself with the general types of questions likely to be found in editions of the GMAT and the reasoning skills, analytical writing skills, and problem-solving strategies that these types of questions demand. This book illustrates various types of questions that appear in the GMAT and explains in detail some of the most effective strategies for mastering these questions.

The most efficient and productive way to use this book is to read first through Chapter 1. Each type of question is briefly described, the directions are given, and the skills each question type measures are outlined. You should pay particular attention to the directions for each question type. This is especially important for the Data Sufficiency questions, which have lengthy and complex directions, and for the

Analytical Writing Assessment, which requires you to discuss the complexities of a given issue and to critique a given argument.

Chapters 3-8 provide detailed illustrations and explanations of individual question types. After you read Chapter 1, you will find the most advantageous way to use the book to study for the multiple-choice portions of the test is to choose a chapter on a particular multiple-choice question type, read carefully the introductory material, and then do the sample test sections in that chapter. As you take the sample test sections, follow the directions and time specifications given. When you complete a sample test section, use the answer key that follows it to check your responses. Then review the sample test section carefully, spending as much time as is necessary to familiarize yourself with the range of questions or problems presented in the sample test section.

The chapter on the Analytical Writing Assessment is somewhat different from those on the multiple-choice questions. It presents examples of the writing tasks that will appear on the test as well as a selection of actual responses written by students. Each response is followed by an explanation of why it was awarded a particular score. You will also see the general scoring guides that readers use to score the responses. The chapter on the Analytical Writing Assessment provides all the information you need to familiarize yourself thoroughly with the kinds of writing tasks that you will see on the GMAT as well as with the standards that will be used in judging your responses.

You may find it useful to read through all of Chapter 2, Math Review, before working through Chapters 3, Problem Solving, and 4,

Data Sufficiency, or you may wish to use Chapter 2 as a reference as you work on Chapters 3 and 4. However, since Chapter 2 is intended to provide you with a comprehensive review of the basic mathematical concepts used in the quantitative sections of the GMAT, you may find it valuable to read through the chapter as a whole.

The introductory material, sample test sections, and answer keys to the sample test sections in Chapter 5, Reading Comprehension, Chapter 6, Critical Reasoning, and Chapter 7, Sentence Correction, should be approached in the way suggested above. The explanatory materials for Reading Comprehension and Critical Reasoning have been written as thorough explanations of the reasoning and problem-solving challenges each question type presents. Demonstrating strategies for successfully meeting these challenges, regardless of the particular content of the questions or problems that appear in a specific edition of the GMAT, is the objective of these explanations.

After you complete the review and practice built into each chapter you should turn to Chapter 9, which includes three authentic GMAT tests. It will be most helpful in preparing yourself to take the GMAT if you regard the tests in Chapter 9 as facsimiles of the test you will take for scoring. (**Note:** Form C, which was administered prior to October 1994, lacks the Analytical Writing Assessment.) Time yourself on each section, and follow the directions exactly as given.

Following each test reprinted in Chapter 9 is an answer key, information about scoring and score interpretation, and an explanation for every multiple-choice question on that test. Guidelines for the use of GMAT scores are also given.

---

*The material in *The Official Guide for GMAT Review* is intended to familiarize you with the types of questions found on the GMAT. Although the questions on the sample test sections in chapters 3-8 represent the general nature of the questions on the test, it is possible that a type of question not illustrated by and explained in the *Guide* may appear on the GMAT. It is also possible that material illustrated by and explained in the *Guide* may not appear on the test.

1 Description of the Graduate Management Admission Test

The Graduate Management Admission Test is designed to help graduate schools assess the qualifications of applicants for advanced study in business and management. The test can be used by both schools and students in evaluating verbal and mathematical skills as well as general knowledge and preparation for graduate study. Note, however, that GMAT scores should be considered as only one of several indicators of ability.

Format

The current GMAT test is made up of nine separately timed sections. Seven of these sections are composed of multiple-choice questions. Each multiple-choice question offers five choices from which the examinee is to select the best answer. Two of the sections consist of equally weighted but different writing tasks.

Every form of the test contains one section of trial multiple-choice questions that are needed for pretesting and equating purposes. These questions, however, are not identified, and you should do your best on all questions. The answers to trial questions are not counted in your test score.

While research and experience have shown that the use of a large number of short, multiple-choice questions is an effective and reliable way of providing a fair and valid evaluation of certain skills among a wide variety of people with different backgrounds, both the Graduate Management Admission Council and Educational Testing Service are aware of the limits of the multiple-choice format, particularly in measuring an applicant's ability to explain and analyze complex issues or to develop a detailed and appropriate critique of an argument. In order to measure these latter skills directly, the Analytical Writing Assessment was introduced into the GMAT test.

Content

It is important to recognize that the GMAT evaluates skills and abilities that develop over relatively long periods of time. Although the sections are basically verbal or mathematical, the complete test provides one method of measuring overall ability. The GMAT does not test specific knowledge obtained in college course work, and it does not seek to measure achievements in any specific areas of study.

The Graduate Management Admission Council recognizes that questions arise concerning techniques for taking standardized examinations such as the GMAT, and it is hoped that the descriptions, sample test sections, and explanations given here, along with the authentic tests, will give you a practical familiarity with both the concepts and techniques required by GMAT questions.

The material on the following pages provides a general description and brief discussion of the objectives and techniques for each question type. Following this test are a math review designed to help you review basic mathematical skills useful in the Problem Solving and Data Sufficiency sections of the GMAT and six chapters, one for each question type, that present sample test sections with answer keys and detailed explanations of the specific question types and of all questions and answers from the sample test sections. (The sample test sections are made up of questions that have appeared in the actual GMAT. There is, of course, no answer key for the writing tasks.) Methods of determining the best answer to a particular kind of question as well as explanations of the different kinds of questions appearing in any one section are also represented in these chapters.

Chapter 9 contains three authentic GMAT tests. (Form C lacks the Analytical Writing Assessment because it was administered before October 1994.) The tests are followed by answer keys, explanations for each question, and scoring information (including scoring information for the Analytical Writing Assessment), which explains how GMAT scores are calculated and interpreted.

Problem Solving Questions

This section of the GMAT is designed to test (1) basic mathematical skills, (2) understanding of elementary mathematical concepts, and (3) the ability to reason quantitatively and to solve quantitative problems. Approximately half the problems in the test are in a mathematical setting; the remainder are based on "real life" situations.

WHAT IS MEASURED

Problem Solving questions test your ability to understand verbal descriptions of situations and to solve problems using arithmetic, elementary algebra, or commonly known concepts of geometry.

The directions for Problem Solving questions read as follows:

Directions: In this section solve each problem, using any available space on the page for scratchwork. Then indicate the best of the answer choices given.

Numbers: All numbers used are real numbers.

Figures: Figures that accompany problems in this section are intended to provide information useful in solving the problems. They are drawn as accurately as possible EXCEPT when it is stated in a specific problem that its figure is not drawn to scale. All figures lie in a plane unless otherwise indicated.

Data Sufficiency Questions

Each of the problems in the Data Sufficiency section of the GMAT consists of a question, often accompanied by some initial information, and two statements, labeled (1) and (2), containing additional information. You must decide whether sufficient information to answer the question is given by either (1) or (2) individually or—if not—by both combined.

These are the directions that you will find for the Data Sufficiency section of the GMAT. Read them carefully.

Directions: Each of the data sufficiency problems below consists of a question and two statements, labeled (1) and (2), in which certain data are given. You have to decide whether the data given in the statements are sufficient for answering the question. Using the data given in the statements plus your knowledge of mathematics and everyday facts (such as the number of days in July or the meaning of *counterclockwise*), you are to fill in oval

A if statement (1) ALONE is sufficient, but statement (2) alone is not sufficient to answer the question asked;

B if statement (2) ALONE is sufficient, but statement (1) alone is not sufficient to answer the question asked;

C if BOTH statements (1) and (2) TOGETHER are sufficient to answer the question asked, but NEITHER statement ALONE is sufficient;

D if EACH statement ALONE is sufficient to answer the question asked;

E if statements (1) and (2) TOGETHER are NOT sufficient to answer the question asked, and additional data specific to the problem are needed.

Numbers: All numbers used are real numbers.

Figures: A figure in a data sufficiency problem will conform to the information given in the question, but will not necessarily conform to the additional information given in statements (1) and (2).

You may assume that lines shown as straight are straight and that angle measures are greater than zero.

You may assume that the positions of points, angles, regions, etc., exist in the order shown.

All figures lie in a plane unless otherwise indicated.

Note: In questions that ask for the value of a quantity, the data given in the statements are sufficient only when it is possible to determine exactly one numerical value for the quantity.

Example:

In ΔPQR, what is the value of x?

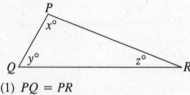

(1) $PQ = PR$
(2) $y = 40$

Explanation: According to statement (1), $PQ = PR$; therefore, ΔPQR is isosceles and $y = z$. Since $x + y + z = 180$, it follows that $x + 2y = 180$. Since statement (1) does not give a value for y, you cannot answer the question using statement (1) alone. According to statement (2), $y = 40$; therefore, $x + z = 140$. Since statement (2) does not give a value for z, you cannot answer the question using statement (2) alone. Using both statements together, since $x + 2y = 180$ and the value of y is given, you can find y and z; therefore, you can find the value of x. Therefore, the answer is C.

WHAT IS MEASURED

Data Sufficiency questions are designed to measure your ability to analyze a quantitative problem, to recognize which information is relevant, and to determine at what point there is sufficient information to solve the problem.

Reading Comprehension Questions

The Reading Comprehension section is made up of several reading passages about which you will be asked interpretive, applicative, and inferential questions. The passages are up to 350 words long, and they discuss topics from the social sciences, the physical or biological sciences, and such business-related fields as marketing, economics, and human resource management. Because every Reading Comprehension section includes passages from several different content areas, you will probably be generally familiar with some of the material; however, neither the passages nor the questions assume detailed knowledge of the topics discussed.

WHAT IS MEASURED

Reading Comprehension questions measure your ability to understand, analyze, and apply information and concepts presented in written form. All questions are to be answered on the basis of what is stated or implied in the reading material, and no specific knowledge of the material is required. Reading Comprehension therefore, evaluates your ability to

● understand words and statements in the reading passages (Questions of this type are not vocabulary questions. These questions test your understanding of and ability to use specialized terms as well as your understanding of the English language. You may also find that questions of this type ask about the overall meaning of a passage).

- understand the logical relationships between significant points and concepts in the reading passages (For example, such questions may ask you to determine the strong and weak points of an argument or to evaluate the importance of arguments and ideas in a passage).
- draw inferences from facts and statements in the reading passages (The inference questions will ask you to consider factual statements or information and, on the basis of that information, reach a general conclusion).
- understand and follow the development of quantitative concepts as they are presented in verbal material (This may involve the interpretation of numerical data or the use of simple arithmetic to reach conclusions about material in a passage.)

The directions for Reading Comprehension questions read as follows:

Directions: Each passage in this group is followed by questions based on its content. After reading a passage, choose the best answer to each question and fill in the corresponding oval on the answer sheet. Answer all questions following a passage on the basis of what is <u>stated</u> or <u>implied</u> in that passage.

Critical Reasoning Questions

The Critical Reasoning section of the GMAT is designed to test the reasoning skills involved (1) in making arguments, (2) in evaluating arguments, and (3) in formulating or evaluating a plan of action. Most of the questions are based on a separate argument or set of statements; occasionally, two or three questions are based on the same argument or set of statements. The materials on which questions are based are drawn from a variety of sources. No familiarity with the subject matter of those materials is presupposed.

WHAT IS MEASURED

Critical Reasoning questions are designed to provide one measure of your ability to reason effectively in the areas of

- argument construction (Questions in this category may ask you to recognize such things as the basic structure of an argument; properly drawn conclusions; underlying assumptions; well-supported explanatory hypotheses; parallels between structurally similar arguments).
- argument evaluation (Questions in this category may ask you to analyze a given argument and to recognize such things as factors that would strengthen, or weaken, the given argument; reasoning errors committed in making that argument; aspects of the method by which the argument proceeds).
- formulating and evaluating a plan of action (Questions in this category may ask you to recognize such things as the relative appropriateness, effectiveness, or efficiency of different plans of action; factors that would strengthen, or weaken, the prospects of success for a proposed plan of action; assumptions underlying a proposed plan of action.)

The directions for Critical Reasoning questions read as follows:

Directions: For each question in this section, select the best of the answer choices given.

Sentence Correction Questions

Sentence Correction questions ask you which of the five choices best expresses an idea or relationship. The questions will require you to be familiar with the stylistic conventions and grammatical rules of standard written English and to demonstrate your ability to improve incorrect or ineffective expressions.

WHAT IS MEASURED

Sentence Correction questions test two broad aspects of language proficiency:

1. *Correct expression.* A correct sentence is grammatically and structurally sound. It conforms to all the rules of standard written English (for example: noun-verb agreement, noun-pronoun agreement, pronoun consistency, pronoun case, and verb tense sequence). Further, a correct sentence will not have dangling, misplaced, or improperly formed modifiers, will not have unidiomatic or inconsistent expressions, and will not have faults in parallel construction.

2. *Effective expression.* An effective sentence expresses an idea or relationship clearly and concisely as well as grammatically. This does not mean that the choice with the fewest and simplest words is necessarily the best answer. It means that there are no superfluous words or needlessly complicated expressions in the best choice.

In addition, an effective sentence uses proper diction. (Diction refers to the standard dictionary meanings of words and the appropriateness of words in context.) In evaluating the diction of a sentence, you must be able to recognize whether the words are well chosen, accurate, and suitable for the context.

The directions for Sentence Correction questions read as follows:

Directions: In each of the following sentences, some part of the sentence or the entire sentence is underlined. Beneath each sentence you will find five ways of phrasing the underlined part. The first of these repeats the original; the other four are different. If you think the original is the best of these answer choices, choose answer A; otherwise choose one of the others. Select the best version and fill in the corresponding oval on your answer sheet.

This is a test of correctness and effectiveness of expression. In choosing answers, follow the requirements of standard written English; that is, pay attention to grammar, choice of words, and sentence construction. Choose the answer that produces the most effective sentence; this answer should be clear and exact, without awkwardness, ambiguity, redundancy, or grammatical error.

Examples:
A thunderclap is a complex acoustic signal as a result of rapid expansion of heated air in the path of a lightning flash.

(A) as a result of
(B) caused as a result of
(C) resulting because of the
(D) resulting from the
(E) that results because there is

In choice A, *is a . . . . signal as a result of* is incorrect. It is the thunderclap that results from the expansion; its being a signal is irrelevant. In choice B, it is superfluous to use both *caused* and *result*, and it is also superfluous to use both *result* and *because* in choices C and E. In choice C, *because of* is not the correct preposition to use after *resulting*; *from* is correct and is used in the best answer, D.

Ever since the Civil War, the status of women was a live social issue in this country.

(A) Ever since the Civil War, the status of women was
(B) Since the Civil War, women's status was
(C) Ever since the Civil War, the status of women has been
(D) Even at the time of the Civil War, the status of women has been
(E) From the times of the Civil War, the status of women has been

In choice A, the verb following *women* should be *has been*, not *was*, because *ever since* denotes a period of time continuing from the past into the present. For the same reason, *was* is inappropriately used with *since* in

choice B. In choice D, *even at* changes the meaning of the original sentence substantially and does not fit with *has been*; *was* is correct with *even at*. In choice E, *times* is incorrect; the standard phrase is *from the time of*. C is the best answer.

Analytical Writing Assessment

The Analytical Writing Assessment, consists of two thirty-minute writing tasks, "Analysis of an Issue" and "Analysis of an Argument." For the Analysis of an Issue task, you will need to analyze a given issue or opinion and then explain your point of view on the subject by citing relevant reasons and/or examples drawn from your experience, observations, or reading. For the Analysis of an Argument task, you will need to analyze the reasoning behind a given argument and then write a critique of that argument. You may, for example, consider what questionable assumptions underlie the thinking, what alternative explanations or counter-examples might weaken the conclusion, or what sort of evidence could help strengthen or refute the argument.

WHAT IS MEASURED

The Analytical Writing Assessment is designed as a direct measure of your ability to think critically and to communicate your ideas. More specifically, the Analysis of an Issue task tests your ability to explore the complexities of an issue or opinion and, if appropriate, to take a position informed by your understanding of those complexities. The Analysis of an Argument task tests your ability to formulate an appropriate and constructive critique of a specific conclusion based upon a specific line of thinking.

The issue and argument that you will find on the test concern topics of general interest, some related to

business and some pertaining to a variety of other subjects. It is important to note, however, that none presupposes any specific knowledge of business or of other specific content areas: only your capacity to write analytically is being assessed. College and university faculty members from various subject matter areas, including but not confined to management education, will evaluate how well you write. To qualify as GMAT readers, they must first demonstrate their ability to evaluate a large number of sample responses accurately and reliably, according to GMAT standards and scoring criteria. Once qualified, they will consider both the overall quality of your ideas about the issue and argument presented and your overall ability to organize, develop, and express those ideas; to provide relevant supporting reasons and examples; and to control the elements of standard written English. (In considering the elements of standard written English, readers are trained to be sensitive and fair in evaluating the responses of ESL [English as a Second Language] candidates.)

The directions for the two writing tasks in the Analytical Writing Assessment read as follows:

Directions for Analysis of an Issue: In this section, you will need to analyze the issue presented below and explain your views on it. The question has no "correct" answer. Instead, you should consider various perspectives as you develop your own position on the issue.

Read the statement and the instructions that follow it, and then make any notes in your test booklet that will help you plan your response. Begin writing your response on the separate answer document. Make sure that you use the answer document that goes with this writing task.

General Test-Taking Suggestions

1. Although the GMAT stresses accuracy more than speed, it is important to use the allotted time wisely. You will be able to do so if you are familiar with the mechanics of the test and the kinds of materials, questions, and directions in the test. Therefore, become familiar with the formats and requirements of each section of the test.

2. After you become generally familiar with all question types, use the individual chapters on each question type in this book (Chapters 3-8), which include sample test sections and detailed explanations, to prepare yourself for the actual GMAT tests in Chapter 9. (As noted elsewhere in this *Guide*, the actual GMAT tests were all administered before the Analytical Writing Assessment existed and so do not contain this section.) When taking the tests, try to follow all the requirements specified in the directions and keep within the time limits. While these tests are useful for familiarization, they cannot be used to predict your performance on the actual test.

3. Read all test directions carefully. Since many answer sheets give indications that the examinees do not follow directions, this suggestion is particularly important. The directions explain exactly what each section requires in order to answer each question type. If you read hastily, you may miss important instructions and seriously jeopardize your scores.

4. In the multiple-choice sections, answer as many questions as possible, but avoid random guessing. Your GMAT scores for these sections will be based on the number of questions you answer correctly minus a fraction of the number you answer incorrectly. Therefore, it is unlikely that mere guessing on the multiple-choice questions will improve your scores significantly, and it does take time. However, if you have some knowledge of a question and can eliminate at least one of the answer choices as wrong, your chance of getting the best answer is improved, and it will be to your advantage to answer the question. If you know nothing at all about a particular question, it is probably better to skip it. The number of omitted questions will not be subtracted.

   The best way to approach the two writing tasks comprising the Analytical Writing Assessment is to take a few minutes to think about each question and plan a response before you begin writing. Take care to organize your ideas and develop them fully, but leave time to reread your response and make any revisions that you think would improve it.

5. Take a watch to the examination and be sure to note the time limit for each section. Since each question in the multiple-choice sections has the same weight, it is not wise to spend too much time on one question if that causes you to neglect other questions.

6. In all sections of the test, both multiple-choice and writing, make every effort to pace yourself. Work steadily and as rapidly as possible without being careless.

7. A wise practice in handling multiple-choice sections of the GMAT is to answer the questions you are sure of first. Then, if time permits, go back and attempt the more difficult questions.

8. On all sections of the test, multiple-choice and writing, read each question carefully and thoroughly. Before answering a question, determine exactly what is being asked. Never skim a question or, in the case of a multiple-choice question, the possible answers. Skimming may cause you to miss important information or nuances in the question.

9. Do not become upset if you cannot answer a question in a multiple-choice section. A person can do very well without answering every question or finishing every section. No one is expected to get a perfect score.

10. When you take the test, you will mark your answers for the multiple choice sections on a separate answer sheet. As you go through the test, be sure that the number of each answer on the answer sheet matches the corresponding question number in the test book. Your answer sheet may contain space

for more answers or questions than there are in the test book. Do not be concerned, but be careful. Indicate each of your answers with a dark mark that completely fills the response position on the answer sheet. Light or partial marks may not be properly read by the scoring machine. Indicate only one response to each question, and erase all unintended marks completely.

For the Analytical Writing Assessment, you will be given a separate answer document for each writing task. Be sure to write your responses on the answer document that goes with that task: the scorers will not see anything you write in the test book in which the writing task questions are printed. When writing, feel free to cross out or insert words, but please write legibly.

GMAT: Test Specifications

All editions of the GMAT are constructed to measure the same skills and meet the same specifications. Thus, each section of the test is constructed according to established specifications for every edition of the GMAT. These specifications include definite requirements for the number of questions, the points tested by each question, the kinds of questions, and the difficulty of each question.

Because the various editions of the test inevitably differ somewhat in difficulty, they are made equivalent to each other by statistical methods. This equating process makes it possible to assure that all reported scores of a given value denote approximately the same level of ability regardless of the edition being used or of the particular group taking the test at a given time.

Since equating, strictly speaking, cannot be carried out for different editions of the Analytical Writing Assessment, comparability between tests is maintained by keeping as many factors as possible consistent in scoring across scoring sessions. Thus, the academic profile of the scorers remains the same, as do the general scoring guides they use. The training they receive before each scoring session is fully standardized, and the accuracy of each scorer is closely monitored during each scoring session. And, finally, statistical analyses are conducted to study the correlation between scores on the writing tasks and scores on those multiple-choice sections of the GMAT that measure related skills.

Test Development Process

Educational Testing Service professional staff responsible for developing the verbal and writing measures of the GMAT have backgrounds and advanced degrees in the humanities, in measurement, or in writing assessment. Those responsible for the quantitative portion have advanced degrees in mathematics or related fields.

Standardized procedures have been developed to guide the test-generation process, to assure high-quality test material, to avoid idiosyncratic questions, and to encourage development of test material that is widely appropriate.

An important part of the development of test material is the review process. Each question, whether writing task or multiple-choice question, as well as any stimulus material on which questions are based, must be reviewed by several independent critics. In appropriate cases (and such cases include all writing tasks), questions are also reviewed by experts outside ETS who can bring fresh perspectives to bear on the questions in terms of actual content or in terms of sensitivity to minority and women's concerns.

After all the questions have been reviewed and revised as appropriate, the multiple-choice questions are assembled into clusters suitable for trial during actual administrations of the GMAT. In this manner, new questions are tried out, under standard testing conditions, by representative samples of GMAT examinees. Questions being tried out do not affect examinees' scores but are themselves evaluated: they are analyzed statistically for usefulness and weaknesses. The questions that perform satisfactorily become part of a pool of questions from which future editions of the GMAT can be assembled; those that do not are rewritten to correct the flaws and tried out again—or discarded.

In contrast to the multiple-choice questions, the writing tasks are not tried out during actual administrations of the GMAT: this would be impractical. Instead, the writing tasks are pretested on first-year business school students — students who not so long ago were GMAT candidates themselves and who are therefore representative of the GMAT test-taking population. The responses are read at a pretest scoring session to determine which writing tasks are clear and accessible to examinees, which can be successfully completed within the allotted half-hour, and which discriminate fairly and reliably (i.e., they are not skewed in some way so as to disadvantage certain examinees, and they produce scores all along the scoring scale). Only those tasks that perform well in the pretest scoring sessions become part of the pool from which editions of the Analytical Writing Assessment can be assembled.

In preparing those sections of the GMAT that will contribute to the scoring process, the test assembler uses only questions that have been successfully tried out or pretested. The test assembler considers not only each question's characteristics but also the relationship of the question to the entire group of questions with respect to the test specifications discussed above. When the test has been assembled, it is reviewed by a second test specialist and by the test development coordinator for the GMAT.

After satisfactory resolution of any points raised in these reviews, the test goes to a test editor. The test editor's review is likely to result in further suggestions for change, and the test assembler must decide how these suggested changes will be handled. If a suggested change yields an editorial improvement, without jeopardizing content integrity, the change is adopted; otherwise, new wording is sought that will meet the dual concerns of content integrity and editorial style. The review process is continued at each stage of test assembly and copy preparation, down to careful scrutiny of the final proof immediately prior to printing.

All reviewers except the editor and proofreader must attempt to answer each multiple-choice question without the help of the answer key. Thus, for the multiple-choice sections of the GMAT, each reviewer "takes the test," uninfluenced by knowledge of what the question writer or test assembler believed each answer should be. The answer key is certified as official only after at least three reviewers have agreed independently on the best answer for each question.

The extensive, careful procedure described here has been developed over the years to assure that every question in any new edition of the GMAT is appropriate and useful and that the combination of questions that make up the new edition is satisfactory. Nevertheless, the appraisal is

not complete until after the new edition has been administered during a national test administration and the multiple-choice questions have been subjected to a rigorous process of analysis to see whether each question yields the expected result. This further appraisal sometimes reveals that a multiple-choice question is not satisfactory after all; it may prove to be ambiguous, or require information beyond the scope of the test, or be otherwise unsuitable. Answers to such questions are not used in computing scores.

2 Math Review

Although this chapter provides a review of some of the mathematical concepts of arithmetic, algebra, and geometry, it is not intended to be a textbook. You should use this chapter to familiarize yourself with the kinds of topics that are tested in the GMAT. You may wish to consult an arithmetic, algebra, or geometry book for a more detailed discussion of some of the topics.

The topics that are covered in Section A, arithmetic, include:

1. Properties of integers
2. Fractions
3. Decimals
4. Real numbers
5. Ratio and proportion
6. Percents
7. Powers and roots of numbers
8. Descriptive statistics
9. Sets
10. Counting methods
11. Discrete probability

The content of Section B, algebra, does not extend beyond what is usually covered in a first-year high school algebra course. The topics included are:

1. Simplifying algebraic expressions
2. Equations
3. Solving linear equations with one unknown
4. Solving two linear equations with two unknowns
5. Solving equations by factoring
6. Solving quadratic equations
7. Exponents
8. Inequalities
9. Absolute value
10. Functions

Section C, geometry, is limited primarily to measurement and intuitive geometry or spatial visualization. Extensive knowledge of theorems and the ability to construct proofs, skills that are usually developed in a formal geometry course, are not tested. The topics included in this section are:

1. Lines
2. Intersecting lines and angles
3. Perpendicular lines
4. Parallel lines
5. Polygons (convex)
6. Triangles
7. Quadrilaterals
8. Circles
9. Rectangular solids and cylinders
10. Coordinate geometry

Section D, word problems, presents examples of and solutions to the following types of word problems:

1. Rate
2. Work
3. Mixture
4. Interest
5. Discount
6. Profit
7. Sets
8. Geometry
9. Measurement
10. Data interpretation

A. Arithmetic

1. PROPERTIES OF INTEGERS

An *integer* is any number in the set $\{\ldots -3, -2, -1, 0, 1, 2, 3, \ldots\}$. If x and y are integers and $x \neq 0$, then x is a *divisor (factor)* of y provided that $y = xn$ for some integer n. In this case, y is also said to be *divisible* by x or to be a *multiple* of x. For example, 7 is a divisor or factor of 28 since $28 = (7)(4)$, but 8 is not a divisor of 28 since there is no integer n such that $28 = 8n$.

If x and y are positive integers, there exist unique integers q and r, called the *quotient* and *remainder*, respectively, such that $y = xq + r$ and $0 \leq r < x$. For example, when 28 is divided by 8, the quotient is 3 and the remainder is 4 since $28 = (8)(3) + 4$. Note that y is divisible by x if and only if the remainder r is 0; for example, 32 has a remainder of 0 when divided by 8 because 32 is divisible by 8. Also, note that when a smaller integer is divided by a larger integer, the quotient is 0 and the remainder is the smaller integer. For example, 5 divided by 7 has the quotient 0 and the remainder 5 since $5 = (7)(0) + 5$.

Any integer that is divisible by 2 is an *even integer*; the set of even integers is $\{\ldots -4, -2, 0, 2, 4, 6, 8, \ldots\}$. Integers that are not divisible by 2 are *odd integers*; $\{\ldots -3, -1, 1, 3, 5, \ldots\}$ is the set of odd integers.

If at least one factor of a product of integers is even, then the product is even; otherwise the product is odd. If two integers are both even or both odd, then their sum and their difference are even. Otherwise, their sum and their difference are odd.

A *prime* number is a positive integer that has exactly two different positive divisors, 1 and itself. For example, 2, 3, 5, 7, 11, and 13 are prime numbers, but 15 is not, since 15 has four different positive divisors, 1, 3, 5, and 15. The number 1 is not a prime number, since it has only one positive divisor. Every integer greater than 1 is either prime or can be uniquely expressed as a product of prime factors. For example, $14 = (2)(7)$, $81 = (3)(3)(3)(3)$, and $484 = (2)(2)(11)(11)$.

The numbers $-2, -1, 0, 1, 2, 3, 4, 5$ are *consecutive integers*. Consecutive integers can be represented by $n, n + 1, n + 2, n + 3, \ldots$, where n is an integer. The numbers $0, 2, 4, 6, 8$ are *consecutive even integers*, and $1, 3, 5, 7, 9$ are *consecutive odd integers*. Consecutive even integers can be represented by $2n, 2n + 2, 2n + 4, \ldots$, and consecutive odd integers can be represented by $2n + 1, 2n + 3, 2n + 5, \ldots$, where n is an integer.

Properties of the integer 1. If n is any number, then $1 \cdot n = n$, and for any number $n \neq 0$, $n \cdot \dfrac{1}{n} = 1$. The number 1 can be expressed in many ways; for example, $\dfrac{n}{n} = 1$ for any number $n \neq 0$. Multiplying or dividing an expression by 1, in any form, does not change the value of that expression.

Properties of the integer 0. The integer 0 is neither positive nor negative. If n is any number, then $n + 0 = n$ and $n \cdot 0 = 0$. Division by 0 is not defined.

2. FRACTIONS

In a fraction $\frac{n}{d}$, n is the *numerator* and d is the *denominator*. The denominator of a fraction can never be 0, because division by 0 is not defined.

Two fractions are said to be *equivalent* if they represent the same number. For example, $\frac{8}{36}$ and $\frac{14}{63}$ are equivalent since they both represent the number $\frac{2}{9}$. In each case, the faction is reduced to lowest terms by dividing both numerator and denominator by their *greatest common divisor* (gcd). The gcd of 8 and 36 is 4 and the gcd of 14 and 63 is 7.

Addition and subtraction of fractions. Two fractions with the same denominator can be added or subtracted by performing the required operation with the numerators, leaving the denominators the same. For example, $\frac{3}{5}+\frac{4}{5}=\frac{3+4}{5}=\frac{7}{5}$, and $\frac{5}{7}-\frac{2}{7}=\frac{5-2}{7}=\frac{3}{7}$. If two fractions do not have the same denominator, express them as equivalent fractions with the same denominator. For example, to add $\frac{3}{5}$ and $\frac{4}{7}$, mutliply the numerator and denominator of the first fraction by 7 and the numerator and denominator of the second fraction by 5, obtaining $\frac{21}{35}$ and $\frac{20}{35}$, respectively;

$$\frac{21}{35}+\frac{20}{35}=\frac{41}{35}.$$

For the new denominator, choosing the *least common multiple* (lcm) of the denominators usually lessens the work. For $\frac{2}{3}+\frac{1}{6}$, the lcm of 3 and 6 is 6 (not $3 \times 6 = 18$), so

$$\frac{2}{3}+\frac{1}{6}=\frac{2}{3}\cdot\frac{2}{2}+\frac{1}{6}=\frac{4}{6}+\frac{1}{6}=\frac{5}{6}.$$

Multiplication and division of fractions. To multiply two fractions, simply multiply the two numerators and multiply the two denominators. For example, $\frac{2}{3}\times\frac{4}{7}=\frac{2\times4}{3\times7}=\frac{8}{21}.$

To divide by a fraction, invert the divisor (that is, find its *reciprocal*) and multiply. For example $\frac{2}{3}\div\frac{4}{7}=\frac{2}{3}\times\frac{7}{4}=\frac{14}{12}=\frac{7}{6}.$

In the problem above, the reciprocal of $\frac{4}{7}$ is $\frac{7}{4}$. In general, the reciprocal of a fraction $\frac{n}{d}$ is $\frac{d}{n}$, where n and d are not zero.

Mixed numbers. A number that consists of a whole number and a fraction, for example, $7\frac{2}{3}$, is a mixed number: $7\frac{2}{3}$ means $7 + \frac{2}{3}$.

To change a mixed number into a fraction, multiply the whole number by the denominator of the fraction and add this number to the numerator of the fraction; then put the result over the denominator of the fraction. For example,

$$7\frac{2}{3} = \frac{(3 \times 7) + 2}{3} = \frac{23}{3}.$$

3. DECIMALS

In the decimal system, the position of the period or *decimal point* determines the place value of the digits. For example, the digits in the number 7,654.321 have the following place values:

Thousands		Hundreds	Tens	Ones or units		Tenths	Hundredths	Thousandths
7	,	6	5	4	.	3	2	1

Some examples of decimals follow.

$$0.321 = \frac{3}{10} + \frac{2}{100} + \frac{1}{1,000} = \frac{321}{1,000}$$

$$0.0321 = \frac{0}{10} + \frac{3}{100} + \frac{2}{1,000} + \frac{1}{10,000} = \frac{321}{10,000}$$

$$1.56 = 1 + \frac{5}{10} + \frac{6}{100} = \frac{156}{100}$$

Sometimes decimals are expressed as the product of a number with only one digit to the left of the decimal point and a power of 10. This is called *scientific notation*. For example, 231 can be written as 2.31×10^2 and 0.0231 can be written as 2.31×10^{-2}. When a number is expressed in scientific notation, the exponent of the 10 indicates the number of places that the decimal point is to be moved in the number that is to be mutliplied by a power of 10 in order to obtain the product. The decimal point is moved to the right if the exponent is positive and to the left if the exponent is negative. For example, 20.13×10^3 is equal to 20,130 and 1.91×10^{-4} is equal to 0.000191.

Addition and subtraction of decimals. To add or subtract two decimals, the decimal points of both numbers should be lined up. If one of the numbers has fewer digits to the right of the decimal point than the other, zeros may be inserted to the right of the last digit. For example, to add 17.6512 and 653.27, set up the numbers in a column and add:

$$
\begin{array}{r}
17.6512 \\
+653.2700 \\
\hline
670.9212
\end{array}
$$

Likewise for 653.27 minus 17.6512:

$$
\begin{array}{r}
653.2700 \\
-17.6512 \\
\hline
635.6188
\end{array}
$$

Multiplication of decimals. To multiply decimals, multiply the numbers as if they were whole numbers and then insert the decimal point in the product so that the number of digits to the right of the decimal point is equal to the sum of the numbers of digits to the right of the decimal points in the numbers being multiplied. For example:

$$
\begin{array}{r}
2.09 \\
\times\ 1.3 \\
\hline
627 \\
209 \\
\hline
2.717
\end{array}
$$

(2 digits to the right)
(1 digit to the right)

(2 + 1 = 3 digits to the right)

Division of decimals. To divide a number (the dividend) by a decimal (the divisor), move the decimal point of the divisor to the right until the divisor is a whole number. Then move the decimal point of the dividend the same number of places to the right, and divide as you would by a whole number. The decimal point in the quotient will be directly above the decimal point in the new dividend. For example, to divide 698.12 by 12.4:

$$12.4\overline{)698.12}$$

will be replaced by

$$124\overline{)6981.2}$$

and the division would proceed as follows:

$$
\begin{array}{r}
56.3 \\
124\overline{)6981.2} \\
620 \\
\hline
781 \\
744 \\
\hline
372 \\
372 \\
\hline
0
\end{array}
$$

4. REAL NUMBERS

All *real* numbers correspond to points on the number line and all points on the number line correspond to real numbers. All real numbers except zero are either positive or negative.

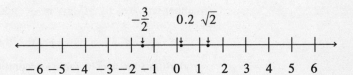

On a number line, numbers corresponding to points to the left of zero are negative and numbers corresponding to points to the right of zero are positive. For any two numbers on the number line, the number to the left is less than the number to the right; for example,

$-4 < -3$, $-\dfrac{3}{2} < -1$, and $1 < \sqrt{2} < 2$.

To say that the number n is between 1 and 4 on the number line means that $n > 1$ and $n < 4$, that is, $1 < n < 4$. If n is "between 1 and 4, inclusive," then $1 \leq n \leq 4$.

The distance between a number and zero on the number line is called the *absolute value* of the number. Thus 3 and −3 have the same absolute value, 3, since they are both three units from zero. The absolute value of 3 is denoted $|3|$. Examples of absolute values of numbers are

$$|-5| = |5| = 5, \quad \left|-\frac{7}{2}\right| = \frac{7}{2}, \quad \text{and} \quad |0| = 0.$$

Note that the absolute value of any nonzero number is positive.

Here are some properties of real numbers that are used frequently. If x, y, and z are real numbers, then

(1) $x + y = y + x$ and $xy = yx$.

For example, $8 + 3 = 3 + 8 = 11$, and $(17)(5) = (5)(17) = 85$.

(2) $(x + y) + z = x + (y + z)$ and $(xy)z = x(yz)$.

For example, $(7 + 5) + 2 = 7 + (5 + 2) = 7 + (7) = 14$,

and $(5\sqrt{3})(\sqrt{3}) = 5(\sqrt{3}\sqrt{3}) = (5)(3) = 15$.

(3) $x(y + z) = xy + xz$.

For example, $718(36) + 718(64) = 718(36 + 64) = 718(100) = 71,800$.

(4) If x and y are both positive, then $x + y$ and xy are positive.

(5) If x and y are both negative, then $x + y$ is negative and xy is positive.

(6) If x is positive and y is negative, then xy is negative.

(7) If $xy = 0$, then $x = 0$ or $y = 0$. For example, $3y = 0$ implies $y = 0$.

(8) $|x + y| \leq |x| + |y|$. For example, if $x = 10$ and $y = 2$,

then $|x + y| = |12| = 12 = |x| + |y|$; and if $x = 10$

and $y = -2$, then $|x + y| = |8| = 8 < 12 = |x| + |y|$.

5. RATIO AND PROPORTION

The *ratio* of the number a to the number b $(b \neq 0)$ is $\frac{a}{b}$.

A ratio may be expressed or represented in several ways. For example, the ratio of 2 to 3 can be written as 2 to 3, 2:3, or $\frac{2}{3}$. The order of the terms of a ratio is important. For example, the ratio of the number of months with exactly 30 days to the number with exactly 31 days is $\frac{4}{7}$, not $\frac{7}{4}$.

A *proportion* is a statement that two ratios are equal; for example, $\frac{2}{3} = \frac{8}{12}$ is a proportion. One way to solve a proportion involving an unknown is to cross multiply, obtaining a new equality. For example, to solve for n in the proportion $\frac{2}{3} = \frac{n}{12}$, cross multiply, obtaining $24 = 3n$; then divide both sides by 3, to get $n = 8$.

6. PERCENTS

Percent means *per hundred* or *number out of 100*. A percent can be represented as a fraction with a denominator of 100, or as a decimal. For example, $37\% = \frac{37}{100} = 0.37$.

To find a certain percent of a number, multiply the number by the percent expressed as a decimal or fraction. For example:

$$20\% \text{ of } 90 = 0.20 \times 90 = 18$$

or

$$20\% \text{ of } 90 = \frac{20}{100} \times 90 = \frac{1}{5} \times 90 = 18.$$

Percents greater than 100%. Percents greater than 100% are represented by numbers greater than 1. For example:

$$300\% = \frac{300}{100} = 3$$

$$250\% \text{ of } 80 = 2.5 \times 80 = 200.$$

Percents less than 1%. The percent 0.5% means $\frac{1}{2}$ of 1 percent. For example, 0.5% of 12 is equal to $0.005 \times 12 = 0.06$.

Percent change. Often a problem will ask for the percent increase or decrease from one quantity to another quantity. For example, "If the price of an item increases from $24 to $30, what is the percent increase in price?" To find the percent increase, first find the amount of the increase; then divide this increase by the original amount, and express this quotient as a percent. In the example above, the percent increase would be found in the following way: the amount of the increase is $(30 - 24) = 6$.

Therefore, the percent increase is $\frac{6}{24} = 0.25 = 25\%$.

Likewise, to find the percent decrease (for example, the price of an item is reduced from $30 to $24), first find the amount of the decrease; then divide this decrease by the original amount, and express this quotient as a percent. In the example above, the amount of decrease is $(30 - 24) = 6$. Therefore, the percent decrease is $\frac{6}{30} = 0.20 = 20\%$.

Note that the percent increase from 24 to 30 is not the same as the percent decrease from 30 to 24.

In the following example, the increase is greater than 100 percent: If the cost of a certain house in 1983 was 300 percent of its cost in 1970, by what percent did the cost increase?

If n is the cost in 1970, then the percent increase is equal to $\frac{3n - n}{n} = \frac{2n}{n} = 2$, or 200 percent.

7. POWERS AND ROOTS OF NUMBERS

When a number k is to be used n times as a factor in a product, it can be expressed as k^n, which means the nth power of k. For example, $2^2 = 2 \times 2 = 4$ and $2^3 = 2 \times 2 \times 2 = 8$ are powers of 2.

Squaring a number that is greater than 1, or raising it to a higher power, results in a larger number; squaring a number between 0 and 1 results in a smaller number. For example:

$3^2 = 9$ $\qquad\qquad$ $(9 > 3)$

$\left(\frac{1}{3}\right)^2 = \frac{1}{9}$ $\qquad$ $\left(\frac{1}{9} < \frac{1}{3}\right)$

$(0.1)^2 = 0.01$ $\qquad$ $(0.01 < 0.1)$

A *square root* of a number n is a number that, when squared, is equal to n. The square root of a negative number is not a real number. Every positive number n has two square roots, one positive and the other negative, but $\sqrt{n}$ denotes the positive number whose square is n. For example, $\sqrt{9}$ denotes 3. The two square roots of 9 are $\sqrt{9} = 3$ and $-\sqrt{9} = -3$.

Every real number r has exactly one real *cube root*, which is the number s such that $s^3 = r$. The real cube root of r is denoted by $\sqrt[3]{r}$. Since $2^3 = 8$, $\sqrt[3]{8} = 2$. Similarly, $\sqrt[3]{-8} = -2$, because $(-2)^3 = -8$.

8. DESCRIPTIVE STATISTICS

A list of numbers, or numerical data, can be described by various statistical measures. One of the most common of these measures is the *average*, or *(arithmetic) mean*, which locates a type of "center" for the data. The average of n numbers is defined as the sum of the n numbers divided by n. For example, the average of 6, 4, 7, 10, and 4 is $\dfrac{6+4+7+10+4}{5} = \dfrac{31}{5} = 6.2$.

The *median* is another type of center for a list of numbers. To calculate the median of n numbers, first order the numbers from least to greatest; if n is odd, the median is defined as the middle number, while if n is even, the median is defined as the average of the two middle numbers. In the example above, the numbers, in order, are 4, 4, 6, 7, 10, and the median is 6, the middle number. For the numbers 4, 6, 6, 8, 9, 12, the median is $\dfrac{6+8}{2} = 7$. Note that the mean of these numbers is 7.5. The median of a set of data can be less than, equal to, or greater than the mean. Note that for a large set of data (for example, the salaries of 800 company employees), it is often true that about half of the data is less than the median and about half of the data is greater than the median; but this is not always the case, as the following data show.

$$3, 5, 7, 7, 7, 7, 7, 7, 8, 9, 9, 9, 9, 10, 10$$

Here the median is 7, but only $\dfrac{2}{15}$ of the data is less than the median.

The *mode* of a list of numbers is the number that occurs most frequently in the list. For example, the mode of 1, 3, 6, 4, 3, 5 is 3. A list of numbers may have more than one mode. For example, the list 1, 2, 3, 3, 3, 5, 7, 10, 10, 10, 20 has two modes, 3 and 10.

The degree to which numerical data are spread out or dispersed can be measured in many ways. The simplest measure of dispersion is the *range*, which is defined as the greatest value in the numerical data minus the least value. For example, the range of 11, 10, 5, 13, 21 is $21 - 5 = 16$. Note how the range depends on only two values in the data.

One of the most common measures of dispersion is the *standard deviation*. Generally speaking, the greater the data are spread away form the mean, the greater the standard deviation. The standard deviation of n numbers can be calculated as follows: (1) find the arithmetic mean, (2) find the differences between the mean and each of the n numbers, (3) square each of the differences, (4) find the average of the squared differences, and (5) take the nonnegative square root of this average. Shown below is this calculation for the data 0, 7, 8, 10, 10, which have arithmetic mean 7.

x	$x - 7$	$(x - 7)^2$
0	−7	49
7	0	0
8	1	1
10	3	9
10	3	9
Total		68

Standard deviation: $\sqrt{\dfrac{68}{5}} \approx 3.7$

Notice that the standard deviation depends on every data value, although it depends most on values that are farthest from the mean. This is why a distribution with data grouped closely around the mean will have a smaller standard deviation than will data spread far from the mean. To illustrate this, compare the data 6, 6, 6.5, 7.5, 9, which also have mean 7. Note that the numbers in the second set of data seem to be grouped more closely around the mean of 7 than the numbers in the first set. This is reflected in the standard deviation, which is less for the second set (approximately 1.1) than for the first set (approximately 3.7).

There are many ways to display numerical data that show how the data are distributed. One simple way is with a *frequency distribution*, which is useful for data that have values occurring with varying frequencies. For example, the 20 numbers

$$
\begin{array}{cccccccccc}
-4 & 0 & 0 & -3 & -2 & -1 & -1 & 0 & -1 & -4 \\
-1 & -5 & 0 & -2 & 0 & -5 & -2 & 0 & 0 & -1
\end{array}
$$

are displayed below in a frequency distribution by listing each different value x and the frequency f with which x occurs.

Data Value x	Frequency f
−5	2
−4	2
−3	1
−2	3
−1	5
0	7
Total	20

From the frequency distribution, one can readily compute descriptive statistics:

Mean: $\dfrac{(-5)(2) + (-4)(2) + (-3)(1) + (-2)(3) + (-1)(5) + (0)(7)}{20} = -1.6$

Median: −1 (the average of the 10th and 11th numbers)

Mode: 0 (the number that occurs most frequently)

Range: $0 - (-5) = 5$

Standard deviation:

$$
\sqrt{\dfrac{(-5 + 1.6)^2(2) + (-4 + 1.6)^2(2) + \ldots + (0 + 1.6)^2(7)}{20}} \approx 1.7
$$

9. SETS

In mathematics a *set* is a collection of numbers or other objects. The objects are called the *elements* of the set. If S is a set having a finite number of elements, then the number of elements is denoted by $|S|$. Such a set is often defined by listing its elements; for example, $S = \{-5, 0, 1\}$ is a set with $|S| = 3$. The order in which the elements are listed in a set does not matter; thus $\{-5, 0, 1\} = \{0, 1, -5\}$. If all the elements of a set S are also elements of a set T, then S is a *subset* of T; for example, $S = \{-5, 0, 1\}$ is a subset of $T = \{-5, 0, 1, 4, 10\}$.

For any two sets A and B, the *union* of A and B is the set of all elements that are in A *or* in B *or* in both. The *intersection* of A and B is the set of all elements that are both in A *and* in B. The union is denoted by $A \cup B$ and the intersection is denoted by $A \cap B$. As an example, if $A = \{3, 4\}$ and $B = \{4, 5, 6\}$, then $A \cup B = \{3, 4, 5, 6\}$ and $A \cap B = \{4\}$. Two sets that have no elements in common are said to be *disjoint* or *mutually exclusive*.

The relationship between sets is often illustrated with a *Venn diagram* in which sets are represented by regions in a plane. For two sets S and T that are not disjoint and neither is a subset of the other, the intersection $S \cap T$ is represented by the shaded region of the diagram below.

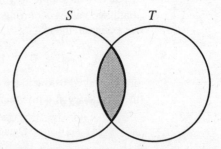

This diagram illustrates a fact about any two finite sets S and T: the number of elements in their union equals the sum of their individual numbers of elements minus the number of elements in their intersection (because the latter are counted twice in the sum); more concisely,

$$|S \cup T| = |S| + |T| - |S \cap T|.$$

This counting method is called the general addition rule for two sets. As a special case, if S and T are disjoint, then

$$|S \cup T| = |S| + |T|$$

since $|S \cup T| = 0$.

10. COUNTING METHODS

There are some useful methods for counting objects and sets of objects without actually listing the elements to be counted. The following principle of multiplication is fundamental to these methods.

If an object is to be chosen from a set of m objects and a second object is to be chosen from a different set of n objects, then there are mn ways of choosing both objects simultaneously.

As an example, suppose the objects are items on a menu. If a meal consists of one entree and one dessert and there are 5 entrees and 3 desserts on the menu, then there are $5 \times 3 = 15$ different meals that can be ordered from the menu. As another example, each time a coin is flipped, there are two possible outcomes, heads and tails. If an experiment consists of 8 consecutive coin flips, then the experiment has 2^8 possible outcomes, where each of these outcomes is a list of heads and tails in some order.

A symbol that is often used with the multiplication principle is the *factorial*. If n is an integer greater than 1, then n factorial, denoted by the symbol $n!$, is defined as the product of all the integers from 1 to n. Therefore,

$$2! = (1)(2) = 2,$$
$$3! = (1)(2)(3) = 6,$$
$$4! = (1)(2)(3)(4) = 24, \text{ etc.}$$

Also, by definition, $0! = 1! = 1$.

The factorial is useful for counting the number of ways that a set of objects can be ordered. If a set of n objects is to be ordered from 1st to nth, then there are n choices for the 1st object, $n-1$ choices for the 2nd object, $n-2$ choices for the 3rd object, and so on, until there is only 1 choice for the nth object. Thus, by the multiplication principle, the number of ways of ordering the n objects is

$$n(n-1)(n-2) \cdots (3)(2)(1) = n!.$$

For example, the number of ways of ordering the letters A, B, and C is 3!, or 6:

ABC, ACB, BAC, BCA, CAB, and CBA.

These orderings are called the *permutations* of the letters A, B, and C.

A permutation can be thought of as a selection process in which objects are selected one by one in a certain order. If the order of selection is not relevant and only k objects are to be selected from a larger set of n objects, a different counting method is employed. Specifically, consider a set of n objects from which a complete selection of k objects is to be made without regard to order, where $0 \leq k \leq n$. Then the number of possible complete selections of k objects is called the number of *combinations* of n objects taken k at a time and is denoted by $\binom{n}{k}$. The value of $\binom{n}{k}$ is given by

$$\binom{n}{k} = \frac{n!}{k!\,(n-k)!}.$$

Note that $\binom{n}{k}$ is the number of k-element subsets of a set with n elements. For example, if $S = \{A, B, C, D, E\}$, then the number of 2-element subsets of S, or the number of combinations of 5 letters taken 2 at a time, is $\binom{5}{2} = \frac{5!}{2!\,3!} = \frac{120}{(2)(6)} = 10$.

The subsets are {A, B}, {A, C}, {A, D}, {A, E}, {B, C}, {B, D}, {B, E}, {C, D}, {C, E,}, and {D, E}. Note that $\binom{5}{2} = 10 = \binom{5}{3}$, since every 2-element subset chosen from a set of 5 elements corresponds to a unique 3-element subset consisting of the elements *not* chosen. In general,

$$\binom{n}{k} = \binom{n}{n-k}.$$

11. DISCRETE PROBABILITY

Many of the ideas discussed in the preceding three topics are important to the study of discrete probability. Discrete probability is concerned with *experiments* that have a finite number of *outcomes*. Given such an experiment, an *event* is a particular set of outcomes. For example, rolling a number cube with faces numbered 1 to 6 (similar to a 6-sided die) is an experiment with 6 possible outcomes: 1, 2, 3, 4, 5, or 6. One event in this experiment is that the outcome is 4, denoted {4}; another event is that the outcome is an odd number: {1, 3, 5}.

The probability than an event E occurs, denoted by $P(E)$, is a number between 0 and 1, inclusive. If E has no outcomes, then E is *impossible* and $P(E) = 0$; if E is the set of all possible outcomes of the experiment, then E is *certain* to occur and $P(E) = 1$. Otherwise, E is possible but uncertain, and $0 < P(E) < 1$. If F is a subset of E, then $P(F) \leq P(E)$. In the example above, if the probability of each of the 6 outcomes is the same, then the probability of each outcome is $\frac{1}{6}$, and the outcomes are said to be *equally likely*. For experiments in which all of the individual outcomes are equally likely, the probability of an event E is

$$P(E) = \frac{\text{The number of outcomes in } E}{\text{The total number of possible outcomes}}.$$

In the example, the probability that the outcome is an odd number is

$$P(\{1, 3, 5\}) = \frac{|\{1, 3, 5\}|}{6} = \frac{3}{6}.$$

Given an experiment with events E and F, the following events are defined.

"*not E*" is the set of outcomes that are not outcomes in E;

"*E or F*" is the set of outcomes in E or F or both, that is, $E \cup F$;

"*E and F*" is the set of outcomes in both E and F, that is, $E \cap F$.

The probability that E does not occur is $P(\text{not } E) = 1 - P(E)$. The probability that "*E or F*" occurs is

$$P(E \text{ or } F) = P(E) + P(F) - P(E \text{ and } F),$$

using the general addition rule at the end of Section A.9. For the number cube, if E is the event that the outcome is an odd number, {1, 3, 5}, and F is the event that the outcome is a prime number, {2, 3, 5}, then $P(E \text{ and } F) = P(\{3, 5\}) = \frac{2}{6}$, and so

$$P(E \text{ or } F) = P(E) + P(F) - P(E \text{ and } F) = \frac{3}{6} + \frac{3}{6} - \frac{2}{6} = \frac{4}{6}.$$

Note that the event "E or F" is $E \cup F = \{1, 2, 3, 5\}$, and hence $P(E \text{ or } F) =$
$\frac{|\{1, 2, 3, 5\}|}{6} = \frac{4}{6}.$

If the event "E and F" is impossible (that is, $E \cap F$ has no outcomes), then E and F are said to be *mutually exclusive* events, and $P(E \text{ and } F) = 0$. Then the general addition rule is reduced to

$$P(E \text{ or } F) = P(E) + P(F).$$

This is the special addition rule for the probability of two mutually exclusive events.

Two events A and B are said to be *independent* if the occurrence of either event does not alter the probability that the other event occurs. For one roll of the number cube, let $A = \{2, 4, 6\}$ and let $B = \{5, 6\}$. Then the probability that A occurs is

$P(A) = \frac{|A|}{6} = \frac{3}{6} = \frac{1}{2}$, while, *presuming B occurs*, the probability that A occurs is

$$\frac{|A \cap B|}{|B|} = \frac{|\{6\}|}{|\{5, 6\}|} = \frac{1}{2}.$$

Similarly, the probability that B occurs is $P(B) = \frac{|B|}{6} = \frac{2}{6} = \frac{1}{3}$, while, *presuming A occurs*, the probability that B occurs is

$$\frac{|B \cap A|}{|A|} = \frac{|\{6\}|}{|\{2, 4, 6\}|} = \frac{1}{3}.$$

Thus, the occurrence of either event does not affect the probability that the other event occurs. Therefore, A and B are independent.

The following multiplication rule holds for any independent events E and F:

$$P(E \text{ and } F) = P(E)P(F).$$

For the independent events A and B above,

$$P(A \text{ and } B) = P(A)P(B)$$

$$= \left(\frac{1}{2}\right)\left(\frac{1}{3}\right) = \left(\frac{1}{6}\right).$$

Note that the event "A and B" is $A \cap B = \{6\}$, and hence $P(A \text{ and } B) = P(\{6\}) = \frac{1}{6}$. It follows from the general addition rule and the multiplication rule above that if E and F are independent, then

$$P(E \text{ or } F) = P(E) + P(F) - P(E)P(F).$$

For a final example of some of these rules, consider an experiment with events A, B, and C for which $P(A) = 0.23$, $P(B) = 0.40$, and $P(C) = 0.85$. Also, suppose that events A and B are mutually exclusive and events B and C are independent. Then

$$\begin{aligned} P(A \text{ or } B) &= P(A) + P(B) \quad \text{(since } A \text{ and } B \text{ are mutually exclusive)} \\ &= 0.23 + 0.40 \\ &= 0.63 \\ P(B \text{ or } C) &= P(B) + P(C) - P(B)P(C) \quad \text{(by independence)} \\ &= 0.40 + 0.85 - (0.40)(0.85) \\ &= 0.91 \end{aligned}$$

Note that $P(A$ or $C)$ and $P(A$ and $C)$ cannot be determined using the information given. But it can be determined that A and C are *not* mutually exclusive since $P(A) + P(C) = 1.08$, which is greater than 1, and therefore cannot equal $P(A$ or $C)$; from this it follows that $P(A$ and $C) \geq 0.08$. One can also deduce that $P(A$ and $C) \leq P(A) = 0.23$, since $A \cap C$ is a subset of A, and that $P(A$ or $C) \geq P(C) = 0.85$ since C is a subset of $A \cup C$. Thus, one can conclude that $0.85 \leq P(A$ or $C) \leq 1$ and $0.08 \leq P(A$ and $C) \leq 0.23$.

B. Algebra

Algebra is based on the operations of arithmetic and on the concept of an *unknown quantity,* or *variable.* Letters such as x or n are used to represent unknown quantities. For example, suppose Pam has 5 more pencils than Fred. If F represents the number of pencils that Fred has, then the number of pencils that Pam has is $F + 5$. As another example, if Jim's present salary S is increased by 7%, then his new salary is $1.07S$. A combination of letters and arithmetic operations, such as $F + 5$, $\dfrac{3x^2}{2x - 5}$, and $19x^2 - 6x + 3$, is called an *algebraic expression.*

The expression $19x^2 - 6x + 3$ consists of the *terms* $19x^2, -6x$, and 3, where 19 is the *coefficient* of $x^2, -6$ is the coefficient of x^1, and 3 is a *constant term* (or coefficient of $x^0 = 1$). Such an expression is called a *second degree* (or *quadratic*) *polynomial in* x since the highest power of x is 2. The expression $F + 5$ is a *first degree* (or *linear*) *polynomial in* F since the highest power of F is 1. The expression $\dfrac{3x^2}{2x - 5}$ is not a polynomial because it is not a sum of terms that are each powers of x multiplied by coefficients.

1. SIMPLIFYING ALGEBRAIC EXPRESSIONS

Often when working with algebraic expressions, it is necessary to simplify them by factoring or combining *like* terms. For example, the expression $6x + 5x$ is equivalent to $(6 + 5)x$, or $11x$. In the expression $9x - 3y$, 3 is a factor common to both terms: $9x - 3y = 3(3x - y)$. In the expression $5x^2 + 6y$, there are no like terms and no common factors.

If there are common factors in the numerator and denominator of an expression, they can be divided out, provided that they are not equal to zero.

For example, if $x \neq 3$, then $\dfrac{x - 3}{x - 3}$ is equal to 1; therefore,

$$\begin{aligned} \frac{3xy - 9y}{x - 3} &= \frac{3y(x - 3)}{x - 3} \\ &= (3y)(1) \\ &= 3y. \end{aligned}$$

To multiply two algebraic expressions, each term of one expression is multiplied by each term of the other expression. For example:

$$(3x - 4)(9y + x) = 3x(9y + x) - 4(9y + x)$$
$$= (3x)(9y) + (3x)(x) + (-4)(9y) + (-4)(x)$$
$$= 27xy + 3x^2 - 36y - 4x$$

An algebraic expression can be evaluated by substituting values of the unknowns in the expression. For example, if $x = 3$ and $y = -2$, then $3xy - x^2 + y$ can be evaluated as

$$3(3)(-2) - (3)^2 + (-2) = -18 - 9 - 2 = -29.$$

2. EQUATIONS

A major focus of algebra is to solve equations involving algebraic expressions. Some examples of such equations are

$$5x - 2 = 9 - x \quad \text{(a linear equation with one unknown)}$$
$$3x + 1 = y - 2 \quad \text{(a linear equation with two unknowns)}$$
$$5x^2 + 3x - 2 = 7x \quad \text{(a quadratic equation with one unknown)}$$
$$\frac{x(x - 3)(x^2 + 5)}{x - 4} = 0$$

(an equation that is factored on one side with 0 on the other).

The *solutions* of an equation with one or more unknowns are those values that make the equation true, or "satisfy the equation," when they are substituted for the unknowns of the equation. An equation may have no solution or one or more solutions. If two or more equations are to be solved together, the solutions must satisfy all of the equations simultaneously.

Two equations having the same solution(s) are *equivalent equations*. For example, the equations

$$2 + x = 3$$
$$4 + 2x = 6$$

each have the unique solution $x = 1$. Note that the second equation is the first equation multiplied by 2. Similarly, the equations

$$3x - y = 6$$
$$6x - 2y = 12$$

have the same solutions, although in this case each equation has infinitely many solutions. If any value is assigned to x, then $3x - 6$ is a corresponding value for y that will satisfy both equations; for example, $x = 2$ and $y = 0$ is a solution to both equations, as is $x = 5$ and $y = 9$.

3. SOLVING LINEAR EQUATIONS WITH ONE UNKNOWN

To solve a linear equation with one unknown (that is, to find the value of the unknown that satisfies the equation), the unknown should be isolated on one side of the equation. This can be done by performing the same mathematical operations on both sides of the equation. Remember that if the same number is added to or subtracted from both sides of the equation, this does not change the equality; likewise, multiplying or dividing both sides by the same nonzero number does not change the equality. For example, to solve the equation $\dfrac{5x - 6}{3} = 4$ for x, the variable x can be isolated using the following steps:

$$\frac{5x - 6}{3} = 4$$
$$5x - 6 = 12 \quad \text{(multiplying by 3)}$$
$$5x = 12 + 6 = 18 \quad \text{(adding 6)}$$
$$x = \frac{18}{5} \quad \text{(dividing by 5)}$$

The solution, $\dfrac{18}{5}$, can be checked by substituting it for x in the original equation to determine whether it satisfies that equation:

$$\frac{5\left(\dfrac{18}{5}\right) - 6}{3} = \frac{18 - 6}{3} = \frac{12}{3} = 4.$$

Therefore, $x = \dfrac{18}{5}$ is the solution.

4. SOLVING TWO LINEAR EQUATIONS WITH TWO UNKNOWNS

For two linear equations with two unknowns, if the equations are equivalent, then there are infinitely many solutions to the equations, as illustrated at the end of Section B.2. If the equations are not equivalent, then they have either one unique solution or no solution. The latter case is illustrated by the two equations:

$$3x + 4y = 17$$
$$6x + 8y = 35$$

Note that $3x + 4y = 17$ implies $6x + 8y = 34$, which contradicts the second equation. Thus, no values of x and y can simultaneously satisfy both equations.

There are several methods of solving two linear equations in two unknowns. With any method, if a contradiction is reached, then the equations have no solution; if a trivial equation such as $0 = 0$ is reached, then the equations are equivalent and have infinitely many solutions. Otherwise, a unique solution can be found.

One way to solve for the two unknowns is to express one of the unknowns in terms of the other using one of the equations, and then substitute the expression into the remaining equation to obtain an equation with one unknown. This equation can be solved and the value of the unknown substituted into either of the original equations to find the value of the other unknown. For example, the following two equations can be solved for x and y.

$$(1) \quad 3x + 2y = 11$$
$$(2) \quad x - y = 2$$

In equation (2), $x = 2 + y$. Substitute $2 + y$ in equation (1) for x:

$$3(2 + y) + 2y = 11$$
$$6 + 3y + 2y = 11$$
$$6 + 5y = 11$$
$$5y = 5$$
$$y = 1$$

If $y = 1$, then $x = 2 + 1 = 3$.

There is another way to solve for x and y by eliminating one of the unknowns. This can be done by making the coefficients of one of the unknowns the same (disregarding the sign) in both equations and either adding the equations or subtracting one equation from the other. For example, to solve the equations

$$(1) \quad 6x + 5y = 29$$
$$(2) \quad 4x - 3y = -6$$

by this method, multiply equation (1) by 3 and equation (2) by 5 to get

$$18x + 15y = 87$$
$$20x - 15y = -30.$$

Adding the two equations eliminates y, yielding $38x = 57$, or $x = \dfrac{3}{2}$. Finally, substituting $\dfrac{3}{2}$ for x in one of the equations gives $y = 4$. These answers can be checked by substituting both values into both of the original equations.

5. SOLVING EQUATIONS BY FACTORING

Some equations can be solved by factoring. To do this, first add or subtract expressions to bring all the expressions to one side of the equation, with 0 on the other side. Then try to factor the nonzero side into a product of expressions. If this is possible, then using property (7) in Section A.4 each of the factors can be set equal to 0, yielding several simpler equations that possibly can be solved. The solutions of the simpler equations will be solutions of the factored equation. As an example, consider the equation $x^3 - 2x^2 + x = -5\,(x - 1)^2$:

$$x^3 - 2x^2 + x + 5(x - 1)^2 = 0$$
$$x(x^2 - 2x + 1) + 5(x - 1)^2 = 0$$
$$x(x - 1)^2 + 5(x - 1)^2 = 0$$
$$(x + 5)(x - 1)^2 = 0$$

$$x + 5 = 0 \quad \text{or} \quad (x - 1)^2 = 0$$
$$x = -5 \quad \text{or} \quad x = 1.$$

For another example, consider $\dfrac{x(x - 3)(x^2 + 5)}{x - 4} = 0$. A fraction equals 0 if and only if its numerator equals 0. Thus, $x(x - 3)(x^2 + 5) = 0$:

$$x = 0 \quad \text{or} \quad x - 3 = 0 \quad \text{or} \quad x^2 + 5 = 0$$
$$x = 0 \quad \text{or} \quad x = 3 \quad \text{or} \quad x^2 + 5 = 0.$$

But $x^2 + 5 = 0$ has no real solution since $x^2 + 5 > 0$ for every real number. Thus, the solutions are 0 and 3.

The solutions of an equation are also called the *roots* of the equation. These roots can be checked by substituting them into the original equation to determine whether they satisfy the equation.

6. SOLVING QUADRATIC EQUATIONS

The standard form for a *quadratic equation* is

$$ax^2 + bx + c = 0,$$

where a, b, and c are real numbers and $a \neq 0$; for example:

$$x^2 + 6x + 5 = 0,$$
$$3x^2 - 2x = 0, \text{ and}$$
$$x^2 + 4 = 0.$$

Some quadratic equations can easily be solved by factoring. For example:

(1) $x^2 + 6x + 5 = 0$
      $(x + 5)(x + 1) = 0$
      $x + 5 = 0 \text{ or } x + 1 = 0$
      $x = -5 \text{ or } x = -1$

(2) $3x^2 - 3 = 8x$
      $3x^2 - 8x - 3 = 0$
      $(3x + 1)(x - 3) = 0$
      $3x + 1 = 0 \text{ or } x - 3 = 0$
      $x = -\dfrac{1}{3} \text{ or } x = 3$

A quadratic equation has at most two real roots and may have just one or even no real root. For example, the equation $x^2 - 6x + 9 = 0$ can be expressed as $(x - 3)^2 = 0$, or $(x - 3)(x - 3) = 0$; thus the only root is 3. The equation $x^2 + 4 = 0$ has no real root; since the square of any real number is greater than or equal to zero, $x^2 + 4$ must be greater than zero.

An expression of the form $a^2 - b^2$ can be factored as $(a - b)(a + b)$.

For example, the quadratic equation $9x^2 - 25 = 0$ can be solved as follows.

$$(3x - 5)(3x + 5) = 0$$
$$3x - 5 = 0 \text{ or } 3x + 5 = 0$$
$$x = \frac{5}{3} \text{ or } x = -\frac{5}{3}$$

If a quadratic expression is not easily factored, then its roots can always be found using the *quadratic formula*: If $ax^2 + bx + c = 0$ $(a \neq 0)$, then the roots are

$$x = \frac{-b + \sqrt{b^2 - 4ac}}{2a} \quad \text{and} \quad x = \frac{-b - \sqrt{b^2 - 4ac}}{2a}.$$

These are two distinct real numbers unless $b^2 - 4ac \leq 0$. If $b^2 - 4ac = 0$; then these two expressions for x are equal to $-\dfrac{b}{2a}$, and the equation has only one root. If $b^2 - 4ac < 0$, then $\sqrt{b^2 - 4ac}$ is not a real number and the equation has no real roots.

To solve the quadratic equation $x^2 - 7x + 8 = 0$ using the graduate formula, note that $a = 1$, $b = -7$, and $c = 8$, and hence the roots are

$$x = \frac{7 + \sqrt{49 - 4(1)(8)}}{2(1)} = \frac{7 + \sqrt{17}}{2} \approx 5.6 \text{ and } x = \frac{7 - \sqrt{17}}{2} \approx 1.4.$$

7. EXPONENTS

A positive integer exponent of a number or a variable indicates a product, and the positive integer is the number of times that the number or variable is a factor in the product. For example, x^5 means $(x)(x)(x)(x)(x)$; that is, x is a factor in the product 5 times.

Some rules about exponents follow.

Let x and y be any positive numbers, and let r and s be any positive integers.

(1) $(x^r)(x^s) = x^{(r+s)}$; for example, $(2^2)(2^3) = 2^{(2+3)} = 2^5 = 32$.

(2) $\dfrac{x^r}{x^s} = x^{r-s}$; for example, $\dfrac{4^5}{4^2} = 4^{5-2} = 4^3 = 64$.

(3) $(x^r)(y^r) = (xy)^r$; for example, $(3^3)(4^3) = 12^3 = 1,728$.

(4) $\left(\dfrac{x}{y}\right)^r = \dfrac{x^r}{y^r}$; for example, $\left(\dfrac{2}{3}\right)^3 = \dfrac{2^3}{3^3} = \dfrac{8}{27}$.

(5) $(x^r)^s = x^{rs} = (x^s)^r$; for example, $(x^3)^4 = x^{12} = (x^4)^3$.

(6) $x^{-r} = \dfrac{1}{x^r}$; for example, $3^{-2} = \dfrac{1}{3^2} = \dfrac{1}{9}$.

(7) $x^0 = 1$; for example, $6^0 = 1$.

(8) $x^{\frac{r}{s}} = \left(x^{\frac{1}{s}}\right)^r = \left(x^r\right)^{\frac{1}{s}} = \sqrt[s]{x^r}$; for example, $8^{\frac{2}{3}} = \left(8^{\frac{1}{3}}\right)^2 = \left(8^2\right)^{\frac{1}{3}} = \sqrt[3]{8^2} = \sqrt[3]{64}$

$= 4$ and $9^{\frac{1}{2}} = \sqrt{9} = 3$.

It can be shown that rules 1-6 also apply when r and s are not integers and are not positive, that is, when r and s are any real numbers.

8. INEQUALITIES

An *inequality* is a statement that uses one of the following symbols:

$\neq$	not equal to
$>$	greater than
$\geq$	greater than or equal to
$<$	less than
$\leq$	less than or equal to

Some examples of inequalities are $5x - 3 < 9$, $6x \geq y$, and $\frac{1}{2} < \frac{3}{4}$. Solving a linear inequality with one unknown is similar to solving an equation; the unknown is isolated on one side of the inequality. As in solving an equation, the same number can be added to or subtracted from both sides of the inequality, or both sides of an inequality can be multiplied or divided by a positive number without changing the truth of the inequality. However, multiplying or dividing an inequality by a negative number reverses the order of the inequality. For example, $6 > 2$, but $(-1)(6) < (-1)(2)$.

To solve the inequality $3x - 2 > 5$ for x, isolate x by using the following steps:

$$3x - 2 > 5$$
$$3x > 7 \quad \text{(adding 2 to both sides)}$$
$$x > \frac{7}{3} \quad \text{(dividing both sides by 3)}$$

To solve the inequality $\frac{5x - 1}{-2} < 3$ for x, isolate x by using the following steps:

$$\frac{5x - 1}{-2} < 3$$
$$5x - 1 > -6 \quad \text{(multiplying both sides by } -2)$$
$$5x > -5 \quad \text{(adding 1 to both sides)}$$
$$x > -1 \quad \text{(dividing both sides by 5)}$$

9. ABSOLUTE VALUE

The absolute value of x, denoted $|x|$, is defined to be x if $x \geq 0$ and $-x$ if $x < 0$. Note that $\sqrt{x^2}$ denotes the nonnegative square root of x^2, and so $\sqrt{x^2} = |x|$.

10. FUNCTIONS

An algebraic expression in one variable can be used to define a *function* of that variable. A function is denoted by a letter such as f or g along with the variable in the expression. For example, the expression $x^3 - 5x^2 + 2$ defines a function f that can be denoted by

$$f(x) = x^3 - 5x^2 + 2.$$

The expression $\frac{2z + 7}{\sqrt{z + 1}}$ defines a function g that can be denoted by

$$g(z) = \frac{2z + 7}{\sqrt{z + 1}}.$$

The symbols "$f(x)$" or "$g(z)$" do not represent products; each is merely the symbol for an expression, and is read "f of x" or "g of z."

Function notation provides a short way of writing the result of substituting a value for a variable. If $x = 1$ is substituted in the first expression, the result can be written $f(1) = -2$, and $f(1)$ is called the "value of f at $x = 1$." Similarly, if $z = 0$ is substituted in the second expression, then the value of g at $z = 0$ is $g(0) = 7$.

Once a function $f(x)$ is defined, it is useful to think of the variable x as an input and $f(x)$ as the corresponding output. In any function there can be no more than one output for a given input. However, more than one input can give the same output; for example, if $h(x) = |x + 3|$, then $h(-4) = 1 = h(-2)$.

The set of all allowable inputs for a function is called the *domain* of the function. For f and g defined above, the domain of f is the set of all real numbers and the domain of g is the set of all numbers greater than -1. The domain of any function can be arbitrarily specified, as in the function defined by "$h(x) = 9x - 5$ for $0 \leq x \leq 10$." Without such a restriction, the domain is assumed to be all values of x that result in a real number when substituted into the function.

The domain of a function can consist of only the positive integers and possibly 0. For example,

$$a(n) = n^2 + \frac{n}{5} \text{ for } n = 0, 1, 2, 3, \ldots .$$

Such a function is called a *sequence* and $a(n)$ is denoted by a_n. The value of the sequence a_n at $n = 3$ is $a_3 = 3^2 + \frac{3}{5} = 9.6$. As another example, consider the sequence defined by $b_n = (-1)^n (n!)$ for $n = 1, 2, 3, \ldots .$ A sequence like this is often indicated by listing its values in the order $b_1, b_2, b_3, \ldots, b_n, \ldots$ as follows:

$$-1, 2, -6, \ldots, (-1)^n (n!), \ldots ,$$

and $(-1)^n (n!)$ is called the nth term of the sequence.

C. Geometry

1. LINES

In geometry, the word "line" refers to a straight line that extends without end in both directions.

The line above can be referred to as line PQ or line ℓ. The part of the line from P to Q is called a *line segment*. P and Q are the *endpoints* of the segment. The notation PQ is used to denote both the segment and the length of the segment. The intention of the notation can be determined from the context.

2. INTERSECTING LINES AND ANGLES

If two lines intersect, the opposite angles are called *vertical angles* and have the same measure. In the figure

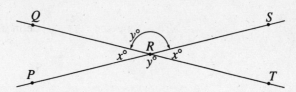

$\angle PRQ$ and $\angle SRT$ are vertical angles and $\angle QRS$ and $\angle PRT$ are vertical angles. Also, $x + y = 180$ since PRS is a straight line.

3. PERPENDICULAR LINES

An angle that has a measure of 90° is a *right angle*. If two lines intersect at right angles, the lines are *perpendicular*. For example:

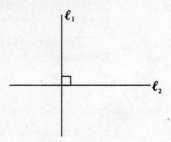

ℓ_1 and ℓ_2 above are perpendicular, denoted by $\ell_1 \perp \ell_2$. A right angle symbol in an angle of intersection indicates that the lines are perpendicular.

4. PARALLEL LINES

If two lines that are in the same plane do not intersect, the two lines are *parallel*. In the figure

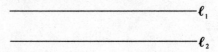

lines ℓ_1 and ℓ_2 are parallel, denoted by $\ell_1 \parallel \ell_2$. If two parallel lines are intersected by a third line, as shown below, then the angle measures are related as indicated, where $x + y = 180$.

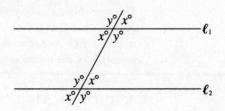

5. POLYGONS (CONVEX)

A *polygon* is a closed plane figure formed by three or more line segments, called the *sides* of the polygon. Each side intersects exactly two other sides at their endpoints. The points of intersection of the sides are *vertices*. The term "polygon" will be used to mean a convex polygon, that is, a polygon in which each interior angle has a measure of less than 180°.

The following figures are polygons:

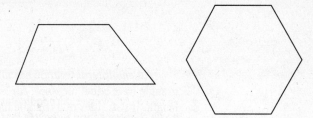

The following figures are not polygons:

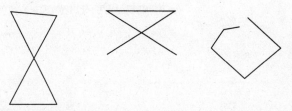

A polygon with three sides is a *triangle*; with four sides, a *quadrilateral*; with five sides, a *pentagon*; and with six sides, a *hexagon*.

The sum of the interior angle measures of a triangle is 180°. In general, the sum of the interior angle measures of a polygon with n sides is equal to $(n - 2)180°$. For example, this sum for a pentagon is $(5 - 2)180 = (3)180 = 540$ degrees.

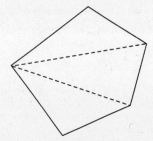

Note that a pentagon can be partitioned into three triangles and therefore the sum of the angle measures can be found by adding the sum of the angle measures of three triangles.

The *perimeter* of a polygon is the sum of the lengths of its sides.

The commonly used phrase "area of a triangle" (or any other plane figure) is used to mean the area of the region enclosed by that figure.

6. TRIANGLES

There are several special types of triangles with important properties. But one property that all triangles share is that the sum of the lengths of any two of the sides is greater than the length of the third side, as illustrated below.

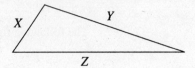

$$x + y > z, \quad x + z > y, \quad \text{and} \quad y + z > x.$$

An *equilateral* triangle has all sides of equal length. All angles of an equilateral triangle have equal measure. An *isosceles* triangle has at least two sides of the same length. If two sides of a triangle have the same length, then the two angles opposite those sides have the same measure. Conversely, if two angles of a triangle have the same measure, then the sides opposite those angles have the same length. In isoceles triangle PQR below, $x = y$ since $PQ = QR$.

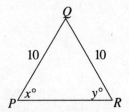

A triangle that has a right angle is a *right* triangle. In a right triangle, the side opposite the right angle is the *hypotenuse*, and the other two sides are the *legs*. An important theorem concerning right triangles is the *Pythagorean theorem*, which states: In a right triangle, the square of the length of the hypotenuse is equal to the sum of the squares of the lengths of the legs.

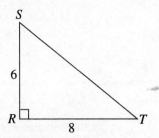

In the figure above, ΔRST is a right triangle, so $(RS)^2 + (RT)^2 = (ST)^2$. Here, $RS = 6$ and $RT = 8$, so $ST = 10$, since $6^2 + 8^2 = 36 + 64 = 100 = (ST)^2$ and $ST = \sqrt{100}$. Any triangle in which the lengths of the sides are in the ratio 3:4:5 is a right triangle. In general, if a, b, and c are the lengths of the sides of a triangle and $a^2 + b^2 = c^2$, then the triangle is a right triangle.

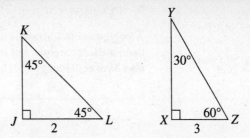

In 45°-45°-90° triangles, the lengths of the sides are in the ratio $1:1:\sqrt{2}$. For example, in $\triangle JKL$, if $JL = 2$, then $JK = 2$ and $KL = 2\sqrt{2}$. In 30°-60°-90° triangles, the lengths of the sides are in the ratio $1:\sqrt{3}:2$. For example, in $\triangle XYZ$, if $XZ = 3$, then $XY = 3\sqrt{3}$ and $YZ = 6$.

The *altitude* of a triangle is the segment drawn from a vertex perpendicular to the side opposite that vertex. Relative to that vertex and altitude, the opposite side is called the *base*.

The area of a triangle is equal to:

$$\frac{\text{(the length of the altitude)} \times \text{(the length of the base)}}{2}$$

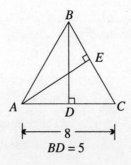

In $\triangle ABC$, BD is the altitude to base AC and AE is the altitude to base BC. The area of $\triangle ABC$ is equal to

$$\frac{BD \times AC}{2} = \frac{5 \times 8}{2} = 20.$$

The area is also equal to $\frac{AE \times BC}{2}$. If $\triangle ABC$ above is isosceles and $AB = BC$, then altitude BD bisects the base; that is, $AD = DC = 4$. Similarly, any altitude of an equilateral triangle bisects the side to which it is drawn.

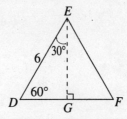

In equilateral triangle DEF, if $DE = 6$, then $DG = 3$ and $EG = 3\sqrt{3}$. The area of $\triangle DEF$ is equal to $\frac{3\sqrt{3} \times 6}{2} = 9\sqrt{3}$.

7. QUADRILATERALS

A polygon with four sides is a *quadrilateral*. A quadrilateral in which both pairs of opposite sides are parallel is a *parallelogram*. The opposite sides of a parallelogram also have equal length.

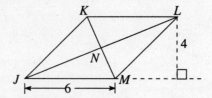

In parallelogram *JKLM*, *JK* ∥ *LM* and *JK* = *LM*; *KL* ∥ *JM* and *KL* = *JM*.

The diagonals of a parallelogram bisect each other (that is, *KN* = *NM* and *JN* = *NL*).

The area of a parallelogram is equal to

(the length of the altitude) × (the length of the base).

The area of *JKLM* is equal to $4 \times 6 = 24$.

A parallelogram with right angles is a *rectangle*, and a rectangle with all sides of equal length is a *square*.

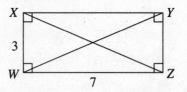

The perimeter of *WXYZ* = $2(3) + 2(7) = 20$ and the area of *WXYZ* is equal to $3 \times 7 = 21$. The diagonals of a rectangle are equal; therefore $WY = XZ = \sqrt{9 + 49} = \sqrt{58}$.

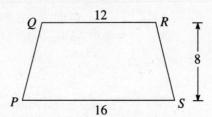

A quadrilateral with two sides that are parallel, as shown above, is a *trapezoid*. The area of trapezoid *PQRS* may be calculated as follows:

$$\frac{1}{2}(\text{sum of bases})(\text{height}) = \frac{1}{2}(QR + PS)(8) = \frac{1}{2}(28 \times 8) = 112.$$

8. CIRCLES

A *circle* is a set of points in a plane that are all located the same distance from a fixed point (the *center* of the circle).

A *chord* of a circle is a line segment that has its endpoints on the circle. A chord that passes through the center of the circle is a *diameter* of the circle. A *radius* of a circle is a segment from the center of the circle to a point on the circle. The words "diameter" and "radius" are also used to refer to the lengths of these segments.

The *circumference* of a circle is the distance around the circle. If r is the radius of the circle, then the circumference is equal to $2\pi r$, where π is approximately $\frac{22}{7}$ or 3.14. The *area* of a circle of radius r is equal to πr^2.

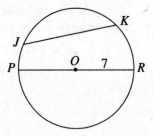

In the circle above, O is the center of the circle and JK and PR are chords. PR is a diameter and OR is a radius. If $OR = 7$, then the circumference of the circle is $2\pi(7) = 14\pi$ and the area of the circle is $\pi(7)^2 = 49\pi$.

The number of degrees of arc in a circle (or the number of degrees in a complete revolution) is 360.

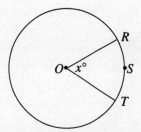

In the circle with center O above, the length of arc RST is $\frac{x}{360}$ of the circumference of the circle; for example, if $x = 60$, then arc RST has length $\frac{1}{6}$ of the circumference of the circle.

A line that has exactly one point in common with a circle is said to be *tangent* to the circle, and that common point is called the *point of tangency*. A radius or diameter with an endpoint at the point of tangency is perpendicular to the tangent line, and, conversely, a line that is perpendicular to a diameter at one of its endpoints is tangent to the circle at that endpoint.

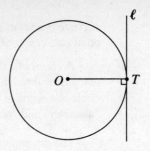

The line ℓ above is tangent to the circle and radius OT is perpendicular to ℓ.

If each vertex of a polygon lies on a circle, then the polygon is *inscribed* in the circle and the circle is *circumscribed* about the polygon. If each side of a polygon is tangent to a circle, then the polygon is *circumscribed* about the circle and the circle is *inscribed* in the polygon.

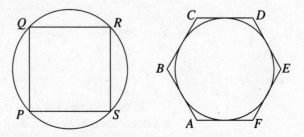

In the figure above, quadrilateral *PQRS* is inscribed in a circle and hexagon *ABCDEF* is circumscribed about a circle.

If a triangle is inscribed in a circle so that one of its sides is a diameter of the circle, then the triangle is a right triangle.

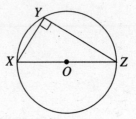

In the circle above, *XZ* is a diameter and the measure of $\angle XYZ$ is 90°.

9. RECTANGULAR SOLIDS AND CYLINDERS

A *rectangular solid* is a three-dimensional figure formed by six rectangular surfaces, as shown below. Each rectangular surface is a *face*. Each solid or dotted line segment is an *edge*, and each point at which the edges meet is a *vertex*. A rectangular solid has six faces, twelve edges, and eight vertices. Opposite faces are parallel rectangles that have the same dimensions. A rectangular solid in which all edges are of equal length is a *cube*.

The *surface area* of a rectangular solid is equal to the sum of the areas of all the faces. The *volume* is equal to

$$(\text{length}) \times (\text{width}) \times (\text{height});$$
in other words, (area of base) × (height).

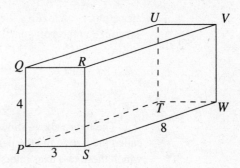

In the rectangular solid above, the dimensions are 3, 4, and 8. The surface area is equal to $2(3 \times 4) + 2(3 \times 8) + 2(4 \times 8) = 136$. The volume is equal to $3 \times 4 \times 8 = 96$.

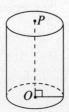

The figure above is a right circular *cylinder*. The two bases are circles of the same size with centers O and P, respectively, and altitude (height) OP is perpendicular to the bases. The surface area of a right circular cylinder with a base of radius r and height h is equal to $2(\pi r^2) + 2\pi rh$ (the sum of the areas of the two bases plus the area of the curved surface).

The volume of a cylinder is equal to $\pi r^2 h$, that is,

$$(\text{area of base}) \times (\text{height}).$$

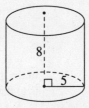

In the cylinder above, the surface area is equal to

$$2(25\pi) + 2\pi(5)(8) = 130\pi,$$

and the volume is equal to

$$25\pi(8) = 200\pi.$$

10. COORDINATE GEOMETRY

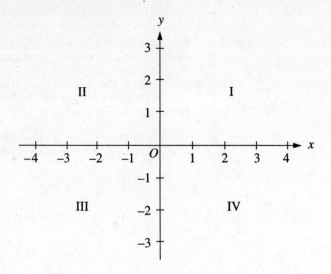

The figure above shows the (rectangular) *coordinate plane*. The horizontal line is called the *x-axis* and the perpendicular vertical line is called the *y-axis*. The point at which these two axes intersect, designated O, is called the *origin*. The axes divide the plane into four quadrants, I, II, III, and IV, as shown.

Each point in the plane has an *x-coordinate* and a *y-coordinate*. A point is identified by an ordered pair (x, y) of numbers in which the x-coordinate is the first number and the y-coordinate is the second number.

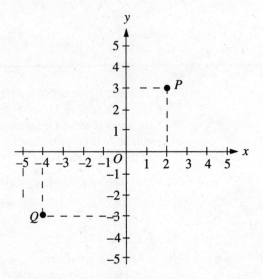

In the graph above, the (x, y) coordinates of point P are $(2, 3)$ since P is 2 units to the right of the y-axis (that is, $x = 2$) and 3 units above the x-axis (that is, $y = 3$). Similarly, the (x, y) coordinates of point Q are $(-4, -3)$. The origin O has coordinates $(0, 0)$.

One way to find the distance between two points in the coordinate plane is to use the Pythagorean theorem.

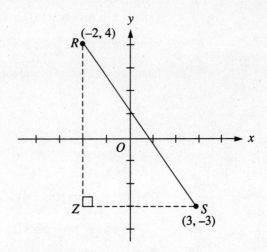

To find the distance between points R and S using the Pythagorean theorem, draw the triangle as shown. Note that Z has (x, y) coordinates $(-2, -3)$, $RZ = 7$, and $ZS = 5$. Therefore, the distance between R and S is equal to

$$\sqrt{7^2 + 5^2} = \sqrt{74}.$$

For a line in the coordinate plane, the coordinates of each point on the line satisfy a linear equation of the form $y = mx + b$ (or the form $x = a$ if the line is vertical).

For example, each point on the line below satisfies the equation $y = -\dfrac{1}{2}x + 1$. One can verify this for the points $(-2, 2)$, $(2, 0)$, and $(0, 1)$ by substituting the respective coordinates for x and y in the equation.

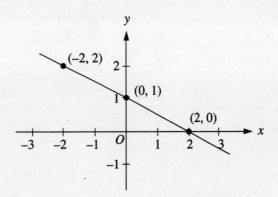

In the equation $y = mx + b$ of a line, the coefficient m is the *slope* of the line and the constant term b is the *y-intercept* of the line. For any two points on the line, the slope is defined to be the ratio of the difference in the y-coordinates to the difference in the x-coordinates. Using $(-2, 2)$ and $(2, 0)$ above, the slope is

$$\frac{\text{The difference in the } y\text{-coordinates}}{\text{The difference in the } x\text{-coordinates}} = \frac{0 - 2}{2 - (-2)} = \frac{-2}{4} = -\frac{1}{2}.$$

The y-intercept is the y-coordinate of the point at which the line intersects the y-axis. For the line above, the y-intercept is 1, and this is the resulting value of y when x is set equal to 0 in the equation $y = -\frac{1}{2}x + 1$. The *x-intercept* is the x-coordinate of the point at which the line intersects the x-axis. The x-intercept can be found by setting $y = 0$ and solving for x. For the line $y = -\frac{1}{2}x + 1$, this gives

$$-\frac{1}{2}x + 1 = 0$$

$$-\frac{1}{2}x = -1$$

$$x = 2.$$

Thus, the x-intercept is 2.

Given any two points (x_1, y_1) and (x_2, y_2) with $x_1 \neq x_2$, the equation of the line passing through these points can be found by applying the definition of slope. Since the slope is $m = \frac{y_2 - y_1}{x_2 - x_1}$, then using a point known to be on the line, say (x_1, y_1), any point (x, y) on the line must satisfy $\frac{y - y_1}{x - x_1} = m$, or $y - y_1 = m(x - x_1)$. (Using (x_2, y_2) as the known point would yield an equivalent equation.) For example, consider the points $(-2, 4)$ and $(3, -3)$ on the line below.

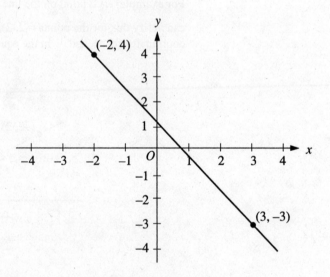

The slope of this line is $\frac{-3 - 4}{3 - (-2)} = \frac{-7}{5}$, so an equation of this line can be found using the point $(3, -3)$ as follows:

$$y - (-3) = -\frac{7}{5}(x - 3)$$

$$y + 3 = -\frac{7}{5}x + \frac{21}{5}$$

$$y = -\frac{7}{5}x + \frac{6}{5}.$$

The y-intercept is $\frac{6}{5}$. The *x-intercept* can be found as follows:

$$0 = -\frac{7}{5}x + \frac{6}{5}$$

$$\frac{7}{5}x = \frac{6}{5}$$

$$x = \frac{6}{7}.$$

Both of these intercepts can be seen on the graph.

If the slope of a line is negative, the line slants downward from left to right; if the slope is positive, the line slants upward. If the slope is 0, the line is horizontal; the equation of such a line is of the form $y = b$ since $m = 0$. For a vertical line, slope is not defined, and the equation is of the form $x = a$, where a is the x-intercept.

There is a connection between graphs of lines in the coordinate plane and solutions of two linear equations with two unknowns. If two linear equations with unknowns x and y have a unique solution, then the graphs of the equations are two lines that intersect in one point, which is the solution. If the equations are equivalent, then they represent the same line with infinitely many points or solutions. If the equations have no solution, then they represent parallel lines, which do not intersect.

There is also a connection between functions (see Section B.5) and the coordinate plane. If a function is graphed in the coordinate plane, the function can be understood in different and useful ways. Consider the function defined by

$$f(x) = -\frac{7}{5}x + \frac{6}{5}.$$

If the value of the function, $f(x)$, is equated with the variable y, then the graph of the function in the xy-coordinate plane is simply the graph of the equation

$$y = -\frac{7}{5}x + \frac{6}{5}$$

shown above. Similarly, any function $f(x)$ can be graphed by equating y with the value of the function:

$$y = f(x).$$

So for any x in the domain of the function f, the point with coordinates $(x, f(x))$ is on the graph of f, and the graph consists entirely of these points.

As another example, consider a quadratic polynomial function defined by $f(x) = x^2 - 1$. One can plot several points $(x, f(x))$ on the graph to understand the connection between a function and its graph:

x	$f(x)$
−2	3
−1	0
0	−1
1	0
2	3

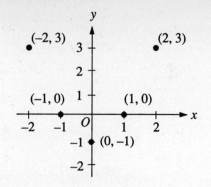

If all of the points were graphed for $-2 \le x \le 2$, then the graph would appear as follows.

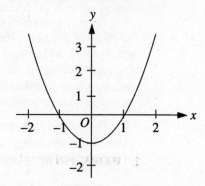

The graph of a quadratic function is called a *parabola* and always has the shape of the curve above, although it may be upside down or have a greater or lesser width. Note that the roots of the equation $f(x) = x^2 - 1 = 0$ are $x = 1$ and $x = -1$; these coincide with the x-intercepts since x-intercepts are found by setting $y = 0$ and solving for x. Also, the y-intercept is $f(0) = -1$ since this is the value of y corresponding to $x = 0$. For any function f, the x-intercepts are the solutions of the equation $f(x) = 0$ and the y-intercept is the value $f(0)$.

D. Word Problems

Many of the principles discussed in this chapter are used to solve word problems. The following discussion of word problems illustrates some of the techniques and concepts used in solving such problems.

1. RATE PROBLEMS

The distance that an object travels is equal to the product of the average speed at which it travels and the amount of time it takes to travel that distance, that is,

$$\text{Rate} \times \text{Time} = \text{Distance.}$$

Example 1: If a car travels at an average speed of 70 kilometers per hour for 4 hours, how many kilometers does it travel?

Solution: Since rate × time = distance, simply multiply 70 km/hour × 4 hours. Thus, the car travels 280 kilometers in 4 hours.

To determine the average rate at which an object travels, divide the total distance traveled by the total amount of traveling time.

Example 2: On a 400-mile trip, car X traveled half the distance at 40 miles per hour and the other half at 50 miles per hour. What was the average speed of car X?

Solution: First it is necessary to determine the amount of traveling time. During the first 200 miles, the car traveled at 40 mph; therefore, it took $\frac{200}{40} = 5$ hours to travel the first 200 miles. During the second 200 miles, the car traveled at 50 mph; therefore, it took $\frac{200}{50} = 4$ hours to travel the second 200 miles. Thus, the average speed of car X was $\frac{400}{9} = 44\frac{4}{9}$ mph. Note that the average speed is *not* $\frac{40+50}{2} = 45$.

Some rate problems can be solved by using ratios.

Example 3: If 5 shirts cost $44, then, at this rate, what is the cost of 8 shirts?

Solution: If c is the cost of the 8 shirts, then $\frac{5}{44} = \frac{8}{c}$. Cross multiplication results in the equation

$$5c = 8 \times 44 = 352$$
$$c = \frac{352}{5} = 70.40$$

The 8 shirts cost $70.40.

2. WORK PROBLEMS

In a work problem, the rates at which certain persons or machines work alone are usually given, and it is necessary to compute the rate at which they work together (or vice versa).

The basic formula for solving work problems is: $\frac{1}{r} + \frac{1}{s} = \frac{1}{h}$, where r and s are, for example, the number of hours it takes Rae and Sam, respectively, to complete a job when working alone, and h is the number of hours it takes Rae and Sam to do the job when working together. The reasoning is that in 1 hour Rae does $\frac{1}{r}$ of the job, Sam does $\frac{1}{s}$ of the job, and Rae and Sam together do $\frac{1}{h}$ of the job.

Example 1: If machine X can produce 1,000 bolts in 4 hours and machine Y can produce 1,000 bolts in 5 hours, in how many hours can machines X and Y, working together at these constant rates, produce 1,000 bolts?

Solution:
$$\frac{1}{4} + \frac{1}{5} = \frac{1}{h}$$
$$\frac{5}{20} + \frac{4}{20} = \frac{1}{h}$$
$$\frac{9}{20} = \frac{1}{h}$$
$$9h = 20$$
$$h = \frac{20}{9} = 2\frac{2}{9} \text{ hours}$$

Working together, machines X and Y can produce 1,000 bolts in $2\frac{2}{9}$ hours.

Example 2: If Art and Rita can do a job in 4 hours when working together at their respective constant rates and Art can do the job alone in 6 hours, in how many hours can Rita do the job alone?

Solution:

$$\frac{1}{6} + \frac{1}{R} = \frac{1}{4}$$

$$\frac{R+6}{6R} = \frac{1}{4}$$

$$4R + 24 = 6R$$

$$24 = 2R$$

$$12 = R$$

Working alone, Rita can do the job in 12 hours.

3. MIXTURE PROBLEMS

In mixture problems, substances with different characteristics are combined, and it is necessary to determine the characteristics of the resulting mixture.

Example 1: If 6 pounds of nuts that cost $1.20 per pound are mixed with 2 pounds of nuts that cost $1.60 per pound, what is the cost per pound of the mixture?

Solution: The total cost of the 8 pounds of nuts is

$$6(\$1.20) + 2(\$1.60) = \$10.40.$$

The cost per pound is $\dfrac{\$10.40}{8} = \$1.30.$

Example 2: How many liters of a solution that is 15 percent salt must be added to 5 liters of a solution that is 8 percent salt so that the resulting solution is 10 percent salt?

Solution: Let *n* represent the number of liters of the 15% solution. The amont of salt in the 15% solution [0.15*n*] plus the amount of salt in the 8% solution [(0.08)(5)] must be equal to the amount of salt in the 10% mixture [0.10 (*n* + 5)]. Therefore,

$$0.15n + 0.08(5) = 0.10(n + 5)$$

$$15n + 40 = 10n + 50$$

$$5n = 10$$

$$n = 2 \text{ liters.}$$

Two liters of the 15% salt solution must be added to the 8% solution to obtain the 10% solution.

4. INTEREST PROBLEMS

Interest can be computed in two basic ways. With simple annual interest, the interest is computed on the principal only and is equal to (principle) × (interest rate) × (time). If interest is compounded, then interest is computed on the principal as well as on any interest already earned.

Example 1: If $8,000 is invested at 6 percent simple annual interest, how much interest is earned after 3 months?

Solution: Since the annual interest rate is 6%, the interest for 1 year is

$(0.06)(\$8,000) = \$480.$ The interest earned in 3 months is $\dfrac{3}{12}(\$480) = \$120.$

Example 2: If $10,000 is invested at 10 percent annual interest, compounded semiannually, what is the balance after 1 year?

Solution: The balance after the first 6 months would be

10,000 + (10,000)(0.05) = 10,500 dollars. The balance after one year would be
10,500 + (10,500)(0.05) = 11,025 dollars.

Note that the interest rate for each 6-month period is 5%, which is half of the 10% annual rate. The balance after one year can also be expressed as

$$10,000 \left(1 + \frac{0.10}{2}\right)^2 \text{ dollars.}$$

5. DISCOUNT

If a price is discounted by n percent, then the price becomes $(100 - n)$ percent of the original price.

Example 1: A certain customer paid $24 for a dress. If that price represented a 25 percent discount on the original price of the dress, what was the original price of the dress?

Solution: If p is the original price of the dress, then $0.75p$ is the discounted price and $0.75p = 24, or $p = 32. The original price of the dress was $32.

Example 2: The price of an item is discounted by 20 percent and then this reduced price is discounted by an additional 30 percent. These two discounts are equal to an overall discount of what percent?

Solution: If p is the original price of the item, then $0.8p$ is the price after the first discount. The price after the second discount is $(0.7)(0.8)p = 0.56p$. This represents an overall discount of 44 percent (100% – 56%).

6. PROFIT

Gross profit is equal to revenues minus expenses, or selling price minus cost.

Example: A certain appliance costs a merchant $30. At what price should the merchant sell the appliance in order to make a gross profit of 50 percent of the cost of the appliance?

Solution: If s is the selling price of the appliance, then $s - 30 = (0.5)(30)$, or $s = 45. The merchant should sell the appliance for $45.

7. SETS

If S is the set of numbers 1, 2, 3, and 4, you can write $S = \{1, 2, 3, 4\}$. Sets can also be represented by Venn diagrams. That is, the relationship among the members of sets can be represented by circles.

Example 1: Each of 25 people is enrolled in history, mathematics, or both. If 20 are enrolled in history and 18 are enrolled in mathematics, how many are enrolled in both history and mathematics?

Solution: The 25 people can be divided into three sets: those who study history only, those who study mathematics only, and those who study history and mathematics. Thus a Venn diagram may be drawn as follows, where n is the number of people enrolled in both courses, $20 - n$ is the number enrolled in history only, and $18 - n$ is the number enrolled in mathematics only.

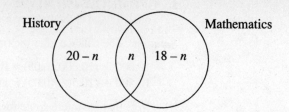

History   Mathematics

$20 - n$ n $18 - n$

Since there is a total of 25 people, $(20 - n) + n + (18 - n) = 25$, or $n = 13$. Thirteen people are enrolled in both history and mathematics. Note that $20 + 18 - 13 = 25$, which is the general addition rule for two sets.
(See Section A.9.)

Example 2: In a certain production lot, 40 percent of the toys are red and the remaining toys are green. Half of the toys are small and half are large. If 10 percent of the toys are red and small, and 40 toys are green and large, how many of the toys are red and large?

Solution: For this kind of problem, it is helpful to organize the information in a table:

	Red	Green	Total
Small	10%		50%
Large			50%
Total	40%	60%	100%

The numbers in the table are the percents given. The following percents can be computed on the basis of what is given:

	Red	Green	Total
Small	10%	40%	50%
Large	30%	20%	50%
Total	40%	60%	100%

Since 20% of the number of toys (n) are green and large, $0.20n = 40$ (40 toys are green and large), or $n = 200$. Therefore, 30% of the 200 toys, or $(0.3)(200) = 60$, are red and large.

8. GEOMETRY PROBLEMS

The following is an example of a word problem involving geometry.

Example:

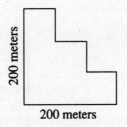

The figure above shows an aerial view of a piece of land. If all angles shown are right angles, what is the perimeter of the piece of land?

Solution: For reference, label the figure as

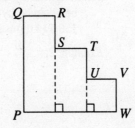

If all the angles are right angles, then $QR + ST + UV = PW$, and $RS + TU + VW = PQ$. Hence, the perimeter of the land is $2PW + 2PQ = 2 \times 200 + 2 \times 200 = 800$ meters.

9. MEASUREMENT PROBLEMS

Some questions on the GMAT involve metric units of measure, whereas others involve English units of measure. However, except for units of time, if a question requires conversion from one unit of measure to another, the relationship between those units will be given.

Example: A train travels at a constant rate of 25 meters per second. How many kilometers does it travel in 5 minutes? (1 kilometer = 1,000 meters)

Solution: In 1 minute the train travels (25)(60) = 1,500 meters, so in 5 minutes it travels 7,500 meters. Since 1 kilometer = 1,000 meters, it follows that 7,500 meters equals $\frac{7,500}{1,000}$, or 7.5 kilometers.

10. DATA INTERPRETATION

Occasionally a question or set of questions will be based on data provided in a table or graph. Some examples of tables and graphs are given below.

Example 1:

POPULATION BY AGE GROUP
(in thousands)

Age	Population
17 years and under	63,376
18-44 years	86,738
45-64 years	43,845
65 years and over	24,054

How many people are 44 years old or younger?

Solution: The figures in the table are given in thousands. The answer in thousands can be obtained by adding 63,376 thousand and 86,738 thousand. The result is 150,114 thousand, which is 150,114,000.

Example 2:

AVERAGE TEMPERATURE AND PRECIPITATION IN CITY *X*

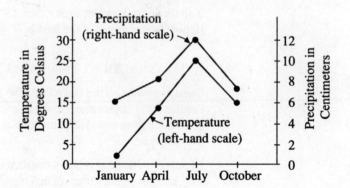

What are the average temperature and precipitation in City *X* during April?

Solution: Note that the scale on the left applies to the temperature line graph and the one on the right applies to the precipitation line graph. According to the graph, during April the average temperature is approximately 14° Celsius and the average precipitation is 8 centimenters.

Example 3:

DISTRIBUTION OF AL'S WEEKLY NET SALARY

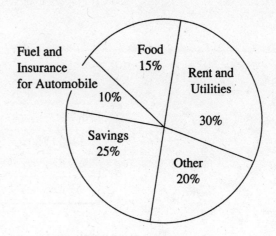

Weekly Net Salary: $350

To how many of the categories listed was at least $80 of Al's weekly net salary allocated?

Solution: In the circle, graph the relative sizes of the sectors are proportional to their corresponding values and the sum of the percents given is 100%. Note that $\frac{80}{350}$ is approximately 23%, so at least $80 was allocated to each of 2 categories — Rent and Utilities, and Savings — since their allocations are each greater than 23%.

3 Problem Solving

In these questions you are to solve each problem and select the best of the five answer choices given. The mathematics required to answer the questions does not extend beyond that assumed to be common to the mathematics background of all examinees.

The following pages include test-taking strategies, eight sample test sections (with answer keys), and detailed explanations of every problem on the sample test sections. These explanations present possible problem-solving strategies for the problems.

Test-Taking Strategies for Problem Solving

1. Pacing yourself is very important. Take a watch with you and consult it from time to time. Work as carefully as possible, but do not spend valuable time checking answers or pondering over problems that you find difficult. Make a check mark in your test book next to the troublesome problems or those problems you feel you should double-check. When you have completed the section, go back and spend the remaining time on those difficult problems. Remember, each question has the same weight.

2. Space is available in the test book for scratchwork. Working a problem out in writing may help you avoid errors in solving the problem. If diagrams or figures are not presented, it may help if your draw your own.

3. Read each question carefully to determine what information is given and what is being asked. For word problems, take one step at a time, reading each sentence carefully and translating the information into equations.

4. Before attempting to answer a question, scan the answer choices; otherwise you may waste time putting answers in a form that is not given (for example, putting an answer in the form $\frac{\sqrt{2}}{2}$ when the options are given in the form $\frac{1}{\sqrt{2}}$ or finding the answer in decimal form, such as 0.25, when the choices are given in fractional form, such as $\frac{1}{4}$).

5. For questions that require approximations, scan the answer choices to get some idea of the required closeness of approximation; otherwise, you may waste time on long computations where a short mental process would serve as well (for example, taking 48 percent of a number instead of half the number).

6. If you cannot solve a problem but you can eliminate some of the answer choices as being unlikely, you should guess. If the answer choices are equally plausible, you should not guess. Remember, a percentage of the wrong answers will be subtracted from the number of right answers to compensate for guessing, but the number of omitted questions will not be subtracted.

When you take the sample test sections, use the answer spaces on pages 61 and 62 to mark your answers.

Answer Spaces for Problem Solving Sample Test Sections

Sample Test Section 1

	A	B	C	D	E			A	B	C	D	E			A	B	C	D	E			A	B	C	D	E
1	Ⓐ	Ⓑ	Ⓒ	Ⓓ	Ⓔ		5	Ⓐ	Ⓑ	Ⓒ	Ⓓ	Ⓔ		9	Ⓐ	Ⓑ	Ⓒ	Ⓓ	Ⓔ		13	Ⓐ	Ⓑ	Ⓒ	Ⓓ	Ⓔ
2	Ⓐ	Ⓑ	Ⓒ	Ⓓ	Ⓔ		6	Ⓐ	Ⓑ	Ⓒ	Ⓓ	Ⓔ		10	Ⓐ	Ⓑ	Ⓒ	Ⓓ	Ⓔ		14	Ⓐ	Ⓑ	Ⓒ	Ⓓ	Ⓔ
3	Ⓐ	Ⓑ	Ⓒ	Ⓓ	Ⓔ		7	Ⓐ	Ⓑ	Ⓒ	Ⓓ	Ⓔ		11	Ⓐ	Ⓑ	Ⓒ	Ⓓ	Ⓔ		15	Ⓐ	Ⓑ	Ⓒ	Ⓓ	Ⓔ
4	Ⓐ	Ⓑ	Ⓒ	Ⓓ	Ⓔ		8	Ⓐ	Ⓑ	Ⓒ	Ⓓ	Ⓔ		12	Ⓐ	Ⓑ	Ⓒ	Ⓓ	Ⓔ		16	Ⓐ	Ⓑ	Ⓒ	Ⓓ	Ⓔ

Sample Test Section 2

	A	B	C	D	E			A	B	C	D	E			A	B	C	D	E			A	B	C	D	E
1	Ⓐ	Ⓑ	Ⓒ	Ⓓ	Ⓔ		5	Ⓐ	Ⓑ	Ⓒ	Ⓓ	Ⓔ		9	Ⓐ	Ⓑ	Ⓒ	Ⓓ	Ⓔ		13	Ⓐ	Ⓑ	Ⓒ	Ⓓ	Ⓔ
2	Ⓐ	Ⓑ	Ⓒ	Ⓓ	Ⓔ		6	Ⓐ	Ⓑ	Ⓒ	Ⓓ	Ⓔ		10	Ⓐ	Ⓑ	Ⓒ	Ⓓ	Ⓔ		14	Ⓐ	Ⓑ	Ⓒ	Ⓓ	Ⓔ
3	Ⓐ	Ⓑ	Ⓒ	Ⓓ	Ⓔ		7	Ⓐ	Ⓑ	Ⓒ	Ⓓ	Ⓔ		11	Ⓐ	Ⓑ	Ⓒ	Ⓓ	Ⓔ		15	Ⓐ	Ⓑ	Ⓒ	Ⓓ	Ⓔ
4	Ⓐ	Ⓑ	Ⓒ	Ⓓ	Ⓔ		8	Ⓐ	Ⓑ	Ⓒ	Ⓓ	Ⓔ		12	Ⓐ	Ⓑ	Ⓒ	Ⓓ	Ⓔ		16	Ⓐ	Ⓑ	Ⓒ	Ⓓ	Ⓔ

Sample Test Section 3

	A	B	C	D	E			A	B	C	D	E			A	B	C	D	E			A	B	C	D	E
1	Ⓐ	Ⓑ	Ⓒ	Ⓓ	Ⓔ		5	Ⓐ	Ⓑ	Ⓒ	Ⓓ	Ⓔ		9	Ⓐ	Ⓑ	Ⓒ	Ⓓ	Ⓔ		13	Ⓐ	Ⓑ	Ⓒ	Ⓓ	Ⓔ
2	Ⓐ	Ⓑ	Ⓒ	Ⓓ	Ⓔ		6	Ⓐ	Ⓑ	Ⓒ	Ⓓ	Ⓔ		10	Ⓐ	Ⓑ	Ⓒ	Ⓓ	Ⓔ		14	Ⓐ	Ⓑ	Ⓒ	Ⓓ	Ⓔ
3	Ⓐ	Ⓑ	Ⓒ	Ⓓ	Ⓔ		7	Ⓐ	Ⓑ	Ⓒ	Ⓓ	Ⓔ		11	Ⓐ	Ⓑ	Ⓒ	Ⓓ	Ⓔ		15	Ⓐ	Ⓑ	Ⓒ	Ⓓ	Ⓔ
4	Ⓐ	Ⓑ	Ⓒ	Ⓓ	Ⓔ		8	Ⓐ	Ⓑ	Ⓒ	Ⓓ	Ⓔ		12	Ⓐ	Ⓑ	Ⓒ	Ⓓ	Ⓔ		16	Ⓐ	Ⓑ	Ⓒ	Ⓓ	Ⓔ

Sample Test Section 4

	A	B	C	D	E			A	B	C	D	E			A	B	C	D	E			A	B	C	D	E
1	Ⓐ	Ⓑ	Ⓒ	Ⓓ	Ⓔ		5	Ⓐ	Ⓑ	Ⓒ	Ⓓ	Ⓔ		9	Ⓐ	Ⓑ	Ⓒ	Ⓓ	Ⓔ		13	Ⓐ	Ⓑ	Ⓒ	Ⓓ	Ⓔ
2	Ⓐ	Ⓑ	Ⓒ	Ⓓ	Ⓔ		6	Ⓐ	Ⓑ	Ⓒ	Ⓓ	Ⓔ		10	Ⓐ	Ⓑ	Ⓒ	Ⓓ	Ⓔ		14	Ⓐ	Ⓑ	Ⓒ	Ⓓ	Ⓔ
3	Ⓐ	Ⓑ	Ⓒ	Ⓓ	Ⓔ		7	Ⓐ	Ⓑ	Ⓒ	Ⓓ	Ⓔ		11	Ⓐ	Ⓑ	Ⓒ	Ⓓ	Ⓔ		15	Ⓐ	Ⓑ	Ⓒ	Ⓓ	Ⓔ
4	Ⓐ	Ⓑ	Ⓒ	Ⓓ	Ⓔ		8	Ⓐ	Ⓑ	Ⓒ	Ⓓ	Ⓔ		12	Ⓐ	Ⓑ	Ⓒ	Ⓓ	Ⓔ		16	Ⓐ	Ⓑ	Ⓒ	Ⓓ	Ⓔ

Sample Test Section 5

	A	B	C	D	E			A	B	C	D	E			A	B	C	D	E			A	B	C	D	E
1	Ⓐ	Ⓑ	Ⓒ	Ⓓ	Ⓔ		5	Ⓐ	Ⓑ	Ⓒ	Ⓓ	Ⓔ		9	Ⓐ	Ⓑ	Ⓒ	Ⓓ	Ⓔ		13	Ⓐ	Ⓑ	Ⓒ	Ⓓ	Ⓔ
2	Ⓐ	Ⓑ	Ⓒ	Ⓓ	Ⓔ		6	Ⓐ	Ⓑ	Ⓒ	Ⓓ	Ⓔ		10	Ⓐ	Ⓑ	Ⓒ	Ⓓ	Ⓔ		14	Ⓐ	Ⓑ	Ⓒ	Ⓓ	Ⓔ
3	Ⓐ	Ⓑ	Ⓒ	Ⓓ	Ⓔ		7	Ⓐ	Ⓑ	Ⓒ	Ⓓ	Ⓔ		11	Ⓐ	Ⓑ	Ⓒ	Ⓓ	Ⓔ		15	Ⓐ	Ⓑ	Ⓒ	Ⓓ	Ⓔ
4	Ⓐ	Ⓑ	Ⓒ	Ⓓ	Ⓔ		8	Ⓐ	Ⓑ	Ⓒ	Ⓓ	Ⓔ		12	Ⓐ	Ⓑ	Ⓒ	Ⓓ	Ⓔ		16	Ⓐ	Ⓑ	Ⓒ	Ⓓ	Ⓔ

Sample Test Section 6

1 Ⓐ Ⓑ Ⓒ Ⓓ Ⓔ   5 Ⓐ Ⓑ Ⓒ Ⓓ Ⓔ   9 Ⓐ Ⓑ Ⓒ Ⓓ Ⓔ   13 Ⓐ Ⓑ Ⓒ Ⓓ Ⓔ
2 Ⓐ Ⓑ Ⓒ Ⓓ Ⓔ   6 Ⓐ Ⓑ Ⓒ Ⓓ Ⓔ   10 Ⓐ Ⓑ Ⓒ Ⓓ Ⓔ   14 Ⓐ Ⓑ Ⓒ Ⓓ Ⓔ
3 Ⓐ Ⓑ Ⓒ Ⓓ Ⓔ   7 Ⓐ Ⓑ Ⓒ Ⓓ Ⓔ   11 Ⓐ Ⓑ Ⓒ Ⓓ Ⓔ   15 Ⓐ Ⓑ Ⓒ Ⓓ Ⓔ
4 Ⓐ Ⓑ Ⓒ Ⓓ Ⓔ   8 Ⓐ Ⓑ Ⓒ Ⓓ Ⓔ   12 Ⓐ Ⓑ Ⓒ Ⓓ Ⓔ   16 Ⓐ Ⓑ Ⓒ Ⓓ Ⓔ

Sample Test Section 7

1 Ⓐ Ⓑ Ⓒ Ⓓ Ⓔ   5 Ⓐ Ⓑ Ⓒ Ⓓ Ⓔ   9 Ⓐ Ⓑ Ⓒ Ⓓ Ⓔ   13 Ⓐ Ⓑ Ⓒ Ⓓ Ⓔ
2 Ⓐ Ⓑ Ⓒ Ⓓ Ⓔ   6 Ⓐ Ⓑ Ⓒ Ⓓ Ⓔ   10 Ⓐ Ⓑ Ⓒ Ⓓ Ⓔ   14 Ⓐ Ⓑ Ⓒ Ⓓ Ⓔ
3 Ⓐ Ⓑ Ⓒ Ⓓ Ⓔ   7 Ⓐ Ⓑ Ⓒ Ⓓ Ⓔ   11 Ⓐ Ⓑ Ⓒ Ⓓ Ⓔ   15 Ⓐ Ⓑ Ⓒ Ⓓ Ⓔ
4 Ⓐ Ⓑ Ⓒ Ⓓ Ⓔ   8 Ⓐ Ⓑ Ⓒ Ⓓ Ⓔ   12 Ⓐ Ⓑ Ⓒ Ⓓ Ⓔ   16 Ⓐ Ⓑ Ⓒ Ⓓ Ⓔ

Sample Test Section 8

1 Ⓐ Ⓑ Ⓒ Ⓓ Ⓔ   5 Ⓐ Ⓑ Ⓒ Ⓓ Ⓔ   9 Ⓐ Ⓑ Ⓒ Ⓓ Ⓔ   13 Ⓐ Ⓑ Ⓒ Ⓓ Ⓔ
2 Ⓐ Ⓑ Ⓒ Ⓓ Ⓔ   6 Ⓐ Ⓑ Ⓒ Ⓓ Ⓔ   10 Ⓐ Ⓑ Ⓒ Ⓓ Ⓔ   14 Ⓐ Ⓑ Ⓒ Ⓓ Ⓔ
3 Ⓐ Ⓑ Ⓒ Ⓓ Ⓔ   7 Ⓐ Ⓑ Ⓒ Ⓓ Ⓔ   11 Ⓐ Ⓑ Ⓒ Ⓓ Ⓔ   15 Ⓐ Ⓑ Ⓒ Ⓓ Ⓔ
4 Ⓐ Ⓑ Ⓒ Ⓓ Ⓔ   8 Ⓐ Ⓑ Ⓒ Ⓓ Ⓔ   12 Ⓐ Ⓑ Ⓒ Ⓓ Ⓔ   16 Ⓐ Ⓑ Ⓒ Ⓓ Ⓔ

Sample Test Section 9

1 Ⓐ Ⓑ Ⓒ Ⓓ Ⓔ   5 Ⓐ Ⓑ Ⓒ Ⓓ Ⓔ   9 Ⓐ Ⓑ Ⓒ Ⓓ Ⓔ   13 Ⓐ Ⓑ Ⓒ Ⓓ Ⓔ
2 Ⓐ Ⓑ Ⓒ Ⓓ Ⓔ   6 Ⓐ Ⓑ Ⓒ Ⓓ Ⓔ   10 Ⓐ Ⓑ Ⓒ Ⓓ Ⓔ   14 Ⓐ Ⓑ Ⓒ Ⓓ Ⓔ
3 Ⓐ Ⓑ Ⓒ Ⓓ Ⓔ   7 Ⓐ Ⓑ Ⓒ Ⓓ Ⓔ   11 Ⓐ Ⓑ Ⓒ Ⓓ Ⓔ   15 Ⓐ Ⓑ Ⓒ Ⓓ Ⓔ
4 Ⓐ Ⓑ Ⓒ Ⓓ Ⓔ   8 Ⓐ Ⓑ Ⓒ Ⓓ Ⓔ   12 Ⓐ Ⓑ Ⓒ Ⓓ Ⓔ   16 Ⓐ Ⓑ Ⓒ Ⓓ Ⓔ

Sample Test Section 10

1 Ⓐ Ⓑ Ⓒ Ⓓ Ⓔ   5 Ⓐ Ⓑ Ⓒ Ⓓ Ⓔ   9 Ⓐ Ⓑ Ⓒ Ⓓ Ⓔ   13 Ⓐ Ⓑ Ⓒ Ⓓ Ⓔ
2 Ⓐ Ⓑ Ⓒ Ⓓ Ⓔ   6 Ⓐ Ⓑ Ⓒ Ⓓ Ⓔ   10 Ⓐ Ⓑ Ⓒ Ⓓ Ⓔ   14 Ⓐ Ⓑ Ⓒ Ⓓ Ⓔ
3 Ⓐ Ⓑ Ⓒ Ⓓ Ⓔ   7 Ⓐ Ⓑ Ⓒ Ⓓ Ⓔ   11 Ⓐ Ⓑ Ⓒ Ⓓ Ⓔ   15 Ⓐ Ⓑ Ⓒ Ⓓ Ⓔ
4 Ⓐ Ⓑ Ⓒ Ⓓ Ⓔ   8 Ⓐ Ⓑ Ⓒ Ⓓ Ⓔ   12 Ⓐ Ⓑ Ⓒ Ⓓ Ⓔ   16 Ⓐ Ⓑ Ⓒ Ⓓ Ⓔ

PROBLEM SOLVING SAMPLE TEST SECTION 1

Time — 25 minutes

16 Questions

Directions: In this section solve each problem, using any available space on the page for scratchwork. Then indicate the best of the answer choices given.

Numbers: All numbers used are real numbers.

Figures: Figures that accompany problems in this section are intended to provide infomation useful in solving the problems. They are drawn as accurately as possible EXCEPT when it is stated in a specific problem that its figure is not drawn to scale. All figures lie in a plane unless otherwise indicated.

1. If Mario was 32 years old 8 years ago, how old was he x years ago?

(A) $x - 40$
(B) $x - 24$
(C) $40 - x$
(D) $24 - x$
(E) $24 + x$

2. Running at the same constant rate, 6 identical machines can produce a total of 270 bottles per minute. At this rate, how many bottles could 10 such machines produce in 4 minutes?

(A)   648
(B)   1,800
(C)   2,700
(D) 10,800
(E) 64,800

3. Three business partners, Q, R, and S, agree to divide their total profit for a certain year in the ratios $2 : 5 : 8$, respectively. If Q's share was $4,000, what was the total profit of the business partners for the year?

(A) $26,000
(B) $30,000
(C) $52,000
(D) $60,000
(E) $300,000

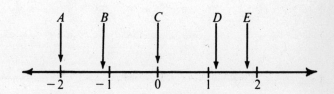

4. Of the five coordinates associated with points A, B, C, D, and E on the number line above, which has the greatest absolute value?

(A) A
(B) B
(C) C
(D) D
(E) E

GO ON TO THE NEXT PAGE.

5. A restaurant meal cost $35.50 and there was no tax. If the tip was more than 10 percent but less than 15 percent of the cost of the meal, then the total amount paid must have been between

(A) $40 and $42
(B) $39 and $41
(C) $38 and $40
(D) $37 and $39
(E) $36 and $37

6. Harriet wants to put up fencing around three sides of her rectangular yard and leave a side of 20 feet unfenced. If the yard has an area of 680 square feet, how many feet of fencing does she need?

(A) 34
(B) 40
(C) 68
(D) 88
(E) 102

7. If $u > t$, $r > q$, $s > t$, and $t > r$, which of the following must be true?

   I. $u > s$
  II. $s > q$
 III. $u > r$

(A) I only
(B) II only
(C) III only
(D) I and II
(E) II and III

8. Increasing the original price of an article by 15 percent and then increasing the new price by 15 percent is equivalent to increasing the original price by

(A) 32.25%
(B) 31.00%
(C) 30.25%
(D) 30.00%
(E) 22.50%

9. If k is an integer and 0.0010101×10^k is greater than 1,000, what is the least possible value of k ?

(A) 2
(B) 3
(C) 4
(D) 5
(E) 6

GO ON TO THE NEXT PAGE.

10. If $\left(b - 3\right)\left(4 + \dfrac{2}{b}\right) = 0$ and $b \neq 3$, then $b =$

(A) -8

(B) -2

(C) $-\dfrac{1}{2}$

(D) $\dfrac{1}{2}$

(E) 2

11. In a weight-lifting competition, the total weight of Joe's two lifts was 750 pounds. If twice the weight of his first lift was 300 pounds more than the weight of his second lift, what was the weight, in pounds, of his <u>first</u> lift?

(A) 225
(B) 275
(C) 325
(D) 350
(E) 400

12. One hour after Yolanda started walking from X to Y, a distance of 45 miles, Bob started walking along the same road from Y to X. If Yolanda's walking rate was 3 miles per hour and Bob's was 4 miles per hour, how many miles had Bob walked when they met?

(A) 24
(B) 23
(C) 22
(D) 21
(E) 19.5

13. The average (arithmetic mean) of 6 numbers is 8.5. When one number is discarded, the average of the remaining numbers becomes 7.2. What is the discarded number?

(A) 7.8
(B) 9.8
(C) 10.0
(D) 12.4
(E) 15.0

GO ON TO THE NEXT PAGE.

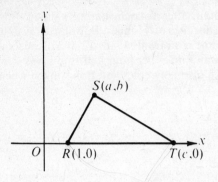

14. In the rectangular coordinate system above, the area of $\triangle RST$ is

(A) $\dfrac{bc}{2}$

(B) $\dfrac{b(c-1)}{2}$

(C) $\dfrac{c(b-1)}{2}$

(D) $\dfrac{a(c-1)}{2}$

(E) $\dfrac{c(a-1)}{2}$

15. Which of the following equations has a root in common with $x^2 - 6x + 5 = 0$?

(A) $x^2 + 1 = 0$
(B) $x^2 - x - 2 = 0$
(C) $x^2 - 10x - 5 = 0$
(D) $2x^2 - 2 = 0$
(E) $x^2 - 2x - 3 = 0$

16. One inlet pipe fills an empty tank in 5 hours. A second inlet pipe fills the same tank in 3 hours. If both pipes are used together, how long will it take to fill $\dfrac{2}{3}$ of the tank?

(A) $\dfrac{8}{15}$ hr

(B) $\dfrac{3}{4}$ hr

(C) $\dfrac{5}{4}$ hr

(D) $\dfrac{15}{8}$ hr

(E) $\dfrac{8}{3}$ hr

STOP

IF YOU FINISH BEFORE TIME IS CALLED, YOU MAY CHECK YOUR WORK ON THIS SECTION ONLY.
DO NOT TURN TO ANY OTHER SECTION IN THE TEST.

Answer Key for Sample Test Section 1

PROBLEM SOLVING

1.	C	9.	E
2.	B	10.	C
3.	B	11.	D
4.	A	12.	A
5.	B	13.	E
6.	D	14.	B
7.	E	15.	D
8.	A	16.	C

Explanatory Material: Problem Solving

The following discussion is intended to familiarize you with the most efficient and effective approaches to the kinds of problems common to Problem Solving. The questions on the sample tests in this chapter are generally representative of the kinds of problems you will encounter in this section of the GMAT. Remember that it is the problem-solving strategy that is important, not the specific details of a particular problem.

Sample Test Section 1

1. **If Mario was 32 years old 8 years ago, how old was he x years ago?**

   (A) $x - 40$
   (B) $x - 24$
   (C) $40 - x$
   (D) $24 - x$
   (E) $24 + x$

Since Mario was 32 years old 8 years ago, his age now is $32 + 8 = 40$. x years ago, Mario was x years younger, so his age then was $40 - x$. Thus, the best answer is C.

2. **Running at the same constant rate, 6 identical machines can produce a total of 270 bottles per minute. At this rate, how many bottles could 10 such machines produce in 4 minutes?**

   (A) 648
   (B) 1,800
   (C) 2,700
   (D) 10,800
   (E) 64,800

The production rate of each machine is $\frac{270}{6} = 45$ bottles per minute. The production rate for 10 machines is $45(10) = 450$ bottles per minute. Therefore, the 10 machines can produce $450(4) = 1,800$ bottles in 4 minutes. The best answer is B.

3. **Three business partners, Q, R, and S, agree to divide their total profit for a certain year in the ratios $2 : 5 : 8$, respectively. If Q's share was $4,000, what was the total profit of the business partners for the year?**

   (A) $26,000
   (B) $30,000
   (C) $52,000
   (D) $60,000
   (E) $300,000

Based on the ratios $2 : 5 : 8$, the total profit T was divided as follows: $\frac{2}{15}T$ was given to Q, $\frac{5}{15}T$ was given to R, and $\frac{8}{15}T$ was given to S. Since $\frac{2}{15}T = \$4,000$, $T = \frac{15}{2}(4,000) = \$30,000$.

Therefore, the best answer is B.

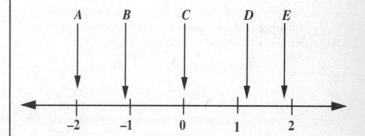

4. **Of the five coordinates associated with points A, B, C, D, and E on the number line above, which has the greatest absolute value?**

   (A) A
   (B) B
   (C) C
   (D) D
   (E) E

The absolute value of a number x may be thought of as the distance between x and 0 on the number line. By inspection of the five points, the coordinate of point A is farthest from 0 and thus has the greatest absolute value. Therefore, the best answer is A.

5. **A restaurant meal cost $35.50 and there was no tax. If the tip was more than 10 percent but less than 15 percent of the cost of the meal, then the total amount paid must have been between**

   (A) $40 and $42
   (B) $39 and $41
   (C) $38 and $40
   (D) $37 and $39
   (E) $36 and $37

If P is the total amount paid, then P must be greater than $\$35.50(1.1)$ but less than $\$35.50(1.15)$. That is, P is between $39.05 and $40.825. It follows that P must be between $39 and $41, which is choice B. Each of the other choices excludes a possible value of P. Thus, the best answer is B.

6. Harriet wants to put up fencing around three sides of her rectangular yard and leave a side of 20 feet unfenced. If the yard has an area of 680 square feet, how many feet of fencing does she need?

(A) 34
(B) 40
(C) 68
(D) 88
(E) 102

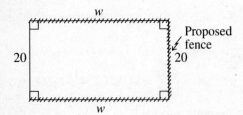

The diagram above shows the rectangular yard with the known dimension, 20 feet, and the unknown dimension, w feet. The area of the yard is $20w = 680$ square feet, so $w = \dfrac{680}{20} = 34$ feet. The length of fencing needed is then $34 + 20 + 34 = 88$ feet. Thus, the best answer is D.

7. If $u > t, r > q, s > t,$ and $t > r,$ which of the following must be true?

I. $u > s$
II. $s > q$
III. $u > r$

(A) I only
(B) II only
(C) III only
(D) I and II
(E) II and III

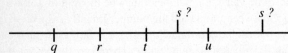

The number line shown above is based on the given inequalities and may be helpful when I, II, and III are considered.

    I. It may be that $q = 0, r = 1, t = 2, u = 3,$ and $s = 4,$ so that $u > s$ is not necessarily true.

    II. Since $s > t, t > r,$ and $r > q,$ it follows that $s > q.$

    III. Since $u > t$ and $t > r,$ it follows that $u > r.$

Since II and III must be true, the best answer is E.

8. Increasing the original price of an article by 15 percent and then increasing the new price by 15 percent is equivalent to increasing the original price by

(A) 32.25%
(B) 31.00%
(C) 30.25%
(D) 30.00%
(E) 22.50%

If p is the original price, then the 15 percent increase in price results in a price of $1.15p$. The next 15 percent increase in price results in a price of $1.15(1.15p)$, or $1.3225p$. Thus, the price increased by $1.3225p - p = 0.3225p$, or 32.25% of p. The best answer is A.

9. If k is an integer and 0.0010101×10^k is greater than 1,000, what is the least possible value of k ?

(A) 2
(B) 3
(C) 4
(D) 5
(E) 6

Since 0.0010101 is being multiplied by the kth power of 10, k is the number of decimal places that the decimal point in 0.0010101 will move to the right (if $k > 0$) in the product 0.0010101×10^k. By inspection, 6 is the least number of decimal places that the decimal point must move to the right in order for the product to be greater than 1,000. Thus, the best answer is E.

10. If $(b - 3)\left(4 + \dfrac{2}{b}\right) = 0$ and $b \neq 3,$ then $b =$

(A) -8

(B) -2

(C) $-\dfrac{1}{2}$

(D) $\dfrac{1}{2}$

(E) 2

Since $(b - 3)\left(4 + \dfrac{2}{b}\right) = 0$, it follows that either $b - 3 = 0$ or $4 + \dfrac{2}{b} = 0$. That is, either $b = 3$ or $b = -\dfrac{1}{2}$. But $b \neq 3$ is given, so $b = -\dfrac{1}{2}$, and the best answer is C.

11. In a weight-lifting competition, the total weight of Joe's two lifts was 750 pounds. If twice the weight of his first lift was 300 pounds more than the weight of his second lift, what was the weight, in pounds, of his <u>first</u> lift?

(A) 225
(B) 275
(C) 325
(D) 350
(E) 400

Let F and S be the weights, in pounds, of Joe's first and second lifts, respectively. Then $F + S = 750$ and $2F = S + 300$. The second equation may be written as $S = 2F - 300$, and $2F - 300$ may be substituted for S in the first equation to get $F + (2F - 300) = 750$. Thus, $3F = 1{,}050$, or $F = 350$ pounds, and the best answer is D.

12. One hour after Yolanda started walking from X to Y, a distance of 45 miles, Bob started walking along the same road from Y to X. If Yolanda's walking rate was 3 miles per hour and Bob's was 4 miles per hour, how many miles had Bob walked when they met?

(A) 24
(B) 23
(C) 22
(D) 21
(E) 19.5

Let t be the number of hours that Bob had walked when he met Yolanda. Then, when they met, Bob had walked $4t$ miles and Yolanda had walked $3(t + 1)$ miles. These distances must sum to 45 miles, so $4t + 3(t + 1) = 45$, which may be solved for t as follows.

$$4t + 3(t + 1) = 45$$
$$4t + 3t + 3 = 45$$
$$7t = 42$$
$$t = 6 \text{ (hours)}$$

Therefore, Bob had walked $4t = 4(6) = 24$ miles when they met. The best answer is A.

13. The average (arithmetic mean) of 6 numbers is 8.5. When one number is discarded, the average of the remaining numbers becomes 7.2. What is the discarded number?

(A) 7.8
(B) 9.8
(C) 10.0
(D) 12.4
(E) 15.0

The sum of the 6 numbers is $6(8.5) = 51.0$; the sum of the 5 remaining numbers is $5(7.2) = 36.0$. Thus, the discarded number must be $51.0 - 36.0 = 15.0$, and the best answer is E.

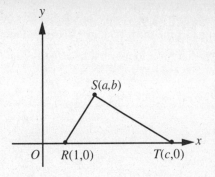

14. In the rectangular coordinate system above, the area of $\triangle RST$ is

(A) $\dfrac{bc}{2}$

(B) $\dfrac{b(c - 1)}{2}$

(C) $\dfrac{c(b - 1)}{2}$

(D) $\dfrac{a(c - 1)}{2}$

(E) $\dfrac{c(a - 1)}{2}$

If segment RT is chosen as the base of $\triangle RST$, then the height is b, the y-coordinate of point S. Since $RT = c - 1$ (the difference between the x-coordinates of R and T), the area of $\triangle RST$ is $\frac{1}{2}(RT)b = \frac{1}{2}(c - 1)b$, and the best answer is B.

15. Which of the following equations has a root in common with $x^2 - 6x + 5 = 0$?

(A) $x^2 + 1 = 0$
(B) $x^2 - x - 2 = 0$
(C) $x^2 - 10x - 5 = 0$
(D) $2x^2 - 2 = 0$
(E) $x^2 - 2x - 3 = 0$

Since $x^2 - 6x + 5 = (x - 5)(x - 1)$, the roots of $x^2 - 6x + 5 = 0$ are 1 and 5. When these two values are substituted in each of the five choices to determine whether or not they satisfy the equation, only in choice D does a value satisfy the equation, namely, $2(1)^2 - 2 = 0$. Thus, the best answer is D.

16. One inlet pipe fills an empty tank in 5 hours. A second inlet pipe fills the same tank in 3 hours. If both pipes are used together, how long will it take to fill $\frac{2}{3}$ of the tank?

(A) $\frac{8}{15}$ hr

(B) $\frac{3}{4}$ hr

(C) $\frac{5}{4}$ hr

(D) $\frac{15}{8}$ hr

(E) $\frac{8}{3}$ hr

Since the first pipe fills $\frac{1}{5}$ of the tank in one hour and the second pipe fills $\frac{1}{3}$ of the tank in one hour, together they fill $\frac{1}{5} + \frac{1}{3} = \frac{8}{15}$ of the tank in one hour. At this rate, if t is the number of hours needed to fill $\frac{2}{3}$ of the tank, then $\frac{8}{15}t = \frac{2}{3}$, or $t = \frac{2}{3}\left(\frac{15}{8}\right) = \frac{5}{4}$ hours. Thus, the best answer is C.

PROBLEM SOLVING SAMPLE TEST SECTION 2

Time — 25 minutes

16 Questions

<u>Directions:</u> In this section solve each problem, using any available space on the page for scratchwork. Then indicate the best of the answer choices given.

<u>Numbers:</u> All numbers used are real numbers.

<u>Figures:</u> Figures that accompany problems in this section are intended to provide infomation useful in solving the problems. They are drawn as accurately as possible EXCEPT when it is stated in a specific problem that its figure is not drawn to scale. All figures lie in a plane unless otherwise indicated.

1. During the first week of September, a shoe retailer sold 10 pairs of a certain style of oxfords at $35.00 a pair. If, during the second week of September, 15 pairs were sold at the sale price of $27.50 a pair, by what amount did the revenue from weekly sales of these oxfords increase during the second week?

   (A) $62.50
   (B) $75.00
   (C) $112.50
   (D) $137.50
   (E) $175.00

2. The number $2 - 0.5$ is how many times the number $1 - 0.5$?

   (A) 2
   (B) 2.5
   (C) 3
   (D) 3.5
   (E) 4

3. If $x = -1$, then $-(x^4 + x^3 + x^2 + x) =$

   (A) -10
   (B) -4
   (C) 0
   (D) 4
   (E) 10

4. Coins are dropped into a toll box so that the box is being filled at the rate of approximately 2 cubic feet per hour. If the empty rectangular box is 4 feet long, 4 feet wide, and 3 feet deep, approximately how many hours does it take to fill the box?

   (A) 4
   (B) 8
   (C) 16
   (D) 24
   (E) 48

5. $\left(\dfrac{1}{5}\right)^2 - \left(\dfrac{1}{5}\right)\left(\dfrac{1}{4}\right) =$

   (A) $-\dfrac{1}{20}$

   (B) $-\dfrac{1}{100}$

   (C) $\dfrac{1}{100}$

   (D) $\dfrac{1}{20}$

   (E) $\dfrac{1}{5}$

GO ON TO THE NEXT PAGE.

-71-

6. A club collected exactly $599 from its members. If each member contributed at least $12, what is the greatest number of members the club could have?

(A) 43
(B) 44
(C) 49
(D) 50
(E) 51

7. A union contract specifies a 6 percent salary increase plus a $450 bonus for each employee. For a certain employee, this is equivalent to an 8 percent salary increase. What was this employee's salary before the new contract?

(A) $21,500
(B) $22,500
(C) $23,500
(D) $24,300
(E) $25,000

8. If n is a positive integer and $k + 2 = 3^n$, which of the following could NOT be a value of k?

(A) 1
(B) 4
(C) 7
(D) 25
(E) 79

9. Elena purchased brand X pens for $4.00 apiece and brand Y pens for $2.80 apiece. If Elena purchased a total of 12 of these pens for $42.00, how many brand X pens did she purchase?

(A) 4
(B) 5
(C) 6
(D) 7
(E) 8

GO ON TO THE NEXT PAGE.

10. If the length and width of a rectangular garden plot were each increased by 20 percent, what would be the percent increase in the area of the plot?

(A) 20%
(B) 24%
(C) 36%
(D) 40%
(E) 44%

11. The population of a bacteria culture doubles every 2 minutes. Approximately how many minutes will it take for the population to grow from 1,000 to 500,000 bacteria?

(A) 10
(B) 12
(C) 14
(D) 16
(E) 18

12. When 10 is divided by the positive integer n, the remainder is $n - 4$. Which of the following could be the value of n?

(A) 3
(B) 4
(C) 7
(D) 8
(E) 12

13. For a light that has an intensity of 60 candles at its source, the intensity in candles, S, of the light at a point d feet from the source is given by the formula $S = \dfrac{60k}{d^2}$, where k is a constant. If the intensity of the light is 30 candles at a distance of 2 feet from the source, what is the intensity of the light at a distance of 20 feet from the source?

(A) $\dfrac{3}{10}$ candle

(B) $\dfrac{1}{2}$ candle

(C) $1\dfrac{1}{3}$ candles

(D) 2 candles

(E) 3 candles

GO ON TO THE NEXT PAGE.

14. If x and y are prime numbers, which of the following CANNOT be the sum of x and y?

(A) 5
(B) 9
(C) 13
(D) 16
(E) 23

15. Of the 3,600 employees of Company X, $\frac{1}{3}$ are clerical. If the clerical staff were to be reduced by $\frac{1}{3}$, what percent of the total number of the remaining employees would then be clerical?

(A) 25%
(B) 22.2%
(C) 20%
(D) 12.5%
(E) 11.1%

16. In which of the following pairs are the two numbers reciprocals of each other?

I. 3 and $\frac{1}{3}$

II. $\frac{1}{17}$ and $\frac{-1}{17}$

III. $\sqrt{3}$ and $\frac{\sqrt{3}}{3}$

(A) I only
(B) II only
(C) I and II
(D) I and III
(E) II and III

STOP

**IF YOU FINISH BEFORE TIME IS CALLED, YOU MAY CHECK YOUR WORK ON THIS SECTION ONLY.
DO NOT TURN TO ANY OTHER SECTION IN THE TEST.**

Answer Key for Sample Test Section 2

PROBLEM SOLVING

1. A	9. D
2. C	10. E
3. C	11. E
4. D	12. C
5. B	13. A
6. C	14. E
7. B	15. A
8. B	16. D

Explanatory Material:
Problem Solving Sample Test Section 2

1. During the first week of September, a shoe retailer sold 10 pairs of a certain style of oxfords at $35.00 a pair. If, during the second week of September, 15 pairs were sold at the sale price of $27.50 a pair, by what amount did the revenue from weekly sales of these oxfords increase during the second week?

   (A) $62.50
   (B) $75.00
   (C) $112.50
   (D) $137.50
   (E) $175.00

The total sales revenue from the oxfords during the first week was 10($35.00) = $350.00, and during the second week it was 15($27.50) = $412.50. Thus, the increase in sales revenue was $412.50 − $350.00 = $62.50, and the best answer is A.

2. The number $2 - 0.5$ is how many times the number $1 - 0.5$?

   (A) 2
   (B) 2.5
   (C) 3
   (D) 3.5
   (E) 4

Since $2 - 0.5 = 1.5$ and $1 - 0.5 = 0.5$, the number $2 - 0.5$ is $\frac{1.5}{0.5} = 3$ times the number $1 - 0.5$. Thus, the best answer is C.

3. If $x = -1$, then $-(x^4 + x^3 + x^2 + x) =$

   (A) −10
   (B) −4
   (C) 0
   (D) 4
   (E) 10

$-((-1)^4 + (-1)^3 + (-1)^2 + (-1)) = -(1 - 1 + 1 - 1) = -0 = 0$. The best answer is C.

4. Coins are dropped into a toll box so that the box is being filled at the rate of approximately 2 cubic feet per hour. If the empty rectangular box is 4 feet long, 4 feet wide, and 3 feet deep, approximately how many hours does it take to fill the box?

   (A) 4
   (B) 8
   (C) 16
   (D) 24
   (E) 48

The volume of the toll box is (4)(4)(3) = 48 cubic feet. Since the box is filled at the rate of 2 cubic feet per hour, it takes $\frac{48}{2} = 24$ hours to fill the box. Thus, the best answer is D.

5. $\left(\frac{1}{5}\right)^2 - \left(\frac{1}{5}\right)\left(\frac{1}{4}\right) =$

   (A) $-\frac{1}{20}$
   (B) $-\frac{1}{100}$
   (C) $\frac{1}{100}$
   (D) $\frac{1}{20}$
   (E) $\frac{1}{5}$

$\left(\frac{1}{5}\right)^2 - \left(\frac{1}{5}\right)\left(\frac{1}{4}\right) = \frac{1}{25} - \frac{1}{20} = \frac{4}{100} - \frac{5}{100} = -\frac{1}{100}$. Thus, the best answer is B.

6. A club collected exactly $599 from its members. If each member contributed at least $12, what is the greatest number of members the club could have?

   (A) 43
   (B) 44
   (C) 49
   (D) 50
   (E) 51

If n is the number of members in the club, then at least $12n$ dollars, but perhaps more, was contributed. Thus, $12n \leq 599$, or $n \leq \frac{599}{12} = 49\frac{11}{12}$. Since n is a whole number, the greatest possible value of n is 49. Therefore, the best answer is C.

-75-

7. A union contract specifies a 6 percent salary increase plus a \$450 bonus for each employee. For a certain employee, this is equivalent to an 8 percent salary increase. What was this employee's salary before the new contract?

(A) \$21,500
(B) \$22,500
(C) \$23,500
(D) \$24,300
(E) \$25,000

If S is the employee's salary before the new contract, then the increase in the employee's earnings is \$450 plus 6 percent of S, or $\$450 + 0.06S$. Since this increase is 8 percent of S, it follows that $\$450 + 0.06S = 0.08S$, or $0.02S = \$450$, so that $S = \dfrac{\$450}{0.02} = \$22,500$. Thus, the best answer is B.

8. If n is a positive integer and $k + 2 = 3^n$, which of the following could NOT be a value of k ?

(A) 1
(B) 4
(C) 7
(D) 25
(E) 79

As each of the choices is substituted for k, the sum $k + 2$ can be examined to determine whether or not it is a power of 3. The sums corresponding to A-E are 3, 6, 9, 27, and 81, respectively. Note that $3 = 3^1$, $9 = 3^2$, $27 = 3^3$, and $81 = 3^4$, but 6 is not a power of 3. So 4 cannot be a value of k, whereas 1, 7, 25, and 79 can be values of k. Thus, the best answer is B.

Alternatively, since any power of 3 must be odd, $k = 3^n - 2$ must also be odd and $k = 4$ is not possible.

9. Elena purchased brand X pens for \$4.00 apiece and brand Y pens for \$2.80 apiece. If Elena purchased a total of 12 of these pens for \$42.00, how many brand X pens did she purchase?

(A) 4
(B) 5
(C) 6
(D) 7
(E) 8

Let x denote the number of brand X pens Elena purchased. Then the number of brand Y pens she purchased was $12 - x$ and the total cost of the pens was $4x + 2.80(12 - x) = 42.00$ dollars. This equation can be solved as follows.

$$4x + 2.80(12 - x) = 42.00$$
$$4x + 33.60 - 2.80x = 42.00$$
$$1.20x = 8.40$$
$$x = 7$$

Thus, the best answer is D.

10. If the length and width of a rectangular garden plot were each increased by 20 percent, what would be the percent increase in the area of the plot?

(A) 20%
(B) 24%
(C) 36%
(D) 40%
(E) 44%

If the length and width are L and W, respectively, then the increased length and width are $1.2L$ and $1.2W$, respectively. Thus, the increased area is $(1.2L)(1.2W) = 1.44LW$, and the percent increase in area is 44%. The best answer is therefore E.

11. The population of a bacteria culture doubles every 2 minutes. Approximately how many minutes will it take for the population to grow from 1,000 to 500,000 bacteria?

(A) 10
(B) 12
(C) 14
(D) 16
(E) 18

After each successive 2-minute period, the bacteria population is 2,000, 4,000, 8,000, 16,000, 32,000, 64,000, 128,000, 256,000, and then 512,000. Therefore, after eight 2-minute periods, or 16 minutes, the population is only 256,000; and after nine 2-minute periods, or 18 minutes, the population is just over 500,000. Thus, the best answer is E.

Alternatively, if n denotes the number of 2-minute periods it takes for the population to grow from 1,000 to 500,000, then $2^n(1,000) = 500,000$, or $2^n = 500$. Since $2^4 = 16$, $2^8 = 16^2 = 256$, and $2^9 = 2(256) = 512$, the value of n is approximately 9. Thus, the approximate time is $2(9) = 18$ minutes.

12. When 10 is divided by the positive integer n, the remainder is $n - 4$. Which of the following could be the value of n ?

(A) 3
(B) 4
(C) 7
(D) 8
(E) 12

One way to answer the question is to examine each option to see which one satisfies the specified divisibility conditions. A: If $n = 3$, then $n - 4 = -1$; but 10 divided by 3 has remainder 1. B: If $n = 4$, then $n - 4 = 0$; but 10 divided by 4 has remainder 2. C: If $n = 7$, then $n - 4 = 3$, which does equal the remainder when 10 is divided by 7. That neither D nor E gives a possible value of n can be shown in the manner used for A and B. Thus, the best answer is C.

An alternative solution, which does not involve extensive checking of each option, is to first write the divisibility condition as the equation $10 = nq + (n - 4)$, where q denotes the quotient. Then,

$$14 = nq + n = n(q + 1),$$

so n must be a divisor of 14. Also, $n - 4 \geq 0$, or $n \geq 4$. Thus, $n = 7$ or $n = 14$.

13. For a light that has an intensity of 60 candles at its source, the intensity in candles, S, of the light at a point d feet from the source is given by the formula $S = \dfrac{60k}{d^2}$, where k is a constant. If the intensity of the light is 30 candles at a distance of 2 feet from the source, what is the intensity of the light at a distance of 20 feet from the source?

(A) $\dfrac{3}{10}$ candle

(B) $\dfrac{1}{2}$ candle

(C) $1\dfrac{1}{3}$ candles

(D) 2 candles

(E) 3 candles

In order to compute $S = \dfrac{60k}{d^2}$ when $d = 20$, the value of the constant k must be determined. Since $S = 30$ candles when $d = 2$ feet, substituting these values into the formula yields $30 = \dfrac{60k}{2^2}$, or $k = 2$. Therefore, when $d = 20$ feet, the intensity is $S = \dfrac{60(2)}{20^2} = \dfrac{120}{400} = \dfrac{3}{10}$ candle. Thus, the best answer is A.

14. If x and y are prime numbers, which of the following CANNOT be the sum of x and y ?

(A) 5
(B) 9
(C) 13
(D) 16
(E) 23

Note that $5 = 2 + 3$, $9 = 2 + 7$, $13 = 2 + 11$, and $16 = 5 + 11$, so that each of choices A-D may be expressed as a sum of two prime numbers. However, if $23 = x + y$, then either x or y (but not both) must be even. Since 2 is the only even prime number, either $x = 2$ and $y = 21$, or $x = 21$ and $y = 2$. Since 21 is not prime, 23 cannot be expressed as the sum of two prime numbers, and the best answer is E.

15. Of the 3,600 employees of Company X, $\dfrac{1}{3}$ are clerical. If the clerical staff were to be reduced by $\dfrac{1}{3}$, what percent of the total number of the remaining employees would then be clerical?

(A) 25%
(B) 22.2%
(C) 20%
(D) 12.5%
(E) 11.1%

The number of clerical employees is $\dfrac{1}{3}(3,600) = 1,200$. As a result of the proposed reduction, the number of clerical employees would be reduced by $\dfrac{1}{3}(1,200) = 400$ and consequently would equal $1,200 - 400 = 800$. The total number of employees would then be $3,600 - 400 = 3,200$. Hence, the percent of clerical employees would then be $\dfrac{800}{3,200} = \dfrac{1}{4} = 25\%$. Thus, the best answer is A.

16. In which of the following pairs are the two numbers reciprocals of each other?

I. 3 and $\dfrac{1}{3}$

II. $\dfrac{1}{17}$ and $\dfrac{-1}{17}$

III. $\sqrt{3}$ and $\dfrac{\sqrt{3}}{3}$

(A) I only
(B) II only
(C) I and II
(D) I and III
(E) II and III

Two numbers are reciprocals of each other if and only if their product is 1. Since $3\left(\dfrac{1}{3}\right) = 1$, $\left(\dfrac{1}{17}\right)\left(-\dfrac{1}{17}\right) = -\dfrac{1}{289} \neq 1$, and $\sqrt{3}\left(\dfrac{\sqrt{3}}{3}\right) = \dfrac{3}{3} = 1$, only in I and III are the two numbers reciprocals of each other. Thus, the best answer is D.

PROBLEM SOLVING SAMPLE TEST SECTION 3

Time — 25 minutes

16 Questions

Directions: In this section solve each problem, using any available space on the page for scratchwork. Then indicate the best of the answer choices given.

Numbers: All numbers used are real numbers.

Figures: Figures that accompany problems in this section are intended to provide information useful in solving the problems. They are drawn as accurately as possible EXCEPT when it is stated in a specific problem that its figure is not drawn to scale. All figures lie in a plane unless otherwise indicated.

1. What is 45 percent of $\frac{7}{12}$ of 240 ?

  (A) 63
  (B) 90
  (C) 108
  (D) 140
  (E) 311

2. If x books cost \$5 each and y books cost \$8 each, then the average (arithmetic mean) cost, in dollars per book, is equal to

  (A) $\dfrac{5x + 8y}{x + y}$

  (B) $\dfrac{5x + 8y}{xy}$

  (C) $\dfrac{5x + 8y}{13}$

  (D) $\dfrac{40xy}{x + y}$

  (E) $\dfrac{40xy}{13}$

GO ON TO THE NEXT PAGE.

3. If $\frac{1}{2}$ of the money in a certain trust fund was invested in stocks, $\frac{1}{4}$ in bonds, $\frac{1}{5}$ in a mutual fund, and the remaining $10,000 in a government certificate, what was the total amount of the trust fund?

(A) $100,000
(B) $150,000
(C) $200,000
(D) $500,000
(E) $2,000,000

4. Marion rented a car for $18.00 plus $0.10 per mile driven. Craig rented a car for $25.00 plus $0.05 per mile driven. If each drove d miles and each was charged exactly the same amount for the rental, then d equals

(A) 100
(B) 120
(C) 135
(D) 140
(E) 150

5. Machine A produces bolts at a uniform rate of 120 every 40 seconds, and machine B produces bolts at a uniform rate of 100 every 20 seconds. If the two machines run simultaneously, how many seconds will it take for them to produce a total of 200 bolts?

(A) 22
(B) 25
(C) 28
(D) 32
(E) 56

6. $\dfrac{3.003}{2.002} =$

(A) 1.05
(B) 1.50015
(C) 1.501
(D) 1.5015
(E) 1.5

GO ON TO THE NEXT PAGE.

Questions 7-9 refer to the following graph.

AVERAGE COSTS OF OPERATING SUBCOMPACT, COMPACT, AND
MIDSIZE CARS IN THE UNITED STATES, 1982–1986

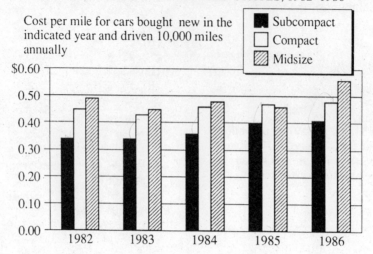

7. In 1982 the approximate average cost of operating a subcompact car for 10,000 miles was

(A) $360
(B) $3,400
(C) $4,100
(D) $4,500
(E) $4,900

8. In 1984 the average cost of operating a subcompact car was approximately what percent less than the average cost of operating a midsized car?

(A) 12%
(B) 20%
(C) 25%
(D) 33%
(E) 48%

9. For each of the years shown, the average cost per mile of operating a compact car minus the average cost per mile of operating a subcompact car was between

(A) $0.12 and $0.18
(B) $0.10 and $0.15
(C) $0.09 and $0.13
(D) $0.06 and $0.12
(E) $0.05 and $0.08

GO ON TO THE NEXT PAGE.

10. What is the decimal equivalent of $\left(\dfrac{1}{5}\right)^5$?

(A) 0.00032
(B) 0.0016
(C) 0.00625
(D) 0.008
(E) 0.03125

11. Two hundred gallons of fuel oil are purchased at $0.91 per gallon and are consumed at a rate of $0.70 worth of fuel per hour. At this rate, how many hours are required to consume the 200 gallons of fuel oil?

(A) 140
(B) 220
(C) 260
(D) 322
(E) 330

12. If $\dfrac{4 - x}{2 + x} = x$, what is the value of $x^2 + 3x - 4$?

(A) −4
(B) −1
(C) 0
(D) 1
(E) 2

13. If $b < 2$ and $2x - 3b = 0$, which of the following must be true?

(A) $x > -3$
(B) $x < 2$
(C) $x = 3$
(D) $x < 3$
(E) $x > 3$

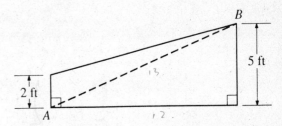

14. The trapezoid shown in the figure above represents a cross section of the rudder of a ship. If the distance from A to B is 13 feet, what is the area of the cross section of the rudder in square feet?

(A) 39
(B) 40
(C) 42
(D) 45
(E) 46.5

GO ON TO THE NEXT PAGE.

15. $\dfrac{(-1.5)(1.2) - (4.5)(0.4)}{30} =$

(A) -1.2
(B) -0.12
(C) 0
(D) 0.12
(E) 1.2

16. If n is a positive integer, then $n(n + 1)(n + 2)$ is

(A) even only when n is even
(B) even only when n is odd
(C) odd whenever n is odd
(D) divisible by 3 only when n is odd
(E) divisible by 4 whenever n is even

STOP

IF YOU FINISH BEFORE TIME IS CALLED, YOU MAY CHECK YOUR WORK ON THIS SECTION ONLY.
DO NOT TURN TO ANY OTHER SECTION IN THE TEST.

Answer Key for Sample Test Section 3

PROBLEM SOLVING

1. A	9. D
2. A	10. A
3. C	11. C
4. D	12. C
5. B	13. D
6. E	14. C
7. B	15. B
8. C	16. E

Explanatory Material:
Problem Solving Sample Test Section 3

1. What is 45 percent of $\frac{7}{12}$ of 240 ?

   (A) 63
   (B) 90
   (C) 108
   (D) 140
   (E) 311

Since 45 percent is $\frac{45}{100} = \frac{9}{20}$, 45 percent of $\frac{7}{12}$ of 240 is $\left(\frac{9}{20}\right)\left(\frac{7}{12}\right)(240) = 63$. The best answer is A.

2. If x books cost \$5 each and y books cost \$8 each, then the average (arithmetic mean) cost, in dollars per book, is equal to

   (A) $\dfrac{5x + 8y}{x + y}$

   (B) $\dfrac{5x + 8y}{xy}$

   (C) $\dfrac{5x + 8y}{13}$

   (D) $\dfrac{40xy}{x + y}$

   (E) $\dfrac{40xy}{13}$

The total number of books is $x + y$, and their total cost is $5x + 8y$ dollars. Therefore, the average cost per book is $\frac{5x + 8y}{x + y}$ dollars. The best answer is A.

3. If $\frac{1}{2}$ of the money in a certain trust fund was invested in stocks, $\frac{1}{4}$ in bonds, $\frac{1}{5}$ in a mutual fund, and the remaining \$10,000 in a government certificate, what was the total amount of the trust fund?

   (A) \$100,000
   (B) \$150,000
   (C) \$200,000
   (D) \$500,000
   (E) \$2,000,000

Since $\frac{1}{2} + \frac{1}{4} + \frac{1}{5} = \frac{19}{20}$, then $\frac{19}{20}$ of the trust fund was invested in stocks, bonds, and a mutual fund. Thus, if F is the dollar amount of the trust fund, the remaining $\frac{1}{20}$ of F is \$10,000. That is, $\frac{1}{20}F = \$10,000$, or $F = \$200,000$. The best answer is therefore C.

4. Marion rented a car for \$18.00 plus \$0.10 per mile driven. Craig rented a car for \$25.00 plus \$0.05 per mile driven. If each drove d miles and each was charged exactly the same amount for the rental, then d equals

   (A) 100
   (B) 120
   (C) 135
   (D) 140
   (E) 150

Marion's total rental charge was $18.00 + 0.10d$ dollars, and Craig's total rental charge was $25.00 + 0.05d$ dollars. Since these amounts are the same, $18.00 + 0.10d = 25.00 + 0.05d$, which implies $0.05d = 7.00$, or $d = \frac{7.00}{0.05} = 140$ miles. Thus, the best answer is D.

5. Machine A produces bolts at a uniform rate of 120 every 40 seconds, and machine B produces bolts at a uniform rate of 100 every 20 seconds. If the two machines run simultaneously, how many seconds will it take for them to produce a total of 200 bolts?

(A) 22
(B) 25
(C) 28
(D) 32
(E) 56

Machine A produces $\frac{120}{40} = 3$ bolts per second and machine B produces $\frac{100}{20} = 5$ bolts per second. Running simultaneously, they produce 8 bolts per second. At this rate, they will produce 200 bolts in $\frac{200}{8} = 25$ seconds. The best answer is therefore B.

6. $\frac{3.003}{2.002} =$

(A) 1.05
(B) 1.50015
(C) 1.501
(D) 1.5015
(E) 1.5

$\frac{3.003}{2.002} = \frac{3(1.001)}{2(1.001)} = \frac{3}{2} = 1.5$

The best answer is E.

Questions 7-9 refer to the following graph.

AVERAGE COSTS OF OPERATING SUBCOMPACT, COMPACT, AND MIDSIZE CARS IN THE UNITED STATES, 1982–1986

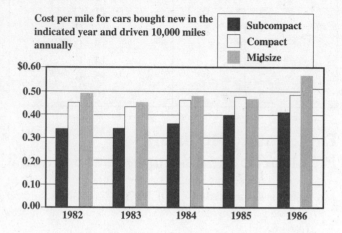

7. In 1982 the approximate average cost of operating a subcompact car for 10,000 miles was

(A) $360
(B) $3,400
(C) $4,100
(D) $4,500
(E) $4,900

According to the bar graph, the average cost per mile of operating a subcompact car in 1982 was about $0.34. Thus, the cost of operating the car for 10,000 miles was approximately $0.34(10,000) = $3,400. The best answer is B.

8. In 1984 the average cost of operating a subcompact car was approximately what percent less than the average cost of operating a midsized car?

(A) 12%
(B) 20%
(C) 25%
(D) 33%
(E) 48%

According to the bars shown for 1984, the average operating cost per mile for a subcompact car was approximately $0.36, or $0.12 less than the $0.48 per mile for a midsized car. Thus, in 1984 the operating cost for a subcompact car was approximately $\frac{0.12}{0.48} = 25\%$ less than the operating cost for a midsized car. The best answer is C.

9. For each of the years shown, the average cost per mile of operating a compact car minus the average cost per mile of operating a subcompact car was between

(A) $0.12 and $0.18
(B) $0.10 and $0.15
(C) $0.09 and $0.13
(D) $0.06 and $0.12
(E) $0.05 and $0.08

The differences in the average operating cost per mile between a subcompact car and a compact car may be estimated from the bar graph. For the consecutive years 1982-1986, the differences were approximately $0.11, $0.09, $0.10, $0.07, and $0.07, respectively. Only choice D gives a range that includes all of these amounts. Thus, the best answer is D.

Alternatively, inspection of the bar graph reveals that the largest difference was about $0.11 (in 1982) and the smallest difference was about $0.07 (in 1985 or 1986). Only choice D gives a range that includes these extreme values, and thus the differences for all five years.

10. What is the decimal equivalent of $\left(\dfrac{1}{5}\right)^5$?

(A) 0.00032
(B) 0.0016
(C) 0.00625
(D) 0.008
(E) 0.03125

$$\left(\frac{1}{5}\right)^5 = (0.2)^5 = (0.2)(0.2)(0.2)(0.2)(0.2) = 0.00032$$

The best answer is A.

11. Two hundred gallons of fuel oil are purchased at $0.91 per gallon and are consumed at a rate of $0.70 worth of fuel per hour. At this rate, how many hours are required to consume the 200 gallons of fuel oil?

(A) 140
(B) 220
(C) 260
(D) 322
(E) 330

The total worth of the 200 gallons of fuel oil is $0.91(200) = $182.00. The time required to consume the $182.00 worth of fuel at a rate of $0.70 worth of fuel per hour is $\dfrac{\$182.00}{\$0.70} = 260$ hours. Therefore, the best answer is C.

12. If $\dfrac{4-x}{2+x} = x$, what is the value of $x^2 + 3x - 4$?

(A) −4
(B) −1
(C) 0
(D) 1
(E) 2

Multiplying both sides of $\dfrac{4-x}{2+x} = x$ by $2 + x$ yields

$4 - x = x(2 + x) = 2x + x^2$, or $x^2 + 3x - 4 = 0$. Thus, the value of $x^2 + 3x - 4$ is 0, and the best answer is C.

13. If $b < 2$ and $2x - 3b = 0$, which of the following must be true?

(A) $x > -3$
(B) $x < 2$
(C) $x = 3$
(D) $x < 3$
(E) $x > 3$

It follows from $2x - 3b = 0$ that $b = \dfrac{2}{3}x$. So $b < 2$ implies

$\dfrac{2}{3}x < 2$, or $x < 2\left(\dfrac{3}{2}\right)$, which means $x < 3$ (choice D). Since

none of the other choices must be true (although $x > -3$ and $x < 2$ could be true), the best answer is D.

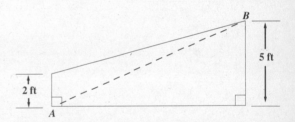

14. The trapezoid shown in the figure above represents a cross section of the rudder of a ship. If the distance from A to B is 13 feet, what is the area of the cross section of the rudder in square feet?

(A) 39
(B) 40
(C) 42
(D) 45
(E) 46.5

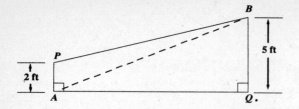

From the figure above, the area of the trapezoidal cross section is $\frac{1}{2}(AP + BQ)(AQ) = \frac{1}{2}(2 + 5)(AQ) = \frac{7}{2}(AQ)$. Since $AB = 13$ feet, using the Pythagorean theorem,

$AQ = \sqrt{13^2 - 5^2} = \sqrt{144} = 12$ feet. Thus, the area is

$\frac{7}{2}(12) = 42$ square feet, and the best answer is C.

Alternatively, the areas of the two triangles may be added together. If AP is taken as the base of $\triangle APB$ and BQ is taken as the base of $\triangle BQA$, then the height of both triangles is AQ. Thus, the area of the trapezoid is

$\frac{1}{2}(AP)(AQ) + \frac{1}{2}(BQ)(AQ) = \frac{1}{2}(2)(12) + \frac{1}{2}(5)(12) = 42$

square feet.

15. $\dfrac{(-1.5)(1.2) - (4.5)(0.4)}{30} =$

   (A) −1.2
   (B) −0.12
   (C) 0
   (D) 0.12
   (E) 1.2

One way to reduce the expression is

$\dfrac{(-1.5)(1.2) - (4.5)(0.4)}{30} = \dfrac{-1.80 - 1.80}{30} = \dfrac{-3.60}{30} = -0.12.$

Another way is

$\dfrac{(-1.5)(1.2) - (4.5)(0.4)}{30} = -\dfrac{15(12) + 45(4)}{3,000} = -\dfrac{12 + 3(4)}{200}$

$= -\dfrac{24}{200} = -\dfrac{12}{100} = -0.12.$

The best answer is B.

16. If n is a positive integer, then $n(n + 1)(n + 2)$ is

   (A) even only when n is even
   (B) even only when n is odd
   (C) odd whenever n is odd
   (D) divisible by 3 only when n is odd
   (E) divisible by 4 whenever n is even

If n is a positive integer, then either n is even or n is odd (and thus $n + 1$ is even). In either case, the product $n(n + 1)(n + 2)$ is even. Thus, each of choices A, B, and C is false. Since $n(n + 1)(n + 2)$ is divisible by 3 when n is 6 (or any even multiple of 3), choice D is false. If n is even, then $n + 2$ is even as well; thus, $n(n + 1)(n + 2)$ is divisible by 4 since even numbers are divisible by 2. The best answer is therefore E.

PROBLEM SOLVING SAMPLE TEST SECTION 4

Time — 25 minutes

16 Questions

Directions: In this section solve each problem, using any available space on the page for scratchwork. Then indicate the best of the answer choices given.

Numbers: All numbers used are real numbers.

Figures: Figures that accompany problems in this section are intended to provide information useful in solving the problems. They are drawn as accurately as possible EXCEPT when it is stated in a specific problem that its figure is not drawn to scale. All figures lie in a plane unless otherwise indicated.

1. If Jack had twice the amount of money that he has, he would have exactly the amount necessary to buy 3 hamburgers at $0.96 apiece and 2 milk shakes at $1.28 apiece. How much money does Jack have?

(A) $1.60
(B) $2.24
(C) $2.72
(D) $3.36
(E) $5.44

2. If a photocopier makes 2 copies in $\frac{1}{3}$ second, then, at the same rate, how many copies does it make in 4 minutes?

(A) 360
(B) 480
(C) 576
(D) 720
(E) 1,440

3. The price of a certain television set is discounted by 10 percent, and the reduced price is then discounted by 10 percent. This series of successive discounts is equivalent to a single discount of

(A) 20%
(B) 19%
(C) 18%
(D) 11%
(E) 10%

4. If $\dfrac{2}{1 + \dfrac{2}{y}} = 1$, then $y =$

(A) -2

(B) $-\dfrac{1}{2}$

(C) $\dfrac{1}{2}$

(D) 2

(E) 3

GO ON TO THE NEXT PAGE.

5. If a rectangular photograph that is 10 inches wide by 15 inches long is to be enlarged so that the width will be 22 inches and the ratio of width to length will be unchanged, then the length, in inches, of the enlarged photograph will be

(A) 33
(B) 32
(C) 30
(D) 27
(E) 25

6. If m is an integer such that $(-2)^{2m} = 2^{9-m}$, then $m =$

(A) 1
(B) 2
(C) 3
(D) 4
(E) 6

7. If $0 \leqq x \leqq 4$ and $y < 12$, which of the following CANNOT be the value of xy?

(A) -2
(B) 0
(C) 6
(D) 24
(E) 48

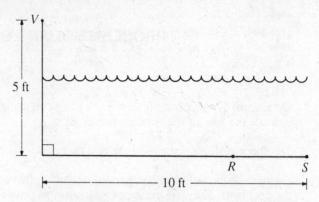

8. In the figure above, V represents an observation point at one end of a pool. From V, an object that is actually located on the bottom of the pool at point R appears to be at point S. If $VR = 10$ feet, what is the distance RS, in feet, between the actual position and the perceived position of the object?

(A) $10 - 5\sqrt{3}$

(B) $10 - 5\sqrt{2}$

(C) 2

(D) $2\frac{1}{2}$

(E) 4

GO ON TO THE NEXT PAGE.

-88-

9. If the total payroll expense of a certain business in year Y was \$84,000, which was 20 percent more than in year X, what was the total payroll expense in year X?

(A) \$70,000
(B) \$68,320
(C) \$64,000
(D) \$60,000
(E) \$52,320

10. If a, b, and c are consecutive positive integers and $a < b < c$, which of the following must be true?

   I. $c - a = 2$

   II. abc is an even integer.

   III. $\dfrac{a + b + c}{3}$ is an integer.

(A) I only
(B) II only
(C) I and II only
(D) II and III only
(E) I, II, and III

11. A straight pipe 1 yard in length was marked off in fourths and also in thirds. If the pipe was then cut into separate pieces at each of these markings, which of the following gives all the different lengths of the pieces, in fractions of a yard?

(A) $\dfrac{1}{6}$ and $\dfrac{1}{4}$ only

(B) $\dfrac{1}{4}$ and $\dfrac{1}{3}$ only

(C) $\dfrac{1}{6}$, $\dfrac{1}{4}$, and $\dfrac{1}{3}$

(D) $\dfrac{1}{12}$, $\dfrac{1}{6}$, and $\dfrac{1}{4}$

(E) $\dfrac{1}{12}$, $\dfrac{1}{6}$, and $\dfrac{1}{3}$

12. What is the least integer that is a sum of three different primes each greater than 20?

(A) 69
(B) 73
(C) 75
(D) 79
(E) 83

13. A tourist purchased a total of \$1,500 worth of traveler's checks in \$10 and \$50 denominations. During the trip the tourist cashed 7 checks and then lost all of the rest. If the number of \$10 checks cashed was one more or one less than the number of \$50 checks cashed, what is the minimum possible value of the checks that were lost?

(A) \$1,430
(B) \$1,310
(C) \$1,290
(D) \$1,270
(E) \$1,150

GO ON TO THE NEXT PAGE.

-89-

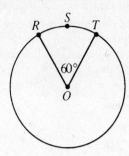

14. If the circle above has center O and circumference 18π, then the perimeter of sector $RSTO$ is

(A) $3\pi + 9$
(B) $3\pi + 18$
(C) $6\pi + 9$
(D) $6\pi + 18$
(E) $6\pi + 24$

15. If each of the following fractions were written as a repeating decimal, which would have the longest sequence of different digits?

(A) $\dfrac{2}{11}$

(B) $\dfrac{1}{3}$

(C) $\dfrac{41}{99}$

(D) $\dfrac{2}{3}$

(E) $\dfrac{23}{37}$

16. Today Rose is twice as old as Sam and Sam is 3 years younger than Tina. If Rose, Sam, and Tina are all alive 4 years from today, which of the following must be true on that day?

   I. Rose is twice as old as Sam.
  II. Sam is 3 years younger than Tina.
 III. Rose is older than Tina.

(A) I only
(B) II only
(C) III only
(D) I and II
(E) II and III

STOP

IF YOU FINISH BEFORE TIME IS CALLED, YOU MAY CHECK YOUR WORK ON THIS SECTION ONLY.
DO NOT TURN TO ANY OTHER SECTION IN THE TEST.

PROBLEM SOLVING

1. C	9. A
2. E	10. E
3. B	11. D
4. D	12. E
5. A	13. D
6. C	14. B
7. E	15. E
8. A	16. B

Explanatory Material:
Problem Solving Sample Test Section 4

1. If Jack had twice the amount of money that he has, he would have exactly the amount necessary to buy 3 hamburgers at $0.96 apiece and 2 milk shakes at $1.28 apiece. How much money does Jack have?

   (A) $1.60
   (B) $2.24
   (C) $2.72
   (D) $3.36
   (E) $5.44

Let J be the amount of money Jack has. Then

$2J = 3(\$0.96) + 2(\$1.28) = \$5.44$. So $J = \frac{1}{2}(\$5.44) = \$2.72$,

and the best answer is C.

2. If a photocopier makes 2 copies in $\frac{1}{3}$ second, then, at the same rate, how many copies does it make in 4 minutes?

   (A)   360
   (B)   480
   (C)   576
   (D)   720
   (E) 1,440

The photocopier makes copies at the rate of 2 copies in $\frac{1}{3}$

second, or 6 copies per second. Since 4 minutes equals 240 seconds, the photocopier makes $6(240) = 1,440$ copies in 4 minutes. Therefore, the best answer is E.

3. The price of a certain television set is discounted by 10 percent, and the reduced price is then discounted by 10 percent. This series of successive discounts is equivalent to a single discount of

   (A) 20%
   (B) 19%
   (C) 18%
   (D) 11%
   (E) 10%

If P is the original price of the television set, then $0.9P$ is the price after the first discount, and $0.9(0.9P) = 0.81P$ is the price after the second discount. Thus, the original price is discounted by 19% (100% – 81%), and the best answer is B.

4. If $\dfrac{2}{1+\dfrac{2}{y}} = 1$, then $y =$

   (A)   –2

   (B) $-\dfrac{1}{2}$

   (C) $\dfrac{1}{2}$

   (D)   2

   (E)   3

Since $\dfrac{2}{1+\dfrac{2}{y}} = 1$, $1 + \dfrac{2}{y} = 2$. Thus, $\dfrac{2}{y} = 1$, or $y = 2$, and the best

answer is D.

5. If a rectangular photograph that is 10 inches wide by 15 inches long is to be enlarged so that the width will be 22 inches and the ratio of width to length will be unchanged, then the length, in inches, of the enlarged photograph will be

   (A) 33
   (B) 32
   (C) 30
   (D) 27
   (E) 25

The ratio of width to length of the original photograph is

$\dfrac{10}{15} = \dfrac{2}{3}$. If x is the length of the enlarged photograph, in

inches, then $\dfrac{2}{3} = \dfrac{22}{x}$ since the ratio of width to length will be

unchanged. Thus, $x = 33$ inches, and the best answer is A.

6. If m is an integer such that $(-2)^{2m} = 2^{9-m}$, then $m =$

   (A) 1
   (B) 2
   (C) 3
   (D) 4
   (E) 6

Since $(-2)^{2m} = ((-2)^2)^m = 4^m = 2^{2m}$, it follows that $2^{2m} = 2^{9-m}$. The exponents must be equal, so that $2m = 9 - m$, or $m = 3$. The best answer is therefore C.

7. If $0 \leq x \leq 4$ and $y < 12$, which of the following CANNOT be the value of xy ?

(A) –2
(B) 0
(C) 6
(D) 24
(E) 48

Each of choices A, B, and C can be a value of xy. For if $x = 1$, then $xy = y$, and each of these choices is less than 12. If $x = 4$ and $y = 6$, then $xy = 24$, so that choice D also gives a possible value of xy. In choice E, if $xy = 48$, then for all values of x such that $0 < x \leq 4$, it follows that $y \geq 12$, which contradicts $y < 12$. Thus, 48 cannot be the value of xy, and the best answer is E.

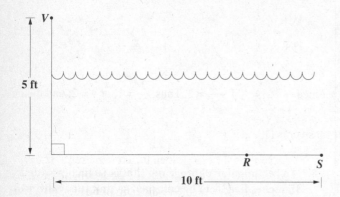

8. In the figure above, V represents an observation point at one end of a pool. From V, an object that is actually located on the bottom of the pool at point R appears to be at point S. If $VR = 10$ feet, what is the distance RS, in feet, between the actual position and the perceived position of the object?

(A) $10 - 5\sqrt{3}$

(B) $10 - 5\sqrt{2}$

(C) 2

(D) $2\frac{1}{2}$

(E) 4

Let P be the point 5 feet directly below V. P is the vertex of the right angle indicated in the figure, and $\triangle VPR$ is thus a right triangle. Then, by the Pythagorean theorem, $PR = \sqrt{10^2 - 5^2} = \sqrt{75} = 5\sqrt{3}$. Thus, $RS = PS - PR = 10 - 5\sqrt{3}$, and the best answer is A.

9. If the total payroll expense of a certain business in year Y was $84,000, which was 20 percent more than in year X, what was the total payroll expense in year X ?

(A) $70,000
(B) $68,320
(C) $64,000
(D) $60,000
(E) $52,320

If p is the total payroll expense in year X, then $1.2p = \$84,000$, so that $p = \dfrac{\$84,000}{1.2} = \$70,000$. Thus, the best answer is A.

10. If a, b, and c are consecutive positive integers and $a < b < c$, which of the following must be true?

  I. $c - a = 2$

  II. abc is an even integer.

  III. $\dfrac{a + b + c}{3}$ is an integer.

(A) I only
(B) II only
(C) I and II only
(D) II and III only
(E) I, II, and III

Since a, b, and c are consecutive integers and $a < b < c$, it follows that $b = a + 1$ and $c = a + 2$. Statement I follows from $c = a + 2$. Concerning statement II, if a is even, then abc is even; if a is odd, then b is even so that abc is even. In either case, abc is even, so statement II must be true. In statement III, $\dfrac{a + b + c}{3} = \dfrac{a + (a + 1) + (a + 2)}{3} = \dfrac{3a + 3}{3} = a + 1 = b$, which is an integer. Therefore, statement III must be true, and the best answer is E.

11. A straight pipe 1 yard in length was marked off in fourths and also in thirds. If the pipe was then cut into separate pieces at each of these markings, which of the following gives all the different lengths of the pieces, in fractions of a yard?

(A) $\dfrac{1}{6}$ and $\dfrac{1}{4}$ only

(B) $\dfrac{1}{4}$ and $\dfrac{1}{3}$ only

(C) $\dfrac{1}{6}, \dfrac{1}{4}$, and $\dfrac{1}{3}$

(D) $\dfrac{1}{12}, \dfrac{1}{6}$, and $\dfrac{1}{4}$

(E) $\dfrac{1}{12}, \dfrac{1}{6}$, and $\dfrac{1}{3}$

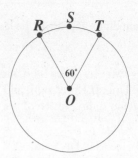

The number line above illustrates the markings on the pipe. Since the pipe is cut at the five markings, six pieces of pipe are produced having lengths, in yards,
$$\frac{1}{4} - 0 = \frac{1}{4}, \quad \frac{1}{3} - \frac{1}{4} = \frac{1}{12}, \quad \frac{1}{2} - \frac{1}{3} = \frac{1}{6}, \quad \frac{2}{3} - \frac{1}{2} = \frac{1}{6},$$
$$\frac{3}{4} - \frac{2}{3} = \frac{1}{12}, \text{ and } 1 - \frac{3}{4} = \frac{1}{4}. \text{ The different lengths of the}$$
pieces are therefore $\frac{1}{12}$, $\frac{1}{6}$, and $\frac{1}{4}$ yard, and the best answer is D.

12. **What is the least integer that is a sum of three different primes each greater than 20?**

   (A) 69
   (B) 73
   (C) 75
   (D) 79
   (E) 83

The three smallest primes that are each greater than 20 are 23, 29, and 31, and their sum is 83. Since any other set of three primes, each greater than 20, would include a prime greater than 31 but no prime less than 23, the corresponding sum would be greater than 83. Thus, 83 is the least such sum, and the best answer is E.

13. **A tourist purchased a total of $1,500 worth of traveler's checks in $10 and $50 denominations. During the trip the tourist cashed 7 checks and then lost all of the rest. If the number of $10 checks cashed was one more or one less than the number of $50 checks cashed, what is the minimum possible value of the checks that were lost?**

   (A) $1,430
   (B) $1,310
   (C) $1,290
   (D) $1,270
   (E) $1,150

Let t be the number of $10 traveler's checks that were cashed and let f be the number of $50 traveler's checks that were cashed. Then $t + f = 7$, and either $t = f + 1$ or $t = f - 1$. Thus, either $t = 4$ and $f = 3$, or $t = 3$ and $f = 4$. In the first case, the value of the lost checks would have been
$1,500 - t(\$10) - f(\$50) = \$1,500 - \$40 - \$150 = \$1,310$;
whereas, in the second case, the value would have been
$1,500 - \$30 - \$200 = \$1,270$. Since the lesser of these amounts is $1,270, the best answer is D.

Alternatively, note that the minimum possible value of the lost checks corresponds to the maximum possible value of the checks that were cashed. Thus, $t = 3$ and $f = 4$, and the minimum possible value of the lost checks is
$$\$1,500 - \$30 - \$200 = \$1,270.$$

14. **If the circle above has center O and circumference 18π, then the perimeter of sector $RSTO$ is**

   (A) $3\pi + 9$
   (B) $3\pi + 18$
   (C) $6\pi + 9$
   (D) $6\pi + 18$
   (E) $6\pi + 24$

If r is the radius of the circle, then the circumference is $2\pi r = 18\pi$, so that $r = 9$. The ratio of the length of arc RST to the circumference is the same as the ratio of 60° to 360°. Thus, the length of arc RST is $\frac{60}{360}(18\pi) = 3\pi$, and, consequently, the perimeter of sector $RSTO$ is $3\pi + r + r = 3\pi + 18$. The best answer is therefore B.

15. **If each of the following fractions were written as a repeating decimal, which would have the longest sequence of different digits?**

   (A) $\frac{2}{11}$

   (B) $\frac{1}{3}$

   (C) $\frac{41}{99}$

   (D) $\frac{2}{3}$

   (E) $\frac{23}{37}$

As repeating decimals, choices A-E are $\frac{2}{11} = 0.181818\ldots$,

$\frac{1}{3} = 0.333\ldots$, $\frac{41}{99} = 0.414141\ldots$, $\frac{2}{3} = 0.666\ldots$,

and $\frac{23}{37} = 0.621621621\ldots$, respectively. The longest

sequence of different digits appears in the last decimal, so the best answer is E.

16. Today Rose is twice as old as Sam and Sam is 3 years younger than Tina. If Rose, Sam, and Tina are all alive 4 years from today, which of the following must be true on that day?

    I. Rose is twice as old as Sam.
   II. Sam is 3 years younger than Tina.
  III. Rose is older than Tina.

  (A) I only
  (B) II only
  (C) III only
  (D) I and II
  (E) II and III

When considering the relationships between people's ages, it may be helpful to keep in mind the fact that the difference between two ages remains constant from one year to the next, but their ratio does not. Thus, statement I need not be true, whereas statement II must be true. For statement III, if R, S, and T denote the respective ages of Rose, Sam, and Tina today, then $R = 2S$ and $S = T - 3$, so that $R = 2(T - 3)$. Thus, $R > T$ if and only if $2(T - 3) > T$, or $T > 6$. Therefore, statement III need not be true, and the best answer is B.

PROBLEM SOLVING SAMPLE TEST SECTION 5

Time — 25 minutes

16 Questions

Directions: In this section solve each problem, using any available space on the page for scratchwork. Then indicate the best of the answer choices given.

Numbers: All numbers used are real numbers.

Figures: Figures that accompany problems in this section are intended to provide information useful in solving the problems. They are drawn as accurately as possible EXCEPT when it is stated in a specific problem that its figure is not drawn to scale. All figures lie in a plane unless otherwise indicated.

1. The average (arithmetic mean) of 6, 8, and 10 equals the average of 7, 9, and

   (A) 5
   (B) 7
   (C) 8
   (D) 9
   (E) 11

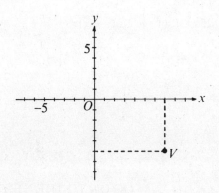

2. In the figure above, the coordinates of point V are

   (A) $(-7, 5)$
   (B) $(-5, 7)$
   (C) $(5, 7)$
   (D) $(7, 5)$
   (E) $(7, -5)$

3. Tickets for all but 100 seats in a 10,000-seat stadium were sold. Of the tickets sold, 20 percent were sold at half price and the remaining tickets were sold at the full price of $2. What was the total revenue from ticket sales?

   (A) $15,840
   (B) $17,820
   (C) $18,000
   (D) $19,800
   (E) $21,780

4. In a mayoral election, Candidate X received $\frac{1}{3}$ more votes than Candidate Y, and Candidate Y received $\frac{1}{4}$ fewer votes than Candidate Z. If Candidate Z received 24,000 votes, how many votes did Candidate X receive?

   (A) 18,000
   (B) 22,000
   (C) 24,000
   (D) 26,000
   (E) 32,000

GO ON TO THE NEXT PAGE.

5. René earns $8.50 per hour on days other than Sundays and twice that rate on Sundays. Last week she worked a total of 40 hours, including 8 hours on Sunday. What were her earnings for the week?

(A) $272
(B) $340
(C) $398
(D) $408
(E) $476

6. In a shipment of 120 machine parts, 5 percent were defective. In a shipment of 80 machine parts, 10 percent were defective. For the two shipments combined, what percent of the machine parts were defective?

(A) 6.5%
(B) 7.0%
(C) 7.5%
(D) 8.0%
(E) 8.5%

7. $\dfrac{2\frac{3}{5} - 1\frac{2}{3}}{\frac{2}{3} - \frac{3}{5}} =$

(A) 16
(B) 14
(C) 3
(D) 1
(E) −1

8. If $x = -1$, then $\dfrac{x^4 - x^3 + x^2}{x - 1} =$

(A) $-\dfrac{3}{2}$

(B) $-\dfrac{1}{2}$

(C) 0

(D) $\dfrac{1}{2}$

(E) $\dfrac{3}{2}$

9. Which of the following equations is NOT equivalent to $25x^2 = y^2 - 4$?

(A) $25x^2 + 4 = y^2$

(B) $75x^2 = 3y^2 - 12$

(C) $25x^2 = (y + 2)(y - 2)$

(D) $5x = y - 2$

(E) $x^2 = \dfrac{y^2 - 4}{25}$

GO ON TO THE NEXT PAGE.

10. A toy store regularly sells all stock at a discount of 20 percent to 40 percent. If an additional 25 percent were deducted from the discount price during a special sale, what would be the lowest possible price of a toy costing $16 before any discount?

(A) $5.60
(B) $7.20
(C) $8.80
(D) $9.60
(E) $15.20

11. If there are 664,579 prime numbers among the first 10 million positive integers, approximately what percent of the first 10 million positive integers are prime numbers?

(A) 0.0066%
(B) 0.066%
(C) 0.66%
(D) 6.6%
(E) 66%

12. A bank customer borrowed $10,000, but received y dollars less than this due to discounting. If there was a separate $25 service charge, then, in terms of y, the service charge was what fraction of the amount that the customer received?

(A) $\dfrac{25}{10,000 - y}$

(B) $\dfrac{25}{10,000 - 25y}$

(C) $\dfrac{25y}{10,000 - y}$

(D) $\dfrac{y - 25}{10,000 - y}$

(E) $\dfrac{25}{10,000 - (y - 25)}$

13. An airline passenger is planning a trip that involves three connecting flights that leave from Airports A, B, and C, respectively. The first flight leaves Airport A every hour, beginning at 8:00 a.m., and arrives at Airport B $2\frac{1}{2}$ hours later. The second flight leaves Airport B every 20 minutes, beginning at 8:00 a.m., and arrives at Airport C $1\frac{1}{6}$ hours later. The third flight leaves Airport C every hour, beginning at 8:45 a.m. What is the least total amount of time the passenger must spend between flights if all flights keep to their schedules?

(A) 25 min
(B) 1 hr 5 min
(C) 1 hr 15 min
(D) 2 hr 20 min
(E) 3 hr 40 min

GO ON TO THE NEXT PAGE.

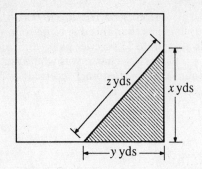

16. Jack is now 14 years older than Bill. If in 10 years Jack will be twice as old as Bill, how old will Jack be in 5 years?

(A) 9
(B) 19
(C) 21
(D) 23
(E) 33

14. The shaded portion of the rectangular lot shown above represents a flower bed. If the area of the bed is 24 square yards and $x = y + 2$, then z equals

(A) $\sqrt{13}$

(B) $2\sqrt{13}$

(C) 6

(D) 8

(E) 10

15. How many multiples of 4 are there between 12 and 96, inclusive?

(A) 21
(B) 22
(C) 23
(D) 24
(E) 25

STOP

IF·YOU FINISH BEFORE TIME IS CALLED, YOU MAY CHECK YOUR WORK ON THIS SECTION ONLY.
DO NOT TURN TO ANY OTHER SECTION IN THE TEST.

Answer Key for Sample Test Section 5

PROBLEM SOLVING

Explanatory Material:
Problem Solving Sample Test Section 5

1. The average (arithmetic mean) of 6, 8, and 10 equals the average of 7, 9, and

   (A) 5
   (B) 7
   (C) 8
   (D) 9
   (E) 11

The average of 6, 8, and 10 is $\frac{6+8+10}{3} = 8$, which equals

the average of 7, 9, and x. Thus, $\frac{7+9+x}{3} = 8$, $16 + x = 24$,

and $x = 8$. The best answer is therefore C.

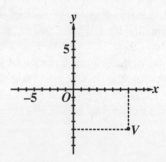

2. In the figure above, the coordinates of point V are

   (A) $(-7, 5)$
   (B) $(-5, 7)$
   (C) $(5, 7)$
   (D) $(7, 5)$
   (E) $(7, -5)$

The x-coordinate of V is 7 and the y-coordinate of V is –5. Thus, the coordinates, (x,y), of V are $(7, -5)$, and the best answer is E. Alternatively, since point V lies in quadrant IV, the x-coordinate of V is positive, and the y-coordinate of V is negative. Only choice E meets these conditions and is, therefore, the best answer.

3. Tickets for all but 100 seats in a 10,000-seat stadium were sold. Of the tickets sold, 20 percent were sold at half price and the remaining tickets were sold at the full price of $2. What was the total revenue from ticket sales?

   (A) $15,840
   (B) $17,820
   (C) $18,000
   (D) $19,800
   (E) $21,780

The number of tickets sold was 10,000 – 100 = 9,900. If 20 percent of the tickets were sold at half price, then 80 percent were sold at full price. Total revenue was therefore $0.2(9,900)(\$1.00) + 0.8(9,900)(\$2.00) = \$17,820$. The best answer is B.

4. In a mayoral election, Candidate X received $\frac{1}{3}$ more votes than Candidate Y, and Candidate Y received $\frac{1}{4}$ fewer votes than Candidate Z. If Candidate Z received 24,000 votes, how many votes did Candidate X receive?

   (A) 18,000
   (B) 22,000
   (C) 24,000
   (D) 26,000
   (E) 32,000

If x, y, and z are the number of votes received by candidates X, Y, and Z, respectively, then $x = \frac{4}{3}\, y$, $y = \frac{3}{4}\, z$, and $z = 24,000$.

By substitution, $y = \left(\frac{3}{4}\right)(24,000) = 18,000$ and

$x = \left(\frac{4}{3}\right)(18,000) = 24,000$. Candidate X received a total of

24,000 votes, and the best answer is C. Alternatively, and

more directly, $x = \left(\frac{4}{3}\right)\left(\frac{3}{4}\right)z = z = 24,000$.

5. René earns $8.50 per hour on days other than Sundays and twice that rate on Sundays. Last week she worked a total of 40 hours, including 8 hours on Sunday. What were her earnings for the week?

   (A) $272
   (B) $340
   (C) $398
   (D) $408
   (E) $476

René worked a total of 32 hours at $8.50 per hour during the week, and 8 hours on Sunday at $17.00 per hour. Her total earnings for the week were 32($8.50) + 8($17) = $408. The best answer is D.

6. In a shipment of 120 machine parts, 5 percent were defective. In a shipment of 80 machine parts, 10 percent were defective. For the two shipments combined, what percent of the machine parts were defective?

   (A) 6.5%
   (B) 7.0%
   (C) 7.5%
   (D) 8.0%
   (E) 8.5%

In the combined shipments, there was a total of 200 machine parts, of which $0.05(120) + 0.1(80) = 6 + 8 = 14$ were defective. The percent of machine parts that were defective in the two shipments combined was $\frac{14}{200} = \frac{7}{100} = 7\%$. The best answer is therefore B.

7. $\dfrac{2\frac{3}{5} - 1\frac{2}{3}}{\frac{2}{3} - \frac{3}{5}} =$

   (A) 16
   (B) 14
   (C) 3
   (D) 1
   (E) −1

$$\frac{2\frac{3}{5} - 1\frac{2}{3}}{\frac{2}{3} - \frac{3}{5}} = \frac{\frac{13}{5} - \frac{5}{3}}{\frac{2}{3} - \frac{3}{5}} = \frac{\frac{39 - 25}{15}}{\frac{10 - 9}{15}} = \frac{\frac{14}{15}}{\frac{1}{15}} = \frac{14}{15} \times \frac{15}{1} = 14.$$

The best answer is B.

8. If $x = -1$, then $\dfrac{x^4 - x^3 + x^2}{x - 1} =$

   (A) $-\dfrac{3}{2}$

   (B) $-\dfrac{1}{2}$

   (C) 0

   (D) $\dfrac{1}{2}$

   (E) $\dfrac{3}{2}$

Substituting the value −1 for x in the expression results in $\dfrac{(-1)^4 - (-1)^3 + (-1)^2}{-1 - 1} = \dfrac{1 - (-1) + 1}{-2} = -\dfrac{3}{2}$. The best answer is A.

9. Which of the following equations is NOT equivalent to $25x^2 = y^2 - 4$?

   (A) $25x^2 + 4 = y^2$
   (B) $75x^2 = 3y^2 - 12$
   (C) $25x^2 = (y + 2)(y - 2)$
   (D) $5x = y - 2$
   (E) $x^2 = \dfrac{y^2 - 4}{25}$

Choice A is obtained by adding 4 to both sides of the equation $25x^2 = y^2 - 4$. Choice B is obtained by multiplying both sides of the original equation by 3, while choice C is equivalent because $y^2 - 4 = (y + 2)(y - 2)$. Choice E is obtained by dividing both sides of the original equation by 25. By the process of elimination, the answer must be D. Squaring both sides of $5x = y - 2$, choice D, gives $25x^2 = y^2 - 4y + 4$, which is NOT equivalent to the original equation. Therefore, the best answer is D.

10. A toy store regularly sells all stock at a discount of 20 percent to 40 percent. If an additional 25 percent were deducted from the discount price during a special sale, what would be the lowest possible price of a toy costing $16 before any discount?

(A) $5.60
(B) $7.20
(C) $8.80
(D) $9.60
(E) $15.20

The lowest possible price is paid when the maximum discount is received, so the lowest possible regular price is $16 – 0.40($16) = $9.60. With an additional 25 percent discount, the lowest possible price is $9.60 – 0.25($9.60) = $7.20. The best answer is B.

Alternatively, the lowest possible price to be paid for the item can be calculated by realizing that if you are being given a discount of 40 percent you are paying 60 percent of the listed price of the item. If an additional 25 percent discount is offered on the item, the price of the item becomes (0.75)(0.60)($16) = $7.20.

11. If there are 664,579 prime numbers among the first 10 million positive integers, approximately what percent of the first 10 million positive integers are prime numbers?

(A) 0.0066%
(B) 0.066%
(C) 0.66%
(D) 6.6%
(E) 66%

The ratio of 664,579 to 10 million is approximately 660,000 to 10,000,000 or $\frac{66}{1,000} = 0.066 = 6.6\%$. The best answer is therefore D.

12. A bank customer borrowed $10,000, but received y dollars less than this due to discounting. If there was a separate $25 service charge, then, in terms of y, the service charge was what fraction of the amount that the customer received?

(A) $\frac{25}{10,000 - y}$

(B) $\frac{25}{10,000 - 25y}$

(C) $\frac{25y}{10,000 - y}$

(D) $\frac{y - 25}{10,000 - y}$

(E) $\frac{25}{10,000 - (y - 25)}$

The amount of money the customer received was $(10,000 - y)$ dollars. The $25 service charge as a fraction of the amount received was, therefore, $\frac{25}{10,000 - y}$. The best answer is A.

13. An airline passenger is planning a trip that involves three connecting flights that leave from Airports A, B, and C, respectively. The first flight leaves Airport A every hour, beginning at 8:00 a.m., and arrives at Airport B $2\frac{1}{2}$ hours later. The second flight leaves Airport B every 20 minutes, beginning at 8:00 a.m., and arrives at Airport C $1\frac{1}{6}$ hours later. The third flight leaves Airport C every hour, beginning at 8:45 a.m. What is the least total amount of time the passenger must spend between flights if all flights keep to their schedules?

(A) 25 min
(B) 1 hr 5 min
(C) 1 hr 15 min
(D) 2 hr 20 min
(E) 3 hr 40 min

Regardless of the time of departure from Airport A, arrival at Airport B will be at 30 minutes past the hour. Flights leave Airport B on the hour, and at either 20 or 40 minutes past the hour. Therefore, the earliest a passenger from Airport A could leave Airport B would be at 40 minutes past the hour with a 10-minute wait between flights. The flight from Airport B to Airport C takes $1\frac{1}{6}$ hours or 1 hour 10 minutes. A flight taken at 40 minutes past the hour would arrive at Airport C at 50 minutes past the hour, causing the passenger to have missed the flight from Airport C by 5 minutes. The passenger therefore has a 55-minute wait, and the least total amount of time the passenger must spend between flights is $10 + 55 = 65$ minutes, or 1 hour 5 minutes. The best answer is B.

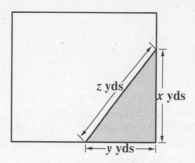

14. The shaded portion of the rectangular lot shown above represents a flower bed. If the area of the bed is 24 square yards and $x = y + 2$, then z equals

(A) $\sqrt{13}$
(B) $2\sqrt{13}$
(C) 6
(D) 8
(E) 10

-101-

The area of the triangular flower bed can be found by the formula $A = \frac{1}{2}$ (altitude)(base) or $24 = \frac{1}{2}(x)(y) = \frac{1}{2}(y + 2)(y)$. Thus, $y^2 + 2y = 48$ or $y^2 + 2y - 48 = 0$. Factoring yields $(y + 8)(y - 6) = 0$, and $y = 6$ since the length must be positive. The altitude x of the region is $6 + 2 = 8$, and the flower bed is a 6-8-10 right triangle. The hypotenuse, z, can be found by using the Pythagorean theorem. The best answer is therefore E.

15. **How many multiples of 4 are there between 12 and 96, inclusive?**

   (A) 21
   (B) 22
   (C) 23
   (D) 24
   (E) 25

The most direct way to find the number of multiples of 4 between 12 and 96, inclusive, would be to write every multiple of 4 starting with 12 (i.e., 12, 16, 20, 24,. . . , 96), but this is very time-consuming and leaves many opportunities for error. Another approach would be to note that in each group of 4 consecutive integers there is one multiple of 4. Between 12 and 96, inclusive, there are 85 numbers that, when divided by 4, yield 21 groups of 4 with 1 number remaining that must be considered independently. In the 21 groups of 4, there are 21 multiples of 4 and the remaining number, 96, is also a multiple of 4. The total number of multiples of 4 between 12 and 96, inclusive, is thus $21 + 1 = 22$. The best answer is B.

   Alternatively, since $12 = 3 \times 4$ and $96 = 24 \times 4$, the number of multiples of 4 between 12 and 96, inclusive, is the same as the number of integers between 3 and 24, inclusive, namely, 22.

16. **Jack is now 14 years older than Bill. If in 10 years Jack will be twice as old as Bill, how old will Jack be in 5 years?**

   (A) 9
   (B) 19
   (C) 21
   (D) 23
   (E) 33

Let j and b be Jack's and Bill's current ages. Then $j = b + 14$ and $j + 10 = 2(b + 10)$. By substitution, $b + 14 + 10 = 2(b + 10)$, and $b + 24 = 2b + 20$. Therefore, $b = 4$ and $j = 18$, and Jack's age in 5 years is $18 + 5 = 23$. The best answer is D.

PROBLEM SOLVING SAMPLE TEST SECTION 6

Time — 25 minutes

16 Questions

Directions: In this section solve each problem, using any available space on the page for scratchwork. Then indicate the best of the answer choices given.

Numbers: All numbers used are real numbers.

Figures: Figures that accompany problems in this section are intended to provide information useful in solving the problems. They are drawn as accurately as possible EXCEPT when it is stated in a specific problem that its figure is not drawn to scale. All figures lie in a plane unless otherwise indicated.

1. In Country X a returning tourist may import goods with a total value of $500 or less tax free, but must pay an 8 percent tax on the portion of the total value in excess of $500. What tax must be paid by a returning tourist who imports goods with a total value of $730 ?

    (A) $58.40
    (B) $40.00
    (C) $24.60
    (D) $18.40
    (E) $16.00

2. Which of the following is greater than $\frac{2}{3}$?

    (A) $\frac{33}{50}$

    (B) $\frac{8}{11}$

    (C) $\frac{3}{5}$

    (D) $\frac{13}{27}$

    (E) $\frac{5}{8}$

3. A rope 40 feet long is cut into two pieces. If one piece is 18 feet longer than the other, what is the length, in feet, of the shorter piece?

    (A) 9
    (B) 11
    (C) 18
    (D) 22
    (E) 29

4. If 60 percent of a rectangular floor is covered by a rectangular rug that is 9 feet by 12 feet, what is the area, in square feet, of the floor?

    (A) 65
    (B) 108
    (C) 180
    (D) 270
    (E) 300

GO ON TO THE NEXT PAGE.

5. The Earth travels around the Sun at a speed of approximately 18.5 miles per second. This approximate speed is how many miles per hour?

(A)   1,080
(B)   1,160
(C)   64,800
(D)   66,600
(E) 3,996,000

6. A collection of books went on sale, and $\frac{2}{3}$ of them were sold for $2.50 each. If none of the 36 remaining books were sold, what was the total amount received for the books that were sold?

(A) $180
(B) $135
(C) $90
(D) $60
(E) $54

7. If "basis points" are defined so that 1 percent is equal to 100 basis points, then 82.5 percent is how many basis points greater than 62.5 percent?

(A)   0.02
(B)   0.2
(C)   20
(D)   200
(E) 2,000

8. The amounts of time that three secretaries worked on a special project are in the ratio of 1 to 2 to 5. If they worked a combined total of 112 hours, how many hours did the secretary who worked the longest spend on the project?

(A) 80
(B) 70
(C) 56
(D) 16
(E) 14

GO ON TO THE NEXT PAGE.

9. If the quotient $\frac{a}{b}$ is positive, which of the following must be true?

(A) $a > 0$

(B) $b > 0$

(C) $ab > 0$

(D) $a - b > 0$

(E) $a + b > 0$

10. If $8^{2x+3} = 2^{3x+6}$, then $x =$

(A) -3
(B) -1
(C) 0
(D) 1
(E) 3

11. Of the following, the closest approximation to

$$\sqrt{\frac{5.98(601.5)}{15.79}} \text{ is}$$

(A) 5
(B) 15
(C) 20
(D) 25
(E) 225

12. Which of the following CANNOT be the greatest common divisor of two positive integers x and y?

(A) 1
(B) x
(C) y
(D) $x - y$
(E) $x + y$

13. An empty pool being filled with water at a constant rate takes 8 hours to fill to $\frac{3}{5}$ of its capacity. How much more time will it take to finish filling the pool?

(A) 5 hr 30 min
(B) 5 hr 20 min
(C) 4 hr 48 min
(D) 3 hr 12 min
(E) 2 hr 40 min

GO ON TO THE NEXT PAGE.

-105-

14. A positive number x is multiplied by 2, and this product is then divided by 3. If the positive square root of the result of these two operations equals x, what is the value of x?

(A) $\frac{9}{4}$

(B) $\frac{3}{2}$

(C) $\frac{4}{3}$

(D) $\frac{2}{3}$

(E) $\frac{1}{2}$

15. A tank contains 10,000 gallons of a solution that is 5 percent sodium chloride by volume. If 2,500 gallons of water evaporate from the tank, the remaining solution will be approximately what percent sodium chloride?

(A) 1.25%
(B) 3.75%
(C) 6.25%
(D) 6.67%
(E) 11.7%

16. A certain grocery purchased x pounds of produce for p dollars per pound. If y pounds of the produce had to be discarded due to spoilage and the grocery sold the rest for s dollars per pound, which of the following represents the gross profit on the sale of the produce?

(A) $(x - y)s - xp$
(B) $(x - y)p - ys$
(C) $(s - p)y - xp$
(D) $xp - ys$
(E) $(x - y)(s - p)$

STOP

IF YOU FINISH BEFORE TIME IS CALLED, YOU MAY CHECK YOUR WORK ON THIS SECTION ONLY.
DO NOT TURN TO ANY OTHER SECTION IN THE TEST.

Answer Key for Sample Test Section 6

PROBLEM SOLVING

1. D	9. C
2. B	10. B
3. B	11. B
4. C	12. E
5. D	13. B
6. A	14. D
7. E	15. D
8. B	16. A

Explanatory Material:
Problem Solving Sample Test Section 6

1. **In Country X a returning tourist may import goods with a total value of $500 or less tax free, but must pay an 8 percent tax on the portion of the total value in excess of $500. What tax must be paid by a returning tourist who imports goods with a total value of $730 ?**

   (A) $58.40
   (B) $40.00
   (C) $24.60
   (D) $18.40
   (E) $16.00

   The tourist must pay tax on $730 – $500 = $230. The amount of the tax is 0.08($230) = $18.40. The best answer is therefore D.

2. **Which of the following is greater than $\frac{2}{3}$?**

   (A) $\dfrac{33}{50}$

   (B) $\dfrac{8}{11}$

   (C) $\dfrac{3}{5}$

   (D) $\dfrac{13}{27}$

   (E) $\dfrac{5}{8}$

One way to determine which of the options given is a value greater than $\frac{2}{3}$ is to establish equivalent fractions. In choice A, $\frac{33}{50} < \frac{2}{3}$ because $\frac{99}{150} < \frac{100}{150}$. In B, $\frac{8}{11} > \frac{2}{3}$ because $\frac{24}{33} > \frac{22}{33}$. In C, $\frac{3}{5} < \frac{2}{3}$ because $\frac{9}{15} < \frac{10}{15}$; in D, $\frac{13}{27} < \frac{2}{3}$ because $\frac{13}{27} < \frac{18}{27}$; and in E, $\frac{5}{8} < \frac{2}{3}$ because $\frac{15}{24} < \frac{16}{24}$. Therefore, the best answer is B.

Alternatively, convert the fractions to decimal form: $\frac{2}{3} = 0.666666\ldots$, $\frac{33}{50} = 0.66$, $\frac{8}{11} = 0.727272\ldots$, $\frac{3}{5} = 0.6$, $\frac{13}{27} = 0.481481\ldots$, and $\frac{5}{8} = 0.625$. Thus, by comparing decimal equivalents, only $\frac{8}{11}$ is greater than $\frac{2}{3}$.

3. **A rope 40 feet long is cut into two pieces. If one piece is 18 feet longer than the other, what is the length, in feet, of the shorter piece?**

   (A) 9
   (B) 11
   (C) 18
   (D) 22
   (E) 29

   Let x be the length of the shorter piece of rope, and let $x + 18$ be the length of the longer piece. Then $x + (x + 18) = 40$, which yields $2x + 18 = 40$, and $x = 11$. The best answer is B.

4. **If 60 percent of a rectangular floor is covered by a rectangular rug that is 9 feet by 12 feet, what is the area, in square feet, of the floor?**

   (A) 65
   (B) 108
   (C) 180
   (D) 270
   (E) 300

   The area of the rug is (9)(12) = 108 square feet, which is 60 percent of x, the total area of the floor. Thus, 108 = 0.6x, or $x = \frac{108}{0.6} = 180$. The best answer is therefore C.

5. The Earth travels around the Sun at a speed of approximately 18.5 miles per second. This approximate speed is how many miles per hour?

   (A)   1,080
   (B)   1,160
   (C)   64,800
   (D)   66,600
   (E)   3,996,000

There are 60 seconds in one minute, and 60 minutes in one hour. In one hour the Earth travels $18.5 \times 60 \times 60 = 66,600$ miles, and the best answer is D.

6. A collection of books went on sale, and $\frac{2}{3}$ of them were sold for $2.50 each. If none of the 36 remaining books were sold, what was the total amount received for the books that were sold?

   (A) $180
   (B) $135
   (C) $90
   (D) $60
   (E) $54

Since $\frac{2}{3}$ of the books in the collection were sold, $\frac{1}{3}$ were not sold. The 36 unsold books represent $\frac{1}{3}$ of the total number of books in the collection, and $\frac{2}{3}$ of the total number of books equals 2(36) or 72. The total proceeds of the sale was 72($2.50) or $180. The best answer is therefore A.

7. If "basis points" are defined so that 1 percent is equal to 100 basis points, then 82.5 percent is how many basis points greater than 62.5 percent?

   (A)   0.02
   (B)   0.2
   (C)   20
   (D)   200
   (E)   2,000

There is a difference of 20 percent between 82.5 percent and 62.5 percent. If 1 percent equals 100 basis points, then 20 percent equals 20(100) or 2,000 basis points. The best answer is E.

8. The amounts of time that three secretaries worked on a special project are in the ratio of 1 to 2 to 5. If they worked a combined total of 112 hours, how many hours did the secretary who worked the longest spend on the project?

   (A)   80
   (B)   70
   (C)   56
   (D)   16
   (E)   14

Since the ratio of hours worked by the secretaries on the project is 1 to 2 to 5, the third secretary spent the longest time on the project, that is, $\frac{5}{8}(112)$ or 70 hours. The best answer is therefore B.

9. If the quotient $\frac{a}{b}$ is positive, which of the following must be true?

   (A) $a > 0$
   (B) $b > 0$
   (C) $ab > 0$
   (D) $a - b > 0$
   (E) $a + b > 0$

If the quotient $\frac{a}{b}$ is positive, then either $a > 0$ and $b > 0$, or $a < 0$ and $b < 0$. It follows that answer choices A and B need not be true. Choice C must be true, because the product of two positive or two negative numbers is positive. Finally, $2 - 3 = -1$ and $-2 + (-1) = -3$ show that choices D and E, respectively, need not be true. The best answer is therefore C.

10. If $8^{2x+3} = 2^{3x+6}$, then $x =$

   (A) -3
   (B) -1
   (C)   0
   (D)   1
   (E)   3

Since $8^{2x+3} = (2^3)^{2x+3} = 2^{6x+9}$, it follows, by equating exponents, that $6x + 9 = 3x + 6$, or $x = -1$. The best answer is therefore B.

11. Of the following, the closest approximation to

    $\sqrt{\dfrac{5.98(601.5)}{15.79}}$ is

   (A)   5
   (B)   15
   (C)   20
   (D)   25
   (E)   225

The value of the expression under the square root sign is approximately $\frac{6(600)}{16} = 225$. Since $225 = 15^2$, $\sqrt{225} = 15$, and the best answer is B.

12. Which of the following CANNOT be the greatest common divisor of two positive integers x and y ?

   (A)   1
   (B) x
   (C) y
   (D) $x - y$
   (E) $x + y$

Each answer choice except E can be the greatest common divisor (g.c.d.) of two positive integers. For example, if $x = 3$ and $y = 2$, then x and y have g.c.d. 1, which equals $x - y$, eliminating A and D. If the two numbers are 2 and 4, then the g.c.d. is 2, which can be x or y, eliminating B and C. However, the greatest common divisor of two positive integers cannot be greater than either one of the integers individually, so the best answer is E.

13. An empty pool being filled with water at a constant rate takes 8 hours to fill to $\frac{3}{5}$ of its capacity. How much more time will it take to finish filling the pool?

   (A) 5 hr 30 min
   (B) 5 hr 20 min
   (C) 4 hr 48 min
   (D) 3 hr 12 min
   (E) 2 hr 40 min

If t is the total time required to fill the entire pool, then $\frac{3}{5}t = 8$.

Thus, $t = \frac{40}{3} = 13\frac{1}{3}$ hours, or 13 hours 20 minutes. It will

therefore take 13 hours 20 minutes – 8 hours = 5 hours 20 minutes to finish filling the pool, and the best answer is B.

14. A positive number x is multiplied by 2, and this product is then divided by 3. If the positive square root of the result of these two operations equals x, what is the value of x ?

   (A) $\frac{9}{4}$

   (B) $\frac{3}{2}$

   (C) $\frac{4}{3}$

   (D) $\frac{2}{3}$

   (E) $\frac{1}{2}$

The value of x must satisfy the equation $\sqrt{\frac{2x}{3}}$. Squaring both sides of the equation and multiplying by 3 yields $2x = 3x^2$, and, since $x > 0$, it follows that $x = \frac{2}{3}$. The best answer is therefore D.

15. A tank contains 10,000 gallons of a solution that is 5 percent sodium chloride by volume. If 2,500 gallons of water evaporate from the tank, the remaining solution will be approximately what percent sodium chloride?

   (A) 1.25%
   (B) 3.75%
   (C) 6.25%
   (D) 6.67%
   (E) 11.7%

The amount of sodium chloride in the tank is $0.05 \times 10,000$ or 500 gallons. After the evaporation of the water, the total amount of solution is $10,000 - 2,500 = 7,500$ gallons, and 500 gallons of sodium chloride remain. The percent of sodium chloride is thus $\frac{500}{7,500} = 6.67$ percent. The best answer is D.

Alternatively, this problem can be approached as an inverse proportion. The original solution contains 5 percent sodium chloride by volume in 10,000 gallons. As water evaporates from the tank, the concentration of sodium chloride in the solution will increase. If x is the fraction of sodium chloride in the remaining solution, then $\frac{10,000}{7,500} = \frac{x}{0.05}$. Solving for x gives $\frac{(0.05)(10,000)}{7,500} = 0.0667$, which equals 6.67 percent.

16. A certain grocery purchased x pounds of produce for p dollars per pound. If y pounds of the produce had to be discarded due to spoilage and the grocery sold the rest for s dollars per pound, which of the following represents the gross profit on the sale of the produce?

   (A) $(x - y)s - xp$
   (B) $(x - y)p - ys$
   (C) $(s - p)y - xp$
   (D) $xp - ys$
   (E) $(x - y)(s - p)$

The grocery paid xp dollars for the produce. The grocery sold $(x - y)$ pounds of the produce for s dollars per pound, and so the total income was $(x - y)s$ dollars. The gross profit, or income minus cost, was therefore $(x - y)s - xp$. The best answer is A.

PROBLEM SOLVING SAMPLE TEST SECTION 7

Time — 25 minutes

16 Questions

Directions: In this section solve each problem, using any available space on the page for scratchwork. Then indicate the best of the answer choices given.

Numbers: All numbers used are real numbers.

Figures: Figures that accompany problems in this section are intended to provide information useful in solving the problems. They are drawn as accurately as possible EXCEPT when it is stated in a specific problem that its figure is not drawn to scale. All figures lie in a plane unless otherwise indicated.

1. If $x + 5y = 16$ and $x = -3y$, then $y =$

   (A) -24
   (B) -8
   (C) -2
   (D) 2
   (E) 8

2. An empty swimming pool with a capacity of 5,760 gallons is filled at the rate of 12 gallons per minute. How many hours does it take to fill the pool to capacity?

   (A) 8
   (B) 20
   (C) 96
   (D) 480
   (E) 720

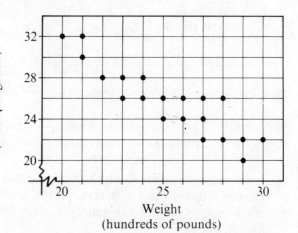

Weight
(hundreds of pounds)

3. The dots on the graph above indicate the weights and fuel efficiency ratings for 20 cars. How many of the cars weigh more than 2,500 pounds and also get more than 22 miles per gallon?

   (A) Three
   (B) Five
   (C) Eight
   (D) Ten
   (E) Eleven

GO ON TO THE NEXT PAGE.

-110-

4. $\dfrac{90 - 8(20 \div 4)}{\frac{1}{2}} =$

(A) 25
(B) 50
(C) 100
(D) 116
(E) 170

5. If a, b, and c are nonzero numbers and $a + b = c$, which of the following is equal to 1 ?

(A) $\dfrac{a - b}{c}$

(B) $\dfrac{a - c}{b}$

(C) $\dfrac{b - c}{a}$

(D) $\dfrac{b - a}{c}$

(E) $\dfrac{c - b}{a}$

6. Bill's school is 10 miles from his home. He travels 4 miles from school to football practice, and then 2 miles to a friend's house. If he is then x miles from home, what is the range of possible values for x ?

(A) $2 \le x \le 10$
(B) $4 \le x \le 10$
(C) $4 \le x \le 12$
(D) $4 \le x \le 16$
(E) $6 \le x \le 16$

7. Three machines, individually, can do a certain job in 4, 5, and 6 hours, respectively. What is the greatest part of the job that can be done in one hour by two of the machines working together at their respective rates?

(A) $\dfrac{11}{30}$

(B) $\dfrac{9}{20}$

(C) $\dfrac{3}{5}$

(D) $\dfrac{11}{15}$

(E) $\dfrac{5}{6}$

8. In 1985, 45 percent of a document storage facility's 60 customers were banks, and in 1987, 25 percent of its 144 customers were banks. What was the percent increase from 1985 to 1987 in the number of bank customers the facility had?

(A) 10.7%

(B) 20%

(C) 25%

(D) $33\frac{1}{3}\%$

(E) $58\frac{1}{3}\%$

GO ON TO THE NEXT PAGE.

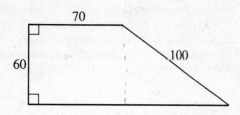

9. What is the perimeter of the figure above?

(A) 380
(B) 360
(C) 330
(D) 300
(E) 230

10. A committee is composed of w women and m men. If 3 women and 2 men are added to the committee, and if one person is selected at random from the enlarged committee, then the probability that a woman is selected can be represented by

(A) $\dfrac{w}{m}$

(B) $\dfrac{w}{w + m}$

(C) $\dfrac{w + 3}{m + 2}$

(D) $\dfrac{w + 3}{w + m + 3}$

(E) $\dfrac{w + 3}{w + m + 5}$

11. Last year Carlos saved 10 percent of his annual earnings. This year he earned 5 percent more than last year and he saved 12 percent of his annual earnings. The amount saved this year was what percent of the amount saved last year?

(A) 122%
(B) 124%
(C) 126%
(D) 128%
(E) 130%

12. Jan lives x floors above the ground floor of a high-rise building. It takes her 30 seconds per floor to walk down the steps and 2 seconds per floor to ride the elevator. If it takes Jan the same amount of time to walk down the steps to the ground floor as to wait for the elevator for 7 minutes and ride down, then x equals

(A) 4
(B) 7
(C) 14
(D) 15
(E) 16

GO ON TO THE NEXT PAGE.

13. A corporation that had \$115.19 billion in profits for the year paid out \$230.10 million in employee benefits. Approximately what percent of the profits were the employee benefits? (1 billion $= 10^9$)

    (A) 50%
    (B) 20%
    (C) 5%
    (D) 2%
    (E) 0.2%

Questions 14-15 refer to the following definition.

   For any positive integer n, $n > 1$, the "length" of n is the number of positive primes (not necessarily distinct) whose product is n. For example, the length of 50 is 3 since $50 = (2)(5)(5)$.

14. Which of the following integers has length 3 ?

    (A) 3
    (B) 15
    (C) 60
    (D) 64
    (E) 105

15. What is the greatest possible length of a positive integer less than 1,000 ?

    (A) 10
    (B) 9
    (C) 8
    (D) 7
    (E) 6

16. A dealer originally bought 100 identical batteries at a total cost of q dollars. If each battery was sold at 50 percent above the original cost per battery, then, in terms of q, for how many dollars was each battery sold?

    (A) $\dfrac{3q}{200}$

    (B) $\dfrac{3q}{2}$

    (C) $150q$

    (D) $\dfrac{q}{100} + 50$

    (E) $\dfrac{150}{q}$

STOP

IF YOU FINISH BEFORE TIME IS CALLED, YOU MAY CHECK YOUR WORK ON THIS SECTION ONLY.
DO NOT TURN TO ANY OTHER SECTION IN THE TEST.

Answer Key for Sample Test Section 7

PROBLEM SOLVING

1. E	9. A
2. A	10. E
3. B	11. C
4. C	12. D
5. E	13. E
6. D	14. E
7. B	15. B
8. D	16. A

Explanatory Material: Problem Solving Sample Test Section 7

1. If $x + 5y = 16$ and $x = -3y$, then $y =$

   (A) -24
   (B) -8
   (C) -2
   (D) 2
   (E) 8

Substituting the second equation into the first equation yields
$$(-3y) + 5y = 16$$
$$2y = 16$$
$$y = 8.$$
Thus, the best answer is E.

2. **An empty swimming pool with a capacity of 5,760 gallons is filled at the rate of 12 gallons per minute. How many hours does it take to fill the pool to capacity?**

   (A) 8
   (B) 20
   (C) 96
   (D) 480
   (E) 720

Since the pool fills at the rate of 12 gallons per minute, the number of minutes required to fill the pool is $5760 \div 12 = 480$ minutes. The number of hours required to fill the pool is $\frac{480}{60}$, or 8. The best answer is A.

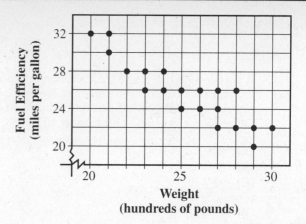

Weight
(hundreds of pounds)

3. **The dots on the graph above indicate the weights and fuel efficiency ratings for 20 cars. How many of the cars weigh more than 2,500 pounds and also get more than 22 miles per gallon?**

   (A) Three
   (B) Five
   (C) Eight
   (D) Ten
   (E) Eleven

Count the number of dots to the right of 25 and above 22 as shown on the graph below. The dots on the vertical line at 25 and those on the horizontal line at 22 are not included. Thus, the best answer is B.

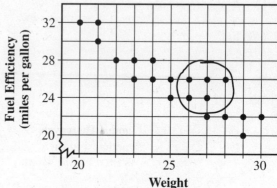

Weight
(hundreds of pounds)

4. $\dfrac{90 - 8(20 \div 4)}{\frac{1}{2}} =$

   (A) 25
   (B) 50
   (C) 100
   (D) 116
   (E) 170

$$\frac{90 - 8(20 \div 4)}{\frac{1}{2}} = \frac{90 - 8(5)}{\frac{1}{2}}$$

$$= \frac{90 - 40}{\frac{1}{2}}$$

$$= \frac{50}{\frac{1}{2}}$$

$$= 50 \times 2$$

$$= 100$$

The best answer is C.

5. If a, b, and c are nonzero numbers and $a + b = c$, which of the following is equal to 1 ?

(A) $\dfrac{a - b}{c}$

(B) $\dfrac{a - c}{b}$

(C) $\dfrac{b - c}{a}$

(D) $\dfrac{b - a}{c}$

(E) $\dfrac{c - b}{a}$

For any fraction equal to 1, the numerator and the denominator must be equal. Using the relationship $a + b = c$ to express the denominator of each fraction in terms of the variables in the numerator, the fractions are

(A) $\dfrac{a - b}{a + b}$ (B) $\dfrac{a - c}{c - a}$ (C) $\dfrac{b - c}{c - b}$ (D) $\dfrac{b - a}{a + b}$ (E) $\dfrac{c - b}{c - b}$

Only choice E has the numerator and denominator equal. Thus, the best answer is E.

6. Bill's school is 10 miles from his home. He travels 4 miles from school to football practice, and then 2 miles to a friend's house. If he is then x miles from home, what is the range of possible values for x ?

(A) $2 \le x \le 10$
(B) $4 \le x \le 10$
(C) $4 \le x \le 12$
(D) $4 \le x \le 16$
(E) $6 \le x \le 16$

A diagram is helpful to solve this problem. The value of x will be greatest if Bill's home (H), school (S), football practice (P), and friend's house (F) are laid out as shown below in Figure 1 with $x = 10 + 4 + 2 = 16$ miles. The value of x will be least if Bill's home, school, football practice, and friend's house are situated as shown below in Figure 2 with $x = 10 - 6 = 4$ miles.

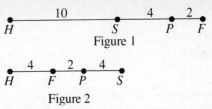

Figure 1

Figure 2

Thus, the best answer is D.

7. Three machines, individually, can do a certain job in 4, 5, and 6 hours, respectively. What is the greatest part of the job that can be done in one hour by two of the machines working together at their respective rates?

(A) $\dfrac{11}{30}$

(B) $\dfrac{9}{20}$

(C) $\dfrac{3}{5}$

(D) $\dfrac{11}{15}$

(E) $\dfrac{5}{6}$

In one hour these machines can do $\dfrac{1}{4}$, $\dfrac{1}{5}$, and $\dfrac{1}{6}$ of the job, respectively. Since the third machine does the smallest part of the job in one hour and only two machines are to be used, the third machine should be eliminated. Therefore, the first two machines will complete $\dfrac{1}{4} + \dfrac{1}{5} = \dfrac{9}{20}$ of the job in one hour. The best answer is B.

8. In 1985, 45 percent of a document storage facility's 60 customers were banks, and in 1987, 25 percent of its 144 customers were banks. What was the percent increase from 1985 to 1987 in the number of bank customers the facility had?

(A) 10.7%
(B) 20%
(C) 25%
(D) $33\dfrac{1}{3}\%$
(E) $58\dfrac{1}{3}\%$

In 1985, the number of banks using the storage facility was $0.45(60) = 27$ banks. In 1987, the number of banks using the storage facility was $0.25(144) = 36$ banks. Between 1985 and 1987, the number of banks increased by 9. Since 27 was the number that was increased, the percent increase equals $\dfrac{9}{27} = \dfrac{1}{3}$, which is $33\dfrac{1}{3}\%$. Thus, the best answer is D.

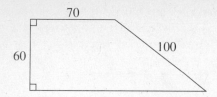

9. What is the perimeter of the figure above?

(A) 380
(B) 360
(C) 330
(D) 300
(E) 230

The figure below shows how the problem can be approached by partitioning the trapezoid into a rectangle and a triangle.

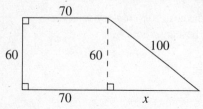

The two pieces of the lower horizontal line segment are 70 and x. From the Pythagorean theorem, $x^2 + 60^2 = 100^2$, $x^2 = 6,400$, and $x = 80$. The length of the lower horizontal line is $70 + 80 = 150$; therefore, the perimeter of the figure is $60 + 70 + 100 + 150 = 380$. The best answer is A.

10. A committee is composed of w women and m men. If 3 women and 2 men are added to the committee, and if one person is selected at random from the enlarged committee, then the probability that a woman is selected can be represented by

(A) $\dfrac{w}{m}$

(B) $\dfrac{w}{w+m}$

(C) $\dfrac{w+3}{m+2}$

(D) $\dfrac{w+3}{w+m+3}$

(E) $\dfrac{w+3}{w+m+5}$

With the additional people the committee has a total of $w + 3$ women and $m + 2$ men for a total of $w + m + 5$ people. The probability that a woman is selected is

$$\frac{\text{the number of women}}{\text{the total number of members}} = \frac{w+3}{w+m+5}$$

Thus, the best answer is E.

11. Last year Carlos saved 10 percent of his annual earnings. This year he earned 5 percent more than last year and he saved 12 percent of his annual earnings. The amount saved this year was what percent of the amount saved last year?

(A) 122%
(B) 124%
(C) 126%
(D) 128%
(E) 130%

If x represents the amount of Carlos' annual earnings last year, then $1.05x$ would represent his earnings this year. The amount Carlos saved last year was $0.10x$, and the amount saved this year is $0.12(1.05x) = 0.126x$. The amount saved this year as a percent of the amount saved last year is

$$\frac{0.126x}{0.1x} = 1.26 = 126\%$$

The best answer is C.

12. Jan lives x floors above the ground floor of a highrise building. It takes her 30 seconds per floor to walk down the steps and 2 seconds per floor to ride the elevator. If it takes Jan the same amount of time to walk down the steps to the ground floor as to wait for the elevator for 7 minutes and ride down, then x equals

(A) 4
(B) 7
(C) 14
(D) 15
(E) 16

Since Jan lives x floors above the ground floor and it takes her 30 seconds per floor to walk and 2 seconds per floor to ride, it takes $30x$ seconds to walk down and $2x$ seconds to ride down after waiting 7 minutes (420 seconds) for the elevator. Thus, $30x = 2x + 420$; $x = 15$. The best answer is D.

13. A corporation that had \$115.19 billion in profits for the year paid out \$230.10 million in employee benefits. Approximately what percent of the profits were the employee benefits? (1 billion $= 10^9$)

(A) 50%
(B) 20%
(C) 5%
(D) 2%
(E) 0.2%

The employee benefits as a fraction of profits is $\dfrac{230.10 \times 10^6}{115.19 \times 10^9}$, which is approximately $\dfrac{230}{155 \times 10^3} = \dfrac{2}{1,000} = 0.2\%$. Thus, the best answer is E.

Questions 14–15 refer to the following definition.

For any positive integer n, $n > 1$, the "length" of n is the number of positive primes (not necessarily distinct) whose product is n. For example, the length of 50 is 3 since $50 = (2)(5)(5)$.

14. Which of the following integers has length 3 ?

(A)   3
(B)   15
(C)   60
(D)   64
(E) 105

To solve this problem it is necessary to factor each number into its primes and determine its "length" until the number of "length" 3 is found. It is obvious that 3 and 15 have lengths 1 and 2, respectively, and

$60 = (5)(3)(2)(2)$ has length 4
$64 = (2)(2)(2)(2)(2)(2)$ has length 6
$105 = (5)(3)(7)$ has length 3

Therefore, the best answer is E.

15. What is the greatest possible length of a positive integer less than 1,000 ?

(A) 10
(B)   9
(C)   8
(D)   7
(E)   6

A positive integer less than 1,000 with greatest possible "length" would be the positive number with the greatest number of prime factors with a product less than 1,000. The greatest number of factors can be obtained by using the smallest prime number, 2, as a factor as many times as possible. Since $2^9 = 512$ and $2^{10} = 1024$, the greatest possible "length" is 9. The best answer is B.

16. A dealer originally bought 100 identical batteries at a total cost of q dollars. If each battery was sold at 50 percent above the original cost per battery, then, in terms of q, for how many dollars was each battery sold?

(A) $\dfrac{3q}{200}$

(B) $\dfrac{3q}{2}$

(C) $150q$

(D) $\dfrac{q}{100} + 50$

(E) $\dfrac{150}{q}$

The cost per battery (in dollars) is $\dfrac{q}{100}$. Since the selling price is 150% of the cost, each battery sells for $\dfrac{150}{100} \times \dfrac{q}{100} = \dfrac{3q}{200}$ dollars. The best answer is A.

PROBLEM SOLVING SAMPLE TEST SECTION 8

Time — 25 minutes

16 Questions

<u>Directions:</u> In this section solve each problem, using any available space on the page for scratchwork. Then indicate the best of the answer choices given.

<u>Numbers:</u> All numbers used are real numbers.

<u>Figures:</u> Figures that accompany problems in this section are intended to provide information useful in solving the problems. They are drawn as accurately as possible EXCEPT when it is stated in a specific problem that its figure is not drawn to scale. All figures lie in a plane unless otherwise indicated.

1. If the population of a certain country increases at the rate of one person every 15 seconds, by how many persons does the population increase in 20 minutes?

   (A) 80
   (B) 100
   (C) 150
   (D) 240
   (E) 300

2. The value of $-3 - (-10)$ is how much greater than the value of $-10 - (-3)$?

   (A) 0
   (B) 6
   (C) 7
   (D) 14
   (E) 26

3. For an agricultural experiment, 300 seeds were planted in one plot and 200 were planted in a second plot. If exactly 25 percent of the seeds in the first plot germinated and exactly 35 percent of the seeds in the second plot germinated, what percent of the total number of seeds germinated?

   (A) 12%
   (B) 26%
   (C) 29%
   (D) 30%
   (E) 60%

4. If $\frac{a}{b} = \frac{2}{3}$, which of the following is NOT true?

   (A) $\frac{a + b}{b} = \frac{5}{3}$

   (B) $\frac{b}{b - a} = 3$

   (C) $\frac{a - b}{b} = \frac{1}{3}$

   (D) $\frac{2a}{3b} = \frac{4}{9}$

   (E) $\frac{a + 3b}{a} = \frac{11}{2}$

5. On the number line, if $r < s$, if p is halfway between r and s, and if t is halfway between p and r, then $\frac{s - t}{t - r} =$

   (A) $\frac{1}{4}$　(B) $\frac{1}{3}$　(C) $\frac{4}{3}$　(D) 3　(E) 4

GO ON TO THE NEXT PAGE.

6. Coins are to be put into 7 pockets so that each pocket contains at least one coin. At most 3 of the pockets are to contain the same number of coins, and no two of the remaining pockets are to contain an equal number of coins. What is the least possible number of coins needed for the pockets?

(A) 7
(B) 13
(C) 17
(D) 22
(E) 28

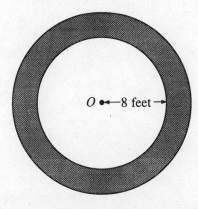

O ◄—8 feet—►

7. The figure above shows a circular flower bed, with its center at O, surrounded by a circular path that is 3 feet wide. What is the area of the path, in square feet?

(A) 25π (B) 38π (C) 55π (D) 57π (E) 64π

	Brand X	Brand Y
Miles per Gallon	40	36
Cost per Gallon	$0.80	$0.75

8. The table above gives the gasoline costs and consumption rates for a certain car driven at 50 miles per hour, using each of two brands of gasoline. How many miles further can the car be driven at this speed on $12 worth of brand X gasoline than on $12 worth of brand Y gasoline?

(A) 20   (B) 24   (C) 84   (D) 100   (E) 104

9. If $1 were invested at 8 percent interest compounded annually, the total value of the investment, in dollars, at the end of 6 years would be

(A) $(1.8)^6$
(B) $(1.08)^6$
(C) $6(1.08)$
(D) $1 + (0.08)^6$
(E) $1 + 6(0.08)$

GO ON TO THE NEXT PAGE.

10. A furniture store sells only two models of desks, model A and model B. The selling price of model A is \$120, which is 30 percent of the selling price of model B. If the furniture store sells 2,000 desks, $\frac{3}{4}$ of which are model B, what is the furniture store's total revenue from the sale of desks?

(A) \$114,000
(B) \$186,000
(C) \$294,000
(D) \$380,000
(E) \$660,000

11. How many minutes does it take John to type y words if he types at the rate of x words per minute?

(A) $\frac{x}{y}$ (B) $\frac{y}{x}$ (C) xy (D) $\frac{60x}{y}$ (E) $\frac{y}{60x}$

12. The weights of four packages are 1, 3, 5, and 7 pounds, respectively. Which of the following CANNOT be the total weight, in pounds, of any combination of the packages?

(A) 9
(B) 10
(C) 12
(D) 13
(E) 14

13. $\sqrt{(16)(20) + (8)(32)} =$

(A) $4\sqrt{20}$
(B) 24
(C) 25
(D) $4\sqrt{20} + 8\sqrt{2}$
(E) 32

14. The positive integer n is divisible by 25. If $\sqrt{n}$ is greater than 25, which of the following could be the value of $\frac{n}{25}$?

(A) 22
(B) 23
(C) 24
(D) 25
(E) 26

GO ON TO THE NEXT PAGE.

-120-

15. If x and y are different integers and $x^2 = xy$, which of the following must be true?

    I. $x = 0$
   II. $y = 0$
  III. $x = -y$

(A) I only
(B) II only
(C) III only
(D) I and III only
(E) I, II, and III

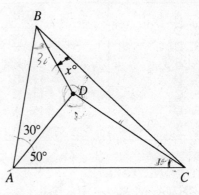

Note: Figure not drawn to scale.

16. In the figure above, $DA = DB = DC$. What is the value of x ?

(A) 10
(B) 20
(C) 30
(D) 40
(E) 50

STOP

**IF YOU FINISH BEFORE TIME IS CALLED, YOU MAY CHECK YOUR WORK ON THIS SECTION ONLY.
DO NOT TURN TO ANY OTHER SECTION IN THE TEST.**

Answer Key for Sample Test Section 8

PROBLEM SOLVING

1. A	9. B
2. D	10. E
3. C	11. B
4. B̶C	12. E
5. D	13. B
6. C	14. E
7. D	15. A
8. B	16. A

Explanatory Material:
Problem Solving Sample Test Section 8

1. **If the population of a certain country increases at the rate of one person every 15 seconds, by how many persons does the population increase in 20 minutes?**

   (A) 80
   (B) 100
   (C) 150
   (D) 240
   (E) 300

Since the population increases at the rate of 1 person every 15 seconds, it increases by 4 people every 60 seconds, that is, by 4 people every minute. Thus, in 20 minutes the population increases by $20 \times 4 = 80$ people. The best answer is A.

2. **The value of $-3 - (-10)$ is how much greater than the value of $-10 - (-3)$?**

   (A) 0
   (B) 6
   (C) 7
   (D) 14
   (E) 26

The value of $-3 - (-10)$ is $-3 + 10 = 7$, and the value of $-10 - (-3)$ is $-10 + 3 = -7$. The difference is $7 - (-7) = 7 + 7 = 14$. Thus, the value of the first expression is 14 more than the value of the second. The best answer is D.

3. **For an agricultural experiment, 300 seeds were planted in one plot and 200 were planted in a second plot. If exactly 25 percent of the seeds in the first plot germinated and exactly 35 percent of the seeds in the second plot germinated, what percent of the total number of seeds germinated?**

   (A) 12%
   (B) 26%
   (C) 29%
   (D) 30%
   (E) 60%

In the first plot 25% of 300 seeds germinated, so $0.25 \times 300 = 75$ seeds germinated. In the second plot, 35% of 200 seeds germinated, so $0.35 \times 200 = 70$ seeds germinated. Since $75 + 70 = 145$ seeds germinated out of a total of $300 + 200 = 500$ seeds, the percent of seeds that germinated is $\frac{145}{500} \times 100\%$, or 29%. Thus, the best answer is C.

4. **If $\frac{a}{b} = \frac{2}{3}$, which of the following is NOT true?**

   (A) $\dfrac{a + b}{b} = \dfrac{5}{3}$

   (B) $\dfrac{b}{b - a} = 3$

   (C) $\dfrac{a - b}{b} = \dfrac{1}{3}$

   (D) $\dfrac{2a}{3b} = \dfrac{4}{9}$

   (E) $\dfrac{a + 3b}{a} = \dfrac{11}{2}$

One approach is to express the left side of each of the choices in terms of $\frac{a}{b}$. Thus, A is true since $\frac{a + b}{b} = \frac{a}{b} + 1 = \frac{2}{3} + 1 = \frac{5}{3}$. D and E can be shown to be true in a similar manner. One way to see that B is true is to first invert both sides, that is, show that $\frac{b - a}{b} = \frac{1}{3}$. This is true since $\frac{b - a}{b} = \frac{b}{b} - \frac{a}{b} = 1 - \frac{2}{3} = \frac{1}{3}$. Thus, B is true. On the other hand, C is not true since $\frac{a - b}{b} = \frac{a}{b} - \frac{b}{b} = \frac{2}{3} - 1 = -\frac{1}{3}$, not $\frac{1}{3}$.

5. **On the number line, if $r < s$, if p is halfway between r and s, and if t is halfway between p and r, then $\dfrac{s - t}{t - r} =$**

   (A) $\dfrac{1}{4}$ (B) $\dfrac{1}{3}$ (C) $\dfrac{4}{3}$ (D) 3   (E) 4

The figure above shows the relative positions of the numbers $r, t, p,$ and s on the number line, where x denotes the length of the line segment from r to t. Thus, $\frac{s - t}{t - r} = \frac{x + 2x}{x} = \frac{3x}{x} = 3$. The best answer is D.

-122-

6. Coins are to be put into 7 pockets so that each pocket contains at least one coin. At most 3 of the pockets are to contain the same number of coins, and no two of the remaining pockets are to contain an equal number of coins. What is the least possible number of coins needed for the pockets?

   (A) 7
   (B) 13
   (C) 17
   (D) 22
   (E) 28

To determine the least possible number of coins needed, the smallest possible number of coins should be placed in each pocket, subject to the constraints of the problem. Thus, one coin should be put in three of the pockets, 2 coins in the fourth pocket, 3 coins in the fifth, 4 coins in the sixth, and 5 coins in the seventh. The least possible number of coins is therefore $1 + 1 + 1 + 2 + 3 + 4 + 5 = 17$, so the best answer is C.

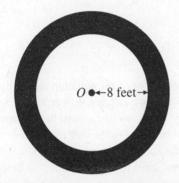

7. The figure above shows a circular flower bed, with its center at O, surrounded by a circular path that is 3 feet wide. What is the area of the path, in square feet?

   (A) 25π (B) 38π (C) 55π (D) 57π (E) 64π

Since the path is 3 feet wide, its outer boundary forms a circle with a radius of $8 + 3 = 11$ feet. The area of the path can be found by finding the area of a circle with a radius of 11 feet and subtracting the area of a circle with a radius of 8 feet. The area of the path is therefore $\pi(11)^2 - \pi(8)^2 = (121 - 64)\pi = 57\pi$ square feet. Thus, the best answer is D.

	Brand X	Brand Y
Miles per Gallon	40	36
Cost per Gallon	$0.80	$0.75

8. The table above gives the gasoline costs and consumption rates for a certain car driven at 50 miles per hour, using each of two brands of gasoline. How many miles further can the car be driven at this speed on $12 worth of brand X gasoline than on $12 worth of brand Y gasoline?

   (A) 20   (B) 24   (C) 84   (D) 100   (E) 104

$12.00 worth of brand X gasoline is $\frac{12.00}{0.80} = 15$ gallons. Since the car gets 40 miles per gallon on brand X, the car would be able to go $(40)(15) = 600$ miles. On the other hand, $12.00 worth of brand Y gasoline is $\frac{12.00}{0.75} = 16$ gallons. Since the car gets 36 miles per gallon using brand Y, the car would be able to go $(36)(16) = 576$ miles. Therefore, the car would be able to go $600 - 576 = 24$ more miles with brand X. The best answer is B.

9. If $1 were invested at 8 percent interest compounded annually, the total value of the investment, in dollars, at the end of 6 years would be

   (A) $(1.8)^6$
   (B) $(1.08)^6$
   (C) $6(1.08)$
   (D) $1 + (0.08)^6$
   (E) $1 + 6(0.08)$

Since the 8 percent interest is compounded annually, each year 0.08 times the investment is added to the investment. This is the same as multiplying the investment by 1.08. Therefore, after six years the initial investment of $1 is $(1)(1.08)^6 = (1.08)^6$ dollars. Thus, the best answer is B.

10. A furniture store sells only two models of desks, model A and model B. The selling price of model A is $120, which is 30 percent of the selling price of model B. If the furniture store sells 2,000 desks, $\frac{3}{4}$ of which are model B, what is the furniture store's total revenue from the sale of desks?

   (A) $114,000
   (B) $186,000
   (C) $294,000
   (D) $380,000
   (E) $660,000

The number of model B desks sold was $\frac{3}{4}(2,000) = 1,500$, so the number of model A desks sold was $2,000 - 1,500 = 500$. Since the price of model A is $120 and this is 30 percent of the price of model *B*, the price of model *B* is $\frac{\$120}{0.3} = \$400$.

Thus, the total revenue from the sales of the desks is
$500(\$120) + 1,500(\$400) = \$60,000 + \$600,000 = \$660,000$.
The best answer is E.

11. **How many minutes does it take John to type *y* words if he types at the rate of *x* words per minute?**

(A) $\frac{x}{y}$ (B) $\frac{y}{x}$ (C) xy (D) $\frac{60x}{y}$ (E) $\frac{y}{60x}$

Let *m* represent the number of minutes John types. John types *x* words a minute for *m* minutes, so he would type a total of $xm = y$ words. Dividing both sides of the equation by *x* yields $m = y/x$. Thus, the best answer is B.

12. **The weights of four packages are 1, 3, 5, and 7 pounds, respectively. Which of the following CANNOT be the total weight, in pounds, of any combination of the packages?**

(A) 9
(B) 10
(C) 12
(D) 13
(E) 14

For each of choices A-D there is a combination of the packages that gives that total: (A) $9 = 1 + 3 + 5$, (B) $10 = 3 + 7$, (C) $12 = 5 + 7$, and (D) $13 = 1 + 5 + 7$. On the other hand, no combination of the packages weighs 14 pounds, since the total weight of the four packages is $1 + 3 + 5 + 7 = 16$ pounds, and there is no combination of packages weighing 2 pounds, whose removal would result in a combination weighing 14 pounds. The best answer is E.

13. $\sqrt{(16)(20) + (8)(32)} =$

(A) $4\sqrt{20}$
(B) 24
(C) 25
(D) $4\sqrt{20} + 8\sqrt{2}$
(E) 32

$\sqrt{(16)(20) + (8)(32)} = \sqrt{320 + 256} = \sqrt{576} = 24$
Thus, the best answer is B.

Alternatively, since $(16)(20) + (8)(32) = (16)(20) + (8)(2)(16)$
$= (16)(20 + 16)$
$= (16)(36),$
it follows that
$\sqrt{(16)(20) + (8)(32)} = \sqrt{(16)(36)} = (4)(6) = 24.$

14. **The positive integer *n* is divisible by 25. If $\sqrt{n}$ is greater than 25, which of the following could be the value of $\frac{n}{25}$?**

(A) 22
(B) 23
(C) 24
(D) 25
(E) 26

If $\sqrt{n} > 25$, then $n > 25^2$, so $n > 625$. Hence $\frac{n}{25} > \frac{625}{25} = 25$. Since only choice E is greater than 25, the best answer is E.

15. **If *x* and *y* are different integers and $x^2 = xy$, which of the following must be true?**

I. $x = 0$
II. $y = 0$
III. $x = -y$

(A) I only
(B) II only
(C) III only
(D) I and III only
(E) I, II, and III

If $x \neq 0$, then both sides of the equation can be divided by *x*, resulting in $x = y$. Thus, either $x = 0$ or $x = y$. Since it is given that $x \neq y$, it follows that *x* must be 0. Therefore, statement I must be true. On the other hand, the values $x = 0$ and $y = 3$ clearly satisfy $x^2 = xy$ but do not satisfy II or III, so II and III do not have to be true. Thus, the best answer is A.

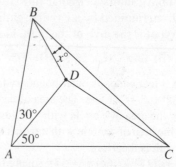

Note: Figure not drawn to scale.

16. **In the figure above, $DA = DB = DC$. What is the value of *x*?**

(A) 10
(B) 20
(C) 30
(D) 40
(E) 50

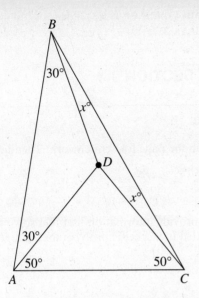

Since $DA = DB = DC$, the interior triangles are all isosceles, and thus the other angles of $\triangle ABC$ have degree measures as indicated in the figure above (drawn to scale). Since the measures of the three angles of a triangle always add up to $180°$, it follows that

$$80 + (30 + x) + (50 + x) = 180$$
$$160 + 2x = 180$$
$$2x = 20$$
$$x = 10.$$

Thus, the best answer is A.

PROBLEM SOLVING SAMPLE TEST SECTION 9

Time — 25 minutes

16 Questions

Directions: In this section solve each problem, using any available space on the page for scratchwork. Then indicate the best of the answer choices given.

Numbers: All numbers used are real numbers.

Figures: Figures that accompany problems in this section are intended to provide information useful in solving the problems. They are drawn as accurately as possible EXCEPT when it is stated in a specific problem that its figure is not drawn to scale. All figures lie in a plane unless otherwise indicated.

1. In the figure above, the sum of the three numbers in the horizontal row equals the product of the three numbers in the vertical column. What is the value of xy?

   (A) 6
   (B) 15
   (C) 35
   (D) 75
   (E) 90

2. For telephone calls between two particular cities, a telephone company charges $0.40 per minute if the calls are placed between 5:00 a.m. and 9:00 p.m. and $0.25 per minute if the calls are placed between 9:00 p.m. and 5:00 a.m. If the charge for a call between the two cities placed at 1:00 p.m. was $10.00, how much would a call of the same duration have cost if it had been placed at 11:00 p.m. ?

   (A) $3.75
   (B) $6.25
   (C) $9.85
   (D) $10.00
   (E) $16.00

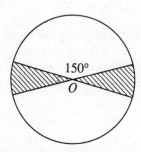

3. If O is the center of the circle above, what fraction of the circular region is shaded?

   (A) $\dfrac{1}{12}$

   (B) $\dfrac{1}{9}$

   (C) $\dfrac{1}{6}$

   (D) $\dfrac{1}{4}$

   (E) $\dfrac{1}{3}$

GO ON TO THE NEXT PAGE.

-126-

4. If a compact disc that usually sells for $12.95 is on sale for $9.95, then the percent decrease in price is closest to

(A) 38%
(B) 31%
(C) 30%
(D) 29%
(E) 23%

5. $$\cfrac{1}{1 + \cfrac{1}{2 + \cfrac{1}{3}}} =$$

(A) $\dfrac{3}{10}$

(B) $\dfrac{7}{10}$

(C) $\dfrac{6}{7}$

(D) $\dfrac{10}{7}$

(E) $\dfrac{10}{3}$

6. A fruit-salad mixture consists of apples, peaches, and grapes in the ratio 6 : 5 : 2, respectively, by weight. If 39 pounds of the mixture is prepared, the mixture includes how many more pounds of apples than grapes?

(A) 15
(B) 12
(C) 9
(D) 6
(E) 4

GO ON TO THE NEXT PAGE.

7. If $\dfrac{3}{x} = 2$ and $\dfrac{y}{4} = 3$, then $\dfrac{3 + y}{x + 4} =$

(A) $\dfrac{10}{9}$

(B) $\dfrac{3}{2}$

(C) $\dfrac{20}{11}$

(D) $\dfrac{30}{11}$

(E) 5

8. $\left(1 + \sqrt{5}\right)\left(1 - \sqrt{5}\right) =$

(A) -4
(B) 2
(C) 6
(D) $-4 - 2\sqrt{5}$
(E) $6 - 2\sqrt{5}$

9. Starting from point O on a flat school playground, a child walks 10 yards due north, then 6 yards due east, and then 2 yards due south, arriving at point P. How far apart, in yards, are points O and P?

(A) 18
(B) 16
(C) 14
(D) 12
(E) 10

10. A certain car increased its average speed by 5 miles per hour in each successive 5-minute interval after the first interval. If in the first 5-minute interval its average speed was 20 miles per hour, how many miles did the car travel in the third 5-minute interval?

(A) 1.0
(B) 1.5
(C) 2.0
(D) 2.5
(E) 3.0

GO ON TO THE NEXT PAGE.

11. Lois has x dollars more than Jim has, and together they have a total of y dollars. Which of the following represents the number of dollars that Jim has?

(A) $\dfrac{y - x}{2}$

(B) $y - \dfrac{x}{2}$

(C) $\dfrac{y}{2} - x$

(D) $2y - x$

(E) $y - 2x$

13. A certain population of bacteria doubles every 10 minutes. If the number of bacteria in the population initially was 10^4, what was the number in the population 1 hour later?

(A) $2(10^4)$

(B) $6(10^4)$

(C) $(2^6)(10^4)$

(D) $(10^6)(10^4)$

(E) $(10^4)^6$

GO ON TO THE NEXT PAGE.

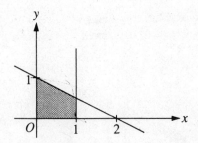

12. In the rectangular coordinate system above, the shaded region is bounded by straight lines. Which of the following is NOT an equation of one of the boundary lines?

(A) $x = 0$
(B) $y = 0$
(C) $x = 1$
(D) $x - y = 0$
(E) $x + 2y = 2$

14. During a certain season, a team won 80 percent of its first 100 games and 50 percent of its remaining games. If the team won 70 percent of its games for the entire season, what was the total number of games that the team played?

(A) 180
(B) 170
(C) 156
(D) 150
(E) 105

15. If Juan takes 11 seconds to run y yards, how many seconds will it take him to run x yards at the same rate?

(A) $\dfrac{11x}{y}$

(B) $\dfrac{11y}{x}$

(C) $\dfrac{x}{11y}$

(D) $\dfrac{11}{xy}$

(E) $\dfrac{xy}{11}$

16. Which of the following fractions has the greatest value?

(A) $\dfrac{6}{(2^2)(5^2)}$

(B) $\dfrac{1}{(2^3)(5^2)}$

(C) $\dfrac{28}{(2^2)(5^3)}$

(D) $\dfrac{62}{(2^3)(5^3)}$

(E) $\dfrac{122}{(2^4)(5^3)}$

S T O P

IF YOU FINISH BEFORE TIME IS CALLED, YOU MAY CHECK YOUR WORK ON THIS SECTION ONLY.
DO NOT TURN TO ANY OTHER SECTION IN THE TEST.

Answer Key for Sample Test Section 9

PROBLEM SOLVING

1. A	9. E
2. B	10. D
3. C	11. A
4. E	12. D
5. B	13. C
6. B	14. D
7. D	15. A
8. A	16. D

Explanatory Material:
Problem Solving Sample Test Section 9

1. In the figure above, the sum of the three numbers in the horizontal row equals the product of the three numbers in the vertical column. What is the value of xy ?

   (A)   6
   (B)   15
   (C)   35
   (D)   75
   (E)   90

The sum of the three numbers in the horizontal row is
37 + 38 + 15, or 90. The product of the three numbers in the vertical column is $15xy$. Thus, $15xy = 90$, or $xy = 6$, and the best answer is A.

2. For telephone calls between two particular cities, a telephone company charges $0.40 per minute if the calls are placed between 5:00 a.m. and 9:00 p.m. and $0.25 per minute if the calls are placed between 9:00 p.m. and 5:00 a.m. If the charge for a call between the two cities placed at 1:00 p.m. was $10.00, how much would a call of the same duration have cost if it had been placed at 11:00 p.m.?

   (A) $3.75
   (B) $6.25
   (C) $9.85
   (D) $10.00
   (E) $16.00

The ratio of the charge per minute for a call placed at
11:00 p.m. to the charge per minute for a call placed at 1:00 p.m.
is $\dfrac{\$0.25}{\$0.40}$, or $\dfrac{5}{8}$. Therefore, if the charge for a call placed at
1:00 p.m. is $10.00, the charge for a call of the same duration
placed at 11:00 p.m. would be $\left(\dfrac{5}{8}\right)(\$10.00)$, or $6.25, and the
best answer is B.

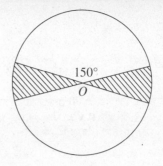

3. If O is the center of the circle above, what fraction of the circular region is shaded?

   (A) $\dfrac{1}{12}$

   (B) $\dfrac{1}{9}$

   (C) $\dfrac{1}{6}$

   (D) $\dfrac{1}{4}$

   (E) $\dfrac{1}{3}$

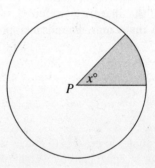

If P is the center of the circle above, then the fraction of the
area of the circular region that is shaded is $\dfrac{x}{360}$. Since vertical
angles are equal, the sum of the central angles of the two
shaded regions is $360° - 2(150)°$, or $60°$. Therefore, $\dfrac{60}{360} = \dfrac{1}{6}$
of the circular region is shaded, and the best answer is C.

4. If a compact disc that usually sells for $12.95 is on sale for $9.95, then the percent decrease in price is closest to

   (A)   38%
   (B)   31%
   (C)   30%
   (D)   29%
   (E)   23%

The percent decrease in the price of an item =

$$\frac{\text{the decrease in the cost of the item}}{\text{the original price of the item}} .$$

Thus, the percent decrease in the price of a compact disc is
$\dfrac{12.95 - 9.95}{12.95}$, or $\dfrac{3}{12.95}$, which is a little less than $\dfrac{3.0}{12.50}$ or
24 percent. Thus, the best answer is E.

-131-

5. $\dfrac{1}{1+\dfrac{1}{2+\dfrac{1}{3}}} =$

   (A) $\dfrac{3}{10}$

   (B) $\dfrac{7}{10}$

   (C) $\dfrac{6}{7}$

   (D) $\dfrac{10}{7}$

   (E) $\dfrac{10}{3}$

$$\frac{1}{1+\dfrac{1}{2+\dfrac{1}{3}}} = \frac{1}{1+\dfrac{1}{\dfrac{7}{3}}} = \frac{1}{1+\dfrac{3}{7}} = \frac{1}{\dfrac{10}{7}} = \frac{7}{10}$$

Thus, the best answer is B.

6. A fruit-salad mixture consists of apples, peaches, and grapes in the ratio 6:5:2, respectively, by weight. If 39 pounds of the mixture is prepared, the mixture includes how many more pounds of apples than grapes?

   (A) 15
   (B) 12
   (C) 9
   (D) 6
   (E) 4

Since the ratio of apples to peaches to grapes is 6:5:2, for each $6 + 5 + 2$ or 13 equal parts by weight of the mixture, 6 parts are apples and 2 parts are grapes. There are then $\dfrac{6}{13}(39) = 18$ pounds of apples and $\dfrac{2}{13}(39) = 6$ pounds of grapes. Therefore, there are $18 - 6 = 12$ more pounds of apples than grapes in 39 pounds of the mixture. The best answer is B.

7. If $\dfrac{3}{x} = 2$ and $\dfrac{y}{4} = 3$, then $\dfrac{3+y}{x+4} =$

   (A) $\dfrac{10}{9}$

   (B) $\dfrac{3}{2}$

   (C) $\dfrac{20}{11}$

   (D) $\dfrac{30}{11}$

   (E) 5

Since $\dfrac{3}{x} = 2$ and $\dfrac{y}{4} = 3$, it follows that $x = \dfrac{3}{2}$ and $y = 12$.

Thus, $\dfrac{3+y}{x+4} = \dfrac{3+12}{\dfrac{3}{2}+4} = \dfrac{15}{\dfrac{11}{2}} = \dfrac{30}{11}$, and the best answer is D.

8. $\left(1 + \sqrt{5}\right)\left(1 - \sqrt{5}\right) =$

   (A) -4
   (B) 2
   (C) 6
   (D) $-4 - 2\sqrt{5}$
   (E) $6 - 2\sqrt{5}$

$$(1 + \sqrt{5})(1 - \sqrt{5}) = 1^2 + \sqrt{5} - \sqrt{5} - (\sqrt{5})^2$$
$$= 1^2 - (\sqrt{5})^2 = 1 - 5 = -4$$

Thus, the best answer is A.

9. Starting from point O on a flat school playground, a child walks 10 yards due north, then 6 yards due east, and then 2 yards due south, arriving at point P. How far apart, in yards, are points O and P?

   (A) 18
   (B) 16
   (C) 14
   (D) 12
   (E) 10

The figure below represents the information given in the question.

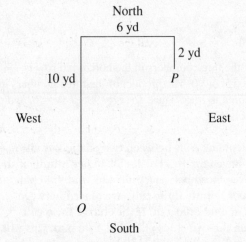

Next, two lines can be drawn; one from P perpendicular to the line representing the child's walk due north, and the other connecting O and P.

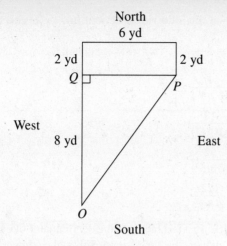

North
6 yd

2 yd   2 yd

Q

P

West

8 yd   East

O

South

OPQ is a right triangle, $QP = 6$ yards, and
$OQ = (10 - 2)$ yards $= 8$ yards. Thus, by the
Pythagorean theorem $OP = \sqrt{6^2 + 8^2} = \sqrt{100} = 10$ yards,
and the best answer is E.

10. **A certain car increased its average speed by 5 miles
per hour in each successive 5-minute interval after the
first interval. If in the first 5-minute interval its
average speed was 20 miles per hour, how many miles
did the car travel in the third 5-minute interval?**

    (A)   1.0
    (B)   1.5
    (C)   2.0
    (D)   2.5
    (E)   3.0

In the first 5-minute interval the car's average speed was
20 miles per hour, and the car's average speed increased by
5 miles per hour in each successive 5-minute interval. Thus,
the average speed was 25 miles per hour in the second
5-minute interval and 30 miles per hour in the third 5-minute
interval. Since 5 minutes is $\frac{1}{12}$ of an hour, the car traveled
$\frac{1}{12}(30)$, or 2.5, miles in the third 5-minute interval, and the
best answer is D.

11. **Lois has x dollars more than Jim has, and together
they have a total of y dollars. Which of the following
represents the number of dollars that Jim has?**

    (A) $\dfrac{y - x}{2}$

    (B) $y - \dfrac{x}{2}$

    (C) $\dfrac{y}{2} - x$

    (D) $2y - x$

    (E) $y - 2x$

If J is the number of dollars that Jim has, then Lois has
$J + x$ dollars. Thus, the amount, y, that they have together
is $J + (J + x)$. So $y = J + (J + x) = 2J + x$, $J = \dfrac{y - x}{2}$,
and the best answer is A.

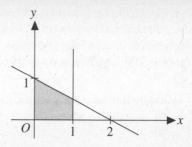

12. **In the rectangular coordinate system above, the
shaded region is bounded by straight lines. Which of
the following is NOT an equation of one of the
boundary lines?**

    (A) $x = 0$
    (B) $y = 0$
    (C) $x = 1$
    (D) $x - y = 0$
    (E) $x + 2y = 2$

The equation of the x-axis is $y = 0$. The equations of the
y-axis and the line one unit to the right of the y-axis are $x = 0$
and $x = 1$, respectively. Thus, the answer key cannot be A, B,
or C. The top boundary line passes through the point (2,0).
To lie on a line this point must satisfy the equation of that line.
Substituting in D yields $2 - 0 = 0$, which is not a true
statement. Thus, $x - y = 0$ is NOT an equation of one of the
boundary lines and the best answer is D.

13. **A certain population of bacteria doubles every
10 minutes. If the number of bacteria in the
population initially was 10^4, what was the number
in the population 1 hour later?**

    (A) $2(10^4)$
    (B) $6(10^4)$
    (C) $(2^6)(10^4)$
    (D) $(10^6)(10^4)$
    (E) $(10^4)^6$

If the population of bacteria doubles every 10 minutes, it
doubles 6 times in an hour. The population after 10 minutes
was $(2)(10^4)$ and after 20 minutes was $(2)(2)(10^4)$, or $(2^2)(10^4)$.
Continuing to multiply by 2 each time the population doubles,
it follows that the population after an hour is $(2^6)(10^4)$, and the
best answer is C.

14. **During a certain season, a team won 80 percent of its
first 100 games and 50 percent of its remaining games.
If the team won 70 percent of its games for the entire
season, what was the total number of games that the
team played?**

    (A)   180
    (B)   170
    (C)   156
    (D)   150
    (E)   105

Let G equal the number of games played by the team this season. Expressed algebraically, 80 percent of its first 100 games and 50 percent of its remaining games is $(0.80)(100) + 0.50(G - 100)$ and 70 percent of its games is $0.70G$. Thus,

$$0.70G = (0.80)(100) + 0.50(G - 100)$$
$$0.70G = 80 + 0.50G - 50$$
$$0.20G = 30$$
$$G = 150$$

Therefore, the team played 150 games and the best answer is D.

15. If Juan takes 11 seconds to run y yards, how many seconds will it take him to run x yards at the same rate?

(A) $\dfrac{11x}{y}$

(B) $\dfrac{11y}{x}$

(C) $\dfrac{x}{11y}$

(D) $\dfrac{11}{xy}$

(E) $\dfrac{xy}{11}$

If Juan takes 11 seconds to run y yards, it takes him $\dfrac{11}{y}$ seconds to run 1 yard. Therefore, it takes him $x\left(\dfrac{11}{y}\right) = \dfrac{11x}{y}$ seconds to run x yards and the best answer is A.

Alternatively, recall that rate $\times$ time $=$ distance.

Therefore, if Juan takes 11 seconds to run y yards he runs at a rate of $\dfrac{y}{11}$ yards per second. So, to run x yards he takes $\dfrac{x}{\frac{y}{11}} = \dfrac{11x}{y}$ seconds.

16. Which of the following fractions has the greatest value?

(A) $\dfrac{6}{(2^2)(5^2)}$

(B) $\dfrac{1}{(2^3)(5^2)}$

(C) $\dfrac{28}{(2^2)(5^3)}$

(D) $\dfrac{62}{(2^3)(5^3)}$

(E) $\dfrac{122}{(2^4)(5^3)}$

Notice that $(2^2)(5^2)$ is a factor of the denominator of each of the answer choices. Factoring it out will make comparison of the sizes of the fractions easier.

(A) $\dfrac{6}{(2^2)(5^2)} = 6 \times \dfrac{1}{(2^2)(5^2)}$

(B) $\dfrac{1}{(2^3)(5^2)} = \dfrac{1}{2} \times \dfrac{1}{(2^2)(5^2)}$

(C) $\dfrac{28}{(2^2)(5^3)} = \dfrac{28}{5} \times \dfrac{1}{(2^2)(5^2)}$

(D) $\dfrac{62}{(2^3)(5^3)} = \dfrac{62}{(2)(5)} \times \dfrac{1}{(2^2)(5^2)} = \dfrac{31}{5} \times \dfrac{1}{(2^2)(5^2)}$

(E) $\dfrac{122}{(2^4)(5^3)} = \dfrac{122}{(2^2)(5)} \times \dfrac{1}{(2^2)(5^2)} = \dfrac{61}{10} \times \dfrac{1}{(2^2)(5^2)}$

Of these fractions, the one with the greatest factor preceding $\dfrac{1}{(2^2)(5^2)}$ is $\dfrac{31}{5} \times \dfrac{1}{(2^2)(5^2)}$. Thus, the best answer is D.

PROBLEM SOLVING SAMPLE TEST SECTION 10

Time — 25 minutes

16 Questions

Directions: In this section solve each problem, using any available space on the page for scratchwork. Then indicate the best of the answer choices given.

Numbers: All numbers used are real numbers.

Figures: Figures that accompany problems in this section are intended to provide information useful in solving the problems. They are drawn as accurately as possible EXCEPT when it is stated in a specific problem that its figure is not drawn to scale. All figures lie in a plane unless otherwise indicated.

1. $\dfrac{\frac{1}{2} + \frac{1}{3}}{\frac{1}{4}} =$

(A) $\dfrac{1}{12}$

(B) $\dfrac{5}{24}$

(C) $\dfrac{2}{3}$

(D) $\dfrac{9}{4}$

(E) $\dfrac{10}{3}$

2. John has 10 pairs of matched socks. If he loses 7 individual socks, what is the greatest number of pairs of matched socks he can have left?

(A) 7
(B) 6
(C) 5
(D) 4
(E) 3

3. Last year's receipts from the sale of candy on Valentine's Day totaled 385 million dollars, which represented 7 percent of total candy sales for the year. Candy sales for the year totaled how many million dollars?

(A)   55
(B)   550
(C)   2,695
(D)   5,500
(E) 26,950

4. How many minutes does it take to travel 120 miles at 400 miles per hour?

(A)   3

(B) $3\frac{1}{3}$

(C) $8\frac{2}{3}$

(D) 12

(E) 18

GO ON TO THE NEXT PAGE.

5. If $1 + \dfrac{1}{x} = 2 - \dfrac{2}{x}$, then $x =$

(A) -1

(B) $\dfrac{1}{3}$

(C) $\dfrac{2}{3}$

(D) 2

(E) 3

6. Last year, for every 100 million vehicles that traveled on a certain highway, 96 vehicles were involved in accidents. If 3 billion vehicles traveled on the highway last year, how many of those vehicles were involved in accidents? (1 billion = 1,000,000,000)

(A)   288
(B)   320
(C)   2,880
(D)   3,200
(E) 28,800

7. If the perimeter of a rectangular garden plot is 34 feet and its area is 60 square feet, what is the length of each of the longer sides?

(A) 5 ft
(B) 6 ft
(C) 10 ft
(D) 12 ft
(E) 15 ft

8. What is the least positive integer that is divisible by each of the integers 1 through 7, inclusive?

(A)   420
(B)   840
(C) 1,260
(D) 2,520
(E) 5,040

GO ON TO THE NEXT PAGE.

9. Thirty percent of the members of a swim club have passed the lifesaving test. Among the members who have <u>not</u> passed the test, 12 have taken the preparatory course and 30 have not taken the course. How many members are there in the swim club?

(A) 60
(B) 80
(C) 100
(D) 120
(E) 140

10. For all numbers s and t, the operation $*$ is defined by $s * t = (s - 1)(t + 1)$. If $(-2) * x = -12$, then $x =$

(A) 2
(B) 3
(C) 5
(D) 6
(E) 11

11. In an increasing sequence of 10 consecutive integers, the sum of the first 5 integers is 560. What is the sum of the last 5 integers in the sequence?

(A) 585
(B) 580
(C) 575
(D) 570
(E) 565

12. A certain manufacturer produces items for which the production costs consist of annual fixed costs totaling $130,000 and variable costs averaging $8 per item. If the manufacturer's selling price per item is $15, how many items must the manufacturer produce and sell to earn an annual profit of $150,000 ?

(A) 2,858
(B) 18,667
(C) 21,429
(D) 35,000
(E) 40,000

GO ON TO THE NEXT PAGE.

13. How many two-element subsets of $\{1, 2, 3, 4\}$ are there that do not contain the pair of elements 2 and 4 ?

(A) One
(B) Two
(C) Four
(D) Five
(E) Six

14. In a certain company, the ratio of the number of managers to the number of production-line workers is 5 to 72. If 8 additional production-line workers were to be hired, the ratio of the number of managers to the number of production-line workers would be 5 to 74. How many managers does the company have?

(A) 5
(B) 10
(C) 15
(D) 20
(E) 25

15. If $(x - 1)^2 = 400,$ which of the following could be the value of $x - 5$?

(A) 15
(B) 14
(C) -24
(D) -25
(E) -26

16. Salesperson A's compensation for any week is $360 plus 6 percent of the portion of A's total sales above $1,000 for that week. Salesperson B's compensation for any week is 8 percent of B's total sales for that week. For what amount of total weekly sales would both salespeople earn the same compensation?

(A) $21,000
(B) $18,000
(C) $15,000
(D) $4,500
(E) $4,000

STOP

IF YOU FINISH BEFORE TIME IS CALLED, YOU MAY CHECK YOUR WORK ON THIS SECTION ONLY.
DO NOT TURN TO ANY OTHER SECTION IN THE TEST.

Answer Key for Sample Test Section 10

PROBLEM SOLVING

1. E	9. A
2. B	10. B
3. D	11. A
4. E	12. E
5. E	13. D
6. C	14. D
7. D	15. C
8. A	16. C

Explanatory Material: Problem Solving Sample Test Section 10

1. $\dfrac{\dfrac{1}{2} + \dfrac{1}{3}}{\dfrac{1}{4}} =$

   (A) $\dfrac{1}{12}$

   (B) $\dfrac{5}{24}$

   (C) $\dfrac{2}{3}$

   (D) $\dfrac{9}{4}$

   (E) $\dfrac{10}{3}$

This complex fraction can be simplified by multiplying numerator and denominator by the lowest common denominator, 12.

$$\frac{\frac{1}{2} + \frac{1}{3}}{\frac{1}{4}} = \frac{\left(\frac{1}{2} + \frac{1}{3}\right) \times 12}{\frac{1}{4} \times 12} = \frac{6+4}{3} = \frac{10}{3}$$

Thus, the best answer is E.

2. John has 10 pairs of matched socks. If he loses 7 individual socks, what is the greatest number of pairs of matched socks he can have left?

   (A) 7
   (B) 6
   (C) 5
   (D) 4
   (E) 3

If John loses 7 individual socks, they could belong to either 4, 5, 6, or 7 different pairs. Therefore, the greatest possible number of pairs of matched socks is $10 - 4 = 6$. Thus, the best answer is B.

   Alternatively, since there were 20 socks altogether, there are $20 - 7 = 13$ socks left, which could be at most 6 pairs.

3. Last year's receipts from the sale of candy on Valentine's Day totaled 385 million dollars, which represented 7 percent of total candy sales for the year. Candy sales for the year totaled how many million dollars?

   (A)   55
   (B)   550
   (C) 2,695
   (D) 5,500
   (E) 26,950

Let x represent the number of millions of dollars spent on candy for the year. Since the Valentine's Day receipts are 7% of the year's receipts, $0.07x = 385$. Solving the equation yields 5,500 million dollars. The best answer is D.

4. How many minutes does it take to travel 120 miles at 400 miles per hour?

   (A) 3

   (B) $3\dfrac{1}{3}$

   (C) $8\dfrac{2}{3}$

   (D) 12

   (E) 18

The number of minutes it takes to travel 120 miles at 400 miles per hour can be found by completing the computation

$$\frac{120 \text{ miles} \times 60 \text{ minutes/hour}}{400 \text{ miles/hour}} = 18 \text{ minutes.}$$ Therefore, the best answer is E.

5. If $1 + \dfrac{1}{x} = 2 - \dfrac{2}{x}$, then $x =$

   (A) -1

   (B) $\dfrac{1}{3}$

   (C) $\dfrac{2}{3}$

   (D) 2

   (E) 3

Multiplying both sides of the equation by x yields $x + 1 = 2x - 2$; and combining like terms leaves $x = 3$. The best answer is E.

6. Last year, for every 100 million vehicles that traveled on a certain highway, 96 vehicles were involved in accidents. If 3 billion vehicles traveled on the highway last year, how many of those vehicles were involved in accidents? (1 billion = 1,000,000,000)

   (A) 288
   (B) 320
   (C) 2,880
   (D) 3,200
   (E) 28,800

The problem states that on a certain highway 96 vehicles out of each 100 million were involved in accidents. Since 3 billion vehicles is equivalent to 3,000 million, the number of vehicles that were involved in accidents last year was $\dfrac{96}{100 \text{ million}} \times 3,000 \text{ million} = 2,880$ vehicles. Thus, the best answer is C.

7. If the perimeter of a rectangular garden plot is 34 feet and its area is 60 square feet, what is the length of each of the longer sides?

   (A) 5 ft
   (B) 6 ft
   (C) 10 ft
   (D) 12 ft
   (E) 15 ft

Let x represent the width of the rectangular garden and y the length of the garden. Since the garden has perimeter 34 feet and area 60 square feet, it follows that $2x + 2y = 34$ and $xy = 60$. Dividing the first equation by 2 gives $x + y = 17$; thus, the problem reduces to finding two numbers whose product is 60 and whose sum is 17. It can be seen by inspection that the two numbers are 5 and 12, so $y = 12$. Therefore, the best answer is D.

8. What is the least positive integer that is divisible by each of the integers 1 through 7, inclusive?

   (A)   420
   (B)   840
   (C) 1,260
   (D) 2,520
   (E) 5,040

A number that is divisible by 1, 2, 3, 4, 5, 6, and 7 must contain 2, 3, 4, 5, 6, and 7 as factors. The least positive integer is achieved by assuring there is no duplication of factors. Since 2 and 3 are factors of 6, they are not included as factors of our least positive integer. Because 4 contains two factors of 2, and 6 contains only one factor of 2, the number must contain a second factor of 2. The number is $(2)(5)(6)(7) = 420$. Thus, the best answer is A.

9. Thirty percent of the members of a swim club have passed the lifesaving test. Among the members who have **not** passed the test, 12 have taken the preparatory course and 30 have not taken the course. How many members are there in the swim club?

   (A)   60
   (B)   80
   (C) 100
   (D) 120
   (E) 140

If 30 percent of the members of the swim club have passed the lifesaving test, then 70 percent have not. Among the members who have not passed the test, 12 have taken the course and 30 have not, for a total of 42 members. If x represents the number of members in the swim club, $0.70x = 42$, so $x = 60$. The best answer is A.

10. For all numbers s and t, the operation $*$ is defined by $s * t = (s - 1)(t + 1)$. If $(-2) * x = -12$, then $x =$

   (A)   2
   (B)   3
   (C)   5
   (D)   6
   (E) 11

Since $s * t = (s - 1)(t + 1)$ and $(-2) * x = (-12)$, $(-2) * x = (-2 - 1)(x + 1) = -12$. Solving $(-3)(x + 1) = -12$ for x yields $x = 3$. Therefore, the best answer is B.

11. In an increasing sequence of 10 consecutive integers, the sum of the first 5 integers is 560. What is the sum of the last 5 integers in the sequence?

   (A) 585
   (B) 580
   (C) 575
   (D) 570
   (E) 565

If $x, x + 1, x + 2, x + 3$, and $x + 4$ are the first five consecutive integers and their sum is 560, then $5x + 10 = 560$, so $x = 110$. The sixth through tenth consecutive numbers are represented by $x + 5, x + 6, x + 7, x + 8$, and $x + 9$; so their sum is $5x + 35 = 5(110) + 35 = 585$. Thus, the best answer is A.

Alternatively, note that the sixth number is 5 more than the first, the seventh is 5 more than the second, and so on; so the sum of the last five integers is $5(5) = 25$ more than the sum of the first five consecutive integers. Therefore, the sum of the last 5 integers is $560 + 25 = 585$.

12. **A certain manufacturer produces items for which the production costs consist of annual fixed costs totaling $130,000 and variable costs averaging $8 per item. If the manufacturer's selling price per item is $15, how many items must the manufacturer produce and sell to earn an annual profit of $150,000 ?**

   (A)   2,858
   (B)   18,667
   (C)   21,429
   (D)   35,000
   (E)   40,000

Let x represent the number of items produced. The manufacturer's profit, $P(x)$, is determined by subtracting cost from revenue, that is, $P(x) = R(x) - C(x)$. Since $R(x) = 15x$ dollars, $C(x) = 8x + 130,000$ dollars, and $P(x) = \$150,000$, $15x - (8x + 130,000) = 150,000$. Solving this equation yields $x = 40,000$. Therefore, the best answer is E.

13. **How many two-element subsets of $\{1, 2, 3, 4\}$ are there that do not contain the pair of elements 2 and 4 ?**

   (A)   One
   (B)   Two
   (C)   Four
   (D)   Five
   (E)   Six

This problem can be solved by finding the difference between the total number of two-element subsets and the number that contain both 2 and 4. There is only one two-element subset that contains both 2 and 4. The total number of two-element subsets is $\dfrac{(4)(3)}{2} = 6$; therefore, the difference is five. Thus, the best answer is D.

Alternatively, the two-element subsets of $\{1, 2, 3, 4\}$ are $\{1, 2\}, \{1, 3\}, \{1, 4\}, \{2, 3\}, \{2, 4\}$, and $\{3, 4\}$. There are 5 two-element subsets that do not contain both 2 and 4.

14. **In a certain company, the ratio of the number of managers to the number of production-line workers is 5 to 72. If 8 additional production-line workers were to be hired, the ratio of the number of managers to the number of production-line workers would be 5 to 74. How many managers does the company have?**

   (A)   5
   (B)   10
   (C)   15
   (D)   20
   (E)   25

If m represents the number of managers and p represents the number of production-line workers, then the ratio of managers to production-line workers is $\dfrac{m}{p} = \dfrac{5}{72}$. With 8 additional production-line workers, $p + 8$ represents the new number of production-line workers and the new ratio is $\dfrac{m}{p+8} = \dfrac{5}{74}$. The two ratios form the system of two equations $5p - 72m = 0$ and $5p - 74m = -40$. Subtracting the two equations to eliminate p yields $m = 20$. Therefore, the best answer is D.

15. **If $(x - 1)^2 = 400$, which of the following could be the value of $x - 5$?**

   (A)   15
   (B)   14
   (C) -24
   (D) -25
   (E) -26

Since $(x - 1)^2 = 400$, $(x - 1) = 20$ or -20; so $x = 21$ or -19. Thus, $x - 5 = 16$ or -24. The best answer is C.

16. **Salesperson A's compensation for any week is $360 plus 6 percent of the portion of A's total sales above $1,000 for that week. Salesperson B's compensation for any week is 8 percent of B's total sales for that week. For what amount of total weekly sales would both salespeople earn the same compensation?**

   (A) $21,000
   (B) $18,000
   (C) $15,000
   (D) $4,500
   (E) $4,000

Let x represent the total weekly sales amount at which both salespersons earn the same compensation. Salesperson B's compensation is represented by $0.08x$ and Salesperson A's compensation is represented by $360 + 0.06(x - 1,000)$. Solving the equation $0.08x = 360 + 0.06(x - 1,000)$ yields $x = 15,000$. Therefore, the best answer is C.

4 Data Sufficiency

In this section of the GMAT, you are to classify each problem according to the five fixed answer choices, rather than find a solution to the problem. Each problem consists of a question and two statements. You are to decide whether the information in each statement alone is sufficient to answer the question or, if neither is, whether the information in the two statements together is sufficient.

The following pages include test-taking strategies, sample test sections (with answer keys), and detailed explanations of every problem from the sample test sections. These explanations present possible problem-solving strategies for the examples.

Test-Taking Strategies for Data Sufficiency

1. Do not waste valuable time solving a problem; you are only to determine whether sufficient information is given to solve the problem. After you have considered statement (1), make a check mark next to (1) if you can determine the answer and a cross mark if you cannot. Be sure to disregard all the information learned from statement (1) while considering statement (2). This is very difficult to do and often results in erroneously choosing answer C when the answer should be B or choosing B when the answer should be C. Suppose statement (2) alone is sufficient. Then a check mark next to (1) indicates that D is the correct answer; a cross mark next to (1) indicates that B is correct. Suppose statement (2) alone is not sufficient. A check mark next to (1) indicates that A is the correct answer; a cross mark next to (1) indicates that you must now consider whether the two statements taken together give sufficient information; if they do, the answer is C; if not, the answer is E.

2. If you determine that the information in statement (1) is sufficient to answer the question, the answer is necessarily either A or D. If you are not sure about statement (1) but you know that statement (2) alone is sufficient, the answer is necessarily either B or D. If neither statement taken alone is sufficient, the answer is either C or E. Thus, if you have doubts about certain portions of the information given but are relatively sure about other portions, you can logically eliminate two or three options and more than double your chances of guessing correctly.

3. Remember that when you are determining whether there is sufficient information to answer a question of the form, "What is the value of y?" the information given must be sufficient to find one and only one value for y. Being able to determine minimum or maximum values or an answer of the form $y = x + 2$ is not sufficient, because such answers constitute a range of values rather than "the value of y."

4. When geometric figures are involved, be very careful not to make unwarranted assumptions based on the figures. A triangle may appear to be isosceles, but can you detect the difference in the lengths of segments 1.8 inches long and 1.85 inches long? Furthermore, the figures are not necessarily drawn to scale; they are generalized figures showing little more than intersecting line segments and the betweenness of points, angles, and regions.

When you take the sample test sections, use the answer spaces on page 145 to mark your answers.

Answer Spaces for Data Sufficiency Sample Test Sections

Sample Test Section 1

1 Ⓐ Ⓑ Ⓒ Ⓓ Ⓔ	6 Ⓐ Ⓑ Ⓒ Ⓓ Ⓔ	11 Ⓐ Ⓑ Ⓒ Ⓓ Ⓔ	16 Ⓐ Ⓑ Ⓒ Ⓓ Ⓔ
2 Ⓐ Ⓑ Ⓒ Ⓓ Ⓔ	7 Ⓐ Ⓑ Ⓒ Ⓓ Ⓔ	12 Ⓐ Ⓑ Ⓒ Ⓓ Ⓔ	17 Ⓐ Ⓑ Ⓒ Ⓓ Ⓔ
3 Ⓐ Ⓑ Ⓒ Ⓓ Ⓔ	8 Ⓐ Ⓑ Ⓒ Ⓓ Ⓔ	13 Ⓐ Ⓑ Ⓒ Ⓓ Ⓔ	18 Ⓐ Ⓑ Ⓒ Ⓓ Ⓔ
4 Ⓐ Ⓑ Ⓒ Ⓓ Ⓔ	9 Ⓐ Ⓑ Ⓒ Ⓓ Ⓔ	14 Ⓐ Ⓑ Ⓒ Ⓓ Ⓔ	19 Ⓐ Ⓑ Ⓒ Ⓓ Ⓔ
5 Ⓐ Ⓑ Ⓒ Ⓓ Ⓔ	10 Ⓐ Ⓑ Ⓒ Ⓓ Ⓔ	15 Ⓐ Ⓑ Ⓒ Ⓓ Ⓔ	20 Ⓐ Ⓑ Ⓒ Ⓓ Ⓔ

Sample Test Section 2

1 Ⓐ Ⓑ Ⓒ Ⓓ Ⓔ	6 Ⓐ Ⓑ Ⓒ Ⓓ Ⓔ	11 Ⓐ Ⓑ Ⓒ Ⓓ Ⓔ	16 Ⓐ Ⓑ Ⓒ Ⓓ Ⓔ
2 Ⓐ Ⓑ Ⓒ Ⓓ Ⓔ	7 Ⓐ Ⓑ Ⓒ Ⓓ Ⓔ	12 Ⓐ Ⓑ Ⓒ Ⓓ Ⓔ	17 Ⓐ Ⓑ Ⓒ Ⓓ Ⓔ
3 Ⓐ Ⓑ Ⓒ Ⓓ Ⓔ	8 Ⓐ Ⓑ Ⓒ Ⓓ Ⓔ	13 Ⓐ Ⓑ Ⓒ Ⓓ Ⓔ	18 Ⓐ Ⓑ Ⓒ Ⓓ Ⓔ
4 Ⓐ Ⓑ Ⓒ Ⓓ Ⓔ	9 Ⓐ Ⓑ Ⓒ Ⓓ Ⓔ	14 Ⓐ Ⓑ Ⓒ Ⓓ Ⓔ	19 Ⓐ Ⓑ Ⓒ Ⓓ Ⓔ
5 Ⓐ Ⓑ Ⓒ Ⓓ Ⓔ	10 Ⓐ Ⓑ Ⓒ Ⓓ Ⓔ	15 Ⓐ Ⓑ Ⓒ Ⓓ Ⓔ	20 Ⓐ Ⓑ Ⓒ Ⓓ Ⓔ

Sample Test Section 3

1 Ⓐ Ⓑ Ⓒ Ⓓ Ⓔ	6 Ⓐ Ⓑ Ⓒ Ⓓ Ⓔ	11 Ⓐ Ⓑ Ⓒ Ⓓ Ⓔ	16 Ⓐ Ⓑ Ⓒ Ⓓ Ⓔ
2 Ⓐ Ⓑ Ⓒ Ⓓ Ⓔ	7 Ⓐ Ⓑ Ⓒ Ⓓ Ⓔ	12 Ⓐ Ⓑ Ⓒ Ⓓ Ⓔ	17 Ⓐ Ⓑ Ⓒ Ⓓ Ⓔ
3 Ⓐ Ⓑ Ⓒ Ⓓ Ⓔ	8 Ⓐ Ⓑ Ⓒ Ⓓ Ⓔ	13 Ⓐ Ⓑ Ⓒ Ⓓ Ⓔ	18 Ⓐ Ⓑ Ⓒ Ⓓ Ⓔ
4 Ⓐ Ⓑ Ⓒ Ⓓ Ⓔ	9 Ⓐ Ⓑ Ⓒ Ⓓ Ⓔ	14 Ⓐ Ⓑ Ⓒ Ⓓ Ⓔ	19 Ⓐ Ⓑ Ⓒ Ⓓ Ⓔ
5 Ⓐ Ⓑ Ⓒ Ⓓ Ⓔ	10 Ⓐ Ⓑ Ⓒ Ⓓ Ⓔ	15 Ⓐ Ⓑ Ⓒ Ⓓ Ⓔ	20 Ⓐ Ⓑ Ⓒ Ⓓ Ⓔ

Sample Test Section 4

1 Ⓐ Ⓑ Ⓒ Ⓓ Ⓔ	6 Ⓐ Ⓑ Ⓒ Ⓓ Ⓔ	11 Ⓐ Ⓑ Ⓒ Ⓓ Ⓔ	16 Ⓐ Ⓑ Ⓒ Ⓓ Ⓔ
2 Ⓐ Ⓑ Ⓒ Ⓓ Ⓔ	7 Ⓐ Ⓑ Ⓒ Ⓓ Ⓔ	12 Ⓐ Ⓑ Ⓒ Ⓓ Ⓔ	17 Ⓐ Ⓑ Ⓒ Ⓓ Ⓔ
3 Ⓐ Ⓑ Ⓒ Ⓓ Ⓔ	8 Ⓐ Ⓑ Ⓒ Ⓓ Ⓔ	13 Ⓐ Ⓑ Ⓒ Ⓓ Ⓔ	18 Ⓐ Ⓑ Ⓒ Ⓓ Ⓔ
4 Ⓐ Ⓑ Ⓒ Ⓓ Ⓔ	9 Ⓐ Ⓑ Ⓒ Ⓓ Ⓔ	14 Ⓐ Ⓑ Ⓒ Ⓓ Ⓔ	19 Ⓐ Ⓑ Ⓒ Ⓓ Ⓔ
5 Ⓐ Ⓑ Ⓒ Ⓓ Ⓔ	10 Ⓐ Ⓑ Ⓒ Ⓓ Ⓔ	15 Ⓐ Ⓑ Ⓒ Ⓓ Ⓔ	20 Ⓐ Ⓑ Ⓒ Ⓓ Ⓔ

Sample Test Section 5

1 Ⓐ Ⓑ Ⓒ Ⓓ Ⓔ	6 Ⓐ Ⓑ Ⓒ Ⓓ Ⓔ	11 Ⓐ Ⓑ Ⓒ Ⓓ Ⓔ	16 Ⓐ Ⓑ Ⓒ Ⓓ Ⓔ
2 Ⓐ Ⓑ Ⓒ Ⓓ Ⓔ	7 Ⓐ Ⓑ Ⓒ Ⓓ Ⓔ	12 Ⓐ Ⓑ Ⓒ Ⓓ Ⓔ	17 Ⓐ Ⓑ Ⓒ Ⓓ Ⓔ
3 Ⓐ Ⓑ Ⓒ Ⓓ Ⓔ	8 Ⓐ Ⓑ Ⓒ Ⓓ Ⓔ	13 Ⓐ Ⓑ Ⓒ Ⓓ Ⓔ	18 Ⓐ Ⓑ Ⓒ Ⓓ Ⓔ
4 Ⓐ Ⓑ Ⓒ Ⓓ Ⓔ	9 Ⓐ Ⓑ Ⓒ Ⓓ Ⓔ	14 Ⓐ Ⓑ Ⓒ Ⓓ Ⓔ	19 Ⓐ Ⓑ Ⓒ Ⓓ Ⓔ
5 Ⓐ Ⓑ Ⓒ Ⓓ Ⓔ	10 Ⓐ Ⓑ Ⓒ Ⓓ Ⓔ	15 Ⓐ Ⓑ Ⓒ Ⓓ Ⓔ	20 Ⓐ Ⓑ Ⓒ Ⓓ Ⓔ

DATA SUFFICIENCY SAMPLE TEST SECTION 1

Time — 25 minutes

20 Questions

Directions: Each of the data sufficiency problems below consists of a question and two statements, labeled (1) and (2), in which certain data are given. You have to decide whether the data given in the statements are <u>sufficient</u> for answering the question. Using the data given in the statements <u>plus</u> your knowledge of mathematics and everyday facts (such as the number of days in July or the meaning of *counterclockwise*), you are to fill in oval

- A if statement (1) ALONE is sufficient, but statement (2) alone is not sufficient to answer the question asked;
- B if statement (2) ALONE is sufficient, but statement (1) alone is not sufficient to answer the question asked;
- C if BOTH statements (1) and (2) TOGETHER are sufficient to answer the question asked, but NEITHER statement ALONE is sufficient;
- D if EACH statement ALONE is sufficient to answer the question asked;
- E if statements (1) and (2) TOGETHER are NOT sufficient to answer the question asked, and additional data specific to the problem are needed.

Numbers: All numbers used are real numbers.

Figures: A figure in a data sufficiency problem will conform to the information given in the question, but will not necessarily conform to the additional information given in statements (1) and (2).

You may assume that lines shown as straight are straight and that angle measures are greater than zero.

You may assume that the positions of points, angles, regions, etc., exist in the order shown.

All figures lie in a plane unless otherwise indicated.

Note: In questions that ask for the value of a quantity, the data given in the statements are sufficient only when it is possible to determine exactly one numerical value for the quantity.

Example:

In $\triangle PQR$, what is the value of x ?

(1) $PQ = PR$

(2) $y = 40$

Explanation: According to statement (1), $PQ = PR$; therefore, $\triangle PQR$ is isosceles and $y = z$. Since $x + y + z = 180$, it follows that $x + 2y = 180$. Since statement (1) does not give a value for y, you cannot answer the question using statement (1) alone. According to statement (2), $y = 40$; therefore, $x + z = 140$. Since statement (2) does not give a value for z, you cannot answer the question using statement (2) alone. Using both statements together, since $x + 2y = 180$ and the value of y is given, you can find the value of x. Therefore, the answer is C.

GO ON TO THE NEXT PAGE.

A Statement (1) ALONE is sufficient, but statement (2) alone is not sufficient.
B Statement (2) ALONE is sufficient, but statement (1) alone is not sufficient.
C BOTH statements TOGETHER are sufficient, but NEITHER statement ALONE is sufficient.
D EACH statement ALONE is sufficient.
E Statements (1) and (2) TOGETHER are NOT sufficient.

1. At a certain picnic, each of the guests was served either a single scoop or a double scoop of ice cream. How many of the guests were served a double scoop of ice cream?

   (1) At the picnic, 60 percent of the guests were served a double scoop of ice cream.

   (2) A total of 120 scoops of ice cream were served to all the guests at the picnic.

2. By what percent was the price of a certain candy bar increased?

   (1) The price of the candy bar was increased by 5 cents.

   (2) The price of the candy bar after the increase was 45 cents.

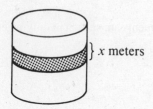 } x meters

3. A circular tub has a band painted around its circumference, as shown above. What is the surface area of this painted band?

   (1) $x = 0.5$
   (2) The height of the tub is 1 meter.

4. Is it true that $a > b$?

   (1) $2a > 2b$

   (2) $a + c > b + c$

5. A thoroughly blended biscuit mix includes only flour and baking powder. What is the ratio of the number of grams of baking powder to the number of grams of flour in the mix?

   (1) Exactly 9.9 grams of flour is contained in 10 grams of the mix.

   (2) Exactly 0.3 gram of baking powder is contained in 30 grams of the mix.

GO ON TO THE NEXT PAGE.

-148-

A   Statement (1) ALONE is sufficient, but statement (2) alone is not sufficient.
B   Statement (2) ALONE is sufficient, but statement (1) alone is not sufficient.
C   BOTH statements TOGETHER are sufficient, but NEITHER statement ALONE is sufficient.
D   EACH statement ALONE is sufficient.
E   Statements (1) and (2) TOGETHER are NOT sufficient.

6. If a real estate agent received a commission of 6 percent of the selling price of a certain house, what was the selling price of the house?

   (1)   The selling price minus the real estate agent's commission was $84,600.

   (2)   The selling price was 250 percent of the original purchase price of $36,000.

7. What is the value of $|x|$?

   (1) $x = -|x|$
   (2) $x^2 = 4$

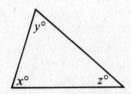

8. What is the value of z in the triangle above?

   (1) $x + y = 139$
   (2) $y + z = 108$

9. A certain bakery sells rye bread in 16-ounce loaves and 24-ounce loaves, and all loaves of the same size sell for the same price per loaf regardless of the number of loaves purchased. What is the price of a 24-ounce loaf of rye bread in this bakery?

   (1)   The total price of a 16-ounce loaf and a 24-ounce loaf of this bread is $2.40.

   (2)   The total price of two 16-ounce loaves and one 24-ounce loaf of this bread is $3.40.

10. If $\dfrac{\sqrt{x}}{y} = n$, what is the value of x ?

   (1) $yn = 10$
   (2) $y = 40$ and $n = \dfrac{1}{4}$

GO ON TO THE NEXT PAGE.

A Statement (1) ALONE is sufficient, but statement (2) alone is not sufficient.
B Statement (2) ALONE is sufficient, but statement (1) alone is not sufficient.
C BOTH statements TOGETHER are sufficient, but NEITHER statement ALONE is sufficient.
D EACH statement ALONE is sufficient.
E Statements (1) and (2) TOGETHER are NOT sufficient.

11. If m and n are consecutive positive integers, is m greater than n?

(1) $m - 1$ and $n + 1$ are consecutive positive integers.

(2) m is an even integer.

12. Paula and Sandy were among those people who sold raffle tickets to raise money for Club X. If Paula and Sandy sold a total of 100 of the tickets, how many of the tickets did Paula sell?

(1) Sandy sold $\frac{2}{3}$ as many of the raffle tickets as Paula did.

(2) Sandy sold 8 percent of all the raffle tickets sold for Club X.

13. Is the integer n odd?

(1) n is divisible by 3.

(2) n is divisible by 5.

$$3.2\square\,\triangle 6$$

14. If $\square$ and $\triangle$ each represent single digits in the decimal above, what digit does $\square$ represent?

(1) When the decimal is rounded to the nearest tenth, 3.2 is the result.

(2) When the decimal is rounded to the nearest hundredth, 3.24 is the result.

15. A certain company currently has how many employees?

(1) If 3 additional employees are hired by the company and all of the present employees remain, there will be at least 20 employees in the company.

(2) If no additional employees are hired by the company and 3 of the present employees resign, there will be fewer than 15 employees in the company.

GO ON TO THE NEXT PAGE.

A Statement (1) ALONE is sufficient, but statement (2) alone is not sufficient.
B Statement (2) ALONE is sufficient, but statement (1) alone is not sufficient.
C BOTH statements TOGETHER are sufficient, but NEITHER statement ALONE is sufficient.
D EACH statement ALONE is sufficient.
E Statements (1) and (2) TOGETHER are NOT sufficient.

16. If x is equal to one of the numbers $\frac{1}{4}$, $\frac{3}{8}$, or $\frac{2}{5}$, what is the value of x?

(1) $\frac{1}{4} < x < \frac{1}{2}$

(2) $\frac{1}{3} < x < \frac{3}{5}$

17. If a, b, and c are integers, is $a - b + c$ greater than $a + b - c$?

(1) b is negative.

(2) c is positive.

18. If $x + 2y + 1 = y - x$, what is the value of x?

(1) $y^2 = 9$

(2) $y = 3$

19. If n is an integer, then n is divisible by how many positive integers?

(1) n is the product of two different prime numbers.

(2) n and 2^3 are each divisible by the same number of positive integers.

20. How many miles long is the route from Houghton to Callahan?

(1) It will take 1 hour less time to travel the entire route at an average rate of 55 miles per hour than at an average rate of 50 miles per hour.

(2) It will take 11 hours to travel the first half of the route at an average rate of 25 miles per hour.

STOP

IF YOU FINISH BEFORE TIME IS CALLED, YOU MAY CHECK YOUR WORK ON THIS SECTION ONLY.
DO NOT TURN TO ANY OTHER SECTION IN THE TEST.

Answer Key for Sample Test Section 1

DATA SUFFICIENCY

1.	C	11.	A
2.	C	12.	A
3.	E	13.	E
4.	D	14.	E
5.	D	15.	C
6.	D	16.	E
7.	B	17.	C
8.	A	18.	B
9.	C	19.	D
10.	D	20.	D

Explanatory Material: Data Sufficiency

The following discussion of Data Sufficiency is intended to familiarize you with the most efficient and effective approaches to the kinds of problems common to Data Sufficiency. The problems on the sample test sections in this chapter are generally representative of the kinds of questions you will encounter in this section of the GMAT. Remember that it is the problem-solving strategy that is important, not the specific details of a particular question.

Sample Test Section 1

1. At a certain picnic, each of the guests was served either a single scoop or a double scoop of ice cream. How many of the guests were served a double scoop of ice cream?

   (1) At the picnic, 60 percent of the guests were served a double scoop of ice cream.

   (2) A total of 120 scoops of ice cream were served to all the guests at the picnic.

Statement (1) alone is not sufficient because the total number of guests is unknown. Thus, the answer must be B, C, or E. Statement (2) alone is not sufficient since there is no information indicating how the 120 scoops were divided into single-scoop and double-scoop servings. Thus, the answer must be C or E. From (1) the ratio of the number of guests who were served a single scoop to the number of guests who were served a double scoop can be determined and can be used with (2) to determine the number of guests who were served a double scoop. Thus, the best answer is C. (It may be helpful to set up equations to determine whether there is sufficient information given in (1) and (2) for answering the question, but it is not actually necessary to solve the equations.)

2. By what percent was the price of a certain candy bar increased?

   (1) The price of the candy bar was increased by 5 cents.

   (2) The price of the candy bar after the increase was 45 cents.

In (1), only the increase in price is given, and both the original and final prices are unknown. Thus, the percent increase cannot be determined from (1) alone, and the answer must be B, C, or E. In (2), only the final price is given, so the percent increase cannot be determined from (2) alone, and the answer must be C or E. From (1) and (2) together, the amount of the increase is known and the price before the increase can be computed. Therefore, the percent increase can be determined, and the best answer is C.

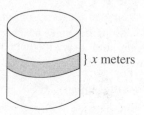

} x meters

3. A circular tub has a band painted around its circumference, as shown above. What is the surface area of this painted band?

   (1) $x = 0.5$

   (2) The height of the tub is 1 meter.

The surface area of the band is the product of the circumference of the band and the width of the band. In (1) the width of the band is given, but the circumference is unknown, so the surface area cannot be determined. Therefore, (1) alone is not sufficient, and the answer must be B, C, or E. In (2) the height of the tub is given, which has no relation to the circumference or the width of the band. Thus, (2) is not sufficient, with or without (1), so the best answer is E.

4. Is it true that $a > b$?

   (1) $2a > 2b$

   (2) $a + c > b + c$

In (1), when both sides of $2a > 2b$ are divided by 2, the result is $a > b$. Thus, (1) alone is sufficient, and the answer must be A or D. In (2), when c is subtracted from both sides of $a + c > b + c$, the result is $a > b$. Thus, (2) alone is also sufficient, and the best answer is D.

5. A thoroughly blended biscuit mix includes only flour and baking powder. What is the ratio of the number of grams of baking powder to the number of grams of flour in the mix?

(1) Exactly 9.9 grams of flour is contained in 10 grams of the mix.
(2) Exactly 0.3 gram of baking powder is contained in 30 grams of the mix.

In any amount of the mix, once both ingredient amounts are known, their ratio can be determined. (This ratio must be the same in any amount of the mix since the mix is thoroughly blended.) Each of statements (1) and (2) alone gives the amount of one ingredient in some amount of the mix, so the amount of the other ingredient can be determined. Thus, each of (1) and (2) alone is sufficient, and the best answer is D.

6. If a real estate agent received a commission of 6 percent of the selling price of a certain house, what was the selling price of the house?

(1) The selling price minus the real estate agent's commission was $84,600.
(2) The selling price was 250 percent of the original purchase price of $36,000.

From (1) it follows that $84,600 is 94% (100% – 6%) of the selling price, and thus the selling price, $\frac{\$84,600}{0.94}$, can be determined. Therefore, (1) alone is sufficient, and the answer must be A or D. From (2) it follows that the selling price is 2.5($36,000). Thus, (2) alone is also sufficient, and the best answer is D.

7. What is the value of $|x|$?

(1) $x = -|x|$
(2) $x^2 = 4$

From (1) all that can be determined is that x is negative (or 0) since $|x|$, the absolute value of x, is always positive (or 0). Thus, (1) alone is not sufficient, and the answer must be B, C, or E. From (2) it can be determined that $x = \pm2$; in either case $|x| = 2$. Since (2) alone is sufficient to determine the value of $|x|$, the best answer is B.

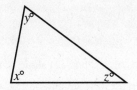

8. What is the value of z in the triangle above?

(1) $x + y = 139$
(2) $y + z = 108$

Note that, as in any triangle, $x + y + z = 180$. Using (1), the value 139 can be substituted for $x + y$ in $x + y + z = 180$ to obtain the value of z. Thus, (1) alone is sufficient, and the answer must be A or D. When the equation in (2) is combined with $x + y + z = 180$, all that can be deduced is the value of x. Thus, (2) alone is not sufficient, and the best answer is A.

9. A certain bakery sells rye bread in 16-ounce loaves and 24-ounce loaves, and all loaves of the same size sell for the same price per loaf regardless of the number of loaves purchased. What is the price of a 24-ounce loaf of rye bread in this bakery?

(1) The total price of a 16-ounce loaf and a 24-ounce loaf of this bread is $2.40.
(2) The total price of two 16-ounce loaves and one 24-ounce loaf of this bread is $3.40.

Let s and t be the prices of a 16-ounce loaf and a 24-ounce loaf, respectively. According to (1), $s + t = \$2.40$. Since t cannot be determined without knowing s, statement (1) alone is not sufficient, and the answer must be B, C, or E. Similarly, according to (2), $2s + t = \$3.40$, so t cannot be determined. Therefore, (2) alone is not sufficient, and the answer must be C or E. Using both equations from (1) and (2), $t = \$2.40 - s = \$3.40 - 2s$, from which s, and thus t, can be determined. The best answer is therefore C.

10. If $\frac{\sqrt{x}}{y} = n$, what is the value of x ?

(1) $yn = 10$
(2) $y = 40$ and $n = \frac{1}{4}$

Note that $\frac{\sqrt{x}}{y} = n$ is equivalent to $\sqrt{x} = yn$ (if $y \neq 0$). From this information and (1), $\sqrt{x} = yn = 10$, and x can be determined. Therefore, the answer must be A or D. From (2), $yn = (40)\left(\frac{1}{4}\right) = 10$, as in (1). Therefore, (2) alone is also sufficient and the best answer is D.

11. If m and n are consecutive positive integers, is m greater than n ?

   (1) $m - 1$ and $n + 1$ are consecutive positive integers.
   (2) m is an even integer.

Note that for two consecutive integers the larger must be 1 more than the smaller. That (1) alone is sufficient can probably be seen most easily by considering particular values for m and n. For example, if $m = 4$, then $n = 3$ or 5 since m and n are consecutive. Then $m - 1 = 3$ and $n + 1 = 4$ or 6. Since $m - 1$ and $n + 1$ are consecutive, $n = 3$ and $m > n$. More generally, since m and n are consecutive, either $m = n + 1$ or $n = m + 1$. But, if $n = m + 1$, then $n + 1 = m + 2$, which is 3 more than $m - 1$, contradicting the fact that $m - 1$ and $n + 1$ are consecutive integers. Thus, $m = n + 1$, or $m > n$, and the answer must be A or D. Because the fact given in (2) that m is even is irrelevant, the best answer is A.

12. Paula and Sandy were among those people who sold raffle tickets to raise money for Club X. If Paula and Sandy sold a total of 100 of the tickets, how many of the tickets did Paula sell?

   (1) Sandy sold $\frac{2}{3}$ as many of the raffle tickets as Paula did.
   (2) Sandy sold 8 percent of all the raffle tickets sold for Club X.

If Paula sold p tickets and Sandy sold s tickets, then $p + s = 100$. According to (1), $s = \frac{2}{3}p$. The value of p can be determined by solving both equations simultaneously.

Therefore, the answer must be A or D. From (2) the number of raffle tickets that Sandy (and thus Paula) sold cannot be determined since the total number of raffle tickets sold is unknown. Thus, (2) alone is not sufficient, and the best answer is A.

13. Is the integer n odd?

   (1) n is divisible by 3.
   (2) n is divisible by 5.

In statement (1), n is divisible by 3, but n may be even or odd as the examples $n = 6$ and $n = 9$ show. Similarly, in statement (2), n is divisible by 5, but it may be even or odd as the examples $n = 10$ and $n = 15$ show. Since neither statement alone is sufficient, the answer must be C or E. From (1) and (2) together, n must be divisible by 15, and the examples $n = 30$ and $n = 45$ show that n may be even or odd. Thus, the best answer is E.

$$3.2\,\square\ \Delta 6$$

14. If $\square$ and Δ each represent single digits in the decimal above, what digit does $\square$ represent?

   (1) When the decimal is rounded to the nearest tenth, 3.2 is the result.
   (2) When the decimal is rounded to the nearest hundredth, 3.24 is the result.

From (1) the decimal must have been rounded down since the tenths digit is 2 in both $3.2\,\square\,\Delta 6$ and 3.2. Hence, $\square$ represents 0, 1, 2, 3, or 4. Since it cannot be determined from (1) alone what digit $\square$ represents, the answer must be B, C, or E. From (2), $\square$ can represent 3 or 4, depending upon the value of Δ. For example, both 3.2376 and 3.2416, when rounded to the nearest hundredth, are 3.24. Since (2) alone is not sufficient, the answer must be C or E, and since the numbers 3.2376 and 3.2416 also satisfy (1) and (2) together, the best answer is E.

15. A certain company currently has how many employees?

   (1) If 3 additional employees are hired by the company and all of the present employees remain, there will be at least 20 employees in the company.
   (2) If no additional employees are hired by the company and 3 of the present employees resign, there will be fewer than 15 employees in the company.

Let n be the current number of employees. According to (1), $n + 3 \geq 20$, or $n \geq 17$, which gives a range of possible values of n. Thus, (1) alone is not sufficient, and the answer must be B, C, or E. According to (2), $n - 3 < 15$, or $n < 18$, which also gives a range for n. Thus, (2) alone is not sufficient, and the answer must be C or E. From (1) and (2) together, the value of n can be determined to be 17. Therefore, the best answer is C.

16. If x is equal to one of the numbers $\frac{1}{4}$, $\frac{3}{8}$, or $\frac{2}{5}$, what is the value of x ?

   (1) $\frac{1}{4} < x < \frac{1}{2}$
   (2) $\frac{1}{3} < x < \frac{3}{5}$

In decimal form, $\frac{1}{4} = 0.25$, $\frac{3}{8} = 0.375$, and $\frac{2}{5} = 0.4$, and statement (1) can be written as $0.25 < x < 0.5$, so that both $\frac{3}{8}$ and $\frac{2}{5}$ are possible values of x. Thus, (1) alone is not sufficient, and the answer must be B, C, or E. Statement (2) can be written as $0.333 \ldots < x < 0.6$, so that both $\frac{3}{8}$ and $\frac{2}{5}$ are possible values of x. Thus, (2) alone is not sufficient, and the answer must be C or E. When both (1) and (2) are considered, it follows that $0.333 \ldots < x < 0.5$, so that, again, $\frac{3}{8}$ and $\frac{2}{5}$ are both possible values of x. Therefore, the best answer is E.

17. If a, b, and c are integers, is $a - b + c$ greater than $a + b - c$?

   (1) b is negative.
   (2) c is positive.

The inequality, $a - b + c > a + b - c$, is equivalent to $-b + c > b - c$, which is equivalent to $2c > 2b$, or $c > b$. Thus, the simpler inequality, $c > b$, may be considered. In (1), $b < 0$ is not sufficient to determine whether $c > b$ since no information is given about c. Hence, the answer must be B, C, or E. Similarly, in (2), $c > 0$ is not sufficient since no information is given about b, and so the answer must be C or E. Using (1) and (2) together, $b < 0 < c$, so that $c > b$, or equivalently, $a - b + c > a + b - c$. Thus, the best answer is C.

18. If $x + 2y + 1 = y - x$, what is the value of x ?

   (1) $y^2 = 9$
   (2) $y = 3$

The equation $x + 2y + 1 = y - x$ is equivalent to $2x = -y - 1$, or $x = -\frac{1}{2}(y + 1)$. Thus, the value of x can be determined if and only if the value of y is known. From (1) it follows that $y = 3$ or $y = -3$, so that x has two possible values as well. Thus, (1) alone is not sufficient, and the answer must be B, C, or E. In (2) the value of y is given; therefore, the value of x can be determined. Thus, (2) alone is sufficient, and the best answer is B.

19. If n is an integer, then n is divisible by how many positive integers?

   (1) n is the product of two different prime numbers.
   (2) n and 2^3 are each divisible by the same number of positive integers.

According to (1), $n = pq$, where both p and q are prime numbers and $p \neq q$. Thus, n is divisible by the positive integers 1, p, q, pq, and no others. Statement (1) alone is therefore sufficient to determine the number of positive divisors of n, and the answer must be A or D. Since $2^3 = 8$ and the number of positive divisors of 8 can be determined, statement (2) alone is also sufficient, and the best answer is D.

20. How many miles long is the route from Houghton to Callahan?

   (1) It will take 1 hour less time to travel the entire route at an average rate of 55 miles per hour than at an average rate of 50 miles per hour.
   (2) It will take 11 hours to travel the first half of the route at an average rate of 25 miles per hour.

Using the standard formula rate $\times$ time = distance, or $rt = d$, it can be determined from (1) that $d = 50t$ and $d = 55(t - 1)$, where t is the time it takes to travel the entire route at an average rate of 50 miles per hour. These equations can be solved simultaneously for t, and then d can be determined. Therefore, (1) alone is sufficient, and the answer must be A or D. Statement (2) can be expressed as $\frac{d}{2} = 25(11)$, which can be solved for d. Thus, statement (2) alone is also sufficient, and the best answer is D.

DATA SUFFICIENCY SAMPLE TEST SECTION 2

Time — 25 minutes

20 Questions

Directions: Each of the data sufficiency problems below consists of a question and two statements, labeled (1) and (2), in which certain data are given. You have to decide whether the data given in the statements are <u>sufficient</u> for answering the question. Using the data given in the statements <u>plus</u> your knowledge of mathematics and everyday facts (such as the number of days in July or the meaning of *counterclockwise*), you are to fill in oval

    A   if statement (1) ALONE is sufficient, but statement (2) alone is not sufficient to answer the question asked;

    B   if statement (2) ALONE is sufficient, but statement (1) alone is not sufficient to answer the question asked;

    C   if BOTH statements (1) and (2) TOGETHER are sufficient to answer the question asked, but NEITHER statement ALONE is sufficient;

    D   if EACH statement ALONE is sufficient to answer the question asked;

    E   if statements (1) and (2) TOGETHER are NOT sufficient to answer the question asked, and additional data specific to the problem are needed.

Numbers: All numbers used are real numbers.

Figures: A figure in a data sufficiency problem will conform to the information given in the question, but will not necessarily conform to the additional information given in statements (1) and (2).

           You may assume that lines shown as straight are straight and that angle measures are greater than zero.

           You may assume that the positions of points, angles, regions, etc., exist in the order shown.

           All figures lie in a plane unless otherwise indicated.

Note: In questions that ask for the value of a quantity, the data given in the statements are sufficient only when it is possible to determine exactly one numerical value for the quantity.

Example:

In $\triangle PQR$, what is the value of x?

  (1) $PQ = PR$

  (2) $y = 40$

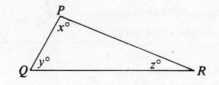

Explanation: According to statement (1), $PQ = PR$; therefore, $\triangle PQR$ is isosceles and $y = z$. Since $x + y + z = 180$, it follows that $x + 2y = 180$. Since statement (1) does not give a value for y, you cannot answer the question using statement (1) alone. According to statement (2), $y = 40$; therefore, $x + z = 140$. Since statement (2) does not give a value for z, you cannot answer the question using statement (2) alone. Using both statements together, since $x + 2y = 180$ and the value of y is given, you can find the value of x. Therefore, the answer is C.

GO ON TO THE NEXT PAGE.

A Statement (1) ALONE is sufficient, but statement (2) alone is not sufficient.
B Statement (2) ALONE is sufficient, but statement (1) alone is not sufficient.
C BOTH statements TOGETHER are sufficient, but NEITHER statement ALONE is sufficient.
D EACH statement ALONE is sufficient.
E Statements (1) and (2) TOGETHER are NOT sufficient.

1. If x and y are positive, what is the value of x?

(1) $x = 3.927y$

(2) $y = 2.279$

2. John and David each received a salary increase. Which one received the greater dollar increase?

(1) John's salary increased 8 percent.

(2) David's salary increased 5 percent.

3. Carlotta can drive from her home to her office by one of two possible routes. If she must also return by one of these routes, what is the distance of the shorter route?

(1) When she drives from her home to her office by the shorter route and returns by the longer route, she drives a total of 42 kilometers.

(2) When she drives both ways, from her home to her office and back, by the longer route, she drives a total of 46 kilometers.

4. If r and s are positive integers, r is what percent of s?

(1) $r = \frac{3}{4}s$

(2) $r \div s = \frac{75}{100}$

5. A shirt and a pair of gloves cost a total of $41.70. How much does the pair of gloves cost?

(1) The shirt costs twice as much as the gloves.

(2) The shirt costs $27.80.

GO ON TO THE NEXT PAGE.

A   Statement (1) ALONE is sufficient, but statement (2) alone is not sufficient.
B   Statement (2) ALONE is sufficient, but statement (1) alone is not sufficient.
C   BOTH statements TOGETHER are sufficient, but NEITHER statement ALONE is sufficient.
D   EACH statement ALONE is sufficient.
E   Statements (1) and (2) TOGETHER are NOT sufficient.

6. What is the number of 360-degree rotations that a bicycle wheel made while rolling 100 meters in a straight line without slipping?

   (1) The diameter of the bicycle wheel, including the tire, was 0.5 meter.

   (2) The wheel made twenty 360-degree rotations per minute.

7. What is the value of the sum of a list of n odd integers?

   (1) $n = 8$

   (2) The square of the number of integers on the list is 64.

8. If a certain animated cartoon consists of a total of 17,280 frames on film, how many minutes will it take to run the cartoon?

   (1) The cartoon runs without interruption at the rate of 24 frames per second.

   (2) It takes 6 times as long to run the cartoon as it takes to rewind the film, and it takes a total of 14 minutes to do both.

9. What was the average number of miles per gallon of gasoline for a car during a certain trip?

   (1) The total cost of the gasoline used by the car for the 180-mile trip was $12.00.

   (2) The cost of the gasoline used by the car for the trip was $1.20 per gallon.

10. If x and y are positive, is $\frac{x}{y}$ greater than 1 ?

   (1) $xy > 1$

   (2) $x - y > 0$

GO ON TO THE NEXT PAGE.

A   Statement (1) ALONE is sufficient, but statement (2) alone is not sufficient.
B   Statement (2) ALONE is sufficient, but statement (1) alone is not sufficient.
C   BOTH statements TOGETHER are sufficient, but NEITHER statement ALONE is sufficient.
D   EACH statement ALONE is sufficient.
E   Statements (1) and (2) TOGETHER are NOT sufficient.

11. In $\triangle PQR$, if $PQ = x$, $QR = x + 2$, and $PR = y$, which of the three angles of $\triangle PQR$ has the greatest degree measure?

(1) $y = x + 3$

(2) $x = 2$

12. Is the prime number p equal to 37 ?

(1) $p = n^2 + 1$, where n is an integer.

(2) p^2 is greater than 200.

13. The only contents of a parcel are 25 photographs and 30 negatives. What is the total weight, in ounces, of the parcel's contents?

(1) The weight of each photograph is 3 times the weight of each negative.

(2) The total weight of 1 of the photographs and 2 of the negatives is $\frac{1}{3}$ ounce.

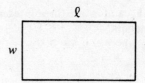

14. If ℓ and w represent the length and width, respectively, of the rectangle above, what is the perimeter?

(1) $2\ell + w = 40$

(2) $\ell + w = 25$

15. What is the ratio of x to y ?

(1) x is 4 more than twice y.

(2) The ratio of $0.5x$ to $2y$ is 3 to 5.

GO ON TO THE NEXT PAGE.

A   Statement (1) ALONE is sufficient, but statement (2) alone is not sufficient.
B   Statement (2) ALONE is sufficient, but statement (1) alone is not sufficient.
C   BOTH statements TOGETHER are sufficient, but NEITHER statement ALONE is sufficient.
D   EACH statement ALONE is sufficient.
E   Statements (1) and (2) TOGETHER are NOT sufficient.

16. If x, y, and z are three integers, are they consecutive integers?

   (1) $z - x = 2$

   (2) $x < y < z$

17. What is the value of x ?

   (1) $-(x + y) = x - y$

   (2) $x + y = 2$

18. A sum of $200,000 from a certain estate was divided among a spouse and three children. How much of the estate did the youngest child receive?

   (1) The spouse received $\frac{1}{2}$ of the sum from the estate, and the oldest child received $\frac{1}{4}$ of the remainder.

   (2) Each of the two younger children received $12,500 more than the oldest child and $62,500 less than the spouse.

19. If the Lincoln Library's total expenditure for books, periodicals, and newspapers last year was $35,000, how much of the expenditure was for books?

   (1) The expenditure for newspapers was 40 percent greater than the expenditure for periodicals.

   (2) The total of the expenditure for periodicals and newspapers was 25 percent less than the expenditure for books.

20. The symbol $\triangledown$ represents one of the following operations: addition, subtraction, multiplication, or division. What is the value of $3 \triangledown 2$?

   (1) $0 \triangledown 1 = 1$

   (2) $1 \triangledown 0 = 1$

STOP

IF YOU FINISH BEFORE TIME IS CALLED. YOU MAY CHECK YOUR WORK ON THIS SECTION ONLY. DO NOT TURN TO ANY OTHER SECTION IN THE TEST.

Answer Key for Sample Test Section 2

DATA SUFFICIENCY

1. C	11. A
2. E	12. E
3. C	13. C
4. D	14. B
5. D	15. B
6. A	16. C
7. E	17. A
8. D	18. B
9. C	19. B
10. B	20. A

Explanatory Material:
Data Sufficiency Sample Test Section 2

1. If x and y are positive, what is the value of x ?

   (1) $x = 3.927y$
   (2) $y = 2.279$

Statement (1) indicates that the value of x is 3.927 times the value of y, and statement (2) gives the value of y. Therefore, (1) and (2) together are sufficient to determine the value of x, but neither statement alone is sufficient, and so the best answer is C.

2. John and David each received a salary increase. Which one received the greater dollar increase?

   (1) John's salary increased 8 percent.
   (2) David's salary increased 5 percent.

In (1) there is no information about David's salary and in (2) there is no information about John's salary; thus, neither statement alone is sufficient, and the answer must be C or E. Since (1) and (2) together give only the percentage increases in salary, it cannot be determined which person received the greater dollar increase. For example, if John's salary was the larger salary, then his salary increase would evidently be the greater amount; however, if David's salary was more than $\frac{8}{5}$ times John's salary, then David's salary increase would be the greater amount. Therefore, (1) and (2) together are not sufficient, and the best answer is E.

3. Carlotta can drive from her home to her office by one of two possible routes. If she must also return by one of these routes, what is the distance of the shorter route?

   (1) When she drives from her home to her office by the shorter route and returns by the longer route, she drives a total of 42 kilometers.

   (2) When she drives both ways, from her home to her office and back, by the longer route, she drives a total of 46 kilometers.

Statement (1) alone is not sufficient because only the sum of the distances of the two routes is given and there are infinitely many pairs of numbers with a given sum. Thus, the answer must be B, C, or E. From (2) the distance of the longer route can be found, but there is no information about the distance of the shorter route. Statement (2) alone is therefore not sufficient, so the answer must be C or E. From (1) and (2) together, the distance of the shorter route can be determined $(42 - \frac{46}{2})$, and the best answer is C.

4. If r and s are positive integers, r is what percent of s ?

   (1) $r = \frac{3}{4}s$

   (2) $r \div s = \frac{75}{100}$

To determine r as a percent of s it suffices to know the ratio of r to s, since any ratio can be converted to an equivalent ratio with denominator 100. Since (1) and (2) both give the ratio of r to s, each alone is sufficient, and the best answer is D.

5. A shirt and a pair of gloves cost a total of $41.70. How much does the pair of gloves cost?

   (1) The shirt costs twice as much as the gloves.
   (2) The shirt costs $27.80.

From (1) it can be determined that the total cost of the shirt and gloves is three times the cost of the gloves alone; in other words, the gloves cost one third as much as the shirt and gloves together. Thus, (1) alone is sufficient, and the answer must be A or D. Since the cost of the gloves is the difference between the total cost, $41.70, and the cost of the shirt, statement (2) alone is also sufficient. The best answer is therefore D.

6. **What is the number of 360-degree rotations that a bicycle wheel made while rolling 100 meters in a straight line without slipping?**

    (1) The diameter of the bicycle wheel, including the tire, was 0.5 meter.
    (2) The wheel made twenty 360-degree rotations per minute.

For each 360-degree rotation, the wheel has traveled a distance equal to its circumference. Thus, the number of 360-degree rotations is equal to the number of times the circumference of the wheel can be laid out along the straight-line path that is 100 meters long; so it suffices to know the size of the wheel. From (1) the circumference of the wheel can be determined. Thus, (1) alone is sufficient, and the answer must be A or D. Statement (2) gives the speed at which the wheel is traveling; however, the size of the wheel cannot be determined, and (2) alone is not sufficient. Therefore, the best answer is A.

7. **What is the value of the sum of a list of n odd integers?**

    (1) $n = 8$
    (2) The square of the number of integers on the list is 64.

Statements (1) and (2) give only the number of integers in the list. Since additional information is needed to determine the sum of the integers (for example, their average), the best answer is E.

8. **If a certain animated cartoon consists of a total of 17,280 frames on film, how many minutes will it take to run the cartoon?**

    (1) The cartoon runs without interruption at the rate of 24 frames per second.
    (2) It takes 6 times as long to run the cartoon as it takes to rewind the film, and it takes a total of 14 minutes to do both.

From (1) it can be determined that it takes $\frac{17,280}{24 \times 60}$ minutes to run the cartoon. Thus, (1) alone is sufficient, and the answer must be A or D. From (2) it can be determined that the time it takes to run the cartoon is $\frac{6}{7}$ of the 14 minutes it takes both to run the cartoon and to rewind the film, and so (2) alone is also sufficient. The best answer is therefore D.

9. **What was the average number of miles per gallon of gasoline for a car during a certain trip?**

    (1) The total cost of the gasoline used by the car for the 180-mile trip was $12.00.
    (2) The cost of the gasoline used by the car for the trip was $1.20 per gallon.

Statement (1) gives the number of miles the car traveled; however, the number of gallons of gasoline used cannot be determined, since only the total cost of the gasoline used is given. Thus, (1) alone is not sufficient, and the answer must be B, C, or E. Statement (2) alone is obviously not sufficient, but it gives the additional information needed in (1) to determine the number of gallons of gasoline used. Once the number of miles traveled and the number of gallons used are known, the average number of miles per gallon can be determined. Therefore, (1) and (2) together are sufficient, and the best answer is C.

10. **If x and y are positive, is $\frac{x}{y}$ greater than 1 ?**

    (1) $xy > 1$
    (2) $x - y > 0$

Since $y > 0$, it follows that $\frac{x}{y} > 1$ if and only if $x > y$. Thus, to answer the question it suffices to determine whether $x > y$. In (1) there are innumerable pairs of different numbers x and y whose product xy is greater than 1, and the larger number in each such pair can be either x or y. Thus, (1) alone is not sufficient, and the answer must be B, C, or E. In (2), $x - y > 0$ is equivalent to $x > y$, so (2) alone is sufficient. The best answer is B.

11. **In $\triangle PQR$, if $PQ = x$, $QR = x + 2$, and $PR = y$, which of the three angles of $\triangle PQR$ has the greatest degree measure?**

    (1) $y = x + 3$
    (2) $x = 2$

In any triangle, the largest angle is opposite the longest side. To determine the longest side it suffices to determine whether $y > x + 2$. Since $x + 3 > x + 2$, it follows from (1) that $y > x + 2$. Statement (1) alone is therefore sufficient, and the answer must be A or D. From (2) it follows that $PQ = 2$ and $QR = 4$. Thus, y can be any value between 2 and 6; it follows that $y > x$, but it cannot be concluded that $y > x + 2$. Statement (2) alone is therefore not sufficient, so the best answer is A.

12. Is the prime number p equal to 37 ?

(1) $p = n^2 + 1$, where n is an integer.

(2) p^2 is greater than 200.

In (1) the expression $n^2 + 1$ can represent a prime number less than 37, equal to 37, or greater than 37, depending on the value of n. For example, if $n = 4$, then $4^2 + 1 = 17$; if $n = 6$, then $6^2 + 1 = 37$; if $n = 10$, then $10^2 + 1 = 101$; and 17, 37, and 101 are all prime numbers. Thus, (1) alone is not sufficient, and the answer must be B, C, or E. Since $14^2 = 196$ and $15^2 = 225$, it follows from (2) that $p > 14$, so that p might or might not equal 37. Thus, (2) alone is not sufficient, and the answer must be C or E. The values of p for $n = 4$ and for $n = 6$ given above show that (1) and (2) together are not sufficient, and the best answer is E.

13. The only contents of a parcel are 25 photographs and 30 negatives. What is the total weight, in ounces, of the parcel's contents?

(1) The weight of each photograph is 3 times the weight of each negative.

(2) The total weight of 1 of the photographs and 2 of the negatives is $\frac{1}{3}$ ounce.

Let p and n denote the weight, in ounces, of a photograph and a negative, respectively. Then the total weight of the parcel's contents can be written as $25p + 30n$. The information in (1) can be written as $p = 3n$. By substituting $3n$ for p in the expression $25p + 30n$, it can be seen that the resulting expression depends on n. Thus, (1) alone is not sufficient, and the answer must be B, C, or E. The information in (2) can be written as $p + 2n = \frac{1}{3}$ and is, similarly, not sufficient. Thus, the answer must be C or E. The two linear equations summarizing the information in (1) and (2) can be solved simultaneously for p and n, so that statements (1) and (2) together are sufficient. The best answer is therefore C.

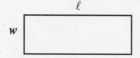

14. If ℓ and w represent the length and width, respectively, of the rectangle above, what is the perimeter?

(1) $2\ell + w = 40$

(2) $\ell + w = 25$

The formula for the perimeter of a rectangle is $P = 2\ell + 2w = 2(\ell + w)$, where ℓ and w represent the length and width, respectively. The perimeter can therefore be determined once $\ell + w$ is known. The value of $\ell + w$ cannot be determined from (1), since $2\ell + w = 40$ is equivalent to $\ell + w = 40 - \ell$, which depends on ℓ. Thus, (1) alone is not sufficient, and the answer must be B, C, or E. However, (2) alone is sufficient because $\ell + w$ is known, and the best answer is B.

15. What is the ratio of x to y ?

(1) x is 4 more than twice y.

(2) The ratio of $0.5x$ to $2y$ is 3 to 5.

Statement (1) can be expressed as $x = 2y + 4$, which is not sufficient since $\dfrac{x}{y} = 2 + \dfrac{4}{y}$, showing that $\dfrac{x}{y}$ depends on y. Thus, the answer must be B, C, or E. Statement (2) can be expressed as $\dfrac{0.5x}{2y} = \dfrac{3}{5}$; so $\dfrac{x}{y} = \dfrac{3}{5} \div \dfrac{0.5}{2}$. Therefore, (2) alone is sufficient, and the best answer is B.

16. If x, y, and z are three integers, are they consecutive integers?

(1) $z - x = 2$

(2) $x < y < z$

From (1) it follows that there is exactly one integer between x and z, but there is no information about y. Thus, (1) alone is not sufficient, and the answer must be B, C, or E. Statement (2) alone is not sufficient because there could be other integers between x and z besides y, so the answer must be C or E. From (1) and (2) together, it follows that y is the unique integer between x and z; that is, $y = x + 1$ and $z = y + 1$, and the integers are consecutive. The best answer is therefore C.

17. What is the value of x ?

(1) $-(x + y) = x - y$

(2) $x + y = 2$

In (1) the equation $-(x + y) = x - y$ can be written as $-x - y = x - y$, which reduces to $-x = x$. The expression $-x$ denotes the additive inverse of x. Because 0 is the only number that is equal to its additive inverse, it follows that $x = 0$, and (1) alone is sufficient. Alternatively, $-x = x$ can be written as $2x = 0$ so that $x = 0$. Thus, the answer must be A or D. In (2) the value of x depends on the value of y, so (2) alone is not sufficient. The best answer is therefore A.

18. A sum of $200,000 from a certain estate was divided among a spouse and three children. How much of the estate did the youngest child receive?

    (1)   The spouse received $\frac{1}{2}$ of the sum from the estate, and the oldest child received $\frac{1}{4}$ of the remainder.

    (2)   Each of the two younger children received $12,500 more than the oldest child and $62,500 less than the spouse.

From (1) the combined amount of the estate that the two younger children received can be determined, but not the individual amount received by either of them. Thus, (1) alone is not sufficient, and the answer must be B, C, or E. In (2) the amount of the estate received by the oldest child and by the spouse can each be expressed in terms of the amount, x, received by each of the two younger children. An equation expressing the sum of $200,000 in terms of x can then be set up and solved for x. It follows that (2) alone is sufficient, so the best answer is B.

19. If the Lincoln Library's total expenditure for books, periodicals, and newspapers last year was $35,000, how much of the expenditure was for books?

    (1)   The expenditure for newspapers was 40 percent greater than the expenditure for periodicals.

    (2)   The total of the expenditure for periodicals and newspapers was 25 percent less than the expenditure for books.

Let b, p, and n denote the expenditure, in dollars, for books, periodicals, and newspapers, respectively. Then $b + p + n = 35,000$. In (1) it follows that $n = 1.4p$, so $b + 2.4p = 35,000$. Since the value of b cannot be determined, (1) alone is not sufficient, and the answer must be B, C, or E. In (2) it follows that $p + n = 0.75b$. Then $0.75b$ can be substituted for $p + n$ in the equation $b + p + n = 35,000$, resulting in an equation involving b alone. Since the value of b can be determined by solving this equation, (2) alone is sufficient, and the best answer is B.

20. The symbol $\triangledown$ represents one of the following operations: addition, subtraction, multiplication, or division. What is the value of $3 \triangledown 2$?

    (1) $0 \triangledown 1 = 1$
    (2) $1 \triangledown 0 = 1$

Since $0 + 1 = 1$, $0 - 1 = -1$, $0 \times 1 = 0$, and $0 \div 1 = 0$, it follows from (1) that $\triangledown$ represents addition, so the value of $3 \triangledown 2$ can be determined. Thus, (1) alone is sufficient, and the answer must be A or D. Since $1 + 0 = 1$, $1 - 0 = 1$, $1 \times 0 = 0$, and $1 \div 0$ is undefined, it follows from (2) that $\triangledown$ could represent either addition or subtraction, so $3 \triangledown 2$ could equal 5 or 1. Thus, (2) alone is not sufficient, and the best answer is A.

DATA SUFFICIENCY SAMPLE TEST SECTION 3

Time — 25 minutes

20 Questions

Directions: Each of the data sufficiency problems below consists of a question and two statements, labeled (1) and (2), in which certain data are given. You have to decide whether the data given in the statements are sufficient for answering the question. Using the data given in the statements plus your knowledge of mathematics and everyday facts (such as the number of days in July or the meaning of *counterclockwise*), you are to fill in oval

A   if statement (1) ALONE is sufficient, but statement (2) alone is not sufficient to answer the question asked;

B   if statement (2) ALONE is sufficient, but statement (1) alone is not sufficient to answer the question asked;

C   if BOTH statements (1) and (2) TOGETHER are sufficient to answer the question asked, but NEITHER statement ALONE is sufficient;

D   if EACH statement ALONE is sufficient to answer the question asked;

E   if statements (1) and (2) TOGETHER are NOT sufficient to answer the question asked, and additional data specific to the problem are needed.

Numbers: All numbers used are real numbers.

Figures: A figure in a data sufficiency problem will conform to the information given in the question, but will not necessarily conform to the additional information given in statements (1) and (2).

You may assume that lines shown as straight are straight and that angle measures are greater than zero.

You may assume that the positions of points, angles, regions, etc., exist in the order shown.

All figures lie in a plane unless otherwise indicated.

Note: In questions that ask for the value of a quantity, the data given in the statements are sufficient only when it is possible to determine exactly one numerical value for the quantity.

Example:

In $\triangle PQR$, what is the value of x ?

(1) $PQ = PR$

(2) $y = 40$

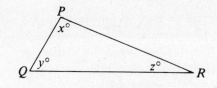

Explanation: According to statement (1), $PQ = PR$; therefore, $\triangle PQR$ is isosceles and $y = z$. Since $x + y + z = 180$, it follows that $x + 2y = 180$. Since statement (1) does not give a value for y, you cannot answer the question using statement (1) alone. According to statement (2), $y = 40$; therefore, $x + z = 140$. Since statement (2) does not give a value for z, you cannot answer the question using statement (2) alone. Using both statements together, since $x + 2y = 180$ and the value of y is given, you can find the value of x. Therefore, the answer is C.

GO ON TO THE NEXT PAGE.

A Statement (1) ALONE is sufficient, but statement (2) alone is not sufficient.
B Statement (2) ALONE is sufficient, but statement (1) alone is not sufficient.
C BOTH statements TOGETHER are sufficient, but NEITHER statement ALONE is sufficient.
D EACH statement ALONE is sufficient.
E Statements (1) and (2) TOGETHER are NOT sufficient.

1. The regular price for canned soup was reduced during a sale. How much money could one have saved by purchasing a dozen 7-ounce cans of soup at the reduced price rather than at the regular price?

   (1) The regular price for the 7-ounce cans was 3 for a dollar.

   (2) The reduced price for the 7-ounce cans was 4 for a dollar.

2. If on a fishing trip Jim and Tom each caught some fish, which one caught more fish?

   (1) Jim caught $\frac{2}{3}$ as many fish as Tom.

   (2) After Tom stopped fishing, Jim continued fishing until he had caught 12 fish.

3. If $5x + 3y = 17$, what is the value of x ?

   (1) x is a positive integer.

   (2) $y = 4x$

4. Yesterday Nan parked her car at a certain parking garage that charges more for the first hour than for each additional hour. If Nan's total parking charge at the garage yesterday was \$3.75, for how many hours of parking was she charged?

   (1) Parking charges at the garage are \$0.75 for the first hour and \$0.50 for each additional hour or fraction of an hour.

   (2) If the charge for the first hour had been \$1.00, Nan's total parking charge would have been \$4.00.

5. If r and s are integers, is $r + s$ divisible by 3 ?

   (1) s is divisible by 3.

   (2) r is divisible by 3.

GO ON TO THE NEXT PAGE.

A   Statement (1) ALONE is sufficient, but statement (2) alone is not sufficient.
B   Statement (2) ALONE is sufficient, but statement (1) alone is not sufficient.
C   BOTH statements TOGETHER are sufficient, but NEITHER statement ALONE is sufficient.
D   EACH statement ALONE is sufficient.
E   Statements (1) and (2) TOGETHER are NOT sufficient.

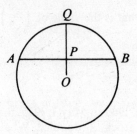

6. What is the radius of the circle above with center O?

(1) The ratio of OP to PQ is 1 to 2.

(2) P is the midpoint of chord AB.

7. A certain 4-liter solution of vinegar and water consists of x liters of vinegar and y liters of water. How many liters of vinegar does the solution contain?

(1) $\frac{x}{4} = \frac{3}{8}$

(2) $\frac{y}{4} = \frac{5}{8}$

8. Is $x < 0$?

(1) $-2x > 0$

(2) $x^3 < 0$

9. Of the 230 single-family homes built in City X last year, how many were occupied at the end of the year?

(1) Of all single-family homes in City X, 90 percent were occupied at the end of last year.

(2) A total of 7,200 single-family homes in City X were occupied at the end of last year.

10. Does the product $jkmn$ equal 1?

(1) $\frac{jk}{mn} = 1$

(2) $j = \frac{1}{k}$ and $m = \frac{1}{n}$

GO ON TO THE NEXT PAGE.

A Statement (1) ALONE is sufficient, but statement (2) alone is not sufficient.
B Statement (2) ALONE is sufficient, but statement (1) alone is not sufficient.
C BOTH statements TOGETHER are sufficient, but NEITHER statement ALONE is sufficient.
D EACH statement ALONE is sufficient.
E Statements (1) and (2) TOGETHER are NOT sufficient.

11. How many of the boys in a group of 100 children have brown hair?

(1) Of the children in the group, 60 percent have brown hair.

(2) Of the children in the group, 40 are boys.

12. Is the perimeter of square S greater than the perimeter of equilateral triangle T?

(1) The ratio of the length of a side of S to the length of a side of T is $4 : 5$.

(2) The sum of the lengths of a side of S and a side of T is 18.

13. If p and q are positive integers and $pq = 24$, what is the value of p?

(1) $\frac{q}{6}$ is an integer.

(2) $\frac{p}{2}$ is an integer.

14. If $x \neq 0$, what is the value of $\left(\frac{x^p}{x^q}\right)^4$?

(1) $p = q$

(2) $x = 3$

15. From May 1, 1960 to May 1, 1975, the closing price of a share of stock X doubled. What was the closing price of a share of stock X on May 1, 1960 ?

(1) From May 1, 1975, to May 1, 1984, the closing price of a share of stock X doubled.

(2) From May 1, 1975, to May 1, 1984, the closing price of a share of stock X increased by $4.50.

GO ON TO THE NEXT PAGE.

A   Statement (1) ALONE is sufficient, but statement (2) alone is not sufficient.
B   Statement (2) ALONE is sufficient, but statement (1) alone is not sufficient.
C   BOTH statements TOGETHER are sufficient, but NEITHER statement ALONE is sufficient.
D   EACH statement ALONE is sufficient.
E   Statements (1) and (2) TOGETHER are NOT sufficient.

16. If d is a positive integer, is $\sqrt{d}$ an integer?

   (1) d is the square of an integer.

   (2) $\sqrt{d}$ is the square of an integer.

17. If Q is an integer between 10 and 100, what is the value of Q ?

   (1) One of Q's digits is 3 more than the other, and the sum of its digits is 9.

   (2) $Q < 50$

18. If digit h is the hundredths' digit in the decimal $d = 0.2h6$, what is the value of d, rounded to the nearest tenth?

   (1) $d < \dfrac{1}{4}$

   (2) $h < 5$

19. What is the value of $x^2 - y^2$?

   (1) $x - y = y + 2$

   (2) $x - y = \dfrac{1}{x + y}$

20. If $\circ$ represents one of the operations $+$, $-$, and $\times$, is $k \circ (\ell + m) = (k \circ \ell) + (k \circ m)$ for all numbers k, ℓ, and m ?

   (1) $k \circ 1$ is not equal to $1 \circ k$ for some numbers k.

   (2) $\circ$ represents subtraction.

S T O P

**IF YOU FINISH BEFORE TIME IS CALLED, YOU MAY CHECK YOUR WORK ON THIS SECTION ONLY.
DO NOT TURN TO ANY OTHER SECTION IN THE TEST.**

Answer Key for Sample Test Section 3

DATA SUFFICIENCY

1.	C	11.	E
2.	A	12.	A
3.	B	13.	E
4.	A	14.	A
5.	C	15.	C
6.	E	16.	D
7.	D	17.	C
8.	D	18.	D
9.	E	19.	B
10.	B	20.	D

Explanatory Material: Data Sufficiency Sample Test Section 3

1. The regular price for canned soup was reduced during a sale. How much money could one have saved by purchasing a dozen 7-ounce cans of soup at the reduced price rather than at the regular price?

    (1) The regular price for the 7-ounce cans was 3 for a dollar.

    (2) The reduced price for the 7-ounce cans was 4 for a dollar.

The saving is the difference between the regular price of a dozen cans and their reduced price. Since (1) gives no information about the reduced price, (1) alone is not sufficient to determine the saving, and the answer must be B, C, or E. Statement (2) alone gives no information about the regular price. Therefore, (2) alone is not sufficient, and the answer must be C or E. From (1) and (2) together, both prices can be computed, and the saving can be determined. Therefore, the best answer is C.

2. If on a fishing trip Jim and Tom each caught some fish, which one caught more fish?

    (1) Jim caught $\frac{2}{3}$ as many fish as Tom.

    (2) After Tom stopped fishing, Jim continued fishing until he had caught 12 fish.

Statement (1) indicates that Jim caught fewer fish than Tom. Therefore, (1) alone is sufficient to answer the question, and the answer must be A or D. Statement (2) gives no information about the number of fish Tom caught. Therefore, (2) alone is not sufficient, and the best answer is A.

3. If $5x + 3y = 17$, what is the value of x ?

    (1) x is a positive integer.

    (2) $y = 4x$

Statement (1) alone is not sufficient because it gives no information about the value of y. Thus, the answer must be B, C, or E. From (2) it follows that $5x + 3(4x) = 17$, which can be solved for x. Therefore, the best answer is B.

4. Yesterday Nan parked her car at a certain parking garage that charges more for the first hour than for each additional hour. If Nan's total parking charge at the garage yesterday was $3.75, for how many hours of parking was she charged?

    (1) Parking charges at the garage are $0.75 for the first hour and $0.50 for each additional hour or fraction of an hour.

    (2) If the charge for the first hour had been $1.00, Nan's total parking charge would have been $4.00.

Statement (1) gives the charge for the first hour and for subsequent hours. From this information, together with the total charge that is given, the number of hours after the first hour can be computed. Thus, the answer must be A or D. From statement (2) the charge for the first hour can be determined; however, there is no information about charges after the first hour. Therefore, (2) alone is not sufficient, and the best answer is A.

5. If r and s are integers, is $r + s$ divisible by 3 ?

    (1) s is divisible by 3.

    (2) r is divisible by 3.

One approach to answering this question is to choose values for r and s. In statement (1), for example, let $s = 6$, which is divisible by 3. Then, $r + s$ is divisible by 3 if $r = 9$ but not if $r = 10$, and similarly for statement (2). In more general terms, $r + s$ is divisible by 3 if both r and s are divisible by 3. If either r or s is not divisible by 3, then $r + s$ might or might not be divisible by 3. Since neither (1) alone nor (2) alone gives information about both r and s, neither statement alone is sufficient, and the answer must be C or E. Statements (1) and (2) together state that both r and s are divisible by 3, however, so the best answer is C.

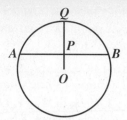

6. What is the radius of the circle above with center O ?

   (1) The ratio of OP to PQ is 1 to 2.
   (2) P is the midpoint of chord AB.

From statement (1) it can be concluded only that the radius is 3 times the length of OP. Since there are many possible lengths of OP and PQ that would have a ratio of 1 to 2, statement (1) alone is not sufficient, and the answer must be B, C, or E. Similarly, knowing that P is the midpoint of chord AB is of no help in determining the radius, so (2) alone is not sufficient. Therefore, the answer must be C or E. Statements (1) and (2) together do not give the length of any line segment shown in the circle, so they are not sufficient to determine the radius. Thus, the best answer is E.

7. A certain 4-liter solution of vinegar and water consists of x liters of vinegar and y liters of water. How many liters of vinegar does the solution contain?

   (1) $\dfrac{x}{4} = \dfrac{3}{8}$

   (2) $\dfrac{y}{4} = \dfrac{5}{8}$

Statement (1) can be solved for x, so (1) alone is sufficient. Therefore, the answer must be A or D. Statement (2) can be solved for y. Since $x + y = 4$, substituting the value of y in the equation will give the value of x. Thus, statement (2) alone is also sufficient, and the best answer is D.

8. Is $x < 0$?

   (1) $-2x > 0$
   (2) $x^3 < 0$

A negative number times a positive number is negative, whereas a negative number times a negative number is positive. Thus, from statement (1) it can be determined that x must be negative, since -2 times x is positive. Therefore, (1) alone is sufficient, and the answer must be A or D. Statement (2) alone is also sufficient, since the cube of a positive number is positive and the cube of a negative number is negative. Therefore, each statement alone is sufficient, and the best answer is D.

9. Of the 230 single-family homes built in City X last year, how many were occupied at the end of the year?

   (1) Of all single-family homes in City X, 90 percent were occupied at the end of last year.
   (2) A total of 7,200 single-family homes in City X were occupied at the end of last year.

Statement (1) does not give the percentage of homes built last year that were occupied. Any number of the 230 homes could be included in the 90 percent of the total. Therefore, the answer must be B, C, or E. Similarly, any number of the 230 homes could be included in the total, and (2) alone is not sufficient. Therefore, the answer must be C or E. From (1) and (2) together, only the total number of single-family homes can be determined. Thus, the best answer is E.

10. Does the product $jkmn$ equal 1 ?

    (1) $\dfrac{jk}{mn} = 1$

    (2) $j = \dfrac{1}{k}$ and $m = \dfrac{1}{n}$

From statement (1) it can be determined only that $jk = mn$. Since this information is not sufficient, the answer must be B, C, or E. From (2) alone, it can be determined that $jk = 1$ and $mn = 1$, so $jkmn = 1$. Thus, (2) alone is sufficient, and the best answer is B.

11. How many of the boys in a group of 100 children have brown hair?

    (1) Of the children in the group, 60 percent have brown hair.
    (2) Of the children in the group, 40 are boys.

From statement (1), only the total number of children who have brown hair can be determined, so (1) alone is not sufficient. Therefore, the answer must be B, C, or E. Clearly (2) alone is not sufficient because nothing is said about brown hair. Therefore, the answer must be C or E. From statements (1) and (2) together, only the total number of children who have brown hair and the number of boys in the group are known. Thus, (1) and (2) together are not sufficient, and the best answer is E.

12. Is the perimeter of square S greater than the perimeter of equilateral triangle T ?

   (1) The ratio of the length of a side of S to the length of a side of T is 4 : 5.

   (2) The sum of the lengths of a side of S and a side of T is 18.

In considering (1), let the length of each side of S be $4x$ and the length of each side of T be $5x$, which is consistent with the ratio given. Thus, the perimeter of S is $4(4x)$ and the perimeter of T is $3(5x)$, and statement (1) alone is sufficient. Thus, the answer must be A or D. Statement (2) alone is not sufficient because there are many pairs of numbers whose sum is 18, and for some of these pairs the perimeter of S is less than that of T, while for other pairs it is greater. The best answer is A.

13. If p and q are positive integers and $pq = 24$, what is the value of p ?

   (1) $\dfrac{q}{6}$ is an integer.

   (2) $\dfrac{p}{2}$ is an integer.

There are four pairs of positive integers whose product is 24: 1 and 24, 2 and 12, 3 and 8, and 4 and 6. From statement (1) the possible values of q are 24, 12, and 6, and there is a value of p corresponding to each of these three values. Thus, statement (1) alone is not sufficient, and the answer must be B, C, or E. From (2), the possible values of p are 2, 4, 6, 8, 12, and 24. Thus, (2) alone is not sufficient, and the answer must be C or E. From (1) and (2) together, it can be determined only that q can be either 12 or 6, so p can be either 2 or 4. Thus, (1) and (2) together are not sufficient, and the best answer is E.

14. If $x \neq 0$, what is the value of $\left(\dfrac{x^p}{x^q}\right)^4$?

   (1) $p = q$
   (2) $x = 3$

From statement (1) it follows, by substitution, that $\dfrac{x^p}{x^q} = 1$,

and thus (1) alone is sufficient to determine the value of

$\left(\dfrac{x^p}{x^q}\right)^4$. Therefore, the answer must be A or D. Statement (2)

alone is not sufficient because it gives no information about

the values of p and q. Thus, the best answer is A.

15. From May 1, 1960 to May 1, 1975, the closing price of a share of stock X doubled. What was the closing price of a share of stock X on May 1, 1960 ?

   (1) From May 1, 1975, to May 1, 1984, the closing price of a share of stock X doubled.

   (2) From May 1, 1975, to May 1, 1984, the closing price of a share of stock X increased by \$4.50.

Neither statement (1) alone nor statement (2) alone gives any information about the price from 1960 to 1975. Thus, the answer must be C or E. From statements (1) and (2) together, the closing price of a share of the stock on May 1, 1975, can be determined (\$4.50) and the closing price on May 1, 1960, can be determined (half of \$4.50). Therefore, (1) and (2) together are sufficient, and the best answer is C.

16. If d is a positive integer, is $\sqrt{d}$ an integer?

   (1) d is the square of an integer.
   (2) $\sqrt{d}$ is the square of an integer.

Statement (1) can be expressed as $d = x^2$, where x is a nonzero

integer. Then $\sqrt{d} = \sqrt{x^2}$ equals x or $-x$, depending on

whether x is positive or negative, respectively. In either case,

$\sqrt{d}$ is an integer. For example, $\sqrt{10^2} = 10$ and

$\sqrt{(-4)^2} = \sqrt{16} = 4 = -(-4)$. Therefore, (1) alone is sufficient,

and the answer must be A or D. In (2) the square of an integer

must also be an integer. Thus, (2) alone is also sufficient, and

the best answer is D.

17. If Q is an integer between 10 and 100, what is the value of Q ?

   (1) One of Q's digits is 3 more than the other, and the sum of its digits is 9.

   (2) $Q < 50$

If x and y are the digits of Q, statement (1) can be expressed as $x = y + 3$ and $x + y = 9$, which can be solved for x and y. It is also possible to see that only the numbers 36 and 63 satisfy (1) without actually setting up equations, but the order of the digits is not known regardless of the method used. Thus, (1) alone is not sufficient, and the answer must be B, C, or E. Clearly, (2) alone is not sufficient because it only narrows the range of possible values of Q. Therefore, the answer must be C or E. When the two possible values of Q are considered and it is noted that only one of the values is less than 50, it can be seen that (1) and (2) together are sufficient to determine the value of Q, and the best answer is C.

18. If digit h is the hundredths' digit in the decimal $d = 0.2h6$, what is the value of d, rounded to the nearest tenth?

(1) $d < \frac{1}{4}$

(2) $h < 5$

The value of d, rounded to the nearest tenth, is 0.3 for $h \geq 5$ and 0.2 for $h < 5$. Statement (1) can be written $d < 0.250$, so $h < 5$. Thus, (1) alone is sufficient, and the answer must be A or D. Statement (2) gives the information that $h < 5$ directly, so (2) alone is also sufficient. The best answer is D.

19. What is the value of $x^2 - y^2$?

(1) $x - y = y + 2$

(2) $x - y = \frac{1}{x + y}$

From statement (1) it can be determined only that $x = 2y + 2$ and that $x^2 - y^2 = (2y + 2)^2 - y^2$, which depends on the value of y. Thus, (1) alone is not sufficient to determine the value of $x^2 - y^2$, and the answer must be B, C, or E. Statement (2) can be rewritten $(x - y)(x + y) = 1$, or $x^2 - y^2 = 1$. Therefore, (2) alone is sufficient, and the best answer is B.

20. If ∘ represents one of the operations +, –, and ×, is $k \circ (\ell + m) = (k \circ \ell) + (k \circ m)$ for all numbers k, ℓ, and m ?

(1) $k \circ 1$ is not equal to $1 \circ k$ for some numbers k.

(2) ∘ represents subtraction.

Since $k \circ 1 = 1 \circ k$ for both + and × (i.e., $k + 1 = 1 + k$ and $k \times 1 = 1 \times k$ for all values of k), according to statement (1), ∘ must represent subtraction. Thus, it can be determined whether $k - (\ell + m) = (k - \ell) + (k - m)$ holds for all k, ℓ, and m. Note, however, that it is not actually necessary to answer this question, only to see that the answer can be determined. Thus, (1) alone is sufficient, and the answer must be A or D. Because statement (2) gives the information directly that ∘ represents subtraction, (2) alone is also sufficient, and the best answer is D.

DATA SUFFICIENCY SAMPLE TEST SECTION 4

Time — 25 minutes

20 Questions

Directions: Each of the data sufficiency problems below consists of a question and two statements, labeled (1) and (2), in which certain data are given. You have to decide whether the data given in the statements are <u>sufficient</u> for answering the question. Using the data given in the statements <u>plus</u> your knowledge of mathematics and everyday facts (such as the number of days in July or the meaning of *counterclockwise*), you are to fill in oval

A   if statement (1) ALONE is sufficient, but statement (2) alone is not sufficient to answer the question asked;

B   if statement (2) ALONE is sufficient, but statement (1) alone is not sufficient to answer the question asked;

C   if BOTH statements (1) and (2) TOGETHER are sufficient to answer the question asked, but NEITHER statement ALONE is sufficient;

D   if EACH statement ALONE is sufficient to answer the question asked;

E   if statements (1) and (2) TOGETHER are NOT sufficient to answer the question asked, and additional data specific to the problem are needed.

Numbers: All numbers used are real numbers.

Figures: A figure in a data sufficiency problem will conform to the information given in the question, but will not necessarily conform to the additional information given in statements (1) and (2).

You may assume that lines shown as straight are straight and that angle measures are greater than zero.

You may assume that the positions of points, angles, regions, etc., exist in the order shown.

All figures lie in a plane unless otherwise indicated.

Note: In questions that ask for the value of a quantity, the data given in the statements are sufficient only when it is possible to determine exactly one numerical value for the quantity.

Example:

In $\triangle PQR$, what is the value of x?

(1) $PQ = PR$

(2) $y = 40$

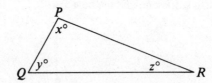

Explanation: According to statement (1), $PQ = PR$; therefore, $\triangle PQR$ is isosceles and $y = z$. Since $x + y + z = 180$, it follows that $x + 2y = 180$. Since statement (1) does not give a value for y, you cannot answer the question using statement (1) alone. According to statement (2), $y = 40$; therefore, $x + z = 140$. Since statement (2) does not give a value for z, you cannot answer the question using statement (2) alone. Using both statements together, since $x + 2y = 180$ and the value of y is given, you can find the value of x. Therefore, the answer is C.

GO ON TO THE NEXT PAGE.

A   Statement (1) ALONE is sufficient, but statement (2) alone is not sufficient.
B   Statement (2) ALONE is sufficient, but statement (1) alone is not sufficient.
C   BOTH statements TOGETHER are sufficient, but NEITHER statement ALONE is sufficient.
D   EACH statement ALONE is sufficient.
E   Statements (1) and (2) TOGETHER are NOT sufficient.

1. Committee member W wants to schedule a one-hour meeting on Thursday for himself and three other committee members, X, Y, and Z. Is there a one-hour period on Thursday that is open for all four members?

   (1) On Thursday W and X have an open period from 9:00 a.m. to 12:00 noon.

   (2) On Thursday Y has an open period from 10:00 a.m. to 1:00 p.m. and Z has an open period from 8:00 a.m. to 11:00 a.m.

2. If Jack's and Kate's annual salaries in 1985 were each 10 percent higher than their respective annual salaries in 1984, what was Jack's annual salary in 1984?

   (1) The sum of Jack's and Kate's annual salaries in 1984 was $50,000.

   (2) The sum of Jack's and Kate's annual salaries in 1985 was $55,000.

3. What is the value of x?

   (1) $x + 1 = 2 - 3x$

   (2) $\frac{1}{2x} = 2$

4. How many newspapers were sold at a certain newsstand today?

   (1) A total of 100 newspapers were sold at the newsstand yesterday, 10 fewer than twice the number sold today.

   (2) The number of newspapers sold at the newsstand yesterday was 45 more than the number sold today.

5. How much did a certain telephone call cost?

   (1) The call lasted 53 minutes.

   (2) The cost for the first 3 minutes was 5 times the cost for each additional minute.

6. A certain expressway has exits J, K, L, and M, in that order. What is the road distance from exit K to exit L?

   (1) The road distance from exit J to exit L is 21 kilometers.

   (2) The road distance from exit K to exit M is 26 kilometers.

GO ON TO THE NEXT PAGE.

A   Statement (1) ALONE is sufficient, but statement (2) alone is not sufficient.
B   Statement (2) ALONE is sufficient, but statement (1) alone is not sufficient.
C   BOTH statements TOGETHER are sufficient, but NEITHER statement ALONE is sufficient.
D   EACH statement ALONE is sufficient.
E   Statements (1) and (2) TOGETHER are NOT sufficient.

7. Two cars, S and T, each traveled a distance of 50 miles. Did car S use more gasoline than car T?

   (1) Cars S and T traveled the entire distance at the rates of 55 miles per hour and 50 miles per hour, respectively.

   (2) For the entire distance, car S traveled 20 miles per gallon of gasoline and car T traveled 25 miles per gallon of gasoline.

8. If n is a positive integer, is n odd?

   (1) $3n$ is odd.

   (2) $n + 3$ is even.

9. Does $2m - 3n = 0$?

   (1) $m \neq 0$

   (2) $6m = 9n$

10. If $xy < 3$, is $x < 1$?

   (1) $y > 3$

   (2) $x < 3$

11. Each of the eggs in a bowl is dyed red, or green, or blue. If one egg is to be removed at random, what is the probability that the egg will be green?

   (1) There are 5 red eggs in the bowl.

   (2) The probability that the egg will be blue is $\frac{1}{3}$.

12. Is the average (arithmetic mean) of x and y greater than 20?

   (1) The average (arithmetic mean) of $2x$ and $2y$ is 48.

   (2) $x = 3y$

GO ON TO THE NEXT PAGE.

A   Statement (1) ALONE is sufficient, but statement (2) alone is not sufficient.
B   Statement (2) ALONE is sufficient, but statement (1) alone is not sufficient.
C   BOTH statements TOGETHER are sufficient, but NEITHER statement ALONE is sufficient.
D   EACH statement ALONE is sufficient.
E   Statements (1) and (2) TOGETHER are NOT sufficient.

13. Marcia's bucket can hold a maximum of how many liters of water?

   (1) The bucket currently contains 9 liters of water.

   (2) If 3 liters of water are added to the bucket when it is half full of water, the amount of water in the bucket will increase by $\frac{1}{3}$.

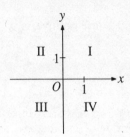

16. If $ab \neq 0$, in what quadrant of the coordinate system above does point (a, b) lie?

   (1) (b, a) lies in quadrant IV.

   (2) $(a, -b)$ lies in quadrant III.

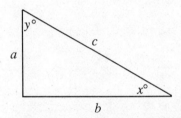

14. In the triangle above, does $a^2 + b^2 = c^2$?

   (1) $x + y = 90$
   (2) $x = y$

15. What is the value of the positive integer n?

   (1) $n^4 < 25$
   (2) $n \neq n^2$

17. From 1984 to 1987, the value of foreign goods consumed annually in the United States increased by what percent?

   (1) In 1984 the value of foreign goods consumed constituted 19.8 percent of the total value of goods consumed in the United States that year.

   (2) In 1987 the value of foreign goods consumed constituted 22.7 percent of the total value of goods consumed in the United States that year.

GO ON TO THE NEXT PAGE.

A   Statement (1) ALONE is sufficient, but statement (2) alone is not sufficient.
B   Statement (2) ALONE is sufficient, but statement (1) alone is not sufficient.
C   BOTH statements TOGETHER are sufficient, but NEITHER statement ALONE is sufficient.
D   EACH statement ALONE is sufficient.
E   Statements (1) and (2) TOGETHER are NOT sufficient.

18. If x, y, and z are positive, is $x = \dfrac{y}{z^2}$?

(1) $z = \dfrac{y}{xz}$

(2) $z = \sqrt{\dfrac{y}{x}}$

19. If x and y are positive integers and $x^y = x^{2y-3}$, what is the value of x^y?

(1) $x = 2$
(2) $x^3 = 8$

20. If k and n are integers, is n divisible by 7?

(1) $n - 3 = 2k$
(2) $2k - 4$ is divisible by 7.

STOP

**IF YOU FINISH BEFORE TIME IS CALLED, YOU MAY CHECK YOUR WORK ON THIS SECTION ONLY.
DO NOT TURN TO ANY OTHER SECTION IN THE TEST.**

Answer Key for Sample Test Section 4

DATA SUFFICIENCY

1. C	11. E
2. E	12. A
3. D	13. B
4. A	14. A
5. E	15. C
6. E	16. D
7. B	17. E
8. D	18. D
9. B	19. D
10. A	20. C

Explanatory Material: Data Sufficiency Sample Test Section 4

1. Committee member W wants to schedule a one-hour meeting on Thursday for himself and three other committee members, X, Y, and Z. Is there a one-hour period on Thursday that is open for all four members?

   (1) On Thursday W and X have an open period from 9:00 a.m. to 12:00 noon.
   (2) On Thursday Y has an open period from 10:00 a.m. to 1:00 p.m. and Z has an open period from 8:00 a.m. to 11:00 a.m.

Statement (1) alone is not sufficient, since it gives no information about Y and Z. Thus, the answer must be B, C, or E. Similarly, statement (2) alone is not sufficient, since it gives no information about W and X. Therefore, the answer must be C or E. From statements (1) and (2) together, it can be determined that all four committee members have an open one-hour period from 10:00 a.m. to 11:00 a.m. Thus, the best answer is C.

2. If Jack's and Kate's annual salaries in 1985 were each 10 percent higher than their respective annual salaries in 1984, what was Jack's annual salary in 1984 ?

   (1) The sum of Jack's and Kate's annual salaries in 1984 was $50,000.
   (2) The sum of Jack's and Kate's annual salaries in 1985 was $55,000.

Statement (1) alone is not sufficient because it gives only the total salaries for Jack and Kate. Thus, the answer must be B, C, or E. From statement (2) alone, it can be determined only that the sum of Jack's and Kate's salaries in 1984 was $55,000 \div 1.1 = \$50,000$, which was given directly in (1). Since statements (1) and (2) give the same information, taken together they still do not provide enough information to determine Jack's salary in 1984. Thus, the best answer is E.

3. What is the value of x ?

   (1) $x + 1 = 3x$
   (2) $\dfrac{1}{2x} = 2$

Each equation, taken separately, can be solved for a unique value of x. Therefore, the best answer is D.

4. How many newspapers were sold at a certain newsstand today?

   (1) A total of 100 newspapers were sold at the newsstand yesterday, 10 fewer than twice the number sold today.
   (2) The number of newspapers sold at the newsstand yesterday was 45 more than the number sold today.

Let t be the number of newspapers sold today. Then statement (1) can be translated as $100 = 2t - 10$, which can be solved for t. Therefore, the answer must be A or D. From statement (2) alone, it can be determined only that the number of newspapers sold yesterday was $t + 45$. Since the number sold yesterday is not known, t cannot be determined and the best answer is A.

5. How much did a certain telephone call cost?

   (1) The call lasted 53 minutes.
   (2) The cost for the first 3 minutes was 5 times the cost for each additional minute.

The cost of the call depends on the duration of the call and the telephone rates. Since statement (1) gives only the duration, it is not sufficient. Therefore, the answer must be B, C, or E. Since statement (2) gives relative rather than actual rates, statement (2) alone is not sufficient, and the answer must be C or E. If c is the cost for the first 3 minutes, then statements (1) and (2) taken together imply that the cost of the call is $c + \dfrac{c}{5}(50)$. Since the value of c cannot be determined, the best answer is E.

6. A certain expressway has exits J, K, L, and M, in that order. What is the road distance from exit K to exit L ?

   (1) The road distance from exit J to exit L is 21 kilometers.
   (2) The road distance from exit K to exit M is 26 kilometers.

Let JK, KL, and LM be the distances between adjacent exits. From statement (1), it can be determined only that $KL = 21 - JK$. Therefore, the answer must be B, C, or E. Similarly, from statement (2), it can be determined only that $KL = 26 - LM$, and the answer must be C or E. Statements (1) and (2) taken together do not provide any of the distances JK, LM, or JM, any of which would give the needed information to find KL. Thus, the best answer is E.

7. Two cars, *S* and *T*, each traveled a distance of 50 miles. Did car *S* use more gasoline than car *T* ?

   (1) Cars *S* and *T* traveled the entire distance at the rates of 55 miles per hour and 50 miles per hour, respectively.

   (2) For the entire distance, car *S* traveled 20 miles per gallon of gasoline and car *T* traveled 25 miles per gallon of gasoline.

From statement (1), it can be determined only that *T* traveled more slowly and thus took more time to make the trip than *S*. Therefore, the answer must be B, C, or E. From statement (2), it can be determined that *S* traveled fewer miles per gallon and thus used more gasoline to travel the same distance than *T*. The best answer is B.

8. If *n* is a positive integer, is *n* odd?

   (1) $3n$ is odd.
   (2) $n + 3$ is even.

Statement (1) implies that *n* is odd, for if *n* were even, any multiple of *n* would be even. Therefore, the answer must be A or D. Statement (2) also implies that *n* is odd, since 3 less than any even number is an odd number. Since either (1) or (2), taken separately, is sufficient to answer the question, the best answer is D.

9. Does $2m - 3n = 0$?

   (1) $m \neq 0$
   (2) $6m = 9n$

The question is equivalent to the question, "Does $2m = 3n$?" Statement (1) alone is not sufficient since it does not give any information about the relationship between *m* and *n*. Therefore, the answer must be B, C, or E. Statement (2) is equivalent to $2m = 3n$, so it is sufficient to answer the question. The best answer is B.

10. If $xy < 3$, is $x < 1$?

   (1) $y > 3$
   (2) $x < 3$

Statement (1) and the information that $xy < 3$ are sufficient to determine that $x < 1$. For if it were true that $x \geq 1$ and $y > 3$, then $xy > 3$, which is not the case. Therefore, the answer must be A or D. Statement (2) alone does not give sufficient information. For example, if $y = 1$, then *x* can be any number less than 3, so it is possible that $x \leq 1$ or $x > 1$. The best answer is A.

11. Each of the eggs in a bowl is dyed red, or green, or blue. If one egg is to be removed at random, what is the probability that the egg will be green?

   (1) There are 5 red eggs in the bowl.

   (2) The probability that the egg will be blue is $\frac{1}{3}$.

To determine the probability that the egg removed is green, one must know the number of green eggs and the total number of eggs, or know what proportion of the eggs are green. None of this information is provided by either statement. Therefore, the answer must be C or E. From statements (1) and (2) together, it can be determined only that the probability is less than $\frac{2}{3}$. The best answer is E.

12. Is the average (arithmetic mean) of *x* and *y* greater than 20 ?

   (1) The average (arithmetic mean) of $2x$ and $2y$ is 48.
   (2) $x = 3y$

According to statement (1), $\frac{2x + 2y}{2} = 48$ and so $\frac{x + y}{2} = 24$, which is greater than 20. Therefore, the answer must be either A or D. Statement (2) alone implies that the average of *x* and *y* equals $\frac{x + y}{2} = \frac{3y + y}{2} = 2y$. Since the value of *y* is not known, it can be determined whether $2y > 20$. The best answer is A.

13. Marcia's bucket can hold a maximum of how many liters of water?

   (1) The bucket currently contains 9 liters of water.
   (2) If 3 liters of water are added to the bucket when it is half full of water, the amount of water in the bucket will increase by $\frac{1}{3}$.

Statement (1) is not sufficient since it implies only that the bucket will hold at least 9 liters. Therefore, the answer must be B, C, or E. With respect to statement (2), if *c* is the capacity of Marcia's bucket and the addition of 3 liters of water increases the volume of the water from $\frac{1}{2}c$ to $\frac{4}{3}\left(\frac{1}{2}c\right)$, then $\frac{4}{3}\left(\frac{1}{2}c\right) - \frac{1}{2}c = 3$, which can be solved for *c*. The best answer is B.

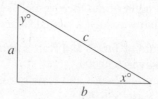

14. In the triangle above, does $a^2 + b^2 = c^2$?

   (1) $x + y = 90$
   (2) $x = y$

The Pythagorean theorem states that $a^2 + b^2 = c^2$ for any right triangle with legs of lengths *a* and *b* and hypotenuse of length *c*. Statement (1) implies that the triangle is a right triangle since the degree measure of the unmarked angle is $180 - (x + y) = 90$. Therefore, $a^2 + b^2 = c^2$ and the answer must be A or D. Statement (2) alone is not sufficient, since $x = y$ does not provide enough information to determine that the largest angle measures 90 degrees. The best answer is A.

15. What is the value of the positive integer n ?

(1) $n^4 < 25$
(2) $n \neq n^2$

Statement (1) alone is not sufficient, for if $n^4 < 25$, then $n = 1$ or $n = 2$, since $1^4 = 1$ and $2^4 = 16$, and $n \geq 3$ implies $n^4 \geq 81$. Therefore, the answer must be B, C, or E. Statement (2) implies only that n is not equal to 1. Statements (1) and (2) together are sufficient, since eliminating $n = 1$ leaves $n = 2$. The best answer is C.

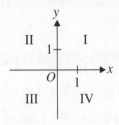

16. If $ab \neq 0$, in what quadrant of the coordinate system above does point (a, b) lie?

(1) (b, a) lies in quadrant IV.
(2) $(a, -b)$ lies in quadrant III.

With respect to statement (1), if (b, a) lies in quadrant IV, then $b > 0$ and $a < 0$, which implies that (a, b) lies in quadrant II. Therefore, the answer must be A or D. With respect to statement (2), if $(a, -b)$ lies in quadrant III, then $a < 0$, $-b < 0$, and $b > 0$. Again, $a < 0$ and $b > 0$ imply that (a, b) lies in quadrant II. The best answer is D.

17. From 1984 to 1987, the value of foreign goods consumed annually in the United States increased by what percent?

(1) In 1984 the value of foreign goods consumed constituted 19.8 percent of the total value of goods consumed in the United States that year.
(2) In 1987 the value of foreign goods consumed constituted 22.7 percent of the total value of goods consumed in the United States that year.

To compute the percent increase, the values of foreign goods consumed in both 1984 and 1987 must be known. Each statement gives only the value of foreign goods as a percentage of the total value of goods consumed in one of the years. Thus, the answer must be C or E. Since statements (1) and (2) together do not provide the values of goods consumed in 1984 and 1987, either total or foreign, they do not give sufficient information to answer the question. Thus, the best answer is E.

18. If x, y, and z are positive, is $x = \dfrac{y}{z^2}$?

(1) $z = \dfrac{y}{xz}$

(2) $z = \sqrt{\dfrac{y}{x}}$

With respect to statement (1), since x, y, and z are positive, both sides of the equation can be multiplied by $\dfrac{x}{z}$ to produce the identical equation $x = \dfrac{y}{z^2}$. Thus, the answer must be A or D. Statement (2) is also an equivalent equation, which can be seen by squaring both sides of the equation and then solving for x. Since each statement gives sufficient information, the best answer is D.

19. If x and y are positive integers and $x^y = x^{2y-3}$, what is the value of x^y ?

(1) $x = 2$
(2) $x^3 = 8$

If $x^y = x^{2y-3}$, then $y = 2y - 3$, or $y = 3$. To determine x^y, or x^3, one only needs the value of x. Statement (1) gives the value of x, and the value of x can be found from statement (2). Thus, the best answer is D.

20. If k and n are integers, is n divisible by 7 ?

(1) $n - 3 = 2k$
(2) $2k - 4$ is divisible by 7.

Statement (1) alone is not sufficient since it implies only that $n = 2k + 3$, which could be any odd number. Therefore, the answer must be B, C, or E. Statement (2) alone is not sufficient since it does not give any information about n. Therefore, the answer must be C or E. Statement (2) does imply that $2k - 4 = 7x$, where x is an integer. Also note that $2k + 3$, from (1), can be expressed as $(2k - 4) + 7$. Thus, combining the information in (1) and (2), $n = 2k + 3 = (2k - 4) + 7$, which is divisible by 7 since it is the sum of two terms, each of which is divisible by 7. The best answer is C.

DATA SUFFICIENCY SAMPLE TEST SECTION 5

Time — 25 minutes

20 Questions

<u>Directions</u>: Each of the data sufficiency problems below consists of a question and two statements, labeled (1) and (2), in which certain data are given. You have to decide whether the data given in the statements are <u>sufficient</u> for answering the question. Using the data given in the statements <u>plus</u> your knowledge of mathematics and everyday facts (such as the number of days in July or the meaning of *counterclockwise*), you are to fill in oval

A if statement (1) ALONE is sufficient, but statement (2) alone is not sufficient to answer the question asked;

B if statement (2) ALONE is sufficient, but statement (1) alone is not sufficient to answer the question asked;

C if BOTH statements (1) and (2) TOGETHER are sufficient to answer the question asked, but NEITHER statement ALONE is sufficient;

D if EACH statement ALONE is sufficient to answer the question asked;

E if statements (1) and (2) TOGETHER are NOT sufficient to answer the question asked, and additional data specific to the problem are needed.

<u>Numbers</u>: All numbers used are real numbers.

<u>Figures</u>: A figure in a data sufficiency problem will conform to the information given in the question, but will not necessarily conform to the additional information given in statements (1) and (2).

You may assume that lines shown as straight are straight and that angle measures are greater than zero.

You may assume that the positions of points, angles, regions, etc., exist in the order shown.

All figures lie in a plane unless otherwise indicated.

<u>Note</u>: In questions that ask for the value of a quantity, the data given in the statements are sufficient only when it is possible to determine exactly one numerical value for the quantity.

<u>Example</u>:

In $\triangle PQR$, what is the value of x ?

(1) $PQ = PR$

(2) $y = 40$

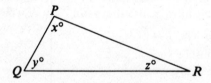

<u>Explanation</u>: According to statement (1), $PQ = PR$; therefore, $\triangle PQR$ is isosceles and $y = z$. Since $x + y + z = 180$, it follows that $x + 2y = 180$. Since statement (1) does not give a value for y, you cannot answer the question using statement (1) alone. According to statement (2), $y = 40$; therefore, $x + z = 140$. Since statement (2) does not give a value for z, you cannot answer the question using statement (2) alone. Using both statements together, since $x + 2y = 180$ and the value of y is given, you can find the value of x. Therefore, the answer is C.

GO ON TO THE NEXT PAGE.

A   Statement (1) ALONE is sufficient, but statement (2) alone is not sufficient.
B   Statement (2) ALONE is sufficient, but statement (1) alone is not sufficient.
C   BOTH statements TOGETHER are sufficient, but NEITHER statement ALONE is sufficient.
D   EACH statement ALONE is sufficient.
E   Statements (1) and (2) TOGETHER are NOT sufficient.

1. A total of 9 women and 12 men reside in the 21 apartments that are in a certain apartment building, one person to each apartment. If a poll taker is to select one of the apartments at random, what is the probability that the resident of the apartment selected will be a woman who is a student?

   (1) Of the women, 4 are students.

   (2) Of the women, 5 are not students.

2. Is x greater than 1.8 ?

   (1) $x > 1.7$
   (2) $x > 1.9$

3. Hoses X and Y simultaneously fill an empty swimming pool that has a capacity of 50,000 liters. If the flow in each hose is independent of the flow in the other hose, how many hours will it take to fill the pool?

   (1) Hose X alone would take 28 hours to fill the pool.

   (2) Hose Y alone would take 36 hours to fill the pool.

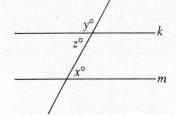

4. In the figure above, if lines k and m are parallel, what is the value of x ?

   (1) $y = 120$
   (2) $z = 60$

5. If x and y are integers, what is the value of y ?

   (1) $xy = 27$
   (2) $x = y^2$

GO ON TO THE NEXT PAGE.

A   Statement (1) ALONE is sufficient, but statement (2) alone is not sufficient.
B   Statement (2) ALONE is sufficient, but statement (1) alone is not sufficient.
C   BOTH statements TOGETHER are sufficient, but NEITHER statement ALONE is sufficient.
D   EACH statement ALONE is sufficient.
E   Statements (1) and (2) TOGETHER are NOT sufficient.

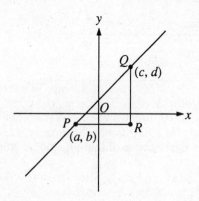

6. In the figure above, segments PR and QR are each parallel to one of the rectangular coordinate axes. Is the ratio of the length of QR to the length of PR equal to 1 ?

   (1) $c = 3$ and $d = 4$.

   (2) $a = -2$ and $b = -1$.

7. In a school election, if each of the 900 voters voted for either Edith or José (but not both), what percent of the female voters in this election voted for José?

   (1) Eighty percent of the female voters voted for Edith.

   (2) Sixty percent of the male voters voted for José.

8. During week W, how much did it cost, per mile, for the gasoline used by car X?

   (1) During week W, car X used gasoline that cost $1.24 per gallon.

   (2) During week W, car X was driven 270 miles.

9. If r and s are integers, is r divisible by 7 ?

   (1) The product rs is divisible by 7.

   (2) s is not divisible by 7.

10. If $\frac{m}{n} = \frac{5}{3}$, what is the value of $m + n$?

   (1) $m > 0$

   (2) $2m + n = 26$

11. If P and Q are each circular regions, what is the radius of the larger of these regions?

   (1) The area of P plus the area of Q is equal to 90π.

   (2) The larger circular region has a radius that is 3 times the radius of the smaller circular region.

GO ON TO THE NEXT PAGE.

A Statement (1) ALONE is sufficient, but statement (2) alone is not sufficient.
B Statement (2) ALONE is sufficient, but statement (1) alone is not sufficient.
C BOTH statements TOGETHER are sufficient, but NEITHER statement ALONE is sufficient.
D EACH statement ALONE is sufficient.
E Statements (1) and (2) TOGETHER are NOT sufficient.

12. Is z less than 0 ?

   (1) $xy > 0$ and $yz < 0$.
   (2) $x > 0$

13. If the total price of n equally priced shares of a certain stock was $12,000, what was the price per share of the stock?

   (1) If the price per share of the stock had been $1 more, the total price of the n shares would have been $300 more.
   (2) If the price per share of the stock had been $2 less, the total price of the n shares would have been 5 percent less.

14. What is the ratio of $x : y : z$?

   (1) $z = 1$ and $xy = 32$.
   (2) $\dfrac{x}{y} = 2$ and $\dfrac{z}{y} = \dfrac{1}{4}$.

15. What is Ricky's age now?

   (1) Ricky is now twice as old as he was exactly 8 years ago.
   (2) Ricky's sister Teresa is now 3 times as old as Ricky was exactly 8 years ago.

16. Is $xy > 5$?

   (1) $1 \leq x \leq 3$ and $2 \leq y \leq 4$.
   (2) $x + y = 5$

17. In year X, 8.7 percent of the men in the labor force were unemployed in June compared with 8.4 percent in May. If the number of men in the labor force was the same for both months, how many men were unemployed in June of that year?

   (1) In May of year X, the number of unemployed men in the labor force was 3.36 million.
   (2) In year X, 120,000 more men in the labor force were unemployed in June than in May.

18. If the average (arithmetic mean) of 4 numbers is 50, how many of the numbers are greater than 50 ?

   (1) None of the four numbers is equal to 50.
   (2) Two of the numbers are equal to 25.

GO ON TO THE NEXT PAGE.

A   Statement (1) ALONE is sufficient, but statement (2) alone is not sufficient.
B   Statement (2) ALONE is sufficient, but statement (1) alone is not sufficient.
C   BOTH statements TOGETHER are sufficient, but NEITHER statement ALONE is sufficient.
D   EACH statement ALONE is sufficient.
E   Statements (1) and (2) TOGETHER are NOT sufficient.

19. On Monday morning a certain machine ran continuously at a uniform rate to fill a production order. At what time did it completely fill the order that morning?

(1) The machine began filling the order at 9:30 a.m.

(2) The machine had filled $\frac{1}{2}$ of the order by 10:30 a.m. and $\frac{5}{6}$ of the order by 11:10 a.m.

20. If $n + k = m$, what is the value of k?

(1) $n = 10$

(2) $m + 10 = n$

STOP

**IF YOU FINISH BEFORE TIME IS CALLED, YOU MAY CHECK YOUR WORK ON THIS SECTION ONLY.
DO NOT TURN TO ANY OTHER SECTION IN THE TEST.**

Answer Key for Sample Test Section 5

DATA SUFFICIENCY

1. D	11. C
2. B	12. C
3. C	13. D
4. D	14. B
5. C	15. A
6. C	16. E
7. A	17. D
8. E	18. E
9. C	19. B
10. B	20. B

Explanatory Material: Data Sufficiency Sample Test Section 5

1. **A total of 9 women and 12 men reside in the 21 apartments that are in a certain apartment building, one person to each apartment. If a poll taker is to select one of the apartments at random, what is the probability that the resident of the apartment selected will be a woman who is a student?**

   (1) Of the women, 4 are students.
   (2) Of the women, 5 are not students.

The probability that the person selected will be a woman who is a student is equal to:

$$\frac{\text{the number of women students}}{\text{the total number of people in the apartments}}.$$

Statement (1) says the number of women students is 4, and since the total number of people in the apartments is known to be 21, statement (1) alone is sufficient. Thus, the answer must be A or D. Statement (2) is also sufficient, since if 5 women are not students and there are 9 women altogether, then $9 - 5 = 4$ women must be students. Since each of the statements alone is sufficient, the best answer is D.

2. **Is x greater than 1.8 ?**

   (1) $x > 1.7$
   (2) $x > 1.9$

Statement (1) alone is not sufficient to determine whether $x > 1.8$, because x could be a number between 1.7 and 1.8. Thus, the answer must be B, C, or E. Statement (2), together with the fact that $1.9 > 1.8$, implies that $x > 1.8$. Thus, (2) alone is sufficient. The best answer is B.

3. **Hoses X and Y simultaneously fill an empty swimming pool that has a capacity of 50,000 liters. If the flow in each hose is independent of the flow in the other hose, how many hours will it take to fill the pool?**

   (1) Hose X alone would take 28 hours to fill the pool.
   (2) Hose Y alone would take 36 hours to fill the pool.

Clearly neither statement (1) nor (2) alone is sufficient, since information about the filling rate for both hoses is needed. Thus, the answer must be C or E. Since hose X fills the pool in 28 hours, hose X fills $\frac{1}{28}$ of the pool in 1 hour. Since hose Y fills the pool in 36 hours, hose Y fills $\frac{1}{36}$ of the pool in 1 hour. Therefore, together they fill $\frac{1}{28} + \frac{1}{36} = \frac{4}{63}$ of the pool in 1 hour, so the time it will take them to fill the pool can be found by solving for t in $\frac{4}{63}(t) = 1$. Note that it is not actually necessary to do any of the computations. Since the two statements together are sufficient, the best answer is C.

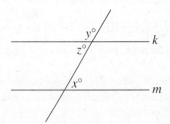

4. **In the figure above, if lines k and m are parallel, what is the value of x ?**

   (1) $y = 120$
   (2) $z = 60$

Because y and z are the degree measures of supplementary angles, statement (1) alone implies that $z = 180 - 120 = 60$. Since z and x are the degree measures of alternate interior angles, it follows that $z = x = 60$. Hence, statement (1) alone is sufficient and the answer must be A or D. Statement (2) implies that $x = 60$ also, since z and x must be equal, as stated above. Therefore, each statement alone is sufficient, and the best answer is D.

5. **If x and y are integers, what is the value of y ?**

   (1) $xy = 27$
   (2) $x = y^2$

Statement (1) alone is not sufficient to determine the value of y, since different pairs of integers could have the product 27, i.e., $(-3)(-9)$ or $(1)(27)$. Thus, the answer must be B, C, or E. Clearly statement (2), which states that $x = y^2$, does not determine the value of y, since x could have many different values. Hence, the answer must be C or E. From (2), if y^2 is substituted for x in statement (1), the result, $y^3 = 27$, implies that $y = 3$. Thus, both (1) and (2) together are sufficient to determine the value of y. The best answer is C.

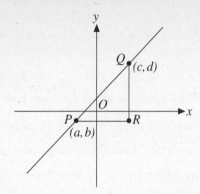

6. In the figure above, segments PR and QR are each parallel to one of the rectangular coordinate axes. Is the ratio of the length of QR to the length of PR equal to 1?

   (1) $c = 3$ and $d = 4$.
   (2) $a = -2$ and $b = -1$.

Note that the ratio of QR to PR is the slope of the line. Since two points are necessary to determine a line, and thus its slope, (1) and (2) together are sufficient, but neither alone is sufficient. Therefore, the best answer is C.

7. In a school election, if each of the 900 voters voted for either Edith or José (but not both), what percent of the female voters in this election voted for José?

   (1) Eighty percent of the female voters voted for Edith.
   (2) Sixty percent of the male voters voted for José.

Statement (1) is sufficient, since if 80 percent of the female voters voted for Edith, then $100\% - 80\% = 20\%$ of the female voters voted for José. Thus, the answer must be A or D. Statement (2) alone is not sufficient to answer the question, since it gives no information about female voters. Therefore, the best answer is A.

8. During week W, how much did it cost, per mile, for the gasoline used by car X?

   (1) During week W, car X used gasoline that cost $1.24 per gallon.
   (2) During week W, car X was driven 270 miles.

Statement (1) is not sufficient, because it does not specify how many gallons of gasoline were bought or how many miles were driven. Thus, the answer must be B, C, or E. Statement (2) is also not sufficient since it does not specify how much money was spent on gasoline. Thus, the answer must be C or E. Since it is not known either how many gallons of gasoline were bought or the total amount spent on gasoline for the week, the two statements together are not sufficient to answer the question. The best answer is E.

9. If r and s are integers, is r divisible by 7?

   (1) The product rs is divisible by 7.
   (2) s is not divisible by 7.

If a product rs is divisible by the prime number 7, then either r is divisible by 7 or s is divisible by 7. Hence, statement (1) alone implies that either r or s is divisible by 7, but it is not sufficient to determine that r is divisible by 7. Therefore, the answer must be B, C, or E. Statement (2) alone is clearly not sufficient, since no information is given about r. Hence, the answer must be C or E. The two statements together are sufficient: If rs is divisible by 7 and s is not divisible by 7, then r is divisible by 7. Thus, the best answer is C.

10. If $\dfrac{m}{n} = \dfrac{5}{3}$, what is the value of $m + n$?

   (1) $m > 0$
   (2) $2m + n = 26$

Statement (1) alone is not sufficient since m and n could be any positive numbers in the ratio 5:3, e.g., 10 and 6 or 5 and 3. Thus, the answer must be B, C, or E. However, statement (2) alone is sufficient, since the equation in the question together with statement (2) form two equations in two unknowns, which can be solved. The values of n, m, and $n + m$ can then be determined. Therefore, the best answer is B.

11. If P and Q are each circular regions, what is the radius of the larger of these regions?

   (1) The area of P plus the area of Q is equal to 90π.
   (2) The larger circular region has a radius that is 3 times the radius of the smaller circular region.

Let r represent the radius of the smaller circular region, and let R represent the radius of the larger circular region. Then statement (1) implies that $\pi r^2 + \pi R^2 = 90\pi$, which is not enough to determine R. Therefore, the answer must be B, C, or E. Statement (2) implies that $R = 3r$, which by itself is clearly not enough to determine R. Hence, the answer is either C or E. If $R/3$ is substituted for r in $\pi r^2 + \pi R^2 = 90\pi$, the result is a single equation in R, which does determine R. Thus, the two statements together are sufficient, and the best answer is C.

12. Is z less than 0?

   (1) $xy > 0$ and $yz < 0$.
   (2) $x > 0$

Statement (1) is not sufficient to answer the question since both of the sets of values $x = 1$, $y = 1$, $z = -1$ and $x = -1$, $y = -1$, $z = 1$ are consistent with statement (1). Hence, the answer must be B, C, or E. Statement (2) alone is clearly not sufficient since it gives no information about z. Therefore, the answer must be C or E. The two statements together are sufficient. Since $xy > 0$ and $x > 0$, y must be positive; since $yz > 0$ and $y > 0$, z must be negative. Thus, the best answer is C.

13. If the total price of *n* equally priced shares of a certain stock was $12,000, what was the price per share of the stock?

(1) If the price per share of the stock had been $1 more, the total price of the *n* shares would have been $300 more.
(2) If the price per share of the stock had been $2 less, the total price of the *n* shares would have been 5 percent less.

Since the price per share of the stock is $\dfrac{\$12,000}{n}$, it suffices to determine the value of *n*. Statement (1) says that if the price of each of the *n* shares of the stock had been $1 more, the total increase would have been $300, or $n(\$1) = \$300$. It follows that $n = 300$, and statement (1) alone is sufficient. Thus, the answer must be A or D. Similarly, statement (2) says that if the price of each of the *n* shares had been reduced by $2, the total reduction in price would have been $0.05(\$12,000)$, or $2n = 0.05(\$12,000)$. Since the value of *n* can be determined from this equation, statement (2) alone is also sufficient, and the best answer is D.

14. What is the ratio of $x : y : z$?

(1) $z = 1$ and $xy = 32$.
(2) $\dfrac{x}{y} = 2$ and $\dfrac{z}{y} = \dfrac{1}{4}$.

Statement (1) alone is clearly not sufficient to answer the question. For example, if $x = 4$ and $y = 8$, the ratio is 4:8:1, but if $x = 16$ and $y = 2$, then the ratio is 16:2:1. Thus, the answer must be B, C, or E. Statement (2) alone is sufficient, since multiplying the two equations by *y* yields $x = 2y$ and $z = \dfrac{1}{4}y$. Therefore, the ratio is $2y : y : \dfrac{1}{4}y = 2 : 1 : \dfrac{1}{4}$. The best answer is B.

15. What is Ricky's age now?

(1) Ricky is now twice as old as he was exactly 8 years ago.
(2) Ricky's sister Teresa is now 3 times as old as Ricky was exactly 8 years ago.

Let *r* stand for Ricky's age now. Statement (1) implies that $r = 2(r - 8)$, so $r = 16$. Hence, statement (1) alone is sufficient, and the answer must be A or D. Letting *t* represent Teresa's age now, statement (2) implies that $t = 3(r - 8)$, which is not enough to determine Ricky's age. Thus, the best answer is A.

16. Is $xy > 5$?

(1) $1 \leq x \leq 3$ and $2 \leq y \leq 4$.
(2) $x + y = 5$

Statement (1) alone is not sufficient, since the product *xy* could be as small as $(1)(2) = 2$ or as large as $(3)(4) = 12$. Therefore, the answer must be B, C, or E. Statement (2) alone is not sufficient since if *x* were 1, *y* would be 4 and $xy = 4$; but if *x* were 2, *y* would be 3 and $xy = 6$. Hence, the answer must be C or E. Both statements together are not sufficient since both of the examples $x = 1, y = 4$ and $x = 2, y = 3$ are consistent with both statements. Therefore, the best answer is E.

17. In year *X*, 8.7 percent of the men in the labor force were unemployed in June compared with 8.4 percent in May. If the number of men in the labor force was the same for both months, how many men were unemployed in June of that year?

(1) In May of year *X*, the number of unemployed men in the labor force was 3.36 million.
(2) In year *X*, 120,000 more men in the labor force were unemployed in June than in May.

Since 8.7 percent of the men in the labor force were unemployed in June, the number of unemployed men could be calculated if the total number of men in the labor force were known. Let *t* represent the total number of men in the labor force. Statement (1) implies that $(8.4\%)t = 3,360,000$, from which the value of *t* can be determined. Therefore, statement (1) alone is sufficient, and the answer must be A or D.

Statement (2) implies that $(8.7\% - 8.4\%)t = 120,000$. Since this can be solved for *t*, statement (2) alone is also sufficient to answer the question. The best answer is D.

18. If the average (arithmetic mean) of 4 numbers is 50, how many of the numbers are greater than 50?

(1) None of the four numbers is equal to 50.
(2) Two of the numbers are equal to 25.

If the four numbers were 25, 25, 26, and 124, their average would be 50 and they would satisfy both statement (1) and statement (2). But if the four numbers were 25, 25, 75, and 75, their average would also be 50 and they would also satisfy both statement (1) and statement (2). Since in the first case only one number is greater than 50 and in the second case two of the numbers are greater than 50, both statements together are not sufficient to answer the question. Thus, the best answer is E.

19. On Monday morning a certain machine ran continuously at a uniform rate to fill a production order. At what time did it completely fill the order that morning?

    (1)   The machine began filling the order at 9:30 a.m.

    (2)   The machine had filled $\frac{1}{2}$ of the order by 10:30 a.m. and $\frac{5}{6}$ of the order by 11:10 a.m.

Statement (1) is clearly not sufficient, since it merely states what time the machine began filling the order. Hence, the answer must be B, C, or E. From statement (2) it can be concluded that $\frac{5}{6} - \frac{1}{2} = \frac{1}{3}$ of the order was filled in 40 minutes; so the entire order was completely filled in $3 \times 40 = 120$ minutes, or 2 hours. Since half of the order was filled by 10:30 a.m., the entire order was filled by 11:30 a.m.. Thus, statement (2) alone is sufficient, and the best answer is B.

20. If $n + k = m$, what is the value of k?

    (1) $n = 10$
    (2) $m + 10 = n$

It is given that $n + k = m$, so $k = m - n$. Thus, it suffices to determine the value of $m - n$. Clearly statement (1) alone is not sufficient because no information involving m is given. Thus, the answer must be B, C, or E. Statement (2) can be expressed as $m - n = -10$; so $k = -10$. Statement (2) alone is therefore sufficient, and the best answer is B.

5 Reading Comprehension

There are six kinds of Reading Comprehension questions, each of which tests a different reading skill. The following pages include descriptions of the various question types, test-taking strategies, sample test sections (with answer keys), and detailed explanations of every question on the sample test sections. The explanations further illustrate the ways in which Reading Comprehension questions evaluate basic reading skills.

Reading Comprehension questions include:

1. **Questions that ask about the main idea of a passage**
   Each Reading Comprehension passage in the GMAT is a unified whole — that is, the individual sentences and paragraphs support and develop one main idea or central point. Sometimes you will be told the central point in the passage itself, and sometimes it will be necessary for you to determine the central point from the overall organization or development of the passage. You may be asked in this kind of question to recognize a correct restatement, or paraphrase, of the main idea of a passage; to identify the author's primary purpose, or objective, in writing the passage; or to assign a title that summarizes briefly and pointedly the main idea developed in the passage.

2. **Questions that ask about the supporting ideas presented in a passage**
   These questions measure your ability to comprehend the supporting ideas in a passage and to differentiate those supporting ideas from the main idea. The questions also measure your ability to differentiate ideas that are *explicitly stated* in a passage from ideas that are *implied* by the author but are not explicitly stated. You may be asked about facts cited in a passage, or about the specific content of arguments presented by the author in support of his or her views, or about descriptive details used to support or elaborate on the main idea. Whereas questions about the main idea ask you to determine the meaning of a passage *as a whole*, questions about supporting ideas ask you to determine the meanings of individual sentences and paragraphs that *contribute* to the meaning of the passage as a whole. One way to think about these questions is to see them as questions asking for the main point of *one small part* of the passage.

3. **Questions that ask for inferences based on information presented in a passage**
   These questions ask about ideas that are not explicitly stated in a passage but are *strongly implied* by the author. Unlike questions about supporting details, which ask about information that is directly stated in a passage, inference questions ask about ideas or meanings that must be inferred from information that is directly stated. Authors can make their points in indirect ways, suggesting ideas without actually stating them. These questions measure your ability to infer an author's intended meaning in parts of a passage where the meaning is only suggested. The questions do not ask about meanings or implications that are remote from the passage but about meanings that are developed indirectly or implications specifically suggested by the author. To answer these questions, you may have to carry statements made by the author one step beyond their literal meanings, or recognize the *opposite* of a statement made by the author, or identify the intended meaning of a word used figuratively in a passage. If a passage explicitly states an effect, for example, you may be asked to infer its cause. If the author compares two phenomena, you may be asked to

infer the basis for the comparison. You may be asked to infer the characteristics of an old policy from an explicit description of a new one. When you read a passage, therefore, you should concentrate not only on the explicit meaning of the author's words, but also on the more subtle meaning implied by those words.

4. **Questions that ask how information given in a passage can be applied to a context outside the passage itself**
These questions measure your ability to discern the relationships between situations or ideas presented by the author and other situations or ideas that might parallel those in the passage. In this kind of question, you may be asked to identify a hypothetical situation that is comparable to a situation presented in the passage, or to select an example that is similar to an example provided in the passage, or to apply ideas given in the passage to a situation not mentioned by the author, or to recognize ideas that the author would probably agree or disagree with on the basis of statements made in the passage. Unlike inference questions, these questions use ideas or situations *not* taken from the passage. Ideas and situations given in a question are *like* those given in the passage, and they parallel ideas and situations given in the passage. Therefore, to answer the question, you must do more than recall what you read. You must recognize the essential attributes of ideas and situations presented in the passage when they appear in different words and in an entirely new context.

5. **Questions that ask about the logical structure of a passage**
These questions ask you to analyze and evaluate the organization and the logic of a passage. They may ask how a passage is constructed: for instance, does it define, does it compare or contrast, does it present a new idea, does it refute an idea. They may also ask how the author persuades readers to accept his or her assertions, or about the reason behind the author's use of any particular supporting detail. You may also be asked to identify assumptions that the author is making, to assess the strengths and weaknesses of the author's arguments, or to recognize appropriate counter-arguments. These questions measure your ability not only to comprehend a passage but to evaluate it critically. However, it is important for you to realize that these questions do not rely on any kind of formal logic, nor do they require that you be familiar with specific terms of logic or argumentation. You can answer these questions using only the information in the passage and careful reasoning.

6. **Questions that about the style and tone of a passage**
These questions ask about the language of a passage and about the ideas in a passage that may be expressed through its language. You may be asked to deduce the author's attitude toward an idea, a fact, or a situation from the words that he or she uses to describe it. You may also be asked to select a word that accurately describes the tone of a passage — for instance, "critical," "questioning," "objective," or "enthusiastic." To answer this type of question, you will have to consider the language of the passage as a whole: it takes more than one pointed critical word to make the tone of an entire passage "critical." Sometimes, these questions ask what audience the passage was probably intended for or what type of publication it probably appeared in. Style and tone questions may apply to one small part of the passage or to the passage as a whole. To answer them, you must ask yourself what meanings are contained in the words of a passage beyond their literal meanings. Were such words selected because of their emotional content, or because a particular audience would expect to hear them? Remember, these questions measure your ability to discern meaning expressed by the author through his or her choice of words.

Test-Taking Strategies for Reading Comprehension

1. You should not expect to be completely familiar with any of the material presented in Reading Comprehension passages. You may find some passages easier to understand than others, but all passages are designed to present a challenge. If you have some familiarity with the material being presented in a passage, do not let this knowledge influence your choice of answers to the questions. Answer all questions on the basis of what is *stated or implied* in the passage itself.

2. Since the questions require specific and detailed understanding of the material in a passage, analyze each passage carefully the first time you read it. Even if you read at a relatively slow rate, you should be able to read the passages in about 6 minutes and will have about 24 minutes left for answering the questions. You should, of course, be sure to allow sufficient time to work on each passage and its questions. There are other ways of approaching Reading Comprehension passages: some test-takers prefer to skim the passages the first time through or even to read the questions before reading the passages. You should choose the method most suitable for you.

3. Underlining parts of a passage may be helpful to you. Focus on key words and phrases and try to follow exactly the development of separate ideas. In the margins, note where each important idea, argument, or set of related facts begins. Make every effort to avoid losing the sense of what is being discussed. If you become lost, you will have to go back over the material, and that wastes time. Keep the following in mind:

   - Note how each fact relates to an idea or an argument.
   - Note where the passage moves from one idea to the next.
   - Separate main ideas from supporting ideas.
   - Determine what conclusions are reached and why.

4. Read the questions carefully, making certain that you understand what is being asked. An answer choice may be incorrect, even though it accurately restates information given in the passage, if it does not answer the question. If you need to, refer back to the passage for clarification.

5. Read all the choices carefully. Never assume that you have selected the best answer without first reading all the choices.

6. Select the choice that best answers the question in terms of the information given in the passage. Do not rely on outside knowledge of the material for answering the questions.

7. Remember that understanding, not speed, is the critical factor in reading comprehension.

When you take the sample test sections, use the answer spaces on page 195 to mark your answers.

Answer Spaces for Reading Comprehension Sample Test Sections

Sample Test Section 1

1 Ⓐ Ⓑ Ⓒ Ⓓ Ⓔ		6 Ⓐ Ⓑ Ⓒ Ⓓ Ⓔ		11 Ⓐ Ⓑ Ⓒ Ⓓ Ⓔ		16 Ⓐ Ⓑ Ⓒ Ⓓ Ⓔ
2 Ⓐ Ⓑ Ⓒ Ⓓ Ⓔ		7 Ⓐ Ⓑ Ⓒ Ⓓ Ⓔ		12 Ⓐ Ⓑ Ⓒ Ⓓ Ⓔ		17 Ⓐ Ⓑ Ⓒ Ⓓ Ⓔ
3 Ⓐ Ⓑ Ⓒ Ⓓ Ⓔ		8 Ⓐ Ⓑ Ⓒ Ⓓ Ⓔ		13 Ⓐ Ⓑ Ⓒ Ⓓ Ⓔ		18 Ⓐ Ⓑ Ⓒ Ⓓ Ⓔ
4 Ⓐ Ⓑ Ⓒ Ⓓ Ⓔ		9 Ⓐ Ⓑ Ⓒ Ⓓ Ⓔ		14 Ⓐ Ⓑ Ⓒ Ⓓ Ⓔ		
5 Ⓐ Ⓑ Ⓒ Ⓓ Ⓔ		10 Ⓐ Ⓑ Ⓒ Ⓓ Ⓔ		15 Ⓐ Ⓑ Ⓒ Ⓓ Ⓔ		

Sample Test Section 2

1 Ⓐ Ⓑ Ⓒ Ⓓ Ⓔ		6 Ⓐ Ⓑ Ⓒ Ⓓ Ⓔ		11 Ⓐ Ⓑ Ⓒ Ⓓ Ⓔ		16 Ⓐ Ⓑ Ⓒ Ⓓ Ⓔ
2 Ⓐ Ⓑ Ⓒ Ⓓ Ⓔ		7 Ⓐ Ⓑ Ⓒ Ⓓ Ⓔ		12 Ⓐ Ⓑ Ⓒ Ⓓ Ⓔ		17 Ⓐ Ⓑ Ⓒ Ⓓ Ⓔ
3 Ⓐ Ⓑ Ⓒ Ⓓ Ⓔ		8 Ⓐ Ⓑ Ⓒ Ⓓ Ⓔ		13 Ⓐ Ⓑ Ⓒ Ⓓ Ⓔ		18 Ⓐ Ⓑ Ⓒ Ⓓ Ⓔ
4 Ⓐ Ⓑ Ⓒ Ⓓ Ⓔ		9 Ⓐ Ⓑ Ⓒ Ⓓ Ⓔ		14 Ⓐ Ⓑ Ⓒ Ⓓ Ⓔ		
5 Ⓐ Ⓑ Ⓒ Ⓓ Ⓔ		10 Ⓐ Ⓑ Ⓒ Ⓓ Ⓔ		15 Ⓐ Ⓑ Ⓒ Ⓓ Ⓔ		

Sample Test Section 3

1 Ⓐ Ⓑ Ⓒ Ⓓ Ⓔ		6 Ⓐ Ⓑ Ⓒ Ⓓ Ⓔ		11 Ⓐ Ⓑ Ⓒ Ⓓ Ⓔ		16 Ⓐ Ⓑ Ⓒ Ⓓ Ⓔ
2 Ⓐ Ⓑ Ⓒ Ⓓ Ⓔ		7 Ⓐ Ⓑ Ⓒ Ⓓ Ⓔ		12 Ⓐ Ⓑ Ⓒ Ⓓ Ⓔ		17 Ⓐ Ⓑ Ⓒ Ⓓ Ⓔ
3 Ⓐ Ⓑ Ⓒ Ⓓ Ⓔ		8 Ⓐ Ⓑ Ⓒ Ⓓ Ⓔ		13 Ⓐ Ⓑ Ⓒ Ⓓ Ⓔ		18 Ⓐ Ⓑ Ⓒ Ⓓ Ⓔ
4 Ⓐ Ⓑ Ⓒ Ⓓ Ⓔ		9 Ⓐ Ⓑ Ⓒ Ⓓ Ⓔ		14 Ⓐ Ⓑ Ⓒ Ⓓ Ⓔ		
5 Ⓐ Ⓑ Ⓒ Ⓓ Ⓔ		10 Ⓐ Ⓑ Ⓒ Ⓓ Ⓔ		15 Ⓐ Ⓑ Ⓒ Ⓓ Ⓔ		

Sample Test Section 4

1 Ⓐ Ⓑ Ⓒ Ⓓ Ⓔ		6 Ⓐ Ⓑ Ⓒ Ⓓ Ⓔ		11 Ⓐ Ⓑ Ⓒ Ⓓ Ⓔ		16 Ⓐ Ⓑ Ⓒ Ⓓ Ⓔ
2 Ⓐ Ⓑ Ⓒ Ⓓ Ⓔ		7 Ⓐ Ⓑ Ⓒ Ⓓ Ⓔ		12 Ⓐ Ⓑ Ⓒ Ⓓ Ⓔ		17 Ⓐ Ⓑ Ⓒ Ⓓ Ⓔ
3 Ⓐ Ⓑ Ⓒ Ⓓ Ⓔ		8 Ⓐ Ⓑ Ⓒ Ⓓ Ⓔ		13 Ⓐ Ⓑ Ⓒ Ⓓ Ⓔ		18 Ⓐ Ⓑ Ⓒ Ⓓ Ⓔ
4 Ⓐ Ⓑ Ⓒ Ⓓ Ⓔ		9 Ⓐ Ⓑ Ⓒ Ⓓ Ⓔ		14 Ⓐ Ⓑ Ⓒ Ⓓ Ⓔ		
5 Ⓐ Ⓑ Ⓒ Ⓓ Ⓔ		10 Ⓐ Ⓑ Ⓒ Ⓓ Ⓔ		15 Ⓐ Ⓑ Ⓒ Ⓓ Ⓔ		

Sample Test Section 5

1 Ⓐ Ⓑ Ⓒ Ⓓ Ⓔ		6 Ⓐ Ⓑ Ⓒ Ⓓ Ⓔ		11 Ⓐ Ⓑ Ⓒ Ⓓ Ⓔ		16 Ⓐ Ⓑ Ⓒ Ⓓ Ⓔ
2 Ⓐ Ⓑ Ⓒ Ⓓ Ⓔ		7 Ⓐ Ⓑ Ⓒ Ⓓ Ⓔ		12 Ⓐ Ⓑ Ⓒ Ⓓ Ⓔ		17 Ⓐ Ⓑ Ⓒ Ⓓ Ⓔ
3 Ⓐ Ⓑ Ⓒ Ⓓ Ⓔ		8 Ⓐ Ⓑ Ⓒ Ⓓ Ⓔ		13 Ⓐ Ⓑ Ⓒ Ⓓ Ⓔ		18 Ⓐ Ⓑ Ⓒ Ⓓ Ⓔ
4 Ⓐ Ⓑ Ⓒ Ⓓ Ⓔ		9 Ⓐ Ⓑ Ⓒ Ⓓ Ⓔ		14 Ⓐ Ⓑ Ⓒ Ⓓ Ⓔ		
5 Ⓐ Ⓑ Ⓒ Ⓓ Ⓔ		10 Ⓐ Ⓑ Ⓒ Ⓓ Ⓔ		15 Ⓐ Ⓑ Ⓒ Ⓓ Ⓔ		

READING COMPREHENSION SAMPLE TEST SECTION 1

Time — 25 minutes

18 Questions

Directions: Each passage in this group is followed by questions based on its content. After reading a passage, choose the best answer to each question and fill in the corresponding oval on the answer sheet. Answer all questions following a passage on the basis of what is stated or implied in that passage.

Caffeine, the stimulant in coffee, has been called "the most widely used psychoactive substance on Earth." Snyder, Daly, and Bruns have recently proposed that
Line caffeine affects behavior by countering the activity in
(5) the human brain of a naturally occurring chemical called adenosine. Adenosine normally depresses neuron firing in many areas of the brain. It apparently does this by inhibiting the release of neurotransmitters, chemicals that carry nerve impulses from one neuron to the next.
(10) Like many other agents that affect neuron firing, adenosine must first bind to specific receptors on neuronal membranes. There are at least two classes of these receptors, which have been designated A_1 and A_2. Snyder et al propose that caffeine, which is struc-
(15) turally similar to adenosine, is able to bind to both types of receptors, which prevents adenosine from attaching there and allows the neurons to fire more readily than they otherwise would.

For many years, caffeine's effects have been attri-
(20) buted to its inhibition of the production of phosphodi-esterase, an enzyme that breaks down the chemical called cyclic AMP. A number of neurotransmitters exert their effects by first increasing cyclic AMP concentra-tions in target neurons. Therefore, prolonged periods at
(25) the elevated concentrations, as might be brought about by a phosphodiesterase inhibitor, could lead to a greater amount of neuron firing and, consequently, to behav-ioral stimulation. But Snyder et al point out that the caffeine concentrations needed to inhibit the production
(30) of phosphodiesterase in the brain are much higher than those that produce stimulation. Moreover, other com-pounds that block phosphodiesterase's activity are not stimulants.

To buttress their case that caffeine acts instead by pre-
(35) venting adenosine binding, Snyder et al compared the stimulatory effects of a series of caffeine derivatives with their ability to dislodge adenosine from its receptors in the brains of mice. "In general," they reported, "the ability of the compounds to compete at the receptors
(40) correlates with their ability to stimulate locomotion in the mouse; i.e., the higher their capacity to bind at the receptors, the higher their ability to stimulate locomo-tion." Theophylline, a close structural relative of caffeine and the major stimulant in tea, was one of the most
(45) effective compounds in both regards.

There were some apparent exceptions to the general correlation observed between adenosine-receptor binding and stimulation. One of these was a compound called 3-isobutyl-1-methylxanthine (IBMX), which bound very

(50) well but actually depressed mouse locomotion. Snyder et al suggest that this is not a major stumbling block to their hypothesis. The problem is that the compound has mixed effects in the brain, a not unusual occurrence with psychoactive drugs. Even caffeine, which is generally
(55) known only for its stimulatory effects, displays this property, depressing mouse locomotion at very low concentrations and stimulating it at higher ones.

1. The primary purpose of the passage is to

    (A) discuss a plan for investigation of a phe-nomenon that is not yet fully understood
    (B) present two explanations of a phenomenon and reconcile the differences between them
    (C) summarize two theories and suggest a third theory that overcomes the problems encoun-tered in the first two
    (D) describe an alternative hypothesis and provide evidence and arguments that support it
    (E) challenge the validity of a theory by exposing the inconsistencies and contradictions in it

2. According to Snyder et al, caffeine differs from adenosine in that caffeine

    (A) stimulates behavior in the mouse and in humans, whereas adenosine stimulates behavior in humans only
    (B) has mixed effects in the brain, whereas adenosine has only a stimulatory effect
    (C) increases cyclic AMP concentrations in target neurons, whereas adenosine decreases such concentrations
    (D) permits release of neurotransmitters when it is bound to adenosine receptors, whereas adenosine inhibits such release
    (E) inhibits both neuron firing and the production of phosphodiesterase when there is a suffi-cient concentration in the brain, whereas adenosine inhibits only neuron firing

GO ON TO THE NEXT PAGE.

3. In response to experimental results concerning IBMX, Snyder et al contended that it is not uncommon for psychoactive drugs to have

(A) mixed effects in the brain
(B) inhibitory effects on enzymes in the brain
(C) close structural relationships with caffeine
(D) depressive effects on mouse locomotion
(E) the ability to dislodge caffeine from receptors in the brain

4. According to Snyder et al, all of the following compounds can bind to specific receptors in the brain EXCEPT

(A) IBMX
(B) caffeine
(C) adenosine
(D) theophylline
(E) phosphodiesterase

5. Snyder et al suggest that caffeine's ability to bind to A_1 and A_2 receptors can be at least partially attributed to which of the following?

(A) The chemical relationship between caffeine and phosphodiesterase
(B) The structural relationship between caffeine and adenosine
(C) The structural similarity between caffeine and neurotransmitters
(D) The ability of caffeine to stimulate behavior
(E) The natural occurrence of caffeine and adenosine in the brain

6. The author quotes Snyder et al in lines 38-43 most probably in order to

(A) reveal some of the assumptions underlying their theory
(B) summarize a major finding of their experiments
(C) point out that their experiments were limited to the mouse
(D) indicate that their experiments resulted only in general correlations
(E) refute the objections made by supporters of the older theory

GO ON TO THE NEXT PAGE.

Archaeology as a profession faces two major problems. First, it is the poorest of the poor. Only paltry sums are available for excavating and even less is available for publishing the results and preserving the sites once excavated. Yet archaeologists deal with priceless objects every day. Second, there is the problem of illegal excavation, resulting in museum-quality pieces being sold to the highest bidder.

I would like to make an outrageous suggestion that would at one stroke provide funds for archaeology and reduce the amount of illegal digging. I would propose that scientific archaeological expeditions and governmental authorities sell excavated artifacts on the open market. Such sales would provide substantial funds for the excavation and preservation of archaeological sites and the publication of results. At the same time, they would break the illegal excavator's grip on the market, thereby decreasing the inducement to engage in illegal activities.

You might object that professionals excavate to acquire knowledge, not money. Moreover, ancient artifacts are part of our global cultural heritage, which should be available for all to appreciate, not sold to the highest bidder. I agree. Sell nothing that has unique artistic merit or scientific value. But, you might reply, everything that comes out of the ground has scientific value. Here we part company. Theoretically, you may be correct in claiming that every artifact has potential scientific value. Practically, you are wrong.

I refer to the thousands of pottery vessels and ancient lamps that are essentially duplicates of one another. In one small excavation in Cyprus, archaeologists recently uncovered 2,000 virtually indistinguishable small jugs in a single courtyard. Even precious royal seal impressions known as *l'melekh* handles have been found in abundance—more than 4,000 examples so far.

The basements of museums are simply not large enough to store the artifacts that are likely to be discovered in the future. There is not enough money even to catalogue the finds; as a result, they cannot be found again and become as inaccessible as if they had never been discovered. Indeed, with the help of a computer, sold artifacts could be more accessible than are the pieces stored in bulging museum basements. Prior to sale, each could be photographed and the list of the purchasers could be maintained on the computer. A purchaser could even be required to agree to return the piece if it should become needed for scientific purposes.

It would be unrealistic to suggest that illegal digging would stop if artifacts were sold on the open market. But the demand for the clandestine product would be substantially reduced. Who would want an unmarked pot when another was available whose provenance was known, and that was dated stratigraphically by the professional archaeologist who excavated it?

7. The primary purpose of the passage is to propose

(A) an alternative to museum display of artifacts
(B) a way to curb illegal digging while benefiting the archaeological profession
(C) a way to distinguish artifacts with scientific value from those that have no such value
(D) the governmental regulation of archaeological sites
(E) a new system for cataloguing duplicate artifacts

8. The author implies that all of the following statements about duplicate artifacts are true EXCEPT:

(A) A market for such artifacts already exists.
(B) Such artifacts seldom have scientific value.
(C) There is likely to be a continuing supply of such artifacts.
(D) Museums are well supplied with examples of such artifacts.
(E) Such artifacts frequently exceed in quality those already catalogued in museum collections.

9. Which of the following is mentioned in the passage as a disadvantage of storing artifacts in museum basements?

(A) Museum officials rarely allow scholars access to such artifacts.
(B) Space that could be better used for display is taken up for storage.
(C) Artifacts discovered in one excavation often become separated from each other.
(D) Such artifacts are often damaged by variations in temperature and humidity.
(E) Such artifacts often remain uncatalogued and thus cannot be located once they are put in storage.

GO ON TO THE NEXT PAGE.

10. The author mentions the excavation in Cyprus (lines 31-34) to emphasize which of the following points?

(A) Ancient lamps and pottery vessels are less valuable, although more rare, than royal seal impressions.
(B) Artifacts that are very similar to each other present cataloguing difficulties to archaeologists.
(C) Artifacts that are not uniquely valuable, and therefore could be sold, are available in large quantities.
(D) Cyprus is the most important location for unearthing large quantities of salable artifacts.
(E) Illegal sales of duplicate artifacts are widespread, particularly on the island of Cyprus.

11. The author's argument concerning the effect of the official sale of duplicate artifacts on illegal excavation is based on which of the following assumptions?

(A) Prospective purchasers would prefer to buy authenticated artifacts.
(B) The price of illegally excavated artifacts would rise.
(C) Computers could be used to trace sold artifacts.
(D) Illegal excavators would be forced to sell only duplicate artifacts.
(E) Money gained from selling authenticated artifacts could be used to investigate and prosecute illegal excavators.

12. The author anticipates which of the following initial objections to the adoption of his proposal?

(A) Museum officials will become unwilling to store artifacts.
(B) An oversupply of salable artifacts will result and the demand for them will fall.
(C) Artifacts that would have been displayed in public places will be sold to private collectors.
(D) Illegal excavators will have an even larger supply of artifacts for resale.
(E) Counterfeiting of artifacts will become more commonplace.

GO ON TO THE NEXT PAGE.

(This passage is excerpted from material published in 1980.)

Federal efforts to aid minority businesses began in the 1960's when the Small Business Administration (SBA) began making federally guaranteed loans and government-sponsored management and technical assistance
(5) available to minority business enterprises. While this program enabled many minority entrepreneurs to form new businesses, the results were disappointing, since managerial inexperience, unfavorable locations, and capital shortages led to high failure rates. Even 15
(10) years after the program was implemented, minority business receipts were not quite two percent of the national economy's total receipts.

Recently federal policymakers have adopted an approach intended to accelerate development of the
(15) minority business sector by moving away from directly aiding small minority enterprises and toward supporting larger, growth-oriented minority firms through intermediary companies. In this approach, large corporations participate in the development of successful and stable
(20) minority businesses by making use of government-sponsored venture capital. The capital is used by a participating company to establish a Minority Enterprise Small Business Investment Company or MESBIC. The MESBIC then provides capital and guidance to minority
(25) businesses that have potential to become future suppliers or customers of the sponsoring company.

MESBIC's are the result of the belief that providing established firms with easier access to relevant management techniques and more job-specific experience, as
(30) well as substantial amounts of capital, gives those firms a greater opportunity to develop sound business foundations than does simply making general management experience and small amounts of capital available. Further, since potential markets for the minority busi
(35) nesses already exist through the sponsoring companies, the minority businesses face considerably less risk in terms of location and market fluctuation. Following early financial and operating problems, sponsoring corporations began to capitalize MESBIC's far above
(40) the legal minimum of $500,000 in order to generate sufficient income and to sustain the quality of management needed. MESBIC's are now emerging as increasingly important financing sources for minority enterprises.
(45) Ironically, MESBIC staffs, which usually consist of Hispanic and Black professionals, tend to approach investments in minority firms more pragmatically than do many MESBIC directors, who are usually senior managers from sponsoring corporations. The latter
(50) often still think mainly in terms of the "social responsibility approach" and thus seem to prefer deals that are riskier and less attractive than normal investment criteria would warrant. Such differences in viewpoint have produced uneasiness among many minority staff members,

(55) who feel that minority entrepreneurs and businesses should be judged by established business considerations. These staff members believe their point of view is closer to the original philosophy of MESBIC's and they are concerned that, unless a more prudent course is fol
(60) lowed, MESBIC directors may revert to policies likely to re-create the disappointing results of the original SBA approach.

13. Which of the following best states the central idea of the passage?

    (A) The use of MESBIC's for aiding minority entrepreneurs seems to have greater potential for success than does the original SBA approach.
    (B) There is a crucial difference in point of view between the staff and directors of some MESBIC's.
    (C) After initial problems with management and marketing, minority businesses have begun to expand at a steady rate.
    (D) Minority entrepreneurs wishing to form new businesses now have several equally successful federal programs on which to rely.
    (E) For the first time since 1960, large corporations are making significant contributions to the development of minority businesses.

14. According to the passage, the MESBIC approach differs from the SBA approach in that MESBIC's

    (A) seek federal contracts to provide markets for minority businesses
    (B) encourage minority businesses to provide markets for other minority businesses
    (C) attempt to maintain a specified rate of growth in the minority business sector
    (D) rely on the participation of large corporations to finance minority businesses
    (E) select minority businesses on the basis of their location

15. Which of the following does the author cite to support the conclusion that the results of the SBA program were disappointing?

    (A) The small number of new minority enterprises formed as a result of the program
    (B) The small number of minority enterprises that took advantage of the management and technical assistance offered under the program
    (C) The small percentage of the nation's business receipts earned by minority enterprises following the program's implementation
    (D) The small percentage of recipient minority enterprises that were able to repay federally guaranteed loans made under the program
    (E) The small number of minority enterprises that chose to participate in the program

GO ON TO THE NEXT PAGE.

16. Which of the following statements about the SBA program can be inferred from the passage?

(A) The maximum term for loans made to recipient businesses was 15 years.
(B) Business loans were considered to be more useful to recipient businesses than was management and technical assistance.
(C) The anticipated failure rate for recipient businesses was significantly lower than the rate that actually resulted.
(D) Recipient businesses were encouraged to relocate to areas more favorable for business development.
(E) The capitalization needs of recipient businesses were assessed and then provided for adequately.

17. The author refers to the "financial and operating problems" (line 38) encountered by MESBIC's primarily in order to

(A) broaden the scope of the discussion to include the legal considerations of funding MESBIC's through sponsoring companies
(B) call attention to the fact that MESBIC's must receive adequate funding in order to function effectively
(C) show that sponsoring companies were willing to invest only $500,000 of government-sponsored venture capital in the original MESBIC's
(D) compare SBA and MESBIC limits on minimum funding
(E) refute suggestions that MESBIC's have been only marginally successful

18. The author's primary objective in the passage is to

(A) disprove the view that federal efforts to aid minority businesses have been ineffective
(B) explain how federal efforts to aid minority businesses have changed since the 1960's
(C) establish a direct link between the federal efforts to aid minority businesses made before the 1960's and those made in the 1980's
(D) analyze the basis for the belief that job-specific experience is more useful to minority businesses than is general management experience
(E) argue that the "social responsibility approach" to aiding minority businesses is superior to any other approach

STOP

IF YOU FINISH BEFORE TIME IS CALLED, YOU MAY CHECK YOUR WORK ON THIS SECTION ONLY.
DO NOT TURN TO ANY OTHER SECTION IN THE TEST.

Answer Key for Sample Test Section 1

READING COMPREHENSION

1. D	10. C
2. D	11. A
3. A	12. C
4. E	13. A
5. B	14. D
6. B	15. C
7. B	16. C
8. E	17. B
9. E	18. B

Explanatory Material: Reading Comprehension

The following discussion of Reading Comprehension is intended to familiarize you with the most efficient and effective approaches to the kinds of problems common to Reading Comprehension. The particular questions on the sample test sections in this chapter are generally representative of the kinds of questions you will encounter in this section of the GMAT. Remember that it is the problem-solving strategy that is important, not the specific details of a particular question.

Sample Test Section 1

1. The primary purpose of the passage is to

(A) discuss a plan for investigation of a phenomenon that is not yet fully understood
(B) present two explanations of a phenomenon and reconcile the differences between them
(C) summarize two theories and suggest a third theory that overcomes the problems encountered in the first two
(D) describe an alternative hypothesis and provide evidence and arguments that support it
(E) challenge the validity of a theory by exposing the inconsistencies and contradictions in it

The best answer is D. This question requires you to identify the primary concern of the passage as a whole. The first paragraph presents a recent hypothesis about how caffeine affects behavior. The second paragraph describes an earlier and widely accepted hypothesis about how caffeine affects behavior, and then presents evidence that is not consistent with that hypothesis. The third and fourth paragraphs return to the newer hypothesis introduced in the first paragraph and provide "evidence and arguments" that support this alternative hypothesis.

2. According to Snyder et al, caffeine differs from adenosine in that caffeine

(A) stimulates behavior in the mouse and in humans, whereas adenosine stimulates behavior in humans only
(B) has mixed effects in the brain, whereas adenosine has only a stimulatory effect
(C) increases cyclic AMP concentrations in target neurons, whereas adenosine decreases such concentrations
(D) permits release of neurotransmitters when it is bound to adenosine receptors, whereas adenosine inhibits such release
(E) inhibits both neuron firing and the production of phosphodiesterase when there is a sufficient concentration in the brain, whereas adenosine inhibits only neuron firing

The best answer is D. Lines 6-12 state that adenosine "depresses neuron firing" by binding to specific receptors on neuronal membranes, which in turn inhibits the release of neurotransmitters. Lines 14-18 describe Snyder et al's hypothesis about caffeine. They propose that caffeine binds to specific receptors on neuronal membranes, which prevents adenosine from binding to those receptors and "allows the neurons to fire more readily than they otherwise would." Therefore, according to Snyder et al, caffeine differs from adenosine in that caffeine permits neurotransmitter release when it is bound to adenosine receptors, whereas adenosine inhibits neurotransmitter release.

3. In response to experimental results concerning IBMX, Snyder et al contended that it is not uncommon for psychoactive drugs to have

(A) mixed effects in the brain
(B) inhibitory effects on enzymes in the brain
(C) close structural relationships with caffeine
(D) depressive effects on mouse locomotion
(E) the ability to dislodge caffeine from receptors in the brain

The best answer is A. The effects of IBMX are discussed in the last paragraph of the passage. IBMX apparently binds to adenosine-specific receptors on neuronal membranes, but, in contrast to the other caffeine derivatives that Snyder et al experimented with, IBMX depresses rather than stimulates mouse locomotion. Snyder et al respond to this experimental result by stating that IBMX has "mixed effects in the brain, a not unusual occurrence with psychoactive drugs" (lines 53-54).

4. According to Snyder et al, all of the following compounds can bind to specific receptors in the brain EXCEPT

(A) IBMX
(B) caffeine
(C) adenosine
(D) theophylline
(E) phosphodiesterase

The best answer is E. This question asks you to identify which compound, according to Snyder et al, does NOT bind to specific receptors in the brain. The last paragraph describes IBMX (A) as a compound that binds to specific receptors in the brain. Lines 14-18 describe Snyder et al's proposal that caffeine (B) can bind to specific receptors in the brain. Lines 6-12 state that adenosine (C) inhibits neuron firing by binding to specific receptors in the brain. Lines 43-45 mention theophylline (D) as an example of a caffeine derivative that binds to specific receptors in the brain. Phosphodiesterase (E), identified as an "enzyme that breaks down the chemical called cyclic AMP" (lines 21-22), is the only compound that is not identified as one that binds to specific receptors in the brain.

5. Snyder et al suggest that caffeine's ability to bind to A_1 and A_2 receptors can be at least partially attributed to which of the following?

(A) The chemical relationship between caffeine and phosphodiesterase
(B) The structural relationship between caffeine and adenosine
(C) The structural similarity between caffeine and neurotransmitters
(D) The ability of caffeine to stimulate behavior
(E) The natural occurrence of caffeine and adenosine in the brain

The best answer is B. This question asks you to identify information that is suggested rather than directly stated in the passage. To answer it, first look for the location in the passage of the information specified in the question. The A_1 and A_2 receptors are mentioned in lines 12-14. Lines 14-18 go on to describe Snyder et al's hypothesis about the effects of caffeine on behavior. They propose that caffeine, "which is structurally similar to adenosine," is able to bind to A_1 and A_2 receptors in the brain, the same receptors that adenosine normally binds to. Thus, the passage suggests that the structural relationship between caffeine and adenosine may be partially responsible for caffeine's ability to bind to A_1 and A_2 receptors.

6. The author quotes Snyder et al in lines 38-43 most probably in order to

(A) reveal some of the assumptions underlying their theory
(B) summarize a major finding of their experiments
(C) point out that their experiments were limited to the mouse
(D) indicate that their experiments resulted only in general correlations
(E) refute the objections made by supporters of the older theory

The best answer is B. This question asks you to identify the function of a quotation in the third paragraph of the passage. The third paragraph provides evidence for Snyder et al's hypothesis by discussing experiments they conducted on mice. The quotation in lines 38-43 "summarizes" the findings of these experiments. Snyder et al found that a number of caffeine derivatives are able to bind to specific receptors in the brains of mice just as adenosine does, and that the derivatives that are most successful at stimulating locomotion are also the most successful in competing with adenosine in binding at the receptors. This finding is "major" in that it supports their hypothesis that the stimulative effects of caffeine are a result of its ability to compete with adenosine.

7. The primary purpose of the passage is to propose

(A) an alternative to museum display of artifacts
(B) a way to curb illegal digging while benefiting the archaeological profession
(C) a way to distinguish artifacts with scientific value from those that have no such value
(D) the governmental regulation of archaeological sites
(E) a new system for cataloguing duplicate artifacts

The best answer is B. The first paragraph identifies two major problems faced by the archaeological profession: inadequate funding and illegal digging. Lines 9-11 indicate that the author is going to suggest how to remedy both problems, thereby benefiting the archaeological profession. The author proceeds to propose allowing the sale of excavated artifacts (lines 11-14) and to explain how this would solve both problems (lines 14-19). The author then supports the proposal by countering possible objections to it, and in the last paragraph explains how the proposal would curb illegal digging (lines 51-55). Thus, the way information is organized in the passage indicates that the author's purpose is to suggest that allowing the sale of excavated artifacts would provide funds for the archaeological profession and curb illegal digging.

8. The author implies that all of the following statements about duplicate artifacts are true EXCEPT:

(A) A market for such artifacts already exists.
(B) Such artifacts seldom have scientific value.
(C) There is likely to be a continuing supply of such artifacts.
(D) Museums are well supplied with examples of such artifacts.
(E) Such artifacts frequently exceed in quality those already catalogued in museum collections.

The best answer is E. The question requires you to identify the answer choice that CANNOT be inferred from the passage. Choice A asserts that potential purchasers for duplicate artifacts exist; this is implied in lines 51-55, which suggest that purchasers would prefer legally acquired duplicate artifacts, thereby reducing demand for clandestine products. Choice B is implied in lines 25-31, which deny the practical scientific value of duplicate artifacts. Choice C is implied in lines 37-39, which express doubt about storing all the artifacts that "are likely to be discovered in the future." Choice D is implied by the reference to "pieces stored in bulging museum basements" (line 44). Nothing in the passage implies that duplicate artifacts exceed museum objects in quality (choice E).

9. Which of the following is mentioned in the passage as a disadvantage of storing artifacts in museum basements?

(A) Museum officials rarely allow scholars access to such artifacts.
(B) Space that could be better used for display is taken up for storage.
(C) Artifacts discovered in one excavation often become separated from each other.
(D) Such artifacts are often damaged by variations in temperature and humidity.
(E) Such artifacts often remain uncatalogued and thus cannot be located once they are put in storage.

The best answer is E. The disadvantages of storing artifacts in museum basements are discussed in the fifth paragraph. Lines 39-42 state that "There is not enough money . . . to catalogue the finds" and declare that as a result stored objects cannot be located. The fact that such objects become "inaccessible" (line 41) is clearly connected to the problems in cataloguing, not to museum policy toward scholars, as choice A states. No mention is made of the situations discussed in choices B, C, and D.

10. The author mentions the excavation in Cyprus (lines 31-34) to emphasize which of the following points?

(A) Ancient lamps and pottery vessels are less valuable, although more rare, than royal seal impressions.
(B) Artifacts that are very similar to each other present cataloguing difficulties to archaeologists.
(C) Artifacts that are not uniquely valuable, and therefore could be sold, are available in large quantities.
(D) Cyprus is the most important location for unearthing large quantities of salable artifacts.
(E) Illegal sales of duplicate artifacts are widespread, particularly on the island of Cyprus.

The best answer is C. In lines 27-29, the author refutes the assertion that every object excavated has potential scientific value and therefore should not be sold. In lines 30-31, the author defines those objects that do not have scientific value: "the thousands of pottery vessels . . . that are essentially duplicates of one another." The Cyprus excavation appears in the next sentence as an example of one location in which such duplicate artifacts have been found in large quantities. The reference to "2,000 virtually indistinguishable small jugs" highlights the profusion and uniformity of the Cyprus finds. Thus, the excavation is mentioned in order to emphasize the ready availability of objects that lack unique value and therefore could be sold.

11. The author's argument concerning the effect of the official sale of duplicate artifacts on illegal excavation is based on which of the following assumptions?

(A) Prospective purchasers would prefer to buy authenticated artifacts.
(B) The price of illegally excavated artifacts would rise.
(C) Computers could be used to trace sold artifacts.
(D) Illegal excavators would be forced to sell only duplicate artifacts.
(E) Money gained from selling authenticated artifacts could be used to investigate and prosecute illegal excavators.

The best answer is A. The author's argument concerning the effect of the official sale of duplicate artifacts on illegal excavation appears in lines 51-52, in which the author predicts that such official sale would reduce demand for "the clandestine product." The rhetorical question that follows (lines 52-55) indicates that the author finds it unlikely that any purchaser would prefer objects of unknown provenance to objects of known origin, or, to rephrase, the author assumes that most people would prefer to purchase objects of authenticated provenance, as choice A states. The author's argument concerning the effect of such sales on illegal excavation does not assume any of the other answer choices.

12. The author anticipates which of the following initial objections to the adoption of his proposal?

(A) Museum officials will become unwilling to store artifacts.

(B) An oversupply of salable artifacts will result and the demand for them will fall.

(C) Artifacts that would have been displayed in public places will be sold to private collectors.

(D) Illegal excavators will have an even larger supply of artifacts for resale.

(E) Counterfeiting of artifacts will become more commonplace.

The best answer is C. The author begins the third paragraph by saying "You might object . . ." in order to anticipate possible objections to the adoption of his proposal. In the next sentence the author asserts that "ancient artifacts . . . should be available for all to appreciate, not sold to the highest bidder" (lines 21-24), acknowledging an opponent's fear that individuals might be allowed to purchase objects that ought to be displayed in public institutions. This objection is paraphrased in choice C. Choice A alludes to a situation that shows the benefits, not the drawbacks, of the author's proposal; B, D, and E describe situations that are not discussed in the passage.

13. Which of the following best states the central idea of the passage?

(A) The use of MESBIC's for aiding minority entrepreneurs seems to have greater potential for success than does the original SBA approach.

(B) There is a crucial difference in point of view between the staff and directors of some MESBIC's.

(C) After initial problems with management and marketing, minority businesses have begun to expand at a steady rate.

(D) Minority entrepreneurs wishing to form new businesses now have several equally successful federal programs on which to rely.

(E) For the first time since 1960, large corporations are making significant contributions to the development of minority businesses.

The best answer is A. The passage begins by indicating that the results of the SBA approach to aiding minority entrepreneurs "were disappointing" (line 7). Lines 42-44 state that "MESBIC's are now emerging as increasingly important financing sources for minority enterprises." Much of the passage is devoted to supporting the author's view that MESBIC's have the greater potential for success, and the last sentence in the passage confirms this view. Choice B accurately restates a point made by the author, that differences exist between staff and directors of MESBIC's, but the point is not central to the author's discussion. The statements in C, D, and E are not supported by information in the passage.

14. According to the passage, the MESBIC approach differs from the SBA approach in that MESBIC's

(A) seek federal contracts to provide markets for minority businesses

(B) encourage minority businesses to provide markets for other minority businesses

(C) attempt to maintain a specified rate of growth in the minority business sector

(D) rely on the participation of large corporations to finance minority businesses

(E) select minority businesses on the basis of their location

The best answer is D. In the second paragraph, the author describes the MESBIC approach as one in which "large corporations participate in the development of successful and stable minority businesses by making use of government-sponsored venture capital" (lines 18-21). There is no indication in the passage that the SBA approach relies on the participation of large corporations. Although any of the other answer choices might actually be true of MESBIC's, there is no information in the passage that confirms that these statements are correct.

15. Which of the following does the author cite to support the conclusion that the results of the SBA program were disappointing?

(A) The small number of new minority enterprises formed as a result of the program

(B) The small number of minority enterprises that took advantage of the management and technical assistance offered under the program

(C) The small percentage of the nation's business receipts earned by minority enterprises following the program's implementation

(D) The small percentage of recipient minority enterprises that were able to repay federally guaranteed loans made under the program

(E) The small number of minority enterprises that chose to participate in the program

The best answer is C. The author concludes that the results of the SBA approach "were disappointing" (line 7) and then supports the conclusion by citing the fact that "Even 15 years after the program was implemented, minority business receipts were not quite two percent of the national economy's total receipts" (lines 9-12). The statements in A, B, D, and E are not supported by the information in the passage.

16. Which of the following statements about the SBA program can be inferred from the passage?

(A) The maximum term for loans made to recipient businesses was 15 years.

(B) Business loans were considered to be more useful to recipient businesses than was management and technical assistance.

(C) The anticipated failure rate for recipient businesses was significantly lower than the rate that actually resulted.

(D) Recipient businesses were encouraged to relocate to areas more favorable for business development.

(E) The capitalization needs of recipient businesses were assessed and then provided for adequately.

The best answer is C. This question asks you to draw an inference about the SBA program. Although the passage does not actually state that the failure rate for SBA recipient businesses was higher than anticipated, in the first paragraph the author does state that the results of the SBA program were disappointing, in part because of the high failure rate among SBA-sponsored businesses. From this it can be inferred that the anticipated failure rate was lower than the actual rate. There is no information in the passage to suggest that A, B, D, and E could be true.

17. The author refers to the "financial and operating problems" (line 38) encountered by MESBIC's primarily in order to

(A) broaden the scope of the discussion to include the legal considerations of funding MESBIC's through sponsoring companies

(B) call attention to the fact that MESBIC's must receive adequate funding in order to function effectively

(C) show that sponsoring companies were willing to invest only $500,000 of government-sponsored venture capital in the original MESBIC's

(D) compare SBA and MESBIC limits on minimum funding

(E) refute suggestions that MESBIC's have been only marginally successful

The best answer is B. The reference in line 38 to "financial and operating problems" appears in the context of a discussion of why corporations came to capitalize MESBIC's "far above the legal minimum of $500,000." The problems are cited to illustrate the reasons that MESBIC's need more than the minimum funding required by law, and thus call attention to this need. The reference is not primarily concerned with legal considerations as suggested in A, or with a comparison with SBA funding limits as suggested in D. The $500,000 mentioned in the passage is the *minimum* level of funding required, not a maximum as suggested in C. There is no suggestion in the passage that MESBIC's have been only marginally successful; thus, choice E is not correct.

18. The author's primary objective in the passage is to

(A) disprove the view that federal efforts to aid minority businesses have been ineffective

(B) explain how federal efforts to aid minority businesses have changed since the 1960's

(C) establish a direct link between the federal efforts to aid minority businesses made before the 1960's and those made in the 1980's

(D) analyze the basis for the belief that job-specific experience is more useful to minority businesses than is general management experience

(E) argue that the "social responsibility approach" to aiding minority businesses is superior to any other approach

The best answer is B. The passage describes efforts undertaken in the 1960's to aid minority businesses and then describes MESBIC's, a newer approach to such efforts. Choice A is not correct because, although the author does suggest that MESBIC's have been effective in aiding minority businesses, there is no indication in the passage that the author's purpose is to disprove the view that federal efforts have been ineffective. Because the passage does not discuss efforts undertaken during the 1980's to aid minority businesses, C cannot be correct. The passage neither attempts to analyze the basis for the belief mentioned in D nor argues that the "social responsibility approach" is the most effective. Therefore, neither D nor E can be correct.

Time — 25 minutes

18 Questions

<u>Directions:</u> Each passage in this group is followed by questions based on its content. After reading a passage, choose the best answer to each question and fill in the corresponding oval on the answer sheet. Answer all questions following a passage on the basis of what is <u>stated</u> or <u>implied</u> in that passage.

The majority of successful senior managers do not closely follow the classical rational model of first clarifying goals, assessing the problem, formulating options, *Line* estimating likelihoods of success, making a decision, (5) and only then taking action to implement the decision. Rather, in their day-by-day tactical maneuvers, these senior executives rely on what is vaguely termed "intuition" to manage a network of interrelated problems that require them to deal with ambiguity, inconsistency, (10) novelty, and surprise; and to integrate action into the process of thinking.

Generations of writers on management have recognized that some practicing managers rely heavily on intuition. In general, however, such writers display a (15) poor grasp of what intuition is. Some see it as the opposite of rationality; others view it as an excuse for capriciousness.

Isenberg's recent research on the cognitive processes of senior managers reveals that managers' intuition is (20) neither of these. Rather, senior managers use intuition in at least five distinct ways. First, they intuitively sense when a problem exists. Second, managers rely on intuition to perform well-learned behavior patterns rapidly. This intuition is not arbitrary or irrational, but is based (25) on years of painstaking practice and hands-on experience that build skills. A third function of intuition is to synthesize isolated bits of data and practice into an integrated picture, often in an "Aha!" experience. Fourth, some managers use intuition as a check on the results (30) of more rational analysis. Most senior executives are familiar with the formal decision analysis models and tools, and those who use such systematic methods for reaching decisions are occasionally leery of solutions suggested by these methods which run counter to their (35) sense of the correct course of action. Finally, managers can use intuition to bypass in-depth analysis and move rapidly to engender a plausible solution. Used in this way, intuition is an almost instantaneous cognitive process in which a manager recognizes familiar patterns. (40) One of the implications of the intuitive style of executive management is that "thinking" is inseparable from acting. Since managers often "know" what is right before they can analyze and explain it, they frequently act first and explain later. Analysis is inextricably tied (45) to action in thinking/acting cycles, in which managers develop thoughts about their companies and organizations not by analyzing a problematic situation and then acting, but by acting and analyzing in close concert.

Given the great uncertainty of many of the manage-(50) ment issues that they face, senior managers often instigate a course of action simply to learn more about an issue. They then use the results of the action to develop a more complete understanding of the issue. One implication of thinking/acting cycles is that action is often (55) part of defining the problem, not just of implementing the solution.

1. According to the passage, senior managers use intuition in all of the following ways EXCEPT to

   (A) speed up the creation of a solution to a problem
   (B) identify a problem
   (C) bring together disparate facts
   (D) stipulate clear goals
   (E) evaluate possible solutions to a problem

2. The passage suggests which of the following about the "writers on management" mentioned in line 12 ?

   (A) They have criticized managers for not following the classical rational model of decision analysis.
   (B) They have not based their analyses on a sufficiently large sample of actual managers.
   (C) They have relied in drawing their conclusions on what managers say rather than on what managers do.
   (D) They have misunderstood how managers use intuition in making business decisions.
   (E) They have not acknowledged the role of intuition in managerial practice.

GO ON TO THE NEXT PAGE

3. Which of the following best exemplifies "an 'Aha!' experience" (line 28) as it is presented in the passage?

(A) A manager risks taking an action whose outcome is unpredictable to discover whether the action changes the problem at hand.

(B) A manager performs well-learned and familiar behavior patterns in creative and uncharacteristic ways to solve a problem.

(C) A manager suddenly connects seemingly unrelated facts and experiences to create a pattern relevant to the problem at hand.

(D) A manager rapidly identifies the methodology used to compile data yielded by systematic analysis.

(E) A manager swiftly decides which of several sets of tactics to implement in order to deal with the contingencies suggested by a problem.

4. According to the passage, the classical model of decision analysis includes all of the following EXCEPT

(A) evaluation of a problem

(B) creation of possible solutions to a problem

(C) establishment of clear goals to be reached by the decision

(D) action undertaken in order to discover more information about a problem

(E) comparison of the probable effects of different solutions to a problem

5. It can be inferred from the passage that which of the following would most probably be one major difference in behavior between Manager X, who uses intuition to reach decisions, and Manager Y, who uses only formal decision analysis?

(A) Manager X analyzes first and then acts; Manager Y does not.

(B) Manager X checks possible solutions to a problem by systematic analysis; Manager Y does not.

(C) Manager X takes action in order to arrive at the solution to a problem; Manager Y does not.

(D) Manager Y draws on years of hands-on experience in creating a solution to a problem; Manager X does not.

(E) Manager Y depends on day-to-day tactical maneuvering; Manager X does not.

6. The passage provides support for which of the following statements?

(A) Managers who rely on intuition are more successful than those who rely on formal decision analysis.

(B) Managers cannot justify their intuitive decisions.

(C) Managers' intuition works contrary to their rational and analytical skills.

(D) Logical analysis of a problem increases the number of possible solutions.

(E) Intuition enables managers to employ their practical experience more efficiently.

GO ON TO THE NEXT PAGE.

Nearly a century ago, biologists found that if they separated an invertebrate animal embryo into two parts at an early stage of its life, it would survive and develop as two normal embryos. This led them to believe that the cells in the early embryo are undetermined in the sense that each cell has the potential to develop in a variety of different ways. Later biologists found that the situation was not so simple. It matters in which plane the embryo is cut. If it is cut in a plane different from the one used by the early investigators, it will not form two whole embryos.

A debate arose over what exactly was happening. Which embryo cells are determined, just when do they become irreversibly committed to their fates, and what are the "morphogenetic determinants" that tell a cell what to become? But the debate could not be resolved because no one was able to ask the crucial questions in a form in which they could be pursued productively. Recent discoveries in molecular biology, however, have opened up prospects for a resolution of the debate. Now investigators think they know at least some of the molecules that act as morphogenetic determinants in early development. They have been able to show that, in a sense, cell determination begins even before an egg is fertilized.

Studying sea urchins, biologist Paul Gross found that an unfertilized egg contains substances that function as morphogenetic determinants. They are located in the cytoplasm of the egg cell; i.e., in that part of the cell's protoplasm that lies outside of the nucleus. In the unfertilized egg, the substances are inactive and are not distributed homogeneously. When the egg is fertilized, the substances become active and, presumably, govern the behavior of the genes they interact with. Since the substances are unevenly distributed in the egg, when the fertilized egg divides, the resulting cells are different from the start and so can be qualitatively different in their own gene activity.

The substances that Gross studied are maternal messenger RNA's—products of certain of the maternal genes. He and other biologists studying a wide variety of organisms have found that these particular RNA's direct, in large part, the synthesis of histones, a class of proteins that bind to DNA. Once synthesized, the histones move into the cell nucleus, where sections of DNA wrap around them to form a structure that resembles beads, or knots, on a string. The beads are DNA segments wrapped around the histones; the string is the intervening DNA. And it is the structure of these beaded DNA strings that guides the fate of the cells in which they are located.

7. It can be inferred from the passage that the morphogenetic determinants present in the early embryo are

(A) located in the nucleus of the embryo cells
(B) evenly distributed unless the embryo is not developing normally
(C) inactive until the embryo cells become irreversibly committed to their final function
(D) identical to those that were already present in the unfertilized egg
(E) present in larger quantities than is necessary for the development of a single individual

8. The main topic of the passage is

(A) the early development of embryos of lower marine organisms
(B) the main contribution of modern embryology to molecular biology
(C) the role of molecular biology in disproving older theories of embryonic development
(D) cell determination as an issue in the study of embryonic development
(E) scientific dogma as a factor in the recent debate over the value of molecular biology

9. According to the passage, when biologists believed that the cells in the early embryo were undetermined, they made which of the following mistakes?

(A) They did not attempt to replicate the original experiment of separating an embryo into two parts.
(B) They did not realize that there was a connection between the issue of cell determination and the outcome of the separation experiment.
(C) They assumed that the results of experiments on embryos did not depend on the particular animal species used for such experiments.
(D) They assumed that it was crucial to perform the separation experiment at an early stage in the embryo's life.
(E) They assumed that different ways of separating an embryo into two parts would be equivalent as far as the fate of the two parts was concerned.

GO ON TO THE NEXT PAGE.

10. It can be inferred from the passage that the initial production of histones after an egg is fertilized takes place

(A) in the cytoplasm
(B) in the maternal genes
(C) throughout the protoplasm
(D) in the beaded portions of the DNA strings
(E) in certain sections of the cell nucleus

11. It can be inferred from the passage that which of the following is dependent on the fertilization of an egg?

(A) Copying of maternal genes to produce maternal messenger RNA's
(B) Synthesis of proteins called histones
(C) Division of a cell into its nucleus and the cytoplasm
(D) Determination of the egg cell's potential for division
(E) Generation of all of a cell's morphogenetic determinants

12. According to the passage, the morphogenetic determinants present in the unfertilized egg cell are which of the following?

(A) Proteins bound to the nucleus
(B) Histones
(C) Maternal messenger RNA's
(D) Cytoplasm
(E) Nonbeaded intervening DNA

GO ON TO THE NEXT PAGE.

In the two decades between 1910 and 1930, over ten percent of the Black population of the United States left the South, where the preponderance of the Black population had been located, and migrated to northern
Line states, with the largest number moving, it is claimed,
(5) between 1916 and 1918. It has been frequently assumed, but not proved, that the majority of the migrants in what has come to be called the Great Migration came from rural areas and were motivated by two concurrent
(10) factors: the collapse of the cotton industry following the boll weevil infestation, which began in 1898, and increased demand in the North for labor following the cessation of European immigration caused by the outbreak of the First World War in 1914. This assump-
(15) tion has led to the conclusion that the migrants' subsequent lack of economic mobility in the North is tied to rural background, a background that implies unfamiliarity with urban living and a lack of industrial skills.

But the question of who actually left the South has
(20) never been rigorously investigated. Although numerous investigations document an exodus from rural southern areas to southern cities prior to the Great Migration, no one has considered whether the same migrants then moved on to northern cities. In 1910 over 600,000
(25) Black workers, or ten percent of the Black work force, reported themselves to be engaged in "manufacturing and mechanical pursuits," the federal census category roughly encompassing the entire industrial sector. The Great Migration could easily have been made up entirely
(30) of this group and their families. It is perhaps surprising to argue that an employed population could be enticed to move, but an explanation lies in the labor conditions then prevalent in the South.

About thirty-five percent of the urban Black popu-
(35) lation in the South was engaged in skilled trades. Some were from the old artisan class of slavery—blacksmiths, masons, carpenters—which had had a monopoly of certain trades, but they were gradually being pushed out by competition, mechanization, and obsolescence.
(40) The remaining sixty-five percent, more recently urbanized, worked in newly developed industries—tobacco, lumber, coal and iron manufacture, and railroads. Wages in the South, however, were low, and Black workers were aware, through labor recruiters and the
(45) Black press, that they could earn more even as unskilled workers in the North than they could as artisans in the South. After the boll weevil infestation, urban Black workers faced competition from the continuing influx of both Black and White rural workers, who were driven
(50) to undercut the wages formerly paid for industrial jobs. Thus, a move north would be seen as advantageous to a group that was already urbanized and steadily employed, and the easy conclusion tying their subsequent economic problems in the North to their rural background comes into question.

13. The author indicates explicitly that which of the following records has been a source of information in her investigation?

(A) United States Immigration Service reports from 1914 to 1930
(B) Payrolls of southern manufacturing firms between 1910 and 1930
(C) The volume of cotton exports between 1898 and 1910
(D) The federal census of 1910
(E) Advertisements of labor recruiters appearing in southern newspapers after 1910

14. In the passage, the author anticipates which of the following as a possible objection to her argument?

(A) It is uncertain how many people actually migrated during the Great Migration.
(B) The eventual economic status of the Great Migration migrants has not been adequately traced.
(C) It is not likely that people with steady jobs would have reason to move to another area of the country.
(D) It is not true that the term "manufacturing and mechanical pursuits" actually encompasses the entire industrial sector.
(E) Of the Black workers living in southern cities, only those in a small number of trades were threatened by obsolescence.

15. According to the passage, which of the following is true of wages in southern cities in 1910?

(A) They were being pushed lower as a result of increased competition.
(B) They had begun to rise so that southern industry could attract rural workers.
(C) They had increased for skilled workers but decreased for unskilled workers.
(D) They had increased in large southern cities but decreased in small southern cities.
(E) They had increased in newly developed industries but decreased in the older trades.

GO ON TO THE NEXT PAGE.

16. The author cites each of the following as possible influences in a Black worker's decision to migrate north in the Great Migration EXCEPT

(A) wage levels in northern cities
(B) labor recruiters
(C) competition from rural workers
(D) voting rights in northern states
(E) the Black press

17. It can be inferred from the passage that the "easy conclusion" mentioned in line 53 is based on which of the following assumptions?

(A) People who migrate from rural areas to large cities usually do so for economic reasons.
(B) Most people who leave rural areas to take jobs in cities return to rural areas as soon as it is financially possible for them to do so.
(C) People with rural backgrounds are less likely to succeed economically in cities than are those with urban backgrounds.
(D) Most people who were once skilled workers are not willing to work as unskilled workers.
(E) People who migrate from their birthplaces to other regions of a country seldom undertake a second migration.

18. The primary purpose of the passage is to

(A) support an alternative to an accepted methodology
(B) present evidence that resolves a contradiction
(C) introduce a recently discovered source of information
(D) challenge a widely accepted explanation
(E) argue that a discarded theory deserves new attention

STOP

IF YOU FINISH BEFORE TIME IS CALLED, YOU MAY CHECK YOUR WORK ON THIS SECTION ONLY. DO NOT TURN TO ANY OTHER SECTION IN THE TEST.

Answer Key for Sample Test Section 2

READING COMPREHENSION

1.	D	10.	A
2.	D	11.	B
3.	C	12.	C
4.	D	13.	D
5.	C	14.	C
6.	E	15.	A
7.	E	16.	D
8.	D	17.	C
9.	E	18.	D

Explanatory Material: Reading Comprehension Sample Test Section 2

1. According to the passage, senior managers use intuition in all of the following ways EXCEPT to

   (A) speed up the creation of a solution to a problem
   (B) identify a problem
   (C) bring together disparate facts
   (D) stipulate clear goals
   (E) evaluate possible solutions to a problem

The best answer is D. The question requires you to recognize which of the choices is NOT mentioned in the passage as a way in which senior managers use intuition. Choice A, speeding up the creation of a solution, is mentioned in lines 36-37, which describe intuition as enabling managers to "move rapidly to engender a plausible solution." B appears in lines 21-22: "they intuitively sense when a problem exists." C is a restatement of the sentence in lines 26-28. E may be gathered from lines 29-30, which state that intuition is used "as a check on the results of more rational analysis"; those results are identified in the next sentence as "solutions." The passage does not mention stipulating goals (choice D).

2. The passage suggests which of the following about the "writers on management" mentioned in line 12 ?

   (A) They have criticized managers for not following the classical rational model of decision analysis.
   (B) They have not based their analyses on a sufficiently large sample of actual managers.
   (C) They have relied in drawing their conclusions on what managers say rather than on what managers do.
   (D) They have misunderstood how managers use intuition in making business decisions.
   (E) They have not acknowledged the role of intuition in managerial practice.

The best answer is D. The author asserts that the writers in question "display a poor grasp of what intuition is" (lines 14-15). The next paragraph presents a view that, according to the author of the passage, characterizes intuition more accurately than the writers on management do. Isenberg's research is specifically described as showing the ways in which managers use intuition (lines 20-21). Therefore, what Isenberg correctly comprehends, and the writers in question misunderstand, is how managers use intuition, as D states.

3. Which of the following best exemplifies "an 'Aha!' experience" (line 28) as it is presented in the passage?

   (A) A manager risks taking an action whose outcome is unpredictable to discover whether the action changes the problem at hand.
   (B) A manager performs well-learned and familiar behavior patterns in creative and uncharacteristic ways to solve a problem.
   (C) A manager suddenly connects seemingly unrelated facts and experiences to create a pattern relevant to the problem at hand.
   (D) A manager rapidly identifies the methodology used to compile data yielded by systematic analysis.
   (E) A manager swiftly decides which of several sets of tactics to implement in order to deal with the contingencies suggested by a problem.

The best answer is C. An "Aha! experience" is said in lines 26-28 to result from the synthesizing of "isolated bits of data and practice into an integrated picture." C is the best example of this kind of process. The connecting of seemingly unrelated facts and experiences mentioned in the answer choice is equivalent to synthesizing "isolated bits of data and practice," and the pattern referred to is comparable to an "integrated picture."

4. According to the passage, the classical model of decision analysis includes all of the following EXCEPT

   (A) evaluation of a problem
   (B) creation of possible solutions to a problem
   (C) establishment of clear goals to be reached by the decision
   (D) action undertaken in order to discover more information about a problem
   (E) comparison of the probable effects of different solutions to a problem

The best answer is D. The question requires you to recognize which of the choices is NOT mentioned in the passage as a component of the classical model of decision analysis. Four of the answer choices are mentioned in the first sentence of the passage, which describes the classical model of analysis: "clarifying goals" (C), "assessing the problem" (A), "formulating options" (B), and "estimating likelihoods of success" (E). Only D, "action undertaken in order to discover more information about a problem," does not appear in the passage.

5. It can be inferred from the passage that which of the following would most probably be one major difference in behavior between Manager X, who uses intuition to reach decisions, and Manager Y, who uses only formal decision analysis?

(A) Manager X analyzes first and then acts; Manager Y does not.
(B) Manager X checks possible solutions to a problem by systematic analysis; Manager Y does not.
(C) Manager X takes action in order to arrive at the solution to a problem; Manager Y does not.
(D) Manager Y draws on years of hands-on experience in creating a solution to a problem; Manager X does not.
(E) Manager Y depends on day-to-day tactical maneuvering; Manager X does not.

The best answer is C. The question requires you to compare behavior based on intuition with behavior based on formal decision analysis. Choice C specifies that the manager who uses intuition incorporates action into the decision-making process, but the manager who uses formal analysis does not. This distinction is made in several places in the passage. Lines 4-5 emphasize that decision-making and action-taking are separate steps in formal decision analysis: "making a decision, and only then taking action." On the other hand, those who use intuition "integrate action into the process of thinking" (lines 10-11). Again, the author mentions that in the intuitive style of management, " 'thinking' is inseparable from acting" (lines 41-42), and "action is often part of defining the problem" (lines 54-55).

6. The passage provides support for which of the following statements?

(A) Managers who rely on intuition are more successful than those who rely on formal decision analysis.
(B) Managers cannot justify their intuitive decisions.
(C) Managers' intuition works contrary to their rational and analytical skills.
(D) Logical analysis of a problem increases the number of possible solutions.
(E) Intuition enables managers to employ their practical experience more efficiently.

The best answer is E. The question requires you to identify a statement that can be inferred from information in the passage but is not explicitly stated. The author asserts that intuitive managers can "move rapidly to engender a plausible solution" (lines 36-37) and that their intuition is based on "experience that builds skills" (lines 25-26). This implies that the combination of skill and rapidity enables managers to employ their practical experience more efficiently, as E states. Choice A cannot be inferred from the passage, which states only that a majority of successful managers are intuitive (lines 1-11), not that their degree of success is greater. B and C are directly contradicted by the passage, and the passage provides no support for D.

7. It can be inferred from the passage that the morphogenetic determinants present in the early embryo are

(A) located in the nucleus of the embryo cells
(B) evenly distributed unless the embryo is not developing normally
(C) inactive until the embryo cells become irreversibly committed to their final function
(D) identical to those that were already present in the unfertilized egg
(E) present in larger quantities than is necessary for the development of a single individual

The best answer is E. The second and third paragraphs of the passage indicate that morphogenetic determinants are substances in the embryo that are activated after the egg has been fertilized and that "tell a cell what to become" (lines 15-16). If, as the author asserts in the first paragraph, biologists have succeeded in dividing an embryo into two parts, each of which survives and develops into a normal embryo, it can be concluded that the quantity of morphogenetic determinants in the early embryo is greater than that required for the development of a single individual. Choices A, B, and C are directly contradicted by information in the passage, and D makes an assertion that cannot be inferred from the passage.

8. The main topic of the passage is

(A) the early development of embryos of lower marine organisms
(B) the main contribution of modern embryology to molecular biology
(C) the role of molecular biology in disproving older theories of embryonic development
(D) cell determination as an issue in the study of embryonic development
(E) scientific dogma as a factor in the recent debate over the value of molecular biology

The best answer is D. In identifying the main topic of the passage, you must consider the passage as a whole. In the first paragraph, the author provides a historical context for the debate described in the second paragraph, concerning when and how the determination of embryo cells takes place. The third and fourth paragraphs provide a specific example of the "Recent discoveries in molecular biology" (line 19) that may lead to the resolution of that debate. C is incorrect because although the passage does indicate that biologists revised their initial belief that early embryo cells are undetermined, this revision is seen as having taken place prior to the "Recent discoveries in molecular biology." Choices A, B, and E do not accurately reflect the content of the passage.

9. According to the passage, when biologists believed that the cells in the early embryo were undetermined, they made which of the following mistakes?

(A) They did not attempt to replicate the original experiment of separating an embryo into two parts.

(B) They did not realize that there was a connection between the issue of cell determination and the outcome of the separation experiment.

(C) They assumed that the results of experiments on embryos did not depend on the particular animal species used for such experiments.

(D) They assumed that it was crucial to perform the separation experiment at an early stage in the embryo's life.

(E) They assumed that different ways of separating an embryo into two parts would be equivalent as far as the fate of the two parts was concerned.

The best answer is E. According to the author, early investigators arrived at the conclusion that the cells of the embryo are undetermined because they "found that if they separated an invertebrate animal embryo into two parts at an early stage of its life, it would survive and develop as two normal embryos" (lines 1-4). However, later biologists discovered that when an embryo was cut in planes different from the one used by the early investigators, it did not form two whole embryos. Because the earlier biologists apparently arrived at their conclusion without attempting to cut an embryo in different planes, it would appear that they assumed, erroneously, that different ways of separating the embryos would not affect the fate of the two embryo parts.

10. It can be inferred from the passage that the initial production of histones after an egg is fertilized takes place

(A) in the cytoplasm
(B) in the maternal genes
(C) throughout the protoplasm
(D) in the beaded portions of the DNA strings
(E) in certain sections of the cell nucleus

The best answer is A. In the third paragraph, the author asserts that substances that function as morphogenetic determinants are located in the cytoplasm of the cell and become active after the cell is fertilized. In the fourth paragraph we learn that these substances are "maternal messenger RNA's" and that they "direct, in large part, the synthesis of histones," which, after being synthesized, "move into the cell nucleus" (lines 39-45). Thus, it can be inferred that after the egg is fertilized, the initial production of histones occurs in the cytoplasm.

11. It can be inferred from the passage that which of the following is dependent on the fertilization of an egg?

(A) Copying of maternal genes to produce maternal messenger RNA's

(B) Synthesis of proteins called histones

(C) Division of a cell into its nucleus and the cytoplasm

(D) Determination of the egg cell's potential for division

(E) Generation of all of a cell's morphogenetic determinants

The best answer is B. Lines 30-34 indicate that substances that function as morphogenetic determinants are inactive in the unfertilized egg and that when the egg is fertilized, they "become active and, presumably, govern the behavior of the genes they interact with." In the fourth paragraph, we learn that these substances exert their control over the fate of the cell by directing "the synthesis of histones." Because these histones cannot be synthesized until the substances that function as morphogenetic determinants become active, and because these substances do not become active until the egg is fertilized, it can be inferred that the synthesis of the histones is dependent on the fertilization of the egg.

12. According to the passage, the morphogenetic determinants present in the unfertilized egg cell are which of the following?

(A) Proteins bound to the nucleus
(B) Histones
(C) Maternal messenger RNA's
(D) Cytoplasm
(E) Nonbeaded intervening DNA

The best answer is C. Lines 26-28 inform us that in his study of sea urchins, Gross "found that an unfertilized egg contains substances that function as morphogenetic determinants." Lines 39-40 assert that the "substances that Gross studied are maternal messenger RNA's," and in lines 41-42 we learn that these maternal messenger RNA's can be found in "a wide variety of organisms." B is incorrect. Although after becoming active these messenger RNA's are said to direct the synthesis of histones, the synthesis of the histones is said to occur after, not before, the egg has been fertilized.

13. The author indicates explicitly that which of the following records has been a source of information in her investigation?

   (A) United States Immigration Service reports from 1914 to 1930
   (B) Payrolls of southern manufacturing firms between 1910 and 1930
   (C) The volume of cotton exports between 1898 and 1910
   (D) The federal census of 1910
   (E) Advertisements of labor recruiters appearing in southern newspapers after 1910

The best answer is D. In lines 24-28, the author states that ten percent of the Black workers in the South were employed in "manufacturing and mechanical pursuits" and then identifies "manufacturing and mechanical pursuits" as the general federal census category for industrial occupations in 1910. Thus, she indicates that she used the federal census as a source of information. Although the author discusses information that may have been included in the records mentioned in A, B, C, and E, she does not "explicitly" identify any of those records as sources used in her investigation.

14. In the passage, the author anticipates which of the following as a possible objection to her argument?

   (A) It is uncertain how many people actually migrated during the Great Migration.
   (B) The eventual economic status of the Great Migration migrants has not been adequately traced.
   (C) It is not likely that people with steady jobs would have reason to move to another area of the country.
   (D) It is not true that the term "manufacturing and mechanical pursuits" actually encompasses the entire industrial sector.
   (E) Of the Black workers living in southern cities, only those in a small number of trades were threatened by obsolescence.

The best answer is C. To answer this question, you must first identify the author's argument. The author argues that it is possible that Black migrants to the North were living and working in urban areas of the South rather than in rural areas, as researchers had previously assumed. In lines 30-33, the author states that it may be "surprising" that an employed population would relocate. Thus, the author anticipates an objection to her argument on the grounds that Black urban workers in the South would have been unlikely to leave an economically secure existence. She meets that objection by stating that "an explanation lies in the labor conditions then prevalent in the South" (lines 32-33), and discusses the low wages that may have motivated Black workers to migrate north for higher pay.

15. According to the passage, which of the following is true of wages in southern cities in 1910?

   (A) They were being pushed lower as a result of increased competition.
   (B) They had begun to rise so that southern industry could attract rural workers.
   (C) They had increased for skilled workers but decreased for unskilled workers.
   (D) They had increased in large southern cities but decreased in small southern cities.
   (E) They had increased in newly developed industries but decreased in the older trades.

The best answer is A. The author discusses wages in southern cities in the third paragraph. Lines 47-50 state that an increase in the number of rural workers who migrated to southern cities after the collapse of the cotton industry led to increased competition for jobs and resulted in wages being pushed lower. There is no indication in the passage that B, C, D, or E was true.

16. The author cites each of the following as possible influences in a Black worker's decision to migrate north in the Great Migration EXCEPT

   (A) wage levels in northern cities
   (B) labor recruiters
   (C) competition from rural workers
   (D) voting rights in northern states
   (E) the Black press

The best answer is D. This question asks you to identify the possible influences that motivated Black workers in their decision to migrate north, and then to recognize which of the choices is NOT mentioned as an influence on Black workers. Choices A, B, C, and E are all discussed in the third paragraph. Lines 48-50 state that "competition from . . . rural workers" (C) resulted in even lower wages in the South. Lines 43-47 state that Black workers were aware through "labor recruiters" (B) and the "Black press" (E) that "wage levels in northern cities" (A) were higher than they were in the South. D — "voting rights in northern states" — is the only option not mentioned in the passage as an influence that may have motivated southern Black workers to move north.

17. It can be inferred from the passage that the "easy conclusion" mentioned in line 53 is based on which of the following assumptions?

(A) People who migrate from rural areas to large cities usually do so for economic reasons.

(B) Most people who leave rural areas to take jobs in cities return to rural areas as soon as it is financially possible for them to do so.

(C) People with rural backgrounds are less likely to succeed economically in cities than are those with urban backgrounds.

(D) Most people who were once skilled workers are not willing to work as unskilled workers.

(E) People who migrate from their birthplaces to other regions of a country seldom undertake a second migration.

The best answer is C. To answer this question, you must first identify the "easy conclusion" mentioned in line 53, which ties Black migrants' "subsequent economic problems in the North to their rural background." This linkage of rural background to economic difficulty after migration to the North is first mentioned in lines 14-18. Here, the author points out that researchers have assumed that Black migrants encountered economic difficulties in northern cities because they were from rural rather than urban backgrounds, and that rural backgrounds imply "unfamiliarity with urban living and a lack of industrial skills." Choice C provides an assumption about the relationship between rural backgrounds and economic difficulty that underlies this conclusion. It states that people with rural backgrounds are more likely to have economic difficulty in urban areas than are people with urban backgrounds. A, B, D, and E can be eliminated because they do not deal with the connection between economic difficulties and rural backgrounds.

18. The primary purpose of the passage is to

(A) support an alternative to an accepted methodology

(B) present evidence that resolves a contradiction

(C) introduce a recently discovered source of information

(D) challenge a widely accepted explanation

(E) argue that a discarded theory deserves new attention

The best answer is D. The first paragraph describes a common assumption about the Great Migration, that the majority of migrants came from rural areas. It also restates the conclusion that is based on this assumption, that the subsequent economic difficulties of Black migrants in the North were a result of their unfamiliarity with urban life. In the second paragraph, the author states that the "question of who actually left the South" (line 19) has never been adequately researched. She goes on to argue that Black migrants may actually have been from urban areas rather than rural areas, and thus that their subsequent economic problems in northern cities were not caused by their rural background. In making this argument, the author is challenging the "widely accepted explanation" presented in the first paragraph.

READING COMPREHENSION SAMPLE TEST SECTION 3

Time — 25 minutes

18 Questions

Directions: Each passage in this group is followed by questions based on its content. After reading a passage, choose the best answer to each question and fill in the corresponding oval on the answer sheet. Answer all questions following a passage on the basis of what is stated or implied in that passage.

In 1896 a Georgia couple suing for damages in the accidental death of their two year old was told that since the child had made no real economic contribution to the family, there was no liability for damages. In contrast,
(5) less than a century later, in 1979, the parents of a three year old sued in New York for accidental-death damages and won an award of $750,000.

The transformation in social values implicit in juxtaposing these two incidents is the subject of Viviana
(10) Zelizer's excellent book, *Pricing the Priceless Child*. During the nineteenth century, she argues, the concept of the "useful" child who contributed to the family economy gave way gradually to the present-day notion of the "useless" child who, though producing no income
(15) for, and indeed extremely costly to, its parents, is yet considered emotionally "priceless." Well established among segments of the middle and upper classes by the mid-1800's, this new view of childhood spread throughout society in the late-nineteenth and early-twentieth
(20) centuries as reformers introduced child-labor regulations and compulsory education laws predicated in part on the assumption that a child's emotional value made child labor taboo.

For Zelizer the origins of this transformation were
(25) many and complex. The gradual erosion of children's productive value in a maturing industrial economy, the decline in birth and death rates, especially in child mortality, and the development of the companionate family (a family in which members were united by
(30) explicit bonds of love rather than duty) were all factors critical in changing the assessment of children's worth. Yet "expulsion of children from the 'cash nexus.' . . . although clearly shaped by profound changes in the economic, occupational, and family structures," Zelizer
(35) maintains, "was also part of a cultural process of 'sacralization' of children's lives." Protecting children from the crass business world became enormously important for late-nineteenth-century middle-class Americans, she suggests; this sacralization was a way of resisting what
(40) they perceived as the relentless corruption of human values by the marketplace.

In stressing the cultural determinants of a child's worth, Zelizer takes issue with practitioners of the new "sociological economics," who have analyzed such tradi-
(45) tionally sociological topics as crime, marriage, education, and health solely in terms of their economic determinants. Allowing only a small role for cultural forces

in the form of individual "preferences," these sociologists tend to view all human behavior as directed primarily by
(50) the principle of maximizing economic gain. Zelizer is highly critical of this approach, and emphasizes instead the opposite phenomenon: the power of social values to transform price. As children became more valuable in emotional terms, she argues, their "exchange" or "sur-
(55) render" value on the market, that is, the conversion of their intangible worth into cash terms, became much greater.

1. It can be inferred from the passage that accidental-death damage awards in America during the nineteenth century tended to be based principally on the

    (A) earnings of the person at time of death
    (B) wealth of the party causing the death
    (C) degree of culpability of the party causing the death
    (D) amount of money that had been spent on the person killed
    (E) amount of suffering endured by the family of the person killed

2. It can be inferred from the passage that in the early 1800's children were generally regarded by their families as individuals who

    (A) needed enormous amounts of security and affection
    (B) required constant supervision while working
    (C) were important to the economic well-being of a family
    (D) were unsuited to spending long hours in school
    (E) were financial burdens assumed for the good of society

GO ON TO THE NEXT PAGE.

-219-

3. Which of the following alternative explanations of the change in the cash value of children would be most likely to be put forward by sociological economists as they are described in the passage?

(A) The cash value of children rose during the nineteenth century because parents began to increase their emotional investment in the upbringing of their children.

(B) The cash value of children rose during the nineteenth century because their expected earnings over the course of a lifetime increased greatly.

(C) The cash value of children rose during the nineteenth century because the spread of humanitarian ideals resulted in a wholesale reappraisal of the worth of an individual.

(D) The cash value of children rose during the nineteenth century because compulsory education laws reduced the supply, and thus raised the costs, of available child labor.

(E) The cash value of children rose during the nineteenth century because of changes in the way negligence law assessed damages in accidental-death cases.

4. The primary purpose of the passage is to

(A) review the literature in a new academic subfield
(B) present the central thesis of a recent book
(C) contrast two approaches to analyzing historical change
(D) refute a traditional explanation of a social phenomenon
(E) encourage further work on a neglected historical topic

5. It can be inferred from the passage that which of the following statements was true of American families over the course of the nineteenth century?

(A) The average size of families grew considerably.
(B) The percentage of families involved in industrial work declined dramatically.
(C) Family members became more emotionally bonded to one another.
(D) Family members spent an increasing amount of time working with each other.
(E) Family members became more economically dependent on each other.

6. Zelizer refers to all of the following as important influences in changing the assessment of children's worth EXCEPT changes in

(A) the mortality rate
(B) the nature of industry
(C) the nature of the family
(D) attitudes toward reform movements
(E) attitudes toward the marketplace

GO ON TO THE NEXT PAGE.

Prior to 1975, union efforts to organize public-sector clerical workers, most of whom are women, were somewhat limited. The factors favoring unionization drives seem to have been either the presence of large numbers
(5) of workers, as in New York City, to make it worth the effort, or the concentration of small numbers in one or two locations, such as a hospital, to make it relatively easy. Receptivity to unionization on the workers' part was also a consideration, but when there were large
(10) numbers involved or the clerical workers were the only unorganized group in a jurisdiction, the multioccupational unions would often try to organize them regardless of the workers' initial receptivity. The strategic reasoning was based, first, on the concern that politi-
(15) cians and administrators might play off unionized against nonunionized workers, and, second, on the conviction that a fully unionized public work force meant power, both at the bargaining table and in the legislature. In localities where clerical workers were few
(20) in number, were scattered in several workplaces, and expressed no interest in being organized, unions more often than not ignored them in the pre-1975 period.

But since the mid-1970's, a different strategy has emerged. In 1977, 34 percent of government clerical
(25) workers were represented by a labor organization, compared with 46 percent of government professionals, 44 percent of government blue-collar workers, and 41 percent of government service workers. Since then, however, the biggest increases in public-sector unioniza-
(30) tion have been among clerical workers. Between 1977 and 1980, the number of unionized government workers in blue-collar and service occupations increased only about 1.5 percent, while in the white-collar occupations the increase was 20 percent and among clerical workers
(35) in particular, the increase was 22 percent.

What accounts for this upsurge in unionization among clerical workers? First, more women have entered the work force in the past few years, and more of them plan to remain working until retirement age. Conse-
(40) quently, they are probably more concerned than their predecessors were about job security and economic benefits. Also, the women's movement has succeeded in legitimizing the economic and political activism of women on their own behalf, thereby producing a more positive atti-
(45) tude toward unions. The absence of any comparable increase in unionization among private-sector clerical workers, however, identifies the primary catalyst—the structural change in the multioccupational public-sector unions themselves. Over the past twenty years, the occu-
(50) pational distribution in these unions has been steadily shifting from predominantly blue-collar to predominantly white-collar. Because there are far more women in white-collar jobs, an increase in the proportion of female members has accompanied the occupational shift
(55) and has altered union policy-making in favor of organizing women and addressing women's issues.

7. According to the passage, the public-sector workers who were most likely to belong to unions in 1977 were

(A) professionals
(B) managers
(C) clerical workers
(D) service workers
(E) blue-collar workers

8. The author cites union efforts to achieve a fully unionized work force (lines 13-19) in order to account for why

(A) politicians might try to oppose public-sector union organizing
(B) public-sector unions have recently focused on organizing women
(C) early organizing efforts often focused on areas where there were large numbers of workers
(D) union efforts with regard to public-sector clerical workers increased dramatically after 1975
(E) unions sometimes tried to organize workers regardless of the workers' initial interest in unionization

9. The author's claim that, since the mid-1970's, a new strategy has emerged in the unionization of public-sector clerical workers (line 23) would be strengthened if the author

(A) described more fully the attitudes of clerical workers toward labor unions
(B) compared the organizing strategies employed by private-sector unions with those of public-sector unions
(C) explained why politicians and administrators sometimes oppose unionization of clerical workers
(D) indicated that the number of unionized public-sector clerical workers was increasing even before the mid-1970's
(E) showed that the factors that favored unionization drives among these workers prior to 1975 have decreased in importance

GO ON TO THE NEXT PAGE.

10. According to the passage, in the period prior to 1975, each of the following considerations helped determine whether a union would attempt to organize a certain group of clerical workers EXCEPT

(A) the number of clerical workers in that group
(B) the number of women among the clerical workers in that group
(C) whether the clerical workers in that area were concentrated in one workplace or scattered over several workplaces
(D) the degree to which the clerical workers in that group were interested in unionization
(E) whether all the other workers in the same jurisdiction as that group of clerical workers were unionized

11. The author states that which of the following is a consequence of the women's movement of recent years?

(A) An increase in the number of women entering the work force
(B) A structural change in multioccupational public-sector unions
(C) A more positive attitude on the part of women toward unions
(D) An increase in the proportion of clerical workers that are women
(E) An increase in the number of women in administrative positions

12. The main concern of the passage is to

(A) advocate particular strategies for future efforts to organize certain workers into labor unions
(B) explain differences in the unionized proportions of various groups of public-sector workers
(C) evaluate the effectiveness of certain kinds of labor unions that represent public-sector workers
(D) analyze and explain an increase in unionization among a certain category of workers
(E) describe and distinguish strategies appropriate to organizing different categories of workers

GO ON TO THE NEXT PAGE.

Milankovitch proposed in the early twentieth century that the ice ages were caused by variations in the Earth's orbit around the Sun. For sometime this theory was considered untestable, largely because there was no suffi-
(5) ciently precise chronology of the ice ages with which the orbital variations could be matched.

To establish such a chronology it is necessary to determine the relative amounts of land ice that existed at various times in the Earth's past. A recent discovery
(10) makes such a determination possible: relative land-ice volume for a given period can be deduced from the ratio of two oxygen isotopes, 16 and 18, found in ocean sediments. Almost all the oxygen in water is oxygen 16, but a few molecules out of every thousand incorporate the
(15) heavier isotope 18. When an ice age begins, the continental ice sheets grow, steadily reducing the amount of water evaporated from the ocean that will eventually return to it. Because heavier isotopes tend to be left behind when water evaporates from the ocean surfaces,
(20) the remaining ocean water becomes progressively enriched in oxygen 18. The degree of enrichment can be determined by analyzing ocean sediments of the period, because these sediments are composed of calcium carbonate shells of marine organisms, shells that were
(25) constructed with oxygen atoms drawn from the surrounding ocean. The higher the ratio of oxygen 18 to oxygen 16 in a sedimentary specimen, the more land ice there was when the sediment was laid down.

As an indicator of shifts in the Earth's climate, the
(30) isotope record has two advantages. First, it is a global record: there is remarkably little variation in isotope ratios in sedimentary specimens taken from different continental locations. Second, it is a more continuous record than that taken from rocks on land. Because of
(35) these advantages, sedimentary evidence can be dated with sufficient accuracy by radiometric methods to establish a precise chronology of the ice ages. The dated isotope record shows that the fluctuations in global ice volume over the past several hundred thousand years
(40) have a pattern: an ice age occurs roughly once every 100,000 years. These data have established a strong connection between variations in the Earth's orbit and the periodicity of the ice ages.

However, it is important to note that other factors,
(45) such as volcanic particulates or variations in the amount of sunlight received by the Earth, could potentially have affected the climate. The advantage of the Milankovitch theory is that it is testable: changes in the Earth's orbit can be calculated and dated by applying Newton's laws
(50) of gravity to progressively earlier configurations of the bodies in the solar system. Yet the lack of information about other possible factors affecting global climate does not make them unimportant.

13. In the passage, the author is primarily interested in

(A) suggesting an alternative to an outdated research method
(B) introducing a new research method that calls an accepted theory into question
(C) emphasizing the instability of data gathered from the application of a new scientific method
(D) presenting a theory and describing a new method to test that theory
(E) initiating a debate about a widely accepted theory

14. The author of the passage would be most likely to agree with which of the following statements about the Milankovitch theory?

(A) It is the only possible explanation for the ice ages.
(B) It is too limited to provide a plausible explanation for the ice ages, despite recent research findings.
(C) It cannot be tested and confirmed until further research on volcanic activity is done.
(D) It is one plausible explanation, though not the only one, for the ice ages.
(E) It is not a plausible explanation for the ice ages, although it has opened up promising possibilities for future research.

15. It can be inferred from the passage that the isotope record taken from ocean sediments would be less useful to researchers if which of the following were true?

(A) It indicated that lighter isotopes of oxygen predominated at certain times.
(B) It had far more gaps in its sequence than the record taken from rocks on land.
(C) It indicated that climate shifts did not occur every 100,000 years.
(D) It indicated that the ratios of oxygen 16 and oxygen 18 in ocean water were not consistent with those found in fresh water.
(E) It stretched back for only a million years.

GO ON TO THE NEXT PAGE.

16. According to the passage, which of the following is true of the ratios of oxygen isotopes in ocean sediments?

(A) They indicate that sediments found during an ice age contain more calcium carbonate than sediments formed at other times.
(B) They are less reliable than the evidence from rocks on land in determining the volume of land ice.
(C) They can be used to deduce the relative volume of land ice that was present when the sediment was laid down.
(D) They are more unpredictable during an ice age than in other climatic conditions.
(E) They can be used to determine atmospheric conditions at various times in the past.

17. It can be inferred from the passage that precipitation formed from evaporated ocean water has

(A) the same isotopic ratio as ocean water
(B) less oxygen 18 than does ocean water
(C) less oxygen 18 than has the ice contained in continental ice sheets
(D) a different isotopic composition than has precipitation formed from water on land
(E) more oxygen 16 than has precipitation formed from fresh water

18. It can be inferred from the passage that calcium carbonate shells

(A) are not as susceptible to deterioration as rocks
(B) are less common in sediments formed during an ice age
(C) are found only in areas that were once covered by land ice
(D) contain radioactive material that can be used to determine a sediment's isotopic composition
(E) reflect the isotopic composition of the water at the time the shells were formed

STOP

**IF YOU FINISH BEFORE TIME IS CALLED, YOU MAY CHECK YOUR WORK ON THIS SECTION ONLY.
DO NOT TURN TO ANY OTHER SECTION IN THE TEST.**

Answer Key for Sample Test Section 3

READING COMPREHENSION

1.	A	10.	B
2.	C	11.	C
3.	B	12.	D
4.	B	13.	D
5.	C	14.	D
6.	D	15.	B
7.	A	16.	C
8.	E	17.	B
9.	E	18.	E

Explanatory Material: Reading Comprehension Sample Test Section 3

1. It can be inferred from the passage that accidental-death damage awards in America during the nineteenth century tended to be based principally on the

   (A) earnings of the person at time of death
   (B) wealth of the party causing the death
   (C) degree of culpability of the party causing the death
   (D) amount of money that had been spent on the person killed
   (E) amount of suffering endured by the family of the person killed

The best answer is A. In the first paragraph, the author cites an accidental-death case from nineteenth-century America in which the absence of economic contribution on the part of a deceased child was ruled sufficient grounds to deny the awarding of damages to the child's parents. The author goes on to discuss how this case typified attitudes that persisted even into the twentieth century. It can be inferred from this that in nineteenth-century America the chief consideration in determining damages in an accidental-death case was the deceased person's earnings. There is no evidence in the passage to suggest that the factors cited in B, C, D, and E were of primary concern in determining accidental-death damages in nineteenth-century America.

2. It can be inferred from the passage that in the early 1800's children were generally regarded by their families as individuals who

   (A) needed enormous amounts of security and affection
   (B) required constant supervision while working
   (C) were important to the economic well-being of a family
   (D) were unsuited to spending long hours in school
   (E) were financial burdens assumed for the good of society

The best answer is C. In the second paragraph, the author describes how during the nineteenth century the concept of the "'useful' child who contributed to the family economy" (lines 12-13) gradually gave way to the present-day notion of the economically "useless" but emotionally "priceless" child; this new view of childhood was "Well established among segments of the middle and upper classes by the mid-1800's" and "spread throughout society in the late-nineteenth and early-twentieth centuries" (lines 16-20). Thus in the early 1800's, prior to the shift in the valuation of children, families valued the role children had to play in the family's economic well-being. Choices A and E describe attitudes more in accord with the present-day view of childhood, and B and D address issues that are not raised in the passage.

3. Which of the following alternative explanations of the change in the cash value of children would be most likely to be put forward by sociological economists as they are described in the passage?

   (A) The cash value of children rose during the nineteenth century because parents began to increase their emotional investment in the upbringing of their children.
   (B) The cash value of children rose during the nineteenth century because their expected earnings over the course of a lifetime increased greatly.
   (C) The cash value of children rose during the nineteenth century because the spread of humanitarian ideals resulted in a wholesale reappraisal of the worth of an individual.
   (D) The cash value of children rose during the nineteenth century because compulsory education laws reduced the supply, and thus raised the costs, of available child labor.
   (E) The cash value of children rose during the nineteenth century because of changes in the way negligence law assessed damages in accidental-death cases.

The best answer is B. According to the author, practitioners of the new "sociological economics" explain sociological phenomena "solely in terms of their economic determinants" and "tend to view all human behavior as directed primarily by the principle of maximizing economic gain" (lines 46-50). Choice B provides just such an economic explanation for the nineteenth-century rise in the cash value of children. Choice A paraphrases Zelizer's own explanation, which is at odds with that of the sociological economists, and C uses social values and emotional factors to explain an even broader revaluation of individual worth. D uses an economic argument to explain the change, but here the economic factors at work are the result of a change in social values. E provides a legal explanation for the change.

4. The primary purpose of the passage is to

   (A) review the literature in a new academic subfield
   (B) present the central thesis of a recent book
   (C) contrast two approaches to analyzing historical change
   (D) refute a traditional explanation of a social phenomenon
   (E) encourage further work on a neglected historical topic

The best answer is B. In the first paragraph, the author contrasts two incidents that are said to exemplify the transformation in social values that forms the subject of Zelizer's book. The second and third paragraphs consist of a brief history of that transformation, as Zelizer presents it, and an account of the factors she considers important in bringing it about. In the last paragraph, the author explains how Zelizer's thesis differs from that of sociological economists. Thus, the passage serves primarily to present the central thesis of Zelizer's book. Choice C is incorrect because although the passage does contrast two approaches, this contrast takes place only in the final paragraph. The other answer choices misrepresent either the author's approach or the subject matter of the passage.

5. It can be inferred from the passage that which of the following statements was true of American families over the course of the nineteenth century?

   (A) The average size of families grew considerably.
   (B) The percentage of families involved in industrial work declined dramatically.
   (C) Family members became more emotionally bonded to one another.
   (D) Family members spent an increasing amount of time working with each other.
   (E) Family members became more economically dependent on each other.

The best answer is C. In the third paragraph, the author cites Zelizer's contention that the new view of childhood that developed in nineteenth-century America was due in part to "the development of the companionate family (a family in which members were united by explicit bonds of love rather than duty)" (lines 28-30). From this it can be inferred that the emotional bonds between family members became increasingly important during this period. There is no information in the passage to support the other answer choices.

6. Zelizer refers to all of the following as important influences in changing the assessment of children's worth EXCEPT changes in

   (A) the mortality rate
   (B) the nature of industry
   (C) the nature of the family
   (D) attitudes toward reform movements
   (E) attitudes toward the marketplace

The best answer is D. Choices A, B, and C are mentioned in lines 25-31 as factors Zelizer regards as "critical in changing the assessment of children's worth"; E is mentioned in lines 36-41, which describe how the "sacralization" of children's lives represented "a way of resisting what they [middle-class Americans] perceived as the relentless corruption of human values by the marketplace." Although reform movements are mentioned in lines 20-23, the passage does not discuss attitudes or changes in attitudes toward those movements. D is therefore *not* among the influences Zelizer is said to regard as important in changing the assessment of children's worth.

7. According to the passage, the public-sector workers who were most likely to belong to unions in 1977 were

   (A) professionals
   (B) managers
   (C) clerical workers
   (D) service workers
   (E) blue-collar workers

The best answer is A. In the second paragraph, the author gives the percentages of workers who were unionized in different categories of the public sector in 1977. Forty-six percent of government professionals were unionized; this is greater than the percentage for any of the other categories of unionized workers from among the listed categories of public-sector workers. Therefore, professionals were more likely to belong to unions than were other public-sector workers.

8. The author cites union efforts to achieve a fully unionized work force (lines 13-19) in order to account for why

  (A) politicians might try to oppose public-sector union
      organizing
  (B) public-sector unions have recently focused on
      organizing women
  (C) early organizing efforts often focused on areas
      where there were large numbers of workers
  (D) union efforts with regard to public-sector clerical
      workers increased dramatically after 1975
  (E) unions sometimes tried to organize workers
      regardless of the workers' initial interest in
      unionization

The best answer is E. In lines 13-19, the author describes the
reasoning behind the multioccupational unions' attempt to
achieve a fully unionized workplace. This reasoning is
provided to explain why "the multioccupational unions would
often try to organize them [clerical workers] regardless of the
workers' initial receptivity" (lines 11-13). Choice A helps to
explain, but is not explained by, the attempt to achieve a fully
unionized work force. An explanation for C is given in lines
3-6; B and D are explained in the second and third paragraphs
of the passage.

9. The author's claim that, since the mid-1970's, a new
strategy has emerged in the unionization of public-
sector clerical workers (line 23) would be strengthened if
the author

  (A) described more fully the attitudes of clerical
      workers toward labor unions
  (B) compared the organizing strategies employed by
      private-sector unions with those of public-sector
      unions
  (C) explained why politicians and administrators
      sometimes oppose unionization of clerical
      workers
  (D) indicated that the number of unionized public-
      sector clerical workers was increasing even
      before the mid-1970's
  (E) showed that the factors that favored unionization
      drives among these workers prior to 1975 have
      decreased in importance

The best answer is E. The question asks what would
strengthen the author's claim that a new strategy for unionization has emerged since the mid-1970's. Line 23 cites the
appearance of the new strategy. The paragraphs that follow
describe the changed circumstances that provided a context for
such new strategies, and lines 52-56 explain precisely how
these changed circumstances created a reason for new unioniz-
ing strategies. The author's claim would be strengthened if it
could be shown not only that there are such new circumstances, but that the old circumstances discussed in the first
paragraph have become less important, further necessitating
the adoption of a new strategy in place of an old strategy
suitable to those older circumstances.

10. According to the passage, in the period prior to 1975,
each of the following considerations helped determine
whether a union would attempt to organize a certain
group of clerical workers EXCEPT

  (A) the number of clerical workers in that group
  (B) the number of women among the clerical workers
      in that group
  (C) whether the clerical workers in that area were
      concentrated in one workplace or scattered
      over several workplaces
  (D) the degree to which the clerical workers in that
      group were interested in unionization
  (E) whether all the other workers in the same
      jurisdiction as that group of clerical workers
      were unionized

The best answer is B. In the first paragraph, the author
describes the considerations relevant to a union's attempt to
organize a certain group of clerical workers prior to 1975.
Choices A, C, D, and E are all cited as important considerations. In line 2, the author notes the fact that most of these
clerical workers were women, but does not suggest that this
was an important consideration for unionizers.

11. The author states that which of the following is a consequence of the women's movement of recent years?

(A) An increase in the number of women entering the work force

(B) A structural change in multioccupational public-sector unions

(C) A more positive attitude on the part of women toward unions

(D) An increase in the proportion of clerical workers that are women

(E) An increase in the number of women in administrative positions

The best answer is C. According to the author, "the women's movement has succeeded in legitimizing the economic and political activism of women on their own behalf," and this in turn has produced in women "a more positive attitude toward unions" (lines 42-45). Although A, B, D, and E describe developments mentioned in the passage, none of these are said to have been a consequence of the women's movement.

12. The main concern of the passage is to

(A) advocate particular strategies for future efforts to organize certain workers into labor unions

(B) explain differences in the unionized proportions of various groups of public-sector workers

(C) evaluate the effectiveness of certain kinds of labor unions that represent public-sector workers

(D) analyze and explain an increase in unionization among a certain category of workers

(E) describe and distinguish strategies appropriate to organizing different categories of workers

The best answer is D. In the first paragraph of the passage, the author asserts that efforts to unionize public-sector clerical workers prior to 1975 were limited and then goes on to describe these limited efforts. In the second paragraph, the author asserts that a new strategy developed after 1975 and cites an increase in union membership among public-sector clerical workers. The author begins the last paragraph by asking what can explain this increase in union membership, and then proceeds to provide an explanation. Thus, the passage is primarily concerned with analyzing and explaining the increase in unionization among public-sector clerical workers.

13. In the passage, the author is primarily interested in

(A) suggesting an alternative to an outdated research method

(B) introducing a new research method that calls an accepted theory into question

(C) emphasizing the instability of data gathered from the application of a new scientific method

(D) presenting a theory and describing a new method to test that theory

(E) initiating a debate about a widely accepted theory

The best answer is D. In the first paragraph, the author describes Milankovitch's theory and explains why the theory previously had been considered untestable. In the second and third paragraphs, the author describes a scientific break-through that has made it possible to test and provide support for Milankovitch's theory. Although the author also mentions other factors that potentially could have affected the Earth's climate, the passage as a whole is concerned primarily with Milankovitch's theory and the scientific method that has been used to test that theory. Choices A, C, and E do not accurately reflect the content of the passage, and, although the passage does describe a new research method as B suggests, this method supports rather than casts doubt on Milankovitch's theory.

14. The author of the passage would be most likely to agree with which of the following statements about the Milankovitch theory?

(A) It is the only possible explanation for the ice ages.

(B) It is too limited to provide a plausible explanation for the ice ages, despite recent research findings.

(C) It cannot be tested and confirmed until further research on volcanic activity is done.

(D) It is one plausible explanation, though not the only one, for the ice ages.

(E) It is not a plausible explanation for the ice ages, although it has opened up promising possibilities for future research.

The best answer is D. In lines 7-13, the author states that a recent discovery has made it possible to establish a precise chronology of the Earth's ice ages. Scientists have used this discovery to test the basic premise of Milankovitch's theory — that the ice ages were caused by variations in the Earth's orbit around the Sun. The author notes in lines 41-43 that the data have established a "strong connection" between orbital variation and ice ages, which confirms the plausibility of Milankovitch's theory. However, one can infer from the last paragraph that the author believes factors other than variations in the Earth's orbit could provide plausible explanations for global climate change.

15. It can be inferred from the passage that the isotope record taken from ocean sediments would be less useful to researchers if which of the following were true?

(A) It indicated that lighter isotopes of oxygen predominated at certain times.

(B) It had far more gaps in its sequence than the record taken from rocks on land.

(C) It indicated that climate shifts did not occur every 100,000 years.

(D) It indicated that the ratios of oxygen 16 and oxygen 18 in ocean water were not consistent with those found in fresh water.

(E) It stretched back for only a million years.

The best answer is B. The author states that one advantage of obtaining an isotopic record from ocean sediment is that the ocean's isotopic record is "a more continuous record than that taken from rocks on land" (lines 33-34). Because a continuous record can indicate more precisely when shifts in the Earth's climate have occurred, the ocean's isotopic record would be less useful if it had more gaps in it than the record taken from rocks. Choice A describes a circumstance that is in fact true, since oxygen 16 is the lighter isotope and, according to the passage, "Almost all the oxygen in water is oxygen 16" (line 13); but this fact clearly has not compromised the usefulness of the ocean's isotopic record as an indicator of climatic shifts. Likewise, E would not diminish its usefulness, since isotopic records showing "flunctuations in global ice volume over the past several hundred thousand years" have been sufficient to determine a meaningful pattern (lines 37-41). If C were shown to be true, Milankovitch's theory would be weakened, but this would not diminish the value of the isotopic record. If D were true, researchers would need to accommodate the inconsistency described in evaluating the isotopic record, but, again, this would not compromise the usefulness of the record itself.

16. According to the passage, which of the following is true of the ratios of oxygen isotopes in ocean sediments?

(A) They indicate that sediments found during an ice age contain more calcium carbonate than sediments formed at other times.

(B) They are less reliable than the evidence from rocks on land in determining the volume of land ice.

(C) They can be used to deduce the relative volume of land ice that was present when the sediment was laid down.

(D) They are more unpredictable during an ice age than in other climatic conditions.

(E) They can be used to determine atmospheric conditions at various times in the past.

The best answer is C. Lines 10-13 state that the relative volume of land ice can be deduced from the ratio of oxygen 18 to oxygen 16 in ocean sediments. Choices A, D, and E are incorrect because there is no information in the passage to support these statements. B is incorrect because it contradicts lines 33-34, in which the author states that ocean sediment provides "a more continuous record than that taken from rocks on land."

17. It can be inferred from the passage that precipitation formed from evaporated ocean water has

    (A) the same isotopic ratio as ocean water
    (B) less oxygen 18 than does ocean water
    (C) less oxygen 18 than has the ice contained in continental ice sheets
    (D) a different isotopic composition than has precipitation formed from water on land
    (E) more oxygen 16 than has precipitation formed from fresh water

The best answer is B. Lines 18-21 state that when water evaporates from the ocean surface, oxygen 18, a heavier isotope than oxygen 16, tends to be left behind in the remaining ocean water. Thus, one can infer that evaporated ocean water would contain less oxygen 18 than would the remaining ocean water. Choice A is incorrect because it contradicts information stated in lines 15-21. C is incorrect because the passage suggests that the water evaporated from the ocean contributes to the growth of continental ice sheets, which should therefore have an isotopic composition similar to that of the precipitation formed from evaporated ocean water. Choices D and E describe information that cannot be inferred from the passage.

18. It can be inferred from the passage that calcium carbonate shells

    (A) are not as susceptible to deterioration as rocks
    (B) are less common in sediments formed during an ice age
    (C) are found only in areas that were once covered by land ice
    (D) contain radioactive material that can be used to determine a sediment's isotopic composition
    (E) reflect the isotopic composition of the water at the time the shells were formed

The best answer is E. Lines 23-26 of the passage state that the calcium carbonate shells of marine organisms are constructed with "oxygen atoms drawn from the surrounding ocean." This water contains varying proportions of oxygen 16 and oxygen 18 and, according to the passage, "becomes progressively enriched in oxygen 18" with the onset of an ice age (lines 15-21). The author states that "The degree of enrichment can be determined by analyzing ocean sediments . . . composed of calcium carbonate shells of marine animals "(lines 21-24). Thus, it can be inferred that the shells of marine organisms would reflect the isotopic composition of the surrounding ocean water at the time when the shells were formed.

Time — 25 minutes

18 Questions

Directions: Each passage in this group is followed by questions based on its content. After reading a passage, choose the best answer to each question and fill in the corresponding oval on the answer sheet. Answer all questions following a passage on the basis of what is <u>stated</u> or <u>implied</u> in that passage.

In contrast to traditional analyses of minority business, the sociological analysis contends that minority business ownership is a group-level phenomenon, in that
Line it is largely dependent upon social-group resources for
(5) its development. Specifically, this analysis indicates that support networks play a critical role in starting and maintaining minority business enterprises by providing owners with a range of assistance, from the informal encouragement of family members and friends to
(10) dependable sources of labor and clientele from the owner's ethnic group. Such self-help networks, which encourage and support ethnic minority entrepreneurs, consist of "primary" institutions, those closest to the individual in shaping his or her behavior and beliefs.
(15) They are characterized by the face-to-face association and cooperation of persons united by ties of mutual concern. They form an intermediate social level between the individual and larger "secondary" institutions based on impersonal relationships. Primary institutions
(20) comprising the support network include kinship, peer, and neighborhood or community subgroups.

A major function of self-help networks is financial support. Most scholars agree that minority business owners have depended primarily on family funds and
(25) ethnic community resources for investment capital. Personal savings have been accumulated, often through frugal living habits that require sacrifices by the entire family and are thus a product of long-term family financial behavior. Additional loans and gifts from relatives,
(30) forthcoming because of group obligation rather than narrow investment calculation, have supplemented personal savings. Individual entrepreneurs do not necessarily rely on their kin because they cannot obtain financial backing from commercial resources. They may actu-
(35) ally avoid banks because they assume that commercial institutions either cannot comprehend the special needs of minority enterprise or charge unreasonably high interest rates.

Within the larger ethnic community, rotating credit
(40) associations have been used to raise capital. These associations are informal clubs of friends and other trusted members of the ethnic group who make regular contributions to a fund that is given to each contributor in rotation. One author estimates that 40 percent of New
(45) York Chinatown firms established during 1900-1950 utilized such associations as their initial source of capital. However, recent immigrants and third or fourth generations of older groups now employ rotating credit

associations only occasionally to raise investment funds.
(50) Some groups, like Black Americans, found other means of financial support for their entrepreneurial efforts. The first Black-operated banks were created in the late nineteenth century as depositories for dues collected from fraternal or lodge groups, which themselves had sprung
(55) from Black churches. Black banks made limited investments in other Black enterprises. Irish immigrants in American cities organized many building and loan associations to provide capital for home construction and purchase. They, in turn, provided work for many Irish
(60) home-building contractor firms. Other ethnic and minority groups followed similar practices in founding ethnic-directed financial institutions.

1. Based on the information in the passage, it would be LEAST likely for which of the following persons to be part of a self-help network?

(A) The entrepreneur's childhood friend
(B) The entrepreneur's aunt
(C) The entrepreneur's religious leader
(D) The entrepreneur's neighbor
(E) The entrepreneur's banker

2. Which of the following illustrates the working of a self-help support network, as such networks are described in the passage?

(A) A public high school offers courses in book-keeping and accounting as part of its open-enrollment adult education program.
(B) The local government in a small city sets up a program that helps teen-agers find summer jobs.
(C) A major commercial bank offers low-interest loans to experienced individuals who hope to establish their own businesses.
(D) A neighborhood-based fraternal organization develops a program of on-the-job training for its members and their friends.
(E) A community college offers county residents training programs that can lead to certification in a variety of technical trades.

GO ON TO THE NEXT PAGE.

3. Which of the following can be inferred from the passage about rotating credit associations?

(A) They were developed exclusively by Chinese immigrants.
(B) They accounted for a significant portion of the investment capital used by Chinese immigrants in New York in the early twentieth century.
(C) Third-generation members of an immigrant group who started businesses in the 1920's would have been unlikely to rely on them.
(D) They were frequently joint endeavors by members of two or three different ethnic groups.
(E) Recent immigrants still frequently turn to rotating credit associations instead of banks for investment capital.

4. The passage best supports which of the following statements?

(A) A minority entrepreneur who had no assistance from family members would not be able to start a business.
(B) Self-help networks have been effective in helping entrepreneurs primarily in the last 50 years.
(C) Minority groups have developed a range of alternatives to standard financing of business ventures.
(D) The financial institutions founded by various ethnic groups owe their success to their unique formal organization.
(E) Successful minority-owned businesses succeed primarily because of the personal strengths of their founders.

5. Which of the following best describes the organization of the second paragraph?

(A) An argument is delineated, followed by a counterargument.
(B) An assertion is made and several examples are provided to illustrate it.
(C) A situation is described and its historical background is then outlined.
(D) An example of a phenomenon is given and is then used as a basis for general conclusions.
(E) A group of parallel incidents is described and the distinctions among the incidents are then clarified.

6. According to the passage, once a minority-owned business is established, self-help networks contribute which of the following to that business?

(A) Information regarding possible expansion of the business into nearby communities
(B) Encouragement of a business climate that is nearly free of direct competition
(C) Opportunities for the business owner to reinvest profits in other minority-owned businesses
(D) Contact with people who are likely to be customers of the new business
(E) Contact with minority entrepreneurs who are members of other ethnic groups

GO ON TO THE NEXT PAGE.

Species interdependence in nature confers many benefits on the species involved, but it can also become a point of weakness when one species involved in the relationship is affected by a catastrophe. Thus, flowering plant species dependent on insect pollination, as opposed to self-pollination or wind pollination, could be endangered when the population of insect-pollinators is depleted by the use of pesticides.

In the forests of New Brunswick, for example, various pesticides have been sprayed in the past 25 years in efforts to control the spruce budworm, an economically significant pest. Scientists have now investigated the effects of the spraying of Matacil, one of the anti-budworm agents that is least toxic to insect-pollinators. They studied Matacil's effects on insect mortality in a wide variety of wild insect species and on plant fecundity, expressed as the percentage of the total flowers on an individual plant that actually developed fruit and bore seeds. They found that the most pronounced mortality after the spraying of Matacil occurred among the smaller bees and one family of flies, insects that were all important pollinators of numerous species of plants growing beneath the tree canopy of forests. The fecundity of plants in one common indigenous species, the red-osier dogwood, was significantly reduced in the sprayed areas as compared to that of plants in control plots where Matacil was not sprayed. This species is highly dependent on the insect-pollinators most vulnerable to Matacil. The creeping dogwood, a species similar to the red-osier dogwood, but which is pollinated by large bees, such as bumblebees, showed no significant decline in fecundity. Since large bees are not affected by the spraying of Matacil, these results add weight to the argument that spraying where the pollinators are sensitive to the pesticide used decreases plant fecundity.

The question of whether the decrease in plant fecundity caused by the spraying of pesticides actually causes a decline in the overall population of flowering plant species still remains unanswered. Plant species dependent solely on seeds for survival or dispersal are obviously more vulnerable to any decrease in plant fecundity that occurs, whatever its cause. If, on the other hand, vegetative growth and dispersal (by means of shoots or runners) are available as alternative reproductive strategies for a species, then decreases in plant fecundity may be of little consequence. The fecundity effects described here are likely to have the most profound impact on plant species with all four of the following characteristics: a short life span, a narrow geographic range, an incapacity for vegetative propagation, and a dependence on a small number of insect-pollinator species. Perhaps we should give special attention to the conservation of such plant species since they lack key factors in their defenses against the environmental disruption caused by pesticide use.

7. Which of the following best summarizes the main point of the passage?

(A) Species interdependence is a point of weakness for some plants, but is generally beneficial to insects involved in pollination.
(B) Efforts to control the spruce budworm have had deleterious effects on the red-osier dogwood.
(C) The use of pesticides may be endangering certain plant species dependent on insects for pollination.
(D) The spraying of pesticides can reduce the fecundity of a plant species, but probably does not affect its overall population stability.
(E) Plant species lacking key factors in their defenses against human environmental disruption will probably become extinct.

8. According to the author, a flowering plant species whose fecundity has declined due to pesticide spraying may not experience an overall population decline if the plant species can do which of the following?

(A) Reproduce itself by means of shoots and runners.
(B) Survive to the end of the growing season.
(C) Survive in harsh climates.
(D) Respond to the fecundity decline by producing more flowers.
(E) Attract large insects as pollinators.

9. The passage suggests that the lack of an observed decline in the fecundity of the creeping dogwood strengthens the researchers' conclusions regarding pesticide use because the

(A) creeping dogwood is a species that does not resemble other forest plants
(B) creeping dogwood is a species pollinated by a broader range of insect species than are most dogwood species
(C) creeping dogwood grows primarily in regions that were not sprayed with pesticide, and so served as a control for the experiment
(D) creeping dogwood is similar to the red-osier dogwood, but its insect pollinators are known to be insensitive to the pesticide used in the study
(E) geographical range of the creeping dogwood is similar to that of the red-osier dogwood, but the latter species relies less on seeds for reproduction

GO ON TO THE NEXT PAGE.

10. The passage suggests that which of the following is true of the forest regions in New Brunswick sprayed with most anti-budworm pesticides other than Matacil?

(A) The fecundity of some flowering plants in those regions may have decreased to an even greater degree than in the regions where Matacil is used.

(B) Insect mortality in those regions occurs mostly among the larger species of insects, such as bumblebees.

(C) The number of seeds produced by common plant species in those regions is probably comparable to the number produced where Matacil is sprayed.

(D) Many more plant species have become extinct in those regions than in the regions where Matacil is used.

(E) The spruce budworm is under better control in those regions than in the regions where Matacil is sprayed.

11. It can be inferred that which of the following is true of plant fecundity as it is defined in the passage?

(A) A plant's fecundity decreases as the percentage of unpollinated flowers on the plant increases.

(B) A plant's fecundity decreases as the number of flowers produced by the plant decreases.

(C) A plant's fecundity increases as the number of flowers produced by the plant increases.

(D) A plant's fecundity is usually low if the plant relies on a small number of insect species for pollination.

(E) A plant's fecundity is high if the plant can reproduce quickly by means of vegetative growth as well as by the production of seeds.

12. It can be inferred from the passage that which of the following plant species would be LEAST likely to experience a decrease in fecundity as a result of the spraying of a pesticide not directly toxic to plants?

(A) A flowering tree pollinated by only a few insect species

(B) A kind of insect-pollinated vine producing few flowers

(C) A wind-pollinated flowering tree that is short-lived

(D) A flowering shrub pollinated by a large number of insect species

(E) A type of wildflower typically pollinated by larger insects

GO ON TO THE NEXT PAGE.

Bernard Bailyn has recently reinterpreted the early history of the United States by applying new social research findings on the experiences of European
Line migrants. In his reinterpretation, migration becomes the
(5) organizing principle for rewriting the history of preindustrial North America. His approach rests on four separate propositions.

The first of these asserts that residents of early modern England moved regularly about their coun-
(10) tryside; migrating to the New World was simply a "natural spillover." Although at first the colonies held little positive attraction for the English—they would rather have stayed home—by the eighteenth century people increasingly migrated to America because they
(15) regarded it as the land of opportunity. Secondly, Bailyn holds that, contrary to the notion that used to flourish in American history textbooks, there was never a typical New World community. For example, the economic and demographic character of early New England towns
(20) varied considerably.

Bailyn's third proposition suggests two general patterns prevailing among the many thousands of migrants: one group came as indentured servants, another came to acquire land. Surprisingly, Bailyn
(25) suggests that those who recruited indentured servants were the driving forces of transatlantic migration. These colonial entrepreneurs helped determine the social character of people who came to preindustrial North America. At first, thousands of unskilled laborers were recruited;
(30) by the 1730's, however, American employers demanded skilled artisans.

Finally, Bailyn argues that the colonies were a half-civilized hinterland of the European culture system. He is undoubtedly correct to insist that the colonies were
(35) part of an Anglo-American empire. But to divide the empire into English core and colonial periphery, as Bailyn does, devalues the achievements of colonial culture. It is true, as Bailyn claims, that high culture in the colonies never matched that in England. But what
(40) of seventeenth-century New England, where the settlers created effective laws, built a distinguished university, and published books? Bailyn might respond that New England was exceptional. However, the ideas and institutions developed by New England Puritans had power-
(45) ful effects on North American culture.

Although Bailyn goes on to apply his approach to some thousands of indentured servants who migrated just prior to the revolution, he fails to link their experience with the political development of the United States.
(50) Evidence presented in his work suggests how we might make such a connection. These indentured servants were treated as slaves for the period during which they had sold their time to American employers. It is not surprising that as soon as they served their time they passed up
(55) good wages in the cities and headed west to ensure their personal independence by acquiring land. Thus, it is in the west that a peculiarly American political culture began, among colonists who were suspicious of authority and intensely antiaristocratic.

13. Which of the following statements about migrants to colonial North America is supported by information in the passage?

(A) A larger percentage of migrants to colonial North America came as indentured servants than as free agents interested in acquiring land.
(B) Migrants who came to the colonies as indentured servants were more successful at making a livelihood than were farmers and artisans.
(C) Migrants to colonial North America were more successful at acquiring their own land during the eighteenth century than during the seventeenth century.
(D) By the 1730's, migrants already skilled in a trade were in more demand by American employers than were unskilled laborers.
(E) A significant percentage of migrants who came to the colonies to acquire land were forced to work as field hands for prosperous American farmers.

14. The author of the passage states that Bailyn failed to

(A) give sufficient emphasis to the cultural and political interdependence of the colonies and England
(B) describe carefully how migrants of different ethnic backgrounds preserved their culture in the United States
(C) take advantage of social research on the experiences of colonists who migrated to colonial North America specifically to acquire land
(D) relate the experience of the migrants to the political values that eventually shaped the character of the United States
(E) investigate the lives of Europeans before they came to colonial North America to determine more adequately their motivations for migrating

15. Which of the following best summarizes the author's evaluation of Bailyn's fourth proposition?

(A) It is totally implausible.
(B) It is partially correct.
(C) It is highly admirable.
(D) It is controversial though persuasive.
(E) It is intriguing though unsubstantiated.

GO ON TO THE NEXT PAGE.

16. According to the passage, Bailyn and the author agree on which of the following statements about the culture of colonial New England?

(A) High culture in New England never equaled the high culture of England.
(B) The cultural achievements of colonial New England have generally been unrecognized by historians.
(C) The colonists imitated the high culture of England, and did not develop a culture that was uniquely their own.
(D) The southern colonies were greatly influenced by the high culture of New England.
(E) New England communities were able to create laws and build a university, but unable to create anything innovative in the arts.

17. According to the passage, which of the following is true of English migrants to the colonies during the eighteenth century?

(A) Most of them were farmers rather than tradespeople or artisans.
(B) Most of them came because they were unable to find work in England.
(C) They differed from other English people in that they were willing to travel.
(D) They expected that the colonies would offer them increased opportunity.
(E) They were generally not as educated as the people who remained in England.

18. The author of the passage is primarily concerned with

(A) comparing several current interpretations of early American history
(B) suggesting that new social research on migration should lead to revisions in current interpretations of early American history
(C) providing the theoretical framework that is used by most historians in understanding early American history
(D) refuting an argument about early American history that has been proposed by social historians
(E) discussing a reinterpretation of early American history that is based on new social research on migration

STOP

IF YOU FINISH BEFORE TIME IS CALLED, YOU MAY CHECK YOUR WORK ON THIS SECTION ONLY.
DO NOT TURN TO ANY OTHER SECTION IN THE TEST.

Answer Key for Sample Test Section 4

READING COMPREHENSION

1. E	10. A
2. D	11. A
3. B	12. C
4. C	13. D
5. B	14. D
6. D	15. B
7. C	16. A
8. A	17. D
9. D	18. E

Explanatory Material: Reading Comprehension Sample Test Section 4

1. Based on the information in the passage, it would be LEAST likely for which of the following persons to be part of a self-help network?

   (A) The entrepreneur's childhood friend
   (B) The entrepreneur's aunt
   (C) The entrepreneur's religious leader
   (D) The entrepreneur's neighbor
   (E) The entrepreneur's banker

The best answer is E. The passage indicates that minority entrepreneurs who participate in self-help networks "may actually avoid banks" (lines 34-35). Thus it would be unlikely that bankers would be part of an entrepreneur's self-help network. Choices A, B, C, and D can be eliminated because they provide examples of members of primary institutions that, according to the passage, would be likely to make up a self-help network. In lines 19-21, primary institutions are defined as "kinship, peer, and neighborhood or community subgroups."

2. Which of the following illustrates the working of a self-help support network, as such networks are described in the passage?

   (A) A public high school offers courses in bookkeeping and accounting as part of its open-enrollment adult education program.
   (B) The local government in a small city sets up a program that helps teenagers find summer jobs.
   (C) A major commercial bank offers low-interest loans to experienced individuals who hope to establish their own businesses.
   (D) A neighborhood-based fraternal organization develops a program of on-the-job training for its members and their friends.
   (E) A community college offers county residents training programs that can lead to certification in a variety of technical trades.

The best answer is D. In lines 13-14, the passage states that self-help networks "consist of 'primary' institutions, those closest to the individual in shaping his or her behavior and beliefs." Lines 20-21 mention "kinship, peer, and neighborhood or community subgroups" as examples of primary institutions. Only D provides an example of a self-help support network that consists of neighbors and friends and is characterized by the "cooperation of persons united by ties of mutual concern" (lines 16-17). Choices A, B, C, and E can be eliminated because schools, banks, and local governments can be regarded as examples of the "'secondary' institutions" mentioned in line 18.

3. Which of the following can be inferred from the passage about rotating credit associations?

   (A) They were developed exclusively by Chinese immigrants.
   (B) They accounted for a significant portion of the investment capital used by Chinese immigrants in New York in the early twentieth century.
   (C) Third-generation members of an immigrant group who started businesses in the 1920's would have been unlikely to rely on them.
   (D) They were frequently joint endeavors by members of two or three different ethnic groups.
   (E) Recent immigrants still frequently turn to rotating credit associations instead of banks for investment capital.

The best answer is B. Lines 44-47 state that it has been estimated that "40 percent of New York Chinatown firms established during 1900-1950" used rotating credit associations as their "initial sources of capital." Thus, it can be inferred that rotating credit associations provided a significant portion of the investment capital used by early twentieth-century Chinese immigrants. Choice A can be eliminated because the passage, although it mentions rotating credit associations in Chinatown, does not indicate that such associations were developed exclusively by Chinese immigrants. Choices C and E can be eliminated because the third paragraph indicates that rotating credit associations were most likely to be used in the early twentieth century (the opposite of what is stated in C) and that recent immigrants would be unlikely to use them. Choice D can be eliminated because joint endeavors between members of ethnic groups are not mentioned in the passage.

4. The passage best supports which of the following statements?

(A) A minority entrepreneur who had no assistance from family members would not be able to start a business.
(B) Self-help networks have been effective in helping entrepreneurs primarily in the last 50 years.
(C) Minority groups have developed a range of alternatives to standard financing of business ventures.
(D) The financial institutions founded by various ethnic groups owe their success to their unique formal organization.
(E) Successful minority-owned businesses succeed primarily because of the personal strengths of their founders.

The best answer is C. The passage is primarily concerned with discussing the ways in which minority entrepreneurs have obtained investment capital: self-help networks and financial institutions founded by immigrants. These methods are alternatives to such standard methods as borrowing from a non-ethnic commercial institution. Choice A can be eliminated because the passage states that minority entrepreneurs rely on neighborhood and community groups and minority-developed financial institutions as well as on family members to start businesses. Choice B can be eliminated because the passage provides no information about the length of time minority entrepreneurs have relied on self-help networks. Choices D and E can be eliminated because the passage does not discuss forms of organization unique to financial institutions founded by ethnic groups or the personal characteristics of minority entrepreneurs.

5. Which of the following best describes the organization of the second paragraph?

(A) An argument is delineated, followed by a counterargument.
(B) An assertion is made and several examples are provided to illustrate it.
(C) A situation is described and its historical background is then outlined.
(D) An example of a phenomenon is given and is then used as a basis for general conclusions.
(E) A group of parallel incidents is described and the distinctions among the incidents are then clarified.

The best answer is B. The second paragraph begins by asserting that minority businesses have primarily relied on self-help networks for investment capital. The rest of the paragraph provides several examples of ways in which minority entrepreneurs have depended on family and community resources for financing businesses. Thus, the second paragraph makes an assertion and then provides

examples to illustrate it. Choice A can be eliminated because the assertion made in the second paragraph is not countered in any way. Choice C can be eliminated because the historical background of self-help networks is not outlined. Choices D and E can be eliminated because the paragraph neither draws general conclusions from the examples it provides nor describes parallel incidents.

6. According to the passage, once a minority-owned business is established, self-help networks contribute which of the following to that business?

(A) Information regrading possible expansion of the business into nearby communities
(B) Encouragement of a business climate that is nearly free of direct competition
(C) Opportunities for the business owner to reinvest profits in other minority-owned businesses
(D) Contact with people who are likely to be customers of the new business
(E) Contact with minority entrepreneurs who are members of other ethnic groups

The best answer is D. The first paragraph states that self-help networks can assist in maintaining minority businesses by providing "clientele from the owner's ethnic group" (lines 10-11). Choices A, B, C, and E can be eliminated because they describe kinds of business assistance that are not discussed in the passage.

7. Which of the following best summarizes the main point of the passage?

(A) Species interdependence is a point of weakness for some plants, but is generally beneficial to insects involved in pollinations.
(B) Efforts to control the spruce budworm have had deleterious effects on the red-osier dogwood.
(C) The use of pesticides may be endangering certain plant species dependent on insects for pollination.
(D) The spraying of pesticides can reduce the fecundity of a plant species, but probably does not affect its overall population stability.
(E) Plant species lacking key factors in their defenses against human environmental disruption will probably become extinct.

The best answer is C. The first paragraph states that plants dependent on insect-pollinators could be endangered if pesticides toxic to such insect-pollinators are used. The second paragraph provides an example of a flowering plant whose fecundity was reduced in areas sprayed with a pesticide toxic to that plant's insect-pollinators. The third paragraph discusses factors that make the overall population of a plant species vulnerable to the use of pesticides. Thus, the passage is primarily concerned with pointing out that pesticides may be endangering flowering plants dependent on insect-pollinators. Choice B accurately describes the effect that the anti-budworm agent Matacil had on the fecundity of the red-osier dogwood, but this detail is presented to support the main point of the passage. Choices A, D, and E do not accurately reflect the content of the passage.

8. According to the author, a flowering plant species whose fecundity has declined due to pesticide spraying may not experience an overall population decline if the plant species can do which of the following?

    (A) Reproduce itself by means of shoots and runners.
    (B) Survive to the end of the growing season.
    (C) Survive in harsh climates.
    (D) Respond to the fecundity decline by producing more flowers.
    (E) Attract large insects as pollinators.

The best answer is A. Lines 42-46 state that if "vegetative growth and dispersal (by means of shoots or runners) are available as alternative strategies for a species," a species' overall population will not necessarily be affected by decreases in fecundity. Although E might seem to be a promising way for a plant species to reverse a decline in fecundity, the author gives no indication that such a survival strategy is possible. Likewise, there is no information in the passage to support B, C, or D.

9. The passage suggests that the lack of an observed decline in the fecundity of the creeping dogwood strengthens the researchers' conclusions regarding pesticide use because the

    (A) creeping dogwood is a species that does not resemble other forest plants
    (B) creeping dogwood is a species pollinated by a broader range of insect species than are most dogwood species
    (C) creeping dogwood grows primarily in regions that were not sprayed with pesticide, and so served as a control for the experiment
    (D) creeping dogwood is similar to the red-osier dogwood, but its insect pollinators are known to be insensitive to the pesticide used in the study
    (E) geographical range of the creeping dogwood is similar to that of the red-osier dogwood, but the latter species relies less on seeds for reproduction

To answer this question, you must first identify the researchers' conclusions regarding pesticide use. At the end of the second paragraph the author cites the researchers' argument that "spraying where the pollinators are sensitive to the pesticide used decreases plant fecundity" (lines 34-35). Researchers based this conclusion in part on the fact that spraying with Matacil had no effect on the fecundity of the creeping dogwood, which is pollinated by large bees that are

"not affected by the spraying of Matacil" (lines 32-33), while the spraying of Matacil did cause a decrease in the fecundity of the red-osier dogwood, which is said to be similar to the creeping dogwood (lines 29-30) but is "highly dependent on the insect-pollinators most vulnerable to Matacil" (lines 28-29). This critical distinction is summarized in D, the best answer to the question.

10. The passage suggests that which of the following is true of the forest regions in New Brunswick sprayed with most anti-budworm pesticides other than Matacil?

    (A) The fecundity of some flowering plants in those regions may have decreased to an even greater degree than in the regions where Matacil is used.
    (B) Insect mortality in those regions occurs mostly among the larger species of insects, such as bumblebees.
    (C) The number of seeds produced by common plant species in those regions is probably comparable to the number produced where Matacil is sprayed.
    (D) Many more plant species have become extinct in those regions than in the regions where Matacil is used.
    (E) The spruce budworm is under better control in those regions than in the regions where Matacil is sprayed.

The best answer is A. Lines 13-14 state that Matacil is "one of the anti-budworm agents that is least toxic to insect-pollinators." However, the second paragraph indicates that Matacil's effects on certain insect pollinators were significant enough to cause declines in the fecundity of some flowering plants. A pesticide more toxic than Matacil would be likely to cause higher mortality rates for certain insect-pollinators; these higher mortality rates would in turn be likely to cause greater decreases in the fecundity of some flowering plants. Choice D is incorrect because the passage does not mention the extinction of plant species resulting from Matacil. Choice E is incorrect because the passage does not discuss the relative effectiveness of Matacil and other anti-budworm agents in controlling the spruce budworm. There is no information in the passage to support choices B and C.

11. It can be inferred that which of the following is true of plant fecundity as it is defined in the passage?

    (A) A plant's fecundity decreases as the percentage of unpollinated flowers on the plant increases.
    (B) A plant's fecundity decreases as the number of flowers produced by the plant decreases.
    (C) A plant's fecundity increases as the number of flowers produced by the plant increases.
    (D) A plant's fecundity is usually low if the plant relies on a small number of insect species for pollination.
    (E) A plant's fecundity is high if the plant can reproduce quickly by means of vegetative growth as well as by the production of seeds.

The best answer is A. Lines 17-19 define plant fecundity as the "percentage of the total flowers on an individual plant that actually developed fruit and bore seeds." The fact that an increased mortality rate among insect-pollinators is linked in the passage to a decrease in the fecundity of certain flowering plants suggests that this decrease is due to the failure of some flowers to become pollinated. Choices B and C are incorrect because the passage indicates that plant fecundity increases or decreases in relation to the percentage of a plant's flowers that bear seeds, not in relation to the number of flowers a plant produces. Choices D and E can be eliminated because the passage does not state that there is a relationship between plant fecundity and the number of insect species that pollinate the plant or the ways in which the plant reproduces.

12. It can be inferred from the passage that which of the following plant species would be LEAST likely to experience a decrease in fecundity as a result of the spraying of a pesticide not directly toxic to plants?

   (A) A flowering tree pollinated by only a few insect species
   (B) A kind of insect-pollinated vine producing few flowers
   (C) A wind-pollinated flowering tree that is short-lived
   (D) A flowering shrub pollinated by a large number of insect species
   (E) A type of wildflower typically pollinated by larger insects

Of the plant species described in the answer choices, the species described in C would be the least likely to experience a decrease in fecundity as a result of the spraying of a pesticide not directly toxic to plants. Lines 4-8 state that plant species that rely on insect pollination rather than wind pollination could experience a decrease in population when pesticides deplete the population of insect-pollinators. Thus, it can be inferred that flowering plant species relying on wind pollination would be unlikely to experience such a decrease when pesticides are used to control insect-pollinators. The plant species described in choices A, B, D, and E may experience decreases in fecundity to various degrees if the pesticides used increase mortality among the insect-pollinators on which the plant species rely.

13. Which of the following statements about migrants to colonial North America is supported by information in the passage?

   (A) A larger percentage of migrants to colonial North America came as indentured servants than as free agents interested in acquiring land.
   (B) Migrants who came to the colonies as indentured servants were more successful at making a livelihood than were farmers and artisans.
   (C) Migrants to colonial North America were more successful at acquiring their own land during the eighteenth century than during the seventeenth century.
   (D) By the 1730's, migrants already skilled in a trade were in more demand by American employers than were unskilled laborers.
   (E) A significant percentage of migrants who came to the colonies to acquire land were forced to work as field hands for prosperous American farmers.

The best answer is D. The third paragraph states that colonial entrepreneurs originally recruited thousands of unskilled laborers to migrate to North America, but that "by the 1730's . . . American employers demanded skilled artisans" (lines 30-31). Thus, by the 1730's skilled migrants were in greater demand by American employers than were unskilled laborers. Choice A can be eliminated because the passage provides no numbers or relative percentages of indentured migrants versus free migrants. Choices B and C can be eliminated because no information is provided on migrants' success at making a livelihood or at becoming landowners. Choice E can be eliminated because the passage does not mention that any migrants were forced to work as fieldhands for prosperous farmers.

14. The author of the passage states that Bailyn failed to

   (A) give sufficient emphasis to the cultural and political interdependence of the colonies and England
   (B) describe carefully how migrants of different ethnic backgrounds preserved their culture in the United States
   (C) take advantage of social research on the experiences of colonists who migrated to colonial North America specifically to acquire land
   (D) relate the experience of the migrants to the political values that eventually shaped the character of the United States
   (E) investigate the lives of Europeans before they came to colonial North America to determine more adequately their motivations for migrating

The best answer is D. In lines 48-49, the author of the passage states that Bailyn fails to link the experience of indentured servants with the political development of the United States, and, in lines 57-59, the author suggests that such colonists, who were "suspicious of authority and intensely antiaristocratic," initiated "a peculiarly American political culture." Thus, the author charges Bailyn with failing to relate the experience of migrants to political values that would shape the character of the United States. Choices A and B can be eliminated because the passage mentions neither political interdependence with England nor the preservation of different ethnic cultures. Choice C is incorrect because Bailyn is described as having employed such research (lines 1-4). None of the statements in the passage supports choice E.

15. Which of the following best summarizes the author's evaluation of Bailyn's fourth proposition?

    (A) It is totally implausible.
    (B) It is partially correct.
    (C) It is highly admirable.
    (D) It is controversial though persuasive.
    (E) It is intriguing though unsubstantiated.

The best answer is B. In the fourth paragraph, the author describes Bailyn's fourth proposition and characterizes one aspect of that proposition as "undoubtedly correct" (line 34) and another as "true" (line 38). However, in lines 35-45, the author criticizes Bailyn for devaluing the achievements of colonial culture and supports that criticism by offering examples of those achievements. Choice A is incorrect because the author agrees in part with Bailyn's fourth proposition. Choices C and D are incorrect because the author criticizes aspects of that proposition, and thus would not evaluate it as either "highly admirable" or "persuasive." Choice E can be eliminated because the author does not evaluate the proposition in terms of its degree of interest.

16. According to the passage, Bailyn and the author agree on which of the following statements about the culture of colonial New England?

    (A) High culture in New England never equaled the high culture of England.
    (B) The cultural achievements of colonial New England have generally been unrecognized by historians.
    (C) The colonists imitated the high culture of England, and did not develop a culture that was uniquely their own.
    (D) The southern colonies were greatly influenced by the high culture of New England.
    (E) New England communities were able to create laws and build a university, but unable to create anything innovative in the arts.

The best answer is A. In lines 38-39, the author of the passage states, "It is true, as Bailyn claims, that high culture in the colonies never matched that in England." Since New England was a part of the American colonies, Bailyn and the author of the passage agree that the culture of New England did not match that of England. Choice B can be eliminated because the author does not discuss historians' general recognition of such cultural achievements. Choice C is incorrect because the author of the passage does not indicate whether Puritan culture was imitative. Choice D can be eliminated because the passage does not discuss the southern colonies as a separate region. Choice E is incorrect because neither Bailyn's nor the author's evaluation of arts in colonial New England is mentioned.

17. According to the passage, which of the following is true of English migrants to the colonies during the eighteenth century?

    (A) Most of them were farmers rather than tradespeople or artisans.
    (B) Most of them came because they were unable to find work in England.
    (C) They differed from other English people in that they were willing to travel.
    (D) They expected that the colonies would offer them increased opportunity.
    (E) They were generally not as educated as the people who remained in England.

The best answer is D. In the discussion of English migrants in the second paragraph, the author of the passage asserts that "by the eighteenth century people increasingly migrated to America because they regarded it as the land of opportunity" (lines 11-15). Choices A and B are incorrect because the specific occupations of these migrants are not mentioned, nor is the employment rate in England mentioned. Choice C is not supported because the passage introduces in lines 8-10 Bailyn's proposition that "residents of early modern England moved regularly about their countryside." Choice E can be eliminated because the passage does not mention the education of either migrants or nonmigrants.

18. The author of the passage is primarily concerned with

(A) comparing several current interpretations of early American history

(B) suggesting that new social research on migration should lead to revisions in current interpretations of early American history

(C) providing the theoretical framework that is used by most historians in understanding early American history

(D) refuting an argument about early American history that has been proposed by social historians

(E) discussing a reinterpretation of early American history that is based on new social research on migration

The best answer is E. Lines 1-4 state that "Bailyn has recently reinterpreted the early history of the United States by applying new social research findings on the experiences of European migrants." The rest of the passage is a consideration, including both description and evaluation, of the four propositions upon which Bailyn's approach rests. Choices A, C, and D are not supported because the passage deals with only one historian's interpretation or theory; in addition, with regard to choice D, the passage takes issue with only one of Bailyn's four propositions. Choice B is incorrect because the passage primarily evaluates Bailyn's work rather than recommending how social research on migration should be utilized.

READING COMPREHENSION SAMPLE TEST SECTION 5

Time — 25 minutes

18 Questions

Directions: Each passage in this group is followed by questions based on its content. After reading a passage, choose the best answer to each question and fill in the corresponding oval on the answer sheet. Answer all questions following a passage on the basis of what is stated or implied in that passage.

Many United States companies have, unfortunately, made the search for legal protection from import competition into a major line of work. Since 1980 the
Line
(5) United States International Trade Commission (ITC) has received about 280 complaints alleging damage from imports that benefit from subsidies by foreign governments. Another 340 charge that foreign companies "dumped" their products in the United States at "less than fair value." Even when no unfair practices
(10) are alleged, the simple claim that an industry has been injured by imports is sufficient grounds to seek relief.

Contrary to the general impression, this quest for import relief has hurt more companies than it has helped. As corporations begin to function globally, they
(15) develop an intricate web of marketing, production, and research relationships. The complexity of these relationships makes it unlikely that a system of import relief laws will meet the strategic needs of all the units under the same parent company.

(20) Internationalization increases the danger that foreign companies will use import relief laws against the very companies the laws were designed to protect. Suppose a United States-owned company establishes an overseas plant to manufacture a product while its competitor
(25) makes the same product in the United States. If the competitor can prove injury from the imports—and that the United States company received a subsidy from a foreign government to build its plant abroad—the United States company's products will be uncompeti-
(30) tive in the United States, since they would be subject to duties.

Perhaps the most brazen case occurred when the ITC investigated allegations that Canadian companies were injuring the United States salt industry by dumping
(35) rock salt, used to de-ice roads. The bizarre aspect of the complaint was that a foreign conglomerate with United States operations was crying for help against a United States company with foreign operations. The "United States" company claiming injury was a subsidiary of a
(40) Dutch conglomerate, while the "Canadian" companies included a subsidiary of a Chicago firm that was the second-largest domestic producer of rock salt.

1. The passage is chiefly concerned with

(A) arguing against the increased internationalization of United States corporations
(B) warning that the application of laws affecting trade frequently has unintended consequences
(C) demonstrating that foreign-based firms receive more subsidies from their governments than United States firms receive from the United States government
(D) advocating the use of trade restrictions for "dumped" products but not for other imports
(E) recommending a uniform method for handling claims of unfair trade practices

2. It can be inferred from the passage that the minimal basis for a complaint to the International Trade Commission is which of the following?

(A) A foreign competitor has received a subsidy from a foreign government.
(B) A foreign competitor has substantially increased the volume of products shipped to the United States.
(C) A foreign competitor is selling products in the United States at less than fair market value.
(D) The company requesting import relief has been injured by the sale of imports in the United States.
(E) The company requesting import relief has been barred from exporting products to the country of its foreign competitor.

GO ON TO THE NEXT PAGE.

3. The last paragraph performs which of the following functions in the passage?

(A) It summarizes the discussion thus far and suggests additional areas for research.
(B) It presents a recommendation based on the evidence presented earlier.
(C) It discusses an exceptional case in which the results expected by the author of the passage were not obtained.
(D) It introduces an additional area of concern not mentioned earlier.
(E) It cites a specific case that illustrates a problem presented more generally in the previous paragraph.

4. The passage warns of which of the following dangers?

(A) Companies in the United States may receive no protection from imports unless they actively seek protection from import competition.
(B) Companies that seek legal protection from import competition may incur legal costs that far exceed any possible gain.
(C) Companies that are United States-owned but operate internationally may not be eligible for protection from import competition under the laws of the countries in which their plants operate.
(D) Companies that are not United States-owned may seek legal protection from import competition under United States import relief laws.
(E) Companies in the United States that import raw materials may have to pay duties on those materials.

5. The passage suggests that which of the following is most likely to be true of United States trade laws?

(A) They will eliminate the practice of "dumping" products in the United States.
(B) They will enable manufacturers in the United States to compete more profitably outside the United States.
(C) They will affect United States trade with Canada more negatively than trade with other nations.
(D) Those that help one unit within a parent company will not necessarily help other units in the company.
(E) Those that are applied to international companies will accomplish their intended result.

6. It can be inferred from the passage that the author believes which of the following about the complaint mentioned in the last paragraph?

(A) The ITC acted unfairly toward the complainant in its investigation.
(B) The complaint violated the intent of import relief laws.
(C) The response of the ITC to the complaint provided suitable relief from unfair trade practices to the complainant.
(D) The ITC did not have access to appropriate information concerning the case.
(E) Each of the companies involved in the complaint acted in its own best interest.

GO ON TO THE NEXT PAGE.

At the end of the nineteenth century, a rising interest in Native American customs and an increasing desire to understand Native American culture prompted ethnologists to begin recording the life stories of Native Americans. Ethnologists had a distinct reason for wanting to hear the stories: they were after linguistic or anthropological data that would supplement their own field observations, and they believed that the personal stories, even of a single individual, could increase their (10) understanding of the cultures that they had been observing from without. In addition many ethnologists at the turn of the century believed that Native American manners and customs were rapidly disappearing, and that it was important to preserve for posterity as (15) much information as could be adequately recorded before the cultures disappeared forever.

There were, however, arguments against this method as a way of acquiring accurate and complete information. Franz Boas, for example, described autobiogra- (20) phies as being "of limited value, and useful chiefly for the study of the perversion of truth by memory," while Paul Radin contended that investigators rarely spent enough time with the tribes they were observing, and inevitably derived results too tinged by the investi- (25) gator's own emotional tone to be reliable.

Even more importantly, as these life stories moved from the traditional oral mode to recorded written form, much was inevitably lost. Editors often decided what elements were significant to the field research on a (30) given tribe. Native Americans recognized that the essence of their lives could not be communicated in English and that events that they thought significant were often deemed unimportant by their interviewers. Indeed, the very act of telling their stories could force (35) Native American narrators to distort their cultures, as taboos had to be broken to speak the names of dead relatives crucial to their family stories.

Despite all of this, autobiography remains a useful tool for ethnological research: such personal reminis- (40) cences and impressions, incomplete as they may be, are likely to throw more light on the working of the mind and emotions than any amount of speculation from an ethnologist or ethnological theorist from another culture.

7. Which of the following best describes the organization of the passage?

(A) The historical backgrounds of two currently used research methods are chronicled.
(B) The validity of the data collected by using two different research methods is compared.
(C) The usefulness of a research method is questioned and then a new method is proposed.
(D) The use of a research method is described and the limitations of the results obtained are discussed.
(E) A research method is evaluated and the changes necessary for its adaptation to other subject areas are discussed.

8. Which of the following is most similar to the actions of nineteenth-century ethnologists in their editing of the life stories of Native Americans?

(A) A witness in a jury trial invokes the Fifth Amendment in order to avoid relating personally incriminating evidence.
(B) A stockbroker refuses to divulge the source of her information on the possible future increase in a stock's value.
(C) A sports announcer describes the action in a team sport with which he is unfamiliar.
(D) A chef purposely excludes the special ingredient from the recipe of his prizewinning dessert.
(E) A politician fails to mention in a campaign speech the similarities in the positions held by her opponent for political office and by herself.

9. According to the passage, collecting life stories can be a useful methodology because

(A) life stories provide deeper insights into a culture than the hypothesizing of academics who are not members of that culture
(B) life stories can be collected easily and they are not subject to invalid interpretations
(C) ethnologists have a limited number of research methods from which to choose
(D) life stories make it easy to distinguish between the important and unimportant features of a culture
(E) the collection of life stories does not require a culturally knowledgeable investigator

GO ON TO THE NEXT PAGE.

10. Information in the passage suggests that which of the following may be a possible way to eliminate bias in the editing of life stories?

(A) Basing all inferences made about the culture on an ethnological theory
(B) Eliminating all of the emotion-laden information reported by the informant
(C) Translating the informant's words into the researcher's language
(D) Reducing the number of questions and carefully specifying the content of the questions that the investigator can ask the informant
(E) Reporting all of the information that the informant provides regardless of the investigator's personal opinion about its intrinsic value

11. The primary purpose of the passage as a whole is to

(A) question an explanation
(B) correct a misconception
(C) critique a methodology
(D) discredit an idea
(E) clarify an ambiguity

12. It can be inferred from the passage that a characteristic of the ethnological research on Native Americans conducted during the nineteenth century was the use of which of the following?

(A) Investigators familiar with the culture under study
(B) A language other than the informant's for recording life stories
(C) Life stories as the ethnologist's primary source of information
(D) Complete transcriptions of informants' descriptions of tribal beliefs
(E) Stringent guidelines for the preservation of cultural data

GO ON TO THE NEXT PAGE.

All of the cells in a particular plant start out with the same complement of genes. How then can these cells differentiate and form structures as different as roots, stems, leaves, and fruits? The answer is that only a small subset of the genes in a particular kind of cell are expressed, or turned on, at a given time. This is accomplished by a complex system of chemical messengers that in plants include hormones and other regulatory molecules. Five major hormones have been identified: auxin, abscisic acid, cytokinin, ethylene, and gibberellin. Studies of plants have now identified a new class of regulatory molecules called oligosaccharins.

Unlike the oligosaccharins, the five well-known plant hormones are pleiotropic rather than specific, that is, each has more than one effect on the growth and development of plants. The five have so many simultaneous effects that they are not very useful in artificially controlling the growth of crops. Auxin, for instance, stimulates the rate of cell elongation, causes shoots to grow up and roots to grow down, and inhibits the growth of lateral shoots. Auxin also causes the plant to develop a vascular system, to form lateral roots, and to produce ethylene.

The pleiotropy of the five well-studied plant hormones is somewhat analogous to that of certain hormones in animals. For example, hormones from the hypothalamus in the brain stimulate the anterior lobe of the pituitary gland to synthesize and release many different hormones, one of which stimulates the release of hormones from the adrenal cortex. These hormones have specific effects on target organs all over the body. One hormone stimulates the thyroid gland, for example, another the ovarian follicle cells, and so forth. In other words, there is a hierarchy of hormones.

Such a hierarchy may also exist in plants. Oligosaccharins are fragments of the cell wall released by enzymes: different enzymes release different oligosaccharins. There are indications that pleiotropic plant hormones may actually function by activating the enzymes that release these other, more specific chemical messengers from the cell wall.

13. According to the passage, the five well-known plant hormones are not useful in controlling the growth of crops because

(A) it is not known exactly what functions the hormones perform
(B) each hormone has various effects on plants
(C) none of the hormones can function without the others
(D) each hormone has different effects on different kinds of plants
(E) each hormone works on only a small subset of a cell's genes at any particular time

14. The passage suggests that the place of hypothalamic hormones in the hormonal hierarchies of animals is similar to the place of which of the following in plants?

(A) Plant cell walls
(B) The complement of genes in each plant cell
(C) A subset of a plant cell's gene complement
(D) The five major hormones
(E) The oligosaccharins

15. The passage suggests that which of the following is a function likely to be performed by an oligosaccharin?

(A) To stimulate a particular plant cell to become part of a plant's root system
(B) To stimulate the walls of a particular cell to produce other oligosaccharins
(C) To activate enzymes that release specific chemical messengers from plant cell walls
(D) To duplicate the gene complement in a particular plant cell
(E) To produce multiple effects on a particular subsystem of plant cells

GO ON TO THE NEXT PAGE.

16. The author mentions specific effects that auxin has on plant development in order to illustrate the

(A) point that some of the effects of plant hormones can be harmful
(B) way in which hormones are produced by plants
(C) hierarchical nature of the functioning of plant hormones
(D) differences among the best-known plant hormones
(E) concept of pleiotropy as it is exhibited by plant hormones

17. According to the passage, which of the following best describes a function performed by oligosaccharins?

(A) Regulating the daily functioning of a plant's cells
(B) Interacting with one another to produce different chemicals
(C) Releasing specific chemical messengers from a plant's cell walls
(D) Producing the hormones that cause plant cells to differentiate to perform different functions
(E) Influencing the development of a plant's cells by controlling the expression of the cells' genes

18. The passage suggests that, unlike the pleiotropic hormones, oligosaccharins could be used effectively to

(A) trace the passage of chemicals through the walls of cells
(B) pinpoint functions of other plant hormones
(C) artificially control specific aspects of the development of crops
(D) alter the complement of genes in the cells of plants
(E) alter the effects of the five major hormones on plant development

STOP

IF YOU FINISH BEFORE TIME IS CALLED, YOU MAY CHECK YOUR WORK ON THIS SECTION ONLY. DO NOT TURN TO ANY OTHER SECTION IN THE TEST.

Answer Key for Sample Test Section 5

READING COMPREHENSION

1.	B	10.	E
2.	D	11.	C
3.	E	12.	B
4.	D	13.	B
5.	D	14.	D
6.	B	15.	A
7.	D	16.	E
8.	C	17.	E
9.	A	18.	C

Explanatory Material: Reading Comprehension Sample Test Section 5

1. The passage is chiefly concerned with

   (A) arguing against the increased internationalization of United States corporations
   (B) warning that the application of laws affecting trade frequently has unintended consequences
   (C) demonstrating that foreign-based firms receive more subsidies from their governments than United States firms receive from the United States government
   (D) advocating the use of trade restrictions for "dumped" products but not for other imports
   (E) recommending a uniform method for handling claims of unfair trade practices

The best answer is B. In the first sentence of the passage, the author characterizes the preoccupation of many United States companies with the search for legal protection from import competition as unfortunate. Then, in lines 12-14, the author explains that the "quest for import relief has hurt more companies than it has helped." The third paragraph discusses one situation in which United States companies might experience such injury — when import relief laws are used against foreign subsidiaries of United States companies — and the last paragraph provides a specific example of this situation. Thus, it can be inferred that the author's primary concern is to warn about possible unintended negative consequences of applying trade laws.

2. It can be inferred from the passage that the minimal basis for a complaint to the International Trade Commission is which of the following?

   (A) A foreign competitor has received a subsidy from a foreign government.
   (B) A foreign competitor has substantially increased the volume of products shipped to the United States.
   (C) A foreign competitor is selling products in the United States at less than fair market value.
   (D) The company requesting import relief has been injured by the sale of imports in the United States.
   (E) The company requesting import relief has been barred from exporting products to the country of its foreign competitor.

The best answer is D. Bases for complaints to the International Trade Commission are discussed in the first paragraph. In lines 3-9 the author mentions the two specific kinds of complaints referred to in choices A and C (about imports benefiting from subsidies provided by foreign governments and about "dumping"), but goes on to conclude the paragraph with the comment that "the simple claim that an industry has been injured by imports is sufficient grounds to seek relief." That a "simple claim" is "sufficient grounds to seek relief" suggests that the minimal basis for a complaint to the ITC is injury from the sale of imports in the United States, as stated in choice D. The situations in choices B and E are not discussed in the passage.

3. The last paragraph performs which of the following functions in the passage?

   (A) It summarizes the discussion thus far and suggests additional areas for research.
   (B) It presents a recommendation based on the evidence presented earlier.
   (C) It discusses an exceptional case in which the results expected by the author of the passage were not obtained.
   (D) It introduces an additional area of concern not mentioned earlier.
   (E) It cites a specific case that illustrates a problem presented more generally in the previous paragraph.

The best answer is E. The last paragraph discusses a specific case in which a United States subsidiary of a Dutch conglomerate accused a Canadian branch of a United States company of "dumping" rock salt in the United States market. This incident is cited as "the most brazen case" (line 32) of the problem stated in lines 20-22 of the previous paragraph: the use of import relief laws by foreign companies against U.S. companies. No recommendations, discussion of unexpected results, or additional areas of research or concern are mentioned in the paragraph. Thus, choices A, B, C, and D are not correct.

4. The passage warns of which of the following dangers?

(A) Companies in the United States may receive no protection from imports unless they actively seek protection from import competition.
(B) Companies that seek legal protection from import competition may incur legal costs that far exceed any possible gain.
(C) Companies that are United States-owned but operate internationally may not be eligible for protection from import competition under the laws of the countries in which their plants operate.
(D) Companies that are not United States-owned may seek legal protection from import competition under United States import relief laws.
(E) Companies in the United States that import raw materials may have to pay duties on those materials.

The best answer is D. The "danger" of import relief laws is stated in lines 20-22: "that foreign companies will use import relief laws against the very companies the laws were designed to protect." Import relief laws are the legal protection referred to in choice D. The passage does not mention the situations described in choices A, B, C, and E.

5. The passage suggests that which of the following is most likely to be true of United States trade laws?

(A) They will eliminate the practice of "dumping" products in the United States.
(B) They will enable manufacturers in the United States to compete more profitably outside the United States.
(C) They will affect United States trade with Canada more negatively than trade with other nations.
(D) Those that help one unit within a parent company will not necessarily help other units in the company.
(E) Those that are applied to international companies will accomplish their intended result.

The best answer is D. In lines 16-19 the author warns that it is "unlikely that a system of import relief laws will meet the strategic needs of all the units under the same parent company." Thus, it can be inferred that the United States trade laws dealing with import relief will not necessarily help all units of a company, as stated in choice D. There is no indication in the passage that United States trade laws are expected to eliminate dumping, as is stated in choice A. Choice E is directly contradicted by the sentence in lines 20-22. There is no discussion in the passage of the situations mentioned in choices B and C.

6. It can be inferred from the passage that the author believes which of the following about the complaint mentioned in the last paragraph?

(A) The ITC acted unfairly toward the complainant in its investigation.
(B) The complaint violated the intent of import relief laws.
(C) The response of the ITC to the complaint provided suitable relief from unfair trade practices to the complainant.
(D) The ITC did not have access to appropriate information concerning the case.
(E) Each of the companies involved in the complaint acted in its own best interest.

The best answer is B. In lines 35-38 the author states that "The bizarre aspect of the complaint was that a foreign conglomerate…was crying for help against a United States company…." It can be inferred from lines 20-22 that import relief laws were designed to protect United States companies from foreign competition. Thus, the lodging of a complaint by a foreign conglomerate against a United States company violated the intent of the laws.

7. Which of the following best describes the organization of the passage?

(A) The historical backgrounds of two currently used research methods are chronicled.
(B) The validity of the data collected by using two different research methods is compared.
(C) The usefulness of a research method is questioned and then a new method is proposed.
(D) The use of a research method is described and the limitations of the results obtained are discussed.
(E) A research method is evaluated and the changes necessary for its adaptation to other subject areas are discussed.

The best answer is D. The first paragraph of the passage identifies a research method (recording life stories) and explains the method's uses. The second and third paragraphs explain limitations of the method's results. The final paragraph explains why the research method is useful despite its limitations. Choices A, B, and C are incorrect because only one research method is discussed, not two. Choice E can be eliminated because the passage does not discuss changing the method or adapting it to any other subject area.

8. Which of the following is most similar to the actions of nineteenth-century ethnologists in their editing of the life stories of Native Americans?

    (A) A witness in a jury trial invokes the Fifth Amendment in order to avoid relating personally incriminating evidence.
    (B) A stockbroker refuses to divulge the source of her information on the possible future increase in a stock's value.
    (C) A sports announcer describes the action in a team sport with which he is unfamiliar.
    (D) A chef purposely excludes the special ingredient from the recipe of his prizewinning dessert.
    (E) A politician fails to mention in a campaign speech the similarities in the positions held by her opponent for political office and by herself.

The best answer is C. Lines 22-23 suggest that ethnologists "rarely spent enough time with the tribes they were observing." Ethnologists who did not spend enough time with tribes they were observing were unlikely to be sufficiently familiar with the culture and customs of those tribes. Such ethnologists nevertheless attempted to describe the lives of tribal members. This attempt can be seen as analogous to the announcer's attempt to describe the actions in a team sport with which he is unfamiliar. Choices A, B, and D can be eliminated because the passage does not suggest that ethnologists deliberately withheld information. Choice E is incorrect because the passage does not mention any common ideas or positions held by both the ethnologists and the Native Americans.

9. According to the passage, collecting life stories can be a useful methodology because

    (A) life stories provide deeper insights into a culture than the hypothesizing of academics who are not members of that culture
    (B) life stories can be collected easily and they are not subject to invalid interpretations
    (C) ethnologists have a limited number of research methods from which to choose
    (D) life stories make it easy to distinguish between the important and unimportant features of a culture
    (E) the collection of life stories does not require a culturally knowledgeable investigator

The best answer is A, which paraphrases the passage's assertion that life stories "are likely to throw more light on the working of the mind and emotions than any amount of speculation from an ethnologist or ethnological theorist from another culture" (lines 40-44). Choice B is incorrect because the passage does not assess the difficulty of collecting life stories, and because the second paragraph discusses ways in which life stories became distorted. Choice C is incorrect because the passage does not specify how many research methods are available to ethnologists. Choice D can be eliminated because the third paragraph mentions distortion arising from ethnologists' failure to recognize significant events in life stories. Choice E is incorrect because the second paragraph suggests that life stories would be more useful if collected by culturally knowledgeable investigators.

10. Information in the passage suggests that which of the following may be a possible way to eliminate bias in the editing of life stories?

    (A) Basing all inferences made about the culture on an ethnological theory
    (B) Eliminating all of the emotion-laden information reported by the informant
    (C) Translating the informant's words into the researcher's language
    (D) Reducing the number of questions and carefully specifying the content of the questions that the investigator can ask the informant
    (E) Reporting all of the information that the informant provides regardless of the investigator's personal opinion about its intrinsic value

The best answer is E. In the third paragraph, the passage asserts that editors made their own decisions about which elements of the Native Americans' life stories were important. It can therefore be inferred from the passage that reporting all of an informant's information would help eliminate bias, because editing had involved subjective judgments about the intrinsic value of the information. Choices A, C, and D can be eliminated because the passage does not attribute bias to failures in adhering to ethnological theory, to translations into the researchers' language, or to problems in the numbers and content of questions posed. Choice B is not supported because the second paragraph criticizes the emotion of the reporter, not that of the informant, for introducing bias.

11. The primary purpose of the passage as a whole is to

    (A) question an explanation
    (B) correct a misconception
    (C) critique a methodology
    (D) discredit an idea
    (E) clarify an ambiguity

The best answer is C. The passage describes a methodology, explains the methodology's intended uses, criticizes the methodology's accurateness and comprehensiveness, and reaffirms the methodology's usefulness despite its limitations. Thus, the primary purpose of the passage is to evaluate or critique a methodology.

12. It can be inferred from the passage that a characteristic of the ethnological research on Native Americans conducted during the nineteenth century was the use of which of the following?

   (A) Investigators familiar with the culture under study
   (B) A language other than the informant's for recording life stories
   (C) Life stories as the ethnologist's primary source of information
   (D) Complete transcriptions of informants' descriptions of tribal beliefs
   (E) Stringent guidelines for the preservation of cultural data

The best answer is B. Lines 30-32 state that "Native Americans recognized that the essence of their lives could not be communicated in English," that is, in the language of the ethnologists recording the life stories. Since this statement supports the idea that "much was inevitably lost," it can be inferred that the informants used a language other than that used to record their life stories. Choice A is incorrect because, in the second paragraph, the investigators are criticized for lacking familiarity with the cultures they studied. Choice C is incorrect because ethnologists recorded life stories to "supplement their own field observations" (lines 7-8). Choice D is incorrect because the passage indicates that life stories were edited; choice E is incorrect because the passage provides no information about guidelines used by the researchers.

13. According to the passage, the five well-known plant hormones are not useful in controlling the growth of crops because

   (A) it is not known exactly what functions the hormones perform
   (B) each hormone has various effects on plants
   (C) none of the hormones can function without the others
   (D) each hormone has different effects on different kinds of plants
   (E) each hormone works on only a small subset of a cell's genes at any particular time

The best answer is B. The passage states that each of the five well-known plant hormones "has more than one effect on the growth and development of plants" (lines 15-16) and that, for this reason "they are not very useful in artificially controlling the growth of crops" (lines 17-18). Choice A is not correct because lines 18-23 describe some of the functions performed by the hormone auxin. Choice E is consistent with information presented in the passage, but by emphasizing the specific effect hormones have at the cellular level rather than the multiplicity of effects they have on the entire plant, E fails to provide the reason stated in the passage that the five hormones are not useful in controlling the growth of crops. Neither C nor D is suggested by anything in the passage.

14. The passage suggests that the place of hypothalamic hormones in the hormonal hierarchies of animals is similar to the place of which of the following in plants?

   (A) Plant cell walls
   (B) The complement of genes in each plant cell
   (C) A subset of a plant cell's gene complement
   (D) The five major hormones
   (E) The oligosaccharins

The best answer is D. According to the passage, "The pleiotropy of the five well-studied plant hormones is somewhat analogous to that of certain hormones in animals" (lines 24-26). The example given involves certain hypothalamic hormones that "stimulate the anterior lobe of the pituitary gland to synthesize and release many different hormones, one of which stimulates the release of hormones from the adrenal cortex" (lines 27-30). These hormones in turn "have specific effects on target organs all over the body" (line 31). This "hierarchy of hormones," as the author calls it, "may also exist in plants" (line 35), where the five pleiotropic hormones may "function by activating the enzymes that release . . . more specific chemical messengers" (lines 39-41). Thus, hypothalamic hormones in animals and the five major hormones in plants occupy a similar place in the respective organisms' hormonal hierarchy.

15. The passage suggests that which of the following is a function likely to be performed by an oligosaccharin?

   (A) To stimulate a particular plant cell to become part of a plant's root system
   (B) To stimulate the walls of a particular cell to produce other oligosaccharins
   (C) To activate enzymes that release specific chemical messengers from plant cell walls
   (D) To duplicate the gene complement in a particular plant cell
   (E) To produce multiple effects on a particular subsystem of plant cells

The best answer is A. The last paragraph characterizes oligosaccharins as "specific chemical messengers" (lines 40-41). The passage indicates that these chemical messengers are "specific" in that, unlike the pleiotropic hormones, they are likely to have particular effects on particular plant cells. Choice A is correct because it is the only answer choice that describes an effect on a specific aspect of plant growth and development: stimulating a particular plant cell to become part of a plant's root system. Choices B and C are incorrect because the last paragraph indicates that enzymes activate the release of oligosaccharins. Choice D is incorrect because, although oligosaccharins do affect the activity of the gene complement of a particular cell, they do not duplicate that complement. Choice E is incorrect because the second paragraph indicates that an oligosaccharin has a specific effect rather than multiple effects on plant cells.

16. The author mentions specific effects that auxin has on plant development in order to illustrate the

   (A) point that some of the effects of plant hormones can be harmful
   (B) way in which hormones are produced by plants
   (C) hierarchical nature of the functioning of plant hormones
   (D) differences among the best-known plant hormones
   (E) concept of pleiotropy as it is exhibited by plant hormones

The best answer is E. The second paragraph states that the five major plant hormones, including auxin, are pleiotropic and indicates that each pleiotropic hormone has "more than one effect on the growth and development of plants" (lines 15-16). The effects of auxin are then listed in detail to provide an example of the different effects a pleiotropic hormone can have on a plant. Thus, the specific effects of auxin are mentioned to illustrate the concept of pleiotropy as it is exhibited by plant hormones. Choice C can be eliminated because the specific effects that auxin has on plant development are not discussed in the context of the hierarchy of hormones. Choices A, B, and D are incorrect because they cite topics that are not discussed in the passage.

17. According to the passage, which of the following best describes a function performed by oligosaccharins?

   (A) Regulating the daily functioning of a plant's cells
   (B) Interacting with one another to produce different chemicals
   (C) Releasing specific chemical messengers from a plant's cell walls
   (D) Producing the hormones that cause plant cells to differentiate to perform different functions
   (E) Influencing the development of a plant's cells by controlling the expression of the cells' genes

The best answer is E. The first paragraph states that plant cells "differentiate and form structures" (line 3) when a "complex system of chemical messengers" (line 7) activates a "small subset of the genes in a particular kind of cell" (lines 5-6). In lines 38-41, the author elaborates on the hormonal system in plants by indicating that the pleiotropic plant hormones activate enzymes, which in turn release oligosaccharins — the "more specific chemical messengers" (lines 40-41). The second paragraph indicates these specific chemical messengers have specific effects on plant development. Thus, the passage indicates that it is the oligosaccharins that directly influence the development of a plant cell by controlling the expression of a plant cell's genes. Choices C and D are incorrect because the oligosaccharins are themselves specific chemical messengers and are not said to produce any hormones. The passage provides no information to support A or B.

18. The passage suggests that, unlike the pleiotropic hormones, oligosaccharins could be used effectively to

   (A) trace the passage of chemicals through the walls of cells
   (B) pinpoint functions of other plant hormones
   (C) artificially control specific aspects of the development of crops
   (D) alter the complement of genes in the cells of plants
   (E) alter the effects of the five major hormones on plant development

The best answer is C. Lines 16-18 state that because each pleiotropic hormone has so many different effects on a plant, pleiotropic hormones "are not very useful in artificially controlling the growth of crops" (lines 17-18). In contrast, the passage indicates that oligosaccharins have specific effects on the growth and development of plants. Thus, in comparison to the pleiotropic hormones, oligosaccharins could potentially be effective in artificially controlling specific aspects of crop development. Choices A, B, D, and E can be eliminated because they describe functions that are not attributed in the passage either to the pleiotropic hormones or to oligosaccharins.

6 Critical Reasoning

In these questions you are to analyze the situation on which each question is based, and then select the answer choice that is the most appropriate response to the question. No specialized knowledge of any particular field is required for answering the questions, and no knowledge of the terminology and of the conventions of formal logic is presupposed. The sample Critical Reasoning test sections that begin on page 259 provide good illustrations of the variety of topics that may be covered, of the kinds of questions that may be asked, and of the level of analysis that will generally be required.

Test-Taking Strategies for Critical Reasoning

1. The set of statements on which a question is based should be read very carefully with close attention to such matters as (1) what is put forward as factual information, (2) what is not said but necessarily follows from what is said, (3) what is claimed to follow from facts that have been put forward, and (4) how well substantiated are any claims to the effect that a particular conclusion follows from the facts that have been put forward. In reading arguments, it is important to attend to the soundness of the reasoning employed; it is not necessary to make a judgment of the actual truth of anything that is put forward as factual information.

2. If a question is based on an argument, be careful to identify clearly which part of the argument is its conclusion. The conclusion does not necessarily come at the end of the text of the argument; it may come somewhere in the middle, or it may even come at the beginning. Be alert to clues in the text that one of the statements made is not simply asserted but is said to follow logically from another statement or other statements in the text.

3. It is important to determine exactly what the question is asking; in fact, you might find it helpful to read the question first, before reading the material on which it is based. For example, an argument may appear to have an obvious flaw, and you may expect to be asked to detect that flaw; but the question may actually ask you to recognize the one among the answer choices that does NOT describe a weakness of the argument.

4. Read all the answer choices carefully. You should not assume that a given answer is the best answer without first reading all the choices.

When you take the sample test sections, use the answer spaces on page 257 to mark your answers.

Answer Spaces for Critical Reasoning Sample Test Sections

Sample Test Section 1

1	Ⓐ Ⓑ Ⓒ Ⓓ Ⓔ	5	Ⓐ Ⓑ Ⓒ Ⓓ Ⓔ	9	Ⓐ Ⓑ Ⓒ Ⓓ Ⓔ	13	Ⓐ Ⓑ Ⓒ Ⓓ Ⓔ
2	Ⓐ Ⓑ Ⓒ Ⓓ Ⓔ	6	Ⓐ Ⓑ Ⓒ Ⓓ Ⓔ	10	Ⓐ Ⓑ Ⓒ Ⓓ Ⓔ	14	Ⓐ Ⓑ Ⓒ Ⓓ Ⓔ
3	Ⓐ Ⓑ Ⓒ Ⓓ Ⓔ	7	Ⓐ Ⓑ Ⓒ Ⓓ Ⓔ	11	Ⓐ Ⓑ Ⓒ Ⓓ Ⓔ	15	Ⓐ Ⓑ Ⓒ Ⓓ Ⓔ
4	Ⓐ Ⓑ Ⓒ Ⓓ Ⓔ	8	Ⓐ Ⓑ Ⓒ Ⓓ Ⓔ	12	Ⓐ Ⓑ Ⓒ Ⓓ Ⓔ	16	Ⓐ Ⓑ Ⓒ Ⓓ Ⓔ

Sample Test Section 2

1	Ⓐ Ⓑ Ⓒ Ⓓ Ⓔ	5	Ⓐ Ⓑ Ⓒ Ⓓ Ⓔ	9	Ⓐ Ⓑ Ⓒ Ⓓ Ⓔ	13	Ⓐ Ⓑ Ⓒ Ⓓ Ⓔ
2	Ⓐ Ⓑ Ⓒ Ⓓ Ⓔ	6	Ⓐ Ⓑ Ⓒ Ⓓ Ⓔ	10	Ⓐ Ⓑ Ⓒ Ⓓ Ⓔ	14	Ⓐ Ⓑ Ⓒ Ⓓ Ⓔ
3	Ⓐ Ⓑ Ⓒ Ⓓ Ⓔ	7	Ⓐ Ⓑ Ⓒ Ⓓ Ⓔ	11	Ⓐ Ⓑ Ⓒ Ⓓ Ⓔ	15	Ⓐ Ⓑ Ⓒ Ⓓ Ⓔ
4	Ⓐ Ⓑ Ⓒ Ⓓ Ⓔ	8	Ⓐ Ⓑ Ⓒ Ⓓ Ⓔ	12	Ⓐ Ⓑ Ⓒ Ⓓ Ⓔ	16	Ⓐ Ⓑ Ⓒ Ⓓ Ⓔ

Sample Test Section 3

1	Ⓐ Ⓑ Ⓒ Ⓓ Ⓔ	5	Ⓐ Ⓑ Ⓒ Ⓓ Ⓔ	9	Ⓐ Ⓑ Ⓒ Ⓓ Ⓔ	13	Ⓐ Ⓑ Ⓒ Ⓓ Ⓔ
2	Ⓐ Ⓑ Ⓒ Ⓓ Ⓔ	6	Ⓐ Ⓑ Ⓒ Ⓓ Ⓔ	10	Ⓐ Ⓑ Ⓒ Ⓓ Ⓔ	14	Ⓐ Ⓑ Ⓒ Ⓓ Ⓔ
3	Ⓐ Ⓑ Ⓒ Ⓓ Ⓔ	7	Ⓐ Ⓑ Ⓒ Ⓓ Ⓔ	11	Ⓐ Ⓑ Ⓒ Ⓓ Ⓔ	15	Ⓐ Ⓑ Ⓒ Ⓓ Ⓔ
4	Ⓐ Ⓑ Ⓒ Ⓓ Ⓔ	8	Ⓐ Ⓑ Ⓒ Ⓓ Ⓔ	12	Ⓐ Ⓑ Ⓒ Ⓓ Ⓔ	16	Ⓐ Ⓑ Ⓒ Ⓓ Ⓔ

Sample Test Section 4

1	Ⓐ Ⓑ Ⓒ Ⓓ Ⓔ	5	Ⓐ Ⓑ Ⓒ Ⓓ Ⓔ	9	Ⓐ Ⓑ Ⓒ Ⓓ Ⓔ	13	Ⓐ Ⓑ Ⓒ Ⓓ Ⓔ
2	Ⓐ Ⓑ Ⓒ Ⓓ Ⓔ	6	Ⓐ Ⓑ Ⓒ Ⓓ Ⓔ	10	Ⓐ Ⓑ Ⓒ Ⓓ Ⓔ	14	Ⓐ Ⓑ Ⓒ Ⓓ Ⓔ
3	Ⓐ Ⓑ Ⓒ Ⓓ Ⓔ	7	Ⓐ Ⓑ Ⓒ Ⓓ Ⓔ	11	Ⓐ Ⓑ Ⓒ Ⓓ Ⓔ	15	Ⓐ Ⓑ Ⓒ Ⓓ Ⓔ
4	Ⓐ Ⓑ Ⓒ Ⓓ Ⓔ	8	Ⓐ Ⓑ Ⓒ Ⓓ Ⓔ	12	Ⓐ Ⓑ Ⓒ Ⓓ Ⓔ	16	Ⓐ Ⓑ Ⓒ Ⓓ Ⓔ

Sample Test Section 5

1	Ⓐ Ⓑ Ⓒ Ⓓ Ⓔ	5	Ⓐ Ⓑ Ⓒ Ⓓ Ⓔ	9	Ⓐ Ⓑ Ⓒ Ⓓ Ⓔ	13	Ⓐ Ⓑ Ⓒ Ⓓ Ⓔ
2	Ⓐ Ⓑ Ⓒ Ⓓ Ⓔ	6	Ⓐ Ⓑ Ⓒ Ⓓ Ⓔ	10	Ⓐ Ⓑ Ⓒ Ⓓ Ⓔ	14	Ⓐ Ⓑ Ⓒ Ⓓ Ⓔ
3	Ⓐ Ⓑ Ⓒ Ⓓ Ⓔ	7	Ⓐ Ⓑ Ⓒ Ⓓ Ⓔ	11	Ⓐ Ⓑ Ⓒ Ⓓ Ⓔ	15	Ⓐ Ⓑ Ⓒ Ⓓ Ⓔ
4	Ⓐ Ⓑ Ⓒ Ⓓ Ⓔ	8	Ⓐ Ⓑ Ⓒ Ⓓ Ⓔ	12	Ⓐ Ⓑ Ⓒ Ⓓ Ⓔ	16	Ⓐ Ⓑ Ⓒ Ⓓ Ⓔ

CRITICAL REASONING SAMPLE TEST SECTION 1

Time — 25 minutes

16 Questions

<u>Directions:</u> For each question in this section, select the best of the answer choices given.

1. Which of the following best completes the passage below?

   In a survey of job applicants, two-fifths admitted to being at least a little dishonest. However, the survey may underestimate the proportion of job applicants who are dishonest, because -------.

   (A) some dishonest people taking the survey might have claimed on the survey to be honest
   (B) some generally honest people taking the survey might have claimed on the survey to be dishonest
   (C) some people who claimed on the survey to be at least a little dishonest may be very dishonest
   (D) some people who claimed on the survey to be dishonest may have been answering honestly
   (E) some people who are not job applicants are probably at least a little dishonest

Questions 2-3 are based on the following.

The average life expectancy for the United States population as a whole is 73.9 years, but children born in Hawaii will live an average of 77 years, and those born in Louisiana, 71.7 years. If a newlywed couple from Louisiana were to begin their family in Hawaii, therefore, their children would be expected to live longer than would be the case if the family remained in Louisiana.

2. Which of the following, if true, would most seriously weaken the conclusion drawn in the passage?

   (A) Insurance company statisticians do not believe that moving to Hawaii will significantly lengthen the average Louisianian's life.
   (B) The governor of Louisiana has falsely alleged that statistics for his state are inaccurate.
   (C) The longevity ascribed to Hawaii's current population is attributable mostly to genetically determined factors.
   (D) Thirty percent of all Louisianians can expect to live longer than 77 years.
   (E) Most of the Hawaiian Islands have levels of air pollution well below the national average for the United States.

3. Which of the following statements, if true, would most significantly strengthen the conclusion drawn in the passage?

   (A) As population density increases in Hawaii, life expectancy figures for that state are likely to be revised downward.
   (B) Environmental factors tending to favor longevity are abundant in Hawaii and less numerous in Louisiana.
   (C) Twenty-five percent of all Louisianians who move to Hawaii live longer than 77 years.
   (D) Over the last decade, average life expectancy has risen at a higher rate for Louisianians than for Hawaiians.
   (E) Studies show that the average life expectancy for Hawaiians who move permanently to Louisiana is roughly equal to that of Hawaiians who remain in Hawaii.

GO ON TO THE NEXT PAGE.

4. Insurance Company X is considering issuing a new policy to cover services required by elderly people who suffer from diseases that afflict the elderly. Premiums for the policy must be low enough to attract customers. Therefore, Company X is concerned that the income from the policies would not be sufficient to pay for the claims that would be made.

Which of the following strategies would be most likely to minimize Company X's losses on the policies?

(A) Attracting middle-aged customers unlikely to submit claims for benefits for many years
(B) Insuring only those individuals who did not suffer any serious diseases as children
(C) Including a greater number of services in the policy than are included in other policies of lower cost
(D) Insuring only those individuals who were rejected by other companies for similar policies
(E) Insuring only those individuals who are wealthy enough to pay for the medical services

5. A program instituted in a particular state allows parents to prepay their children's future college tuition at current rates. The program then pays the tuition annually for the child at any of the state's public colleges in which the child enrolls. Parents should participate in the program as a means of decreasing the cost for their children's college education.

Which of the following, if true, is the most appropriate reason for parents not to participate in the program?

(A) The parents are unsure about which public college in the state the child will attend.
(B) The amount of money accumulated by putting the prepayment funds in an interest-bearing account today will be greater than the total cost of tuition for any of the public colleges when the child enrolls.
(C) The annual cost of tuition at the state's public colleges is expected to increase at a faster rate than the annual increase in the cost of living.
(D) Some of the state's public colleges are contemplating large increases in tuition next year.
(E) The prepayment plan would not cover the cost of room and board at any of the state's public colleges.

6. Company Alpha buys free-travel coupons from people who are awarded the coupons by Bravo Airlines for flying frequently on Bravo airplanes. The coupons are sold to people who pay less for the coupons than they would pay by purchasing tickets from Bravo. This marketing of coupons results in lost revenue for Bravo.

To discourage the buying and selling of free-travel coupons, it would be best for Bravo Airlines to restrict the

(A) number of coupons that a person can be awarded in a particular year
(B) use of the coupons to those who were awarded the coupons and members of their immediate families
(C) days that the coupons can be used to Monday through Friday
(D) amount of time that the coupons can be used after they are issued
(E) number of routes on which travelers can use the coupons

7. The ice on the front windshield of the car had formed when moisture condensed during the night. The ice melted quickly after the car was warmed up the next morning because the defrosting vent, which blows only on the front windshield, was turned on full force.

Which of the following, if true, most seriously jeopardizes the validity of the explanation for the speed with which the ice melted?

(A) The side windows had no ice condensation on them.
(B) Even though no attempt was made to defrost the back window, the ice there melted at the same rate as did the ice on the front windshield.
(C) The speed at which ice on a window melts increases as the temperature of the air blown on the window increases.
(D) The warm air from the defrosting vent for the front windshield cools rapidly as it dissipates throughout the rest of the car.
(E) The defrosting vent operates efficiently even when the heater, which blows warm air toward the feet or faces of the driver and passengers, is on.

GO ON TO THE NEXT PAGE.

8. To prevent some conflicts of interest, Congress could prohibit high-level government officials from accepting positions as lobbyists for three years after such officials leave government service. One such official concluded, however, that such a prohibition would be unfortunate because it would prevent high-level government officials from earning a livelihood for three years.

The official's conclusion logically depends on which of the following assumptions?

(A) Laws should not restrict the behavior of former government officials.
(B) Lobbyists are typically people who have previously been high-level government officials.
(C) Low-level government officials do not often become lobbyists when they leave government service.
(D) High-level government officials who leave government service are capable of earning a livelihood only as lobbyists.
(E) High-level government officials who leave government service are currently permitted to act as lobbyists for only three years.

9. A conservation group in the United States is trying to change the long-standing image of bats as frightening creatures. The group contends that bats are feared and persecuted solely because they are shy animals that are active only at night.

Which of the following, if true, would cast the most serious doubt on the accuracy of the group's contention?

(A) Bats are steadily losing natural roosting places such as caves and hollow trees and are thus turning to more developed areas for roosting.
(B) Bats are the chief consumers of nocturnal insects and thus can help make their hunting territory more pleasant for humans.
(C) Bats are regarded as frightening creatures not only in the United States but also in Europe, Africa, and South America.
(D) Raccoons and owls are shy and active only at night; yet they are not generally feared and persecuted.
(E) People know more about the behavior of other greatly feared animal species, such as lions, alligators, and snakes, than they do about the behavior of bats.

10. Meteorite explosions in the Earth's atmosphere as large as the one that destroyed forests in Siberia, with approximately the force of a twelve-megaton nuclear blast, occur about once a century.

The response of highly automated systems controlled by complex computer programs to unexpected circumstances is unpredictable.

Which of the following conclusions can most properly be drawn, if the statements above are true, about a highly automated nuclear-missile defense system controlled by a complex computer program?

(A) Within a century after its construction, the system would react inappropriately and might accidentally start a nuclear war.
(B) The system would be destroyed if an explosion of a large meteorite occurred in the Earth's atmosphere.
(C) It would be impossible for the system to distinguish the explosion of a large meteorite from the explosion of a nuclear weapon.
(D) Whether the system would respond inappropriately to the explosion of a large meteorite would depend on the location of the blast.
(E) It is not certain what the system's response to the explosion of a large meteorite would be, if its designers did not plan for such a contingency.

GO ON TO THE NEXT PAGE.

Questions 11-12 are based on the following.

The fewer restrictions there are on the advertising of legal services, the more lawyers there are who advertise their services, and the lawyers who advertise a specific service usually charge less for that service than lawyers who do not advertise. Therefore, if the state removes any of its current restrictions, such as the one against advertisements that do not specify fee arrangements, overall consumer legal costs will be lower than if the state retains its current restrictions.

11. If the statements above are true, which of the following must be true?

(A) Some lawyers who now advertise will charge more for specific services if they do not have to specify fee arrangements in the advertisements.
(B) More consumers will use legal services if there are fewer restrictions on the advertising of legal services.
(C) If the restriction against advertisements that do not specify fee arrangements is removed, more lawyers will advertise their services.
(D) If more lawyers advertise lower prices for specific services, some lawyers who do not advertise will also charge less than they currently charge for those services.
(E) If the only restrictions on the advertising of legal services were those that apply to every type of advertising, most lawyers would advertise their services.

12. Which of the following, if true, would most seriously weaken the argument concerning overall consumer legal costs?

(A) The state has recently removed some other restrictions that had limited the advertising of legal services.
(B) The state is unlikely to remove all of the restrictions that apply solely to the advertising of legal services.
(C) Lawyers who do not advertise generally provide legal services of the same quality as those provided by lawyers who do advertise.
(D) Most lawyers who now specify fee arrangements in their advertisements would continue to do so even if the specification were not required.
(E) Most lawyers who advertise specific services do not lower their fees for those services when they begin to advertise.

13. Defense Department analysts worry that the ability of the United States to wage a prolonged war would be seriously endangered if the machine-tool manufacturing base shrinks further. Before the Defense Department publicly connected this security issue with the import quota issue, however, the machine-tool industry raised the national security issue in its petition for import quotas.

Which of the following, if true, contributes most to an explanation of the machine-tool industry's raising the issue above regarding national security?

(A) When the aircraft industries retooled, they provided a large amount of work for tool builders.
(B) The Defense Department is only marginally concerned with the effects of foreign competition on the machine-tool industry.
(C) The machine-tool industry encountered difficulty in obtaining governmental protection against imports on grounds other than defense.
(D) A few weapons important for defense consist of parts that do not require extensive machining.
(E) Several federal government programs have been designed which will enable domestic machine-tool manufacturing firms to compete successfully with foreign toolmakers.

GO ON TO THE NEXT PAGE.

14. Opponents of laws that require automobile drivers and passengers to wear seat belts argue that in a free society people have the right to take risks as long as the people do not harm others as a result of taking the risks. As a result, they conclude that it should be each person's decision whether or not to wear a seat belt.

Which of the following, if true, most seriously weakens the conclusion drawn above?

(A) Many new cars are built with seat belts that automatically fasten when someone sits in the front seat.

(B) Automobile insurance rates for all automobile owners are higher because of the need to pay for the increased injuries or deaths of people not wearing seat belts.

(C) Passengers in airplanes are required to wear seat belts during takeoffs and landings.

(D) The rate of automobile fatalities in states that do not have mandatory seat-belt laws is greater than the rate of fatalities in states that do have such laws.

(E) In automobile accidents, a greater number of passengers who do not wear seat belts are injured than are passengers who do wear seat belts.

15. The cost of producing radios in Country Q is ten percent less than the cost of producing radios in Country Y. Even after transportation fees and tariff charges are added, it is still cheaper for a company to import radios from Country Q to Country Y than to produce radios in Country Y.

The statements above, if true, best support which of the following assertions?

(A) Labor costs in Country Q are ten percent below those in Country Y.

(B) Importing radios from Country Q to Country Y will eliminate ten percent of the manufacturing jobs in Country Y.

(C) The tariff on a radio imported from Country Q to Country Y is less than ten percent of the cost of manufacturing the radio in Country Y.

(D) The fee for transporting a radio from Country Q to Country Y is more than ten percent of the cost of manufacturing the radio in Country Q.

(E) It takes ten percent less time to manufacture a radio in Country Q than it does in Country Y.

16. During the Second World War, about 375,000 civilians died in the United States and about 408,000 members of the United States armed forces died overseas. On the basis of those figures, it can be concluded that it was not much more dangerous to be overseas in the armed forces during the Second World War than it was to stay at home as a civilian.

Which of the following would reveal most clearly the absurdity of the conclusion drawn above?

(A) Counting deaths among members of the armed forces who served in the United States in addition to deaths among members of the armed forces serving overseas

(B) Expressing the difference between the numbers of deaths among civilians and members of the armed forces as a percentage of the total number of deaths

(C) Separating deaths caused by accidents during service in the armed forces from deaths caused by combat injuries

(D) Comparing death rates per thousand members of each group rather than comparing total numbers of deaths

(E) Comparing deaths caused by accidents in the United States to deaths caused by combat in the armed forces

STOP

IF YOU FINISH BEFORE TIME IS CALLED, YOU MAY CHECK YOUR WORK ON THIS SECTION ONLY. DO NOT TURN TO ANY OTHER SECTION IN THE TEST.

Answer Key for Sample Test Section 1

CRITICAL REASONING

1.	A	9.	D
2.	C	10.	E
3.	B	11.	C
4.	A	12.	E
5.	B	13.	C
6.	B	14.	B
7.	B	15.	C
8.	D	16.	D

Explanatory Material: Critical Reasoning

The following discussion of Critical Reasoning is intended to illustrate the variety of ways Critical Reasoning questions may be approached, and to give you an indication of the degree of precision and depth of reasoning that solving these problems will typically require. The particular questions in the sample test sections in this chapter are generally representative of the kinds of questions you will encounter in this section of the GMAT. Remember that the subject matter of a particular question is less important than the reasoning task you are asked to perform.

Sample Test Section 1

1. Which of the following best completes the passage below?

    In a survey of job applicants, two-fifths admitted to being at least a little dishonest. However, the survey may underestimate the proportion of job applicants who are dishonest, because -----.

    (A) some dishonest people taking the survey might have claimed on the survey to be honest
    (B) some generally honest people taking the survey might have claimed on the survey to be dishonest
    (C) some people who claimed on the survey to be at least a little dishonest may be very dishonest
    (D) some people who claimed on the survey to be dishonest may have been answering honestly
    (E) some people who are not job applicants are probably at least a little dishonest

If applicants who are in fact dishonest claimed to be honest, the survey results would show a smaller proportion of dishonest applicants than actually exists. Therefore, A is the best answer.

Choice B is inappropriate because generally honest applicants who claimed to be dishonest could contribute to the overestimation, but not to the underestimation, of dishonest applicants. Choice D is inappropriate because applicants who admitted their dishonesty would not contribute to an underestimation of the proportion of dishonest applicants. Choices C and E are inappropriate because the argument is concerned neither with degrees of dishonesty nor with the honesty of nonapplicants.

Questions 2-3 are based on the following.

The average life expectancy for the United States population as a whole is 73.9 years, but children born in Hawaii will live an average of 77 years, and those born in Louisiana, 71.7 years. If a newlywed couple from Louisiana were to begin their family in Hawaii, therefore, their children would be expected to live longer than would be the case if the family remained in Louisiana.

2. Which of the following, if true, would most seriously weaken the conclusion drawn in the passage?

    (A) Insurance company statisticians do not believe that moving to Hawaii will significantly lengthen the average Louisianian's life.
    (B) The governor of Louisiana has falsely alleged that statistics for his state are inaccurate.
    (C) The longevity ascribed to Hawaii's current population is attributable mostly to genetically determined factors.
    (D) Thirty percent of all Louisianians can expect to live longer than 77 years.
    (E) Most of the Hawaiian Islands have levels of air pollution well below the national average for the United States.

Choice C suggests that a significant proportion of Hawaii's population is genetically predisposed to be long-lived. Since Louisianians are not necessarily so predisposed, and since the Louisianians' children will acquire their genetic characteristics from their parents, not from their birthplace, choice C presents a reason to doubt that Hawaiian-born children of native Louisianians will have an increased life expectancy. Therefore, C is the best answer.

Because the conclusion concerns people born in Hawaii, not the average Louisianian, A does not weaken the conclusion. Because the governor's allegation is false (choice B), it cannot affect the conclusion. Choice D fails to weaken the conclusion because it is consistent with the information given and the conclusion about life expectancy. By suggesting that Hawaii's environment is in one respect particularly healthy, E supports the conclusion.

3. **Which of the following statements, if true, would most significantly strengthen the conclusion drawn in the passage?**

   (A) As population density increases in Hawaii, life expectancy figures for that state are likely to be revised downward.
   (B) Environmental factors tending to favor longevity are abundant in Hawaii and less numerous in Louisiana.
   (C) Twenty-five percent of all Louisianians who move to Hawaii live longer than 77 years.
   (D) Over the last decade, average life expectancy has risen at a higher rate for Louisianians than for Hawaiians.
   (E) Studies show that the average life expectancy for Hawaiians who move permanently to Louisiana is roughly equal to that of Hawaiians who remain in Hawaii.

If B is true, the greater abundance of longevity-promoting environmental factors it mentions is probably at least partly responsible for the higher life expectancy in Hawaii. Children born in Hawaii benefit from these factors from birth, and thus Louisianians who have children in Hawaii increase their children's chances of living longer. Therefore, B is the best answer.

If life expectancy in Hawaii is likely to be falling, as A says, the argument is weakened rather than strengthened. Choices C and E, in the absence of other relevant information, have no bearing on the conclusion; thus, C and E are inappropriate. Choice D is irrelevant, because the information it mentions about rates would already have been incorporated into the statistics cited in the passage.

4. **Insurance Company X is considering issuing a new policy to cover services required by elderly people who suffer from diseases that afflict the elderly. Premiums for the policy must be low enough to attract customers. Therefore, Company X is concerned that the income from the policies would not be sufficient to pay for the claims that would be made.**

   Which of the following strategies would be most likely to minimize Company X's losses on the policies?

   (A) Attracting middle-aged customers unlikely to submit claims for benefits for many years
   (B) Insuring only those individuals who did not suffer any serious diseases as children
   (C) Including a greater number of services in the policy than are included in other policies of lower cost
   (D) Insuring only those individuals who were rejected by other companies for similar policies
   (E) Insuring only those individuals who are wealthy enough to pay for the medical services

Insurance companies can improve the ratio of revenues to claims paid, thus minimizing losses, if they insure as many people belonging to low-risk groups as they can. Because the strategy described in A adds a low-risk group to the pool of policyholders, A is the best answer.

Choice B is irrelevant, since no link is established between childhood diseases and diseases affecting the elderly. Choice C is inappropriate, since increasing the number of services covered is unlikely to minimize losses. Choice D is inappropriate, since it would increase the likelihood that claims against the policy will be made. Because policyholders will file claims against the policy for services covered rather than pay for the cost of the services themselves, E is irrelevant.

5. **A program instituted in a particular state allows parents to prepay their children's future college tuition at current rates. The program then pays the tuition annually for the child at any of the state's public colleges in which the child enrolls. Parents should participate in the program as a means of decreasing the cost for their children's college education.**

   Which of the following, if true, is the most appropriate reason for parents <u>not</u> to participate in the program?

   (A) The parents are unsure about which public college in the state the child will attend.
   (B) The amount of money accumulated by putting the prepayment funds in an interest-bearing account today will be greater than the total cost of tuition for any of the public colleges when the child enrolls.
   (C) The annual cost of tuition at the state's public colleges is expected to increase at a faster rate than the annual increase in the cost of living.
   (D) Some of the state's public colleges are contemplating large increases in tuition next year.
   (E) The prepayment plan would not cover the cost of room and board at any of the state's public colleges.

The passage recommends that parents participate in a tuition prepayment program as a means of decreasing the cost of their children's future college education. If B were true, placing the funds in an interest-bearing account would be more cost-effective than participating in the prepayment program. Therefore B would be a reason for *not* participating and is the best answer.

Neither A nor E is clearly relevant to deciding whether to participate. Since the program applies to whatever public college the child might choose to attend, contingency A is covered by the plan. Regardless of whether the parents participate, the expenses E mentions would not be included in the cost of tuition. Choices C and D, by stating that tuition will increase, provide support for participating in the program.

6. Company Alpha buys free-travel coupons from people who are awarded the coupons by Bravo Airlines for flying frequently on Bravo airplanes. The coupons are sold to people who pay less for the coupons than they would pay by purchasing tickets from Bravo. This marketing of coupons results in lost revenue for Bravo.

To discourage the buying and selling of free-travel coupons, it would be best for Bravo Airlines to restrict the

(A) number of coupons that a person can be awarded in a particular year
(B) use of the coupons to those who were awarded the coupons and members of their immediate families
(C) days that the coupons can be used to Monday through Friday
(D) amount of time that the coupons can be used after they are issued
(E) number of routes on which travelers can use the coupons

Restricting use of the coupons to the immediate families of those awarded them, as B suggests, would make the coupons valueless for anyone else, so that marketing the coupons would no longer be possible. The coupons, however, would still allow the people to whom Bravo gives them to enjoy free travel. Thus, awarding coupons would remain a strong incentive to frequent travel on Bravo. Therefore, B is the best answer.

Choice A, conversely, would do nothing to reduce the resale value of the coupons. Choices C, D, and E all not only fail to prevent Alpha's coupon sales from competing with Bravo's own ticket sales, but also potentially reduce the usefulness of the coupons to the people to whom they are awarded.

7. The ice on the front windshield of the car had formed when moisture condensed during the night. The ice melted quickly after the car was warmed up the next morning because the defrosting vent, which blows only on the front windshield, was turned on full force.

Which of the following, if true, most seriously jeopardizes the validity of the explanation for the speed with which the ice melted?

(A) The side windows had no ice condensation on them.
(B) Even though no attempt was made to defrost the back window, the ice there melted at the same rate as did the ice on the front windshield.
(C) The speed at which ice on a window melts increases as the temperature of the air blown on the window increases.
(D) The warm air from the defrosting vent for the front windshield cools rapidly as it dissipates throughout the rest of the car.
(E) The defrosting vent operates efficiently even when the heater, which blows warm air toward the feet or faces of the driver and passengers, is on.

The speed with which the ice on the windshield melted is attributed to the air blowing full force from the defrosting vent onto the front windshield. This explanation is undermined if, as B states, no attempt was made to defrost the back window and the ice on the back window melted as quickly as did the ice on the windshield. Therefore, B is the best answer.

In the absence of other information, the lack of ice condensation on the side windows that is mentioned in A is irrelevant to the validity of the explanation. Choice C might support the explanation, since the air from the defrosting vent was warm. Neither D nor E gives a reason to doubt that air from the vent caused the ice's melting, and thus neither jeopardizes the explanation's validity.

8. To prevent some conflicts of interest, Congress could prohibit high-level government officials from accepting positions as lobbyists for three years after such officials leave government service. One such official concluded, however, that such a prohibition would be unfortunate because it would prevent high-level government officials from earning a livelihood for three years.

The official's conclusion logically depends on which of the following assumptions?

(A) Laws should not restrict the behavior of former government officials.

(B) Lobbyists are typically people who have previously been high-level government officials.

(C) Low-level government officials do not often become lobbyists when they leave government service.

(D) High-level government officials who leave government service are capable of earning a livelihood only as lobbyists.

(E) High-level government officials who leave government service are currently permitted to act as lobbyists for only three years.

The official argues that prohibiting high-level government officials from accepting positions as lobbyists for three years would prevent the officials from earning a livelihood for that period. This reasoning tacitly excludes the possibility of such officials earning a living through work other than lobbying. Therefore, D, which expresses this tacit assumption, is the best answer.

The official's argument does not depend on assumption A, B, C, or E, since the argument would not be invalidated if some restrictions on the behavior of government officials were desirable (A), or if lobbyists were not typically former high-level government officials (B), or if former low-level government officials did often become lobbyists (C), or if former high-level government officials could act as lobbyists indefinitely (E).

9. A conservation group in the United States is trying to change the long-standing image of bats as frightening creatures. The group contends that bats are feared and persecuted solely because they are shy animals that are active only at night.

Which of the following, if true, would cast the most serious doubt on the accuracy of the group's contention?

(A) Bats are steadily losing natural roosting places such as caves and hollow trees and are thus turning to more developed areas for roosting.

(B) Bats are the chief consumers of nocturnal insects and thus can help make their hunting territory more pleasant for humans.

(C) Bats are regarded as frightening creatures not only in the United States but also in Europe, Africa, and South America.

(D) Raccoons and owls are shy and active only at night; yet they are not generally feared and persecuted.

(E) People know more about the behavior of other greatly feared animal species, such as lions, alligators, and snakes, than they do about the behavior of bats.

The group's contention suggests that animals that are shy and active at night are feared and persecuted for that reason. Choice D establishes that raccoons and owls are shy and active at night, but that they are neither feared nor persecuted. Therefore, D is the best answer.

Although an increasing prevalence of bats might explain the importance of addressing people's fear of bats, A does not address the original causes of that fear. Choices B and E, while relevant to the rationality of people's fear of bats, do not affect the assessment of the accuracy of the group's contention. That bats are feared outside the United States, as C states, does not conflict with the group's explanation for fear of bats in the United States.

10. Meteorite explosions in the Earth's atmosphere as large as the one that destroyed forests in Siberia, with approximately the force of a twelve-megaton nuclear blast, occur about once a century.

The response of highly automated systems controlled by complex computer programs to unexpected circumstances is unpredictable.

Which of the following conclusions can most properly be drawn, if the statements above are true, about a highly automated nuclear-missile defense system controlled by a complex computer program?

(A) Within a century after its construction, the system would react inappropriately and might accidentally start a nuclear war.

(B) The system would be destroyed if an explosion of a large meteorite occurred in the Earth's atmosphere.

(C) It would be impossible for the system to distinguish the explosion of a large meteorite from the explosion of a nuclear weapon.

(D) Whether the system would respond inappropriately to the explosion of a large meteorite would depend on the location of the blast.

(E) It is not certain what the system's response to the explosion of a large meteorite would be, if its designers did not plan for such a contingency.

If the defense system designers did not plan for the contingency of large meteorite explosions, such explosions would, from the system's perspective, be unexpected. The system's response to such explosions is consequently unpredictable. Choice E expresses this inference and is thus the best answer.

Choices A and C cannot be inferred since it is consistent with the stated information that no meteorite explosion will occur within a century and that an appropriately designed nuclear defense system might be able to distinguish nuclear from meteorite explosions. Choices B and D cannot be inferred since there is no information to suggest either that meteorite explosions in the atmosphere would destroy the system or that the location of blasts would determine the appropriateness of the defense system's response.

Questions 11-12 are based on the following.

The fewer restrictions there are on the advertising of legal services, the more lawyers there are who advertise their services, and the lawyers who advertise a specific service usually charge less for that service than lawyers who do not advertise. Therefore, if the state removes any of its current restrictions, such as the one against advertisements that do not specify fee arrangements, overall consumer legal costs will be lower than if the state retains its current restrictions.

11. If the statements above are true, which of the following must be true?

(A) Some lawyers who now advertise will charge more for specific services if they do not have to specify fee arrangements in the advertisements.

(B) More consumers will use legal services if there are fewer restrictions on the advertising of legal services.

(C) If the restriction against advertisements that do not specify fee arrangements is removed, more lawyers will advertise their services.

(D) If more lawyers advertise lower prices for specific services, some lawyers who do not advertise will also charge less than they currently charge for those services.

(E) If the only restrictions on the advertising of legal services were those that apply to every type of advertising, most lawyers would advertise their services.

The supposition in C involves reducing by one the number of restrictions on the advertising of legal services. Any such reduction will, if the stated correlation exists, be accompanied by an increase in the number of lawyers advertising their services, as C predicts. Therefore, C is the best answer.

Choices A, B, D, and E do not follow from the stated information since it is still possible that no lawyers would raise their fees (contrary to A); there would be no increase in the number of consumers using legal services (contrary to B); none of the lawyers who do not advertise would decide to lower their prices (contrary to D); and few lawyers would advertise their legal services (contrary to E).

12. Which of the following, if true, would most seriously weaken the argument concerning overall consumer legal costs?

(A) The state has recently removed some other restrictions that had limited the advertising of legal services.

(B) The state is unlikely to remove all of the restrictions that apply solely to the advertising of legal services.

(C) Lawyers who do not advertise generally provide legal services of the same quality as those provided by lawyers who do advertise.

(D) Most lawyers who now specify fee arrangements in their advertisements would continue to do so even if the specification were not required.

(E) Most lawyers who advertise specific services do not lower their fees for those services when they begin to advertise.

If E is true, the lawyers who begin advertising when the restriction is removed might all be among those who do not lower their fees on beginning to advertise, in which case no decrease in consumer legal costs will occur. Therefore, E weakens the argument and is the best answer.

Since A does not relate the recent removal of restrictions to changes in consumer legal costs, A alone does not weaken the argument. Since the argument is unconcerned with whatever restrictions remain in effect but focuses only on those that will be removed, B does not weaken the argument. Choices C and D are irrelevant to an evaluation of the argument, which is concerned with cost considerations, not with the quality of legal services or the content of lawyers' advertisements.

13. Defense Department analysts worry that the ability of the United States to wage a prolonged war would be seriously endangered if the machine-tool manufacturing base shrinks further. Before the Defense Department publicly connected this security issue with the import quota issue, however, the machine-tool industry raised the national security issue in its petition for import quotas.

Which of the following, if true, contributes most to an explanation of the machine-tool industry's raising the issue above regarding national security?

(A) When the aircraft industries retooled, they provided a large amount of work for tool builders.

(B) The Defense Department is only marginally concerned with the effects of foreign competition on the machine-tool industry.

(C) The machine-tool industry encountered difficulty in obtaining governmental protection against imports on grounds other than defense.

(D) A few weapons important for defense consist of parts that do not require extensive machining.

(E) Several federal government programs have been designed which will enable domestic machine-tool manufacturing firms to compete successfully with foreign toolmakers.

Since the size of the machine-tool manufacturing base presumably has implications in areas beyond national security, one might find it surprising that the industry raised the security issue in its petition. Choice C, the best answer, explains that the industry turned to this issue because others tended to be ineffective in efforts to obtain governmental protection.

Choices A and B, on the other hand, merely explain why the industry might *not* raise the security issue. Choice A suggests that the industry might have raised the issue of jobs instead. Choice B suggests that the part of the government concerned with security is not concerned enough with the industry's import problem to take action. Neither D nor E is relevant to the industry's choice of strategy for securing import quotas.

14. Opponents of laws that require automobile drivers and passengers to wear seat belts argue that in a free society people have the right to take risks as long as the people do not harm others as a result of taking the risks. As a result, they conclude that it should be each person's decision whether or not to wear a seat belt.

Which of the following, if true, most seriously weakens the conclusion drawn above?

(A) Many new cars are built with seat belts that automatically fasten when someone sits in the front seat.

(B) Automobile insurance rates for all automobile owners are higher because of the need to pay for the increased injuries or deaths of people not wearing seat belts.

(C) Passengers in airplanes are required to wear seat belts during takeoffs and landings.

(D) The rate of automobile fatalities in states that do not have mandatory seat-belt laws is greater than the rate of fatalities in states that do have such laws.

(E) In automobile accidents, a greater number of passengers who do not wear seat belts are injured than are passengers who do wear seat belts.

The principle that people are entitled to risk injury provided they do not thereby harm others fails to justify the individual's right to decide not to wear seat belts if it can be shown, as B shows, that that decision does harm others. Therefore, B is the best answer.

The argument implicitly concedes that individuals take risks by not wearing seat belts; therefore, D and E, which simply confirm this concession, do not weaken the conclusion. Choice C cites a requirement analogous to the one at issue, but its existence alone does not bear on the legitimacy of the one at issue. Choice A suggests that the law may be irrelevant in some cases, but it does not address the issue of the law's legitimacy.

15. The cost of producing radios in Country Q is ten percent less than the cost of producing radios in Country Y. Even after transportation fees and tariff charges are added, it is still cheaper for a company to import radios from Country Q to Country Y than to produce radios in Country Y.

The statements above, if true, best support which of the following assertions?

(A) Labor costs in Country Q are ten percent below those in Country Y.

(B) Importing radios from Country Q to Country Y will eliminate ten percent of the manufacturing jobs in Country Y.

(C) The tariff on a radio imported from Country Q to Country Y is less than ten percent of the cost of manufacturing the radio in Country Y.

(D) The fee for transporting a radio from Country Q to Country Y is more than ten percent of the cost of manufacturing the radio in Country Q.

(E) It takes ten percent less time to manufacture a radio in Country Q than it does in Country Y.

If the tariff on importing radios from Country Q to Country Y were as high as ten percent or more of the cost of producing radios in Y, then, contrary to what the passage says, the cost of importing radios from Q to Y would be equal to or more than the cost of producing radios in Y. Thus, the tariff cannot be that high, and C is the best answer.

Choices A and E give possible partial explanations for the cost difference, but neither is supported by the passage because the cost advantage in Q might be attributable to other factors. Choices B and D are both consistent with the information in the passage, but the passage provides no evidence to support them.

16. During the Second World War, about 375,000 civilians died in the United States and about 408,000 members of the United States armed forces died overseas. On the basis of those figures, it can be concluded that it was not much more dangerous to be overseas in the armed forces during the Second World War than it was to stay at home as a civilian.

Which of the following would reveal most clearly the absurdity of the conclusion drawn above?

(A) Counting deaths among members of the armed forces who served in the United States in addition to deaths among members of the armed forces serving overseas

(B) Expressing the difference between the numbers of deaths among civilians and members of the armed forces as a percentage of the total number of deaths

(C) Separating deaths caused by accidents during service in the armed forces from deaths caused by combat injuries

(D) Comparing death rates per thousand members of each group rather than comparing total numbers of deaths

(E) Comparing deaths caused by accidents in the United States to deaths caused by combat in the armed forces

Concluding from the similar numbers of deaths in two groups that the relative danger of death was similar for both groups is absurd if, as here, one group was far smaller. Choice D exposes this absurdity by pointing out the need to compare death rates of the two groups, which would reveal the higher death rate for the smaller group. Therefore, D is the best answer.

Since the conclusion acknowledges the difference between the number of civilian and armed forces deaths, expressing this difference as a percentage, as suggested by B, is beside the point. Choice A is inappropriate because it simply adds a third group to the two being compared. Because cause of death is not at issue, C and E are irrelevant.

CRITICAL REASONING SAMPLE TEST SECTION 2

Time — 25 minutes

16 Questions

<u>Directions:</u> For each question in this section, select the best of the answer choices given.

1. Toughened hiring standards have not been the primary cause of the present staffing shortage in public schools. The shortage of teachers is primarily caused by the fact that in recent years teachers have not experienced any improvements in working conditions and their salaries have not kept pace with salaries in other professions.

Which of the following, if true, would most support the claims above?

(A) Many teachers already in the profession would not have been hired under the new hiring standards.

(B) Today more teachers are entering the profession with a higher educational level than in the past.

(C) Some teachers have cited higher standards for hiring as a reason for the current staffing shortage.

(D) Many teachers have cited low pay and lack of professional freedom as reasons for their leaving the profession.

(E) Many prospective teachers have cited the new hiring standards as a reason for not entering the profession.

2. A proposed ordinance requires the installation in new homes of sprinklers automatically triggered by the presence of a fire. However, a home builder argued that because more than ninety percent of residential fires are extinguished by a household member, residential sprinklers would only marginally decrease property damage caused by residential fires.

Which of the following, if true, would most seriously weaken the home builder's argument?

(A) Most individuals have no formal training in how to extinguish fires.

(B) Since new homes are only a tiny percentage of available housing in the city, the new ordinance would be extremely narrow in scope.

(C) The installation of smoke detectors in new residences costs significantly less than the installation of sprinklers.

(D) In the city where the ordinance was proposed, the average time required by the fire department to respond to a fire was less than the national average.

(E) The largest proportion of property damage that results from residential fires is caused by fires that start when no household member is present.

3. Even though most universities retain the royalties from faculty members' inventions, the faculty members retain the royalties from books and articles they write. Therefore, faculty members should retain the royalties from the educational computer software they develop.

The conclusion above would be more reasonably drawn if which of the following were inserted into the argument as an additional premise?

(A) Royalties from inventions are higher than royalties from educational software programs.

(B) Faculty members are more likely to produce educational software programs than inventions.

(C) Inventions bring more prestige to universities than do books and articles.

(D) In the experience of most universities, educational software programs are more marketable than are books and articles.

(E) In terms of the criteria used to award royalties, educational software programs are more nearly comparable to books and articles than to inventions.

GO ON TO THE NEXT PAGE.

-272-

4. Increases in the level of high-density lipoprotein (HDL) in the human bloodstream lower bloodstream-cholesterol levels by increasing the body's capacity to rid itself of excess cholesterol. Levels of HDL in the bloodstream of some individuals are significantly increased by a program of regular exercise and weight reduction.

Which of the following can be correctly inferred from the statements above?

(A) Individuals who are underweight do not run any risk of developing high levels of cholesterol in the bloodstream.
(B) Individuals who do not exercise regularly have a high risk of developing high levels of cholesterol in the bloodstream late in life.
(C) Exercise and weight reduction are the most effective methods of lowering bloodstream cholesterol levels in humans.
(D) A program of regular exercise and weight reduction lowers cholesterol levels in the bloodstream of some individuals.
(E) Only regular exercise is necessary to decrease cholesterol levels in the bloodstream of individuals of average weight.

5. When limitations were in effect on nuclear-arms testing, people tended to save more of their money, but when nuclear-arms testing increased, people tended to spend more of their money. The perceived threat of nuclear catastrophe, therefore, decreases the willingness of people to postpone consumption for the sake of saving money.

The argument above assumes that

(A) the perceived threat of nuclear catastrophe has increased over the years
(B) most people supported the development of nuclear arms
(C) people's perception of the threat of nuclear catastrophe depends on the amount of nuclear-arms testing being done
(D) the people who saved the most money when nuclear-arms testing was limited were the ones who supported such limitations
(E) there are more consumer goods available when nuclear-arms testing increases

6. Which of the following best completes the passage below?

People buy prestige when they buy a premium product. They want to be associated with something special. Mass-marketing techniques and price-reduction strategies should not be used because _____ .

(A) affluent purchasers currently represent a shrinking portion of the population of all purchasers
(B) continued sales depend directly on the maintenance of an aura of exclusivity
(C) purchasers of premium products are concerned with the quality as well as with the price of the products
(D) expansion of the market niche to include a broader spectrum of consumers will increase profits
(E) manufacturing a premium brand is not necessarily more costly than manufacturing a standard brand of the same product

7. A cost-effective solution to the problem of airport congestion is to provide high-speed ground transportation between major cities lying 200 to 500 miles apart. The successful implementation of this plan would cost far less than expanding existing airports and would also reduce the number of airplanes clogging both airports and airways.

Which of the following, if true, could proponents of the plan above most appropriately cite as a piece of evidence for the soundness of their plan?

(A) An effective high-speed ground-transportation system would require major repairs to many highways and mass-transit improvements.
(B) One-half of all departing flights in the nation's busiest airport head for a destination in a major city 225 miles away.
(C) The majority of travelers departing from rural airports are flying to destinations in cities over 600 miles away.
(D) Many new airports are being built in areas that are presently served by high-speed ground-transportation systems.
(E) A large proportion of air travelers are vacationers who are taking long-distance flights.

GO ON TO THE NEXT PAGE.

Questions 8-9 are based on the following.

If there is an oil-supply disruption resulting in higher international oil prices, domestic oil prices in open-market countries such as the United States will rise as well, whether such countries import all or none of their oil.

8. If the statement above concerning oil-supply disruptions is true, which of the following policies in an open-market nation is most likely to reduce the long-term economic impact on that nation of sharp and unexpected increases in international oil prices?

    (A) Maintaining the quantity of oil imported at constant yearly levels
    (B) Increasing the number of oil tankers in its fleet
    (C) Suspending diplomatic relations with major oil-producing nations
    (D) Decreasing oil consumption through conservation
    (E) Decreasing domestic production of oil

9. Which of the following conclusions is best supported by the statement above?

    (A) Domestic producers of oil in open-market countries are excluded from the international oil market when there is a disruption in the international oil supply.
    (B) International oil-supply disruptions have little, if any, effect on the price of domestic oil as long as an open-market country has domestic supplies capable of meeting domestic demand.
    (C) The oil market in an open-market country is actually part of the international oil market, even if most of that country's domestic oil is usually sold to consumers within its borders.
    (D) Open-market countries that export little or none of their oil can maintain stable domestic oil prices even when international oil prices rise sharply.
    (E) If international oil prices rise, domestic distributors of oil in open-market countries will begin to import more oil than they export.

10. The average normal infant born in the United States weighs between twelve and fourteen pounds at the age of three months. Therefore, if a three-month-old child weighs only ten pounds, its weight gain has been below the United States average.

    Which of the following indicates a flaw in the reasoning above?

    (A) Weight is only one measure of normal infant development.
    (B) Some three-month-old children weigh as much as seventeen pounds.
    (C) It is possible for a normal child to weigh ten pounds at birth.
    (D) The phrase "below average" does not necessarily mean insufficient.
    (E) Average weight gain is not the same as average weight.

11. Red blood cells in which the malarial-fever parasite resides are eliminated from a person's body after 120 days. Because the parasite cannot travel to a new generation of red blood cells, any fever that develops in a person more than 120 days after that person has moved to a malaria-free region is not due to the malarial parasite.

    Which of the following, if true, most seriously weakens the conclusion above?

    (A) The fever caused by the malarial parasite may resemble the fever caused by flu viruses.
    (B) The anopheles mosquito, which is the principal insect carrier of the malarial parasite, has been eradicated in many parts of the world.
    (C) Many malarial symptoms other than the fever, which can be suppressed with antimalarial medication, can reappear within 120 days after the medication is discontinued.
    (D) In some cases, the parasite that causes malarial fever travels to cells of the spleen, which are less frequently eliminated from a person's body than are red blood cells.
    (E) In any region infested with malaria-carrying mosquitoes, there are individuals who appear to be immune to malaria.

GO ON TO THE NEXT PAGE.

12. Fact 1: Television advertising is becoming less effective: the proportion of brand names promoted on television that viewers of the advertising can recall is slowly decreasing.

Fact 2: Television viewers recall commercials aired first or last in a cluster of consecutive commercials far better than they recall commercials aired somewhere in the middle.

Fact 2 would be most likely to contribute to an explanation of fact 1 if which of the following were also true?

(A) The average television viewer currently recalls fewer than half the brand names promoted in commercials he or she saw.
(B) The total time allotted to the average cluster of consecutive television commercials is decreasing.
(C) The average number of hours per day that people spend watching television is decreasing.
(D) The average number of clusters of consecutive commercials per hour of television is increasing.
(E) The average number of television commercials in a cluster of consecutive commercials is increasing.

13. The number of people diagnosed as having a certain intestinal disease has dropped significantly in a rural county this year, as compared to last year. Health officials attribute this decrease entirely to improved sanitary conditions at water-treatment plants, which made for cleaner water this year and thus reduced the incidence of the disease.

Which of the following, if true, would most seriously weaken the health officials' explanation for the lower incidence of the disease?

(A) Many new water-treatment plants have been built in the last five years in the rural county.
(B) Bottled spring water has not been consumed in significantly different quantities by people diagnosed as having the intestinal disease, as compared to people who did not contract the disease.
(C) Because of a new diagnostic technique, many people who until this year would have been diagnosed as having the intestinal disease are now correctly diagnosed as suffering from intestinal ulcers.
(D) Because of medical advances this year, far fewer people who contract the intestinal disease will develop severe cases of the disease.
(E) The water in the rural county was brought up to the sanitary standards of the water in neighboring counties ten years ago.

14. The price the government pays for standard weapons purchased from military contractors is determined by a pricing method called "historical costing." Historical costing allows contractors to protect their profits by adding a percentage increase, based on the current rate of inflation, to the previous year's contractual price.

Which of the following statements, if true, is the best basis for a criticism of historical costing as an economically sound pricing method for military contracts?

(A) The government might continue to pay for past inefficient use of funds.
(B) The rate of inflation has varied considerably over the past twenty years.
(C) The contractual price will be greatly affected by the cost of materials used for the products.
(D) Many taxpayers question the amount of money the government spends on military contracts.
(E) The pricing method based on historical costing might not encourage the development of innovative weapons.

GO ON TO THE NEXT PAGE.

15. Some who favor putting governmental enterprises into private hands suggest that conservation objectives would in general be better served if private environmental groups were put in charge of operating and financing the national park system, which is now run by the government.

Which of the following, assuming that it is a realistic possibility, argues most strongly against the suggestion above?

(A) Those seeking to abolish all restrictions on exploiting the natural resources of the parks might join the private environmental groups as members and eventually take over their leadership.

(B) Private environmental groups might not always agree on the best ways to achieve conservation objectives.

(C) If they wished to extend the park system, the private environmental groups might have to seek contributions from major donors and the general public.

(D) There might be competition among private environmental groups for control of certain park areas.

(E) Some endangered species, such as the California condor, might die out despite the best efforts of the private environmental groups, even if those groups are not hampered by insufficient resources.

16. A recent spate of launching and operating mishaps with television satellites led to a corresponding surge in claims against companies underwriting satellite insurance. As a result, insurance premiums shot up, making satellites more expensive to launch and operate. This, in turn, has added to the pressure to squeeze more performance out of currently operating satellites.

Which of the following, if true, taken together with the information above, best supports the conclusion that the cost of television satellites will continue to increase?

(A) Since the risk to insurers of satellites is spread over relatively few units, insurance premiums are necessarily very high.

(B) When satellites reach orbit and then fail, the causes of failure are generally impossible to pinpoint with confidence.

(C) The greater the performance demands placed on satellites, the more frequently those satellites break down.

(D) Most satellites are produced in such small numbers that no economies of scale can be realized.

(E) Since many satellites are built by unwieldy international consortia, inefficiencies are inevitable.

STOP

**IF YOU FINISH BEFORE TIME IS CALLED, YOU MAY CHECK YOUR WORK ON THIS SECTION ONLY.
DO NOT TURN TO ANY OTHER SECTION IN THE TEST.**

Answer Key for Sample Test Section 2

CRITICAL REASONING

1.	D	9.	C
2.	E	10.	E
3.	E	11.	D
4.	D	12.	E
5.	C	13.	C
6.	B	14.	A
7.	B	15.	A
8.	D	16.	C

Explanatory Material: Critical Reasoning Sample Test Section 2

1. Toughened hiring standards have not been the primary cause of the present staffing shortage in public schools. The shortage of teachers is primarily caused by the fact that in recent years teachers have not experienced any improvements in working conditions and their salaries have not kept pace with salaries in other professions.

   Which of the following, if true, would most support the claims above?

   (A) Many teachers already in the profession would not have been hired under the new hiring standards.
   (B) Today more teachers are entering the profession with a higher educational level than in the past.
   (C) Some teachers have cited higher standards for hiring as a reason for the current staffing shortage.
   (D) Many teachers have cited low pay and lack of professional freedom as reasons for their leaving the profession.
   (E) Many prospective teachers have cited the new hiring standards as a reason for not entering the profession.

The passage rejects one explanation of the shortage of teachers — that it results from toughened hiring standards — and advances an alternative — that it results from deficiencies in pay and working conditions. Choice D provides corroborative evidence for the latter explanation by suggesting that, for many former teachers, poor pay and working conditions were reasons for their quitting the profession. Therefore, D is the best answer.

Choices A, C, and E provide evidence that tends to implicate new hiring standards in the staffing shortage, and thus support the explanation that the passage rejects. Choice B describes what may be a result of the new hiring standards, but it provides no evidence favoring one explanation of the staffing shortage over the other.

2. A proposed ordinance requires the installation in new homes of sprinklers automatically triggered by the presence of a fire. However, a home builder argued that because more than ninety percent of residential fires are extinguished by a household member, residential sprinklers would only marginally decrease property damage caused by residential fires.

   Which of the following, if true, would most seriously weaken the home builder's argument?

   (A) Most individuals have no formal training in how to extinguish fires.
   (B) Since new homes are only a tiny percentage of available housing in the city, the new ordinance would be extremely narrow in scope.
   (C) The installation of smoke detectors in new residences costs significantly less than the installation of sprinklers.
   (D) In the city where the ordinance was proposed, the average time required by the fire department to respond to a fire was less than the national average.
   (E) The largest proportion of property damage that results from residential fires is caused by fires that start when no household member is present.

The home builder reasons from evidence about most residential fires to a conclusion about the effectiveness of sprinklers in preventing property damage. But this reasoning is faulty because of the possibility that most of the property damage results from the minority of fires excluded from the builder's evidence. This possibility is realized if E is true. Thus, E is the best answer.

Because the builder's argument concerns neither the cost of installing sprinklers nor a comparison with fire department performance in other locations, choices C and D are irrelevant. The evidence the home builder cites suggests that formal training (choice A) is not needed in order to extinguish fires. Choice B supports the builder's view that requiring sprinklers would have a limited effect.

3. Even though most universities retain the royalties from faculty members' inventions, the faculty members retain the royalties from books and articles they write. Therefore, faculty members should retain the royalties from the educational computer software they develop.

The conclusion above would be more reasonably drawn if which of the following were inserted into the argument as an additional premise?

(A) Royalties from inventions are higher than royalties from educational software programs.
(B) Faculty members are more likely to produce educational software programs than inventions.
(C) Inventions bring more prestige to universities than do books and articles.
(D) In the experience of most universities, educational software programs are more marketable than are books and articles.
(E) In terms of the criteria used to award royalties, educational software programs are more nearly comparable to books and articles than to inventions.

The passage concludes that, where royalty retention of faculty members' works is concerned, software should be treated as books and articles are, not as inventions are. The conclusion requires an additional premise establishing that software is, in relevant respects, more comparable to books and articles than to inventions. Choice E provides this kind of premise and is therefore the best answer.

Choices A, B, C, and D, conversely, each describe some difference between software and inventions (choices A and B), or between inventions and books and articles (choice C), or between software and books and articles (choice D), but none establishes the required relationship among inventions, software, and books and articles.

4. Increases in the level of high-density lipoprotein (HDL) in the human bloodstream lower bloodstream-cholesterol levels by increasing the body's capacity to rid itself of excess cholesterol. Levels of HDL in the bloodstream of some individuals are significantly increased by a program of regular exercise and weight reduction.

Which of the following can be correctly inferred from the statements above?

(A) Individuals who are underweight do not run any risk of developing high levels of cholesterol in the bloodstream.
(B) Individuals who do not exercise regularly have a high risk of developing high levels of cholesterol in the bloodstream late in life.
(C) Exercise and weight reduction are the most effective methods of lowering bloodstream cholesterol levels in humans.
(D) A program of regular exercise and weight reduction lowers cholesterol levels in the bloodstream of some individuals.
(E) Only regular exercise is necessary to decrease cholesterol levels in the bloodstream of individuals of average weight.

If increased HDL levels cause reduced cholesterol levels and if a certain program increases HDL levels in some individuals, it follows that some individuals who undertake that program achieve reduced cholesterol levels. Choice D is thus correctly inferable and the best answer.

Choice A cannot be correctly inferred because the statements do not establish any connection between being underweight and levels of cholesterol. Neither B nor E is inferable, since there is no indication that exercise alone is either necessary or sufficient to increase HDL levels or to decrease cholesterol levels. Choice C is inappropriate because other methods of cholesterol reduction are not addressed.

5. When limitations were in effect on nuclear-arms testing, people tended to save more of their money, but when nuclear-arms testing increased, people tended to spend more of their money. The perceived threat of nuclear catastrophe, therefore, decreases the willingness of people to postpone consumption for the sake of saving money.

The argument above assumes that

(A) the perceived threat of nuclear catastrophe has increased over the years

(B) most people supported the development of nuclear arms

(C) people's perception of the threat of nuclear catastrophe depends on the amount of nuclear-arms testing being done

(D) the people who saved the most money when nuclear-arms testing was limited were the ones who supported such limitations

(E) there are more consumer goods available when nuclear-arms testing increases

On the basis of an observed correlation between arms testing and people's tendency to save money, the argument concludes that there is a causal connection between a perception of threat and the tendency not to save. That connection cannot be made unless C, linking the perception of threat to the amount of testing being done, is assumed to be true. Therefore, C is the best answer.

The conclusion does not depend on there having been an increase in the perceived threat over time or on how many people supported the development of nuclear arms. Hence, neither A nor B is assumed. Furthermore, the argument does not deal with those who supported arms limitations or with the availability of consumer goods. Thus, D and E are not assumed.

6. Which of the following best completes the passage below?

People buy prestige when they buy a premium product. They want to be associated with something special. Mass-marketing techniques and price-reduction strategies should not be used because _____.

(A) affluent purchasers currently represent a shrinking portion of the population of all purchasers

(B) continued sales depend directly on the maintenance of an aura of exclusivity

(C) purchasers of premium products are concerned with the quality as well as with the price of the products

(D) expansion of the market niche to include a broader spectrum of consumers will increase profits

(E) manufacturing a premium brand is not necessarily more costly than manufacturing a standard brand of the same product

The incomplete passage calls for an explanation of why price-reduction and mass-marketing methods should not be used for premium products. Choice B, which states that sales of these products require that they appear special, provides such an explanation. Therefore, B is the best answer.

No other choice offers an appropriate explanation. Choice C suggests that purchasers of premium products find reduced prices attractive, and it has not been established that the methods affect quality or perception of quality. The diminishing proportion of affluent buyers cited in A argues for using price reductions to attract buyers of lesser means, while D argues for, rather than against, using mass marketing. Choice E is inappropriate, since there is no indication that manufacturing costs are relevant.

7. A cost-effective solution to the problem of airport congestion is to provide high-speed ground transportation between major cities lying 200 to 500 miles apart. The successful implementation of this plan would cost far less than expanding existing airports and would also reduce the number of airplanes clogging both airports and airways.

Which of the following, if true, could proponents of the plan above most appropriately cite as a piece of evidence for the soundness of their plan?

(A) An effective high-speed ground-transportation system would require major repairs to many highways and mass-transit improvements.

(B) One-half of all departing flights in the nation's busiest airport head for a destination in a major city 225 miles away.

(C) The majority of travelers departing from rural airports are flying to destinations in cities over 600 miles away.

(D) Many new airports are being built in areas that are presently served by high-speed ground-transportation systems.

(E) A large proportion of air travelers are vacationers who are taking long-distance flights.

The plan proposes that high-speed ground transportation would be a less expensive solution to airport congestion than would airport expansion. Choice B indicates that between the cities to be served by the plan there is substantial air travel to which ground transportation would represent an alternative. Therefore, B is the best answer.

No other choice could be cited appropriately. Choices A and D both provide some evidence against the plan, A by emphasizing the likely costs of providing high-speed ground transportation, and D by indicating that such an alternative is not by itself a solution to airport congestion. Choices C and E say that there are many travelers for whom the proposed system would actually provide no alternative.

If there is an oil-supply disruption resulting in higher international oil prices, domestic oil prices in open-market countries such as the United States will rise as well, whether such countries import all or none of their oil.

8. If the statement above concerning oil-supply disruptions is true, which of the following policies in an open-market nation is most likely to reduce the long-term economic impact on that nation of sharp and unexpected increases in international oil prices?

   (A) Maintaining the quantity of oil imported at constant yearly levels
   (B) Increasing the number of oil tankers in its fleet
   (C) Suspending diplomatic relations with major oil-producing nations
   (D) Decreasing oil consumption through conservation
   (E) Decreasing domestic production of oil

If the statement about oil-supply disruption is true, domestic oil prices in an open-market country will rise when an oil-supply disruption causes increased international oil prices. A reduction in the amount of oil an open-market country consumes could reduce the economic impact of these increases. Choice D gives a way to reduce oil consumption and is thus the best answer.

None of the other choices is appropriate. Choices A and E describe policies that could actually increase the long-term impact of increases in international oil prices. No relationship is established between the economic impact and either the number of oil tankers (choice B) or diplomatic relations (choice C).

9. Which of the following conclusions is best supported by the statement above?

   (A) Domestic producers of oil in open-market countries are excluded from the international oil market when there is a disruption in the international oil supply.
   (B) International oil-supply disruptions have little, if any, effect on the price of domestic oil as long as an open-market country has domestic supplies capable of meeting domestic demand.
   (C) The oil market in an open-market country is actually part of the international oil market, even if most of that country's domestic oil is usually sold to consumers within its borders.
   (D) Open-market countries that export little or none of their oil can maintain stable domestic oil prices even when international oil prices rise sharply.
   (E) If international oil prices rise, domestic distributors of oil in open-market countries will begin to import more oil than they export.

If the oil market in an open-market country were independent, fluctuations in international oil prices would not affect domestic oil prices. However, if the statement about oil-supply disruption is true, it is evidence that domestic oil prices are dependent on the international market and hence that the domestic oil market is a part of the international oil market. Therefore, C is the best answer.

Choices B and D are not supported, since each contradicts the claim that an international oil-supply disruption will lead to rising oil prices in an open-market nation. Neither are A and E supported, since the statement provides information only about the effect of disruption on oil prices, not domestic producers or distributors.

10. The average normal infant born in the United States weighs between twelve and fourteen pounds at the age of three months. Therefore, if a three-month-old child weighs only ten pounds, its weight gain has been below the United States average.

    Which of the following indicates a flaw in the reasoning above?

    (A) Weight is only one measure of normal infant development.
    (B) Some three-month-old children weigh as much as seventeen pounds.
    (C) It is possible for a normal child to weigh ten pounds at birth.
    (D) The phrase "below average" does not necessarily mean insufficient.
    (E) Average weight gain is not the same as average weight.

The evidence on which the conclusion is based concerns only average weight, but the conclusion concerns average weight gain. Because there is not necessarily a connection between an absolute measurement — such as weight — and a rate of increase — such as weight gain — this argument is flawed. The relevant reasoning error is described in E, which is the best answer.

Neither A nor D identifies a reasoning error in the passage, since the passage makes no claim that weight is the only relevant measure of infant development in general (choice A), and no claim about sufficiency (choice D). Both B and C are consistent with the claims in the passage, and neither identifies a flaw in the argument.

11. **Red blood cells in which the malarial-fever parasite resides are eliminated from a person's body after 120 days. Because the parasite cannot travel to a new generation of red blood cells, any fever that develops in a person more than 120 days after that person has moved to a malaria-free region is not due to the malarial parasite.**

Which of the following, if true, most seriously weakens the conclusion above?

(A) The fever caused by the malarial parasite may resemble the fever caused by flu viruses.

(B) The anopheles mosquito, which is the principal insect carrier of the malarial parasite, has been eradicated in many parts of the world.

(C) Many malarial symptoms other than the fever, which can be suppressed with antimalarial medication, can reappear within 120 days after the medication is discontinued.

(D) In some cases, the parasite that causes malarial fever travels to cells of the spleen, which are less frequently eliminated from a person's body than are red blood cells.

(E) In any region infested with malaria-carrying mosquitoes, there are individuals who appear to be immune to malaria.

The passage concludes that, because the malarial parasite cannot reside in red blood cells for more than 120 days, the malarial parasite cannot cause fever more than 120 days after infection. However, according to D, there is a site in the body where the parasite could reside for more than 120 days after infection. Therefore, D weakens the conclusion and is the best answer.

The resemblance between malarial-fever symptoms and those of other diseases (choice A), the existence of other malarial symptoms (choice C), and the possibility of immunity to malaria (choice E) are irrelevant to the issue of the conditions under which malarial fever can occur. Choice B provides confirmation for the existence of malaria-free regions but does not otherwise bear on the conclusion.

12. **Fact 1: Television advertising is becoming less effective: the proportion of brand names promoted on television that viewers of the advertising can recall is slowly decreasing.**

Fact 2: Television viewers recall commercials aired first or last in a cluster of consecutive commercials far better than they recall commercials aired somewhere in the middle.

Fact 2 would be most likely to contribute to an explanation of fact 1 if which of the following were also true?

(A) The average television viewer currently recalls fewer than half the brand names promoted in commercials he or she saw.

(B) The total time allotted to the average cluster of consecutive television commercials is decreasing.

(C) The average number of hours per day that people spend watching television is decreasing.

(D) The average number of clusters of consecutive commercials per hour of television is increasing.

(E) The average number of television commercials in a cluster of consecutive commercials is increasing.

Because E indicates that the number of commercials in a cluster is increasing, E entails that proportionally more commercials are aired in intermediate positions. Hence, E helps fact 2 explain fact 1 by showing that increasingly more commercials are aired in positions in which viewers find them difficult to recall. E is the best answer.

Choice A testifies to the ineffectiveness of television advertising but does not help fact 2 explain fact 1. Choice B indicates that fact 2 contradicts rather than explains fact 1, since it suggests that the number of commercials per cluster is decreasing. Choices C and D help to explain fact 1— C by describing a change in viewing habits and D by describing a change in programming — but neither relates fact 2 to fact 1.

13. The number of people diagnosed as having a certain intestinal disease has dropped significantly in a rural county this year, as compared to last year. Health officials attribute this decrease entirely to improved sanitary conditions at water-treatment plants, which made for cleaner water this year and thus reduced the incidence of the disease.

Which of the following, if true, would most seriously weaken the health officials' explanation for the lower incidence of the disease?

(A) Many new water-treatment plants have been built in the last five years in the rural county.

(B) Bottled spring water has not been consumed in significantly different quantities by people diagnosed as having the intestinal disease, as compared to people who did not contract the disease.

(C) Because of a new diagnostic technique, many people who until this year would have been diagnosed as having the intestinal disease are now correctly diagnosed as suffering from intestinal ulcers.

(D) Because of medical advances this year, far fewer people who contract the intestinal disease will develop severe cases of the disease.

(E) The water in the rural county was brought up to the sanitary standards of the water in neighboring counties ten years ago.

The health officials' explanation assumes that the decrease in the number of people diagnosed with the disease accurately reflects a diminution in cases of the disease. By pointing out that this assumption is false, C undermines the officials' explanation and thus is the best answer.

Since A supports the view that sanitary conditions have been improving, it tends to support the officials' explanation. So does B, which eliminates a factor that might have differentiated between those contracting and those not contracting the disease and thus rules out an alternative explanation. The reduction of the severity of the diagnosed cases (choice D) does not bear on the officials' explanation. Since the standards in neighboring counties might themselves have been inadequate, E does not weaken the officials' explanation.

14. The price the government pays for standard weapons purchased from military contractors is determined by a pricing method called "historical costing." Historical costing allows contractors to protect their profits by adding a percentage increase, based on the current rate of inflation, to the previous year's contractual price.

Which of the following statements, if true, is the best basis for a criticism of historical costing as an economically sound pricing method for military contracts?

(A) The government might continue to pay for past inefficient use of funds.

(B) The rate of inflation has varied considerably over the past twenty years.

(C) The contractual price will be greatly affected by the cost of materials used for the products.

(D) Many taxpayers question the amount of money the government spends on military contracts.

(E) The pricing method based on historical costing might not encourage the development of innovative weapons.

If the original contractual price for the weapons purchased incorporated an inefficient use of funds, then, since historical costing merely adds to the original price, it preserves these inefficiencies. An economically sound pricing method should at least allow the possibility of reductions in price as such inefficiencies are removed. Hence, A is the best answer.

Because historical costing responds to inflation, both B and C are consistent with the economic soundness of historical costing — B because it refers to the rate of inflation and C because it refers to costs that are reflected in inflation. Choice D offers no grounds for questioning the economic soundness of historical costing in particular. Historical costing applies to standard weapons only, not to the innovative weapons that are mentioned in E.

15. Some who favor putting governmental enterprises into private hands suggest that conservation objectives would in general be better served if private environmental groups were put in charge of operating and financing the national park system, which is now run by the government.

Which of the following, assuming that it is a realistic possibility, argues most strongly against the suggestion above?

(A) Those seeking to abolish all restrictions on exploiting the natural resources of the parks might join the private environmental groups as members and eventually take over their leadership.

(B) Private environmental groups might not always agree on the best ways to achieve conservation objectives.

(C) If they wished to extend the park system, the private environmental groups might have to seek contributions from major donors and the general public.

(D) There might be competition among private environmental groups for control of certain park areas.

(E) Some endangered species, such as the California condor, might die out despite the best efforts of the private environmental groups, even if those groups are not hampered by insufficient resources.

If those seeking to abolish restrictions on exploiting the natural resources of the parks assumed the leadership of a group that was placed in charge of operating the park system, conservation objectives would not be better served. Choice A suggests that such a scenario might result from the proposed policy and is thus the best answer.

Choices C, D, and E list problems that might confront private environmental groups in charge of parks, but they do not give reason to believe that such groups would not be better able to pursue conservation objectives than is the current administration of the park system. Choice B indicates the potential for disagreement among various private environmental groups, but it does not suggest that disagreements could not be resolved.

16. A recent spate of launching and operating mishaps with television satellites led to a corresponding surge in claims against companies underwriting satellite insurance. As a result, insurance premiums shot up, making satellites more expensive to launch and operate. This, in turn, had added to the pressure to squeeze more performance out of currently operating satellites.

Which of the following, if true, taken together with the information above, best supports the conclusion that the cost of television satellites will continue to increase?

(A) Since the risk to insurers of satellites is spread over relatively few units, insurance premiums are necessarily very high.

(B) When satellites reach orbit and then fail, the causes of failure are generally impossible to pinpoint with confidence.

(C) The greater the performance demands placed on satellites, the more frequently those satellites break down.

(D) Most satellites are produced in such small numbers that no economies of scale can be realized.

(E) Since many satellites are built by unwieldy international consortia, inefficiencies are inevitable.

According to the passage, satellite mishaps caused a surge in insurance claims, which, in turn, caused increased insurance premiums. Higher premiums made the satellites more costly, resulting in increased performance demands. If C is true, the greater demands on performance will lead to further increases in costs by increasing the number of mishaps, and thus pushing insurance premiums still higher. Thus, C is the best answer.

Choices A, D, and E all describe factors relevant to costs, but there is no reason to think that the situation described in the passage will cause the costs resulting from these factors to increase. Similarly, the impossibility of pinpointing the causes of failure, mentioned in B, is consistent with the cost of satellites remaining stable.

CRITICAL REASONING SAMPLE TEST SECTION 3

Time — 25 minutes

16 Questions

Directions: For each question in this section, select the best of the answer choices given.

1. Rural households have more purchasing power than do urban or suburban households at the same income level, since some of the income urban and suburban households use for food and shelter can be used by rural households for other needs.

Which of the following inferences is best supported by the statement made above?

(A) The average rural household includes more people than does the average urban or suburban household.
(B) Rural households have lower food and housing costs than do either urban or suburban households.
(C) Suburban households generally have more purchasing power than do either rural or urban households.
(D) The median income of urban and suburban households is generally higher than that of rural households.
(E) All three types of households spend more of their income on food and housing than on all other purchases combined.

2. In 1985 state border colleges in Texas lost the enrollment of more than half, on average, of the Mexican nationals they had previously served each year. Teaching faculties have alleged that this extreme drop resulted from a rise in tuition for international and out-of-state students from $40 to $120 per credit hour.

Which of the following, if feasible, offers the best prospects for alleviating the problem of the drop in enrollment of Mexican nationals as the teaching faculties assessed it?

(A) Providing grants-in-aid to Mexican nationals to study in Mexican universities
(B) Allowing Mexican nationals to study in Texas border colleges and to pay in-state tuition rates, which are the same as the previous international rate
(C) Reemphasizing the goals and mission of the Texas state border colleges as serving both in-state students and Mexican nationals
(D) Increasing the financial resources of Texas colleges by raising the tuition for in-state students attending state institutions
(E) Offering career counseling for those Mexican nationals who graduate from state border colleges and intend to return to Mexico

3. Affirmative action is good business. So asserted the National Association of Manufacturers while urging retention of an executive order requiring some federal contractors to set numerical goals for hiring minorities and women. "Diversity in work force participation has produced new ideas in management, product development, and marketing," the association claimed.

The association's argument as it is presented in the passage above would be most strengthened if which of the following were true?

(A) The percentage of minority and women workers in business has increased more slowly than many minority and women's groups would prefer.
(B) Those businesses with the highest percentages of minority and women workers are those that have been the most innovative and profitable.
(C) Disposable income has been rising as fast among minorities and women as among the population as a whole.
(D) The biggest growth in sales in the manufacturing sector has come in industries that market the most innovative products.
(E) Recent improvements in management practices have allowed many manufacturers to experience enormous gains in worker productivity.

GO ON TO THE NEXT PAGE.

-284-

Questions 4-5 refer to the following.

If the airspace around centrally located airports were restricted to commercial airliners and only those private planes equipped with radar, most of the private-plane traffic would be forced to use outlying airfields. Such a reduction in the amount of private-plane traffic would reduce the risk of midair collision around the centrally located airports.

4. The conclusion drawn in the first sentence depends on which of the following assumptions?

   (A) Outlying airfields would be as convenient as centrally located airports for most pilots of private planes.
   (B) Most outlying airfields are not equipped to handle commercial-airline traffic.
   (C) Most private planes that use centrally located airports are not equipped with radar.
   (D) Commercial airliners are at greater risk of becoming involved in midair collisions than are private planes.
   (E) A reduction in the risk of midair collision would eventually lead to increases in commercial-airline traffic.

5. Which of the following, if true, would most strengthen the conclusion drawn in the second sentence?

   (A) Commercial airliners are already required by law to be equipped with extremely sophisticated radar systems.
   (B) Centrally located airports are experiencing over-crowded airspace primarily because of sharp increases in commercial-airline traffic.
   (C) Many pilots of private planes would rather buy radar equipment than be excluded from centrally located airports.
   (D) The number of midair collisions that occur near centrally located airports has decreased in recent years.
   (E) Private planes not equipped with radar systems cause a disproportionately large number of midair collisions around centrally located airports.

6. Which of the following best completes the passage below?

Established companies concentrate on defending what they already have. Consequently, they tend not to be innovative themselves and tend to underestimate the effects of the innovations of others. The clearest example of this defensive strategy is the fact that -------.

   (A) ballpoint pens and soft-tip markers have eliminated the traditional market for fountain pens, clearing the way for the marketing of fountain pens as luxury or prestige items
   (B) a highly successful automobile was introduced by the same company that had earlier introduced a model that had been a dismal failure
   (C) a once-successful manufacturer of slide rules reacted to the introduction of electronic calculators by trying to make better slide rules
   (D) one of the first models of modern accounting machines, designed for use in the banking industry, was purchased by a public library as well as by banks
   (E) the inventor of a commonly used anesthetic did not intend the product to be used by dentists, who currently account for almost the entire market for that drug

GO ON TO THE NEXT PAGE.

7. Most archaeologists have held that people first reached the Americas less than 20,000 years ago by crossing a land bridge into North America. But recent discoveries of human shelters in South America dating from 32,000 years ago have led researchers to speculate that people arrived in South America first, after voyaging across the Pacific, and then spread northward.

Which of the following, if it were discovered, would be pertinent evidence against the speculation above?

(A) A rock shelter near Pittsburgh, Pennsylvania, contains evidence of use by human beings 19,000 years ago.
(B) Some North American sites of human habitation predate any sites found in South America.
(C) The climate is warmer at the 32,000-year-old South American site than at the oldest known North American site.
(D) The site in South America that was occupied 32,000 years ago was continuously occupied until 6,000 years ago.
(E) The last Ice Age, between 11,500 and 20,000 years ago, considerably lowered worldwide sea levels.

8. In Asia, where palm trees are non-native, the trees' flowers have traditionally been pollinated by hand, which has kept palm fruit productivity unnaturally low. When weevils known to be efficient pollinators of palm flowers were introduced into Asia in 1980, palm fruit productivity increased—by up to fifty percent in some areas—but then decreased sharply in 1984.

Which of the following statements, if true, would best explain the 1984 decrease in productivity?

(A) Prices for palm fruit fell between 1980 and 1984 following the rise in production and a concurrent fall in demand.
(B) Imported trees are often more productive than native trees because the imported ones have left behind their pests and diseases in their native lands.
(C) Rapid increases in productivity tend to deplete trees of nutrients needed for the development of the fruit-producing female flowers.
(D) The weevil population in Asia remained at approximately the same level between 1980 and 1984.
(E) Prior to 1980 another species of insect pollinated the Asian palm trees, but not as efficiently as the species of weevil that was introduced in 1980.

9. Since the mayor's publicity campaign for Greenville's bus service began six months ago, morning automobile traffic into the midtown area of the city has decreased seven percent. During the same period, there has been an equivalent rise in the number of persons riding buses into the midtown area. Obviously, the mayor's publicity campaign has convinced many people to leave their cars at home and ride the bus to work.

Which of the following, if true, casts the most serious doubt on the conclusion drawn above?

(A) Fares for all bus routes in Greenville have risen an average of five percent during the past six months.
(B) The mayor of Greenville rides the bus to City Hall in the city's midtown area.
(C) Road reconstruction has greatly reduced the number of lanes available to commuters in major streets leading to the midtown area during the past six months.
(D) The number of buses entering the midtown area of Greenville during the morning hours is exactly the same now as it was one year ago.
(E) Surveys show that longtime bus riders are no more satisfied with the Greenville bus service than they were before the mayor's publicity campaign began.

GO ON TO THE NEXT PAGE.

10. In the aftermath of a worldwide stock-market crash, Country T claimed that the severity of the stock-market crash it experienced resulted from the accelerated process of denationalization many of its industries underwent shortly before the crash.

Which of the following, if it could be carried out, would be most useful in an evaluation of Country T's assessment of the causes of the severity of its stock-market crash?

(A) Calculating the average loss experienced by individual traders in Country T during the crash

(B) Using economic theory to predict the most likely date of the next crash in Country T

(C) Comparing the total number of shares sold during the worst days of the crash in Country T to the total number of shares sold in Country T just prior to the crash

(D) Comparing the severity of the crash in Country T to the severity of the crash in countries otherwise economically similar to Country T that have not experienced recent denationalization

(E) Comparing the long-term effects of the crash on the purchasing power of the currency of Country T to the immediate, more severe short-term effects of the crash on the purchasing power of the currency of Country T

11. With the emergence of biotechnology companies, it was feared that they would impose silence about proprietary results on their in-house researchers and their academic consultants. This constraint, in turn, would slow the development of biological science and engineering.

Which of the following, if true, would tend to weaken most seriously the prediction of scientific secrecy described above?

(A) Biotechnological research funded by industry has reached some conclusions that are of major scientific importance.

(B) When the results of scientific research are kept secret, independent researchers are unable to build on those results.

(C) Since the research priorities of biotechnology companies are not the same as those of academic institutions, the financial support of research by such companies distorts the research agenda.

(D) To enhance the companies' standing in the scientific community, the biotechnology companies encourage employees to publish their results, especially results that are important.

(E) Biotechnology companies devote some of their research resources to problems that are of fundamental scientific importance and that are not expected to produce immediate practical applications.

12. Some people have questioned the judge's objectivity in cases of sex discrimination against women. But the record shows that in sixty percent of such cases, the judge has decided in favor of the women. This record demonstrates that the judge has not discriminated against women in cases of sex discrimination against women.

The argument above is flawed in that it ignores the possibility that

(A) a large number of the judge's cases arose out of allegations of sex discrimination against women

(B) many judges find it difficult to be objective in cases of sex discrimination against women

(C) the judge is biased against women defendants or plaintiffs in cases that do not involve sex discrimination

(D) the majority of the cases of sex discrimination against women that have reached the judge's court have been appealed from a lower court

(E) the evidence shows that the women should have won in more than sixty percent of the judge's cases involving sex discrimination against women

13. The tobacco industry is still profitable and projections are that it will remain so. In the United States this year, the total amount of tobacco sold by tobacco-farmers has increased, even though the number of adults who smoke has decreased.

Each of the following, if true, could explain the simultaneous increase in tobacco sales and decrease in the number of adults who smoke EXCEPT:

(A) During this year, the number of women who have begun to smoke is greater than the number of men who have quit smoking.

(B) The number of teen-age children who have begun to smoke this year is greater than the number of adults who have quit smoking during the same period.

(C) During this year, the number of nonsmokers who have begun to use chewing tobacco or snuff is greater than the number of people who have quit smoking.

(D) The people who have continued to smoke consume more tobacco per person than they did in the past.

(E) More of the cigarettes made in the United States this year were exported to other countries than was the case last year.

GO ON TO THE NEXT PAGE.

14. Kale has more nutritional value than spinach. But since collard greens have more nutritional value than lettuce, it follows that kale has more nutritional value than lettuce.

Any of the following, if introduced into the argument as an additional premise, makes the argument above logically correct EXCEPT:

(A) Collard greens have more nutritional value than kale.
(B) Spinach has more nutritional value than lettuce.
(C) Spinach has more nutritional value than collard greens.
(D) Spinach and collard greens have the same nutritional value.
(E) Kale and collard greens have the same nutritional value.

15. On the basis of a decrease in the college-age population, many colleges now anticipate increasingly smaller freshman classes each year. Surprised by a 40 percent increase in qualified applicants over the previous year, however, administrators at Nice College now plan to hire more faculty for courses taken by all freshmen.

Which of the following statements about Nice College's current qualified applicants, if true, would strongly suggest that the administrators' plan is flawed?

(A) A substantially higher percentage than usual plan to study for advanced degrees after graduation from college.
(B) According to their applications, their level of participation in extracurricular activities and varsity sports is unusually high.
(C) According to their applications, none of them lives in a foreign country.
(D) A substantially lower percentage than usual rate Nice College as their first choice among the colleges to which they are applying.
(E) A substantially lower percentage than usual list mathematics as their intended major.

16. A researcher discovered that people who have low levels of immune-system activity tend to score much lower on tests of mental health than do people with normal or high immune-system activity. The researcher concluded from this experiment that the immune system protects against mental illness as well as against physical disease.

The researcher's conclusion depends on which of the following assumptions?

(A) High immune-system activity protects against mental illness better than normal immune-system activity does.
(B) Mental illness is similar to physical disease in its effects on body systems.
(C) People with high immune-system activity cannot develop mental illness.
(D) Mental illness does not cause people's immune-system activity to decrease.
(E) Psychological treatment of mental illness is not as effective as is medical treatment.

STOP

IF YOU FINISH BEFORE TIME IS CALLED, YOU MAY CHECK YOUR WORK ON THIS SECTION ONLY.
DO NOT TURN TO ANY OTHER SECTION IN THE TEST.

Answer Key for Sample Test Section 3

CRITICAL REASONING

1. B	9. C
2. B	10. D
3. B	11. D
4. C	12. E
5. E	13. A
6. C	14. A
7. B	15. D
8. C	16. D

Explanatory Material: Critical Reasoning Sample Test Section 3

1. Rural households have more purchasing power than do urban or suburban households at the same income level, since some of the income urban and suburban households use for food and shelter can be used by rural households for other needs.

   Which of the following inferences is best supported by the statement made above?

   (A) The average rural household includes more people than does the average urban or suburban household.
   (B) Rural households have lower food and housing costs than do either urban or suburban households.
   (C) Suburban households generally have more purchasing power than do either rural or urban households.
   (D) The median income of urban and suburban households is generally higher than that of rural households.
   (E) All three types of households spend more of their income on housing than on all other purchases combined.

If the greater purchasing power of rural households results from their having more money left over after meeting basic expenses, it follows, as B says, that those expenses are lower for those households than they are for suburban or urban households at the same income level. Consequently, B is the best answer.

Choice A is not a supported inference, since there is no information to suggest that larger households are not more likely to have either more purchasing power or lower food and shelter expenses. Choices C and D are not supported, since the passage compares only households that share the same income level. Because the relative amounts spent on different types of expenditures are not specified for any of the categories of households, E is not supported.

2. In 1985 state border colleges in Texas lost the enrollment of more than half, on average, of the Mexican nationals they had previously served each year. Teaching faculties have alleged that this extreme drop resulted from a rise in tuition for international and out-of-state students from $40 to $120 per credit hour.

   Which of the following, if feasible, offers the best prospects for alleviating the problem of the drop in enrollment of Mexican nationals as the teaching faculties assessed it?

   (A) Providing grants-in-aid to Mexican nationals to study in Mexican universities
   (B) Allowing Mexican nationals to study in Texas border colleges and to pay in-state tuition rates, which are the same as the previous international rate
   (C) Reemphasizing the goals and mission of the Texas state border colleges as serving both in-state students and Mexican nationals
   (D) Increasing the financial resources of Texas colleges by raising the tuition for in-state students attending state institutions
   (E) Offering career counseling for those Mexican nationals who graduate from state border colleges and intend to return to Mexico

The teaching faculties attribute the drop in enrollment of Mexican nationals to an increase in tuition costs. If the faculties are correct, reducing these costs should halt the drop in enrollment. Choice B offers a plan for reducing these costs and so is the best answer.

Neither C nor D nor E offers a plan that would reduce the costs taken to be responsible for the drop in enrollment. Nor does A offer such a plan: because the problem to be addressed is a drop in enrollment of Mexican nationals at Texas border colleges, providing financial incentive for Mexican nationals to study at Mexican universities, as A suggests, would offer no prospect of alleviating the problem.

3. **Affirmative action is good business. So asserted the National Association of Manufacturers while urging retention of an executive order requiring some federal contractors to set numerical goals for hiring minorities and women. "Diversity in work force participation has produced new ideas in management, product development, and marketing," the association claimed.**

The association's argument as it is presented in the passage above would be most strengthened if which of the following were true?

(A) The percentage of minority and women workers in business has increased more slowly than many minority and women's groups would prefer.

(B) Those businesses with the highest percentages of minority and women workers are those that have been the most innovative and profitable.

(C) Disposable income has been rising as fast among minorities and women as among the population as a whole.

(D) The biggest growth in sales in the manufacturing sector has come in industries that market the most innovative products.

(E) Recent improvements in management practices have allowed many manufacturers to experience enormous gains in worker productivity.

If, as B says, businesses with the highest percentages of minorities and women have been the most profitable, there is reason to believe that, because it increases the level of participation of women and minorities in the work force, affirmative action is good business. Thus, B is the best answer.

Choice A suggests that minority and women's groups have reason to support affirmative action, but it does not indicate that affirmative action is good business. Because there is no indication that the improvement in disposable income noted in C is due to affirmative action, C does not strengthen the argument given for affirmative action. Choice D addresses growth in sales and E addresses improvements in management; neither, however, asserts that these benefits are due to affirmative action.

Questions 4-5 refer to the following.

If the airspace around centrally located airports were restricted to commercial airliners and only those private planes equipped with radar, most of the private-plane traffic would be forced to use outlying airfields. Such a reduction in the amount of private-plane traffic would reduce the risk of midair collision around the centrally located airports.

4. The conclusion drawn in the first sentence depends on which of the following assumptions?

(A) Outlying airfields would be as convenient as centrally located airports for most pilots of private planes.

(B) Most outlying airfields are not equipped to handle commercial-airline traffic.

(C) Most private planes that use centrally located airports are not equipped with radar.

(D) Commercial airliners are at greater risk of becoming involved in midair collisions than are private planes.

(E) A reduction in the risk of midair collision would eventually lead to increases in commercial-airline traffic.

The first sentence concludes that prohibiting private planes that are not radar-equipped from centrally located airports would force most private planes away from those airports. This conclusion cannnot be true unless it is true that, as choice C says, most private planes that use these airports are not radar-equipped. Therefore the first sentence's conclusion assumes choice C, which is thus the best answer.

The conclusion need not assume that outlying airfields are convenient for private planes (choice A), since the restrictions would give planes that are not radar equipped no choice. The conclusion concerns only how the radar requirement would affect the volume of private plane traffic, so choice B, which deals with commercial planes, and choices D and E, which deal with risk of midair collision, need not be assumed.

5. Which of the following, if true, would most strengthen the conclusion drawn in the second sentence?

(A) Commercial airliners are already required by law to be equipped with extremely sophisticated radar systems.

(B) Centrally located airports are experiencing overcrowded airspace primarily because of sharp increases in commercial-airline traffic.

(C) Many pilots of private planes would rather buy radar equipment than be excluded from centrally located airports.

(D) The number of midair collisions that occur near centrally located airports has decreased in recent years.

(E) Private planes not equipped with radar systems cause a disproportionately large number of midair collisions around centrally located airports.

The second sentence concludes that the reduction described in the first sentence would reduce the risk of midair collisions around centrally located airports. According to E, such a reduction would remove precisely the kind of plane that causes a disproportionate number of midair collisions. Thus E is the best answer.

Choices B and C concern the question of whether or not the proposed restrictions would reduce plane traffic, but not the question of whether any resulting reductions would reduce the risk of midair collisions. Because A does not address the question of whether reducing private-plane traffic would reduce the risk of midair collisions, A is inappropriate. That the number of midair collisions has recently decreased is irrelevant to whether the proposed reduction would further reduce collisions, so D is inappropriate.

6. Which of the following best completes the passage below?

Established companies concentrate on defending what they already have. Consequently, they tend not to be innovative themselves and tend to underestimate the effects of the innovations of others. The clearest example of this defensive strategy is the fact that ------.

(A) ballpoint pens and soft-tip markers have eliminated the traditional market for fountain pens, clearing the way for the marketing of fountain pens as luxury or prestige items

(B) a highly successful automobile was introduced by the same company that had earlier introduced a model that had been a dismal failure

(C) a once-successful manufacturer of slide rules reacted to the introduction of electronic calculators by trying to make better slide rules

(D) one of the first models of modern accounting machines, designed for use in the banking industry, was purchased by a public library as well as by banks

(E) the inventor of a commonly used anesthetic did not intend the product to be used by dentists, who currently account for almost the entire market for that drug

Choice C is a clear example of a defensive, noninnovative strategy that underestimates the effects of others' innovations: the slide-rule manufacturer acted as though any advantages offered by the newer and fundamentally different technology of a competing product, the electronic calculator, could be matched by improving the older, more familiar product. Choice C is thus the best answer.

The other choices are not examples of the defensive strategy the author cites. Choices D and E are cases of new products finding unintended users, not of responses to innovations of others; nor does B describe such a response. Choice A presents a case in which innovative products displaced an older product from its traditional market but in so doing made possible a new marketing strategy for the older product.

7. Most archaeologists have held that people first reached the Americas less than 20,000 years ago by crossing a land bridge into North America. But recent discoveries of human shelters in South America dating from 32,000 years ago have led researchers to speculate that people arrived in South America first, after voyaging across the Pacific, and then spread northward.

Which of the following, if it were discovered, would be pertinent evidence against the speculation above?

(A) A rock shelter near Pittsburgh, Pennsylvania, contains evidence of use by human beings 19,000 years ago.
(B) Some North American sites of human habitation predate any sites found in South America.
(C) The climate is warmer at the 32,000-year-old South American site than at the oldest known North American site.
(D) The site in South America that was occupied 32,000 years ago was continuously occupied until 6,000 years ago.
(E) The last Ice Age, between 11,500 and 20,000 years ago, considerably lowered worldwide sea levels.

The reasoning behind the researchers' speculation that people first arrived in South America is that there is no evidence of North American sites that predate the human shelters discovered in South America. If it were discovered that, as B states, some North American sites predate those in South America, the reasoning behind the speculation would no longer hold. Thus, B is the best answer.

The facts related in A and E both involve time periods occurring after those discussed in the passage, and so create no conflict with the speculation. Although C and D describe discoveries about the South American site, neither the relative climates mentioned in C nor the duration of occupation mentioned in D provides evidence against the speculation.

8. In Asia, where palm trees are non-native, the trees' flowers have traditionally been pollinated by hand, which has kept palm fruit productivity unnaturally low. When weevils known to be efficient pollinators of palm flowers were introduced into Asia in 1980, palm fruit productivity increased — by up to fifty percent in some areas — but then decreased sharply in 1984.

Which of the following statements, if true, would best explain the 1984 decrease in productivity?

(A) Prices for palm fruit fell between 1980 and 1984 following the rise in production and a concurrent fall in demand.
(B) Imported trees are often more productive than native trees because the imported ones have left behind their pests and diseases in their native lands.
(C) Rapid increases in productivity tend to deplete trees of nutrients needed for the development of the fruit-producing female flowers.
(D) The weevil population in Asia remained at approximately the same level between 1980 and 1984.
(E) Prior to 1980 another species of insect pollinated the Asian palm trees, but not as efficiently as the species of weevil that was introduced in 1980.

If C is true, the rapid increase in productivity among Asian palm trees after 1980 probably depleted nutrients needed for the development of fruit-producing flowers. Thus C explains why the palms' productivity could subsequently decline, and is the best answer.

Choice A relates a drop in the price of palm fruit to a rise in production and a fall in demand, but it does not explain the subsequent drop in the trees' productivity. Choice B gives no reason for the decrease in productivity of the trees introduced to Asia. Nor does D, since the stability of the weevil population described in D would support stability of palm fruit productivity between 1980 and 1984 rather than a decrease. Because E describes the pollination of the trees prior to 1980, it cannot explain a change occurring in 1984.

9. Since the mayor's publicity campaign for Greenville's bus service began six months ago, morning automobile traffic into the midtown area of the city has decreased seven percent. During the same period, there has been an equivalent rise in the number of persons riding buses into the midtown area. Obviously, the mayor's publicity campaign has convinced many people to leave their cars at home and ride the bus to work.

Which of the following, if true, casts the most serious doubt on the conclusion drawn above?

(A) Fares for all bus routes in Greenville have risen an average of five percent during the past six months.
(B) The mayor of Greenville rides the bus to City Hall in the city's midtown area.
(C) Road reconstruction has greatly reduced the number of lanes available to commuters in major streets leading to the midtown area during the past six months.
(D) The number of buses entering the midtown area of Greenville during the morning hours is exactly the same now as it was one year ago.
(E) Surveys show that longtime bus riders are no more satisfied with the Greenville bus service than they were before the mayor's publicity campaign began.

The passage concludes that the mayor's publicity campaign has persuaded people to ride the bus to work instead of driving, and it cites as evidence the decreased morning automobile traffic and increased bus ridership into the midtown area. But the road reconstruction described in C provides an alternative explanation for this evidence, so C is the best answer.

Choice A eliminates decreased fares as a possible explanation for the increased ridership, so it supports rather than casts doubt on the conclusion. Similarly, (D) and (E) each eliminate a possible explanation: the unchanged number of buses cited in D, and longtime bus riders' attitudes cited in E suggest that the increased ridership is not explained by improved service. The fact that the mayor rides the bus, cited in B, may contribute to the effectiveness of the publicity campaign, but it is irrelevant to assessing whether the campaign caused the increased ridership.

10. In the aftermath of a worldwide stock-market crash, Country T claimed that the severity of the stock market crash it experienced resulted from the accelerated process of denationalization many of its industries underwent shortly before the crash.

Which of the following, if it could be carried out, would be most useful in an evaluation of Country T's assessment of the causes of the severity of its stock-market crash?

(A) Calculating the average loss experienced by individual traders in Country T during the crash
(B) Using economic theory to predict the most likely date of the next crash in Country T
(C) Comparing the total number of shares sold during the worst days of the crash in Country T to the total number of shares sold in Country T just prior to the crash
(D) Comparing the severity of the crash in Country T to the severity of the crash in countries otherwise economically similar to Country T that have not experienced recent denationalization
(E) Comparing the long-term effects of the crash on the purchasing power of the currency of Country T to the immediate, more severe short-term effects of the crash on the purchasing power of the currency of Country T

The comparison suggested in D would be useful in evaluating Country T's assessment of the causes of the severity of its stock market crash. If the severity of the crash is at least as great in the countries that are, except for recent nationalization, economically similar to Country T, Country T's assessment is undermined. If the severity of the crash is not as great in these countries as in Country T, however, the assessment is supported. Thus, D is the best answer.

Choices A, C, and E are not good answers because each concerns only determining the severity of the crash in Country T, not assessing a hypothesis about the causes of the crash. Nor is the date of Country T's next crash relevant to assessing such a hypothesis; thus, B is inappropriate.

11. With the emergence of biotechnology companies, it was feared that they would impose silence about proprietary results on their in-house researchers and their academic consultants. This constraint, in turn, would slow the development of biological science and engineering.

Which of the following, if true, would tend to weaken most seriously the prediction of scientific secrecy described above?

(A) Biotechnological research funded by industry has reached some conclusions that are of major scientific importance.

(B) When the results of scientific research are kept secret, independent researchers are unable to build on those results.

(C) Since the research priorities of biotechnology companies are not the same as those of academic institutions, the financial support of research by such companies distorts the research agenda.

(D) To enhance the companies' standing in the scientific community, the biotechnology companies encourage employees to publish their results, especially results that are important.

(E) Biotechnology companies devote some of their research resources to problems that are of fundamental scientific importance and that are not expected to produce immediate practical applications.

Choice D weakens the prediction of secrecy by establishing that biotechnology companies have a strong motive to encourage their researchers to publicize results. Therefore, D is the best answer.

Neither A nor B nor E provides any reason to expect that the prediction will be or will not be fulfilled. Choices A and B support the argument that developments in biological science and engineering would be slowed if the prediction of secrecy were fulfilled. Choice E, which says that biotechnology companies devote some resources to fundamental problems without immediate practical benefits, is merely consistent with that argument and so does not weaken the prediction. The distortion of the research agenda asserted in C is not relevant to the question of scientific secrecy.

12. Some people have questioned the judge's objectivity in cases of sex discrimination against women. But the record shows that in sixty percent of such cases, the judge has decided in favor of the women. This record demonstrates that the judge has not discriminated against women in cases of sex discrimination against women.

The argument above is flawed in that it ignores the possibility that

(A) a large number of the judge's cases arose out of allegations of sex discrimination against women

(B) many judges find it difficult to be objective in cases of sex discrimination against women

(C) the judge is biased against women defendants or plaintiffs in cases that do not involve sex discrimination

(D) the majority of the cases of sex discrimination against women that have reached the judge's court have been appealed from a lower court

(E) the evidence shows that the women should have won in more than sixty percent of the judge's cases involving sex discrimination against women

The flaw in the argument is that it assumes erroneously that a majority of decisions favorable to women in sex discrimination cases demonstrates absence of discriminatory behavior against women on the part of the judge who made those decisions. Choice E exposes this flaw by pointing out that the judge may well have failed to decide in favor of women in cases where evidence shows that the women should have won. Therefore, E is the best answer.

Choices B and C introduce considerations with no bearing on the reasoning of the argument. Because the argument concerns a particular judge, B is inappropriate; because it concerns cases of a particular type, C is inappropriate. Choices A and D also have no bearing, because the origin of these cases is not at issue in the argument.

13. The tobacco industry is still profitable and projections are that it will remain so. In the United States this year, the total amount of tobacco sold by tobacco-farmers has increased, even though the number of adults who smoke has decreased.

Each of the following, if true, could explain the simultaneous increase in tobacco sales and decrease in the number of adults who smoke EXCEPT:

(A) During this year, the number of women who have begun to smoke is greater than the number of men who have quit smoking.

(B) The number of teen-age children who have begun to smoke this year is greater than the number of adults who have quit smoking during the same period.

(C) During this year, the number of nonsmokers who have begun to use chewing tobacco or snuff is greater than the number of people who have quit smoking.

(D) The people who have continued to smoke consume more tobacco per person than they did in the past.

(E) More of the cigarettes made in the United States this year were exported to other countries than was the case last year.

If the number of men beginning to smoke and the number of women quitting smoking during the year are equal, choice A would result in an increase, not a decrease, in the number of adults who smoke. Hence, A does *not* explain the facts cited and is the best answer.

Given the decrease in the number of adults who smoke, the increase in tobacco sales could be explained by a proportionally greater increase in the nonadults who smoke or the nonsmokers who use tobacco. An increase in total tobacco use by smokers or in the sales of United States tobacco abroad would also explain the facts cited. Thus, because B, C, D, and E could explain the facts cited, none of them can be the best answer.

14. Kale has more nutritional value than spinach. But since collard greens have more nutritional value than lettuce, it follows that kale has more nutritional value than lettuce.

Any of the following, if introduced into the argument as an additional premise, makes the argument above logically correct EXCEPT:

(A) Collard greens have more nutritional value than kale.

(B) Spinach has more nutritional value than lettuce.

(C) Spinach has more nutritional value than collard greens.

(D) Spinach and collard greens have the same nutritional value.

(E) Kale and collard greens have the same nutritional value.

The question asks for an additional premise that does *not* make the argument logically correct. Adding choice A to the information given in the passage leaves open the possibility that, in order of nutritional value, the vegetables rank: collard greens, lettuce, kale, spinach. Because this order is contrary to the conclusion of the argument, A leaves open the possibility that the conclusion of the argument is false; A is thus the best answer.

By contrast, any of choices B, C, D, and E, when added to the information that the nutritional value of kale is greater than that of spinach and that the nutritional value of collard greens is greater than that of lettuce, makes the conclusion — that kale has more nutritional value than lettuce — follow logically.

15. On the basis of a decrease in the college-age population, many colleges now anticipate increasingly smaller freshman classes each year. Surprised by a 40 percent increase in qualified applicants over the previous year, however, administrators at Nice College now plan to hire more faculty for courses taken by all freshmen.

Which of the following statements about Nice College's current qualified applicants, if true, would strongly suggest that the administrators' plan is flawed?

(A) A substantially higher percentage than usual plan to study for advanced degrees after graduation from college.

(B) According to their applications, their level of participation in extracurricular activities and varsity sports is unusually high.

(C) According to their applications, none of them lives in a foreign country.

(D) A substantially lower percentage than usual rate Nice College as their first choice among the colleges to which they are applying.

(E) A substantially lower percentage than usual list mathematics as their intended major.

If, as D states, a substantial percentage of the qualified applicants do not rate Nice College as their first choice, then, provided many of these applicants are accepted at and enroll in the colleges that are their first choices, the increase in applications to Nice College might not result in any increase in the size of its freshman class. So D is the best answer.

Nothing can be determined from A, B, C, or E about the size of the freshman class, so none of these choices is relevant to the question of whether Nice College should hire more faculty to teach courses taken by all freshmen. Thus, these choices are inappropriate.

16. A researcher discovered that people who have low levels of immune-system activity tend to score much lower on tests of mental health than do people with normal or high immune-system activity. The researcher concluded from this experiment that the immune system protects against mental illness as well as against physical disease.

The researcher's conclusion depends on which of the following assumptions?

(A) High immune-system activity protects against mental illness better than normal immune-system activity does.

(B) Mental illness is similar to physical disease in its effects on body systems.

(C) People with high immune-system activity cannot develop mental illness.

(D) Mental illness does not cause people's immune-system activity to decrease.

(E) Psychological treatment of mental illness is not as effective as is medical treatment.

The researcher concludes from the association of low immune-system activity with low mental-health scores that, in effect, immune system activity can inhibit mental illness. If, contrary to D, mental illness can depress immune-system activity, the association mentioned does not support the researcher's conclusion. So D must be assumed.

Normal immune-system activity could protect against mental illness without high-immune system activity offering increased protection, contrary to what A states, or prevention, contrary to what C states, so neither A nor C is assumed. The conclusion does not depend on there being a similarity between mental and physical illness, so B is not assumed; nor does it depend on there being a difference in treatments, so E is not assumed.

CRITICAL REASONING SAMPLE TEST SECTION 4

Time — 25 minutes

16 Questions

Directions: For each question in this section, select the best of the answer choices given.

1. A milepost on the towpath read "21" on the side facing the hiker as she approached it and "23" on its back. She reasoned that the next milepost forward on the path would indicate that she was halfway between one end of the path and the other. However, the milepost one mile further on read "20" facing her and "24" behind.

Which of the following, if true, would explain the discrepancy described above?

(A) The numbers on the next milepost had been reversed.
(B) The numbers on the mileposts indicate kilometers, not miles.
(C) The facing numbers indicate miles to the end of the path, not miles from the beginning.
(D) A milepost was missing between the two the hiker encountered.
(E) The mileposts had originally been put in place for the use of mountain bikers, not for hikers.

2. Airline: Newly developed collision-avoidance systems, although not fully tested to discover potential malfunctions, must be installed immediately in passenger planes. Their mechanical warnings enable pilots to avoid crashes.

Pilots: Pilots will not fly in planes with collision-avoidance systems that are not fully tested. Malfunctioning systems could mislead pilots, causing crashes.

The pilots' objection is most strengthened if which of the following is true?

(A) It is always possible for mechanical devices to malfunction.
(B) Jet engines, although not fully tested when first put into use, have achieved exemplary performance and safety records.
(C) Although collision-avoidance systems will enable pilots to avoid some crashes, the likely malfunctions of the not-fully-tested systems will cause even more crashes.
(D) Many airline collisions are caused in part by the exhaustion of overworked pilots.
(E) Collision-avoidance systems, at this stage of development, appear to have worked better in passenger planes than in cargo planes during experimental flights made over a six-month period.

3. Guitar strings often go "dead"—become less responsive and bright in tone—after a few weeks of intense use. A researcher whose son is a classical guitarist hypothesized that dirt and oil, rather than changes in the material properties of the string, were responsible.

Which of the following investigations is most likely to yield significant information that would help to evaluate the researcher's hypothesis?

(A) Determining if a metal alloy is used to make the strings used by classical guitarists
(B) Determining whether classical guitarists make their strings go dead faster than do folk guitarists
(C) Determining whether identical lengths of string, of the same gauge, go dead at different rates when strung on various brands of guitars
(D) Determining whether a dead string and a new string produce different qualities of sound
(E) Determining whether smearing various substances on new guitar strings causes them to go dead

4. Most consumers do not get much use out of the sports equipment they purchase. For example, seventeen percent of the adults in the United States own jogging shoes, but only forty-five percent of the owners jog more than once a year, and only seventeen percent jog more than once a week.

Which of the following, if true, casts most doubt on the claim that most consumers get little use out of the sports equipment they purchase?

(A) Joggers are most susceptible to sports injuries during the first six months in which they jog.
(B) Joggers often exaggerate the frequency with which they jog in surveys designed to elicit such information.
(C) Many consumers purchase jogging shoes for use in activities other than jogging.
(D) Consumers who take up jogging often purchase an athletic shoe that can be used in other sports.
(E) Joggers who jog more than once a week are often active participants in other sports as well.

GO ON TO THE NEXT PAGE.

5. Two decades after the Emerald River Dam was built, none of the eight fish species native to the Emerald River was still reproducing adequately in the river below the dam. Since the dam reduced the annual range of water temperature in the river below the dam from 50 degrees to 6 degrees, scientists have hypothesized that sharply rising water temperatures must be involved in signaling the native species to begin the reproductive cycle.

Which of the following statements, if true, would most strengthen the scientists' hypothesis?

(A) The native fish species were still able to reproduce only in side streams of the river below the dam where the annual temperature range remains approximately 50 degrees.
(B) Before the dam was built, the Emerald River annually overflowed its banks, creating backwaters that were critical breeding areas for the native species of fish.
(C) The lowest recorded temperature of the Emerald River before the dam was built was 34 degrees, whereas the lowest recorded temperature of the river after the dam was built has been 43 degrees.
(D) Nonnative species of fish, introduced into the Emerald River after the dam was built, have begun competing with the declining native fish species for food and space.
(E) Five of the fish species native to the Emerald River are not native to any other river in North America.

6. It is true that it is against international law to sell plutonium to countries that do not yet have nuclear weapons. But if United States companies do not do so, companies in other countries will.

Which of the following is most like the argument above in its logical structure?

(A) It is true that it is against the police department's policy to negotiate with kidnappers. But if the police want to prevent loss of life, they must negotiate in some cases.
(B) It is true that it is illegal to refuse to register for military service. But there is a long tradition in the United States of conscientious objection to serving in the armed forces.
(C) It is true that it is illegal for a government official to participate in a transaction in which there is an apparent conflict of interest. But if the facts are examined carefully, it will clearly be seen that there was no actual conflict of interest in the defendant's case.
(D) It is true that it is against the law to burglarize people's homes. But someone else certainly would have burglarized that house if the defendant had not done so first.
(E) It is true that company policy forbids supervisors to fire employees without two written warnings. But there have been many supervisors who have disobeyed this policy.

GO ON TO THE NEXT PAGE.

7. In recent years many cabinetmakers have been winning acclaim as artists. But since furniture must be useful, cabinetmakers must exercise their craft with an eye to the practical utility of their product. For this reason, cabinetmaking is not art.

Which of the following is an assumption that supports drawing the conclusion above from the reason given for that conclusion?

(A) Some furniture is made to be placed in museums, where it will not be used by anyone.

(B) Some cabinetmakers are more concerned than others with the practical utility of the products they produce.

(C) Cabinetmakers should be more concerned with the practical utility of their products than they currently are.

(D) An object is not an art object if its maker pays attention to the object's practical utility.

(E) Artists are not concerned with the monetary value of their products.

8. Although custom prosthetic bone replacements produced through a new computer-aided design process will cost more than twice as much as ordinary replacements, custom replacements should still be cost-effective. Not only will surgery and recovery time be reduced, but custom replacements should last longer, thereby reducing the need for further hospital stays.

Which of the following must be studied in order to evaluate the argument presented above?

(A) The amount of time a patient spends in surgery *versus* the amount of time spent recovering from surgery

(B) The amount by which the cost of producing custom replacements has declined with the introduction of the new technique for producing them

(C) The degree to which the use of custom replacements is likely to reduce the need for repeat surgery when compared with the use of ordinary replacements

(D) The degree to which custom replacements produced with the new technique are more carefully manufactured than are ordinary replacements

(E) The amount by which custom replacements produced with the new technique will drop in cost as the production procedures become standardized and applicable on a larger scale

9. Extinction is a process that can depend on a variety of ecological, geographical, and physiological variables. These variables affect different species of organisms in different ways, and should, therefore, yield a random pattern of extinctions. However, the fossil record shows that extinction occurs in a surprisingly definite pattern, with many species vanishing at the same time.

Which of the following, if true, forms the best basis for at least a partial explanation of the patterned extinctions revealed by the fossil record?

(A) Major episodes of extinction can result from widespread environmental disturbances that affect numerous different species.

(B) Certain extinction episodes selectively affect organisms with particular sets of characteristics unique to their species.

(C) Some species become extinct because of accumulated gradual changes in their local environments.

(D) In geologically recent times, for which there is no fossil record, human intervention has changed the pattern of extinctions.

(E) Species that are widely dispersed are the least likely to become extinct.

10. Neither a rising standard of living nor balanced trade, by itself, establishes a country's ability to compete in the international marketplace. Both are required simultaneously since standards of living can rise because of growing trade deficits and trade can be balanced by means of a decline in a country's standard of living.

If the facts stated in the passage above are true, a proper test of a country's ability to be competitive is its ability to

(A) balance its trade while its standard of living rises

(B) balance its trade while its standard of living falls

(C) increase trade deficits while its standard of living rises

(D) decrease trade deficits while its standard of living falls

(E) keep its standard of living constant while trade deficits rise

GO ON TO THE NEXT PAGE.

11. Certain messenger molecules fight damage to the lungs from noxious air by telling the muscle cells encircling the lungs' airways to contract. This partially seals off the lungs. An asthma attack occurs when the messenger molecules are activated unnecessarily, in response to harmless things like pollen or household dust.

Which of the following, if true, points to the most serious flaw of a plan to develop a medication that would prevent asthma attacks by blocking receipt of any messages sent by the messenger molecules referred to above?

(A) Researchers do not yet know how the body produces the messenger molecules that trigger asthma attacks.

(B) Researchers do not yet know what makes one person's messenger molecules more easily activated than another's.

(C) Such a medication would not become available for several years, because of long lead times in both development and manufacture.

(D) Such a medication would be unable to distinguish between messages triggered by pollen and household dust and messages triggered by noxious air.

(E) Such a medication would be a preventative only and would be unable to alleviate an asthma attack once it had started.

12. Since the routine use of antibiotics can give rise to resistant bacteria capable of surviving antibiotic environments, the presence of resistant bacteria in people could be due to the human use of prescription antibiotics. Some scientists, however, believe that most resistant bacteria in people derive from human consumption of bacterially infected meat.

Which of the following statements, if true, would most significantly strengthen the hypothesis of the scientists?

(A) Antibiotics are routinely included in livestock feed so that livestock producers can increase the rate of growth of their animals.

(B) Most people who develop food poisoning from bacterially infected meat are treated with prescription antibiotics.

(C) The incidence of resistant bacteria in people has tended to be much higher in urban areas than in rural areas where meat is of comparable quality.

(D) People who have never taken prescription antibiotics are those least likely to develop resistant bacteria.

(E) Livestock producers claim that resistant bacteria in animals cannot be transmitted to people through infected meat.

13. The recent decline in the value of the dollar was triggered by a prediction of slower economic growth in the coming year. But that prediction would not have adversely affected the dollar had it not been for the government's huge budget deficit, which must therefore be decreased to prevent future currency declines.

Which of the following, if true, would most seriously weaken the conclusion about how to prevent future currency declines?

(A) The government has made little attempt to reduce the budget deficit.

(B) The budget deficit has not caused a slowdown in economic growth.

(C) The value of the dollar declined several times in the year prior to the recent prediction of slower economic growth.

(D) Before there was a large budget deficit, predictions of slower economic growth frequently caused declines in the dollar's value.

(E) When there is a large budget deficit, other events in addition to predictions of slower economic growth sometimes trigger declines in currency value.

14. Which of the following best completes the passage below?

At a recent conference on environmental threats to the North Sea, most participating countries favored uniform controls on the quality of effluents, whether or not specific environmental damage could be attributed to a particular source of effluent. What must, of course, be shown, in order to avoid excessively restrictive controls, is that _____.

(A) any uniform controls that are adopted are likely to be implemented without delay

(B) any substance to be made subject to controls can actually cause environmental damage

(C) the countries favoring uniform controls are those generating the largest quantities of effluents

(D) all of any given pollutant that is to be controlled actually reaches the North Sea at present

(E) environmental damage already inflicted on the North Sea is reversible

GO ON TO THE NEXT PAGE.

15. Traditionally, decision-making by managers that is reasoned step-by-step has been considered preferable to intuitive decision-making. However, a recent study found that top managers used intuition significantly more than did most middle- or lower-level managers. This confirms the alternative view that intuition is actually more effective than careful, methodical reasoning.

The conclusion above is based on which of the following assumptions?

(A) Methodical, step-by-step reasoning is inappropriate for making many real-life management decisions.
(B) Top managers have the ability to use either intuitive reasoning or methodical, step-by-step reasoning in making decisions.
(C) The decisions made by middle- and lower-level managers can be made as easily by using methodical reasoning as by using intuitive reasoning.
(D) Top managers use intuitive reasoning in making the majority of their decisions.
(E) Top managers are more effective at decision-making than middle- or lower-level managers.

16. The imposition of quotas limiting imported steel will not help the big American steel mills. In fact, the quotas will help "mini-mills" flourish in the United States. Those small domestic mills will take more business from the big American steel mills than would have been taken by the foreign steel mills in the absence of quotas.

Which of the following, if true, would cast the most serious doubt on the claim made in the last sentence above?

(A) Quality rather than price is a major factor in determining the type of steel to be used for a particular application.
(B) Foreign steel mills have long produced grades of steel comparable in quality to the steel produced by the big American mills.
(C) American quotas on imported goods have often induced other countries to impose similar quotas on American goods.
(D) Domestic "mini-mills" consistently produce better grades of steel than do the big American mills.
(E) Domestic "mini-mills" produce low-volume, specialized types of steels that are not produced by the big American steel mills.

STOP

IF YOU FINISH BEFORE TIME IS CALLED, YOU MAY CHECK YOUR WORK ON THIS SECTION ONLY.
DO NOT TURN TO ANY OTHER SECTION IN THE TEST.

Answer Key for Sample Test Section 4
CRITICAL REASONING

1.	C	9.	A
2.	C	10.	A
3.	E	11.	D
4.	C	12.	A
5.	A	13.	D
6.	D	14.	B
7.	D	15.	E
8.	C	16.	E

Explanatory Material: Critical Reasoning Sample Test Section 4

1. A milepost on the towpath read "21" on the side facing the hiker as she approached it and "23" on its back. She reasoned that the next milepost forward on the path would indicate that she was halfway between one end of the path and the other. However, the milepost one mile further on read "20" facing her and "24" behind.

   Which of the following, if true, would explain the discrepancy described above?

   (A) The numbers on the next milepost had been reversed.
   (B) The numbers on the mileposts indicate kilometers, not miles.
   (C) The facing numbers indicate miles to the end of the path, not miles from the beginning.
   (D) A milepost was missing between the two the hiker encountered.
   (E) The mileposts had originally been put in place for the use of mountain bikers, not for hikers.

The hiker's reasoning assumes that the number that faced her indicated distance from the path's beginning. The numbers on the second milepost show that this assumption was erroneous. They are, however, the numbers that would be expected if the facing number indicated the distance to the path's end with the number on the back indicating the distance from the beginning. Thus choice C explains the discrepancy and is the best answer.

The next milepost being reversed (choice A) cannot be the explanation, because if the hiker's reasoning were accurate both numbers on the milepost would be 22. The units (choice B) would not affect whether the number became smaller or larger. Nor would a missing milepost (choice D) affect the direction of change. The mode of transportation (choice E) is irrelevant to distance.

2. Airline: Newly developed collision-avoidance systems, although not fully tested to discover potential malfunctions, must be installed immediately in passenger planes. Their mechanical warnings enable pilots to avoid crashes.

   Pilots: Pilots will not fly in planes with collision avoidance systems that are not fully tested. Malfunctioning systems could mislead pilots, causing crashes.

   The pilots' objection is most strengthened if which of the following is true?

   (A) It is always possible for mechanical devices to malfunction.
   (B) Jet engines, although not fully tested when first put into use, have achieved exemplary performance and safety records.
   (C) Although collision-avoidance systems will enable pilots to avoid some crashes, the likely malfunctions of the not-fully-tested systems will cause even more crashes.
   (D) Many airline collisions are caused in part by the exhaustion of overworked pilots.
   (E) Collision-avoidance systems, at this stage of development, appear to have worked better in passenger planes than in cargo planes during experimental flights made over a six-month period.

Choice C states that what the pilots think could happen is likely to happen. Thus, C is the best answer.

Choice A is inappropriate because it says nothing about the malfunctions that most concern the pilots — those that might mislead. Nor does A distinguish tested from not-fully-tested systems. Choice B is inappropriate. The only outcome of using insufficiently tested equipment that might strengthen the pilots' objection is an unfavorable one, but B reports on a favorable outcome. Choice D is inappropriate because it mentions a problem that needs to be addressed whether or not the collision avoidance systems are installed immediately. Choice E is inappropriate because it provides no evidence that any malfunctions were of a sort to mislead pilots and cause crashes.

3. Guitar strings often go "dead" — become less responsive and bright in tone — after a few weeks of intense use. A researcher whose son is a classical guitarist hypothesized that dirt and oil, rather than changes in the material properties of the string, were responsible.

Which of the following investigations is most likely to yield significant information that would help to evaluate the researcher's hypothesis?

(A) Determining if a metal alloy is used to make the strings used by classical guitarists
(B) Determining whether classical guitarists make their strings go dead faster than do folk guitarists
(C) Determining whether identical lengths of string, of the same gauge, go dead at different rates when strung on various brands of guitars
(D) Determining whether a dead string and a new string produce different qualities of sound
(E) Determining whether smearing various substances on new guitar strings causes them to go dead

The hypothesis has two parts: first, that intense use does not bring material changes that cause the string to go dead and, second, that dirt and oil do cause the phenomenon. The experiment suggested in choice E directly tests this hypothesis by contaminating strings that are known to have their original material properties. Thus, E is the best answer.

Because factors associated with style of play (choice B) and brand of guitar (choice C) might affect how the strings become contaminated, no result of the investigations in B and C will allow clear evaluation of the hypothesis. Information about the strings' material (choice A) will need considerable supplementation before its bearing on the hypothesis is clear. The passage already gives the information promised by investigation D.

4. Most consumers do not get much use out of the sports equipment they purchase. For example, seventeen percent of the adults in the United States own jogging shoes, but only forty-five percent of the owners jog more than once a year, and only seventeen percent jog more than once a week.

Which of the following, if true, casts most doubt on the claim that most consumers get little use out of the sports equipment they purchase?

(A) Joggers are most susceptible to sports injuries during the first six months in which they jog.
(B) Joggers often exaggerate the frequency with which they jog in surveys designed to elicit such information.
(C) Many consumers purchase jogging shoes for use in activities other than jogging.
(D) Consumers who take up jogging often purchase an athletic shoe that can be used in other sports.
(E) Joggers who jog more than once a week are often active participants in other sports as well.

The claim that most consumers do not get much use out of the sports equipment they purchase is supported by the infrequency with which jogging shoes are used for jogging. This reasoning overlooks the possibility that jogging shoes are used for other purposes; thus, choice C is the best answer.

Because injured joggers are less likely to use their jogging shoes, choice A is inappropriate. If B is true, joggers use their jogging shoes even less than the study cited states. So choice B is inappropriate. Because the consumers and joggers mentioned in D and E respectively are most likely to be among those who frequently use sports equipment and whose existence the argument concedes, D and E are inappropriate.

5. Two decades after the Emerald River Dam was built, none of the eight fish species native to the Emerald River was still reproducing adequately in the river below the dam. Since the dam reduced the annual range of water temperature in the river below the dam from 50 degrees to 6 degrees, scientists have hypothesized that sharply rising water temperatures must be involved in signaling the native species to begin the reproductive cycle.

Which of the following statements, if true, would most strengthen the scientists' hypothesis?

(A) The native fish species were still able to reproduce only in side streams of the river below the dam where the annual temperature range remains approximately 50 degrees.
(B) Before the dam was built, the Emerald River annually overflowed its banks, creating backwaters that were critical breeding areas for the native species of fish.
(C) The lowest recorded temperature of the Emerald River before the dam was built was 34 degrees, whereas the lowest recorded temperature of the river after the dam was built has been 43 degrees.
(D) Nonnative species of fish, introduced into the Emerald River after the dam was built, have begun competing with the declining native fish species for food and space.
(E) Five of the fish species native to the Emerald River are not native to any other river in North America.

For the hypothesis to be tenable it is important that the fish in streams in the Emerald River area that retain a wide temperature difference have not lost their ability to reproduce. Choice A asserts that these fish could still reproduce, and is thus the best answer.

Choice B undermines the hypothesis by suggesting a completely different hypothesis; choice C tends to support the claim that the temperature variation has lessened, but does not show that this is the right explanation; since D relates a development after the native species began to decline, it does not bear on the hypothesis, which concerns the decline's original cause; and choice E emphasizes the seriousness of the problem, but sheds no light on what causes it.

6. It is true that it is against international law to sell plutonium to countries that do not yet have nuclear weapons. But if United States companies do not do so, companies in other countries will.

Which of the following is most like the argument above in its logical structure?

(A) It is true that it is against the police department's policy to negotiate with kidnappers. But if the police want to prevent loss of life, they must negotiate in some cases.

(B) It is true that it is illegal to refuse to register for military service. But there is a long tradition in the United States of conscientious objection to serving in the armed forces.

(C) It is true that it is illegal for a government official to participate in a transaction in which there is an apparent conflict of interest. But if the facts are examined carefully, it will clearly be seen that there was no actual conflict of interest in the defendant's case.

(D) It is true that it is against the law to burglarize people's homes. But someone else certainly would have burglarized that house if the defendant had not done so first.

(E) It is true that company policy forbids supervisors to fire employees without two written warnings. But there have been many supervisors who have disobeyed this policy.

The argument in the passage acknowledges that a certain action contravenes a law, but it presents an excuse for the action by presupposing that someone will inevitably break this law. Only choice D shares all these features, and is thus the best answer.

In choice A, an excuse is presented for contravening a stated policy. However, unlike in the passage and choice D, there is no presupposition that the policy will inevitably be contravened. Similarly, choices B and E report that illegal activities have occurred, without presupposing that they inevitably will. Choice C describes a case as being one to which the law that is stated is inapplicable.

7. In recent years, many cabinetmakers have been winning acclaim as artists. But since furniture must be useful, cabinetmakers must exercise their craft with an eye to the practical utility of their product. For this reason, cabinetmaking is not art.

Which of the following is an assumption that supports drawing the conclusion above from the reason given for that conclusion?

(A) Some furniture is made to be placed in museums, where it will not be used by anyone.

(B) Some cabinetmakers are more concerned than others with the practical utility of the products they produce.

(C) Cabinetmakers should be more concerned with the practical utility of their products than they currently are.

(D) An object is not an art object if its maker pays attention to the object's practical utility.

(E) Artists are not concerned with the monetary value of their products.

The argument concludes that cabinetmaking is not an art because cabinetmakers must consider the practical utility of their products. If it is true that an object is not a work of art if its maker pays attention to the object's practical utility, as choice D says, the conclusion is supported. Thus, choice D is the best answer.

The argument is concerned with whether or not the cabinetmakers must take the practical utility of their products into consideration, not with either their monetary value (choice E) or what actually happens to them (choice A). The argument is not concerned with the precise degree to which individual cabinetmakers take the practical utility of cabinets into consideration. Thus, neither B nor C is appropriate.

8. Although custom prosthetic bone replacements produced through a new computer-aided design process will cost more than twice as much as ordinary replacements, custom replacements should still be cost-effective. Not only will surgery and recovery time be reduced, but custom replacements should last longer, thereby reducing the need for further hospital stays.

Which of the following must be studied in order to evaluate the argument presented above?

(A) The amount of time a patient spends in surgery *versus* the amount of time spent recovering from surgery
(B) The amount by which the cost of producing custom replacements has declined with the introduction of the new technique for producing them
(C) The degree to which the use of custom replacements is likely to reduce the need for repeat surgery when compared with the use of ordinary replacements
(D) The degree to which custom replacements produced with the new technique are more carefully manufactured than are ordinary replacements
(E) The amount by which custom replacements produced with the new technique will drop in cost as the production procedures become standardized and applicable on a larger scale

Although costly to produce, custom bone replacements are tentatively projected to be cost-effective because of other savings. To evaluate the argument it must be determined whether these savings will compensate for the increased cost. Thus, study of the expected reduction in the need for further hospital stays is needed, and choice C is the best answer.

The argument requires no study of the ratio between surgery and recovery time, so choice A is inappropriate. Past and future changes in cost are irrelevant to evaluating an argument that is based on the currently projected cost, so choices B and E are inappropriate. Finally, since studying the care with which the custom replacements are made does not itself provide information about costs, choice D is also incorrect.

9. Extinction is a process that can depend on a variety of ecological, geographical, and physiological variables. These variables affect different species of organisms in different ways, and should, therefore, yield a random pattern of extinctions. However, the fossil record shows that extinction occurs in a surprisingly definite pattern, with many species vanishing at the same time.

Which of the following, if true, forms the best basis for at least a partial explanation of the patterned extinctions revealed by the fossil record?

(A) Major episodes of extinction can result from widespread environmental disturbances that affect numerous different species.
(B) Certain extinction episodes selectively affect organisms with particular sets of characteristics unique to their species.
(C) Some species become extinct because of accumulated gradual changes in their local environments.
(D) In geologically recent times, for which there is no fossil record, human intervention has changed the pattern of extinctions.
(E) Species that are widely dispersed are the least likely to become extinct.

Choice A, the best answer, asserts that some environmental disturbances can be so widespread as to cause the extinction of numerous species. This fact helps to explain why the fossil record frequently shows many species becoming extinct at the same time, despite the variety of factors that can cause a species to become extinct.

None of the other choices explains how numerous extinctions could have occurred simultaneously in the past. Choice B explains why sometimes only a very limited range of species becomes extinct. Choice C explains how some individual species become extinct. Choice D explains why the modern period is unlike the period of the fossil record, and choice E states which species are least likely to become extinct.

10. Neither a rising standard of living nor balanced trade, by itself, establishes a country's ability to compete in the international marketplace. Both are required simultaneously since standards of living can rise because of growing trade deficits and trade can be balanced by means of a decline in a country's standard of living.

If the facts stated in the passage above are true, a proper test of a country's ability to be competitive is its ability to

(A) balance its trade while its standard of living rises
(B) balance its trade while its standard of living falls
(C) increase trade deficits while its standard of living rises
(D) decrease trade deficits while its standard of living falls
(E) keep its standard of living constant while trade deficits rise

The passage states that a country capable of competing in the international marketplace must balance trade while its standard of living rises. In view of this information, a proper test of a country's ability to compete in the international marketplace will establish that both of these conditions are met simultaneously. Since neither choice B, nor choice C, nor choice D, nor choice E describe tests that incorporate both of these criteria, these answers are inappropriate. Choice A, which describes a test that does, is the best answer.

11. Certain messenger molecules fight damage to the lungs from noxious air by telling the muscle cells encircling the lungs' airways to contract. This partially seals off the lungs. An asthma attack occurs when the messenger molecules are activated unnecessarily, in response to harmless things like pollen or household dust.

Which of the following, if true, points to the most serious flaw of a plan to develop a medication that would prevent asthma attacks by blocking receipt of any messages sent by the messenger molecules referred to above?

(A) Researchers do not yet know how the body produces the messenger molecules that trigger asthma attacks.
(B) Researchers do not yet know what makes one person's messenger molecules more easily activated than another's.
(C) Such a medication would not become available for several years, because of long lead times in both development and manufacture.
(D) Such a medication would be unable to distinguish between messages triggered by pollen and household dust and messages triggered by noxious air.
(E) Such a medication would be a preventative only and would be unable to alleviate an asthma attack once it had started.

The medication to be developed is intended to prevent asthma attacks by suppressing the natural action of certain molecules in the lungs. Choice D asserts that this suppression would occur not only when the molecules' action is superfluous, but also when it is necessary. This would be a serious flaw in the medication, so D is the best answer.

Choices A and B refer to a lack of knowledge about how the messenger molecules are produced or activated, but not about how they act in the lungs. Choice C describes how long the development might take, but does not rule out the possibility of success. Choice E asserts merely that the medication would be unable to do something it was not intended to do.

12. Since the routine use of antibiotics can give rise to resistant bacteria capable of surviving antibiotic environments, the presence of resistant bacteria in people could be due to the human use of prescription antibiotics. Some scientists, however, believe that most resistant bacteria in people derive from human consumption of bacterially infected meat.

Which of the following statements, if true, would most significantly strengthen the hypothesis of the scientists?

(A) Antibiotics are routinely included in livestock feed so that livestock producers can increase the rate of growth of their animals.
(B) Most people who develop food poisoning from bacterially infected meat are treated with prescription antibiotics.
(C) The incidence of resistant bacteria in people has tended to be much higher in urban areas than in rural areas where meat is of comparable quality.
(D) People who have never taken prescription antibiotics are those least likely to develop resistant bacteria.
(E) Livestock producers claim that resistant bacteria in animals cannot be transmitted to people through infected meat.

If livestock are routinely fed antibiotics, as choice A states, meat from livestock is likely to contain the resistant bacteria, since any routine of antibiotics can result in resistant bacteria. Thus, choice A is the best answer.

How cases of food poisoning are treated (choice B) fails to indicate whether the infecting bacteria are resistant bacteria. Choice C suggests that meat consumption is not the primary culprit for the high incidence of resistant bacteria. Choice D tends to support the competing hypothesis that prescription antibiotics are responsible. Choice E asserts that livestock farmers claim that the hypothesis is false, but it provides no basis for evaluating the truth of this claim.

13. The recent decline in the value of the dollar was triggered by a prediction of slower economic growth in the coming year. But that prediction would not have adversely affected the dollar had it not been for the government's huge budget deficit, which must therefore be decreased to prevent future currency declines.

Which of the following, if true, would most seriously weaken the conclusion about how to prevent future currency declines?

(A) The government has made little attempt to reduce the budget deficit.
(B) The budget deficit has not caused a slowdown in economic growth.
(C) The value of the dollar declined several times in the year prior to the recent prediction of slower economic growth.
(D) Before there was a large budget deficit, predictions of slower economic growth frequently caused declines in the dollar's value.
(E) When there is a large budget deficit, other events in addition to predictions of slower economic growth sometimes trigger declines in currency value.

The argument assumes that a particular prediction can cause a currency decline only if accompanied by a large budget deficit. Since choice D states that this prediction can cause a currency decline without a large budget deficit, choice D is the best answer.

That a method is not fully implemented does not imply that the method is ineffective. Thus, choice A is inappropriate. Since no slowdown in economic growth is asserted, what might cause such a slowdown is irrelevant. Thus, choice B is inappropriate. Since C supports the claim that a budget deficit is the underlying cause of the currency decline, C is inappropriate. Choice E is inappropriate because it supports the claim that a decrease in the budget deficit is necessary.

14. Which of the following best completes the passage below?

At a recent conference on environmental threats to the North Sea, most participating countries favored uniform controls on the quality of effluents, whether or not specific environmental damage could be attributed to a particular source of effluent. What must, of course, be shown, in order to avoid excessively restrictive controls, is that _____.

(A) any uniform controls that are adopted are likely to be implemented without delay
(B) any substance to be made subject to controls can actually cause environmental damage
(C) the countries favoring uniform controls are those generating the largest quantities of effluents
(D) all of any given pollutant that is to be controlled actually reaches the North Sea at present
(E) environmental damage already inflicted on the North Sea is reversible

If a substance that causes no environmental damage were subject to controls, those controls would be more restrictive than necessary. Choice B is therefore the best answer.

Ensuring prompt implementation of controls, as choice A claims, is not a necessary part of avoiding excessively restrictive controls. Although it would probably help to avoid excessive restrictions if some of the countries producing the most effluents favored uniform controls, it is not necessary that all such countries do, as choice C claims. Not all of any given pollutant need reach the North Sea, as choice D claims, since at most some needs to. Since the controls can be excessively restrictive even if the damage already inflicted is reversible, choice E is incorrect.

15. Traditionally, decision-making by managers that is reasoned step-by-step has been considered preferable to intuitive decision-making. However, a recent study found that top managers used intuition significantly more than did most middle- or lower-level managers. This confirms the alternative view that intuition is actually more effective than careful, methodical reasoning.

The conclusion above is based on which of the following assumptions?

(A) Methodical, step-by-step reasoning is inappropriate for making many real-life management decisions.
(B) Top managers have the ability to use either intuitive reasoning or methodical, step-by-step reasoning in making decisions.
(C) The decisions made by middle- and lower-level managers can be made as easily by using methodical reasoning as by using intuitive reasoning.
(D) Top managers use intuitive reasoning in making the majority of their decisions.
(E) Top managers are more effective at decision-making than middle- or lower-level managers.

If top managers are not the more effective decision makers, then the fact that they use intuition more often than lower-level managers does not support the conclusion that intuition is more effective. Because the argument must assume E, choice E is the best answer.

To the extent that less effective methods are inappropriate, the passage does not assume A, but argues for it. Since the argument leaves open the possibility of situations in which top managers are unable to use one of the methods, choice B is inappropriate. Since the ease with which a method is implemented is not at issue, choice C is inappropriate. The argument is consistent with managers at all levels using intuition in the minority of decisions made. Thus, choice D is inappropriate.

16. The imposition of quotas limiting imported steel will not help the big American steel mills. In fact, the quotas will help "mini-mills" flourish in the United States. Those small domestic mills will take more business from the big American steel mills than would have been taken by the foreign steel mills in the absence of quotas.

Which of the following, if true, would cast the most serious doubt on the claim made in the last sentence above?

(A) Quality rather than price is a major factor in determining the type of steel to be used for a particular application.

(B) Foreign steel mills have long produced grades of steel comparable in quality to the steel produced by the big American mills.

(C) American quotas on imported goods have often induced other countries to impose similar quotas on American goods.

(D) Domestic "mini-mills" consistently produce better grades of steel than do the big American mills.

(E) Domestic "mini-mills" produce low-volume, specialized types of steels that are not produced by the big American steel mills.

If, as choice E asserts, large and small mills produce different types of steels, increasing sales by small mills need not lead to decreasing sales by large ones. Thus, choice E casts a serious doubt on the claim and is the best answer.

Choice A does not present enough information about the relative quality of steel from foreign and domestic mills to cast any doubt on the claim. Similarly, choice B does not provide enough information about small American mills, nor does choice C provide enough information about the likely consequences of quotas imposed by foreign countries to cast doubt on the claim. Choice D tends to support the claim, since better steel should sell better than poorer steel.

CRITICAL REASONING SAMPLE TEST SECTION 5

Time — 25 minutes

16 Questions

Directions: For each question in this section, select the best of the answer choices given.

1. A drug that is highly effective in treating many types of infection can, at present, be obtained only from the bark of the ibora, a tree that is quite rare in the wild. It takes the bark of 5,000 trees to make one kilogram of the drug. It follows, therefore, that continued production of the drug must inevitably lead to the ibora's extinction.

Which of the following, if true, most seriously weakens the argument above?

(A) The drug made from ibora bark is dispensed to doctors from a central authority.
(B) The drug made from ibora bark is expensive to produce.
(C) The leaves of the ibora are used in a number of medical products.
(D) The ibora can be propagated from cuttings and grown under cultivation.
(E) The ibora generally grows in largely inaccessible places.

2. High levels of fertilizer and pesticides, needed when farmers try to produce high yields of the same crop year after year, pollute water supplies. Experts therefore urge farmers to diversify their crops and to rotate their plantings yearly.

To receive governmental price-support benefits for a crop, farmers must have produced that same crop for the past several years.

The statements above, if true, best support which of the following conclusions?

(A) The rules for governmental support of farm prices work against efforts to reduce water pollution.
(B) The only solution to the problem of water pollution from fertilizers and pesticides is to take farmland out of production.
(C) Farmers can continue to make a profit by rotating diverse crops, thus reducing costs for chemicals, but not by planting the same crop each year.
(D) New farming techniques will be developed to make it possible for farmers to reduce the application of fertilizers and pesticides.
(E) Governmental price supports for farm products are set at levels that are not high enough to allow farmers to get out of debt.

3. Shelby Industries manufactures and sells the same gauges as Jones Industries. Employee wages account for forty percent of the cost of manufacturing gauges at both Shelby Industries and Jones Industries. Shelby Industries is seeking a competitive advantage over Jones Industries. Therefore, to promote this end, Shelby Industries should lower employee wages.

Which of the following, if true, would most weaken the argument above?

(A) Because they make a small number of precision instruments, gauge manufacturers cannot receive volume discounts on raw materials.
(B) Lowering wages would reduce the quality of employee work, and this reduced quality would lead to lowered sales.
(C) Jones Industries has taken away twenty percent of Shelby Industries' business over the last year.
(D) Shelby Industries pays its employees, on average, ten percent more than does Jones Industries.
(E) Many people who work for manufacturing plants live in areas in which the manufacturing plant they work for is the only industry.

GO ON TO THE NEXT PAGE.

-309-

4. Some communities in Florida are populated almost exclusively by retired people and contain few, if any, families with small children. Yet these communities are home to thriving businesses specializing in the rental of furniture for infants and small children.

Which of the following, if true, best reconciles the seeming discrepancy described above?

(A) The businesses specializing in the rental of children's furniture buy their furniture from distributors outside of Florida.
(B) The few children who do reside in these communities all know each other and often make overnight visits to one another's houses.
(C) Many residents of these communities who move frequently prefer renting their furniture to buying it outright.
(D) Many residents of these communities must provide for the needs of visiting grandchildren several weeks a year.
(E) Children's furniture available for rental is of the same quality as that available for sale in the stores.

5. Large national budget deficits do not cause large trade deficits. If they did, countries with the largest budget deficits would also have the largest trade deficits. In fact, when deficit figures are adjusted so that different countries are reliably comparable to each other, there is no such correlation.

If the statements above are all true, which of the following can properly be inferred on the basis of them?

(A) Countries with large national budget deficits tend to restrict foreign trade.
(B) Reliable comparisons of the deficit figures of one country with those of another are impossible.
(C) Reducing a country's national budget deficit will not necessarily result in a lowering of any trade deficit that country may have.
(D) When countries are ordered from largest to smallest in terms of population, the smallest countries generally have the smallest budget and trade deficits.
(E) Countries with the largest trade deficits never have similarly large national budget deficits.

6. "Fast cycle time" is a strategy of designing a manufacturing organization to eliminate bottlenecks and delays in production. Not only does it speed up production, but it also assures quality. The reason is that the bottlenecks and delays cannot be eliminated unless all work is done right the first time.

The claim about quality made above rests on a questionable presupposition that

(A) any flaw in work on a product would cause a bottleneck or delay and so would be prevented from occurring on a "fast cycle" production line
(B) the strategy of "fast cycle time" would require fundamental rethinking of product design
(C) the primary goal of the organization is to produce a product of unexcelled quality, rather than to generate profits for stockholders
(D) "fast cycle time" could be achieved by shaving time off each of the component processes in a production cycle
(E) "fast cycle time" is a concept in business strategy that has not yet been put into practice in a factory

7. Many breakfast cereals are fortified with vitamin supplements. Some of these cereals provide 100 percent of the recommended daily requirement of vitamins. Nevertheless, a well-balanced breakfast, including a variety of foods, is a better source of those vitamins than are such fortified breakfast cereals alone.

Which of the following, if true, would most strongly support the position above?

(A) In many foods, the natural combination of vitamins with other nutrients makes those vitamins more usable by the body than are vitamins added in vitamin supplements.
(B) People who regularly eat cereals fortified with vitamin supplements sometimes neglect to eat the foods in which the vitamins occur naturally.
(C) Foods often must be fortified with vitamin supplements because naturally occurring vitamins are removed during processing.
(D) Unprocessed cereals are naturally high in several of the vitamins that are usually added to fortified breakfast cereals.
(E) Cereals containing vitamin supplements are no harder to digest than similar cereals without added vitamins.

GO ON TO THE NEXT PAGE.

8. Which of the following best completes the passage below?

The more worried investors are about losing their money, the more they will demand a high potential return on their investment; great risks must be offset by the chance of great rewards. This principle is the fundamental one in determining interest rates, and it is illustrated by the fact that -------.

(A) successful investors are distinguished by an ability to make very risky investments without worrying about their money
(B) lenders receive higher interest rates on unsecured loans than on loans backed by collateral
(C) in times of high inflation, the interest paid to depositors by banks can actually be below the rate of inflation
(D) at any one time, a commercial bank will have a single rate of interest that it will expect all of its individual borrowers to pay
(E) the potential return on investment in a new company is typically lower than the potential return on investment in a well-established company

9. A famous singer recently won a lawsuit against an advertising firm for using another singer in a commercial to evoke the famous singer's well-known rendition of a certain song. As a result of the lawsuit, advertising firms will stop using imitators in commercials. Therefore, advertising costs will rise, since famous singers' services cost more than those of their imitators.

The conclusion above is based on which of the following assumptions?

(A) Most people are unable to distinguish a famous singer's rendition of a song from a good imitator's rendition of the same song.
(B) Commercials using famous singers are usually more effective than commercials using imitators of famous singers.
(C) The original versions of some well-known songs are unavailable for use in commercials.
(D) Advertising firms will continue to use imitators to mimic the physical mannerisms of famous singers.
(E) The advertising industry will use well-known renditions of songs in commercials.

10. A certain mayor has proposed a fee of five dollars per day on private vehicles entering the city, claiming that the fee will alleviate the city's traffic congestion. The mayor reasons that, since the fee will exceed the cost of round-trip bus fare from many nearby points, many people will switch from using their cars to using the bus.

Which of the following statements, if true, provides the best evidence that the mayor's reasoning is flawed?

(A) Projected increases in the price of gasoline will increase the cost of taking a private vehicle into the city.
(B) The cost of parking fees already makes it considerably more expensive for most people to take a private vehicle into the city than to take a bus.
(C) Most of the people currently riding the bus do not own private vehicles.
(D) Many commuters opposing the mayor's plan have indicated that they would rather endure traffic congestion than pay a five-dollar-per day fee.
(E) During the average workday, private vehicles owned and operated by people living within the city account for twenty percent of the city's traffic congestion.

GO ON TO THE NEXT PAGE.

11. A group of children of various ages was read stories in which people caused harm, some of those people doing so intentionally, and some accidentally. When asked about appropriate punishments for those who had caused harm, the younger children, unlike the older ones, assigned punishments that did not vary according to whether the harm was done intentionally or accidentally. Younger children, then, do not regard people's intentions as relevant to punishment.

Which of the following, if true, would most seriously weaken the conclusion above?

(A) In interpreting these stories, the listeners had to draw on a relatively mature sense of human psychology in order to tell whether harm was produced intentionally or accidentally.
(B) In these stories, the severity of the harm produced was clearly stated.
(C) Younger children are as likely to produce harm unintentionally as are older children.
(D) The older children assigned punishment in a way that closely resembled the way adults had assigned punishment in a similar experiment.
(E) The younger children assigned punishments that varied according to the severity of the harm done by the agents in the stories.

12. When hypnotized subjects are told that they are deaf and are then asked whether they can hear the hypnotist, they reply, "No." Some theorists try to explain this result by arguing that the selves of hypnotized subjects are dissociated into separate parts, and that the part that is deaf is dissociated from the part that replies.

Which of the following challenges indicates the most serious weakness in the attempted explanation described above?

(A) Why does the part that replies not answer, "Yes"?
(B) Why are the observed facts in need of any special explanation?
(C) Why do the subjects appear to accept the hypnotist's suggestion that they are deaf?
(D) Why do hypnotized subjects all respond the same way in the situation described?
(E) Why are the separate parts of the self the same for all subjects?

Questions 13-14 are based on the following.

The program to control the entry of illegal drugs into the country was a failure in 1987. If the program had been successful, the wholesale price of most illegal drugs would not have dropped substantially in 1987.

13. The argument in the passage depends on which of the following assumptions?

(A) The supply of illegal drugs dropped substantially in 1987.
(B) The price paid for most illegal drugs by the average consumer did not drop substantially in 1987.
(C) Domestic production of illegal drugs increased at a higher rate than did the entry of such drugs into the country.
(D) The wholesale price of a few illegal drugs increased substantially in 1987.
(E) A drop in demand for most illegal drugs in 1987 was not the sole cause of the drop in their wholesale price.

14. The argument in the passage would be most seriously weakened if it were true that

(A) in 1987 smugglers of illegal drugs, as a group, had significantly more funds at their disposal than did the country's customs agents
(B) domestic production of illegal drugs increased substantially in 1987
(C) the author's statements were made in order to embarrass the officials responsible for the drug-control program
(D) in 1987 illegal drugs entered the country by a different set of routes than they did in 1986
(E) the country's citizens spent substantially more money on illegal drugs in 1987 than they did in 1986

GO ON TO THE NEXT PAGE.

15. Excavation of the ancient city of Kourion on the island of Cyprus revealed a pattern of debris and collapsed buildings typical of towns devastated by earthquakes. Archaeologists have hypothesized that the destruction was due to a major earthquake known to have occurred near the island in A.D. 365.

Which of the following, if true, most strongly supports the archaeologists' hypothesis?

(A) Bronze ceremonial drinking vessels that are often found in graves dating from years preceding and following A.D. 365 were also found in several graves near Kourion.
(B) No coins minted after A.D. 365 were found in Kourion, but coins minted before that year were found in abundance.
(C) Most modern histories of Cyprus mention that an earthquake occurred near the island in A.D. 365.
(D) Several small statues carved in styles current in Cyprus in the century between A.D. 300 and 400 were found in Kourion.
(E) Stone inscriptions in a form of the Greek alphabet that was definitely used in Cyprus after A.D. 365 were found in Kourion.

16. Sales of telephones have increased dramatically over the last year. In order to take advantage of this increase, Mammoth Industries plans to expand production of its own model of telephone, while continuing its already very extensive advertising of this product.

Which of the following, if true, provides most support for the view that Mammoth Industries cannot increase its sales of telephones by adopting the plan outlined above?

(A) Although it sells all of the telephones that it produces, Mammoth Industries' share of all telephone sales has declined over the last year.
(B) Mammoth Industries' average inventory of telephones awaiting shipment to retailers has declined slightly over the last year.
(C) Advertising has made the brand name of Mammoth Industries' telephones widely known, but few consumers know that Mammoth Industries owns this brand.
(D) Mammoth Industries' telephone is one of three brands of telephone that have together accounted for the bulk of the last year's increase in sales.
(E) Despite a slight decline in the retail price, sales of Mammoth Industries' telephones have fallen in the last year.

STOP

IF YOU FINISH BEFORE TIME IS CALLED, YOU MAY CHECK YOUR WORK ON THIS SECTION ONLY.
DO NOT TURN TO ANY OTHER SECTION IN THE TEST.

Answer Key for Sample Test Section 5

CRITICAL REASONING

1. D	9. E
2. A	10. B
3. B	11. A
4. D	12. A
5. C	13. E
6. A	14. B
7. A	15. B
8. B	16. E

Explanatory Material: Critical Reasoning Sample Test Section 5

1. A drug that is highly effective in treating many types of infection can, at present, be obtained only from the bark of the ibora, a tree that is quite rare in the wild. It takes the bark of 5,000 trees to make one kilogram of the drug. It follows, therefore, that continued production of the drug must inevitably lead to the ibora's extinction.

   Which of the following, if true, most seriously weakens the argument above?

   (A) The drug made from ibora bark is dispensed to doctors from a central authority.
   (B) The drug made from ibora bark is expensive to produce.
   (C) The leaves of the ibora are used in a number of medical products.
   (D) The ibora can be propagated from cuttings and grown under cultivation.
   (E) The ibora generally grows in largely inaccessible places.

If the ibora can be successfully cultivated, it is possible to continue production of the drug without threatening the ibora with extinction. Therefore, choice D is the best answer.

   If production continues, the method for distributing the drug after it has been produced (choice A) is not likely, on its own, to have consequences for the continued existence of the ibora. Nor is the price of the drug (choice B). If the leaves of the ibora also have a use (choice C), the threat of extinction is strengthened rather than weakened. Finally, if the ibora is largely inaccessible (choice E), this bears on the question of whether production of the drug could continue, not on what would happen if it did continue.

2. High levels of fertilizer and pesticides, needed when farmers try to produce high yields of the same crop year after year, pollute water supplies. Experts therefore urge farmers to diversify their crops and to rotate their plantings yearly.

   To receive governmental price-support benefits for a crop, farmers must have produced that same crop for the past several years.

   The statements above, if true, best support which of the following conclusions?

   (A) The rules for governmental support of farm prices work against efforts to reduce water pollution.
   (B) The only solution to the problem of water pollution from fertilizers and pesticides is to take farmland out of production.
   (C) Farmers can continue to make a profit by rotating diverse crops, thus reducing costs for chemicals, but not by planting the same crop each year.
   (D) New farming techniques will be developed to make it possible for farmers to reduce the application of fertilizers and pesticides.
   (E) Governmental price supports for farm products are set at levels that are not high enough to allow farmers to get out of debt.

Farmers benefit from governmental price supports only when they produce the same crops from year to year. Farmers who wish to receive the benefit of these price supports will be unlikely to reduce water pollution because they will not follow the experts' advice regarding diversification and rotation. Thus, A is the best answer.

   Since the experts' advice is evidently their favored solution, the notion that the sole solution is something else (choice B) is not supported. The statements mention neither farmers' costs and revenues nor developments in farming techniques, and thus support no conclusions about prospects for profits (choice C) or future farming techniques (choice D). Because no information is given about either the amount of price support or farmers' debt, choice E is not supported.

3. Shelby Industries manufactures and sells the same gauges as Jones Industries. Employee wages account for forty percent of the cost of manufacturing gauges at both Shelby Industries and Jones Industries. Shelby Industries is seeking a competitive advantage over Jones Industries. Therefore, to promote this end, Shelby Industries should lower employee wages.

Which of the following, if true, would most weaken the argument above?

(A) Because they make a small number of precision instruments, gauge manufacturers cannot receive volume discounts on raw materials.

(B) Lowering wages would reduce the quality of employee work, and this reduced quality would lead to lowered sales.

(C) Jones Industries has taken away twenty percent of Shelby Industries' business over the last year.

(D) Shelby Industries pays its employees, on average, ten percent more than does Jones Industries.

(E) Many people who work for manufacturing plants live in areas in which the manufacturing plant they work for is the only industry.

According to choice B, the effect of lowering wages is to reduce quality sufficiently to reduce sales. This is a good reason to doubt that wage cuts would give Shelby Industries any competitive advantage, so choice B is the best answer.

Some of the other choices provide good reasons for, rather than against, lowering wages. Choice A implies that reducing the cost of raw materials is not possible, choice D indicates that Shelby Industries' wages are relatively high, and choice E suggests that Shelby Industries would not lose many workers if it did reduce wages. Choice C gives a reason for Shelby Industries to be concerned about its competitive position but no reason to think wage cuts would not improve that position.

4. Some communities in Florida are populated almost exclusively by retired people and contain few, if any, families with small children. Yet these communities are home to thriving businesses specializing in the rental of furniture for infants and small children.

Which of the following, if true, best reconciles the seeming discrepancy described above?

(A) The businesses specializing in the rental of children's furniture buy their furniture from distributors outside of Florida.

(B) The few children who do reside in these communities all know each other and often make overnight visits to one another's houses.

(C) Many residents of these communities who move frequently prefer renting their furniture to buying it outright.

(D) Many residents of these communities must provide for the needs of visiting grandchildren several weeks a year.

(E) Children's furniture available for rental is of the same quality as that available for sale in the stores.

If many residents of these communities host visiting grandchildren several weeks a year, as D states, that in itself might generate sufficient demand for rented children's furniture to support thriving businesses. Thus, D helps reconcile the apparent discrepancy and is the best answer.

The few households mentioned in choice B are unlikely to generate sufficient demand for rental businesses to thrive. Similarly, choices A and E, though they provide information concerning the furniture that is rented in these communities, do not address the prior issue of why there should be such demand for children's furniture. Choice C helps explain why these communities have an unusually high demand for rental furniture, but not why such a demand would extend to children's furniture.

5. Large national budget deficits do not cause large trade deficits. If they did, countries with the largest budget deficits would also have the largest trade deficits. In fact, when deficit figures are adjusted so that different countries are reliably comparable to each other, there is no such correlation.

If the statements above are all true, which of the following can properly be inferred on the basis of them?

(A) Countries with large national budget deficits tend to restrict foreign trade.
(B) Reliable comparisons of the deficit figures of one country with those of another are impossible.
(C) Reducing a country's national budget deficit will not necessarily result in a lowering of any trade deficit that country may have.
(D) When countries are ordered from largest to smallest in terms of population, the smallest countries generally have the smallest budget and trade deficits.
(E) Countries with the largest trade deficits never have similarly large national budget deficits.

The passage asserts that large budget deficits do not cause large trade deficits. If this is so, it is possible that a country with large budget and trade deficits could reduce its budget deficit and yet retain a large trade deficit. Thus, choice C is the best answer.

None of the other choices can be inferred. The passage says nothing about how countries respond to large budget deficits (choice A). The passage states that comparing deficit figures for different countries can be reliable (contrary to choice B). Correlation between deficit size and population size (choice D) is not at issue in the passage. Finally, it is consistent with the passage that countries with the largest trade deficits sometimes have similarly large budget deficits (choice E).

6. "Fast cycle time" is a strategy of designing a manufacturing organization to eliminate bottlenecks and delays in production. Not only does it speed up production, but it also assures quality. The reason is that the bottlenecks and delays cannot be eliminated unless all work is done right the first time.

The claim about quality made above rests on a questionable presupposition that

(A) any flaw in work on a product would cause a bottleneck or delay and so would be prevented from occurring on a "fast cycle" production line
(B) the strategy of "fast cycle time" would require fundamental rethinking of product design
(C) the primary goal of the organization is to produce a product of unexcelled quality, rather than to generate profits for stockholders
(D) "fast cycle time" could be achieved by shaving time off each of the component processes in a production cycle
(E) "fast cycle time" is a concept in business strategy that has not yet been put into practice in a factory

The argument presupposes that, if bottlenecks and delays are eliminated, production work must have been accomplished flawlessly. This presupposition is questionable, since there might well be flaws that do not impede the manufacturing process. The best answer is thus choice A.

None of the other choices is presupposed. The argument is consistent with redesigning the manufacturing process and not the product (choice B). The primary goal might be profits, and quality merely a means to that end (choice C). The argument does not rely on the feasibility of any one method of implementing "fast cycle time" (choice D). Finally, the concept of "fast cycle time" could already have been implemented operationally (choice E).

7. Many breakfast cereals are fortified with vitamin supplements. Some of these cereals provide 100 percent of the recommended daily requirement of vitamins. Nevertheless, a well-balanced breakfast, including a variety of foods, is a better source of those vitamins than are such fortified breakfast cereals alone.

Which of the following, if true, would most strongly support the position above?

(A) In many foods, the natural combination of vitamins with other nutrients makes those vitamins more usable by the body than are vitamins added in vitamin supplements.
(B) People who regularly eat cereals fortified with vitamin supplements sometimes neglect to eat the foods in which the vitamins occur naturally.
(C) Foods often must be fortified with vitamin supplements because naturally occurring vitamins are removed during processing.
(D) Unprocessed cereals are naturally high in several of the vitamins that are usually added to fortified breakfast cereals.
(E) Cereals containing vitamin supplements are no harder to digest than similar cereals without added vitamins.

By pointing out that, when occurring in natural combination with other nutrients, vitamins are more usable by the body than are those same vitamins when added as a supplement, choice A provides reason to believe that a well-balanced breakfast is a better source of vitamins than is a fortified breakfast cereal. A is the best answer.

Choice B does not support the position taken, although the position taken, if correct, is relevant to the people mentioned. Choice E describes a similarity between fortified cereals and other cereals. Choice C provides a reason for adding supplements to processed cereals, and choice D gives information about unprocessed cereals, but neither adds support for the alleged advantage of a well-balanced breakfast over a fortified cereal.

8. Which of the following best completes the passage below?

The more worried investors are about losing their money, the more they will demand a high potential return on their investment; great risks must be offset by the chance of great rewards. This principle is the fundamental one in determining interest rates, and it is illustrated by the fact that - - - - - - - - - -.

(A) successful investors are distinguished by an ability to make very risky investments without worrying about their money
(B) lenders receive higher interest rates on unsecured loans than on loans backed by collateral
(C) in times of high inflation, the interest paid to depositors by banks can actually be below the rate of inflation
(D) at any one time, a commercial bank will have a single rate of interest that it will expect all of its individual borrowers to pay
(E) the potential return on investment in a new company is typically lower than the potential return on investment in a well-established company

Since an unsecured loan is more risky, from the lender's point of view, than a loan backed by collateral, the fact that lenders receive higher interest rates for unsecured loans is an illustration of the principle outlined in the passage. Thus, choice B is the best answer.

None of the other choices gives a clear instance in which increased risk is compensated by the potential for increased return. Choice A does not concern return on investment at all. Choice C is an instance of low return unrelated to risk. In choice D, contrary to the principle, the rate of return remains constant despite possible variations in risk, and choice E also runs counter to the principle if investments in well-established companies entail less risk.

9. A famous singer recently won a lawsuit against an advertising firm for using another singer in a commercial to evoke the famous singer's well-known rendition of a certain song. As a result of the lawsuit, advertising firms will stop using imitators in commercials. Therefore, advertising costs will rise, since famous singers' services cost more than those of their imitators.

The conclusion above is based on which of the following assumptions?

(A) Most people are unable to distinguish a famous singer's rendition of a song from a good imitator's rendition of the same song.
(B) Commercials using famous singers are usually more effective than commercials using imitators of famous singers.
(C) The original versions of some well-known songs are unavailable for use in commercials.
(D) Advertising firms will continue to use imitators to mimic the physical mannerisms of famous singers.
(E) The advertising industry will use well-known renditions of songs in commercials.

If choice E were not assumed, the costs of the services of the famous singers of well-known renditions of songs would not be said to affect advertising costs. Since advertising costs are, however, projected to rise because of the relatively high cost of famous singers' services, choice E is assumed and is the best answer.

Choice A is irrelevant to the argument, since famous singers' services cost more than imitators' anyway. The argument addresses commercials' cost, not their effectiveness, so choice B is not assumed. The argument assumes that some well-known renditions of songs are available, but does not require that any versions be unavailable (choice C). Since the argument states that advertising firms will stop using imitators, choice D is not assumed.

10. A certain mayor has proposed a fee of five dollars per day on private vehicles entering the city, claiming that the fee will alleviate the city's traffic congestion. The mayor reasons that, since the fee will exceed the cost of round-trip bus fare from many nearby points, many people will switch from using their cars to using the bus.

Which of the following statements, if true, provides the best evidence that the mayor's reasoning is flawed?

(A) Projected increases in the price of gasoline will increase the cost of taking a private vehicle into the city.
(B) The cost of parking fees already makes it considerably more expensive for most people to take a private vehicle into the city than to take a bus.
(C) Most of the people currently riding the bus do not own private vehicles.
(D) Many commuters opposing the mayor's plan have indicated that they would rather endure traffic congestion than pay a five-dollar-per day fee.
(E) During the average workday, private vehicles owned and operated by people living within the city account for twenty percent of the city's traffic congestion.

The mayor's reasoning rests on assuming that, if it costs more to travel to the city by car than by bus, people will choose to travel by bus rather than by car. Choice B provides evidence that this assumption is false, and is therefore the best answer.

Choice A does not undermine the mayor's view that the five dollar fee will provide an incentive to switch to buses. Choice C makes it unlikely that the bus system will lose current riders if new riders are attracted. Choice D is inappropriate since many drivers not switching to buses is entirely consistent with many people making the switch. Choice E supports the mayor's proposal by indicating that vehicles entering the city produce most of the city's congestion.

11. A group of children of various ages was read stories in which people caused harm, some of those people doing so intentionally, and some accidentally. When asked about appropriate punishments for those who had caused harm, the younger children, unlike the older ones, assigned punishments that did not vary according to whether the harm was done intentionally or accidentally. Younger children, then, do not regard people's intentions as relevant to punishment

Which of the following, if true, would most seriously weaken the conclusion above?

(A) In interpreting these stories, the listeners had to draw on a relatively mature sense of human psychology in order to tell whether harm was produced intentionally or accidentally.
(B) In these stories, the severity of the harm produced was clearly stated.
(C) Younger children are as likely to produce harm unintentionally as are older children.
(D) The older children assigned punishment in a way that closely resembled the way adults had assigned punishment in a similar experiment.
(E) The younger children assigned punishments that varied according to the severity of the harm done by the agents in the stories.

Choice A, the best answer, indicates that younger children might be unable to tell whether the harm in the stories was produced intentionally. Thus, even if younger children do regard people's intentions as relevant, they might be unable to apply this criterion here. Therefore, A undermines the conclusion's support.

Choices B and E support the conclusion by suggesting that another factor — severity of harm — either possibly (choice B) or actually (choice E) motivated variations in the punishments assigned by younger children. Neither choice C nor choice D affects the conclusion. The conclusion concerns what children recognize about others' behavior, not children's own behavior (choice C). The similarity between older children's and adult's assignments (choice D) leaves open the question of why younger children's assignments differed.

12. When hypnotized subjects are told that they are deaf and are then asked whether they can hear the hypnotist, they reply, "No." Some theorists try to explain this result by arguing that the selves of hypnotized subjects are dissociated into separate parts, and that the part that is deaf is dissociated from the part that replies.

Which of the following challenges indicates the most serious weakness in the attempted explanation described above?

(A) Why does the part that replies not answer, "Yes"?
(B) Why are the observed facts in need of any special explanation?
(C) Why do the subjects appear to accept the hypnotist's suggestion that they are deaf?
(D) Why do hypnotized subjects all respond the same way in the situation described?
(E) Why are the separate parts of the self the same for all subjects?

Since the question elicits a reply, the question was presumably heard, but presumably not by the part that is deaf. The explanation's obvious weakness, therefore, is that it fails to indicate why the part that replies would reply as if it were the part that is deaf. Choice A points to this failure and is the best answer.

Choice B does not challenge the explanation itself, but the need for an explanation in the first place. Choices C and D raise pertinent questions concerning the facts described, but do not address the proffered explanation of those facts. Choice E points to a question to which the attempted explanation gives rise, but does not challenge the adequacy of the explanation.

Questions 13-14 are based on the following.

The program to control the entry of illegal drugs into the country was a failure in 1987. If the program had been successful, the wholesale price of most illegal drugs would not have dropped substantially in 1987.

13. The argument in the passage depends on which of the following assumptions?

(A) The supply of illegal drugs dropped substantially in 1987.
(B) The price paid for most illegal drugs by the average consumer did not drop substantially in 1987.
(C) Domestic production of illegal drugs increased at a higher rate than did the entry of such drugs into the country.
(D) The wholesale price of a few illegal drugs increased substantially in 1987.
(E) A drop in demand for most illegal drugs in 1987 was not the sole cause of the drop in their wholesale price.

The only choice that must be true in order to conclude legitimately from the drop in the wholesale price of illegal drugs that the program was a failure is choice E, the best answer. If the drop in price was caused by a drop in demand, there is no reason to suspect that there has been any increase in supply caused by drugs entering the country.

The other choices can be false without affecting the argument. The supply of illegal drugs need not have dropped (choice A), and the retail price could have dropped (choice B). The entry of illegal drugs could have risen at a higher rate than domestic production (choice C), and no illegal drug need have undergone a substantial price rise (choice D).

14. The argument in the passage would be most seriously weakened if it were true that

    (A) in 1987 smugglers of illegal drugs, as a group, had significantly more funds at their disposal than did the country's customs agents
    (B) domestic production of illegal drugs increased substantially in 1987
    (C) the author's statements were made in order to embarrass the officials responsible for the drug-control program
    (D) in 1987 illegal drugs entered the country by a different set of routes than they did in 1986
    (E) the country's citizens spent substantially more money on illegal drugs in 1987 than they did in 1986

If domestic production of illegal drugs increased substantially, the overall supply could have increased (and the price fallen) without more illegal drugs entering the country, and without any failure of the program. Thus, choice B is the best answer.

None of the other choices weakens the argument. The smugglers' having more money (choice A) suggests that they would have resources to evade controls. The author's intention (choice C) is irrelevant to whether the reasoning the statements express is cogent. A change of routes (choice D) would have increased the chance of the program failing, and an increase in the amount of money spent (choice E) also provides evidence that the program did fail, given the low price levels.

15. Excavation of the ancient city of Kourion on the island of Cyprus revealed a pattern of debris and collapsed buildings typical of towns devastated by earthquakes. Archaeologists have hypothesized that the destruction was due to a major earthquake known to have occurred near the island in A.D. 365.

Which of the following, if true, most strongly supports the archaeologists' hypothesis?

    (A) Bronze ceremonial drinking vessels that are often found in graves dating from years preceding and following A.D. 365 were also found in several graves near Kourion.
    (B) No coins minted after A.D. 365 were found in Kourion, but coins minted before that year were found in abundance.
    (C) Most modern histories of Cyprus mention that an earthquake occurred near the island in A.D. 365.
    (D) Several small statues carved in styles current in Cyprus in the century between A.D. 300 and 400 were found in Kourion.
    (E) Stone inscriptions in a form of the Greek alphabet that was definitely used in Cyprus after A.D. 365 were found in Kourion.

The archaeologists hypothesized that Kourion was devastated by an earthquake known to have occurred in A.D. 365. Since choice B provides evidence that A.D. 365 was the date when life in Kourion was disrupted, B supports the hypothesis that it was the A.D. 365 earthquake that devastated Kourion. Thus, B is the best answer.

By contrast, choices A, D, and E all give information about artifacts found in or used in Kourion, but they do not specifically point to A.D. 365 as the date of the devastation. Thus, A, D, and E are inappropriate. Since choice C supports something already established, namely, that an earthquake occurred in A.D. 365, C is inappropriate.

16. **Sales of telephones have increased dramatically over the last year. In order to take advantage of this increase, Mammoth Industries plans to expand production of its own model of telephone, while continuing its already very extensive advertising of this product.**

Which of the following, if true, provides most support for the view that Mammoth Industries *cannot* increase its sales of telephones by adopting the plan outlined above?

(A) Although it sells all of the telephones that it produces, Mammoth Industries' share of all telephone sales has declined over the last year.

(B) Mammoth Industries' average inventory of telephones awaiting shipment to retailers has declined slightly over the last year.

(C) Advertising has made the brand name of Mammoth Industries' telephones widely known, but few consumers know that Mammoth Industries owns this brand.

(D) Mammoth Industries' telephone is one of three brands of telephone that have together accounted for the bulk of the last year's increase in sales.

(E) Despite a slight decline in the retail price, sales of Mammoth Industries' telephones have fallen in the last year.

Choice E indicates that Mammoth's telephones already fail to participate in the industry trend of higher sales despite heavy advertising. Producing more of the same model would thus be unlikely to generate increased sales for Mammoth, so E is the best answer.

If Mammoth has sold all the telephones it produced, it might increase sales by producing more, even if it has lost market share, as choice A states. Choice D indicates that Mammoth's sales are increasing, and similarly for B if the decrease in inventory results from retailers taking delivery of more telephones. So long as consumers recognize the brand name of Mammoth's telephones, as choice C states, it probably does not matter whether they associate it with Mammoth.

7 Sentence Correction

Sample Sentence Correction test sections begin on page 327; answers to the questions follow the test sections. After the answers are explanations for all the questions. These explanations address types of grammatical and syntactical problems you are likely to encounter in the Sentence Correction section of the GMAT.

Study Suggestions

1. One way to gain familiarity with the basic conventions of standard written English is to read material that reflects standard usage. Suitable material will usually be found in good magazines and nonfiction books, editorials in outstanding newspapers, and the collections of essays used by many college and university writing courses.

2. A general review of basic rules of grammar and practice with writing exercises are also ways of studying for the Sentence Correction section. If you have papers that have been carefully evaluated for grammatical errors, it may be helpful to review the comments and corrections.

Test-Taking Strategies for Sentence Correction

1. Read the entire sentence carefully. Try to understand the specific idea or relationship that the sentence should express.

2. Since the part of the sentence that *may* be incorrect is underlined, concentrate on evaluating the underlined part for errors and possible corrections before reading the answer choices.

3. Read each answer choice carefully. Choice A always repeats the underlined portion of the original sentence. Choose A if you think that the sentence is best as it stands, but only after examining all of the other choices.

4. Try to determine how well each choice corrects whatever you consider wrong with the original sentence.

5. Make sure that you evaluate the sentence and the choices in terms of general clarity, grammatical and idiomatic usage, economy and precision of language, and appropriateness of diction.

6. Read the whole sentence, substituting the choice that you prefer for the underlined part. A choice may be wrong because it does not fit grammatically or structurally with the rest of the sentence. Remember that some sentences will require no corrections. The answer to such sentences should be A.

When you take the sample test sections, use the answer spaces on page 325 to mark your answers.

Answer Spaces for Sentence Correction Sample Test Sections

Sample Test Section 1

1 Ⓐ Ⓑ Ⓒ Ⓓ Ⓔ	7 Ⓐ Ⓑ Ⓒ Ⓓ Ⓔ	13 Ⓐ Ⓑ Ⓒ Ⓓ Ⓔ	19 Ⓐ Ⓑ Ⓒ Ⓓ Ⓔ
2 Ⓐ Ⓑ Ⓒ Ⓓ Ⓔ	8 Ⓐ Ⓑ Ⓒ Ⓓ Ⓔ	14 Ⓐ Ⓑ Ⓒ Ⓓ Ⓔ	20 Ⓐ Ⓑ Ⓒ Ⓓ Ⓔ
3 Ⓐ Ⓑ Ⓒ Ⓓ Ⓔ	9 Ⓐ Ⓑ Ⓒ Ⓓ Ⓔ	15 Ⓐ Ⓑ Ⓒ Ⓓ Ⓔ	21 Ⓐ Ⓑ Ⓒ Ⓓ Ⓔ
4 Ⓐ Ⓑ Ⓒ Ⓓ Ⓔ	10 Ⓐ Ⓑ Ⓒ Ⓓ Ⓔ	16 Ⓐ Ⓑ Ⓒ Ⓓ Ⓔ	22 Ⓐ Ⓑ Ⓒ Ⓓ Ⓔ
5 Ⓐ Ⓑ Ⓒ Ⓓ Ⓔ	11 Ⓐ Ⓑ Ⓒ Ⓓ Ⓔ	17 Ⓐ Ⓑ Ⓒ Ⓓ Ⓔ	
6 Ⓐ Ⓑ Ⓒ Ⓓ Ⓔ	12 Ⓐ Ⓑ Ⓒ Ⓓ Ⓔ	18 Ⓐ Ⓑ Ⓒ Ⓓ Ⓔ	

Sample Test Section 2

1 Ⓐ Ⓑ Ⓒ Ⓓ Ⓔ	7 Ⓐ Ⓑ Ⓒ Ⓓ Ⓔ	13 Ⓐ Ⓑ Ⓒ Ⓓ Ⓔ	19 Ⓐ Ⓑ Ⓒ Ⓓ Ⓔ
2 Ⓐ Ⓑ Ⓒ Ⓓ Ⓔ	8 Ⓐ Ⓑ Ⓒ Ⓓ Ⓔ	14 Ⓐ Ⓑ Ⓒ Ⓓ Ⓔ	20 Ⓐ Ⓑ Ⓒ Ⓓ Ⓔ
3 Ⓐ Ⓑ Ⓒ Ⓓ Ⓔ	9 Ⓐ Ⓑ Ⓒ Ⓓ Ⓔ	15 Ⓐ Ⓑ Ⓒ Ⓓ Ⓔ	21 Ⓐ Ⓑ Ⓒ Ⓓ Ⓔ
4 Ⓐ Ⓑ Ⓒ Ⓓ Ⓔ	10 Ⓐ Ⓑ Ⓒ Ⓓ Ⓔ	16 Ⓐ Ⓑ Ⓒ Ⓓ Ⓔ	22 Ⓐ Ⓑ Ⓒ Ⓓ Ⓔ
5 Ⓐ Ⓑ Ⓒ Ⓓ Ⓔ	11 Ⓐ Ⓑ Ⓒ Ⓓ Ⓔ	17 Ⓐ Ⓑ Ⓒ Ⓓ Ⓔ	
6 Ⓐ Ⓑ Ⓒ Ⓓ Ⓔ	12 Ⓐ Ⓑ Ⓒ Ⓓ Ⓔ	18 Ⓐ Ⓑ Ⓒ Ⓓ Ⓔ	

Sample Test Section 3

1 Ⓐ Ⓑ Ⓒ Ⓓ Ⓔ	7 Ⓐ Ⓑ Ⓒ Ⓓ Ⓔ	13 Ⓐ Ⓑ Ⓒ Ⓓ Ⓔ	19 Ⓐ Ⓑ Ⓒ Ⓓ Ⓔ
2 Ⓐ Ⓑ Ⓒ Ⓓ Ⓔ	8 Ⓐ Ⓑ Ⓒ Ⓓ Ⓔ	14 Ⓐ Ⓑ Ⓒ Ⓓ Ⓔ	20 Ⓐ Ⓑ Ⓒ Ⓓ Ⓔ
3 Ⓐ Ⓑ Ⓒ Ⓓ Ⓔ	9 Ⓐ Ⓑ Ⓒ Ⓓ Ⓔ	15 Ⓐ Ⓑ Ⓒ Ⓓ Ⓔ	21 Ⓐ Ⓑ Ⓒ Ⓓ Ⓔ
4 Ⓐ Ⓑ Ⓒ Ⓓ Ⓔ	10 Ⓐ Ⓑ Ⓒ Ⓓ Ⓔ	16 Ⓐ Ⓑ Ⓒ Ⓓ Ⓔ	22 Ⓐ Ⓑ Ⓒ Ⓓ Ⓔ
5 Ⓐ Ⓑ Ⓒ Ⓓ Ⓔ	11 Ⓐ Ⓑ Ⓒ Ⓓ Ⓔ	17 Ⓐ Ⓑ Ⓒ Ⓓ Ⓔ	
6 Ⓐ Ⓑ Ⓒ Ⓓ Ⓔ	12 Ⓐ Ⓑ Ⓒ Ⓓ Ⓔ	18 Ⓐ Ⓑ Ⓒ Ⓓ Ⓔ	

Sample Test Section 4

1 Ⓐ Ⓑ Ⓒ Ⓓ Ⓔ	7 Ⓐ Ⓑ Ⓒ Ⓓ Ⓔ	13 Ⓐ Ⓑ Ⓒ Ⓓ Ⓔ	19 Ⓐ Ⓑ Ⓒ Ⓓ Ⓔ
2 Ⓐ Ⓑ Ⓒ Ⓓ Ⓔ	8 Ⓐ Ⓑ Ⓒ Ⓓ Ⓔ	14 Ⓐ Ⓑ Ⓒ Ⓓ Ⓔ	20 Ⓐ Ⓑ Ⓒ Ⓓ Ⓔ
3 Ⓐ Ⓑ Ⓒ Ⓓ Ⓔ	9 Ⓐ Ⓑ Ⓒ Ⓓ Ⓔ	15 Ⓐ Ⓑ Ⓒ Ⓓ Ⓔ	21 Ⓐ Ⓑ Ⓒ Ⓓ Ⓔ
4 Ⓐ Ⓑ Ⓒ Ⓓ Ⓔ	10 Ⓐ Ⓑ Ⓒ Ⓓ Ⓔ	16 Ⓐ Ⓑ Ⓒ Ⓓ Ⓔ	22 Ⓐ Ⓑ Ⓒ Ⓓ Ⓔ
5 Ⓐ Ⓑ Ⓒ Ⓓ Ⓔ	11 Ⓐ Ⓑ Ⓒ Ⓓ Ⓔ	17 Ⓐ Ⓑ Ⓒ Ⓓ Ⓔ	
6 Ⓐ Ⓑ Ⓒ Ⓓ Ⓔ	12 Ⓐ Ⓑ Ⓒ Ⓓ Ⓔ	18 Ⓐ Ⓑ Ⓒ Ⓓ Ⓔ	

Sample Test Section 5

1 Ⓐ Ⓑ Ⓒ Ⓓ Ⓔ	7 Ⓐ Ⓑ Ⓒ Ⓓ Ⓔ	13 Ⓐ Ⓑ Ⓒ Ⓓ Ⓔ	19 Ⓐ Ⓑ Ⓒ Ⓓ Ⓔ
2 Ⓐ Ⓑ Ⓒ Ⓓ Ⓔ	8 Ⓐ Ⓑ Ⓒ Ⓓ Ⓔ	14 Ⓐ Ⓑ Ⓒ Ⓓ Ⓔ	20 Ⓐ Ⓑ Ⓒ Ⓓ Ⓔ
3 Ⓐ Ⓑ Ⓒ Ⓓ Ⓔ	9 Ⓐ Ⓑ Ⓒ Ⓓ Ⓔ	15 Ⓐ Ⓑ Ⓒ Ⓓ Ⓔ	21 Ⓐ Ⓑ Ⓒ Ⓓ Ⓔ
4 Ⓐ Ⓑ Ⓒ Ⓓ Ⓔ	10 Ⓐ Ⓑ Ⓒ Ⓓ Ⓔ	16 Ⓐ Ⓑ Ⓒ Ⓓ Ⓔ	22 Ⓐ Ⓑ Ⓒ Ⓓ Ⓔ
5 Ⓐ Ⓑ Ⓒ Ⓓ Ⓔ	11 Ⓐ Ⓑ Ⓒ Ⓓ Ⓔ	17 Ⓐ Ⓑ Ⓒ Ⓓ Ⓔ	
6 Ⓐ Ⓑ Ⓒ Ⓓ Ⓔ	12 Ⓐ Ⓑ Ⓒ Ⓓ Ⓔ	18 Ⓐ Ⓑ Ⓒ Ⓓ Ⓔ	

SENTENCE CORRECTION SAMPLE TEST SECTION 1

Time — 25 minutes

22 Questions

<u>Directions</u>: In each of the following sentences, some part of the sentence or the entire sentence is underlined. Beneath each sentence you will find five ways of phrasing the underlined part. The first of these repeats the original; the other four are different. If you think the original is the best of these answer choices, choose answer A; otherwise choose one of the others. Select the best version and fill in the corresponding oval on your answer sheet.

This is a test of correctness and effectiveness of expression. In choosing answers, follow the requirements of standard written English; that is, pay attention to grammar, choice of words, and sentence construction. Choose the answer that produces the most effective sentence; this answer should be clear and exact, without awkwardness, ambiguity, redundancy, or grammatical error.

1. The Wallerstein study indicates that even after a decade young men and women still experience some of the effects of a divorce <u>occurring when a child</u>.

   (A) occurring when a child
   (B) occurring when children
   (C) that occurred when a child
   (D) that occurred when they were children
   (E) that has occurred as each was a child

2. Since 1981, when the farm depression began, the number of acres overseen by professional farm-management companies <u>have grown from 48 million to nearly 59 million, an area that is about Colorado's size.</u>

   (A) have grown from 48 million to nearly 59 million, an area that is about Colorado's size
   (B) have grown from 48 million to nearly 59 million, about the size of Colorado
   (C) has grown from 48 million to nearly 59 million, an area about the size of Colorado
   (D) has grown from 48 million up to nearly 59 million, an area about the size of Colorado's
   (E) has grown from 48 million up to nearly 59 million, about Colorado's size

3. Some bat caves, like honeybee hives, have residents that take on different duties such as defending the entrance, <u>acting as sentinels and to sound</u> a warning at the approach of danger, and scouting outside the cave for new food and roosting sites.

   (A) acting as sentinels and to sound
   (B) acting as sentinels and sounding
   (C) to act as sentinels and sound
   (D) to act as sentinels and to sound
   (E) to act as a sentinel sounding

4. The only way for growers to salvage frozen citrus is <u>to process them quickly into juice concentrate before they rot when warmer weather returns</u>.

   (A) to process them quickly into juice concentrate before they rot when warmer weather returns
   (B) if they are quickly processed into juice concentrate before warmer weather returns to rot them
   (C) for them to be processed quickly into juice concentrate before the fruit rots when warmer weather returns
   (D) if the fruit is quickly processed into juice concentrate before they rot when warmer weather returns
   (E) to have it quickly processed into juice concentrate before warmer weather returns and rots the fruit

GO ON TO THE NEXT PAGE.

5. Carbon-14 dating reveals that the megalithic monuments in Brittany are nearly 2,000 years <u>as old as any of their supposed</u> Mediterranean predecessors.

(A) as old as any of their supposed
(B) older than any of their supposed
(C) as old as their supposed
(D) older than any of their supposedly
(E) as old as their supposedly

6. In virtually all types of tissue in every animal species, dioxin induces the production of enzymes that are the organism's <u>trying to metabolize, or render harmless, the chemical that is irritating it.</u>

(A) trying to metabolize, or render harmless, the chemical that is irritating it
(B) trying that it metabolize, or render harmless, the chemical irritant
(C) attempt to try to metabolize, or render harmless, such a chemical irritant
(D) attempt to try and metabolize, or render harmless, the chemical irritating it
(E) attempt to metabolize, or render harmless, the chemical irritant

7. Dr. Hakuta's research among Hispanic children in the United States indicates that the more the children use both Spanish and English, <u>their intellectual advantage is greater in skills underlying reading ability and nonverbal logic.</u>

(A) their intellectual advantage is greater in skills underlying reading ability and nonverbal logic
(B) their intellectual advantage is the greater in skills underlaying reading ability and nonverbal logic
(C) the greater their intellectual advantage in skills underlying reading ability and nonverbal logic
(D) in skills that underlay reading ability and nonverbal logic, their intellectual advantage is the greater
(E) in skills underlying reading ability and nonverbal logic, the greater intellectual advantage is theirs

8. Lacking information about energy use, people tend to overestimate the amount of energy used by <u>equipment, such as lights, that are visible and must be turned on and off and underestimate that</u> used by unobtrusive equipment, such as water heaters.

(A) equipment, such as lights, that are visible and must be turned on and off and underestimate that
(B) equipment, such as lights, that are visible and must be turned on and off and underestimate it when
(C) equipment, such as lights, that is visible and must be turned on and off and underestimate it when
(D) visible equipment, such as lights, that must be turned on and off and underestimate that
(E) visible equipment, such as lights, that must be turned on and off and underestimate it when

9. Astronomers at the Palomar Observatory have discovered a distant supernova explosion, one <u>that they believe is</u> a type previously unknown to science.

(A) that they believe is
(B) that they believe it to be
(C) they believe that it is of
(D) they believe that is
(E) they believe to be of

GO ON TO THE NEXT PAGE.

10. However much United States voters may agree that there is waste in government and that the government as a whole spends beyond its means, it is difficult to find broad support for a movement toward a minimal state.

   (A) However much United States voters may agree that
   (B) Despite the agreement among United States voters to the fact
   (C) Although United States voters agree
   (D) Even though United States voters may agree
   (E) There is agreement among United States voters that

11. Based on accounts of various ancient writers, scholars have painted a sketchy picture of the activities of an all-female cult that, perhaps as early as the sixth century B.C., worshipped a goddess known in Latin as Bona Dea, "the good goddess."

   (A) Based on accounts of various ancient writers
   (B) Basing it on various ancient writers' accounts
   (C) With accounts of various ancient writers used for a basis
   (D) By the accounts of various ancient writers they used
   (E) Using accounts of various ancient writers

12. Formulas for cash flow and the ratio of debt to equity do not apply to new small businesses in the same way as they do to established big businesses, because they are growing and are seldom in equilibrium.

   (A) Formulas for cash flow and the ratio of debt to equity do not apply to new small businesses in the same way as they do to established big businesses, because they are growing and are seldom in equilibrium.
   (B) Because they are growing and are seldom in equilibrium, formulas for cash flow and the ratio of debt to equity do not apply to new small businesses in the same way as they do to established big businesses.
   (C) Because they are growing and are seldom in equilibrium, new small businesses are not subject to the same applicability of formulas for cash flow and the ratio of debt to equity as established big businesses.
   (D) Because new small businesses are growing and are seldom in equilibrium, formulas for cash flow and the ratio of debt to equity do not apply to them in the same way as to established big businesses.
   (E) New small businesses are not subject to the applicability of formulas for cash flow and the ratio of debt to equity in the same way as established big businesses, because they are growing and are seldom in equilibrium.

13. State officials report that soaring rates of liability insurance have risen to force cutbacks in the operations of everything from local governments and school districts to day-care centers and recreational facilities.

   (A) rates of liability insurance have risen to force
   (B) rates of liability insurance are a force for
   (C) rates for liability insurance are forcing
   (D) rises in liability insurance rates are forcing
   (E) liability insurance rates have risen to force

GO ON TO THE NEXT PAGE.

14. Paleontologists believe that fragments of a primate jawbone unearthed in Burma and estimated at 40 to 44 million years old provide evidence of a crucial step along the evolutionary path that led to human beings.

   (A) at 40 to 44 million years old provide evidence of
   (B) as being 40 to 44 million years old provides evidence of
   (C) that it is 40 to 44 million years old provides evidence of what was
   (D) to be 40 to 44 million years old provide evidence of
   (E) as 40 to 44 million years old provides evidence of what was

15. In his research paper, Dr. Frosh, medical director of the Payne Whitney Clinic, distinguishes mood swings, which may be violent without their being grounded in mental disease, from genuine manic-depressive psychosis.

   (A) mood swings, which may be violent without their being grounded in mental disease, from genuine manic-depressive psychosis
   (B) mood swings, perhaps violent without being grounded in mental disease, and genuine manic-depressive psychosis
   (C) between mood swings, which may be violent without being grounded in mental disease, and genuine manic-depressive psychosis
   (D) between mood swings, perhaps violent without being grounded in mental disease, from genuine manic-depressive psychosis
   (E) genuine manic-depressive psychosis and mood swings, which may be violent without being grounded in mental disease

16. Unlike a typical automobile loan, which requires a fifteen- to twenty-percent down payment, the lease-loan buyer is not required to make an initial deposit on the new vehicle.

   (A) the lease-loan buyer is not required to make
   (B) with lease-loan buying there is no requirement of
   (C) lease-loan buyers are not required to make
   (D) for the lease-loan buyer there is no requirement of
   (E) a lease-loan does not require the buyer to make

17. Native American burial sites dating back 5,000 years indicate that the residents of Maine at that time were part of a widespread culture of Algonquian-speaking people.

   (A) were part of a widespread culture of Algonquian-speaking people
   (B) had been part of a widespread culture of people who were Algonquian-speaking
   (C) were people who were part of a widespread culture that was Algonquian-speaking
   (D) had been people who were part of a widespread culture that was Algonquian-speaking
   (E) were a people which had been part of a widespread, Algonquian-speaking culture

18. Each of Hemingway's wives—Hadley Richardson, Pauline Pfeiffer, Martha Gelhorn, and Mary Welsh—were strong and interesting women, very different from the often pallid women who populate his novels.

   (A) Each of Hemingway's wives—Hadley Richardson, Pauline Pfeiffer, Martha Gelhorn, and Mary Welsh—were strong and interesting women,
   (B) Hadley Richardson, Pauline Pfeiffer, Martha Gelhorn, and Mary Welsh—each of them Hemingway's wives—were strong and interesting women,
   (C) Hemingway's wives—Hadley Richardson, Pauline Pfeiffer, Martha Gelhorn, and Mary Welsh—were all strong and interesting women,
   (D) Strong and interesting women—Hadley Richardson, Pauline Pfeiffer, Martha Gelhorn, and Mary Welsh—each a wife of Hemingway, was
   (E) Strong and interesting women—Hadley Richardson, Pauline Pfeiffer, Martha Gelhorn, and Mary Welsh—every one of Hemingway's wives were

GO ON TO THE NEXT PAGE.

19. In addition to having more protein than wheat does, the protein in rice is higher quality than that in wheat, with more of the amino acids essential to the human diet.

(A) the protein in rice is higher quality than that in
(B) rice has protein of higher quality than that in
(C) the protein in rice is higher in quality than it is in
(D) rice protein is higher in quality than it is in
(E) rice has a protein higher in quality than

20. An array of tax incentives has led to a boom in the construction of new office buildings; so abundant has capital been for commercial real estate that investors regularly scour the country for areas in which to build.

(A) so abundant has capital been for commercial real estate that
(B) capital has been so abundant for commercial real estate, so that
(C) the abundance of capital for commercial real estate has been such,
(D) such has the abundance of capital been for commercial real estate that
(E) such has been an abundance of capital for commercial real estate,

21. Defense attorneys have occasionally argued that their clients' misconduct stemmed from a reaction to something ingested, but in attributing criminal or delinquent behavior to some food allergy, the perpetrators are in effect told that they are not responsible for their actions.

(A) in attributing criminal or delinquent behavior to some food allergy
(B) if criminal or delinquent behavior is attributed to an allergy to some food
(C) in attributing behavior that is criminal or delinquent to an allergy to some food
(D) if some food allergy is attributed as the cause of criminal or delinquent behavior
(E) in attributing a food allergy as the cause of criminal or delinquent behavior

22. The voluminous personal papers of Thomas Alva Edison reveal that his inventions typically sprang to life not in a flash of inspiration but evolved slowly from previous works.

(A) sprang to life not in a flash of inspiration but evolved slowly
(B) sprang to life not in a flash of inspiration but were slowly evolved
(C) did not spring to life in a flash of inspiration but evolved slowly
(D) did not spring to life in a flash of inspiration but had slowly evolved
(E) did not spring to life in a flash of inspiration but they were slowly evolved

STOP

IF YOU FINISH BEFORE TIME IS CALLED, YOU MAY CHECK YOUR WORK ON THIS SECTION ONLY. DO NOT TURN TO ANY OTHER SECTION IN THE TEST.

-331-

Answer Key for Sample Test Section 1

SENTENCE CORRECTION

1.	D	12.	D
2.	C	13.	C
3.	B	14.	D
4.	E	15.	C
5.	B	16.	E
6.	E	17.	A
7.	C	18.	C
8.	D	19.	B
9.	E	20.	A
10.	A	21.	B
11.	E	22.	C

Explanatory Material: Sentence Correction

The following discussion of Sentence Correction is intended to familiarize you with the most efficient and effective approaches to Sentence Correction. The particular questions on the sample test sections in this chapter are generally representative of the kinds of questions you will encounter in this section of the GMAT. Remember that it is the problem-solving strategy that is important, not the specific details of a particular question.

Sample Test Section 1

1. The Wallerstein study indicates that even after a decade young men and women still experience some of the effects of a divorce occurring when a child.

   (A) occurring when a child
   (B) occurring when children
   (C) that occurred when a child
   (D) that occurred when they were children
   (E) that has occurred as each was a child

Choice D is best. The phrasing *a divorce that occurred when they were children* correctly uses the relative clause *that occurred* to modify *a divorce* and includes a pronoun and verb (*they were*) that refer unambiguously to their antecedent, *men and women*. Choice A incorrectly introduces the *when . . .* phrase with *occur-ring*, thus illogically making *divorce* the grammatical referent of *when a child*; furthermore, the singular *child* does not agree with the plural *men and women*. B replaces *child* with *children* but otherwise fails to correct A's errors of structure and logic, and C corrects only the error created by *occurring*. Choice E includes an incorrect verb tense (*has occurred*) and wrongly replaces *when* with *as*. Also, *each was* does not properly refer to *men and women*.

2. Since 1981, when the farm depression began, the number of acres overseen by professional farm-management companies have grown from 48 million to nearly 59 million, an area that is about Colorado's size.

   (A) have grown from 48 million to nearly 59 million, an area that is about Colorado's size
   (B) have grown from 48 million to nearly 59 million, about the size of Colorado
   (C) has grown from 48 million to nearly 59 million, an area about the size of Colorado
   (D) has grown from 48 million up to nearly 59 million, an area about the size of Colorado's
   (E) has grown from 48 million up to nearly 59 million, about Colorado's size

In choice C, the best answer, *an area about the size of Colorado* clearly describes a rough equivalence between the area of Colorado and the area overseen by the companies. In A and B, the plural verb *have* does not agree with the singular subject *number*. Choice A is also wordy, since *that is* can be deleted without loss of clarity. The absence of *an area* in B and E impairs clarity: the phrase beginning with *about* must modify a noun such as *area* that is logically equivalent to the number of acres given. In D and E *up to* is unidiomatic; the correct expression is *from x to y*. In D, *the size of Colorado's* is unidiomatic, since *of Colorado* forms a complete possessive.

3. Some bat caves, like honeybee hives, have residents that take on different duties such as defending the entrance, acting as sentinels and to sound a warning at the approach of danger, and scouting outside the cave for new food and roosting sites.

   (A) acting as sentinels and to sound
   (B) acting as sentinels and sounding
   (C) to act as sentinels and sound
   (D) to act as sentinels and to sound
   (E) to act as a sentinel sounding

Because the verb phrases used to describe the bats' duties are governed by the phrase *different duties such as*, they should each be expressed in the present participial (or "-ing") form to parallel *defending* and *scouting*. Choices A, C, D, and E all violate parallelism by employing infinitives (*to . . .*) in place of participial phrases. In E the singular *sentinel* is not consistent with *residents*, and the omission of *and* distorts the meaning of the original. Only B, the best answer, preserves the sense of the original, uses the correct idiom, and observes the parallelism required among and within the three main verb phrases.

4. The only way for growers to salvage frozen citrus is <u>to process them quickly into juice concentrate before they rot when warmer weather returns</u>.

   (A) to process them quickly into juice concentrate before they rot when warmer weather returns

   (B) if they are quickly processed into juice concentrate before warmer weather returns to rot them

   (C) for them to be processed quickly into juice concentrate before the fruit rots when warmer weather returns

   (D) if the fruit is quickly processed into juice concentrate before they rot when warmer weather returns

   (E) to have it quickly processed into juice concentrate before warmer weather returns and rots the fruit

For parallelism, the linking verb *is* should link two infinitives: *The only way to salvage . . . is to process*. Choice A begins with an infinitive, but the plural pronouns *them* and *they* do not agree with the singular noun *citrus*. Choices B, C, and D do not begin with an infinitive, and all present pronoun errors: the plural pronouns cannot grammatically refer to *citrus* or *fruit*, nor can they refer to *farmers* without absurdity. The best choice, E, has parallel infinitives and uses *fruit* to refer unambiguously to *citrus*. E also expresses the cause-and-effect relationship between the return of warmer weather and the rotting of the fruit; A, C, and D merely describe these events as contemporaneous.

5. Carbon-14 dating reveals that the megalithic monuments in Brittany are nearly 2,000 years <u>as old as any of their supposed</u> Mediterranean predecessors.

   (A) as old as any of their supposed
   (B) older than any of their supposed
   (C) as old as their supposed
   (D) older than any of their supposedly
   (E) as old as their supposedly

Choices A, C, and E do not state the comparison logically. The expression *as old as* indicates equality of age, but the sentence indicates that the Brittany monuments predate the Mediterranean monuments by 2,000 years. In B, the best choice, *older than* makes this point of comparison clear. B also correctly uses the adjective *supposed*, rather than the adverb *supposedly* used in D and E, to modify the noun phrase *Mediterranean predecessors*.

6. In virtually all types of tissue in every animal species, dioxin induces the production of enzymes that are the organism's <u>trying to metabolize, or render harmless, the chemical that is irritating it</u>.

   (A) trying to metabolize, or render harmless, the chemical that is irritating it

   (B) trying that it metabolize, or render harmless, the chemical irritant

   (C) attempt to try to metabolize, or render harmless, such a chemical irritant

   (D) attempt to try and metabolize, or render harmless, the chemical irritating it

   (E) attempt to metabolize, or render harmless, the chemical irritant

Although an "-ing" verb such as *trying* can sometimes be used as a noun, the phrase *the organism's trying to metabolize* in A is unidiomatic because *trying* is used as the object of *organism's*. In B, *trying that it metabolize* is ungrammatical. The noun *attempt* could follow *organism's*; also, it would parallel the noun *enzymes*, and parallelism is needed here because the sentence uses the linking verb *are* to equate *enzymes* and *attempt*. In C and D, however, *attempt to try* is redundant. Choice E, which says *attempt to metabolize*, is best. The phrase *the chemical irritant* is also the most concise and precise conclusion for the sentence because it clearly refers to the *dioxin* mentioned earlier.

7. Dr. Hakuta's research among Hispanic children in the United States indicates that the more the children use both Spanish and English, <u>their intellectual advantage is greater in skills underlying reading ability and nonverbal logic</u>.

   (A) their intellectual advantage is greater in skills underlying reading ability and nonverbal logic

   (B) their intellectual advantage is the greater in skills underlaying reading ability and nonverbal logic

   (C) the greater their intellectual advantage in skills underlying reading ability and nonverbal logic

   (D) in skills that underlay reading ability and nonverbal logic, their intellectual advantage is the greater

   (E) in skills underlying reading ability and nonverbal logic, the greater intellectual advantage is theirs

The best choice is C. The phrase *the more the children* should be completed by a parallel phrase that begins with a comparative adjective and a noun phrase, as in *the greater their . . . advantage*. Only C correctly completes the structure with a parallel phrase. Choices A, B, D, and E present structures that are unwieldy and awkward in addition to being nonparallel, and that state the relationship between language use and skills development less clearly than C does. Also, *underlaying* in B and *underlay* in D are incorrect; the meaning of this sentence requires the present participle of "underlie," *underlying,* as a modifier of *skills*.

8. Lacking information about energy use, people tend to overestimate the amount of energy used by <u>equipment, such as lights, that are visible and must be turned on and off and underestimate that</u> used by unobtrusive equipment, such as water heaters.

   (A) equipment, such as lights, that are visible and must be turned on and off and underestimate that

   (B) equipment, such as lights, that are visible and must be turned on and off and underestimate it when

   (C) equipment, such as lights, that is visible and must be turned on and off and underestimate it when

   (D) visible equipment, such as lights, that must be turned on and off and underestimate that

   (E) visible equipment, such as lights, that must be turned on and off and underestimate it when

Choices A and B incorrectly use the plural verb *are* with the singular noun *equipment*. In B, C, and E, *when used by* does not parallel *amount . . . used by* and nonsensically suggests that the people are used by the equipment. D, the best choice, correctly parallels *the amount . . . used by* with *that used by*, in which *that* is the pronoun substitute for *amount*. Moreover, D solves the agreement problem of A and B by omitting the *to be* verb used with *visible* and placing *visible* before *equipment*; the phrase *visible equipment* is also parallel with *unobtrusive equipment*.

9. Astronomers at the Palomar Observatory have discovered a distant supernova explosion, one <u>that they believe is</u> a type previously unknown to science.

   (A) that they believe is

   (B) that they believe it to be

   (C) they believe that it is of

   (D) they believe that is

   (E) they believe to be of

Choice E is best. The pronoun *that* in A and B should be deleted, since the pronoun *one* is sufficient to introduce the modifier and the sentence is more fluid without *that*. In B and C, *it* and *that it* are intrusive and ungrammatical: the idiom is "believe x to be y." In the context of this sentence, the infinitive *to be* is more appropriate than the limited present-tense *is* in referring to an event that occurred long ago but has been discovered only recently. Finally, A, B, and D lack *of* and so illogically equate this particular explosion with the whole class of explosions to which it belongs: it is not *a type* but possibly one *of a type*.

10. <u>However much United States voters may agree that</u> there is waste in government and that the government as a whole spends beyond its means, it is difficult to find broad support for a movement toward a minimal state.

   (A) However much United States voters may agree that

   (B) Despite the agreement among United States voters to the fact

   (C) Although United States voters agree

   (D) Even though United States voters may agree

   (E) There is agreement among United States voters that

A is the best choice. Choices B, C, and D incorrectly omit *that* after *agree*; *that* is needed to create the parallel construction *agree that there is waste . . . and that the government . . . spends*. Choice E, though it retains *that*, is grammatically incorrect: because E starts with an independent rather than a subordinate clause and separates its two independent clauses with a comma, it creates a run-on sentence with no logical connection established between the halves. In B, *the agreement . . . to the fact* is unidiomatic, and B, C, and E alter the sense of the original sentence by saying that voters *agree* rather than that they *may agree*.

11. <u>Based on accounts of various ancient writers</u>, scholars have painted a sketchy picture of the activities of an all-female cult that, perhaps as early as the sixth century B.C., worshipped a goddess known in Latin as Bona Dea, "the good goddess."

   (A) Based on accounts of various ancient writers

   (B) Basing it on various ancient writers' accounts

   (C) With accounts of various ancient writers used for a basis

   (D) By the accounts of various ancient writers they used

   (E) Using accounts of various ancient writers

In choice A, the introductory clause beginning *Based on* modifies *scholars*, the noun that immediately follows it: in other words, A says that *scholars* were *based on the accounts of various ancient writers*. Choice B is awkward and imprecise in that the referent for the pronoun *it* is not immediately clear. C and D are also wordy and awkward, and in D *By the accounts . . . they used* is an unidiomatic and roundabout way of saying that scholars used the accounts. E, the best choice, is clear and concise; it correctly uses a present participle (or "-ing" verb) to introduce the modifier describing how the scholars worked.

12. <u>Formulas for cash flow and the ratio of debt to equity</u>
    <u>do not apply to new small businesses in the same way</u>
    <u>as they do to established big businesses, because they</u>
    <u>are growing and are seldom in equilibrium.</u>

    (A) Formulas for cash flow and the ratio of debt to
        equity do not apply to new small businesses in
        the same way as they do to established big
        businesses, because they are growing and are
        seldom in equilibrium.
    (B) Because they are growing and are seldom in
        equilibrium, formulas for cash flow and the ratio
        of debt to equity do not apply to new small
        businesses in the same way as they do to estab-
        lished big businesses.
    (C) Because they are growing and are seldom in
        equilibrium, new small businesses are not subject
        to the same applicability of formulas for cash
        flow and the ratio of debt to equity as established
        big businesses.
    (D) Because new small businesses are growing and
        are seldom in equilibrium, formulas for cash
        flow and the ratio of debt to equity do not
        apply to them in the same way as to established
        big businesses.
    (E) New small businesses are not subject to the
        applicability of formulas for cash flow and the
        ratio of debt to equity in the same way as
        established big businesses, because they are
        growing and are seldom in equilibrium.

In A, the *they* after *because* is ambiguous; it seems illogically
to refer to *Formulas* because *they* and *Formulas* are each the
grammatical subject of a clause and because the previous *they*
refers to *Formulas*. In A and B, *do not apply to . . . in the
same way as they do to* is wordy and awkward. D, the best
choice, says more concisely *in the same way as to*. Also in B,
because *they* refers to *formulas*, the introductory clause states
confusedly that the formulas are growing. In C and E, *subject
to the [same] applicability of . . .* is wordy, awkward, and
imprecise; furthermore, *are* is preferable either before or after
established big businesses to complete the comparison.
Finally, the referent of *they* is not immediately clear in E.

13. State officials report that soaring <u>rates of liability</u>
    <u>insurance have risen to force</u> cutbacks in the opera-
    tions of everything from local governments and school
    districts to day-care centers and recreational facilities.

    (A) rates of liability insurance have risen to force
    (B) rates of liability insurance are a force for
    (C) rates for liability insurance are forcing
    (D) rises in liability insurance rates are forcing
    (E) liability insurance rates have risen to force

In choices A and B, *rates of* is incorrect; when *rates* means
"prices charged," it should be followed by *for*. Also in B, *are
a force for* does not accurately convey the meaning that the
soaring rates are actually forcing cutbacks in the present. In
A and E, it is redundant to say that soaring rates *have risen*.

Similarly, the word *rises* makes D redundant. C, the best choice,
is idiomatic and concise, and it correctly uses the progressive
verb form *are forcing* to indicate an ongoing situation.

14. Paleontologists believe that fragments of a primate
    jawbone unearthed in Burma and estimated <u>at 40 to</u>
    <u>44 million years old provide evidence of</u> a crucial step
    along the evolutionary path that led to human beings.

    (A) at 40 to 44 million years old provide evidence of
    (B) as being 40 to 44 million years old provides
        evidence of
    (C) that it is 40 to 44 million years old provides
        evidence of what was
    (D) to be 40 to 44 million years old provide evidence of
    (E) as 40 to 44 million years old provides evidence of
        what was

D, the best choice, correctly follows *estimated* with *to be*. The
other choices present structures that are not idiomatic when
used in conjunction with *estimated*. Choices B, C, and E all
mismatch the singular verb *provides* with its plural subject,
fragments, and in choices C and E, *what was* is unnecessary
and wordy. In choice C, the use of the verb phrase *estimated
that it is* produces an ungrammatical sentence.

15. In his research paper, Dr. Frosh, medical director of
    the Payne Whitney Clinic, distinguishes <u>mood swings,</u>
    <u>which may be violent without their being grounded in</u>
    <u>mental disease, from genuine manic-depressive</u>
    <u>psychosis.</u>

    (A) mood swings, which may be violent without their
        being grounded in mental disease, from
        genuine manic-depressive psychosis
    (B) mood swings, perhaps violent without being
        grounded in mental disease, and genuine
        manic-depressive psychosis
    (C) between mood swings, which may be violent
        without being grounded in mental disease, and
        genuine manic-depressive psychosis
    (D) between mood swings, perhaps violent without
        being grounded in mental disease, from
        genuine manic-depressive psychosis
    (E) genuine manic-depressive psychosis and mood
        swings, which may be violent without being
        grounded in mental disease

The best choice is C because it uses the idiomatically correct
expression *distinguishes between* x *and* y and because it
provides a structure in which the relative clause beginning
which may be violent clearly modifies *mood swings*. The other
choices use *distinguishes* in unidiomatic constructions.
Additionally, *their* in A is intrusive and unnecessary, and the
modifier of *mood swings* in B and D (*perhaps violent*) is
awkward and less clear than the more developed clause *which
may be violent*.

-335-

16. **Unlike a typical automobile loan, which requires a fifteen- to twenty-percent down payment, <u>the lease-loan buyer is not required to make</u> an initial deposit on the new vehicle.**

   (A) the lease-loan buyer is not required to make
   (B) with lease-loan buying there is no requirement of
   (C) lease-loan buyers are not required to make
   (D) for the lease-loan buyer there is no requirement of
   (E) a lease-loan does not require the buyer to make

Choice E, the best answer, correctly uses a parallel construction to draw a logical comparison: *Unlike a typical automobile loan, . . . a lease-loan . . . .* Choice A illogically compares an *automobile loan*, an inanimate thing, with a *lease-loan buyer*, a person. In choice C, *buyers* makes the comparison inconsistent in number as well as illogical. Choices B and D are syntactically and logically flawed because each attempts to compare the noun *loan* and a prepositional phrase: *with lease-loan buying* in B and *for the lease-loan buyer* in D. Choices B and D are also imprecise and awkward. Finally, choice E is the only option that supplies an active verb form, *does not require*, to parallel *requires*.

17. **Native American burial sites dating back 5,000 years indicate that the residents of Maine at that time <u>were part of a widespread culture of Algonquian-speaking people</u>.**

   (A) were part of a widespread culture of Algonquian-speaking people
   (B) had been part of a widespread culture of people who were Algonquian-speaking
   (C) were people who were part of a widespread culture that was Algonquian-speaking
   (D) had been people who were part of a widespread culture that was Algonquian-speaking
   (E) were a people which had been part of a widespread, Algonquian-speaking culture

Choice A is best because it correctly uses the simple past tense, *the residents . . . at that time were*, and because it is the most concise. In B and D, the replacement of *were* with the past perfect *had been* needlessly changes the original meaning by suggesting that the Native Americans had previously ceased to be part of the widespread culture. All of the choices but A are wordy, and in C, D, and E the word *people* redundantly describes *the residents* rather than the larger group to which the residents belonged. These choices are also imprecise because they state that the *culture*, rather than *people*, spoke the Algonquian language. Choice E displays inconsistent tenses and an error of pronoun reference, *people which*.

18. **<u>Each of Hemingway's wives — Hadley Richardson, Pauline Pfeiffer, Martha Gelhorn, and Mary Welsh — were strong and interesting women,</u> very different from the often pallid women who populate his novels.**

   (A) Each of Hemingway's wives — Hadley Richardson, Pauline Pfeiffer, Martha Gelhorn, and Mary Welsh — were strong and interesting women,
   (B) Hadley Richardson, Pauline Pfeiffer, Martha Gelhorn, and Mary Welsh — each of them Hemingway's wives — were strong and interesting women,
   (C) Hemingway's wives — Hadley Richardson, Pauline Pfeiffer, Martha Gelhorn, and Mary Welsh — were all strong and interesting women,
   (D) Strong and interesting women — Hadley Richardson, Pauline Pfeiffer, Martha Gelhorn, and Mary Welsh — each a wife of Hemingway, was
   (E) Strong and interesting women — Hadley Richardson, Pauline Pfeiffer, Martha Gelhorn, and Mary Welsh — every one of Hemingway's wives were

Each choice but C contains errors of agreement. In both A and E, the singular subject (*each* in A, *every one* in E) does not agree with the plural verb *were*, while in D, the plural subject *women* is mismatched with the singular verb *was*. In B, the subject and verb agree, but the descriptive phrase placed between them creates an illogical statement because *each* cannot be *wives*; *each* can be one of the wives, or a wife. The pronoun constructions in A, B, D, and E are wordy; also, B, D, and E are very awkwardly structured and do not convey the point about Hemingway's wives clearly. Choice C correctly links *wives* with *were*, eliminates the unnecessary pronouns, and provides a clearer structure.

19. **In addition to having more protein than wheat does, <u>the protein in rice is higher quality than that in</u> wheat, with more of the amino acids essential to the human diet.**

   (A) the protein in rice is higher quality than that in
   (B) rice has protein of higher quality than that in
   (C) the protein in rice is higher in quality than it is in
   (D) rice protein is higher in quality than it is in
   (E) rice has a protein higher in quality than

In this sentence, the initial clause modifies the nearest noun, identifying it as the thing being compared with *wheat*. By making *protein* the noun modified, choices A, C, and D illogically compare *wheat* with *protein* and claim that the <u>protein</u> in rice has more protein than wheat does. In C and D, the comparative structure *higher in quality than it is in wheat* absurdly suggests that rice protein contains wheat. B, the best choice, logically compares *wheat* to *rice* by placing the noun *rice* immediately after the initial clause. B also uses *that* to refer to *protein* in making the comparison between the proteins of rice and wheat. Choice E needs either *that in* or *does* after *wheat* to make a complete and logical comparison.

20. An array of tax incentives has led to a boom in the construction of new office buildings; <u>so abundant has capital been for commercial real estate that</u> investors regularly scour the country for areas in which to build.

    (A) so abundant has capital been for commercial real estate that
    (B) capital has been so abundant for commercial real estate, so that
    (C) the abundance of capital for commercial real estate has been such,
    (D) such has the abundance of capital been for commercial real estate that
    (E) such has been an abundance of capital for commercial real estate,

Choice A is best. The construction *so abundant has capital been . . . that* correctly and clearly expresses the relationship between the abundance and the investors' response. In choice B, the repetition of *so* is illogical and unidiomatic. Choices C, D, and E alter somewhat the intended meaning of the sentence; because of its position in these statements, *such* functions to mean "of a kind" rather than to intensify *abundant*. Choice D awkwardly separates *has* and *been*, and the omission of *that* from C and E makes those choices ungrammatical.

21. Defense attorneys have occasionally argued that their clients' misconduct stemmed from a reaction to something ingested, but <u>in attributing criminal or delinquent behavior to some food allergy</u>, the perpetrators are in effect told that they are not responsible for their actions.

    (A) in attributing criminal or delinquent behavior to some food allergy
    (B) if criminal or delinquent behavior is attributed to an allergy to some food
    (C) in attributing behavior that is criminal or delinquent to an allergy to some food
    (D) if some food allergy is attributed as the cause of criminal or delinquent behavior
    (E) in attributing a food allergy as the cause of criminal or delinquent behavior

In choices A, C, and E, *in attributing . . . behavior* modifies *the perpetrators*, producing the illogical statement that the perpetrators rather than the defense attorneys are attributing behavior to food allergies. Choice C is also wordy, and *attributing . . . as* is unidiomatic in E. In the correct form of the expression, one *attributes* x, an effect, *to* y, a cause; or, if a passive construction is used, x *is attributed to* y. D avoids the initial modification error by using a passive construction (in which the attributors are not identified), but *attributed* x *as the cause of* y is unidiomatic. Choice B is best.

22. The voluminous personal papers of Thomas Alva Edison reveal that his inventions typically <u>sprang to life not in a flash of inspiration but evolved slowly</u> from previous works.

    (A) sprang to life not in a flash of inspiration but evolved slowly
    (B) sprang to life not in a flash of inspiration but were slowly evolved
    (C) did not spring to life in a flash of inspiration but evolved slowly
    (D) did not spring to life in a flash of inspiration but had slowly evolved
    (E) did not spring to life in a flash of inspiration but they were slowly evolved

C, the best choice, places *not* and *but* in such a way that the distinction between springing to life in a flash of inspiration and evolving slowly is logically and idiomatically expressed. A and B are faulty because, for grammatical parallelism, *not in a flash . . .* must be followed by *but in . . .* , not by a conjugated form of the verb. Moreover, *were slowly evolved* is incorrect in B because *evolve*, in this sense of the word, cannot be made passive. Choices C, D, and E all correctly place *not* before *spring*. D, however, contains inconsistent verb tenses; E contains the faulty passive and an intrusive *they*.

-337-

SENTENCE CORRECTION SAMPLE TEST SECTION 2

Time — 25 minutes

22 Questions

<u>Directions</u>: In each of the following sentences, some part of the sentence or the entire sentence is underlined. Beneath each sentence you will find five ways of phrasing the underlined part. The first of these repeats the original; the other four are different. If you think the original is the best of these answer choices, choose answer A; otherwise choose one of the others. Select the best version and fill in the corresponding oval on your answer sheet.

This is a test of correctness and effectiveness of expression. In choosing answers, follow the requirements of standard written English; that is, pay attention to grammar, choice of words, and sentence construction. Choose the answer that produces the most effective sentence; this answer should be clear and exact, without awkwardness, ambiguity, redundancy, or grammatical error.

1. A Labor Department study states that the <u>numbers of women employed outside the home grew by more than a thirty-five percent increase</u> in the past decade and accounted for more than sixty-two percent of the total growth in the civilian work force.

    (A) numbers of women employed outside the home grew by more than a thirty-five percent increase
    (B) numbers of women employed outside the home grew more than thirty-five percent
    (C) numbers of women employed outside the home were raised by more than thirty-five percent
    (D) number of women employed outside the home increased by more than thirty-five percent
    (E) number of women employed outside the home was raised by more than a thirty-five percent increase

2. The first decision for most tenants living in a building undergoing <u>being converted to cooperative ownership is if to sign</u> a no-buy pledge with the other tenants.

    (A) being converted to cooperative ownership is if to sign
    (B) being converted to cooperative ownership is whether they should be signing
    (C) being converted to cooperative ownership is whether or not they sign
    (D) conversion to cooperative ownership is if to sign
    (E) conversion to cooperative ownership is whether to sign

3. The end of the eighteenth century saw the emergence of prize-stock breeding, with individual bulls and cows receiving awards, fetching unprecedented prices, and <u>excited</u> enormous interest whenever they were put on show.

    (A) excited
    (B) it excited
    (C) exciting
    (D) would excite
    (E) it had excited

4. Of all the possible disasters that threaten American agriculture, the possibility of an adverse change in climate <u>is maybe the more difficult for analysis.</u>

    (A) is maybe the more difficult for analysis
    (B) is probably the most difficult to analyze
    (C) is maybe the most difficult for analysis
    (D) is probably the more difficult to analyze
    (E) is, it may be, the analysis that is most difficult

GO ON TO THE NEXT PAGE.

5. Published in Harlem, the owner and editor of the *Messenger* were two young journalists, Chandler Owen and A. Philip Randolph, who would later make his reputation as a labor leader.

(A) Published in Harlem, the owner and editor of the *Messenger* were two young journalists, Chandler Owen and A. Philip Randolph, who would later make his reputation as a labor leader.
(B) Published in Harlem, two young journalists, Chandler Owen and A. Philip Randolph, who would later make his reputation as a labor leader, were the owner and editor of the *Messenger*.
(C) Published in Harlem, the *Messenger* was owned and edited by two young journalists, A. Philip Randolph, who would later make his reputation as a labor leader, and Chandler Owen.
(D) The *Messenger* was owned and edited by two young journalists, Chandler Owen and A. Philip Randolph, who would later make his reputation as a labor leader, and published in Harlem.
(E) The owner and editor being two young journalists, Chandler Owen and A. Philip Randolph, who would later make his reputation as a labor leader, the *Messenger* was published in Harlem.

6. The rise in the Commerce Department's index of leading economic indicators suggest that the economy should continue its expansion into the coming months, but that the mixed performance of the index's individual components indicates that economic growth will proceed at a more moderate pace than in the first quarter of this year.

(A) suggest that the economy should continue its expansion into the coming months, but that
(B) suggest that the economy is to continue expansion in the coming months, but
(C) suggests that the economy will continue its expanding in the coming months, but that
(D) suggests that the economy is continuing to expand into the coming months, but that
(E) suggests that the economy will continue to expand in the coming months, but

7. In three centuries—from 1050 to 1350—several million tons of stone were quarried in France for the building of eighty cathedrals, five hundred large churches, and some tens of thousands of parish churches.

(A) for the building of eighty cathedrals, five hundred large churches, and some
(B) in order that they might build eighty cathedrals, five hundred large churches, and some
(C) so as they might build eighty cathedrals, five hundred large churches, and some
(D) so that there could be built eighty cathedrals, five hundred large churches, and
(E) such that they could build eighty cathedrals, five hundred large churches, and

8. What was as remarkable as the development of the compact disc has been the use of the new technology to revitalize, in better sound than was ever before possible, some of the classic recorded performances of the pre-LP era.

(A) What was as remarkable as the development of the compact disc
(B) The thing that was as remarkable as developing the compact disc
(C) No less remarkable than the development of the compact disc
(D) Developing the compact disc has been none the less remarkable than
(E) Development of the compact disc has been no less remarkable as

9. Unlike computer skills or other technical skills, there is a disinclination on the part of many people to recognize the degree to which their analytical skills are weak.

(A) Unlike computer skills or other technical skills, there is a disinclination on the part of many people to recognize the degree to which their analytical skills are weak.
(B) Unlike computer skills or other technical skills, which they admit they lack, many people are disinclined to recognize that their analytical skills are weak.
(C) Unlike computer skills or other technical skills, analytical skills bring out a disinclination in many people to recognize that they are weak to a degree.
(D) Many people, willing to admit that they lack computer skills or other technical skills, are disinclined to recognize that their analytical skills are weak.
(E) Many people have a disinclination to recognize the weakness of their analytical skills while willing to admit their lack of computer skills or other technical skills.

GO ON TO THE NEXT PAGE.

10. Some buildings that were destroyed and heavily damaged in the earthquake last year were constructed in violation of the city's building code.

(A) Some buildings that were destroyed and heavily damaged in the earthquake last year were
(B) Some buildings that were destroyed or heavily damaged in the earthquake last year had been
(C) Some buildings that the earthquake destroyed and heavily damaged last year have been
(D) Last year the earthquake destroyed or heavily damaged some buildings that have been
(E) Last year some of the buildings that were destroyed or heavily damaged in the earthquake had been

11. From the earliest days of the tribe, kinship determined the way in which the Ojibwa society organized its labor, provided access to its resources, and defined rights and obligations involved in the distribution and consumption of those resources.

(A) and defined rights and obligations involved in the distribution and consumption of those resources
(B) defining rights and obligations involved in their distribution and consumption
(C) and defined rights and obligations as they were involved in its distribution and consumption
(D) whose rights and obligations were defined in their distribution and consumption
(E) the distribution and consumption of them defined by rights and obligations

12. A report by the American Academy for the Advancement of Science has concluded that much of the currently uncontrolled dioxins to which North Americans are exposed comes from the incineration of wastes.

(A) much of the currently uncontrolled dioxins to which North Americans are exposed comes
(B) much of the currently uncontrolled dioxins that North Americans are exposed to come
(C) much of the dioxins that are currently uncontrolled and that North Americans are exposed to comes
(D) many of the dioxins that are currently uncontrolled and North Americans are exposed to come
(E) many of the currently uncontrolled dioxins to which North Americans are exposed come

13. In June of 1987, *The Bridge of Trinquetaille*, Vincent van Gogh's view of an iron bridge over the Rhone sold for $20.2 million and it was the second highest price ever paid for a painting at auction.

(A) Rhone sold for $20.2 million and it was
(B) Rhone, which sold for $20.2 million, was
(C) Rhone, was sold for $20.2 million,
(D) Rhone was sold for $20.2 million, being
(E) Rhone, sold for $20.2 million, and was

14. *Bufo marinus* toads, fierce predators that will eat frogs, lizards, and even small birds, are native to South America but were introduced into Florida during the 1930's in an attempt to control pests in the state's vast sugarcane fields.

(A) are native to South America but were introduced into Florida during the 1930's in an attempt to control
(B) are native in South America but were introduced into Florida during the 1930's as attempts to control
(C) are natives of South America but were introduced into Florida during the 1930's in an attempt at controlling
(D) had been native to South America but were introduced to Florida during the 1930's as an attempt at controlling
(E) had been natives of South America but were introduced to Florida during the 1930's as attempts at controlling

15. While some academicians believe that business ethics should be integrated into every business course, others say that students will take ethics seriously only if it would be taught as a separately required course.

(A) only if it would be taught as a separately required course
(B) only if it is taught as a separate, required course
(C) if it is taught only as a course required separately
(D) if it was taught only as a separate and required course
(E) if it would only be taught as a required course, separately

GO ON TO THE NEXT PAGE.

16. Scientists have observed large concentrations of heavy-metal deposits in the upper twenty centimeters of Baltic Sea sediments, which are consistent with the growth of industrial activity there.

(A) Baltic Sea sediments, which are consistent with the growth of industrial activity there
(B) Baltic Sea sediments, where the growth of industrial activity is consistent with these findings
(C) Baltic Sea sediments, findings consistent with its growth of industrial activity
(D) sediments from the Baltic Sea, findings consistent with the growth of industrial activity in the area
(E) sediments from the Baltic Sea, consistent with the growth of industrial activity there

17. For members of the seventeenth-century Ashanti nation in Africa, animal-hide shields with wooden frames were essential items of military equipment, a method to protect warriors against enemy arrows and spears.

(A) a method to protect
(B) as a method protecting
(C) protecting
(D) as a protection of
(E) to protect

18. In metalwork one advantage of adhesive-bonding over spot-welding is that the contact, and hence the bonding, is effected continuously over a broad surface instead of a series of regularly spaced points with no bonding in between.

(A) instead of
(B) as opposed to
(C) in contrast with
(D) rather than at
(E) as against being at

19. Under a provision of the Constitution that was never applied, Congress has been required to call a convention for considering possible amendments to the document when formally asked to do it by the legislatures of two-thirds of the states.

(A) was never applied, Congress has been required to call a convention for considering possible amendments to the document when formally asked to do it
(B) was never applied, there has been a requirement that Congress call a convention for consideration of possible amendments to the document when asked to do it formally
(C) was never applied, whereby Congress is required to call a convention for considering possible amendments to the document when asked to do it formally
(D) has never been applied, whereby Congress is required to call a convention to consider possible amendments to the document when formally asked to do so
(E) has never been applied, Congress is required to call a convention to consider possible amendments to the document when formally asked to do so

20. The current administration, being worried over some foreign trade barriers being removed and our exports failing to increase as a result of deep cuts in the value of the dollar, has formed a group to study ways to sharpen our competitiveness.

(A) being worried over some foreign trade barriers being removed and our exports failing
(B) worrying over some foreign trade barriers being removed, also over the failure of our exports
(C) worried about the removal of some foreign trade barriers and the failure of our exports
(D) in that they were worried about the removal of some foreign trade barriers and also about the failure of our exports
(E) because of its worry concerning the removal of some foreign trade barriers, also concerning the failure of our exports

21. In the minds of many people living in England, before Australia was Australia, it was the antipodes, the opposite pole to civilization, an obscure and unimaginable place that was considered the end of the world.

(A) before Australia was Australia, it was the antipodes
(B) before there was Australia, it was the antipodes
(C) it was the antipodes that was Australia
(D) Australia was what was the antipodes
(E) Australia was what had been known as the antipodes

GO ON TO THE NEXT PAGE.

22. <u>Using a Doppler ultrasound device, fetal heartbeats can be detected by the twelfth week of pregnancy.</u>

(A) Using a Doppler ultrasound device, fetal heartbeats can be detected by the twelfth week of pregnancy.

(B) Fetal heartbeats can be detected by the twelfth week of pregnancy, using a Doppler ultrasound device.

(C) Detecting fetal heartbeats by the twelfth week of pregnancy, a physician can use a Doppler ultrasound device.

(D) By the twelfth week of pregnancy, fetal heartbeats can be detected using a Doppler ultrasound device by a physician.

(E) Using a Doppler ultrasound device, a physician can detect fetal heartbeats by the twelfth week of pregnancy.

STOP

IF YOU FINISH BEFORE TIME IS CALLED, YOU MAY CHECK YOUR WORK ON THIS SECTION ONLY. DO NOT TURN TO ANY OTHER SECTION IN THE TEST.

Answer Key for Sample Test Section 2

SENTENCE CORRECTION

1.	D	12.	E
2.	E	13.	C
3.	C	14.	A
4.	B	15.	B
5.	C	16.	D
6.	E	17.	C
7.	A	18.	D
8.	C	19.	E
9.	D	20.	C
10.	B	21.	A
11.	A	22.	E

Explanatory Material: Sentence Correction Sample Test Section 2

1. **A Labor Department study states that the <u>numbers of women employed outside the home grew by more than a thirty-five percent increase</u> in the past decade and accounted for more than sixty-two percent of the total growth in the civilian work force.**

   (A) numbers of women employed outside the home grew by more than a thirty-five percent increase
   (B) numbers of women employed outside the home grew more than thirty-five percent
   (C) numbers of women employed outside the home were raised by more than thirty-five percent
   (D) number of women employed outside the home increased by more than thirty-five percent
   (E) number of women employed outside the home was raised by more than a thirty-five percent increase

Because a count of women employed outside the home at any given time will be expressed by a single number, the use of the plural noun *numbers* in choices A, B, and C is illogical. In A, the phrase *grew by more than a thirty-five percent increase* is redundant and wordy, since the sense of *increase* is implicit in the verb *grew*. In C and E, the passive verb forms *were raised* and *was raised* are inappropriate because there is no identifiable agent responsible for the raising of the number of women employed. In choice E, *was raised by . . . increase* is redundant. Choice D, which presents the comparison logically and idiomatically, is the best answer.

2. **The first decision for most tenants living in a building undergoing <u>being converted to cooperative ownership is if to sign</u> a no-buy pledge with the other tenants.**

   (A) being converted to cooperative ownership is if to sign
   (B) being converted to cooperative ownership is whether they should be signing
   (C) being converted to cooperative ownership is whether or not they sign
   (D) conversion to cooperative ownership is if to sign
   (E) conversion to cooperative ownership is whether to sign

In A, B, and C, the phrase *being converted* is awkward and redundant, since the sense of process indicated by *being* has already been conveyed by *undergoing*. A and D can be faulted for saying *if* rather than *whether*, since the sentence poses alternative possibilities, to sign or not to sign. Only E, the best choice, idiomatically completes *whether* with an infinitive, *to sign*, that functions as a noun equivalent of *decision*. Choice E also uses the noun *conversion*, which grammatically completes the phrase begun by *undergoing*.

3. **The end of the eighteenth century saw the emergence of prize-stock breeding, with individual bulls and cows receiving awards, fetching unprecedented prices, and <u>excited</u> enormous interest whenever they were put on show.**

   (A) excited
   (B) it excited
   (C) exciting
   (D) would excite
   (E) it had excited

Choice C is best. The third verb phrase in the series describing *bulls and cows* should have the same grammatical form as the first two. Only choice C has a present participle (or "-ing" form) that is parallel with the two preceding verbs, *receiving* and *fetching*. Instead of the present participle, choices A and B use the past tense (*excited*), choice D uses an auxiliary verb (*would excite*), and choice E uses the past perfect tense (*had excited*). Additionally, the incorrect verb tenses in B and E are introduced by a pronoun, *it*, that lacks a logical noun referent.

4. Of all the possible disasters that threaten American agriculture, the possibility of an adverse change in climate <u>is maybe the more difficult for analysis</u>.

   (A) is maybe the more difficult for analysis
   (B) is probably the most difficult to analyze
   (C) is maybe the most difficult for analysis
   (D) is probably the more difficult to analyze
   (E) is, it may be, the analysis that is most difficult

Choice B is the best answer. The sentence compares one thing, *an adverse change in climate*, to all other things in its class — that is, to *all the possible disasters that threaten American agriculture*; therefore, the sentence requires the superlative form of the adjective, *most difficult*, rather than the comparative form, *more difficult*, which appears in choices A and D. In A and C, the use of *maybe* is unidiomatic, and *difficult* should be completed by the infinitive *to analyze*. Choice E is awkwardly phrased and, when inserted into the sentence, produces an illogical structure: *the possibility . . . is . . . the analysis that*.

5. <u>Published in Harlem, the owner and editor of the *Messenger* were two young journalists, Chandler Owen and A. Philip Randolph, who would later make his reputation as a labor leader.</u>

   (A) Published in Harlem, the owner and editor of the *Messenger* were two young journalists, Chandler Owen and A. Philip Randolph, who would later make his reputation as a labor leader.
   (B) Published in Harlem, two young journalists, Chandler Owen and A. Philip Randolph, who would later make his reputation as a labor leader, were the owner and editor of the *Messenger*.
   (C) Published in Harlem, the *Messenger* was owned and edited by two young journalists, A. Philip Randolph, who would later make his reputation as a labor leader, and Chandler Owen.
   (D) The *Messenger* was owned and edited by two young journalists, Chandler Owen and A. Philip Randolph, who would later make his reputation as a labor leader, and published in Harlem.
   (E) The owner and editor being two young journalists, Chandler Owen and A. Philip Randolph, who would later make his reputation as a labor leader, the *Messenger* was published in Harlem.

Choices A and B present dangling modifiers that illogically suggest that Owen and Randolph, rather than the *Messenger*, were published in Harlem. In D, the phrase *and published in Harlem* is too remote from *the Messenger* to modify it effectively. In E, *being* produces an awkward construction, and the placement of the main clause at the end of the sentence is confusing. Only in C, the best answer, is *Published in Harlem* followed immediately by *the Messenger*. Also, C makes it clear that the clause beginning *who* refers to Randolph.

6. The rise in the Commerce Department's index of leading economic indicators <u>suggest that the economy should continue its expansion into the coming months, but that</u> the mixed performance of the index's individual components indicates that economic growth will proceed at a more moderate pace than in the first quarter of this year.

   (A) suggest that the economy should continue its expansion into the coming months, but that
   (B) suggest that the economy is to continue expansion in the coming months, but
   (C) suggests that the economy will continue its expanding in the coming months, but that
   (D) suggests that the economy is continuing to expand into the coming months, but that
   (E) suggests that the economy will continue to expand in the coming months, but

In choices A and B, the verb *suggest* does not agree with its singular subject, *rise*. In context, the phrase *into the coming months* in A and D is not idiomatic; *in the coming months* is preferable. In A, C, and D, the *that* appearing after *but* creates a subordinate clause where an independent clause is needed for the new subject, *mixed performance*. Choice E includes the correct verb form, *suggests*, eliminates *that*, and properly employs the future tense, *will continue to expand*. That this tense is called for is indicated both by the future time to which *the coming months* refers and by the parallel verb form *will proceed* in the nonunderlined part of the sentence. Choice E is best.

7. In three centuries — from 1050 to 1350 — several million tons of stone were quarried in France <u>for the building of eighty cathedrals, five hundred large churches, and some</u> tens of thousands of parish churches.

   (A) for the building of eighty cathedrals, five hundred large churches, and some
   (B) in order that they might build eighty cathedrals, five hundred large churches, and some
   (C) so as they might build eighty cathedrals, five hundred large churches, and some
   (D) so that there could be built eighty cathedrals, five hundred large churches, and
   (E) such that they could build eighty cathedrals, five hundred large churches, and

Choice A is best. The other choices are unidiomatic or unnecessarily wordy, and the pronoun *they*, which appears in B, C, and E, has no grammatical referent.

8. <u>What was as remarkable as the development of the compact disc</u> has been the use of the new technology to revitalize, in better sound than was ever before possible, some of the classic recorded performances of the pre-LP era.

   (A) What was as remarkable as the development of the compact disc
   (B) The thing that was as remarkable as developing the compact disc
   (C) No less remarkable than the development of the compact disc
   (D) Developing the compact disc has been none the less remarkable than
   (E) Development of the compact disc has been no less remarkable as

Besides being wordy, the clauses beginning *What was* in A and *The thing that was* in B cause inconsistencies in verb tense: *the use of the new technology* cannot logically be described by both the present perfect *has been* and the past *was*. In B and D, *developing the compact disc* is not parallel to *the use of new technology to revitalize . . . performances*; in C, the best answer, the noun *development* is parallel to *use*. The phrases *none the less . . . than* in D and *no less . . . as* in E are unidiomatic; the correct form of expression, *no less . . . than*, appears in C, the best choice.

9. <u>Unlike computer skills or other technical skills, there is a disinclination on the part of many people to recognize the degree to which their analytical skills are weak.</u>

   (A) Unlike computer skills or other technical skills, there is a disinclination on the part of many people to recognize the degree to which their analytical skills are weak.
   (B) Unlike computer skills or other technical skills, which they admit they lack, many people are disinclined to recognize that their analytical skills are weak.
   (C) Unlike computer skills or other technical skills, analytical skills bring out a disinclination in many people to recognize that they are weak to a degree.
   (D) Many people, willing to admit that they lack computer skills or other technical skills, are disinclined to recognize that their analytical skills are weak.
   (E) Many people have a disinclination to recognize the weakness of their analytical skills while willing to admit their lack of computer skills or other technical skills.

Choice D is best. Choice A illogically compares *skills* to *a disinclination*; choice B compares *skills* to *many people*. Choice C makes the comparison logical by casting *analytical skills* as the subject of the sentence, but it is awkward and unidiomatic to say *skills bring out a disinclination*. Also in C, the referent of *they* is unclear, and *weak to a degree* changes the meaning of the

original statement. In E, *have a disinclination . . . while willing* is grammatically incomplete, and *admit their lack* should be *admit to their lack*. By making *people* the subject of the sentence, D best expresses the intended contrast, which pertains not so much to skills as to people's willingness to recognize different areas of weakness.

10. <u>Some buildings that were destroyed and heavily damaged in the earthquake last year were</u> constructed in violation of the city's building code.

    (A) Some buildings that were destroyed and heavily damaged in the earthquake last year were
    (B) Some buildings that were destroyed or heavily damaged in the earthquake last year had been
    (C) Some buildings that the earthquake destroyed and heavily damaged last year have been
    (D) Last year the earthquake destroyed or heavily damaged some buildings that have been
    (E) Last year some of the buildings that were destroyed or heavily damaged in the earthquake had been

Choice B is best. Choices A and C illogically state that some buildings were both destroyed *and* damaged; *or* is needed to indicate that each of the buildings suffered either one fate or the other. In using only one verb tense, *were*, A fails to indicate that the buildings were constructed before the earthquake occurred. Choices C and D use the present perfect tense incorrectly, saying in effect that the buildings *have been constructed* after they were destroyed last year. Choice E suggests that the construction of the buildings, rather than the earthquake, occurred last year, thus making the sequence of events unclear. Only B uses verb tenses correctly to indicate that construction of the buildings was completed prior to the earthquake.

11. From the earliest days of the tribe, kinship determined the way in which the Ojibwa society organized its labor, provided access to its resources, <u>and defined rights and obligations involved in the distribution and consumption of those resources.</u>

    (A) and defined rights and obligations involved in the distribution and consumption of those resources
    (B) defining rights and obligations involved in their distribution and consumption
    (C) and defined rights and obligations as they were involved in its distribution and consumption
    (D) whose rights and obligations were defined in their distribution and consumption
    (E) the distribution and consumption of them defined by rights and obligations

Choice A is best. The activities listed are presented as parallel ideas and should thus be expressed in grammatically parallel structures. Choice A correctly uses the simple past tense *defined* to parallel *organized* and *provided*. Choice A also correctly joins the last two parallel phrases with *and* and clearly expresses the relationship of *rights and obligations* to *resources*. Choice C preserves parallelism but is wordy, and *its* has no logical referent. Choices B, D, and E each replace the verb phrase with a subordinate modifier, violating parallelism and making the statements ungrammatical. Furthermore, it is unclear what *defining . . . consumption* in B is intended to modify; in D, *whose* incorrectly attributes *rights and obligations* to *resources*; and E presents *rights and obligations* as defining, rather than as being defined.

12. A report by the American Academy for the Advancement of Science has concluded that <u>much of the currently uncontrolled dioxins to which North Americans are exposed comes</u> from the incineration of wastes.

   (A) much of the currently uncontrolled dioxins to which North Americans are exposed comes
   (B) much of the currently uncontrolled dioxins that North Americans are exposed to come
   (C) much of the dioxins that are currently uncontrolled and that North Americans are exposed to comes
   (D) many of the dioxins that are currently uncontrolled and North Americans are exposed to come
   (E) many of the currently uncontrolled dioxins to which North Americans are exposed come

Choices A, B, and C are flawed because the countable noun *dioxins* should be modified by *many* rather than *much*, which is used with uncountable nouns such as "work" or "happiness." In addition, both A and C incorrectly use the singular verb *comes* with the plural noun *dioxins*. Choices C and D are needlessly wordy, and D requires *that* before *North Americans* to be grammatically complete. Choice E, the best answer, is both grammatically correct and concise.

13. In June of 1987, *The Bridge of Trinquetaille,* Vincent van Gogh's view of an iron bridge over the <u>Rhone sold for $20.2 million and it was</u> the second highest price ever paid for a painting at auction.

   (A) Rhone sold for $20.2 million and it was
   (B) Rhone, which sold for $20.2 million, was
   (C) Rhone, was sold for $20.2 million,
   (D) Rhone was sold for $20.2 million, being
   (E) Rhone, sold for $20.2 million, and was

A comma is needed after *Rhone* in choices A and D to set off the modifying phrase that begins *Vincent . . .*; without the comma, the phrase appears to be part of the main clause, and it is thus unclear what noun should govern the verb *sold*. Furthermore, *it* in A has no logical referent, and *being* in D is not idiomatic. Choices B and E produce the illogical statement that the painting *was the second highest price*. Choice C, the best answer, avoids this problem by using a noun phrase in which *price* clearly refers to *$20.2 million*. And by using a comma after *Rhone* to set off the phrase that modifies *The Bridge of Trinquetaille*, C makes the painting the subject of *was sold*.

14. *Bufo marinus* toads, fierce predators that will eat frogs, lizards, and even small birds, <u>are native to South America but were introduced into Florida during the 1930's in an attempt to control</u> pests in the state's vast sugarcane fields.

   (A) are native to South America but were introduced into Florida during the 1930's in an attempt to control
   (B) are native in South America but were introduced into Florida during the 1930's as attempts to control
   (C) are natives of South America but were introduced into Florida during the 1930's in an attempt at controlling
   (D) had been native to South America but were introduced to Florida during the 1930's as an attempt at controlling
   (E) had been natives of South America but were introduced to Florida during the 1930's as attempts at controlling

Choice A is best. The phrasing *are native to* correctly suggests that the toad species is indigenous to, and still exists in, South America. In B, *native in* is unidiomatic; in C and E, *natives of* illogically suggests that each toad now in Florida hails from South America. In D and E, *had been* inaccurately implies that the toads are no longer native, or indigenous, to South America, and *introduced to Florida* is unidiomatic. Both *as attempts* in B and E and *as an attempt* in D are wrong because the attempt consists not of the toads themselves, but of their introduction into the environment. The correct phrase, *in an attempt*, should be completed by an infinitive (here, *to control*), as in A.

15. While some academicians believe that business ethics should be integrated into every business course, others say that students will take ethics seriously <u>only if it would be taught as a separately required course.</u>

   (A) only if it would be taught as a separately required course
   (B) only if it is taught as a separate, required course
   (C) if it is taught only as a course required separately
   (D) if it was taught only as a separate and required course
   (E) if it would only be taught as a required course, separately

Choice B is best: in sentences expressing a conditional result (*x will happen if y happens*), the verb of the main clause should be in the future tense and the verb of the *if* clause should be in the present indicative. Thus, *is taught* (in B) is consistent with *will take*, whereas *would be taught* (in A and E) and *was taught* (in D) are not. For clarity, *only* in C, D, and E should immediately precede the entire *if* clause that it is meant to modify. Also, the intended meaning is distorted when the adverb *separately* is used to modify *required*, as in A and C, or *taught*, as in E; B correctly uses the adjective *separate* to modify *course*.

16. Scientists have observed large concentrations of heavy-metal deposits in the upper twenty centimeters of Baltic Sea sediments, which are consistent with the growth of industrial activity there.

    (A) Baltic Sea sediments, which are consistent with the growth of industrial activity there
    (B) Baltic Sea sediments, where the growth of industrial activity is consistent with these findings
    (C) Baltic Sea sediments, findings consistent with its growth of industrial activity
    (D) sediments from the Baltic Sea, findings consistent with the growth of industrial activity in the area
    (E) sediments from the Baltic Sea, consistent with the growth of industrial activity there

All of the choices but D contain ambiguities. In A and B the words *which* and *where* appear to refer to *sediments*, and in E it is not clear what *consistent* describes. In A, C, and E, there is no logical place to which *there* or *its* could refer. In D, the best choice, the phrase *sediments from the Baltic Sea* tells where the sediments originate, *findings* provides a noun for *consistent* to modify, and *in the area* clearly identifies where the industrial activity is growing.

17. For members of the seventeenth-century Ashanti nation in Africa, animal-hide shields with wooden frames were essential items of military equipment, a method to protect warriors against enemy arrows and spears.

    (A) a method to protect
    (B) as a method protecting
    (C) protecting
    (D) as a protection of
    (E) to protect

Choice C is best because the participle *protecting* begins a phrase that explains what the shields did. Choices A and B awkwardly use the singular word *method* to refer to *items of military equipment* rather than to the use of such items. Also, a *method of protecting* would be more idiomatic than a *method to protect* in A or a *method protecting* in B. In B and D, *as* is incorrect; also, a *protection* in D has no noun for which it can logically substitute. Choice E is incomplete; *used to protect* would have been acceptable.

18. In metalwork one advantage of adhesive-bonding over spot-welding is that the contact, and hence the bonding, is effected continuously over a broad surface instead of a series of regularly spaced points with no bonding in between.

    (A) instead of
    (B) as opposed to
    (C) in contrast with
    (D) rather than at
    (E) as against being at

The corrected sentence must contrast an effect of spot-welding with an effect of adhesive-bonding. To do so logically and grammatically, it must describe the effects in parallel terms. When inserted into the sentence, D produces the parallel construction *over a broad surface rather than at a series*. Having no word such as *over* or *at* to indicate location, choices A, B, and C fail to complete the parallel and so illogically draw a contrast between *surface* and *series*. In E, *as against being* is a wordy and unidiomatic way to establish the intended contrast. Choice D is best.

19. Under a provision of the Constitution that was never applied, Congress has been required to call a convention for considering possible amendments to the document when formally asked to do it by the legislatures of two-thirds of the states.

    (A) was never applied, Congress has been required to call a convention for considering possible amendments to the document when formally asked to do it
    (B) was never applied, there has been a requirement that Congress call a convention for consideration of possible amendments to the document when asked to do it formally
    (C) was never applied, whereby Congress is required to call a convention for considering possible amendments to the document when asked to do it formally
    (D) has never been applied, whereby Congress is required to call a convention to consider possible amendments to the document when formally asked to do so
    (E) has never been applied, Congress is required to call a convention to consider possible amendments to the document when formally asked to do so

Choices A, B, C, and D contain tense errors (the use of *was never applied* with *has been required* in A, for example), unidiomatic expressions (*call . . . for considering*), and uses of a pronoun (*it*) with no noun referent. By introducing the subordinating conjunction *whereby*, C and D produce sentence fragments. Only E, the best choice, corrects all of these problems. The predicate *has never been applied* refers to a span of time, from the writing of the Constitution to the present, rather than to a past event (as *was* does), and the phrase *is required* indicates that the provision still applies. The phrase *call . . . to consider* is idiomatic, and *to do so* can substitute grammatically for it.

20. The current administration, <u>being worried over some foreign trade barriers being removed and our exports failing</u> to increase as a result of deep cuts in the value of the dollar, has formed a group to study ways to sharpen our competitiveness.

   (A) being worried over some foreign trade barriers being removed and our exports failing
   (B) worrying over some foreign trade barriers being removed, also over the failure of our exports
   (C) worried about the removal of some foreign trade barriers and the failure of our exports
   (D) in that they were worried about the removal of some foreign trade barriers and also about the failure of our exports
   (E) because of its worry concerning the removal of some foreign trade barriers, also concerning the failure of our exports

Choice C is best because its phrasing is parallel and concise. A, D, and E begin with unnecessarily wordy phrases. Choice C also uses the idiomatic expression *worried about* rather than *worried over* (as in A) or *worrying over* (as in B); *worried about* is preferable when describing a condition rather than an action. Whereas C uses compact and parallel noun phrases such as *the removal . . . and the failure . . .* , the other choices employ phrases that are wordy, awkward, or nonparallel. D is also flawed in that the plural pronoun *they* does not agree with the singular noun *administration*.

21. In the minds of many people living in England, <u>before Australia was Australia, it was the antipodes</u>, the opposite pole to civilization, an obscure and unimaginable place that was considered the end of the world.

   (A) before Australia was Australia, it was the antipodes
   (B) before there was Australia, it was the antipodes
   (C) it was the antipodes that was Australia
   (D) Australia was what was the antipodes
   (E) Australia was what had been known as the antipodes

Choice A is best, for A alone makes clear that the land now known as Australia was considered the antipodes before it was developed. In B, *it* has no logical referent, because the previous clause describes a time when there was no Australia. Nor does *it* have a referent in C: substituting *Australia* for *it* produces a nonsensical statement. D is wordy, with the unnecessary *what was*, and imprecise in suggesting that Australia was considered the antipodes after it became Australia. E similarly distorts the original meaning, and the past perfect *had been* is inconsistent with the past tense used to establish a time frame for the rest of the sentence.

22. <u>Using a Doppler ultrasound device, fetal heartbeats can be detected by the twelfth week of pregnancy.</u>

   (A) Using a Doppler ultrasound device, fetal heartbeats can be detected by the twelfth week of pregnancy.
   (B) Fetal heartbeats can be detected by the twelfth week of pregnancy, using a Doppler ultrasound device.
   (C) Detecting fetal heartbeats by the twelfth week of pregnancy, a physician can use a Doppler ultrasound device.
   (D) By the twelfth week of pregnancy, fetal heartbeats can be detected using a Doppler ultrasound device by a physician.
   (E) Using a Doppler ultrasound device, a physician can detect fetal heartbeats by the twelfth week of pregnancy.

Choice A presents a dangling modifier. The phrase beginning the sentence has no noun that it can logically modify and hence cannot fit anywhere in the sentence and make sense. Coming first, it modifies *heartbeats*, the nearest free noun in the main clause; that is, choice A says that the heartbeats are using the Doppler ultrasound device. Choice B contains the same main clause and dangling modifier, now at the end. Contrary to intent, the wording in choice C suggests that physicians can use a Doppler ultrasound device after they detect fetal heartbeats. In choice D the phrase *using . . . device* should follow *physician*, the noun it modifies. Choice E is best.

SENTENCE CORRECTION SAMPLE TEST SECTION 3

Time — 25 minutes

22 Questions

Directions: In each of the following sentences, some part of the sentence or the entire sentence is underlined. Beneath each sentence you will find five ways of phrasing the underlined part. The first of these repeats the original; the other four are different. If you think the original is the best of these answer choices, choose answer A; otherwise choose one of the others. Select the best version and fill in the corresponding oval on your answer sheet.

This is a test of correctness and effectiveness of expression. In choosing answers, follow the requirements of standard written English; that is, pay attention to grammar, choice of words, and sentence construction. Choose the answer that produces the most effective sentence; this answer should be clear and exact, without awkwardness, ambiguity, redundancy, or grammatical error.

1. Delighted by the reported earnings for the first quarter of the fiscal year, it was decided by the company manager to give her staff a raise.

   (A) it was decided by the company manager to give her staff a raise
   (B) the decision of the company manager was to give her staff a raise
   (C) the company manager decided to give her staff a raise
   (D) the staff was given a raise by the company manager
   (E) a raise was given to the staff by the company manager

2. A study commissioned by the Department of Agriculture showed that if calves exercise and associated with other calves, they will require less medication and gain weight quicker than do those raised in confinement.

   (A) associated with other calves, they will require less medication and gain weight quicker than do
   (B) associated with other calves, they require less medication and gain weight quicker than
   (C) associate with other calves, they required less medication and will gain weight quicker than do
   (D) associate with other calves, they have required less medication and will gain weight more quickly than do
   (E) associate with other calves, they require less medication and gain weight more quickly than

3. Displays of the aurora borealis, or "northern lights," can heat the atmosphere over the arctic enough to affect the trajectories of ballistic missiles, induce electric currents that can cause blackouts in some areas and corrosion in north-south pipelines.

   (A) to affect the trajectories of ballistic missiles, induce
   (B) that the trajectories of ballistic missiles are affected, induce
   (C) that it affects the trajectories of ballistic missiles, induces
   (D) that the trajectories of ballistic missiles are affected and induces
   (E) to affect the trajectories of ballistic missiles and induce

4. The golden crab of the Gulf of Mexico has not been fished commercially in great numbers, primarily on account of living at great depths—2,500 to 3,000 feet down.

   (A) on account of living
   (B) on account of their living
   (C) because it lives
   (D) because of living
   (E) because they live

GO ON TO THE NEXT PAGE.

5. The cameras of the Voyager II spacecraft detected six small, previously unseen moons circling Uranus, which doubles to twelve the number of satellites now known as orbiting the distant planet.

(A) which doubles to twelve the number of satellites now known as orbiting
(B) doubling to twelve the number of satellites now known to orbit
(C) which doubles to twelve the number of satellites now known in orbit around
(D) doubling to twelve the number of satellites now known as orbiting
(E) which doubles to twelve the number of satellites now known that orbit

6. As a baby emerges from the darkness of the womb with a rudimentary sense of vision, it would be rated about 20/500, or legally blind if it were an adult with such vision.

(A) As a baby emerges from the darkness of the womb with a rudimentary sense of vision, it would be rated about 20/500, or legally blind if it were an adult with such vision.
(B) A baby emerges from the darkness of the womb with a rudimentary sense of vision that would be rated about 20/500, or legally blind as an adult.
(C) As a baby emerges from the darkness of the womb, its rudimentary sense of vision would be rated about 20/500; qualifying it to be legally blind if an adult.
(D) A baby emerges from the darkness of the womb with a rudimentary sense of vision that would be rated about 20/500; an adult with such vision would be deemed legally blind.
(E) As a baby emerges from the darkness of the womb, its rudimentary sense of vision, which would be deemed legally blind for an adult, would be rated about 20/500.

7. While Jackie Robinson was a Brooklyn Dodger, his courage in the face of physical threats and verbal attacks was not unlike that of Rosa Parks, who refused to move to the back of a bus in Montgomery, Alabama.

(A) not unlike that of Rosa Parks, who refused
(B) not unlike Rosa Parks, who refused
(C) like Rosa Parks and her refusal
(D) like that of Rosa Parks for refusing
(E) as that of Rosa Parks, who refused

8. The rising of costs of data-processing operations at many financial institutions has created a growing opportunity for independent companies to provide these services more efficiently and at lower cost.

(A) The rising of costs
(B) Rising costs
(C) The rising cost
(D) Because the rising cost
(E) Because of rising costs

9. There is no consensus on what role, if any, is played by acid rain in slowing the growth or damaging forests in the eastern United States.

(A) slowing the growth or damaging
(B) the damage or the slowing of the growth of
(C) the damage to or the slowness of the growth of
(D) damaged or slowed growth of
(E) damaging or slowing the growth of

10. Galileo was convinced that natural phenomena, as manifestations of the laws of physics, would appear the same to someone on the deck of a ship moving smoothly and uniformly through the water as a person standing on land.

(A) water as a
(B) water as to a
(C) water; just as it would to a
(D) water, as it would to the
(E) water; just as to the

11. A recent study has found that within the past few years, many doctors had elected early retirement rather than face the threats of lawsuits and the rising costs of malpractice insurance.

(A) had elected early retirement rather than face
(B) had elected early retirement instead of facing
(C) have elected retiring early instead of facing
(D) have elected to retire early rather than facing
(E) have elected to retire early rather than face

GO ON TO THE NEXT PAGE.

12. Architects and stonemasons, huge palace and temple clusters were built by the Maya without benefit of the wheel or animal transport.

   (A) huge palace and temple clusters were built by the Maya without benefit of the wheel or animal transport
   (B) without the benefits of animal transport or the wheel, huge palace and temple clusters were built by the Maya
   (C) the Maya built huge palace and temple clusters without the benefit of animal transport or the wheel
   (D) there were built, without the benefit of the wheel or animal transport, huge palace and temple clusters by the Maya
   (E) were the Maya who, without the benefit of the wheel or animal transport, built huge palace and temple clusters

13. In astronomy the term "red shift" denotes the extent to which light from a distant galaxy has been shifted toward the red, or long-wave, end of the light spectrum by the rapid motion of the galaxy away from the Earth.

   (A) to which light from a distant galaxy has been shifted
   (B) to which light from a distant galaxy has shifted
   (C) that light from a distant galaxy has been shifted
   (D) of light from a distant galaxy shifting
   (E) of the shift of light from a distant galaxy

14. William H. Johnson's artistic debt to Scandinavia is evident in paintings that range from sensitive portraits of citizens in his wife's Danish home, Kerteminde, and awe-inspiring views of fjords and mountain peaks in the western and northern regions of Norway.

   (A) and
   (B) to
   (C) and to
   (D) with
   (E) in addition to

15. In 1978 only half the women granted child support by a court received the amount awarded; at least as much as a million and more others had not any support agreements whatsoever.

   (A) at least as much as a million and more others had not any
   (B) at least as much as more than a million others had no
   (C) more than a million others had not any
   (D) more than a million others had no
   (E) there was at least a million or more others without any

16. According to a recent poll, owning and living in a freestanding house on its own land is still a goal of a majority of young adults, like that of earlier generations.

   (A) like that of earlier generations
   (B) as that for earlier generations
   (C) just as earlier generations did
   (D) as have earlier generations
   (E) as it was of earlier generations

17. The Gorton-Dodd bill requires that a bank disclose to their customers how long they will delay access to funds from deposited checks.

   (A) that a bank disclose to their customers how long they will delay access to funds from deposited checks
   (B) a bank to disclose to their customers how long they will delay access to funds from a deposited check
   (C) that a bank disclose to its customers how long it will delay access to funds from deposited checks
   (D) a bank that it should disclose to its customers how long it will delay access to funds from a deposited check
   (E) that banks disclose to customers how long access to funds from their deposited check is to be delayed

GO ON TO THE NEXT PAGE.

18. Geologists believe that the warning signs for a major earthquake may include sudden fluctuations in local seismic activity, tilting and other deformations of the Earth's crust, changing the measured strain across a fault zone, and varying the electrical properties of underground rocks.

    (A) changing the measured strain across a fault zone, and varying
    (B) changing measurements of the strain across a fault zone, and varying
    (C) changing the strain as measured across a fault zone, and variations of
    (D) changes in the measured strain across a fault zone, and variations in
    (E) changes in measurements of the strain across a fault zone, and variations among

19. Health officials estimate that 35 million Africans are in danger of contracting trypanosomiasis, or "African sleeping sickness," a parasitic disease spread by the bites of tsetse flies.

    (A) are in danger of contracting
    (B) are in danger to contract
    (C) have a danger of contracting
    (D) are endangered by contraction
    (E) have a danger that they will contract

20. Unlike a funded pension system, in which contributions are invested to pay future beneficiaries, a pay-as-you-go approach is the foundation of Social Security.

    (A) a pay-as-you-go approach is the foundation of Social Security
    (B) the foundation of Social Security is a pay-as-you-go approach
    (C) the approach of Social Security is pay-as-you-go
    (D) Social Security's approach is pay-as-you-go
    (E) Social Security is founded on a pay-as-you-go approach

21. Critics of the trend toward privately operated prisons consider corrections facilities to be an integral part of the criminal justice system and question if profits should be made from incarceration.

    (A) to be an integral part of the criminal justice system and question if
    (B) as an integral part of the criminal justice system and they question if
    (C) as being an integral part of the criminal justice system and question whether
    (D) an integral part of the criminal justice system and question whether
    (E) are an integral part of the criminal justice system, and they question whether

22. The Federal Reserve Board's reduction of interest rates on loans to financial institutions is both an acknowledgement of past economic trends and an effort to influence their future direction.

    (A) reduction of interest rates on loans to financial institutions is both an acknowledgement of past economic trends and an effort
    (B) reduction of interest rates on loans to financial institutions is an acknowledgement both of past economic trends as well as an effort
    (C) reduction of interest rates on loans to financial institutions both acknowledge past economic trends and attempt
    (D) reducing interest rates on loans to financial institutions is an acknowledgement both of past economic trends and an effort
    (E) reducing interest rates on loans to financial institutions both acknowledge past economic trends as well as attempt

STOP

IF YOU FINISH BEFORE TIME IS CALLED, YOU MAY CHECK YOUR WORK ON THIS SECTION ONLY. DO NOT TURN TO ANY OTHER SECTION IN THE TEST.

Answer Key for Sample Test Section 3

SENTENCE CORRECTION

1.	C	12.	C
2.	E	13.	A
3.	E	14.	B
4.	C	15.	D
5.	B	16.	E
6.	D	17.	C
7.	A	18.	D
8.	C	19.	A
9.	E	20.	E
10.	B	21.	D
11.	E	22.	A

Explanatory Material: Sentence Correction Sample Test Section 3

1. Delighted by the reported earnings for the first quarter of the fiscal year, <u>it was decided by the company manager to give her staff a raise</u>.

    (A) it was decided by the company manager to give her staff a raise
    (B) the decision of the company manager was to give her staff a raise
    (C) the company manager decided to give her staff a raise
    (D) the staff was given a raise by the company manager
    (E) a raise was given to the staff by the company manager

Grammatically, the participial phrase beginning *delighted* must modify the subject of the main clause. Because it is the manager who was delighted, choice C, in which *the company manager* appears as the subject, is the best answer. Choices A, B, D, and E create illogical statements by using *it, the decision, the staff*, and *a raise*, respectively, as the sentence subject. Use of the passive voice in A, D, and E produces unnecessary wordiness, as does the construction *the decision of the company manager was to* in B.

2. A study commissioned by the Department of Agriculture showed that if calves exercise and <u>associated with other calves, they will require less medication and gain weight quicker than do</u> those raised in confinement.

    (A) associated with other calves, they will require less medication and gain weight quicker than do
    (B) associated with other calves, they require less medication and gain weight quicker than
    (C) associate with other calves, they required less medication and will gain weight quicker than do
    (D) associate with other calves, they have required less medication and will gain weight more quickly than do
    (E) associate with other calves, they require less medication and gain weight more quickly than

Choice E, the best answer, uses the adverbial phrase *more quickly than* to modify the verb phrase *gain weight*. In A, B, and C, *quicker than* is incorrect because an adjective should not be used to modify a verb phrase. E is also the only choice with consistent verb tenses. The first verb in the clauses introduced by *showed that* is *exercise*. A and B incorrectly compound that present tense verb with a past tense verb, *associated*. C and D correctly use *associate*, but C follows with the past tense *required* and D with the present perfect *have required*. Both C and D incorrectly conclude with the future tense *will gain*.

3. Displays of the aurora borealis, or "northern lights," can heat the atmosphere over the arctic enough <u>to affect the trajectories of ballistic missiles, induce</u> electric currents that can cause blackouts in some areas and corrosion in north-south pipelines.

    (A) to affect the trajectories of ballistic missiles, induce
    (B) that the trajectories of ballistic missiles are affected, induce
    (C) that it affects the trajectories of ballistic missiles, induces
    (D) that the trajectories of ballistic missiles are affected and induces
    (E) to affect the trajectories of ballistic missiles and induce

The use of the phrasing *can heat . . . enough to affect* in A and E is more idiomatic than the use of the subordinate clause beginning with *that* in B, C, and D. Also, B produces an illogical and ungrammatical statement by making *induce* parallel with the verb *heat* rather than with the appropriate form of the verb *affect*; C lacks agreement in using the singular pronoun *it* to refer to the plural noun *displays*; and D is faulty because *induces* cannot fit grammatically with any noun in the sentence. Choice A incorrectly separates the two infinitives *to affect* and *[to] induce* with a comma when it should compound them with *and*, as does E, the best choice.

4. The golden crab of the Gulf of Mexico has not been fished commercially in great numbers, primarily <u>on account of living</u> at great depths — 2,500 to 3,000 feet down.

   (A) on account of living
   (B) on account of their living
   (C) because it lives
   (D) because of living
   (E) being they live

As used in choices A, B, and D, the phrases *on account of* and *because of* are unidiomatic; *because*, which appears in C and E, is preferable here since *because* can introduce a complete subordinate clause explaining the reason why the golden crab has not been fished extensively. B and E also produce agreement errors by using the plural pronouns *their* and *they* to refer to the singular noun *crab*. Choice D, like A, fails to provide a noun or pronoun to perform the action of *living*, but even with *its* the phrases would be more awkward and less clear than *it lives*. C, which uses *because* and *it* as the singular subject of a clause, is the best choice.

5. The cameras of the Voyager II spacecraft detected six small, previously unseen moons circling Uranus, <u>which doubles to twelve the number of satellites now known as orbiting</u> the distant planet.

   (A) which doubles to twelve the number of satellites now known as orbiting
   (B) doubling to twelve the number of satellites now known to orbit
   (C) which doubles to twelve the number of satellites now known in orbit around
   (D) doubling to twelve the number of satellites now known as orbiting
   (E) which doubles to twelve the number of satellites now known that orbit

The pronoun *which* should be used to refer to a previously mentioned noun, not to the idea expressed in an entire clause. In A, C, and E, *which* seems to refer to a vague concept involving the detection of moons, but there is no specific noun, such as *detection*, to which it can refer. Also in E, the use of the phrasing *the number . . . now known that orbit* is ungrammatical and unclear. B and D use the correct participial form, *doubling*, to modify the preceding clause, but D, like A, uses *known as orbiting* rather than *known to orbit*, a phrase that is more idiomatic in context. B, therefore, is the best answer.

6. <u>As a baby emerges from the darkness of the womb with a rudimentary sense of vision, it would be rated about 20/500, or legally blind if it were an adult with such vision.</u>

   (A) As a baby emerges from the darkness of the womb with a rudimentary sense of vision, it would be rated about 20/500, or legally blind if it were an adult with such vision.
   (B) A baby emerges from the darkness of the womb with a rudimentary sense of vision that would be rated about 20/500, or legally blind as an adult.
   (C) As a baby emerges from the darkness of the womb, its rudimentary sense of vision would be rated about 20/500; qualifying it to be legally blind if an adult.
   (D) A baby emerges from the darkness of the womb with a rudimentary sense of vision that would be rated about 20/500; an adult with such vision would be deemed legally blind.
   (E) As a baby emerges from the darkness of the womb, its rudimentary sense of vision, which would deemed legally blind for an adult, would be rated about 20/500.

In choice A, *it*, the subject of the main clause, seems to refer to *baby*, the subject of the subordinate clause; thus, A seems to state that the newborn baby, rather than its sense of vision, would be rated 20/500. Similarly, choices B and E use awkward and ambiguous phrasing that suggests that the *sense of vision*, rather than an adult with 20/500 vision, would be considered legally blind. C incorrectly uses the semicolon, which should separate independent clauses, to set off a verb phrase. The phrase *if an adult* in C is also illogical, since it states that a baby could also be an adult. D is the best choice.

7. While Jackie Robinson was a Brooklyn Dodger, his courage in the face of physical threats and verbal attacks was <u>not unlike that of Rosa Parks, who refused</u> to move to the back of a bus in Montgomery, Alabama.

   (A) not unlike that of Rosa Parks, who refused
   (B) not unlike Rosa Parks, who refused
   (C) like Rosa Parks and her refusal
   (D) like that of Rosa Parks for refusing
   (E) as that of Rosa Parks, who refused

Choices B and C present faulty comparisons: in B, Jackie Robinson's courage is compared to Rosa Parks herself, not to her courage, and in C it is compared to both Rosa Parks and her refusal. Choice D does not make clear whether it was Jackie Robinson or Rosa Parks who showed courage in refusing to move to the back of the bus; in fact, saying *for refusing* rather than *who refused* makes it sound as if *courage* moved to the back of the bus. Choice E incorrectly uses *as* rather than *like* to compare two noun phrases. Choice A is best.

-354-

8. The rising of costs of data-processing operations at many financial institutions has created a growing opportunity for independent companies to provide these services more efficiently and at lower cost.

    (A) The rising of costs
    (B) Rising costs
    (C) The rising cost
    (D) Because the rising cost
    (E) Because of rising costs

C is the best choice. In choice A, *The rising of costs* is unidiomatic, and in B *costs . . . has* lacks subject-verb agreement. Choices D and E produce sentence fragments since *Because* makes the clause subordinate rather than independent.

9. There is no consensus on what role, if any, is played by acid rain in slowing the growth or damaging forests in the eastern United States.

    (A) slowing the growth or damaging
    (B) the damage or the slowing of the growth of
    (C) the damage to or the slowness of the growth of
    (D) damaged or slowed growth of
    (E) damaging or slowing the growth of

The corrected sentence must make clear that both *damaging* and *slowing the growth of* refer to *forests*. E is the only choice that does so without introducing errors. In choice A, *of* is required after *growth*. In choices B and C, the use of *the damage* instead of *damaging* produces awkward and wordy constructions, and without *to* after *damage,* B is grammatically incomplete. In C, *the slowness of* does not convey the original sense that the rate of growth has been slowed by acid rain. Choice D also changes the meaning of the sentence by making both *damaged* and *slowed* refer to *growth*.

10. Galileo was convinced that natural phenomena, as manifestations of the laws of physics, would appear the same to someone on the deck of a ship moving smoothly and uniformly through the water as a person standing on land.

    (A) water as a
    (B) water as to a
    (C) water; just as it would to a
    (D) water, as it would to the
    (E) water; just as to the

B, the best choice, uses the idiomatic and grammatically parallel form *the same to X as to Y.* Because A lacks the preposition *to,* it seems to compare the appearance of natural phenomena to that of a person standing on land. C and D unnecessarily repeat *would* and wrongly use the singular *it* to refer to the plural *phenomena.* C and E each contain a faulty semicolon and produce errors in idiom, *the same to X just as [it would] to.* D and E use the definite article *the* where the indefinite article *a* is needed to refer to an unspecified person.

11. A recent study has found that within the past few years, many doctors had elected early retirement rather than face the threats of lawsuits and the rising costs of malpractice insurance.

    (A) had elected early retirement rather than face
    (B) had elected early retirement instead of facing
    (C) have elected retiring early instead of facing
    (D) have elected to retire early rather than facing
    (E) have elected to retire early rather than face

Because the sentence describes a situation that continues into the present, choices A and B are incorrect in using the past perfect *had elected,* which denotes an action completed at a specific time in the past. Also, alternatives presented in the expressions *x rather than y* and *x instead of y* should be parallel in form, but A and B mismatch the noun *retirement* with the verb forms *face* and *facing.* C is faulty because *have elected,* which is correct in tense, cannot idiomatically be followed by a participle such as *retiring.* D correctly follows *have elected* with an infinitive, *to retire,* but, like A and B, fails to maintain parallelism. Only E, the best choice, uses the correct tense, observes parallelism, and is idiomatic.

12. Architects and stonemasons, huge palace and temple clusters were built by the Maya without benefit of the wheel or animal transport.

    (A) huge palace and temple clusters were built by the Maya without benefit of the wheel or animal transport
    (B) without the benefits of animal transport or the wheel, huge palace and temple clusters were built by the Maya
    (C) the Maya built huge palace and temple clusters without the benefit of animal transport or the wheel
    (D) there were built, without the benefit of the wheel or animal transport, huge palace and temple clusters by the Maya
    (E) were the Maya who, without the benefit of the wheel or animal transport, built huge palace and temple clusters

A, B, and D illogically suggest that the *palace and temple clusters* were architects and stonemasons. For the modification to be logical, *Architects and stonemasons* must immediately precede *the Maya,* the noun phrase it is meant to modify. A, B, and D also use the passive verb form *were built,* which produces unnecessary awkwardness and wordiness. E is awkwardly phrased and produces a sentence fragment, because the appositive noun phrase *Architects and stonemasons* cannot serve as the subject of *were the Maya.* C, the best answer, places *the Maya* immediately after its modifier and uses the active verb form *built.*

13. In astronomy the term "red shift" denotes the extent <u>to which light from a distant galaxy has been shifted</u> toward the red, or long-wave, end of the light spectrum by the rapid motion of the galaxy away from the Earth.

(A) to which light from a distant galaxy has been shifted
(B) to which light from a distant galaxy has shifted
(C) that light from a distant galaxy has been shifted
(D) of light from a distant galaxy shifting
(E) of the shift of light from a distant galaxy

Choice A is best because it is idiomatic and because its passive verb construction, *has been shifted*, clearly indicates that the *light* has been acted upon *by the rapid motion*. In B, the active verb *has shifted* suggests that the light, not the motion, is the agency of action, but such a construction leaves the phrase *by the rapid motion of the galaxy away from the Earth* without any logical or grammatical function. In C, the construction *the extent that light* is ungrammatical; *denotes the extent* must be completed by *to which*. D incorrectly employs an active verb, *shifting*, and *extent of light* is imprecise and awkward. E is faulty because it contains no verb to express the action performed by the *rapid motion*.

14. William H. Johnson's artistic debt to Scandinavia is evident in paintings that range from sensitive portraits of citizens in his wife's Danish home, Kerteminde, <u>and</u> awe-inspiring views of fjords and mountain peaks in the western and northern regions of Norway.

(A) and
(B) to
(C) and to
(D) with
(E) in addition to

The construction *range from x* must be completed by *to y*, as in choice B, the best answer: Johnson's paintings *range from . . . portraits . . . to . . . views*. Each of the other choices produces an unidiomatic construction.

15. In 1978 only half the women granted child support by a court received the amount awarded; <u>at least as much as a million and more others had not any</u> support agreements whatsoever.

(A) at least as much as a million and more others had not any
(B) at least as much as more than a million others had no
(C) more than a million others had not any
(D) more than a million others had no
(E) there was at least a million or more others without any

D, the best choice, is idiomatic, clear, and concise. Both A and B incorrectly use *much* rather than *many* to describe the countable noun *others*; *much* should be used with uncountable nouns such as "joy" or "labor." Even if this error were corrected, though, A and B would still be wrong. Because *more than x* necessarily includes the sense of *at least as many as x*, it is redundant and confusing to use elements of both expressions to refer to the same number of women. In A and C, *not any support agreements* is wordy and awkward. Like A and B, E redundantly uses both *at least* and *more*, and it incorrectly links the singular verb *was* with the plural subject *others*.

16. According to a recent poll, owning and living in a freestanding house on its own land is still a goal of a majority of young adults, <u>like that of earlier generations</u>.

(A) like that of earlier generations
(B) as that for earlier generations
(C) just as earlier generations did
(D) as have earlier generations
(E) as it was of earlier generations

The intended comparison should be completed by a clause beginning with *as* and containing a subject and verb that correspond to the subject and verb of the main clause. In E, the best choice, *it* refers unambiguously to the phrasal subject *owning . . . land*, the verb *was* corresponds to *is*, and today's *young adults* are appropriately compared to *earlier generations*. Choices A and B lack a verb corresponding to *is* and a clear referent for *that*. Choices C and D are confusing and illogical because their verbs, *did* and *have*, cannot substitute for *is* in the main clause.

17. The Gorton-Dodd bill requires <u>that a bank disclose to their customers how long they will delay access to funds from deposited checks</u>.

(A) that a bank disclose to their customers how long they will delay access to funds from deposited checks
(B) a bank to disclose to their customers how long they will delay access to funds from a deposited check
(C) that a bank disclose to its customers how long it will delay access to funds from deposited checks
(D) a bank that it should disclose to its customers how long it will delay access to funds from a deposited check
(E) that banks disclose to customers how long access to funds from their deposited check is to be delayed

Choice C is best. In A and B, the plural pronouns *their* and *they* do not agree with the singular noun *bank*. B, like D and E, illogically shifts from the plural *customers* and *funds* to the singular *check*, as if the customers were jointly depositing only one check. In D, *requires a bank that it should* is ungrammatical; *requires that a bank* is the appropriate idiom. In E, the use of the passive construction *is to be delayed* is less informative than the active voice because the passive does not explicitly identify the bank as the agent responsible for the delay.

18. Geologists believe that the warning signs for a major earthquake may include sudden fluctuations in local seismic activity, tilting and other deformations of the Earth's crust, <u>changing the measured strain across a fault zone, and varying</u> the electrical properties of underground rocks.

 (A) changing the measured strain across a fault zone, and varying
 (B) changing measurements of the strain across a fault zone, and varying
 (C) changing the strain as measured across a fault zone, and variations of
 (D) changes in the measured strain across a fault zone, and variations in
 (E) changes in measurements of the strain across a fault zone, and variations among

D, the best choice, describes *the warning signs* in parallel phrases. Despite surface appearances, the nouns *changes* and *variations* are parallel with *tilting*, but the verbal forms *changing* and *varying* in A, B, and C are not: *tilting*, one of the *deformations of the Earth's crust*, is used here as a noun that is parallel to *fluctuations*, whereas *changing* and *varying* are used as verbs indicating some action undertaken. Moreover, these verbs are used incorrectly because the sentence mentions no subject that is performing these actions. B and E illogically state that it is not the *strain* but the *measurements* that portend danger, and *among* in E wrongly suggests a comparison of different electrical properties rather than of different behaviors of the same properties.

19. Health officials estimate that 35 million Africans <u>are in danger of contracting</u> trypanosomiasis, or "African sleeping sickness," a parasitic disease spread by the bites of tsetse flies.

 (A) are in danger of contracting
 (B) are in danger to contract
 (C) have a danger of contracting
 (D) are endangered by contraction
 (E) have a danger that they will contract

Choice A, which is both idiomatic and concise, is best. In choice B, *to contract* is wrong because the phrase *are in danger* must be followed by *of*, not by an infinitive. The phrase *have a danger* is unidiomatic in C. In D, the phrase *by contraction trypanosomiasis* requires *of* after *contraction*; even if this correction were made, though, the passive construction in D would be unnecessarily wordy and also imprecise, because it is the disease more than the act of contracting it that poses the danger. In E, *have a danger* is again unidiomatic, and the *that* clause following the phrase is, within the structure of the sentence, ungrammatical and awkward.

20. Unlike a funded pension system, in which contributions are invested to pay future beneficiaries, <u>a pay-as-you-go approach is the foundation of Social Security</u>.

 (A) a pay-as-you-go approach is the foundation of Social Security
 (B) the foundation of Social Security is a pay-as-you-go approach
 (C) the approach of Social Security is pay-as-you-go
 (D) Social Security's approach is pay-as-you-go
 (E) Social Security is founded on a pay-as-you-go approach

In this sentence, the first noun of the main clause grammatically identifies what is being compared with *a funded pension system*; to be logical, the comparison must be made between comparable things. Only E, the best choice, compares one kind of system of providing for retirees, the *funded pension system*, with another such system, *Social Security*. Choices A, C, and D all illogically compare the pension system with the *approach* taken by Social Security itself. In B, the comparison of *pension system* with *foundation* is similarly flawed.

21. Critics of the trend toward privately operated prisons consider corrections facilities <u>to be an integral part of the criminal justice system and question if</u> profits should be made from incarceration.

 (A) to be an integral part of the criminal justice system and question if
 (B) as an integral part of the criminal justice system and they question if
 (C) as being an integral part of the criminal justice system and question whether
 (D) an integral part of the criminal justice system and question whether
 (E) are an integral part of the criminal justice system, and they question whether

When *consider* means "regard as," as it does in this sentence, its object should be followed immediately by the phrase that identifies or describes that object. Thus, *to be* in A, *as* in B, and *as being* in C produce unidiomatic constructions in the context of the sentence. Also, although *if* and *whether* can be used interchangeably after some verbs, *question if*, which appears in A and B, is unidiomatic, and *they* in B is unnecessary. E also contains the unnecessary *they*, and it uses the ungrammatical construction *consider . . . facilities are*. Grammatically and idiomatically sound, D is the best choice.

22. The Federal Reserve Board's <u>reduction of interest rates on loans to financial institutions is both an acknowledgment of past economic trends and an effort</u> to influence their future direction.

(A) reduction of interest rates on loans to financial institutions is both an acknowledgment of past economic trends and an effort

(B) reduction of interest rates on loans to financial institutions is an acknowledgment both of past economic trends as well as an effort

(C) reduction of interest rates on loans to financial institutions both acknowledge past economic trends and attempt

(D) reducing interest rates on loans to financial institutions is an acknowledgment both of past economic trends and an effort

(E) reducing interest rates on loans to financial institutions both acknowledge past economic trends as well as attempt

Choice A is best. In B, *both* must come before *acknowledgment* if it is to link *acknowledgment* and *effort*; as misplaced here, it creates the unfulfilled expectation that the *reduction of interest rates* will be an acknowledgment of two different things. Moreover, *both . . . as well as . . .* is redundant: the correct idiom is *both x and y*. In C, the plural verbs *acknowledge* and *attempt* do not agree with their singular subject, *reduction*; also, it is imprecise to characterize a *reduction* as performing actions such as acknowledging or attempting. In both D and E, the use of the participle *reducing* rather than the noun *reduction* is awkward. Like B, D misplaces *both*, while E repeats both the redundancy of B and the agreement error of C.

SENTENCE CORRECTION SAMPLE TEST SECTION 4

Time — 25 minutes

22 Questions

<u>Directions</u>: In each of the following sentences, some part of the sentence or the entire sentence is underlined. Beneath each sentence you will find five ways of phrasing the underlined part. The first part of these repeats the original; the other four are different. If you think the original is the best of these answers choices, choose answer A; otherwise, choose one of the others. Select the best version and fill in the corresponding oval on your answer sheet.

This is a test of correctness and effectiveness of expression. In choosing answers, follow the requirements of standard written English; that is, pay attention to grammar, choice of words, and sentence construction. Choose the answer that produces the most effective sentence; this answer should be clear and exact, without awkwardness, ambiguity, redundancy, or grammatical error.

1. Congress is debating a bill requiring certain employers <u>provide workers with unpaid leave so as to</u> care for sick or newborn children.

   (A) provide workers with unpaid leave so as to
   (B) to provide workers with unpaid leave so as to
   (C) provide workers with unpaid leave in order that they
   (D) to provide workers with unpaid leave so that they can
   (E) provide workers with unpaid leave and

2. Often visible as smog, <u>ozone is formed in the atmosphere from</u> hydrocarbons and nitrogen oxides, two major pollutants emitted by automobiles, react with sunlight.

   (A) ozone is formed in the atmosphere from
   (B) ozone is formed in the atmosphere when
   (C) ozone is formed in the atmosphere, and when
   (D) ozone, formed in the atmosphere when
   (E) ozone, formed in the atmosphere from

3. Although she had signed a pledge of abstinence <u>while being an adolescent</u>, Frances Willard was 35 years old before she chose to become a temperance activist.

   (A) while being an adolescent
   (B) while in adolescence
   (C) at the time of her being adolescent
   (D) as being in adolescence
   (E) as an adolescent

4. A President entering the final two years of a second term is <u>likely to be at a severe disadvantage and is often unable to</u> carry out a legislative program.

   (A) likely to be at a severe disadvantage and is often unable to
   (B) likely severely disadvantaged and often unable to
   (C) liable to be severely disadvantaged and cannot often
   (D) liable that he or she is at a severe disadvantage and cannot often
   (E) at a severe disadvantage, often likely to be unable that he or she can

5. The original building and loan associations were organized as limited life funds, whose members made monthly payments on their share <u>subscriptions, then taking turns drawing</u> on the funds for home mortgages.

   (A) subscriptions, then taking turns drawing
   (B) subscriptions, and then taking turns drawing
   (C) subscriptions and then took turns drawing
   (D) subscriptions and then took turns, they drew
   (E) subscriptions and then drew, taking turns

GO ON TO THE NEXT PAGE.

6. The number of undergraduate degrees in engineering awarded by colleges and universities in the United States increased by more than twice from 1978 to 1985.

   (A) increased by more than twice
   (B) increased more than two times
   (C) more than doubled
   (D) was more than doubled
   (E) had more than doubled

7. The British Admiralty and the War Office met in March 1892 to consider a possible Russian attempt to seize Constantinople and how they would have to act militarily to deal with them.

   (A) how they would have to act militarily to deal with them
   (B) how to deal with them if military action would be necessary
   (C) what would be necessary militarily for dealing with such an event
   (D) what military action would be necessary in order to deal with such an event
   (E) the necessity of what kind of military action in order to take for dealing with it

8. Growing competitive pressures may be encouraging auditors to bend the rules in favor of clients; auditors may, for instance, allow a questionable loan to remain on the books in order to maintain a bank's profits on paper.

   (A) clients; auditors may, for instance, allow
   (B) clients, as an instance, to allow
   (C) clients, like to allow
   (D) clients, such as to be allowing
   (E) clients; which might, as an instance, be the allowing of

9. If the proposed expenditures for gathering information abroad are reduced even further, international news reports have been and will continue to diminish in number and quality.

   (A) have been and will continue to diminish
   (B) have and will continue to diminish
   (C) will continue to diminish, as they already did,
   (D) will continue to diminish, as they have already,
   (E) will continue to diminish

10. Gall's hypothesis of there being different mental functions localized in different parts of the brain is widely accepted today.

    (A) of there being different mental functions localized in different parts of the brain is widely accepted today
    (B) of different mental functions that are localized in different parts of the brain is widely accepted today
    (C) that different mental functions are localized in different parts of the brain is widely accepted today
    (D) which is that there are different mental functions localized in different parts of the brain is widely accepted today
    (E) which is widely accepted today is that there are different mental functions localized in different parts of the brain

11. Though the term "graphic design" may suggest laying out corporate brochures and annual reports, they have come to signify widely ranging work, from package designs and company logotypes to signs, book jackets, computer graphics, and film titles.

    (A) suggest laying out corporate brochures and annual reports, they have come to signify widely ranging
    (B) suggest laying out corporate brochures and annual reports, it has come to signify a wide range of
    (C) suggest corporate brochure and annual report layout, it has signified widely ranging
    (D) have suggested corporate brochure and annual report layout, it has signified a wide range of
    (E) have suggested laying out corporate brochures and annual reports, they have come to signify widely ranging

12. The root systems of most flowering perennials either become too crowded, which results in loss in vigor, and spread too far outward, producing a bare center.

    (A) which results in loss in vigor, and spread
    (B) resulting in loss in vigor, or spreading
    (C) with the result of loss of vigor, or spreading
    (D) resulting in loss of vigor, or spread
    (E) with a resulting loss of vigor, and spread

GO ON TO THE NEXT PAGE.

13. George Sand (Aurore Lucile Dupin) was one of the first European writers to consider the rural poor to be legitimate subjects for literature and portray these with sympathy and respect in her novels.

   (A) to be legitimate subjects for literature and portray these
   (B) should be legitimate subjects for literature and portray these
   (C) as being legitimate subjects for literature and portraying them
   (D) as if they were legitimate subjects for literature and portray them
   (E) legitimate subjects for literature and to portray them

14. Salt deposits and moisture threaten to destroy the Mohenjo-Daro excavation in Pakistan, the site of an ancient civilization that flourished at the same time as the civilizations in the Nile delta and the river valleys of the Tigris and Euphrates.

   (A) that flourished at the same time as the civilizations
   (B) that had flourished at the same time as had the civilizations
   (C) that flourished at the same time those had
   (D) flourishing at the same time as those did
   (E) flourishing at the same time as those were

15. In 1973 mortgage payments represented twenty-one percent of an average thirty-year-old male's income; and forty-four percent in 1984.

   (A) income; and forty-four percent in 1984
   (B) income; in 1984 the figure was forty-four percent
   (C) income, and in 1984 forty-four percent
   (D) income, forty-four percent in 1984 was the figure
   (E) income that rose to forty-four percent in 1984

16. In contrast to large steel plants that take iron ore through all the steps needed to produce several different kinds of steel, processing steel scrap into a specialized group of products has enabled small mills to put capital into new technology and remain economically viable.

   (A) processing steel scrap into a specialized group of products has enabled small mills to put capital into new technology and remain
   (B) processing steel scrap into a specialized group of products has enabled small mills to put capital into new technology, remaining
   (C) the processing of steel scrap into a specialized group of products has enabled small mills to put capital into new technology, remaining
   (D) small mills, by processing steel scrap into a specialized group of products, have been able to put capital into new technology and remain
   (E) small mills, by processing steel scrap into a specialized group of products, have been able to put capital into new technology and remained

17. Any medical test will sometimes fail to detect a condition when it is present and indicate that there is one when it is not.

   (A) a condition when it is present and indicate that there is one
   (B) when a condition is present and indicate that there is one
   (C) a condition when it is present and indicate that it is present
   (D) when a condition is present and indicate its presence
   (E) the presence of a condition when it is there and indicate its presence

GO ON TO THE NEXT PAGE.

18. One legacy of Madison Avenue's recent campaign to appeal to people fifty years old and over is the realization that as a person ages, their concerns change as well.

   (A) the realization that as a person ages, their
   (B) the realization that as people age, their
   (C) to realize that when a person ages, his or her
   (D) to realize that when people age, their
   (E) realizing that as people age, their

19. Out of America's fascination with all things antique have grown a market for bygone styles of furniture and fixtures that are bringing back the chaise lounge, the overstuffed sofa, and the claw-footed bathtub.

   (A) things antique have grown a market for bygone styles of furniture and fixtures that are bringing
   (B) things antique has grown a market for bygone styles of furniture and fixtures that is bringing
   (C) things that are antiques has grown a market for bygone styles of furniture and fixtures that bring
   (D) antique things have grown a market for bygone styles of furniture and fixtures that are bringing
   (E) antique things has grown a market for bygone styles of furniture and fixtures that bring

20. Having the right hand and arm being crippled by a sniper's bullet during the First World War, Horace Pippin, a Black American painter, worked by holding the brush in his right hand and guiding its movements with his left.

   (A) Having the right hand and arm being crippled by a sniper's bullet during the First World War
   (B) In spite of his right hand and arm being crippled by a sniper's bullet during the First World War
   (C) Because there had been a sniper's bullet during the First World War that crippled his right hand and arm
   (D) The right hand and arm being crippled by a sniper's bullet during the First World War
   (E) His right hand and arm crippled by a sniper's bullet during the First World War

21. Beyond the immediate cash flow crisis that the museum faces, its survival depends on if it can broaden its membership and leave its cramped quarters for a site where it can store and exhibit its more than 12,000 artifacts.

   (A) if it can broaden its membership and leave
   (B) whether it can broaden its membership and leave
   (C) whether or not it has the capability to broaden its membership and can leave
   (D) its ability for broadening its membership and leaving
   (E) the ability for it to broaden its membership and leave

22. The Emperor Augustus, it appears, commissioned an idealized sculptured portrait, the features of which are so unrealistic as to constitute what one scholar calls an "artificial face."

   (A) so unrealistic as to constitute
   (B) so unrealistic they constituted
   (C) so unrealistic that they have constituted
   (D) unrealistic enough so that they constitute
   (E) unrealistic enough so as to constitute

STOP

IF YOU FINISH BEFORE TIME IS CALLED, YOU MAY CHECK YOUR WORK ON THIS SECTION ONLY. DO NOT TURN TO ANY OTHER SECTION IN THE TEST.

Answer Key for Sample Test Section 4

SENTENCE CORRECTION

1. D	12. D
2. B	13. E
3. E	14. A
4. A	15. B
5. C	16. D
6. C	17. C
7. D	18. B
8. A	19. B
9. E	20. E
10. C	21. B
11. B	22. A

Explanatory Material: Sentence Correction Sample Test Section 4

1. Congress is debating a bill requiring certain employers <u>provide workers with unpaid leave so as to</u> care for sick or newborn children.

   (A) provide workers with unpaid leave so as to
   (B) to provide workers with unpaid leave so as to
   (C) provide workers with unpaid leave in order that they
   (D) to provide workers with unpaid leave so that they can
   (E) provide workers with unpaid leave and

Choices A, C, and E are ungrammatical because, in this context, *requiring . . . employers* must be followed by an infinitive. These options display additional faults: in A, *so as to* fails to specify that the workers receiving the leave will be the people caring for the infants and children; *in order that they*, as used in C, is imprecise and unidiomatic; and E says that the bill being debated would require the employers themselves to care for the children. Choice B offers the correct infinitive, *to provide*, but contains the faulty *so as to*. Choice D is best.

2. Often visible as smog, <u>ozone is formed in the atmosphere from</u> hydrocarbons and nitrogen oxides, two major pollutants emitted by automobiles, react with sunlight.

   (A) ozone is formed in the atmosphere from
   (B) ozone is formed in the atmosphere when
   (C) ozone is formed in the atmosphere, and when
   (D) ozone, formed in the atmosphere when
   (E) ozone, formed in the atmosphere from

In choice A, the construction *from hydrocarbons and nitrogen oxides . . . react* is ungrammatical. In B, the best choice, the conjunction *when* replaces the preposition *from*, producing a grammatical and logical statement. In choice C, the use of the conjunction *and* results in the illogical assertion that the

formation of ozone in the atmosphere happens in addition to, rather than as a result of, its formation when hydrocarbons and nitrogen oxide react with sunlight. Choice D omits the main verb, *is*, leaving a sentence fragment. E compounds the error of D with that of A.

3. Although she had signed a pledge of abstinence <u>while being an adolescent</u>, Frances Willard was 35 years old before she chose to become a temperance activist.

   (A) while being an adolescent
   (B) while in adolescence
   (C) at the time of her being adolescent
   (D) as being in adolescence
   (E) as an adolescent

Choices A, B, and D are unidiomatic. Choice C is awkward and wordy; furthermore, the phrase *at the time of her being adolescent* suggests that Willard's adolescence lasted only for a brief, finite moment rather than for an extended period of time. Choice E, idiomatic and precise, is the best answer.

4. A President entering the final two years of a second term is <u>likely to be at a severe disadvantage and is often unable to</u> carry out a legislative program.

   (A) likely to be at a severe disadvantage and is often unable to
   (B) likely severely disadvantaged and often unable to
   (C) liable to be severely disadvantaged and cannot often
   (D) liable that he or she is at a severe disadvantage and cannot often
   (E) at a severe disadvantage, often likely to be unable that he or she can

Choice A is best. Choice B lacks the necessary infinitive after *likely*. In B and C, *disadvantaged*, which often means "hampered by substandard economic and social conditions," is less precise than *at a disadvantage*. In C and D, *cannot often carry out* suggests that a President with limited time suffers only from an inability to achieve legislative goals frequently, not from a frequent inability to achieve them at all. In C, *liable*, followed by an infinitive, can legitimately be used to express probability with a bad outcome, but C is otherwise flawed as noted. D's *liable* and E's *unable* should be followed by an infinitive rather than by a relative clause beginning with *that*.

5. The original building and loan associations were organized as limited life funds, whose members made monthly payments on their share <u>subscriptions, then taking turns drawing</u> on the funds for home mortgages.

   (A) subscriptions, then taking turns drawing
   (B) subscriptions, and then taking turns drawing
   (C) subscriptions and then took turns drawing
   (D) subscriptions and then took turns, they drew
   (E) subscriptions and then drew, taking turns

The sentence speaks of a sequence of actions in the past: shareholders *made* their monthly payments and subsequently *took* turns drawing on the funds. Choice C, the best answer, uses parallel past-tense verb forms to express this sequence. Choices A and B violate parallelism by using *taking* where *took* is required. The wording in D results in a run-on sentence and does not specify what the members took turns doing. Similarly, E does not specify what the members *drew*, and *taking turns* produces nonsense when combined with the rest of the sentence.

6. The number of undergraduate degrees in engineering awarded by colleges and universities in the United States <u>increased by more than twice</u> from 1978 to 1985.

   (A) increased by more than twice
   (B) increased more than two times
   (C) more than doubled
   (D) was more than doubled
   (E) had more than doubled

Choice A is faulty because an adverb such as *twice* cannot function as an object of the preposition *by*. B distorts the sentence's meaning, stating that the number of engineering degrees conferred increased on more than two distinct occasions. D's passive verb *was . . . doubled* suggests without warrant that some unnamed agent increased the number of engineering degrees. The past perfect tense in E, *had . . . doubled*, is inappropriate unless the increase in engineering degrees is specifically being viewed as having occurred further back in the past than some subsequent event. Choice C is best.

7. The British Admiralty and the War Office met in March 1892 to consider a possible Russian attempt to seize Constantinople and <u>how they would have to act militarily to deal with them.</u>

   (A) how they would have to act militarily to deal with them
   (B) how to deal with them if military action would be necessary
   (C) what would be necessary militarily for dealing with such an event
   (D) what military action would be necessary in order to deal with such an event
   (E) the necessity of what kind of military action in order to take for dealing with it

In choices A and B, the pronoun *them* has no antecedent; furthermore, the *if* clause in B must take *should* rather than *would*. In C, *necessary militarily* is awkward and vague. E is wordy and garbles the meaning with incorrect word order. Choice D is best: its phrasing is clear, grammatical, and idiomatic. Moreover, D is the choice that most closely parallels the construction of the nonunderlined portion of the sentence. The sentence states that the Admiralty and the War Office met to consider *x* and *y*, where *x* is the noun phrase *a possible Russian attempt*. D provides a noun phrase, *military action*, that matches the structure of *x* more closely than do the corresponding noun elements in the other choices.

8. Growing competitive pressures may be encouraging auditors to bend the rules in favor of <u>clients; auditors may, for instance, allow</u> a questionable loan to remain on the books in order to maintain a bank's profits on paper.

   (A) clients; auditors may, for instance, allow
   (B) clients, as an instance, to allow
   (C) clients, like to allow
   (D) clients, such as to be allowing
   (E) clients; which might, as an instance, be the allowing of

The first independent clause of the sentence describes a general situation; in A, the best choice, a second independent clause clearly and grammatically presents an example of this circumstance. Choice B uses *as an instance* ungrammatically: *as an instance* requires *of* to form such idiomatic constructions as "She cited x *as an instance of* y." Also, this construction cannot link infinitives such as *to bend* and *to allow*. The infinitive is again incorrect in C and D. C misuses *like*, a comparative preposition, to introduce an example. D requires *by* in place of *to be*. E, aside from being wordy and imprecise, uses the pronoun *which* to refer vaguely to the whole preceding clause rather than to a specific noun referent.

9. If the proposed expenditures for gathering information abroad are reduced even further, international news reports <u>have been and will continue to diminish</u> in number and quality.

   (A) have been and will continue to diminish
   (B) have and will continue to diminish
   (C) will continue to diminish, as they already did,
   (D) will continue to diminish, as they have already,
   (E) will continue to diminish

Choices A and B fail because the logic of the sentence demands that the verb in the main clause be wholly in the future tense: if *x* happens, *y* will happen. To compound the problem, the auxiliary verbs *have been* in A and *have* in B cannot properly be completed by *to diminish*. C, D, and E supply the correct verb form, but C and D conclude with faulty *as* clauses that are awkward and unnecessary, because *will continue* describes an action begun in the past. E is the best choice.

10. Gall's hypothesis <u>of there being different mental functions localized in different parts of the brain is widely accepted today.</u>

   (A) of there being different mental functions localized in different parts of the brain is widely accepted today

   (B) of different mental functions that are localized in different parts of the brain is widely accepted today

   (C) that different mental functions are localized in different parts of the brain is widely accepted today

   (D) which is that there are different mental functions localized in different parts of the brain is widely accepted today

   (E) which is widely accepted today is that there are different mental functions localized in different parts of the brain

Choices A and B are faulty because a relative clause beginning with *that* is needed to state Gall's hypothesis. The phrase *of there being*, as used in A, is wordy and unidiomatic; in B, *of different mental functions* does not convey Gall's point about those functions. Choices D and E are awkward and wordy, and both use *which* where *that* would be the preferred pronoun for introducing a clause that states Gall's point. Further, the phrasing of E misleadingly suggests that a distinction is being made between this hypothesis and others by Gall that are not widely accepted today. Choice C is best.

11. Though the term "graphic design" may <u>suggest laying out corporate brochures and annual reports, they have come to signify widely ranging</u> work, from package designs and company logotypes to signs, book jackets, computer graphics, and film titles.

   (A) suggest laying out corporate brochures and annual reports, they have come to signify widely ranging

   (B) suggest laying out corporate brochures and annual reports, it has come to signify a wide range of

   (C) suggest corporate brochure and annual report layout, it has signified widely ranging

   (D) have suggested corporate brochure and annual report layout, it has signified a wide range of

   (E) have suggested laying out corporate brochures and annual reports, they have come to signify widely ranging

Choice A contains an agreement error: *the term* requires the singular *it has* in place of the plural *they have*. Furthermore, *widely ranging* is imprecise: graphic design work does not range about widely but rather comprises a *wide range* of activities. Choice C contains *widely ranging* and, like D, fails to use a verb form such as *laying out* to define the activities, instead presenting an awkward noun phrase: *corporate*

brochure and annual report layout. The present perfect tense is used inappropriately in choices C (*has signified*), D (*have suggested . . . has signified*), and E (*have suggested*) to indicate recently completed rather than ongoing action. Additionally, E contains the incorrect *they have* and the imprecise *widely ranging*. Choice B is best.

12. The root systems of most flowering perennials either become too crowded, <u>which results in loss in vigor, and spread</u> too far outward, producing a bare center.

   (A) which results in loss in vigor, and spread

   (B) resulting in loss in vigor, or spreading

   (C) with the result of loss of vigor, or spreading

   (D) resulting in loss of vigor, or spread

   (E) with a resulting loss of vigor, and spread

Choice A misuses *which*: as a relative pronoun, *which* should refer to a specific noun rather than to the action of an entire clause. A also produces the unidiomatic and illogical construction *either . . . and*. Choice B properly uses a verb phrase (*resulting . . .*) instead of *which* to modify the action of the first clause and also correctly completes *either* with *or*, but the verbs following *either* and *or* are not parallel: *spreading* must be *spread* to match *become*. Choice C is flawed by the nonparallel verb *spreading* and the wordy phrase that begins *with the result of*. Choice E is similarly wordy and uses *and* where *or* is required. Choice D — concise, idiomatic, and parallel with the rest of the sentence — is best.

13. George Sand (Aurore Lucile Dupin) was one of the first European writers to consider the rural poor <u>to be legitimate subjects for literature and portray these</u> with sympathy and respect in her novels.

   (A) to be legitimate subjects for literature and portray these

   (B) should be legitimate subjects for literature and portray these

   (C) as being legitimate subjects for literature and portraying them

   (D) as if they were legitimate subjects for literature and portray them

   (E) legitimate subjects for literature and to portray them

When the verb *consider* is used to mean "regard" or "deem," it can be used more economically without the *to be* of choice A; *should be* in choice B, *as being* in choice C, and *as if* in choice D are used unidiomatically with this sense of *consider*, and D carries the unwarranted suggestion that Sand is somehow viewing the rural poor hypothetically. Choice E, therefore, is best: each of the other choices inserts an unnecessary, unidiomatic, or misleading phrase before *legitimate subjects*. Moreover, A and B incorrectly use *these* rather than *them* as the pronoun referring to the poor. In C, *portraying* is not parallel with *to consider*. Only E has *to portray*; although not essential, *to* underscores the parallelism of *portray* and *consider*.

14. Salt deposits and moisture threaten to destroy the Mohenjo-Daro excavation in Pakistan, the site of an ancient civilization that flourished at the same time as the civilizations in the Nile delta and the river valleys of the Tigris and Euphrates.

(A) that flourished at the same time as the civilizations
(B) that had flourished at the same time as had the civilizations
(C) that flourished at the same time those had
(D) flourishing at the same time as those did
(E) flourishing at the same time as those were

Choice A, the best answer, uses the simple past tense *flourished* to describe civilizations existing simultaneously in the past. Choice B wrongly uses the past perfect *had flourished*; past perfect tense indicates action that was completed prior to some other event described in the simple past tense: for example, "Mayan civilization *had ceased* to exist by the time Europeans first *reached* the Americas." Choice C lacks *as* after *time*. In choices C, D, and E, the plural pronoun *those* has no plural noun to which it can refer. In C, *had* signals the incorrect past perfect; *did* in D and *were* in E are awkward and unnecessary. D and E also incorrectly use the present participle *flourishing* where *that flourished* is needed.

15. In 1973 mortgage payments represented twenty-one percent of an average thirty-year-old male's income; and forty-four percent in 1984.

(A) income; and forty-four percent in 1984
(B) income; in 1984 the figure was forty-four percent
(C) income, and in 1984 forty-four percent
(D) income, forty-four percent in 1984 was the figure
(E) income that rose to forty-four percent in 1984

To establish the clearest comparison between circumstances in 1973 and those in 1984, a separate clause is needed to describe each year. Choices A and C, in failing to use separate clauses, are too elliptical and therefore unclear. Choice A also incorrectly uses *and* and a semicolon to separate an independent clause and a phrase. Choice D incorrectly separates two independent clauses with a comma; moreover, the placement of *in 1984* is awkward and confusing. In choice E, *that* refers illogically to *income*, thereby producing the misstatement that income rather than mortgage payments rose to forty-four percent in 1984. Choice B is best; two properly constructed clauses that clearly express the comparison are separated by a semicolon.

16. In contrast to large steel plants that take iron ore through all the steps needed to produce several different kinds of steel, processing steel scrap into a specialized group of products has enabled small mills to put capital into new technology and remain economically viable.

(A) processing steel scrap into a specialized group of products has enabled small mills to put capital into new technology and remain
(B) processing steel scrap into a specialized group of products has enabled small mills to put capital into new technology, remaining
(C) the processing of steel scrap into a specialized group of products has enabled small mills to put capital into new technology, remaining
(D) small mills, by processing steel scrap into a specialized group of products, have been able to put capital into new technology and remain
(E) small mills, by processing steel scrap into a specialized group of products, have been able to put capital into new technology and remained

The logical comparison here is between *large steel plants* and *small mills*. Choices A, B, and C illogically contrast *large steel plants* with *[the] processing [of] steel scrap*. Further, in choices B and C *remaining* is not parallel with *put*; consequently, it is not clear exactly what is *remaining economically viable*. The contrast between large plants and small mills is logically phrased in choices D and E, but *remained* in E is not parallel with *put*. Choice D, the best answer, uses parallel verb forms to complete the construction *have been able to put . . . and remain*.

17. Any medical test will sometimes fail to detect a condition when it is present and indicate that there is one when it is not.

(A) a condition when it is present and indicate that there is one
(B) when a condition is present and indicate that there is one
(C) a condition when it is present and indicate that it is present
(D) when a condition is present and indicate its presence
(E) the presence of a condition when it is there and indicate its presence

Only choice C, the best answer, produces a sentence in which every pronoun *it* refers clearly and logically to the noun *condition*. In choices A and B, the phrase *indicate that there is one* does not grammatically fit with *when it is not* because *it* has no referent. Choices B and D are imprecise in saying that a test will fail to detect *when a condition is present*, since the issue is the presence and not the timing of the condition. Further, *its presence* in D leaves the *it* in *when it is not* without a logical referent: *it* must refer to *condition*, not *presence*. Choice E repeats this error; also, *the presence . . . when it is there* is imprecise and redundant.

18. One legacy of Madison Avenue's recent campaign to appeal to people fifty years old and over is the realization that as a person ages, their concerns change as well.

  (A) the realization that as a person ages, their
  (B) the realization that as people age, their
  (C) to realize that when a person ages, his or her
  (D) to realize that when people age, their
  (E) realizing that as people age, their

In choice A, the plural pronoun *their* does not agree in number with the singular noun *person*. Choices C, D, and E can be faulted for failing to complete the construction *One legacy . . . is* with a noun that matches the noun *legacy*; these choices use verb forms — the infinitive *to realize* or the present participle *realizing* — in place of a noun such as *realization*. Further, *when* in C and D is less precise than *as* in characterizing a prolonged and gradual process such as aging. B is the best answer.

19. Out of America's fascination with all things antique have grown a market for bygone styles of furniture and fixtures that are bringing back the chaise lounge, the overstuffed sofa, and the claw-footed bathtub.

  (A) things antique have grown a market for bygone styles of furniture and fixtures that are bringing
  (B) things antique has grown a market for bygone styles of furniture and fixtures that is bringing
  (C) things that are antiques has grown a market for bygone styles of furniture and fixtures that bring
  (D) antique things have grown a market for bygone styles of furniture and fixtures that are bringing
  (E) antique things has grown a market for bygone styles of furniture and fixtures that bring

Choice B is best. In A and D, *have grown* does not agree with the singular noun *market*. In addition, all of the choices except B use plural verbs after *that*, thus illogically stating either that *bygone styles of furniture and fixtures*, or *fixtures* alone, are reviving the particular pieces mentioned; it is instead *the market* for those styles *that is bringing back* such pieces, as B states. Furthermore, choices C and E, by using the verb form *bring,* fail to convey the ongoing nature of the revival properly described by the progressive verb *is bringing.*

20. Having the right hand and arm being crippled by a sniper's bullet during the First World War, Horace Pippin, a Black American painter, worked by holding the brush in his right hand and guiding its movements with his left.

  (A) Having the right hand and arm being crippled by a sniper's bullet during the First World War
  (B) In spite of his right hand and arm being crippled by a sniper's bullet during the First World War
  (C) Because there had been a sniper's bullet during the First World War that crippled his right hand and arm
  (D) The right hand and arm being crippled by a sniper's bullet during the First World War
  (E) His right hand and arm crippled by a sniper's bullet during the First World War

In E, the best answer, the construction *His right hand . . . crippled* clearly and grammatically modifies the subject of the sentence, *Horace Pippin*. In A, the use of the two participles *Having* and *being* is ungrammatical. Choice B is awkward and changes the meaning of the original statement: the point is that Pippin's method of painting arose because of, not *in spite of*, his injury. Choice C is wordy and awkwardly places the clause beginning *that crippled . . .* so that it appears to modify *the First World War* rather than *bullet*. In choice D, *The* should be *His*, and *being* should be omitted.

21. Beyond the immediate cash flow crisis that the museum faces, its survival depends on if it can broaden its membership and leave its cramped quarters for a site where it can store and exhibit its more than 12,000 artifacts.

  (A) if it can broaden its membership and leave
  (B) whether it can broaden its membership and leave
  (C) whether or not it has the capability to broaden its membership and can leave
  (D) its ability for broadening its membership and leaving
  (E) the ability for it to broaden its membership and leave

Choice A is faulty because it uses the unidiomatic construction *depends on if*; *whether* is required to connect *depends on* with the clause beginning *it can . . . .* Choice C uses *whether or not* where only *whether* is needed, includes the awkward and wordy construction *has the capability to*, and unnecessarily repeats the idea of capability with *can*. Choices D and E use unidiomatic constructions where the phrase *its ability to broaden* is required. Choice B — idiomatic, concise, and correct — is best.

22. The Emperor Augustus, it appears, commissioned an idealized sculpture portrait, the features of which are <u>so unrealistic as to constitute</u> what one scholar calls an "artificial face."

(A) so unrealistic as to constitute
(B) so unrealistic they constituted
(C) so unrealistic that they have constituted
(D) unrealistic enough so that they constitute
(E) unrealistic enough so as to constitute

The verbs *are* and *calls* indicate that the sculpture is being viewed and judged in the present. Thus, neither the past tense verb *constituted* (in B) nor the present perfect verb *have constituted* (in C) is correct; both suggest that the statue's features once constituted an *artificial face* but no longer do so. Also, B would be better if *that* were inserted after *so unrealistic*, although the omission of *that* is not ungrammatical. Choices D and E use unidiomatic constructions with *enough*: *unrealistic enough to constitute* would be idiomatic, but the use of *enough* is imprecise and awkward in this context. Choice A, which uses the clear, concise, and idiomatic construction *so unrealistic as to constitute*, is best.

SENTENCE CORRECTION SAMPLE TEST SECTION 5

Time — 25 minutes

22 Questions

Directions: In each of the following sentences, some part of the sentence or the entire sentence is underlined. Beneath each sentence you will find five ways of phrasing the underlined part. The first part of these repeats the original; the other four are different. If you think the original is the best of these answers choices, choose answer A; otherwise, choose one of the others. Select the best version and fill in the corresponding oval on your answer sheet.

This is a test of correctness and effectiveness of expression. In choosing answers, follow the requirements of standard written English; that is, pay attention to grammar, choice of words, and sentence construction. Choose the answer that produces the most effective sentence; this answer should be clear and exact, without awkwardness, ambiguity, redundancy, or grammatical error.

1. The psychologist William James believed that facial expressions not only provide a visible sign of an emotion, actually contributing to the feeling itself.

   (A) emotion, actually contributing to the feeling itself
   (B) emotion but also actually contributing to the feeling itself
   (C) emotion but also actually contribute to the feeling itself
   (D) emotion; they also actually contribute to the feeling of it
   (E) emotion; the feeling itself is also actually contributed to by them

2. Along with the drop in producer prices announced yesterday, the strong retail sales figures released today seem like it is indicative that the economy, although growing slowly, is not nearing a recession.

   (A) like it is indicative that
   (B) as if to indicate
   (C) to indicate that
   (D) indicative of
   (E) like an indication of

3. The National Transportation Safety Board has recommended the use of fail-safe mechanisms on airliner cargo door latches assuring the doors are properly closed before takeoff and to prevent them from popping open in flight.

   (A) assuring the doors are properly closed
   (B) for the assurance of proper closing
   (C) assuring proper closure
   (D) to assure closing the doors properly
   (E) to assure that the doors are properly closed

4. Iguanas have been an important food source in Latin America since prehistoric times, and it is still prized as a game animal by the campesinos, who typically cook the meat in a heavily spiced stew.

   (A) it is still prized as a game animal
   (B) it is still prized as game animals
   (C) they are still prized as game animals
   (D) they are still prized as being a game animal
   (E) being still prized as a game animal

GO ON TO THE NEXT PAGE.

-369-

5. The financial crash of October 1987 demonstrated that the world's capital markets are integrated more closely than never before and events in one part of the global village may be transmitted to the rest of the village—almost instantaneously.

   (A) integrated more closely than never before and
   (B) closely integrated more than ever before so
   (C) more closely integrated as never before while
   (D) more closely integrated than ever before and that
   (E) more than ever before closely integrated as

6. New theories propose that catastrophic impacts of asteroids and comets may have caused reversals in the Earth's magnetic field, the onset of ice ages, splitting apart continents 80 million years ago, and great volcanic eruptions.

   (A) splitting apart continents
   (B) the splitting apart of continents
   (C) split apart continents
   (D) continents split apart
   (E) continents that were split apart

7. Wisconsin, Illinois, Florida, and Minnesota have begun to enforce statewide bans prohibiting landfills to accept leaves, brush, and grass clippings.

   (A) prohibiting landfills to accept leaves, brush, and grass clippings
   (B) prohibiting that landfills accept leaves, brush, and grass clippings
   (C) prohibiting landfills from accepting leaves, brush, and grass clippings
   (D) that leaves, brush, and grass clippings cannot be accepted in landfills
   (E) that landfills cannot accept leaves, brush, and grass clippings

8. Even though the direct costs of malpractice disputes amounts to a sum lower than one percent of the $541 billion the nation spent on health care last year, doctors say fear of lawsuits plays a major role in health-care inflation.

   (A) amounts to a sum lower
   (B) amounts to less
   (C) amounted to less
   (D) amounted to lower
   (E) amounted to a lower sum

9. Except for a concert performance that the composer himself staged in 1911, Scott Joplin's ragtime opera *Treemonisha* was not produced until 1972, sixty-one years after its completion.

   (A) Except for a concert performance that the composer himself staged
   (B) Except for a concert performance with the composer himself staging it
   (C) Besides a concert performance being staged by the composer himself
   (D) Excepting a concert performance that the composer himself staged
   (E) With the exception of a concert performance with the staging done by the composer himself

10. Students in the metropolitan school district lack math skills to such a large degree as to make it difficult to absorb them into a city economy becoming ever more dependent on information-based industries.

    (A) lack math skills to such a large degree as to make it difficult to absorb them into a city economy becoming
    (B) lack math skills to a large enough degree that they will be difficult to absorb into a city's economy that becomes
    (C) lack of math skills is so large as to be difficult to absorb them into a city's economy that becomes
    (D) are lacking so much in math skills as to be difficult to absorb into a city's economy becoming
    (E) are so lacking in math skills that it will be difficult to absorb them into a city economy becoming

GO ON TO THE NEXT PAGE.

11. The diet of the ordinary Greek in classical times was largely vegetarian—vegetables, fresh cheese, oatmeal, and meal cakes, and meat rarely.

(A) and meat rarely
(B) and meat was rare
(C) with meat as rare
(D) meat a rarity
(E) with meat as a rarity

12. An inventory equal to 90 days sales is as much as even the strongest businesses carry, and then only as a way to anticipate higher prices or ensure against shortages.

(A) as much as even
(B) so much as even
(C) even so much as
(D) even as much that
(E) even so much that

13. The decision by one of the nation's largest banks to admit to $3 billion in potential losses on foreign loans could mean less lending by commercial banks to developing countries and increasing the pressure on multigovernment lenders to supply the funds.

(A) increasing the pressure
(B) the increasing pressure
(C) increased pressure
(D) the pressure increased
(E) the pressure increasing

14. Downzoning, zoning that typically results in the reduction of housing density, allows for more open space in areas where little water or services exist.

(A) little water or services exist
(B) little water or services exists
(C) few services and little water exists
(D) there is little water or services available
(E) there are few services and little available water

15. Reporting that one of its many problems had been the recent extended sales slump in women's apparel, the seven-store retailer said it would start a three-month liquidation sale in all of its stores.

(A) its many problems had been the recent
(B) its many problems has been the recently
(C) its many problems is the recently
(D) their many problems is the recent
(E) their many problems had been the recent

16. Legislation in the Canadian province of Ontario requires of both public and private employers that pay be the same for jobs historically held by women as for jobs requiring comparable skill that are usually held by men.

(A) that pay be the same for jobs historically held by women as for jobs requiring comparable skill that are
(B) that pay for jobs historically held by women should be the same as for a job requiring comparable skills
(C) to pay the same in jobs historically held by women as in jobs of comparable skill that are
(D) to pay the same regardless of whether a job was historically held by women or is one demanding comparable skills
(E) to pay as much for jobs historically held by women as for a job demanding comparable skills

17. It has been estimated that the annual cost to the United States of illiteracy in lost industrial output and tax revenues is at least $20 billion a year.

(A) the annual cost to the United States of illiteracy in lost industrial output and tax revenues is at least $20 billion a year
(B) the annual cost of illiteracy to the United States is at least $20 billion a year because of lost industrial output and tax revenues
(C) illiteracy costs the United States at least $20 billion a year in lost industrial output and tax revenues
(D) $20 billion a year in lost industrial output and tax revenues is the annual cost to the United States of illiteracy
(E) lost industrial output and tax revenues cost the United States at least $20 billion a year because of illiteracy

GO ON TO THE NEXT PAGE.

18. Egyptians are credited as having pioneered embalming methods as long ago as 2650 B.C.

   (A) as having
   (B) with having
   (C) to have
   (D) as the ones who
   (E) for being the ones who

19. Domestic automobile manufacturers have invested millions of dollars into research to develop cars more gasoline-efficient even than presently on the road.

   (A) into research to develop cars more gasoline-efficient even than presently on the road
   (B) into research for developing even more gasoline-efficient cars on the road than at present
   (C) for research for cars to be developed that are more gasoline-efficient even than presently on the road
   (D) in research to develop cars even more gasoline-efficient than those at present on the road
   (E) in research for developing cars that are even more gasoline-efficient than presently on the road

20. Visitors to the park have often looked up into the leafy canopy and saw monkeys sleeping on the branches, whose arms and legs hang like socks on a clothesline.

   (A) saw monkeys sleeping on the branches, whose arms and legs hang
   (B) saw monkeys sleeping on the branches, whose arms and legs were hanging
   (C) saw monkeys sleeping on the branches, with arms and legs hanging
   (D) seen monkeys sleeping on the branches, with arms and legs hanging
   (E) seen monkeys sleeping on the branches, whose arms and legs have hung

21. From the bark of the paper birch tree the Menomini crafted a canoe about twenty feet long and two feet wide, with small ribs and rails of cedar, which could carry four persons or eight hundred pounds of baggage so light that a person could easily portage it around impeding rapids.

   (A) baggage so light
   (B) baggage being so light
   (C) baggage, yet being so light
   (D) baggage, and so light
   (E) baggage yet was so light

22. From the time of its defeat by the Germans in 1940 until its liberation in 1944, France was a bitter and divided country; a kind of civil war raged in the Vichy government between those who wanted to collaborate with the Nazis with those who opposed them.

   (A) between those who wanted to collaborate with the Nazis with those who opposed
   (B) between those who wanted to collaborate with the Nazis and those who opposed
   (C) between those wanting to collaborate with the Nazis with those opposing
   (D) among those who wanted to collaborate with the Nazis and those who opposed
   (E) among those wanting to collaborate with the Nazis with those opposing

STOP

**IF YOU FINISH BEFORE TIME IS CALLED, YOU MAY CHECK YOUR WORK ON THIS SECTION ONLY.
DO NOT TURN TO ANY OTHER SECTION IN THE TEST.**

Answer Key for Sample Test Section 5

SENTENCE CORRECTION

1.	C	12.	A
2.	C	13.	C
3.	E	14.	E
4.	C	15.	A
5.	D	16.	A
6.	B	17.	C
7.	C	18.	B
8.	C	19.	D
9.	A	20.	D
10.	E	21.	E
11.	E	22.	B

Explanatory Material: Sentence Correction Sample Test Section 5

1. The psychologist William James believed that facial expressions not only provide a visible sign of an <u>emotion, actually contributing to the feeling itself.</u>

   (A) emotion, actually contributing to the feeling itself
   (B) emotion but also actually contributing to the feeling itself
   (C) emotion but also actually contribute to the feeling itself
   (D) emotion; they also actually contribute to the feeling of it
   (E) emotion; the feeling itself is also actually contributed to by them

Only C, the best answer, clearly and correctly states that James believed *facial expressions* perform <u>both</u> functions mentioned: the construction *James believed that facial expressions not only x* is completed by *but also y*, where *x* and *y* are grammatically parallel. In A, the absence of *but also y* results in a sentence fragment. In B, *but also contributing* is not parallel to *not only provide*. Choices D and E again lack *but also y*, instead introducing independent clauses that fail to associate the second part of the belief unequivocally with James. Also, the passive construction *is . . . contributed to by them* in E and the phrase *the feeling of it* in D are awkward in context.

2. Along with the drop in producer prices announced yesterday, the strong retail sales figures released today seem <u>like it is indicative that</u> the economy, although growing slowly, is not nearing a recession.

   (A) like it is indicative that
   (B) as if to indicate
   (C) to indicate that
   (D) indicative of
   (E) like an indication of

Choice C, the best answer, offers a concise and idiomatic grammatical sequence: the main verb *seem* is followed by an infinitive (*to indicate*), which is in turn followed by its direct object, a noun clause introduced by the relative pronoun *that*. In A, *seem* is followed by *like*, a preposition improperly used to introduce a clause. Also, *it* either disagrees in number with *figures* or lacks an antecedent altogether. In B, *as if* is introduced awkwardly and (in context) unidiomatically between *seem* and the infinitive. Also, with *that* omitted, B is ungrammatical. Choices D and E, with *of* substituted for *that*, are likewise ungrammatical: *of*, a preposition, can introduce a phrase, but not a clause.

3. The National Transportation Safety Board has recommended the use of fail-safe mechanisms on airliner cargo door latches <u>assuring the doors are properly closed</u> before takeoff and to prevent them from popping open in flight.

   (A) assuring the doors are properly closed
   (B) for the assurance of proper closing
   (C) assuring proper closure
   (D) to assure closing the doors properly
   (E) to assure that the doors are properly closed

The correct choice will include *to assure*, an infinitive parallel to *to prevent*. Thus, A, B, and C are disqualified. Moreover, the participial phrases in A and C (*assuring . . .*), easily construed as adjectives modifying *latches*, are confusing. Choices B and C are additionally faulty because, in omitting the noun *doors*, they fail both to specify what is being closed and to supply an antecedent for the pronoun *them*. D offers the necessary infinitive, but the gerund phrase *closing . . .* imprecisely refers to the act of closing the doors rather than to the condition of the closed doors. Choice E, with its idiomatic and precise noun clause, is the best answer.

4. Iguanas have been an important food source in Latin America since prehistoric times, and it is still prized as a game animal by the campesinos, who typically cook the meat in a heavily spiced stew.

   (A) it is still prized as a game animal
   (B) it is still prized as game animals
   (C) they are still prized as game animals
   (D) they are still prized as being a game animal
   (E) being still prized as a game animal

All nouns and pronouns grammatically referring back to the plural noun *Iguanas* must be plural. Choices A, B, D, and E all produce agreement problems by using singular forms (*it, animal*), leaving C the best choice. In addition, D is awkward and wordy, and E offers a participial phrase (*being . . .*) where the beginning of an independent clause is required.

5. The financial crash of October 1987 demonstrated that the world's capital markets are integrated more closely than never before and events in one part of the global village may be transmitted to the rest of the village — almost instantaneously.

   (A) integrated more closely than never before and
   (B) closely integrated more than ever before so
   (C) more closely integrated as never before while
   (D) more closely integrated than ever before and that
   (E) more than ever before closely integrated as

Choice D, the best answer, produces a clear sentence in which parallel structure (two clauses introduced by *that*) underscores meaning: *the crash demonstrated [1] that markets are integrated and [2] that events may be transmitted.* The other choices lack this parallel structure and contain additional faults. The phrases *more . . . than never* in A and *more . . . as never* in C are both unidiomatic: the idiom is *more than ever.* Choices B, C, and E end with *so, while,* and *as,* respectively: *and that* is needed so that two parallel clauses may be properly joined. Finally, B and E misplace the adverb *more,* which here should come just before *closely*: closer, not more frequent, integration of the world's capital markets is what facilitates the transmission of economic events.

6. New theories propose that catastrophic impacts of asteroids and comets may have caused reversals in the Earth's magnetic field, the onset of ice ages, splitting apart continents 80 million years ago, and great volcanic eruptions.

   (A) splitting apart continents
   (B) the splitting apart of continents
   (C) split apart continents
   (D) continents split apart
   (E) continents that were split apart

The word *splitting* must function as a noun to parallel the other items in the noun series of which it is part: *reversals, onset,* and *eruptions.* In B, the best choice, the definite article *the* clearly signifies that *splitting* is to be taken as a noun. In A, *splitting* introduces a verb phrase that breaks the parallelism of the noun series. In C, the verb *split* is similarly disruptive. Choice D, grammatically vague, resembles C if *split* is a verb and E if *split* is an adjective. In E, *continents* illogically replaces *the splitting* in the series: although the *impacts* in question may have caused continents to split, they did not cause those continents that were split apart 80 million years ago to materialize.

7. Wisconsin, Illinois, Florida, and Minnesota have begun to enforce statewide bans prohibiting landfills to accept leaves, brush, and grass clippings.

   (A) prohibiting landfills to accept leaves, brush, and grass clippings
   (B) prohibiting that landfills accept leaves, brush, and grass clippings
   (C) prohibiting landfills from accepting leaves, brush, and grass clippings
   (D) that leaves, brush, and grass clippings cannot be accepted in landfills
   (E) that landfills cannot accept leaves, brush, and grass clippings

Choice C is the best answer. Either of the following constructions would be idiomatic here: *x forbids y to do z* or *x prohibits y from doing z.* Choices A and B violate idiom; D and E introduce constructions that, in context, are faulty. First of all, both *bans that x cannot be done* and *bans that y cannot do x* are unidiomatic formulations. Secondly, the negative *cannot* after *bans* is illogical.

8. Even though the direct costs of malpractice disputes <u>amounts to a sum lower than</u> one percent of the $541 billion the nation spent on health care last year, doctors say fear of lawsuits plays a major role in health-care inflation.

(A) amounts to a sum lower
(B) amounts to less
(C) amounted to less
(D) amounted to lower
(E) amounted to a lower sum

The correct choice must feature a verb that agrees with the plural noun *costs* and refers to an action completed *last year* (past tense). The verb *amounts* in A and B fulfills neither condition, and *amounts to a sum* in A is redundant. The same redundancy occurs in E, and the construction *a lower sum than* is awkward and imprecise in the context of the sentence. In D, the adjective *lower* is erroneously used in place of the noun *less* as object of the preposition *to*. Choice C is best.

9. <u>Except for a concert performance that the composer himself staged</u> in 1911, Scott Joplin's ragtime opera *Treemonisha* was not produced until 1972, sixty-one years after its completion.

(A) Except for a concert performance that the composer himself staged
(B) Except for a concert performance with the composer himself staging it
(C) Besides a concert performance being staged by the composer himself
(D) Excepting a concert performance that the composer himself staged
(E) With the exception of a concert performance with the staging done by the composer himself

Choice A is best. In B, the participle *staging* inappropriately expresses ongoing rather than completed action, and the prepositional phrase containing this participle (*with . . . it*) is unidiomatic. Likewise, C uses the participle *being* inappropriately. In D, the use of *Excepting* in place of the preposition *Except for* is unidiomatic. Choice E is awkward and wordy.

10. Students in the metropolitan school district <u>lack math skills to such a large degree as to make it difficult to absorb them into a city economy becoming</u> ever more dependent on information-based industries.

(A) lack math skills to such a large degree as to make it difficult to absorb them into a city economy becoming
(B) lack math skills to a large enough degree that they will be difficult to absorb into a city's economy that becomes
(C) lack of math skills is so large as to be difficult to absorb them into a city's economy that becomes
(D) are lacking so much in math skills as to be difficult to absorb into a city's economy becoming
(E) are so lacking in math skills that it will be difficult to absorb them into a city economy becoming

In A, *lack* is modified by a wordy and awkward construction, *to such a large degree as to make it difficult to*. B is similarly flawed, and *to a large enough degree that* is unidiomatic. C is ungrammatical because it uses *lack* as a noun rather than as a verb: the phrase beginning *Students . . .* becomes a dangling element, and *them* refers illogically to *skills* rather than *students*. Additionally, A, B, and C fail to use one or both of the "-ing" forms *are lacking* and *becoming*; these forms are preferable to *lack* and *becomes* in describing progressive and ongoing conditions. D uses the "-ing" forms, but *so much . . . as to be difficult to absorb* is an awkward and unidiomatic verbal modifier. Choice E is best.

11. The diet of the ordinary Greek in classical times was largely vegetarian — vegetables, fresh cheese, oatmeal, and meal cakes, <u>and meat rarely</u>.

(A) and meat rarely
(B) and meat was rare
(C) with meat as rare
(D) meat a rarity
(E) with meat as a rarity

The best answer here must qualify the statement made in the main clause, *The diet . . . was largely vegetarian*: it cannot be treated as part of the list of vegetarian foods. In other words, the best answer must logically and grammatically attach to the main clause when the list is omitted. Choice A fails this test: *The diet . . . was largely vegetarian, and meat rarely*. D fails also, because it lacks a function word such as *with* to link it to the main clause. The wording of choice B is imprecise and ambiguous — for example, it could mean that meat was scarce, or that it was not well done or medium. Choice C is unidiomatic. Clearly phrased, grammatically linked, and idiomatically sound, choice E is best.

12. **An inventory equal to 90 days sales is <u>as much as even</u> the strongest businesses carry, and then only as a way to anticipate higher prices or ensure against shortages.**

   (A) as much as even
   (B) so much as even
   (C) even so much as
   (D) even as much that
   (E) even so much that

The idiomatic form for this type of comparison is *as much as*. Thus, choice A is best. The phrase *so much as* is used unidiomatically in choices B and C; *so much as* is considered idiomatic if it is preceded by a negative, as in "She left not so much as a trace." In choices C, D, and E, *even* is misplaced so that it no longer clearly modifies *the strongest businesses*. Moreover, the use of *that* rather than *as* is unidiomatic in choices D and E.

13. **The decision by one of the nation's largest banks to admit to $3 billion in potential losses on foreign loans could mean less lending by commercial banks to developing countries and <u>increasing the pressure</u> on multigovernment lenders to supply the funds.**

   (A) increasing the pressure
   (B) the increasing pressure
   (C) increased pressure
   (D) the pressure increased
   (E) the pressure increasing

The best answer will complete the phrase *could mean less lending* with a construction that is parallel to *less lending*. Here *less* is an adjective modifying *lending*, which functions as a noun in naming a banking activity. C, the best choice, parallels this *adjective + noun* construction with *increased* [adjective] *pressure* [noun]. Choice A violates parallelism by introducing a phrase in place of the *adjective + noun* construction. Choices D and E also fail to parallel the *adjective + noun* construction. In choice B, the definite article *the* needlessly suggests that some previously mentioned type of pressure is being referred to, and *increasing* implies without warrant that the increase has been continuing for some indefinite period of time, not that it occurs as a consequence of the bank's decision.

14. **Downzoning, zoning that typically results in the reduction of housing density, allows for more open space in areas where <u>little water or services exist.</u>**

   (A) little water or services exist
   (B) little water or services exists
   (C) few services and little water exists
   (D) there is little water or services available
   (E) there are few services and little available water

The adjective *little* modifies "mass nouns" (e.g., *water)*, which refer to some undifferentiated quantity; the adjective *few* modifies "count nouns" (e.g., *services*), which refer to groups made up of distinct members that can be considered individually. Hence, choices A, B, and D are incorrect because *little* cannot

properly modify *services*. Also, since *water* and *services* are being discussed as a pair, they should logically be treated as a compound subject requiring a plural verb; thus, the singular verbs *exists* (in B and C) and *is* (in D) are wrong. Choice E is best: the plural verb *are* is used, and *few* correctly modifies *services*.

15. **Reporting that one of <u>its many problems had been the recent</u> extended sales slump in women's apparel, the seven-store retailer said it would start a three-month liquidation sale in all of its stores.**

   (A) its many problems had been the recent
   (B) its many problems has been the recently
   (C) its many problems is the recently
   (D) their many problems is the recent
   (E) their many problems had been the recent

Choice A is best: the singular pronoun *its* agrees in number with the singular noun referent *retailer*; the past perfect verb form *had been* is used appropriately to refer to action completed prior to the action of the simple past tense *said*; and the adjective *recent* correctly modifies the noun phrase *extended sales slump*. The adverb *recently* in choices B and C distorts the meaning of the sentence by illogically suggesting that what was recent was only the extension of the slump, and not the slump itself. In choices D and E, the plural pronoun *their* does not agree with the singular noun *retailer*.

16. **Legislation in the Canadian province of Ontario requires of both public and private employers <u>that pay be the same for jobs historically held by women as for jobs requiring comparable skill that are</u> usually held by men.**

   (A) that pay be the same for jobs historically held by women as for jobs requiring comparable skill that are
   (B) that pay for jobs historically held by women should be the same as for a job requiring comparable skills
   (C) to pay the same in jobs historically held by women as in jobs of comparable skill that are
   (D) to pay the same regardless of whether a job was historically held by women or is one demanding comparable skills
   (E) to pay as much for jobs historically held by women as for a job demanding comparable skills

Choice A is best. In choice B, *should* is illogical after *requires*, or at least unnecessary, and so is better omitted; in choices B and E, *job* does not agree in number with *jobs*; and in choices B, D, and E, the wording illogically describes the *comparable skills* rather than the *jobs* as being "usually held by men." Choices C, D, and E produce the ungrammatical construction *requires of . . . employers to pay*, in which *of* makes the phrase incorrect. In C, the use of *in* rather than *for* is unidiomatic, and *jobs of comparable skill* confusedly suggests that the jobs rather than the workers possess the skills. In D, the phrase beginning *regardless . . .* is awkward and wordy in addition to being illogical.

17. It has been estimated that the annual cost to the United States of illiteracy in lost industrial output and tax revenues is at least $20 billion a year.

   (A) the annual cost to the United States of illiteracy in lost industrial output and tax revenues is at least $20 billion a year
   (B) the annual cost of illiteracy to the United States is at least $20 billion a year because of lost industrial output and tax revenues
   (C) illiteracy costs the United States at least $20 billion a year in lost industrial output and tax revenues
   (D) $20 billion a year in lost industrial output and tax revenues is the annual cost to the United States of illiteracy
   (E) lost industrial output and tax revenues cost the United States at least $20 billion a year because of illiteracy

In choices A, B, and D, the combined use of *annual* and *a year* is redundant. Choices A, D, and E are awkward and confused because other constructions intrude within the phrase *cost . . . of illiteracy*: for greatest clarity, *cost* should be followed immediately by a phrase (e.g., *of illiteracy*) that identifies the nature of the cost. Choice E is particularly garbled in reversing cause and effect, saying that it is lost output and revenues rather than illiteracy that costs the United States over $20 billion a year. Choice B is wordy and awkward, and idiom requires *in* rather than *because of* to introduce a phrase identifying the constituents of the $20 billion loss. Concise, logically worded, and idiomatic, choice C is best.

18. Egyptians are credited as having pioneered embalming methods as long ago as 2650 B.C.

   (A) as having
   (B) with having
   (C) to have
   (D) as the ones who
   (E) for being the ones who

In English it is idiomatic usage to *credit* someone *with* having done something. Hence, only choice B, the best answer, is idiomatic. The verb *credited* would have to be changed to *regarded* for choices A or D to be idiomatic, to *believed* for choice C to be idiomatic, and to *given credit* for choice E to be idiomatic.

19. Domestic automobile manufacturers have invested millions of dollars into research to develop cars more gasoline-efficient even than presently on the road.

   (A) into research to develop cars more gasoline-efficient even than presently on the road
   (B) into research for developing even more gasoline-efficient cars on the road than at present
   (C) for research for cars to be developed that are more gasoline-efficient even than presently the road
   (D) in research to develop cars even more gasoline-efficient than those at present on the road
   (E) in research for developing cars that are even more gasoline-efficient than presently on the road

Choice D, the best answer, uses the preposition *than* to compare two clearly specified and grammatically parallel terms, the cars the manufacturers hope to develop and *those at present on the road*. In A, the phrase *more gasoline-efficient . . . than presently on the road* does not identify the second term of the comparison. In B, the misuse of modifying phrases produces an ambiguous and awkward statement: *even more gasoline-efficient cars* could refer either to more cars that are efficient or to cars that are more efficient. Choices B, C, and E all use *research for [verb]* where the idiom requires *research to [verb]*. In addition, C awkwardly separates *even* from *more*, and C and E again fail to indicate the second term of the comparison.

20. Visitors to the park have often looked up into the leafy canopy and saw monkeys sleeping on the branches, whose arms and legs hang like socks on a clothesline.

   (A) saw monkeys sleeping on the branches, whose arms and legs hang
   (B) saw monkeys sleeping on the branches, whose arms and legs were hanging
   (C) saw monkeys sleeping on the branches, with arms and legs hanging
   (D) seen monkeys sleeping on the branches, with arms and legs hanging
   (E) seen monkeys sleeping on the branches, whose arms and legs have hung

Choices A, B, and C use *have . . . saw* where *have . . . seen* is required. Choices A, B, and E awkwardly separate the relative clause beginning *whose arms and legs . . .* from *monkeys*, the noun it modifies. Choices A and E also confusingly use the present tense *hang* and the present perfect *have hung*, respectively; neither verb conveys clearly that, at the time the monkeys were spotted sleeping, their arms and legs were hanging in the manner described. Choice D, the best answer, not only forms a correct and clear sentence by supplying the present perfect verb *have . . . seen*, but also solves the problem of the *whose . . .* clause by using the appropriately placed adverbial phrase *with arms and legs hanging . . .* to modify *sleeping*.

21. From the bark of the paper birch tree the Menomini crafted a canoe about twenty feet long and two feet wide, with small ribs and rails of cedar, which could carry four persons or eight hundred pounds of <u>baggage so light</u> that a person could easily portage it around impeding rapids.

   (A) baggage so light
   (B) baggage being so light
   (C) baggage, yet being so light
   (D) baggage, and so light
   (E) baggage yet was so light

Choice E, the best answer, states that although the canoe could transport cargo of considerable weight, it was light: *a canoe . . . which could carry . . . yet was . . . light . . . .* Here, the conjunction *yet* is appropriately and correctly used to link two verb phrases. Choices A and B do not use *yet* with a verb parallel to *could carry* and thus fail to express this contrast. Furthermore, both place adjectival constructions after *baggage*, illogically stating that the *eight hundred pounds of baggage*, rather than the canoe, was light. Choice C supplies *yet* but ungrammatically uses the participle *being* where *was* is required. Similarly, D omits the necessary verb after *and*; and here again, the use of *and* rather than *yet* fails to express the contrast.

22. From the time of its defeat by the Germans in 1940 until its liberation in 1944, France was a bitter and divided country; a kind of civil war raged in the Vichy government <u>between those who wanted to collaborate with the Nazis with those who opposed</u> them.

   (A) between those who wanted to collaborate with the Nazis with those who opposed
   (B) between those who wanted to collaborate with the Nazis and those who opposed
   (C) between those wanting to collaborate with the Nazis with those opposing
   (D) among those who wanted to collaborate with the Nazis and those who opposed
   (E) among those wanting to collaborate with the Nazis with those opposing

Choice B, the best answer, correctly uses the construction *between x and y* to describe the conflict between two opposing groups. Choices A and C each use the ungrammatical *between x with y*. Choices D and E incorrectly use the preposition *among* in place of *between*: *among* is used to describe the relationship of more than two elements, as in "the tension among residents"; *between* is generally used to describe the relationship of two entities. Choice E also repeats the *with* error.

8 Analytical Writing Assessment

In this section of the GMAT, you are to write a 30-minute response to each of two separate writing tasks. One is called "Analysis of an Issue," and the other is called "Analysis of an Argument." The Analysis of an Issue task requires you to consider a given issue or opinion and then explain your point of view on the subject by citing relevant reasons and/or examples based on your experience, observations, or reading. The Analysis of an Argument task requires you to read a brief argument, analyze the reasoning behind the argument, and then write a critique of the argument. The answer documents for each task allow for writing in pencil on three sides of letter-sized (8½ by 11 inch) paper.

The following pages include sample questions exemplifying each of the two writing tasks and actual responses to each of these questions. In each case, the responses illustrate three selected points on the scoring scale, which runs from 6, the highest score, to 1, the lowest (the score of zero [0] is reserved for responses that are illegible or not written on the assigned topic). The three selected points illustrated are 6, 4, and 2, corresponding, respectively, to an outstanding response, an adequate response, and a seriously flawed response. Also included are the general scoring guides used by the scorers in evaluating the responses as well as a specific explanation following each pretest response showing why that response received a particular score.

Test-Taking Strategies for the Analytical Writing Assessment

General

1. Read the question carefully. Make sure you have taken all parts of a question into account before you begin responding to it.

2. Do not start to write immediately. Take a few minutes to think about the question and plan a response before you begin writing. You may find it helpful to write a brief outline or jot down some ideas in the space provided in the test book. Take care to organize your ideas and develop them fully, but leave time to reread your response and make any revisions that you think would improve it.

Analysis of an Issue

1. Although many "analysis of an issue" questions require you to take a position, you should be careful about the way in which you go about doing so. Do not leap to a position: what is being assessed is your ability to think and write critically. Try to show that you recognize and understand the complexities of an issue or an opinion before you take a position. Consider the issue from different perspectives, and think about your own experiences or reading related to the issue. Work your way to a position rather than simply announcing one.

2. While it is essential to illustrate and develop your ideas by means of examples drawn from your observations, experiences, and reading, it is not a good idea simply to catalogue examples. One or two well-chosen, well-developed examples are much more effective than a long list of them.

Analysis of an Argument

1. Your job here is to analyze and critique a line of thinking or reasoning. Get used to asking yourself questions like the following: What questionable assumptions might underlie the thinking? What alternative explanations might be given? What counterexamples might be raised? What additional evidence might prove useful in fully and fairly evaluating the reasoning?

2. Use the opportunity of discussing alternative explanations or counterexamples to introduce illustrations and examples drawn from your observations, experiences, or reading. Again, do not simply list examples; develop them.

3. Your finished response to this writing task should not read like an outline; it should, rather, read like a discussion with full sentences, a coherent organizational scheme, logical transitions between points, and appropriately introduced and developed examples.

ANALYSIS OF AN ISSUE

Time — 30 minutes

Directions: In this section, you will need to analyze the issue presented below and explain your views on it. The question has no "correct" answer. Instead, you should consider various perspectives as you develop your own position on the issue.

Read the statement and the instructions that follow it, and then make any notes in your test booklet that will help you plan your response. Begin writing your response on the separate answer document. Make sure that you use the answer document that goes with this writing task.

"People often complain that products are not made to last. They feel that making products that wear out fairly quickly wastes both natural and human resources. What they fail to see, however, is that such manufacturing practices keep costs down for the consumer and stimulate demand."

Which do you find more compelling, the complaint about products that do not last or the response to it? Explain your position using relevant reasons and/or examples from your own experience, observations, or reading.

NOTES

Use the space below or on the facing page to plan your response. Any writing on these pages will not be evaluated.

GMAT SCORING GUIDE: ANALYSIS OF AN ISSUE

SCORE

6   OUTSTANDING

A 6 paper presents a cogent, well-articulated analysis of the complexities of the issue and demonstrates mastery of the elements of effective writing.

A typical paper in this category

— explores ideas and develops a position on the issue with insightful reasons and/or persuasive examples
— is clearly well organized
— demonstrates superior control of language, including diction and syntactic variety
— demonstrates superior facility with the conventions (grammar, usage, and mechanics) of standard written English but may have minor flaws

5   STRONG

A 5 paper presents a well-developed analysis of the complexities of the issue and demonstrates a strong control of the elements of effective writing.

A typical paper in this category

— develops a position on the issue with well-chosen reasons and/or examples
— is generally well organized
— demonstrates clear control of language, including diction and syntactic variety
— demonstrates facility with the conventions of standard written English but may have minor flaws

4   ADEQUATE

A 4 paper presents a competent analysis of the issue and demonstrates adequate control of the elements of writing.

A typical paper in this category

— develops a position on the issue with relevant reasons and/or examples
— is adequately organized
— demonstrates adequate control of language, including diction and syntax, but may lack syntactic variety
— displays control of the conventions of standard written English but may have some flaws

3 LIMITED

A 3 paper demonstrates some competence in its analysis of the issue and in its control of the elements of writing but is clearly flawed.

A typical paper in this category exhibits *one or more* of the following characteristics:

— is vague or limited in developing a position on the issue
— is poorly organized
— is weak in the use of relevant reasons or examples
— uses language imprecisely and/or lacks sentence variety
— contains occasional major errors or frequent minor errors in grammar, usage, and mechanics

---

2 SERIOUSLY FLAWED

A 2 paper demonstrates serious weaknesses in analytical writing skills.

A typical paper in this category exhibits *one or more* of the following characteristics:

— is unclear or seriously limited in presenting or developing a position on the issue
— is disorganized
— provides few, if any, relevant reasons or examples
— has serious and frequent problems in the use of language and sentence structure
— contains numerous errors in grammar, usage, or mechanics that interfere with meaning

---

1 FUNDAMENTALLY DEFICIENT

A 1 paper demonstrates fundamental deficiencies in analytical writing skills.

A typical paper in this category exhibits *one or more* of the following characteristics:

— provides little evidence of the ability to develop or organize a coherent response to the topic
— has severe and persistent errors in language and sentence structure
— contains a pervasive pattern of errors in grammar, usage, and mechanics that severely interferes with meaning

---

0 Any paper that is totally illegible or obviously not written on the assigned topic receives a score of zero.
NR Any blank paper or nonverbal response receives a score of NR.

Many people feel that products are not made to last, and correspondingly, many natural and human resources are wasted. On the other hand, it can be noted that such manufacturing practices keep costs down and hence stimulate demand. In this discussion, I shall present arguments favoring the former statement and refuting the latter statement.

Products that are not made to last waste a great deal of natural and human resources. The exact amount of wasted natural resources depends on the specific product. For example in the automobile industry, the Yugo is the classic example of an underpriced vehicle that was not made to last. Considering that the average Yugo had (not "has" since they are no longer produced!) a life expectancy of two years and 25,000 miles, it was a terrible waste.

Automobile industry standards today create vehicles that are warrantied for about five years and 50,000 miles. By producing cheap Yugos that last less than half as long as most cars are warrantied, the Yugo producer is wasting valuable natural resources. These same resources could be used by Ford or Toyota to produce an Escort or Tercel that will last twice as long, thereby reducing the usage of natural resources by a factor of two.

Human resources in this example are also wasteful. On the production side, manufacturers of a poor quality automobile, like the Yugo, get no personal or profession satisfaction from the fact that their product is the worst automobile in the United States. This knowledge adversely affects the productivity of the Yugo workers.

Conversely, the workers at the Saturn plants constantly receive positive feedback on their successful products. Saturn prides itself with its reputation for quality and innovation — as is seen in its recent massive recall to fix a defect. This recall was handled so well that Saturn's image was actually bolstered. Had a recall occurred at a Yugo plant, the bad situation would have become even worse.

Another factor in the human resources area is the reaction by the consumer. A great deal of human resources have been wasted by Yugo owners waiting for the dreaded tow truck to show up to haul away the Yugo carcass. Any vehicle owner who is uncertain of his/her vehicle's performance at 7 AM as he/she is about to drive to work, senses a great deal of despair. This is a great waste of human resources for the consumer.

While the consumer senses the waste of natural and human resources in a poor quality product, so does the manufacturer. People who argue that low quality manufacturing processes keep costs low for the consumer and hence stimulate demand should look at the Yugo example. In the mid-1980's the Yugo was by far the cheapest car in the United States at $3995. By 1991, the Yugo was no longer sold here and was synonymous with the word "lemon."

EXPLANATION OF SCORE — 6

The response above is ambitious and somewhat unusual in its focusing on just one example, the lesson of the now defunct Yugo. Responses, especially outstanding ones, typically discuss several different examples that build support for the writer's position on the issue. This sample response, then, should not be taken as necessarily endorsing a one-example writing strategy. What it *does* serve to underscore is how much is to be gained by *developing*, not just *listing*, examples. The strength of the response lies in the organized and thorough way in which it explores the related aspects of the example it cites. The clear organizational scheme (two major points, with the second point subdivided) is readily apparent: Yugo's substandard cars (1) waste natural resources and (2) waste human resources by (a) destroying worker morale and productivity and (b) inconveniencing and upsetting customers. The persuasiveness of the writer's thinking is especially evident in the discussion of the second major point, the waste of human resources. Here the writer not only considers customers as well as workers but also introduces the matter of the Saturn recall in order to show, by contrast with the case of Yugo, how a superior product, satisfied workers, and a company image good for marketing are interrelated.

The response complements its outstanding organizational clarity and thorough development with some syntactic variety and an occasional rhetorical flair (e. g., the image of the despairing Yugo owner waiting for "the dreaded tow truck . . . to haul away the Yugo carcass" in paragraph 6). It is important to point out, however, that the writing is not perfect. For one thing, the opening paragraph is essentially a repeat of the question. In addition, the writing is not — and is not expected to be — entirely free from minor flaws (e. g., "profession satisfaction" [paragraph 4] should obviously be "professional satisfaction," and "Saturn prides itself with" [paragraph 5] should be "Saturn prides itself in"). Nevertheless, these occasional flaws are not serious enough to detract from the general impression that this is an excellent response to the question.

I find the response to the complaint more compelling. Although the complaint is valid, it is most often the case the building a product to last forever will indeed cost more than the average consumer is willing to pay. Creating such a product would require more materials and/or more heavy-duty wear resistant materials which inherently are more expensive. Another factor that would drive costs up is the fact that demand for products would decrease. The demand would decrease since people do not have to replace old products with new product as often. With the increased variable costs for materials combined with a reduction in the production volume associated with lower demand, manufacturers must raise prices to break even or maintain the current level of profits.

Although a few producers may make products to last, it is understandable how these companies can be driven out of existence. If a new competitor enters the market with a similar product that has a shorter life but a substantially lower price, then they will probably steal major portions of the other company's market share. The effects depend heavily upon the consumers' perception of quality and what the customers requirements from the product actually are.

For example, consumers may decide between two types of automobiles. One car may be built to last a long time but may not have the performance or be as comfortable as another car that is cheaper. So most consumers would purchase the cheaper car even though it may not last as long as the heavy-duty car. Consumers may not realize that the more expensive car is of higher quality in the sense that it will last longer and will not be willing to pay the extra cost.

Consumer decisions also depend on what consumers are actually looking for in a product. Consumers typically get tired of driving the same car for many years and want to buy new cars fairly often. This tendency forces producers to keep costs low enough to allow low enough prices for people to buy cars often. People don't want cars to last forever.

In conclusion, producers are in the situation that they're in due to external forces from the consumers. Producers must compete and they have found the best way satisfy the majority of the consumers.

EXPLANATION OF SCORE — 4

This response presents a competent analysis of the issue. It develops its position by explaining some of the ways in which the factors mentioned in the question — manufacturing costs and consumer demand — are affected by making products that do not last very long. By way of illustration, the response cites the example of consumers choosing automobiles. Although this example is relevant, it lacks specificity: no actual types of cars are described in terms of the key issue, durability, and no contrast between more and less durable types is developed to prove a point.

Although the response is competently organized and therefore generally easy to follow in its main lines, its clarity is marred by an awkward transition from the second paragraph to the third. The main idea of the second paragraph is that many consumers will abandon a made-to-last expensive product in favor of a substantially cheaper version with a shorter life. But the last sentence of this paragraph, a sentence that is signally unclear, marks an ill-prepared-for change in the direction of the entire response. "The effects" (the word, used loosely and unclearly, seems to refer to the consumer's final decisions about what to buy) are seen to depend not only upon the simple choice between cost and quality but also upon a complex of new forces — aspects of consumer psychology and "requirements" (consumer needs?) — that now suddenly and puzzlingly face the reader. Although the third and fourth paragraphs go on to develop the writer's views about these new forces, the reader never quite recovers from the sense that the response has abruptly changed course. What is more, the consideration of consumer psychology and "requirements" can cause the writer to stray into side issues. For example, pointing out that customers may choose a car on the basis of performance and comfort rather than durability has no direct bearing on the complaint that products are not made to last.

The wording of this response is generally appropriate, although the language is occasionally awkward, as in "keep costs low enough to allow low enough prices" (paragraph 4) and "producers are in the situation that they're in" (paragraph 5).

I find the response better than the complaint of people. The response seems to originate without much thought involved. It is more of an emotional complaint than one anchored in logic or thought. Yes, it is a waste of human resources but that is without consideration to the benefits: lower costs and stimulated demand. Thus, the response fails to recognize the benefits.

The strength of the response is that it forces the reader to reconsider the complaint. It adds a new dimension to the argument. It, however, fails to adress the issue of wasting human resources. Does this mean the responder agrees with the notion of wasting resources.

In all actuality both the response and complaint as ineffective. The complaint doesn't recognize or address the benefits, like the response doesn't address the issue of wasting resources. The response, however, does bring in a new dimension and thus weakens the argument of the complaint.

EXPLANATION OF SCORE — 2

In this piece of writing, the writer's purpose seems to waver between defending "the response" against "the complaint" and weighing the relative strengths and limitations of both. In addition, the writer offers no new reasons or specific examples and so ends up merely repeating assertions made in "the complaint" and "the response."

The writing is marked throughout by vagueness. The writer's decision to adopt the topic's terms "response" and "complaint" as a convenient shorthand for the two positions articulated leads immediately to a confusing lack of specificity, compounded in the first paragraph by the fact that the two terms are mixed up (e.g., "response" in the second and the fifth sentences is meant to refer to "complaint"). The first paragraph is made even more confusing because the pronouns *it* and *that* lack antecedents in the sentence "Yes, it is a waste of human resources but that is without consideration to the benefits."

The general lack of clarity is aggravated by errors in conventional English grammar and usage, most of them concentrated in paragraph 3. The first sentence begins with a unidiomatic phrase ("In all actuality") and lacks a verb ("both the response and complaint as ineffective"). The second sentence incorrectly uses *like* instead of *just as*: "The complaint doesn't recognize or address . . . like the response doesn't address." In short, the writing fits the description of seriously flawed prose in the scoring guide: it displays "serious and frequent problems in the use of language and sentence structure."

ANALYSIS OF AN ARGUMENT

Time — 30 minutes

Directions: In this section you will be asked to write a critique of the argument presented below. *You are NOT being asked to present your own views on the subject.*

Read the argument and the instructions that follow it, and then make any notes in your test booklet that will help you plan your response. Begin writing your response on the separate answer sheet. Make sure that you use the answer sheet that goes with this writing task.

The following appeared as part of an article in a daily newspaper:

"The computerized on-board warning system that will be installed in commercial airliners will virtually solve the problem of midair plane collisions. One plane's warning system can receive signals from another's transponder — a radio set that signals a plane's course — in order to determine the likelihood of a collision and recommend evasive action."

Discuss how well reasoned you find this argument. In your discussion be sure to analyze the line of reasoning and the use of evidence in the argument. For example, you may need to consider what questionable assumptions underlie the thinking and what alternative explanations or counterexamples might weaken the conclusion. You can also discuss what sort of evidence would strengthen or refute the argument, what changes in the argument would make it more logically sound, and what, if anything, would help you better evaluate its conclusion.

NOTES

Use the space below or on the facing page to plan your response. Any writing on this page will not be evaluated.

GMAT SCORING GUIDE: ANALYSIS OF AN ARGUMENT

SCORE

6   OUTSTANDING

A 6 paper presents a cogent, well-articulated critique of the argument and demonstrates mastery of the elements of effective writing.

A typical paper in this category

— clearly identifies and insightfully analyzes important features of the argument
— develops ideas cogently, organizes them logically, and connects them with clear transitions
— effectively supports the main points of the critique
— demonstrates control of language, including diction and syntactic variety
— demonstrates facility with the conventions of standard written English but may have minor flaws

5   STRONG

A 5 paper presents a well-developed critique of the argument and demonstrates good control of the elements of effective writing.

A typical paper in this category

— clearly identifies important features of the argument and analyzes them in a generally thoughtful way
— develops ideas clearly, organizes them logically, and connects them with appropriate transitions
— sensibly supports the main points of the critique
— demonstrates control of language, including diction and syntactic variety
— demonstrates facility with the conventions of standard written English but may have occasional flaws

4   ADEQUATE

A 4 paper presents a competent critique of the argument and demonstrates adequate control of the elements of writing.

A typical paper in this category

— identifies and capably analyzes important features of the argument
— develops and organizes ideas satisfactorily but may not connect them with transitions
— supports the main points of the critique
— demonstrates sufficient control of language to convey ideas with reasonable clarity
— generally follows the conventions of standard written English but may have some flaws

3 LIMITED

A 3 paper demonstrates some competence in its critique of the argument and in its control of the elements of writing but is plainly flawed.

A typical paper in this category exhibits *one or more* of the following characteristics:

— does not identify or analyze most of the important features of the argument, although some analysis is present
— is limited in the logical development and organization of ideas
— offers support of little relevance and value for points of the critique
— does not convey meaning clearly
— contains occasional major errors or frequent minor errors in grammar, usage, and mechanics

---

2 SERIOUSLY FLAWED

A 2 paper demonstrates serious weaknesses in analytical writing skills.

A typical paper in this category exhibits *one or more* of the following characteristics:

— does not identify or analyze the main features of the argument, but may instead present the writer's own views on the subject
— does not develop ideas or is disorganized
— provides little, if any, relevant or reasonable support
— has serious and frequent problems in the use of language and in sentence structure
— contains numerous errors in grammar, usage, and mechanics that interfere with meaning

---

1 FUNDAMENTALLY DEFICIENT

A 1 paper demonstrates fundamental deficiencies in analytical writing skills.

A typical paper in this category exhibits *more than one* of the following characteristics:

— provides little evidence of the ability to understand and analyze the argument
— provides little evidence of the ability to develop an organized response
— has severe and persistent errors in language and sentence structure
— contains a pervasive pattern of errors in grammar, usage, and mechanics that results in incoherence

---

0   Any paper that is totally illegible or obviously not written on the assigned topic receives a score of zero.
NR Any blank paper or nonverbal response receives a score of NR.

The argument that this warning system will virtually solve the problem of midair plane collisions omits some important concerns that must be addressed to substantiate the argument. The statement that follows the description of what this warning system will do simply describes the system and how it operates. This alone does not constitute a logical argument in favor of the warning system, and it certainly does not provide support or proof of the main argument.

Most conspicuously, the argument does not address the cause of the problem of midair plane collisions, the use of the system by pilots and flight specialists, or who is involved in the midair plane collisions. First, the argument assumes that the cause of the problem is that the planes' courses, the likelihood of collisions, and actions to avoid collisions are unknown or inaccurate. In a weak attempt to support its claim, the argument describes a system that makes all of these things accurately known. But if the cause of the problem of midair plane collisions is that pilots are not paying attention to their computer systems or flight operations, the warning system will not solve the collision problem. Second, the argument never addresses the interface between individuals and the system and how this will affect the warning system's objective of obliterating the problem of collisions. If the pilot or flight specialist does not conform to what the warning system suggests, midair collisions will not be avoided. Finally, if planes other than commercial airliners are involved in the collisions, the problem of these collisions can not be solved by a warning system that will not be installed on non-commercial airliners. The argument also does not address what would happen in the event that the warning system collapses, fails, or does not work properly.

Because the argument leaves out several key issues, it is not sound or persuasive. If it included the items discussed above instead of solely explaining what the system supposedly does, the argument would have been more thorough and convincing.

EXPLANATION OF SCORE — 6

This response is, as the scoring guide requires of a 6, "cogent" and "well articulated": all the points made not only bear directly on the argument to be analyzed but also contribute to a single, integrated development of the writer's critique. The writer begins by making the controlling point that a mere *description* of the warning system's mode of operation cannot serve as a true *argument* proving the system's effectiveness, since the description overlooks several major considerations. The writer then identifies these considerations — what causes midair collisions, how pilots will actually use the commercial airline warning system, what kinds of airplanes are typically involved in midair collisions — and, citing appropriate counterexamples (e.g., what if pilots do not pay attention to their instruments?), explains fully how each oversight undermines the conclusion that the warning system will virtually eliminate midair plane collisions.

Throughout, the writer complements the logically organized development of this critique with good, clear prose that demonstrates the ability not only to control language and vary sentence structure but also to express ideas forcibly (e.g., "the argument never addresses the interface between individuals and the system"). Of course, as in any response written under time constraints, occasional minor flaws can be found. For example, "the argument assumes that the cause of the problem is that the planes' courses, the likelihood of collisions, and actions to avoid collisions are unknown or inaccurate" is wordy and imprecise: how can a *course*, a *likelihood*, or *actions* be *inaccurate*? But flaws such as these, minor and infrequent, do not interfere with the overall clarity and forcefulness of this outstanding response.

The argument is not logically convincing. It does not state whether all planes can receive signals from each other. It does not state whether planes constantly receive signals. If they only receive signals once every certain time interval, collisions will not definitely be prevented. Further if they receive a signal right before they are about to crash, they cannot avoid each other.

The main flaw in the argument is that it assumes that the two planes, upon receiving each other's signals, will know which evasive action to take. For example, the two planes could be going towards each other and then receive the signals. If one turns at an angle to the left and the other turns at an angle to the right, the two planes will still crash. Even if they receive an updated signal, they will not have time to avoid each other.

The following argument would be more sound and persuasive. The new warning system will solve the problem of midair plane collisions. Each plane will receive constant, continual signals from each other. If the two planes are headed in a direction where they will crash, the system will coordinate the signals, and tell one plane to go one way, and the other plane to go another way. The new system will ensure that the two planes will turn in different directions so they don't crash by trying to prevent the original crash. In addition, the two planes will be able to see themselves and the other on a computer screen, to aid in the evasive action.

EXPLANATION OF SCORE — 4

This response competently cites a number of deficiencies in the argument presented: the information given about the nature of the signals sent and received and the evasive action recommended does not warrant the conclusion that the on-board warning system "will virtually solve the problem of midair plane collisions." However, in discussing these insufficiencies in the argument, the response reveals an unevenness in the quality of its reasoning. For example, while it is perfectly legitimate to point out that the argument assumes too much and says too little about the evasive action that will be recommended by the warning system, it is farfetched to suggest that the system might be so poorly designed as to route two approaching airplanes to the same spot. Likewise, while it is fair to question the effectiveness of a warning signal about which the argument says so little, it is not reasonable to assume that the system would be designed to space signals so far apart that they would prove useless. Rather than invent implausibly bad versions of the warning system to prove that it might be ineffective, a stronger response would analyze unexplored possibilities inherent in the information that is given — e.g., the possibility that pilots might not be able to respond quickly and effectively to the radio signals the argument says they will receive when the new system is installed. The "more sound and persuasive argument" in the last paragraph, while an improvement on the original, continues to overlook this possibility and also assumes that other types of aircraft without transponders will pose no problems.

The organization of ideas, while generally sound, is sometimes weakened by needless repetition of the same points, as in sentences 4 and 5 of the last paragraph. The writing contains minor instances of awkwardness (e.g., "Each plane will receive constant, continual signals from each other" in paragraph 3), but is free of flaws that make understanding difficult. However, though the writing is generally clean and clear, the syntax does not show much variety. A few sentences begin with "if" clauses, but almost all the rest, even those that begin with a transitional phrase such as "for example" or "in addition," conform to a "subject, verb, complement" pattern. The first paragraph, in which the second and third sentences begin the same way ("It does not state"), is particularly repetitious.

This argument has no information about air collisions. I think most cases happen in new airports because the air traffic is heavy. In this case sound airport control could solve the problem.

I think this argument is logically reasonable. Its assumption is that plane collisions are caused by planes that don't know each others positions. So pilots can do nothing, if they know each others position through the system it will solve the problem.

If it can provide evidence the problem is lack of knowledge of each others positions, it will be more sound and persuasive.

More information about air collisions is helpful, (the reason for air collisions).

EXPLANATION OF SCORE — 2

This response is seriously flawed in several ways. First of all, it has very little substance. The writer appears to make only one point — that while it seems reasonable to assume that midair collisions would be less likely if pilots were sure of each other's positions, readers cannot adequately judge this assumption without more information about where, why, and how such collisions occur. This point, furthermore, is neither explained by a single reason beyond what is given in the topic nor supported by a single example. Legitimate though it is, it cannot, alone and undeveloped, serve as an adequate response to the argument.

Aside from being undeveloped, the response is confusing. At the outset, it seems to be critical of the argument. The writer begins by pointing to the inadequacy of the information given; then speculates, without evidence, that "most cases happen in new airports"; and then suggests that the problem should be addressed by improving "airport control," not (it is implied) by installing on-board warning systems. After criticizing the argument in the first paragraph, the writer confusingly seems to endorse it in the second. Then, in the remainder of the response, the writer returns to a critical stance.

The general lack of coherence is reflected in the serious and frequent writing problems that make meaning hard to determine — e.g., the elliptical and ungrammatical "So pilots can do nothing, if they know each others position through the system it will solve the problem" (paragraph 2) or "If it can provide evidence the problem is lack of knowledge of each others positions, it will be more sound and persuasive" (paragraph 3). The prose suffers from a variety of basic errors in grammar, usage, and mechanics.

9 Three Authentic Graduate Management Admission Tests

The tests that follow are Graduate Management Admission Tests that have been slightly modified. Form A was administered in March 1995, Form B in June 1995, and Form C in June 1993. The actual test books contained seven multiple-choice sections, one of which consisted of trial questions that were not counted in the scoring. Those trial questions have been omitted from these tests. Test Forms A and B represent the current format of the GMAT, which was revised in October 1994. At that time, the Analytical Writing Assessment (AWA) was added to the test and the multiple-choice sections were shortened. Test Form C is in the old format, with no AWA sections and with longer multiple-choice sections. Although this format of the test is no longer offered, we included this test for those who would like additional practice with the multiple-choice questions. The total testing time for Forms A and B as reproduced here is three hours and thirty-five minutes each and the total testing time for Form C as reproduced here is three hours. The actual test you will take will last about four hours and will include a seventh multiple-choice section with trial questions.

Taking these tests will help you become acquainted with testing procedures and requirements and thereby approach the real test with more assurance. Therefore, you should try to take these tests under conditions similar to those in an actual test administration, observing the time limitations and thinking about each question seriously.

The facsimiles of the GMAT answer documents included before each test may be used for marking your answers to the multiple-choice sections of the tests. After you have taken the tests, compare your answers with the answer keys that follow the tests and determine your scores using the instructions at the end of this chapter. There are no comparable answer keys for the AWA questions. After writing your essays in the allotted time, you may wish to review the scoring guide and sample essays in Chapter 8.

Answer Sheet: Form A

Section 1

1. Ⓐ Ⓑ Ⓒ Ⓓ Ⓔ
2. Ⓐ Ⓑ Ⓒ Ⓓ Ⓔ
3. Ⓐ Ⓑ Ⓒ Ⓓ Ⓔ
4. Ⓐ Ⓑ Ⓒ Ⓓ Ⓔ
5. Ⓐ Ⓑ Ⓒ Ⓓ Ⓔ
6. Ⓐ Ⓑ Ⓒ Ⓓ Ⓔ
7. Ⓐ Ⓑ Ⓒ Ⓓ Ⓔ
8. Ⓐ Ⓑ Ⓒ Ⓓ Ⓔ
9. Ⓐ Ⓑ Ⓒ Ⓓ Ⓔ
10. Ⓐ Ⓑ Ⓒ Ⓓ Ⓔ
11. Ⓐ Ⓑ Ⓒ Ⓓ Ⓔ
12. Ⓐ Ⓑ Ⓒ Ⓓ Ⓔ
13. Ⓐ Ⓑ Ⓒ Ⓓ Ⓔ
14. Ⓐ Ⓑ Ⓒ Ⓓ Ⓔ
15. Ⓐ Ⓑ Ⓒ Ⓓ Ⓔ
16. Ⓐ Ⓑ Ⓒ Ⓓ Ⓔ
17. Ⓐ Ⓑ Ⓒ Ⓓ Ⓔ
18. Ⓐ Ⓑ Ⓒ Ⓓ Ⓔ
19. Ⓐ Ⓑ Ⓒ Ⓓ Ⓔ
20. Ⓐ Ⓑ Ⓒ Ⓓ Ⓔ
21. Ⓐ Ⓑ Ⓒ Ⓓ Ⓔ
22. Ⓐ Ⓑ Ⓒ Ⓓ Ⓔ
23. Ⓐ Ⓑ Ⓒ Ⓓ Ⓔ

Section 2

1. Ⓐ Ⓑ Ⓒ Ⓓ Ⓔ
2. Ⓐ Ⓑ Ⓒ Ⓓ Ⓔ
3. Ⓐ Ⓑ Ⓒ Ⓓ Ⓔ
4. Ⓐ Ⓑ Ⓒ Ⓓ Ⓔ
5. Ⓐ Ⓑ Ⓒ Ⓓ Ⓔ
6. Ⓐ Ⓑ Ⓒ Ⓓ Ⓔ
7. Ⓐ Ⓑ Ⓒ Ⓓ Ⓔ
8. Ⓐ Ⓑ Ⓒ Ⓓ Ⓔ
9. Ⓐ Ⓑ Ⓒ Ⓓ Ⓔ
10. Ⓐ Ⓑ Ⓒ Ⓓ Ⓔ
11. Ⓐ Ⓑ Ⓒ Ⓓ Ⓔ
12. Ⓐ Ⓑ Ⓒ Ⓓ Ⓔ
13. Ⓐ Ⓑ Ⓒ Ⓓ Ⓔ
14. Ⓐ Ⓑ Ⓒ Ⓓ Ⓔ
15. Ⓐ Ⓑ Ⓒ Ⓓ Ⓔ
16. Ⓐ Ⓑ Ⓒ Ⓓ Ⓔ
17. Ⓐ Ⓑ Ⓒ Ⓓ Ⓔ
18. Ⓐ Ⓑ Ⓒ Ⓓ Ⓔ
19. Ⓐ Ⓑ Ⓒ Ⓓ Ⓔ
20. Ⓐ Ⓑ Ⓒ Ⓓ Ⓔ
21. Ⓐ Ⓑ Ⓒ Ⓓ Ⓔ
22. Ⓐ Ⓑ Ⓒ Ⓓ Ⓔ
23. Ⓐ Ⓑ Ⓒ Ⓓ Ⓔ

Section 3

1. Ⓐ Ⓑ Ⓒ Ⓓ Ⓔ
2. Ⓐ Ⓑ Ⓒ Ⓓ Ⓔ
3. Ⓐ Ⓑ Ⓒ Ⓓ Ⓔ
4. Ⓐ Ⓑ Ⓒ Ⓓ Ⓔ
5. Ⓐ Ⓑ Ⓒ Ⓓ Ⓔ
6. Ⓐ Ⓑ Ⓒ Ⓓ Ⓔ
7. Ⓐ Ⓑ Ⓒ Ⓓ Ⓔ
8. Ⓐ Ⓑ Ⓒ Ⓓ Ⓔ
9. Ⓐ Ⓑ Ⓒ Ⓓ Ⓔ
10. Ⓐ Ⓑ Ⓒ Ⓓ Ⓔ
11. Ⓐ Ⓑ Ⓒ Ⓓ Ⓔ
12. Ⓐ Ⓑ Ⓒ Ⓓ Ⓔ
13. Ⓐ Ⓑ Ⓒ Ⓓ Ⓔ
14. Ⓐ Ⓑ Ⓒ Ⓓ Ⓔ
15. Ⓐ Ⓑ Ⓒ Ⓓ Ⓔ
16. Ⓐ Ⓑ Ⓒ Ⓓ Ⓔ
17. Ⓐ Ⓑ Ⓒ Ⓓ Ⓔ
18. Ⓐ Ⓑ Ⓒ Ⓓ Ⓔ
19. Ⓐ Ⓑ Ⓒ Ⓓ Ⓔ
20. Ⓐ Ⓑ Ⓒ Ⓓ Ⓔ
21. Ⓐ Ⓑ Ⓒ Ⓓ Ⓔ
22. Ⓐ Ⓑ Ⓒ Ⓓ Ⓔ
23. Ⓐ Ⓑ Ⓒ Ⓓ Ⓔ

Section 4

1. Ⓐ Ⓑ Ⓒ Ⓓ Ⓔ
2. Ⓐ Ⓑ Ⓒ Ⓓ Ⓔ
3. Ⓐ Ⓑ Ⓒ Ⓓ Ⓔ
4. Ⓐ Ⓑ Ⓒ Ⓓ Ⓔ
5. Ⓐ Ⓑ Ⓒ Ⓓ Ⓔ
6. Ⓐ Ⓑ Ⓒ Ⓓ Ⓔ
7. Ⓐ Ⓑ Ⓒ Ⓓ Ⓔ
8. Ⓐ Ⓑ Ⓒ Ⓓ Ⓔ
9. Ⓐ Ⓑ Ⓒ Ⓓ Ⓔ
10. Ⓐ Ⓑ Ⓒ Ⓓ Ⓔ
11. Ⓐ Ⓑ Ⓒ Ⓓ Ⓔ
12. Ⓐ Ⓑ Ⓒ Ⓓ Ⓔ
13. Ⓐ Ⓑ Ⓒ Ⓓ Ⓔ
14. Ⓐ Ⓑ Ⓒ Ⓓ Ⓔ
15. Ⓐ Ⓑ Ⓒ Ⓓ Ⓔ
16. Ⓐ Ⓑ Ⓒ Ⓓ Ⓔ
17. Ⓐ Ⓑ Ⓒ Ⓓ Ⓔ
18. Ⓐ Ⓑ Ⓒ Ⓓ Ⓔ
19. Ⓐ Ⓑ Ⓒ Ⓓ Ⓔ
20. Ⓐ Ⓑ Ⓒ Ⓓ Ⓔ
21. Ⓐ Ⓑ Ⓒ Ⓓ Ⓔ
22. Ⓐ Ⓑ Ⓒ Ⓓ Ⓔ
23. Ⓐ Ⓑ Ⓒ Ⓓ Ⓔ

Section 5

1. Ⓐ Ⓑ Ⓒ Ⓓ Ⓔ
2. Ⓐ Ⓑ Ⓒ Ⓓ Ⓔ
3. Ⓐ Ⓑ Ⓒ Ⓓ Ⓔ
4. Ⓐ Ⓑ Ⓒ Ⓓ Ⓔ
5. Ⓐ Ⓑ Ⓒ Ⓓ Ⓔ
6. Ⓐ Ⓑ Ⓒ Ⓓ Ⓔ
7. Ⓐ Ⓑ Ⓒ Ⓓ Ⓔ
8. Ⓐ Ⓑ Ⓒ Ⓓ Ⓔ
9. Ⓐ Ⓑ Ⓒ Ⓓ Ⓔ
10. Ⓐ Ⓑ Ⓒ Ⓓ Ⓔ
11. Ⓐ Ⓑ Ⓒ Ⓓ Ⓔ
12. Ⓐ Ⓑ Ⓒ Ⓓ Ⓔ
13. Ⓐ Ⓑ Ⓒ Ⓓ Ⓔ
14. Ⓐ Ⓑ Ⓒ Ⓓ Ⓔ
15. Ⓐ Ⓑ Ⓒ Ⓓ Ⓔ
16. Ⓐ Ⓑ Ⓒ Ⓓ Ⓔ
17. Ⓐ Ⓑ Ⓒ Ⓓ Ⓔ
18. Ⓐ Ⓑ Ⓒ Ⓓ Ⓔ
19. Ⓐ Ⓑ Ⓒ Ⓓ Ⓔ
20. Ⓐ Ⓑ Ⓒ Ⓓ Ⓔ
21. Ⓐ Ⓑ Ⓒ Ⓓ Ⓔ
22. Ⓐ Ⓑ Ⓒ Ⓓ Ⓔ
23. Ⓐ Ⓑ Ⓒ Ⓓ Ⓔ

Section 6

1. Ⓐ Ⓑ Ⓒ Ⓓ Ⓔ
2. Ⓐ Ⓑ Ⓒ Ⓓ Ⓔ
3. Ⓐ Ⓑ Ⓒ Ⓓ Ⓔ
4. Ⓐ Ⓑ Ⓒ Ⓓ Ⓔ
5. Ⓐ Ⓑ Ⓒ Ⓓ Ⓔ
6. Ⓐ Ⓑ Ⓒ Ⓓ Ⓔ
7. Ⓐ Ⓑ Ⓒ Ⓓ Ⓔ
8. Ⓐ Ⓑ Ⓒ Ⓓ Ⓔ
9. Ⓐ Ⓑ Ⓒ Ⓓ Ⓔ
10. Ⓐ Ⓑ Ⓒ Ⓓ Ⓔ
11. Ⓐ Ⓑ Ⓒ Ⓓ Ⓔ
12. Ⓐ Ⓑ Ⓒ Ⓓ Ⓔ
13. Ⓐ Ⓑ Ⓒ Ⓓ Ⓔ
14. Ⓐ Ⓑ Ⓒ Ⓓ Ⓔ
15. Ⓐ Ⓑ Ⓒ Ⓓ Ⓔ
16. Ⓐ Ⓑ Ⓒ Ⓓ Ⓔ
17. Ⓐ Ⓑ Ⓒ Ⓓ Ⓔ
18. Ⓐ Ⓑ Ⓒ Ⓓ Ⓔ
19. Ⓐ Ⓑ Ⓒ Ⓓ Ⓔ
20. Ⓐ Ⓑ Ⓒ Ⓓ Ⓔ
21. Ⓐ Ⓑ Ⓒ Ⓓ Ⓔ
22. Ⓐ Ⓑ Ⓒ Ⓓ Ⓔ
23. Ⓐ Ⓑ Ⓒ Ⓓ Ⓔ

Print your full name here: _____
                        (last)   (first)   (middle)

Graduate
Management
Admission
Council®

Educational Testing Service

Graduate Management Admission Test

NO TEST MATERIAL ON THIS PAGE

ANALYSIS OF AN ARGUMENT

Time—30 minutes

<u>Directions:</u> In this section you will be asked to write a critique of the argument presented below. *You are NOT being asked to present your own views on the subject.*

Read the argument and the instructions that follow it, and then make any notes in your test booklet that will help you plan your response. Begin writing your response on the separate answer sheet. Make sure that you use the answer sheet that goes with this writing task.

The following appeared as part of an article in the business section of a local newspaper.

"Motorcycle X has been manufactured in the United States for over 70 years. Although one foreign company has copied the motorcycle and is selling it for less, the company has failed to attract motorcycle X customers — some say because its product lacks the exceptionally loud noise made by motorcycle X. But there must be some other explanation. After all, foreign cars tend to be quieter than similar American-made cars, but they sell at least as well. Also, television advertisements for motorcycle X highlight its durability and sleek lines, not its noisiness, and the ads typically have voice-overs or rock music rather than engine-roar on the sound track."

Discuss how well reasoned you find this argument. In your discussion be sure to analyze the line of reasoning and the use of evidence in the argument. For example, you may need to consider what questionable assumptions underlie the thinking and what alternative explanations or counterexamples might weaken the conclusion. You can also discuss what sort of evidence would strengthen or refute the argument, what changes in the argument would make it more logically sound, and what, if anything, would help you better evaluate its conclusion.

NOTES

Use the space below or on the facing page to plan your response. Any writing on these pages will not be evaluated.

STOP

**IF YOU FINISH BEFORE TIME IS CALLED, YOU MAY CHECK YOUR WORK ON THIS SECTION ONLY.
DO NOT TURN TO ANY OTHER SECTION IN THE TEST.**

NO TEST MATERIAL ON THIS PAGE.

ANALYSIS OF AN ISSUE

Time—30 minutes

<u>Directions:</u> In this section, you will need to analyze the issue presented below and explain your views on it. The question has no "correct" answer. Instead, you should consider various perspectives as you develop your own position on the issue.

Read the statement and the directions that follow it, and then make any notes in your test booklet that will help you plan your response. Begin writing your response on the separate answer document. Make sure that you use the answer document that goes with this writing task.

"All groups and organizations should function as teams in which everyone makes decisions and shares responsibilities and duties. Giving one person central authority and responsibility for a project or task is not an effective way to get work done."

To what extent do you agree or disagree with the opinion expressed above? Support your views with reasons and/or specific examples drawn from your own work or school experiences, your observations, or your reading.

NOTES

Use the space below or on the facing page to plan your response. Any writing on these pages will not be evaluated.

STOP

IF YOU FINISH BEFORE TIME IS CALLED, YOU MAY CHECK YOUR WORK ON THIS SECTION ONLY.
DO NOT TURN TO ANY OTHER SECTION IN THE TEST.

SECTION 1

Time — 25 minutes

22 Questions

Directions: In each of the following sentences, some part of the sentence or the entire sentence is underlined. Beneath each sentence you will find five ways of phrasing the underlined part. The first of these repeats the original; the other four are different. If you think the original is the best of these answer choices, choose answer A; otherwise, choose one of the others. Select the best version and fill in the corresponding oval on your answer sheet.

This is a test of correctness and effectiveness of expression. In choosing answers, follow the requirements of standard written English; that is, pay attention to grammar, choice of words, and sentence construction. Choose the answer that produces the most effective sentence; this answer should be clear and exact, without awkwardness, ambiguity, redundancy, or grammatical error.

1. Although early soap operas were first aired on evening radio in the 1920's, they had moved to the daytime hours of the 1930's when the evening schedule became crowded with comedians and variety shows.

   (A) were first aired on evening radio in the 1920's, they had moved to the daytime hours of the 1930's
   (B) were first aired on evening radio in the 1920's, they were moved to the daytime hours in the 1930's
   (C) were aired first on evening radio in the 1920's, moving to the daytime hours in the 1930's
   (D) were aired first in the evening on 1920's radio, they moved to the daytime hours of the 1930's
   (E) aired on evening radio first in the 1920's, they were moved to the 1930's in the daytime hours

2. In 1527 King Henry VIII sought to have his marriage to Queen Catherine annulled so as to marry Anne Boleyn.

   (A) so as to marry
   (B) and so could be married to
   (C) to be married to
   (D) so that he could marry
   (E) in order that he would marry

3. The energy source on *Voyager 2* is not a nuclear reactor, in which atoms are actively broken apart; rather a kind of nuclear battery that uses natural radioactive decay to produce power.

   (A) apart; rather
   (B) apart, but rather
   (C) apart, but rather that of
   (D) apart, but that of
   (E) apart; it is that of

4. Seismologists studying the earthquake that struck northern California in October 1989 are still investigating some of its mysteries: the unexpected power of the seismic waves, the upward thrust that threw one man straight into the air, and the strange electromagnetic signals detected hours before the temblor.

   (A) the upward thrust that threw one man straight into the air, and the strange electromagnetic signals detected hours before the temblor
   (B) the upward thrust that threw one man straight into the air, and strange electromagnetic signals were detected hours before the temblor
   (C) the upward thrust threw one man straight into the air, and hours before the temblor strange electromagnetic signals were detected
   (D) one man was thrown straight into the air by the upward thrust, and hours before the temblor strange electromagnetic signals were detected
   (E) one man who was thrown straight into the air by the upward thrust, and strange electromagnetic signals that were detected hours before the temblor

GO ON TO THE NEXT PAGE.

-402-

5. <u>A letter by Mark Twain, written in the same year as *The Adventures of Huckleberry Finn* were published,</u> reveals that Twain provided financial assistance to one of the first Black students at Yale Law School.

(A) A letter by Mark Twain, written in the same year as *The Adventures of Huckleberry Finn* were published,

(B) A letter by Mark Twain, written in the same year of publication as *The Adventures of Huckleberry Finn*,

(C) A letter by Mark Twain, written in the same year that *The Adventures of Huckleberry Finn* was published,

(D) Mark Twain wrote a letter in the same year as he published *The Adventures of Huckleberry Finn* that

(E) Mark Twain wrote a letter in the same year of publication as *The Adventures of Huckleberry Finn* that

6. Two new studies indicate that many people become obese more <u>due to the fact that their bodies burn calories too slowly than overeating.</u>

(A) due to the fact that their bodies burn calories too slowly than overeating

(B) due to their bodies burning calories too slowly than to eating too much

(C) because their bodies burn calories too slowly than that they are overeaters

(D) because their bodies burn calories too slowly than because they eat too much

(E) because of their bodies burning calories too slowly than because of their eating too much

7. As a result of the ground-breaking work of Barbara McClintock, many scientists now believe that all of the information encoded in <u>50,000 to 100,000 of the different genes found in a human cell are contained in merely</u> three percent of the cell's DNA.

(A) 50,000 to 100,000 of the different genes found in a human cell are contained in merely

(B) 50,000 to 100,000 of the human cell's different genes are contained in a mere

(C) the 50,000 to 100,000 different genes found in human cells are contained in merely

(D) 50,000 to 100,000 of human cells' different genes is contained in merely

(E) the 50,000 to 100,000 different genes found in a human cell is contained in a mere

8. <u>So poorly educated and trained are many young recruits to the United States work force that</u> many business executives fear this country will lose its economic preeminence.

(A) So poorly educated and trained are many young recruits to the United States work force that

(B) As poorly educated and trained as many young recruits to the United States work force are,

(C) Because of many young recruits to the United States work force who are so poorly educated and trained,

(D) That many young recruits to the United States work force are so poorly educated and trained is why

(E) Many young recruits to the United States work force who are so poorly educated and trained explains why

GO ON TO THE NEXT PAGE.

9. In the last few years, the number of convicted criminals given community service sentences, which allow the criminals to remain unconfined while they perform specific jobs benefiting the public, have risen dramatically.

(A) sentences, which allow the criminals to remain unconfined while they perform specific jobs benefiting the public, have
(B) sentences, performing specific jobs that benefit the public while being allowed to remain unconfined, have
(C) sentences, performing specific jobs beneficial to the public while they are allowed to remain unconfined, have
(D) sentences which allow them to remain unconfined in their performing of specific jobs beneficial to the public has
(E) sentences allowing them to remain unconfined while performing specific jobs that benefit the public has

10. During the early years of European settlement on a continent that was viewed as "wilderness" by the newcomers, Native Americans, intimately knowing the ecology of the land, were a help in the rescuing of many Pilgrims and pioneers from hardship, or even death.

(A) Native Americans, intimately knowing the ecology of the land, were a help in the rescuing of
(B) Native Americans knew the ecology and the land intimately and this enabled them to help in the rescue of
(C) Native Americans, with their intimate knowledge of the ecology of the land, helped to rescue
(D) having intimate knowledge of the ecology of the land, Native Americans helped the rescue of
(E) knowing intimately the ecology of the land, Native Americans helped to rescue

11. Quasars are so distant that their light has taken billions of years to reach the Earth; consequently, we see them as they were during the formation of the universe.

(A) we see them as they were during
(B) we see them as they had been during
(C) we see them as if during
(D) they appear to us as they did in
(E) they appear to us as though in

12. Because of the enormous research and development expenditures required to survive in the electronics industry, an industry marked by rapid innovation and volatile demand, such firms tend to be very large.

(A) to survive
(B) of firms to survive
(C) for surviving
(D) for survival
(E) for firms' survival

GO ON TO THE NEXT PAGE.

13. <u>Consumers may not think of household cleaning products to be</u> hazardous substances, but many of them can be harmful to health, especially if they are used improperly.

(A) Consumers may not think of household cleaning products to be
(B) Consumers may not think of household cleaning products being
(C) A consumer may not think of their household cleaning products being
(D) A consumer may not think of household cleaning products as
(E) Household cleaning products may not be thought of, by consumers, as

14.   NOT SCORED

15. Archaeologists in Ireland believe that a recently discovered chalice, which dates from the eighth century, was probably buried <u>to keep from</u> being stolen by invaders.

(A) to keep from
(B) to keep it from
(C) to avoid
(D) in order that it would avoid
(E) in order to keep from

16. As measured by the Commerce Department, corporate profits peaked in the fourth quarter of 1988 <u>and have slipped since then, as many companies have been unable to pass on higher costs.</u>

(A) and have slipped since then, as many companies have been unable to pass on higher costs
(B) and have slipped since then, the reason being because many companies have been unable to pass on higher costs
(C) and slipped since then, many companies being unable to pass on higher costs
(D) but, many companies unable to pass on higher costs, they have slipped since then
(E) yet are slipping since then, because many companies were unable to pass on higher costs

GO ON TO THE NEXT PAGE.

17. The recent surge in the number of airplane flights has clogged the nation's air-traffic control system, <u>to lead to 55 percent more delays at airports, and prompts</u> fears among some officials that safety is being compromised.

(A) to lead to 55 percent more delays at airports, and prompts
(B) leading to 55 percent more delay at airports and prompting
(C) to lead to a 55 percent increase in delay at airports and prompt
(D) to lead to an increase of 55 percent in delays at airports, and prompted
(E) leading to a 55-percent increase in delays at airports and prompting

18. Judge Bonham denied a motion <u>to allow members of the jury to go home at the end of each day instead of to confine them to</u> a hotel.

(A) to allow members of the jury to go home at the end of each day instead of to confine them to
(B) that would have allowed members of the jury to go home at the end of each day instead of confined to
(C) under which members of the jury are allowed to go home at the end of each day instead of confining them in
(D) that would allow members of the jury to go home at the end of each day rather than confinement in
(E) to allow members of the jury to go home at the end of each day rather than be confined to

19. In one of the bloodiest battles of the Civil War, fought at Sharpsburg, Maryland, on September 17, 1862, four times as many <u>Americans were killed as</u> would later be killed on the beaches of Normandy during D-Day.

(A) Americans were killed as
(B) Americans were killed than
(C) Americans were killed than those who
(D) more Americans were killed as there
(E) more Americans were killed as those who

20. As a result of medical advances, many people <u>that might at one time have died as children</u> of such infections as diphtheria, pneumonia, or rheumatic fever now live well into old age.

(A) that might at one time have died as children
(B) who might once have died in childhood
(C) that as children might once have died
(D) who in childhood might have at one time died
(E) who, when they were children, might at one time have died

GO ON TO THE NEXT PAGE.

21. Proponents of artificial intelligence say they will be able to make computers that can understand English and other human languages, recognize objects, and reason <u>as an expert does—computers that will be used to diagnose equipment breakdowns, deciding whether to authorize a loan, or other purposes such as these.</u>

    (A) as an expert does—computers that will be used to diagnose equipment breakdowns, deciding whether to authorize a loan, or other purposes such as these
    (B) as an expert does, which may be used for purposes such as diagnosing equipment breakdowns or deciding whether to authorize a loan
    (C) like an expert—computers that will be used for such purposes as diagnosing equipment breakdowns or deciding whether to authorize a loan
    (D) like an expert, the use of which would be for purposes like the diagnosis of equipment breakdowns or the decision whether or not a loan should be authorized
    (E) like an expert, to be used to diagnose equipment breakdowns, deciding whether to authorize a loan or not, or the like

22. <u>Manifestations of Islamic political militancy in the first period of religious reformism were the rise of the Wahhabis in Arabia, the Sanusi in Cyrenaica, the Fulani in Nigeria, the Mahdi in the Sudan, and</u> the victory of the Usuli "mujtahids" in Shiite Iran and Iraq.

    (A) Manifestations of Islamic political militancy in the first period of religious reformism were the rise of the Wahhabis in Arabia, the Sanusi in Cyrenaica, the Fulani in Nigeria, the Mahdi in the Sudan, and
    (B) Manifestations of Islamic political militancy in the first period of religious reformism were shown in the rise of the Wahhabis in Arabia, the Sanusi in Cyrenaica, the Fulani in Nigeria, the Mahdi in the Sudan, and also
    (C) In the first period of religious reformism, manifestations of Islamic political militancy were the rise of the Wahhabis in Arabia, of the Sanusi in Cyrenaica, the Fulani in Nigeria, the Mahdi in the Sudan, and
    (D) In the first period of religious reformism, manifestations of Islamic political militancy were shown in the rise of the Wahhabis in Arabia, the Sanusi in Cyrenaica, the Fulani in Nigeria, the Mahdi in the Sudan, and
    (E) In the first period of religious reformism, Islamic political militancy was manifested in the rise of the Wahhabis in Arabia, the Sanusi in Cyrenaica, the Fulani in Nigeria, and the Mahdi in the Sudan, and in

STOP

IF YOU FINISH BEFORE TIME IS CALLED, YOU MAY CHECK YOUR WORK ON THIS SECTION ONLY.
DO NOT TURN TO ANY OTHER SECTION IN THE TEST.

SECTION 2

Time — 25 minutes

16 Questions

Directions: In this section solve each problem, using any available space on the page for scratchwork. Then indicate the best of the answer choices given.

Numbers: All numbers used are real numbers.

Figures: Figures that accompany problems in this section are intended to provide information useful in solving the problems. They are drawn as accurately as possible EXCEPT when it is stated in a specific problem that its figure is not drawn to scale. All figures lie in a plane unless otherwise indicated.

1. As a salesperson, Phyllis can choose one of two methods of annual payment: either an annual salary of $35,000 with no commission or an annual salary of $10,000 plus a 20 percent commission on her total annual sales. What must her total annual sales be to give her the same annual pay with either method?

(A) $100,000
(B) $120,000
(C) $125,000
(D) $130,000
(E) $132,000

2. A restaurant buys fruit in cans containing $3\frac{1}{2}$ cups of fruit each. If the restaurant uses $\frac{1}{2}$ cup of the fruit in each serving of its fruit compote, what is the least number of cans needed to prepare 60 servings of the compote?

(A) 7
(B) 8
(C) 9
(D) 10
(E) 12

GO ON TO THE NEXT PAGE.

3. If $x > 3{,}000$, then the value of $\dfrac{x}{2x + 1}$ is closest to

(A) $\dfrac{1}{6}$

(B) $\dfrac{1}{3}$

(C) $\dfrac{10}{21}$

(D) $\dfrac{1}{2}$

(E) $\dfrac{3}{2}$

4. Machine A produces 100 parts twice as fast as machine B does. Machine B produces 100 parts in 40 minutes. If each machine produces parts at a constant rate, how many parts does machine A produce in 6 minutes?

(A) 30
(B) 25
(C) 20
(D) 15
(E) 7.5

5. If 18 is 15 percent of 30 percent of a certain number, what is the number?

(A) 9
(B) 36
(C) 40
(D) 81
(E) 400

6. A necklace is made by stringing N individual beads together in the repeating pattern red bead, green bead, white bead, blue bead, and yellow bead. If the necklace design begins with a red bead and ends with a white bead, then N could equal

(A) 16
(B) 32
(C) 44
(D) 54
(E) 68

GO ON TO THE NEXT PAGE.

7. If $x = (0.08)^2$, $y = \dfrac{1}{(0.08)^2}$, and
$z = (1 - 0.08)^2 - 1$, which of the following is true?

(A) $x = y = z$
(B) $y < z < x$
(C) $z < x < y$
(D) $y < x$ and $x = z$.
(E) $x < y$ and $x = z$.

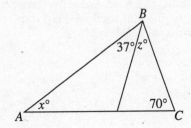

8. In $\triangle ABC$ above, what is x in terms of z ?

(A) $z + 73$
(B) $z - 73$
(C) $70 - z$
(D) $z - 70$
(E) $73 - z$

9. In 1990 a total of x earthquakes occurred worldwide, some but not all of which occurred in Asia. If m of these earthquakes occurred in Asia, which of the following represents the ratio of the number of earthquakes that occurred in Asia to the number that did not occur in Asia?

(A) $\dfrac{x}{m}$

(B) $\dfrac{m}{x}$

(C) $\dfrac{m}{x - m}$

(D) $\dfrac{x}{x - m}$

(E) $1 - \dfrac{m}{x}$

GO ON TO THE NEXT PAGE.

-410-

10. If $\dfrac{x + y}{xy} = 1$, then $y =$

(A) $\dfrac{x}{x - 1}$

(B) $\dfrac{x}{x + 1}$

(C) $\dfrac{x - 1}{x}$

(D) $\dfrac{x + 1}{x}$

(E) x

11. If $\dfrac{1}{2}$ of the air in a tank is removed with each stroke of a vacuum pump, what fraction of the original amount of air has been removed after 4 strokes?

(A) $\dfrac{15}{16}$

(B) $\dfrac{7}{8}$

(C) $\dfrac{1}{4}$

(D) $\dfrac{1}{8}$

(E) $\dfrac{1}{16}$

12. Last year Department Store X had a sales total for December that was 4 times the average (arithmetic mean) of the monthly sales totals for January through November. The sales total for December was what fraction of the sales total for the year?

(A) $\dfrac{1}{4}$

(B) $\dfrac{4}{15}$

(C) $\dfrac{1}{3}$

(D) $\dfrac{4}{11}$

(E) $\dfrac{4}{5}$

13. How many integers n are there such that $1 < 5n + 5 < 25$?

(A) Five
(B) Four
(C) Three
(D) Two
(E) One

GO ON TO THE NEXT PAGE.

14. If the two-digit integers M and N are positive and have the same digits, but in reverse order, which of the following CANNOT be the sum of M and N?

(A) 181
(B) 165
(C) 121
(D) 99
(E) 44

15. Working alone, printers X, Y, and Z can do a certain printing job, consisting of a large number of pages, in 12, 15, and 18 hours, respectively. What is the ratio of the time it takes printer X to do the job, working alone at its rate, to the time it takes printers Y and Z to do the job, working together at their individual rates?

(A) $\frac{4}{11}$

(B) $\frac{1}{2}$

(C) $\frac{15}{22}$

(D) $\frac{22}{15}$

(E) $\frac{11}{4}$

16. In 1985 a company sold a brand of shoes to retailers for a fixed price per pair. In 1986 the number of pairs of the shoes that the company sold to retailers decreased by 20 percent, while the price per pair increased by 20 percent. If the company's revenue from the sale of the shoes in 1986 was $3.0 million, what was the approximate revenue from the sale of the shoes in 1985 ?

(A) $2.4 million
(B) $2.9 million
(C) $3.0 million
(D) $3.1 million
(E) $3.6 million

S T O P

IF YOU FINISH BEFORE TIME IS CALLED, YOU MAY CHECK YOUR WORK ON THIS SECTION ONLY.
DO NOT TURN TO ANY OTHER SECTION IN THE TEST.

SECTION 3

Time—30 minutes

23 Questions

Directions: Each passage in this group is followed by questions based on its content. After reading a passage, choose the best answer to each question and fill in the corresponding oval on the answer sheet. Answer all questions following a passage on the basis of what is <u>stated</u> or <u>implied</u> in that passage.

Joseph Glatthaar's *Forged in Battle* is not the first excellent study of Black soldiers and their White officers in the Civil War, but it uses more soldiers' letters and diaries—
Line including rare material from Black soldiers—and concen-
(5) trates more intensely on Black-White relations in Black regiments than do any of its predecessors. Glatthaar's title expresses his thesis: loyalty, friendship, and respect among White officers and Black soldiers were fostered by the mutual dangers they faced in combat.
(10) Glatthaar accurately describes the government's discriminatory treatment of Black soldiers in pay, promotion, medical care, and job assignments, appropriately emphasizing the campaign by Black soldiers and their officers to get the opportunity to fight. That chance remained limited through-
(15) out the war by army policies that kept most Black units serving in rear-echelon assignments and working in labor battalions. Thus, while their combat death rate was only one-third that of White units, their mortality rate from disease, a major killer in this war, was twice as great.
(20) Despite these obstacles, the courage and effectiveness of several Black units in combat won increasing respect from initially skeptical or hostile White soldiers. As one White officer put it, "they have fought their way into the respect of all the army."
(25) In trying to demonstrate the magnitude of this attitudinal change, however, Glatthaar seems to exaggerate the prewar racism of the White men who became officers in Black regiments. "Prior to the war," he writes of these men, "virtually all of them held powerful racial prejudices."
(30) While perhaps true of those officers who joined Black units for promotion or other self-serving motives, this statement misrepresents the attitudes of the many abolitionists who became officers in Black regiments. Having spent years fighting against the race prejudice endemic in Ameri-
(35) can society, they participated eagerly in this military experiment, which they hoped would help African Americans achieve freedom and postwar civil equality. By current standards of racial egalitarianism, these men's paternalism toward African Americans was racist. But to call their feel-
(40) ings "powerful racial prejudices" is to indulge in generational chauvinism—to judge past eras by present standards.

1. The passage as a whole can best be characterized as which of the following?

(A) An evaluation of a scholarly study
(B) A description of an attitudinal change
(C) A discussion of an analytical defect
(D) An analysis of the causes of a phenomenon
(E) An argument in favor of revising a view

2. According to the author, which of the following is true of Glatthaar's *Forged in Battle* compared with previous studies on the same topic?

(A) It is more reliable and presents a more complete picture of the historical events on which it concentrates than do previous studies.
(B) It uses more of a particular kind of source material and focuses more closely on a particular aspect of the topic than do previous studies.
(C) It contains some unsupported generalizations, but it rightly emphasizes a theme ignored by most previous studies.
(D) It surpasses previous studies on the same topic in that it accurately describes conditions often neglected by those studies.
(E) It makes skillful use of supporting evidence to illustrate a subtle trend that previous studies have failed to detect.

GO ON TO THE NEXT PAGE.

Section 3 starts on page 414.

3. The author implies that the title of Glatthaar's book refers specifically to which of the following?

(A) The sense of pride and accomplishment that Black soldiers increasingly felt as a result of their Civil War experiences

(B) The civil equality that African Americans achieved after the Civil War, partly as a result of their use of organizational skills honed by combat

(C) The changes in discriminatory army policies that were made as a direct result of the performance of Black combat units during the Civil War

(D) The improved interracial relations that were formed by the races' facing of common dangers and their waging of a common fight during the Civil War

(E) The standards of racial egalitarianism that came to be adopted as a result of White Civil War veterans' repudiation of their previous racism

4. The passage mentions which of the following as an important theme that receives special emphasis in Glatthaar's book?

(A) The attitudes of abolitionist officers in Black units

(B) The struggle of Black units to get combat assignments

(C) The consequences of the poor medical care received by Black soldiers

(D) The motives of officers serving in Black units

(E) The discrimination that Black soldiers faced when trying for promotions

5. The passage suggests that which of the following was true of Black units' disease mortality rates in the Civil War?

(A) They were almost as high as the combat mortality rates of White units.

(B) They resulted in part from the relative inexperience of these units when in combat.

(C) They were especially high because of the nature of these units' usual duty assignments.

(D) They resulted in extremely high overall casualty rates in Black combat units.

(E) They exacerbated the morale problems that were caused by the army's discriminatory policies.

6. The author of the passage quotes the White officer in lines 23-24 primarily in order to provide evidence to support the contention that

(A) virtually all White officers initially had hostile attitudes toward Black soldiers

(B) Black soldiers were often forced to defend themselves from physical attacks initiated by soldiers from White units

(C) the combat performance of Black units changed the attitudes of White soldiers toward Black soldiers

(D) White units paid especially careful attention to the performance of Black units in battle

(E) respect in the army as a whole was accorded only to those units, whether Black or White, that performed well in battle

7. Which of the following best describes the kind of error attributed to Glatthaar in lines 25-28 ?

(A) Insisting on an unwarranted distinction between two groups of individuals in order to render an argument concerning them internally consistent

(B) Supporting an argument in favor of a given interpretation of a situation with evidence that is not particularly relevant to the situation

(C) Presenting a distorted view of the motives of certain individuals in order to provide grounds for a negative evaluation of their actions

(D) Describing the conditions prevailing before a given event in such a way that the contrast with those prevailing after the event appears more striking than it actually is

(E) Asserting that a given event is caused by another event merely because the other event occurred before the given event occurred

8. Which of the following actions can best be described as indulging in "generational chauvinism" (lines 40-41) as that practice is defined in the passage?

(A) Condemning a present-day monarch merely because many monarchs have been tyrannical in the past

(B) Clinging to the formal standards of politeness common in one's youth to such a degree that any relaxation of those standards is intolerable

(C) Questioning the accuracy of a report written by an employee merely because of the employee's gender

(D) Deriding the superstitions accepted as "science" in past eras without acknowledging the prevalence of irrational beliefs today

(E) Labeling a nineteenth-century politician as "corrupt" for engaging in once-acceptable practices considered intolerable today

GO ON TO THE NEXT PAGE.

It was once assumed that all living things could be divided into two fundamental and exhaustive categories. Multicellular plants and animals, as well as many unicellular organisms, are eukaryotic—their large, complex cells
Line
(5) have a well-formed nucleus and many organelles. On the other hand, the true bacteria are prokaryotic cells, which are simple and lack a nucleus. The distinction between eukaryotes and bacteria, initially defined in terms of subcellular structures visible with a microscope, was ulti-
(10) mately carried to the molecular level. Here prokaryotic and eukaryotic cells have many features in common. For instance, they translate genetic information into proteins according to the same type of genetic coding. But even where the molecular processes are the same, the details in
(15) the two forms are different and characteristic of the respective forms. For example, the amino acid sequences of various enzymes tend to be typically prokaryotic or eukaryotic. The differences between the groups and the similarities within each group made it seem certain to most biologists
(20) that the tree of life had only two stems. Moreover, arguments pointing out the extent of both structural and functional differences between eukaryotes and true bacteria convinced many biologists that the precursors of the eukaryotes must have diverged from the common ancestor
(25) before the bacteria arose.

Although much of this picture has been sustained by more recent research, it seems fundamentally wrong in one respect. Among the bacteria, there are organisms that are significantly different both from the cells of eukaryotes and
(30) from the true bacteria, and it now appears that there are three stems in the tree of life. New techniques for determining the molecular sequence of the RNA of organisms have produced evolutionary information about the degree to which organisms are related, the time since they diverged
(35) from a common ancestor, and the reconstruction of ancestral versions of genes. These techniques have strongly suggested that although the true bacteria indeed form a large coherent group, certain other bacteria, the archaebacteria, which are also prokaryotes and which resemble true
(40) bacteria, represent a distinct evolutionary branch that far antedates the common ancestor of all true bacteria.

9. The passage is primarily concerned with

(A) detailing the evidence that has led most biologists to replace the trichotomous picture of living organisms with a dichotomous one
(B) outlining the factors that have contributed to the current hypothesis concerning the number of basic categories of living organisms
(C) evaluating experiments that have resulted in proof that the prokaryotes are more ancient than had been expected
(D) summarizing the differences in structure and function found among true bacteria, archaebacteria, and eukaryotes
(E) formulating a hypothesis about the mechanisms of evolution that resulted in the ancestors of the prokaryotes

10. According to the passage, investigations of eukaryotic and prokaryotic cells at the molecular level supported the conclusion that

(A) most eukaryotic organisms are unicellular
(B) complex cells have well-formed nuclei
(C) prokaryotes and eukaryotes form two fundamental categories
(D) subcellular structures are visible with a microscope
(E) prokaryotic and eukaryotic cells have similar enzymes

11. According to the passage, which of the following statements about the two-category hypothesis is likely to be true?

(A) It is promising because it explains the presence of true bacteria-like organisms such as organelles in eukaryotic cells.
(B) It is promising because it explains why eukaryotic cells, unlike prokaryotic cells, tend to form multicellular organisms.
(C) It is flawed because it fails to account for the great variety among eukaryotic organisms.
(D) It is flawed because it fails to account for the similarity between prokaryotes and eukaryotes.
(E) It is flawed because it fails to recognize an important distinction among prokaryotes.

GO ON TO THE NEXT PAGE.

12. It can be inferred from the passage that which of the following have recently been compared in order to clarify the fundamental classifications of living things?

    (A) The genetic coding in true bacteria and that in other prokaryotes
    (B) The organelle structures of archaebacteria, true bacteria, and eukaryotes
    (C) The cellular structures of multicellular organisms and unicellular organisms
    (D) The molecular sequences in eukaryotic RNA, true bacterial RNA, and archaebacterial RNA
    (E) The amino acid sequences in enzymes of various eukaryotic species and those of enzymes in archaebacterial species

13. If the "new techniques" mentioned in line 31 were applied in studies of biological classifications other than bacteria, which of the following is most likely?

    (A) Some of those classifications will have to be reevaluated.
    (B) Many species of bacteria will be reclassified.
    (C) It will be determined that there are four main categories of living things rather than three.
    (D) It will be found that true bacteria are much older than eukaryotes.
    (E) It will be found that there is a common ancestor of the eukaryotes, archaebacteria, and true bacteria.

14. According to the passage, researchers working under the two-category hypothesis were correct in thinking that

    (A) prokaryotes form a coherent group
    (B) the common ancestor of all living things had complex properties
    (C) eukaryotes are fundamentally different from true bacteria
    (D) true bacteria are just as complex as eukaryotes
    (E) ancestral versions of eukaryotic genes functioned differently from their modern counterparts

15. All of the following statements are supported by the passage EXCEPT:

    (A) True bacteria form a distinct evolutionary group.
    (B) Archaebacteria are prokaryotes that resemble true bacteria.
    (C) True bacteria and eukaryotes employ similar types of genetic coding.
    (D) True bacteria and eukaryotes are distinguishable at the subcellular level.
    (E) Amino acid sequences of enzymes are uniform for eukaryotic and prokaryotic organisms.

16. The author's attitude toward the view that living things are divided into three categories is best described as one of

    (A) tentative acceptance
    (B) mild skepticism
    (C) limited denial
    (D) studious criticism
    (E) wholehearted endorsement

GO ON TO THE NEXT PAGE.

Excess inventory, a massive problem for many businesses, has several causes, some of which are unavoidable. Overstocks may accumulate through production overruns or
Line errors. Certain styles and colors prove unpopular. With
(5) some products—computers and software, toys, and books—last year's models are difficult to move even at huge discounts. Occasionally the competition introduces a better product. But in many cases the public's buying tastes simply change, leaving a manufacturer or distributor with
(10) thousands (or millions) of items that the fickle public no longer wants.

One common way to dispose of this merchandise is to sell it to a liquidator, who buys as cheaply as possible and then resells the merchandise through catalogs, discount
(15) stores, and other outlets. However, liquidators may pay less for the merchandise than it cost to make it. Another way to dispose of excess inventory is to dump it. The corporation takes a straight cost write-off on its taxes and hauls the merchandise to a landfill. Although it is hard to believe,
(20) there is a sort of convoluted logic to this approach. It is perfectly legal, requires little time or preparation on the company's part, and solves the problem quickly. The drawback is the remote possibility of getting caught by the news media. Dumping perfectly useful products can turn into a
(25) public relations nightmare. Children living in poverty are freezing and XYZ Company has just sent 500 new snowsuits to the local dump. Parents of young children are barely getting by and QRS Company dumps 1,000 cases of disposable diapers because they have slight imperfections.
(30) The managers of these companies are not deliberately wasteful; they are simply unaware of all their alternatives. In 1976 the Internal Revenue Service provided a tangible incentive for businesses to contribute their products to charity. The new tax law allowed corporations to deduct the
(35) cost of the product donated plus half the difference between cost and fair market selling price, with the proviso that deductions cannot exceed twice cost. Thus, the federal government sanctions—indeed, encourages—an above-cost federal tax deduction for companies that donate inventory to charity.

17. The author mentions each of the following as a cause of excess inventory EXCEPT

(A) production of too much merchandise
(B) inaccurate forecasting of buyers' preferences
(C) unrealistic pricing policies
(D) products' rapid obsolescence
(E) availability of a better product

18. The passage suggests that which of the following is a kind of product that a liquidator who sells to discount stores would be unlikely to wish to acquire?

(A) Furniture
(B) Computers
(C) Kitchen equipment
(D) Baby-care products
(E) Children's clothing

19. The passage provides information that supports which of the following statements?

(A) Excess inventory results most often from insufficient market analysis by the manufacturer.
(B) Products with slight manufacturing defects may contribute to excess inventory.
(C) Few manufacturers have taken advantage of the changes in the federal tax laws.
(D) Manufacturers who dump their excess inventory are often caught and exposed by the news media.
(E) Most products available in discount stores have come from manufacturers' excess-inventory stock.

20. The author cites the examples in lines 25-29 most probably in order to illustrate

(A) the fiscal irresponsibility of dumping as a policy for dealing with excess inventory
(B) the waste-management problems that dumping new products creates
(C) the advantages to the manufacturer of dumping as a policy
(D) alternatives to dumping explored by different companies
(E) how the news media could portray dumping to the detriment of the manufacturer's reputation

GO ON TO THE NEXT PAGE.

21. By asserting that manufacturers "are simply unaware" (line 31), the author suggests which of the following?

(A) Manufacturers might donate excess inventory to charity rather than dump it if they knew about the provision in the federal tax code.
(B) The federal government has failed to provide sufficient encouragement to manufacturers to make use of advantageous tax policies.
(C) Manufacturers who choose to dump excess inventory are not aware of the possible effects on their reputation of media coverage of such dumping.
(D) The manufacturers of products disposed of by dumping are unaware of the needs of those people who would find the products useful.
(E) The manufacturers who dump their excess inventory are not familiar with the employment of liquidators to dispose of overstock.

22. The information in the passage suggests that which of the following, if true, would make donating excess inventory to charity less attractive to manufacturers than dumping?

(A) The costs of getting the inventory to the charitable destination are greater than the above-cost tax deduction.
(B) The news media give manufacturers' charitable contributions the same amount of coverage that they give dumping.
(C) No straight-cost tax benefit can be claimed for items that are dumped.
(D) The fair-market value of an item in excess inventory is 1.5 times its cost.
(E) Items end up as excess inventory because of a change in the public's preferences.

23. Information in the passage suggests that one reason manufacturers might take advantage of the tax provision mentioned in the last paragraph is that

(A) there are many kinds of products that cannot be legally dumped in a landfill
(B) liquidators often refuse to handle products with slight imperfections
(C) the law allows a deduction in excess of the cost of manufacturing the product
(D) media coverage of contributions of excess-inventory products to charity is widespread and favorable
(E) no tax deduction is available for products dumped or sold to a liquidator

STOP

IF YOU FINISH BEFORE TIME IS CALLED, YOU MAY CHECK YOUR WORK ON THIS SECTION ONLY.
DO NOT TURN TO ANY OTHER SECTION IN THE TEST.

SECTION 4

Time—25 minutes

20 Questions

Directions: Each of the data sufficiency problems below consists of a question and two statements, labeled (1) and (2), in which certain data are given. You have to decide whether the data given in the statements are <u>sufficient</u> for answering the question. Using the data given in the statements <u>plus</u> your knowledge of mathematics and everyday facts (such as the number of days in July or the meaning of *counterclockwise*), you are to fill in oval

   A if statement (1) ALONE is sufficient, but statement (2) alone is not sufficient to answer
        the question asked;
   B if statement (2) ALONE is sufficient, but statement (1) alone is not sufficient to answer
        the question asked;
   C if BOTH statements (1) and (2) TOGETHER are sufficient to answer the question asked,
        but NEITHER statement ALONE is sufficient;
   D if EACH statement ALONE is sufficient to answer the question asked;
   E if statements (1) and (2) TOGETHER are NOT sufficient to answer the question asked,
        and additional data specific to the problem are needed.

Numbers: All numbers used are real numbers.

Figures: A figure in a data sufficiency problem will conform to the information given in the question, but will not necessarily conform to the additional information given in statements (1) and (2).

   You may assume that lines shown as straight are straight and that angle measures are greater than zero.

   You may assume that the positions of points, angles, regions, etc., exist in the order shown.

   All figures lie in a plane unless otherwise indicated.

Note: In questions that ask for the value of a quantity, the data given in the statements are sufficient only when it is possible to determine exactly one numerical value for the quantity.

Example:

   In $\triangle PQR$, what is the value of x ?

   (1) $PQ = PR$

   (2) $y = 40$

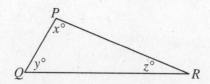

Explanation: According to statement (1), $PQ = PR$; therefore, $\triangle PQR$ is isosceles and $y = z$. Since $x + y + z = 180$, it follows that $x + 2y = 180$. Since statement (1) does not give a value for y, you cannot answer the question using statement (1) alone. According to statement (2), $y = 40$; therefore, $x + z = 140$. Since statement (2) does not give a value for z, you cannot answer the question using statement (2) alone. Using both statements together, since $x + 2y = 180$ and the value of y is given, you can find the value of x. Therefore, the answer is C.

GO ON TO THE NEXT PAGE.

A Statement (1) ALONE is sufficient, but statement (2) alone is not sufficient.
B Statement (2) ALONE is sufficient, but statement (1) alone is not sufficient.
C BOTH statements TOGETHER are sufficient, but NEITHER statement ALONE is sufficient.
D EACH statement ALONE is sufficient.
E Statements (1) and (2) TOGETHER are NOT sufficient.

1. The regular price per eight-ounce can of brand X soup is $0.37, regardless of the number of cans purchased. What amount will be saved on the purchase of 3 eight-ounce cans of brand X soup if the regular price is reduced?

(1) At the reduced price, 3 eight-ounce cans of brand X soup will cost $0.99.

(2) The amount that will be saved on each eight-ounce can of brand X soup purchased at the reduced price is $0.04.

2. Does Joe weigh more than Tim?

(1) Tim's weight is 80 percent of Joe's weight.
(2) Joe's weight is 125 percent of Tim's weight.

3. Is p^2 an odd integer?

(1) p is an odd integer.
(2) $\sqrt{p}$ is an odd integer.

GO ON TO THE NEXT PAGE.

A   Statement (1) ALONE is sufficient, but statement (2) alone is not sufficient.
B   Statement (2) ALONE is sufficient, but statement (1) alone is not sufficient.
C   BOTH statements TOGETHER are sufficient, but NEITHER statement ALONE is sufficient.
D   EACH statement ALONE is sufficient.
E   Statements (1) and (2) TOGETHER are NOT sufficient.

4. What is the value of xy ?

(1) $x + y = 10$

(2) $x - y = 6$

5. Elena receives a salary plus a commission that is equal to a fixed percentage of her sales revenue. What was the total of Elena's salary and commission last month?

(1) Elena's monthly salary is $1,000.

(2) Elena's commission is 5 percent of her sales revenue.

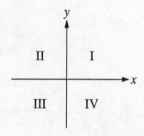

6. Point (x, y) lies in which quadrant of the rectangular coordinate system shown above?

(1) $x + y < 0$

(2) $x = 4$ and $y = -7$.

7. What is the average (arithmetic mean) of x, y, and z ?

(1) $x + y = 5$

(2) $y + z = 7$

8. Chan and Mieko drove separate cars along the entire length of a certain route. If Chan made the trip in 15 minutes, how many minutes did it take Mieko to make the same trip?

(1) Mieko's average speed for the trip was $\frac{3}{4}$ of Chan's average speed.

(2) The route is 14 miles long.

GO ON TO THE NEXT PAGE.

A Statement (1) ALONE is sufficient, but statement (2) alone is not sufficient.
B Statement (2) ALONE is sufficient, but statement (1) alone is not sufficient.
C BOTH statements TOGETHER are sufficient, but NEITHER statement ALONE is sufficient.
D EACH statement ALONE is sufficient.
E Statements (1) and (2) TOGETHER are NOT sufficient.

9. If $xy \neq 0$, is $\frac{x}{y} < 0$?

   (1) $x = -y$
   (2) $-x = -(-y)$

10. What is the value of the two-digit integer x ?

   (1) The sum of the two digits is 3.
   (2) x is divisible by 3.

11. Is the number x between 0.2 and 0.7 ?

   (1) $560x < 280$
   (2) $700x > 280$

GO ON TO THE NEXT PAGE.

A   Statement (1) ALONE is sufficient, but statement (2) alone is not sufficient.
B   Statement (2) ALONE is sufficient, but statement (1) alone is not sufficient.
C   BOTH statements TOGETHER are sufficient, but NEITHER statement ALONE is sufficient.
D   EACH statement ALONE is sufficient.
E   Statements (1) and (2) TOGETHER are NOT sufficient.

12. Is x an integer?

(1) $\frac{x}{2}$ is an integer.

(2) $2x$ is an integer.

13. A swim club that sold only individual and family memberships charged $300 for an individual membership. If the club's total revenue from memberships was $480,000, what was the charge for a family membership?

(1) The revenue from individual memberships was $\frac{1}{4}$ of the total revenue from memberships.

(2) The club sold 1.5 times as many family memberships as individual memberships.

14. If x, y, and z are positive numbers, is $x > y > z$?

(1) $xz > yz$

(2) $yx > yz$

15. Can the positive integer p be expressed as the product of two integers, each of which is greater than 1 ?

(1) $31 < p < 37$

(2) p is odd.

16. Currently there are 50 picture books on each shelf in the children's section of a library. If these books were to be placed on smaller shelves with 30 picture books on each shelf, how many of the smaller shelves would be needed to hold all of these books?

(1) The number of smaller shelves needed is 6 more than the current number of shelves.

(2) Currently there are 9 shelves in the children's section.

GO ON TO THE NEXT PAGE.

A   Statement (1) ALONE is sufficient, but statement (2) alone is not sufficient.
B   Statement (2) ALONE is sufficient, but statement (1) alone is not sufficient.
C   BOTH statements TOGETHER are sufficient, but NEITHER statement ALONE is sufficient.
D   EACH statement ALONE is sufficient.
E   Statements (1) and (2) TOGETHER are NOT sufficient.

17.   Is $y = 6$?

(1) $y^2 = 36$
(2) $y^2 - 7y + 6 = 0$

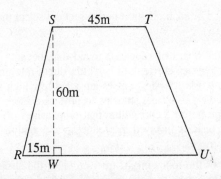

18.   The figure above represents the floor plan of an art gallery that has a lobby and 18 rooms. If Lisa goes from the lobby into room A at the same time that Paul goes from the lobby into room R, and each goes through all of the rooms in succession, entering by one door and exiting by the other, which room will they be in at the same time?

(1)   Lisa spends $2x$ minutes in each room and Paul spends $3x$ minutes in each room.

(2)   Lisa spends 10 minutes less time in each room than Paul does.

19.   Quadrilateral $RSTU$ shown above is a site plan for a parking lot in which side RU is parallel to side ST and RU is longer than ST. What is the area of the parking lot?

(1) $RU = 80$ meters
(2) $TU = 20\sqrt{10}$ meters

20.   If $xy = -6$, what is the value of $xy(x + y)$?

(1) $x - y = 5$
(2) $xy^2 = 18$

STOP

IF YOU FINISH BEFORE TIME IS CALLED, YOU MAY CHECK YOUR WORK ON THIS SECTION ONLY.
DO NOT TURN TO ANY OTHER SECTION IN THE TEST.

SECTION 5

Time — 25 minutes

16 Questions

Directions: For each question in this section, select the best of the answer choices given.

1. The local board of education found that, because the current physics curriculum has little direct relevance to today's world, physics classes attracted few high school students. So to attract students to physics classes, the board proposed a curriculum that emphasizes principles of physics involved in producing and analyzing visual images.

Which of the following, if true, provides the strongest reason to expect that the proposed curriculum will be successful in attracting students?

(A) Several of the fundamental principles of physics are involved in producing and analyzing visual images.
(B) Knowledge of physics is becoming increasingly important in understanding the technology used in today's world.
(C) Equipment that a large producer of photographic equipment has donated to the high school could be used in the proposed curriculum.
(D) The number of students interested in physics today is much lower than the number of students interested in physics 50 years ago.
(E) In today's world the production and analysis of visual images is of major importance in communications, business, and recreation.

2. Many companies now have employee assistance programs that enable employees, free of charge, to improve their physical fitness, reduce stress, and learn ways to stop smoking. These programs increase worker productivity, reduce absenteeism, and lessen insurance costs for employee health care. Therefore, these programs benefit the company as well as the employee.

Which of the following, if true, most significantly strengthens the conclusion above?

(A) Physical fitness programs are often the most popular services offered to employees.
(B) Studies have shown that training in stress management is not effective for many people.
(C) Regular exercise reduces people's risk of heart disease and provides them with increased energy.
(D) Physical injuries sometimes result from entering a strenuous physical fitness program too quickly.
(E) Employee assistance programs require companies to hire people to supervise the various programs offered.

3. Unlike the wholesale price of raw wool, the wholesale price of raw cotton has fallen considerably in the last year. Thus, although the retail price of cotton clothing at retail clothing stores has not yet fallen, it will inevitably fall.

Which of the following, if true, most seriously weakens the argument above?

(A) The cost of processing raw cotton for cloth has increased during the last year.
(B) The wholesale price of raw wool is typically higher than that of the same volume of raw cotton.
(C) The operating costs of the average retail clothing store have remained constant during the last year.
(D) Changes in retail prices always lag behind changes in wholesale prices.
(E) The cost of harvesting raw cotton has increased in the last year.

GO ON TO THE NEXT PAGE.

-426-

4. Small-business groups are lobbying to defeat proposed federal legislation that would substantially raise the federal minimum wage. This opposition is surprising since the legislation they oppose would, for the first time, exempt all small businesses from paying any minimum wage.

Which of the following, if true, would best explain the opposition of small-business groups to the proposed legislation?

(A) Under the current federal minimum-wage law, most small businesses are required to pay no less than the minimum wage to their employees.

(B) In order to attract workers, small companies must match the wages offered by their larger competitors, and these competitors would not be exempt under the proposed laws.

(C) The exact number of companies that are currently required to pay no less than the minimum wage but that would be exempt under the proposed laws is unknown.

(D) Some states have set their own minimum wages— in some cases, quite a bit above the level of the minimum wage mandated by current federal law—for certain key industries.

(E) Service companies make up the majority of small businesses and they generally employ more employees per dollar of revenues than do retail or manufacturing businesses.

5. Reviewer: The book *Art's Decline* argues that European painters today lack skills that were common among European painters of preceding centuries. In this the book must be right, since its analysis of 100 paintings, 50 old and 50 contemporary, demonstrates convincingly that none of the contemporary paintings are executed as skillfully as the older paintings.

Which of the following points to the most serious logical flaw in the reviewer's argument?

(A) The paintings chosen by the book's author for analysis could be those that most support the book's thesis.

(B) There could be criteria other than the technical skill of the artist by which to evaluate a painting.

(C) The title of the book could cause readers to accept the book's thesis even before they read the analysis of the paintings that supports it.

(D) The particular methods currently used by European painters could require less artistic skill than do methods used by painters in other parts of the world.

(E) A reader who was not familiar with the language of art criticism might not be convinced by the book's analysis of the 100 paintings.

6. The pharmaceutical industry argues that because new drugs will not be developed unless heavy development costs can be recouped in later sales, the current 20 years of protection provided by patents should be extended in the case of newly developed drugs. However, in other industries new-product development continues despite high development costs, a fact that indicates that the extension is unnecessary.

Which of the following, if true, most strongly supports the pharmaceutical industry's argument against the challenge made above?

(A) No industries other than the pharmaceutical industry have asked for an extension of the 20-year limit on patent protection.

(B) Clinical trials of new drugs, which occur after the patent is granted and before the new drug can be marketed, often now take as long as 10 years to complete.

(C) There are several industries in which the ratio of research and development costs to revenues is higher than it is in the pharmaceutical industry.

(D) An existing patent for a drug does not legally prevent pharmaceutical companies from bringing to market alternative drugs, provided they are sufficiently dissimilar to the patented drug.

(E) Much recent industrial innovation has occurred in products—for example, in the computer and electronics industries—for which patent protection is often very ineffective.

GO ON TO THE NEXT PAGE.

Questions 7-8 are based on the following.

Bank depositors in the United States are all financially protected against bank failure because the government insures all individuals' bank deposits. An economist argues that this insurance is partly responsible for the high rate of bank failures, since it removes from depositors any financial incentive to find out whether the bank that holds their money is secure against failure. If depositors were more selective, then banks would need to be secure in order to compete for depositors' money.

7. The economist's argument makes which of the following assumptions?

(A) Bank failures are caused when big borrowers default on loan repayments.
(B) A significant proportion of depositors maintain accounts at several different banks.
(C) The more a depositor has to deposit, the more careful he or she tends to be in selecting a bank.
(D) The difference in the interest rates paid to depositors by different banks is not a significant factor in bank failures.
(E) Potential depositors are able to determine which banks are secure against failure.

8. Which of the following, if true, most seriously weakens the economist's argument?

(A) Before the government started to insure depositors against bank failure, there was a lower rate of bank failure than there is now.
(B) When the government did not insure deposits, frequent bank failures occurred as a result of depositors' fears of losing money in bank failures.
(C) Surveys show that a significant proportion of depositors are aware that their deposits are insured by the government.
(D) There is an upper limit on the amount of an individual's deposit that the government will insure, but very few individuals' deposits exceed this limit.
(E) The security of a bank against failure depends on the percentage of its assets that are loaned out and also on how much risk its loans involve.

9. Passengers must exit airplanes swiftly after accidents, since gases released following accidents are toxic to humans and often explode soon after being released. In order to prevent passenger deaths from gas inhalation, safety officials recommend that passengers be provided with smoke hoods that prevent inhalation of the gases.

Which of the following, if true, constitutes the strongest reason <u>not</u> to require implementation of the safety officials' recommendation?

(A) Test evacuations showed that putting on the smoke hoods added considerably to the overall time it took passengers to leave the cabin.
(B) Some airlines are unwilling to buy the smoke hoods because they consider them to be prohibitively expensive.
(C) Although the smoke hoods protect passengers from the toxic gases, they can do nothing to prevent the gases from igniting.
(D) Some experienced flyers fail to pay attention to the safety instructions given on every commercial flight before takeoff.
(E) In many airplane accidents, passengers who were able to reach emergency exits were overcome by toxic gases before they could exit the airplane.

10. In 1960, 10 percent of every dollar paid in automobile insurance premiums went to pay costs arising from injuries incurred in car accidents. In 1990, 50 percent of every dollar paid in automobile insurance premiums went toward such costs, despite the fact that cars were much safer in 1990 than in 1960.

Which of the following, if true, best explains the discrepancy outlined above?

(A) There were fewer accidents in 1990 than in 1960.
(B) On average, people drove more slowly in 1990 than in 1960.
(C) Cars grew increasingly more expensive to repair over the period in question.
(D) The price of insurance increased more rapidly than the rate of inflation between 1960 and 1990.
(E) Health-care costs rose sharply between 1960 and 1990.

GO ON TO THE NEXT PAGE.

11. Caterpillars of all species produce an identical hormone called "juvenile hormone" that maintains feeding behavior. Only when a caterpillar has grown to the right size for pupation to take place does a special enzyme halt the production of juvenile hormone. This enzyme can be synthesized and will, on being ingested by immature caterpillars, kill them by stopping them from feeding.

Which of the following, if true, most strongly supports the view that it would not be advisable to try to eradicate agricultural pests that go through a caterpillar stage by spraying croplands with the enzyme mentioned above?

(A) Most species of caterpillar are subject to some natural predation.
(B) Many agricultural pests do not go through a caterpillar stage.
(C) Many agriculturally beneficial insects go through a caterpillar stage.
(D) Since caterpillars of different species emerge at different times, several sprayings would be necessary.
(E) Although the enzyme has been synthesized in the laboratory, no large-scale production facilities exist as yet.

12. Although aspirin has been proven to eliminate moderate fever associated with some illnesses, many doctors no longer routinely recommend its use for this purpose. A moderate fever stimulates the activity of the body's disease-fighting white blood cells and also inhibits the growth of many strains of disease-causing bacteria.

If the statements above are true, which of the following conclusions is most strongly supported by them?

(A) Aspirin, an effective painkiller, alleviates the pain and discomfort of many illnesses.
(B) Aspirin can prolong a patient's illness by eliminating moderate fever helpful in fighting some diseases.
(C) Aspirin inhibits the growth of white blood cells, which are necessary for fighting some illnesses.
(D) The more white blood cells a patient's body produces, the less severe the patient's illness will be.
(E) The focus of modern medicine is on inhibiting the growth of disease-causing bacteria within the body.

13. Because postage rates are rising, *Home Decorator* magazine plans to maximize its profits by reducing by one half the number of issues it publishes each year. The quality of articles, the number of articles published per year, and the subscription price will not change. Market research shows that neither subscribers nor advertisers will be lost if the magazine's plan is instituted.

Which of the following, if true, provides the strongest evidence that the magazine's profits are likely to decline if the plan is instituted?

(A) With the new postage rates, a typical issue under the proposed plan would cost about one-third more to mail than a typical current issue would.
(B) The majority of the magazine's subscribers are less concerned about a possible reduction in the quantity of the magazine's articles than about a possible loss of the current high quality of its articles.
(C) Many of the magazine's long-time subscribers would continue their subscriptions even if the subscription price were increased.
(D) Most of the advertisers that purchase advertising space in the magazine will continue to spend the same amount on advertising per issue as they have in the past.
(E) Production costs for the magazine are expected to remain stable.

GO ON TO THE NEXT PAGE.

14. A study of marital relationships in which one partner's sleeping and waking cycles differ from those of the other partner reveals that such couples share fewer activities with each other and have more violent arguments than do couples in a relationship in which both partners follow the same sleeping and waking patterns. Thus, mismatched sleeping and waking cycles can seriously jeopardize a marriage.

Which of the following, if true, most seriously weakens the argument above?

(A) Married couples in which both spouses follow the same sleeping and waking patterns also occasionally have arguments that can jeopardize the couple's marriage.

(B) The sleeping and waking cycles of individuals tend to vary from season to season.

(C) The individuals who have sleeping and waking cycles that differ significantly from those of their spouses tend to argue little with colleagues at work.

(D) People in unhappy marriages have been found to express hostility by adopting a different sleeping and waking cycle from that of their spouses.

(E) According to a recent study, most people's sleeping and waking cycles can be controlled and modified easily.

GO ON TO THE NEXT PAGE.

Questions 15-16 are based on the following.

Roland: The alarming fact is that 90 percent of the people in this country now report that they know someone who is unemployed.

Sharon: But a normal, moderate level of unemployment is 5 percent, with 1 out of 20 workers unemployed. So at any given time if a person knows approximately 50 workers, 1 or more will very likely be unemployed.

15. Sharon's argument is structured to lead to which of the following as a conclusion?

(A) The fact that 90% of the people know someone who is unemployed is not an indication that unemployment is abnormally high.

(B) The current level of unemployment is not moderate.

(C) If at least 5% of workers are unemployed, the result of questioning a representative group of people cannot be the percentage Roland cites.

(D) It is unlikely that the people whose statements Roland cites are giving accurate reports.

(E) If an unemployment figure is given as a certain percent, the actual percentage of those without jobs is even higher.

16. Sharon's argument relies on the assumption that

(A) normal levels of unemployment are rarely exceeded

(B) unemployment is not normally concentrated in geographically isolated segments of the population

(C) the number of people who each know someone who is unemployed is always higher than 90% of the population

(D) Roland is not consciously distorting the statistics he presents

(E) knowledge that a personal acquaintance is unemployed generates more fear of losing one's job than does knowledge of unemployment statistics

S T O P

IF YOU FINISH BEFORE TIME IS CALLED, YOU MAY CHECK YOUR WORK ON THIS SECTION ONLY.
DO NOT TURN TO ANY OTHER SECTION IN THE TEST.

SECTION 6

Time — 25 minutes

16 Questions

Directions: In this section solve each problem, using any available space on the page for scratchwork. Then indicate the best of the answer choices given.

Numbers: All numbers used are real numbers.

Figures: Figures that accompany problems in this section are intended to provide information useful in solving the problems. They are drawn as accurately as possible EXCEPT when it is stated in a specific problem that its figure is not drawn to scale. All figures lie in a plane unless otherwise indicated.

1. $\dfrac{(3)(0.072)}{0.54} =$

(A) 0.04
(B) 0.3
(C) 0.4
(D) 0.8
(E) 4.0

2. A car dealer sold x used cars and y new cars during May. If the number of used cars sold was 10 greater than the number of new cars sold, which of the following expresses this relationship?

(A) $x > 10y$
(B) $x > y + 10$
(C) $x > y - 10$
(D) $x = y + 10$
(E) $x = y - 10$

3. What is the maximum number of $1\frac{1}{4}$-foot pieces of wire that can be cut from a wire that is 24 feet long?

(A) 11
(B) 18
(C) 19
(D) 20
(E) 30

4. If each of the two lines ℓ_1 and ℓ_2 is parallel to line ℓ_3, which of the following must be true?

(A) Lines ℓ_1, ℓ_2, and ℓ_3 lie in the same plane.
(B) Lines ℓ_1, ℓ_2, and ℓ_3 lie in different planes.
(C) Line ℓ_1 is parallel to line ℓ_2.
(D) Line ℓ_1 is the same line as line ℓ_2.
(E) Line ℓ_1 is the same line as line ℓ_3.

$$\frac{61.24 \times (0.998)^2}{\sqrt{403}}$$

5. The expression above is approximately equal to

(A) 1
(B) 3
(C) 4
(D) 5
(E) 6

GO ON TO THE NEXT PAGE.

-432-

6. Car X and car Y traveled the same 80-mile route. If car X took 2 hours and car Y traveled at an average speed that was 50 percent faster than the average speed of car X, how many hours did it take car Y to travel the route?

(A) $\dfrac{2}{3}$

(B) 1

(C) $1\dfrac{1}{3}$

(D) $1\dfrac{3}{5}$

(E) 3

7. If the numbers $\dfrac{17}{24}, \dfrac{1}{2}, \dfrac{3}{8}, \dfrac{3}{4},$ and $\dfrac{9}{16}$ were ordered from greatest to least, the middle number of the resulting sequence would be

(A) $\dfrac{17}{24}$

(B) $\dfrac{1}{2}$

(C) $\dfrac{3}{8}$

(D) $\dfrac{3}{4}$

(E) $\dfrac{9}{16}$

8. If a 10 percent deposit that has been paid toward the purchase of a certain product is $110, how much more remains to be paid?

(A) $880
(B) $990
(C) $1,000
(D) $1,100
(E) $1,210

9. Kim purchased n items from a catalog for $8 each. Postage and handling charges consisted of $3 for the first item and $1 for each additional item. Which of the following gives the total dollar amount of Kim's purchase, including postage and handling, in terms of n ?

(A) $8n + 2$
(B) $8n + 4$
(C) $9n + 2$
(D) $9n + 3$
(E) $9n + 4$

GO ON TO THE NEXT PAGE.

10. $\left(\sqrt{7} + \sqrt{7}\right)^2 =$

(A) 98
(B) 49
(C) 28
(D) 21
(E) 14

11. If the average (arithmetic mean) of the four numbers K, $2K + 3$, $3K - 5$, and $5K + 1$ is 63, what is the value of K?

(A) 11

(B) $15\frac{3}{4}$

(C) 22

(D) 23

(E) $25\frac{3}{10}$

12. A rabbit on a controlled diet is fed daily 300 grams of a mixture of two foods, food X and food Y. Food X contains 10 percent protein and food Y contains 15 percent protein. If the rabbit's diet provides exactly 38 grams of protein daily, how many grams of food X are in the mixture?

(A) 100
(B) 140
(C) 150
(D) 160
(E) 200

GO ON TO THE NEXT PAGE.

13. A company that ships boxes to a total of 12 distribution centers uses color coding to identify each center. If either a single color or a pair of two different colors is chosen to represent each center and if each center is uniquely represented by that choice of one or two colors, what is the minimum number of colors needed for the coding? (Assume that the order of the colors in a pair does not matter.)

(A) 4
(B) 5
(C) 6
(D) 12
(E) 24

14. If $x + y = a$ and $x - y = b$, then $2xy =$

(A) $\dfrac{a^2 - b^2}{2}$

(B) $\dfrac{b^2 - a^2}{2}$

(C) $\dfrac{a - b}{2}$

(D) $\dfrac{ab}{2}$

(E) $\dfrac{a^2 + b^2}{2}$

15. A rectangular circuit board is designed to have width w inches, perimeter p inches, and area k square inches. Which of the following equations must be true?

(A) $w^2 + pw + k = 0$

(B) $w^2 - pw + 2k = 0$

(C) $2w^2 + pw + 2k = 0$

(D) $2w^2 - pw - 2k = 0$

(E) $2w^2 - pw + 2k = 0$

16. On a certain road, 10 percent of the motorists exceed the posted speed limit and receive speeding tickets, but 20 percent of the motorists who exceed the posted speed limit do not receive speeding tickets. What percent of the motorists on that road exceed the posted speed limit?

(A) $10\frac{1}{2}\%$

(B) $12\frac{1}{2}\%$

(C) 15%

(D) 22%

(E) 30%

STOP

IF YOU FINISH BEFORE TIME IS CALLED, YOU MAY CHECK YOUR WORK ON THIS SECTION ONLY.
DO NOT TURN TO ANY OTHER SECTION IN THE TEST.

Answer Key: Form A

Section 1	Section 2	Section 3	Section 4	Section 5	Section 6
1. B	1. C	1. A	1. D	1. E	1. C
2. D	2. C	2. B	2. D	2. C	2. D
3. B	3. D	3. D	3. D	3. A	3. C
4. A	4. A	4. B	4. C	4. B	4. C
5. C	5. E	5. C	5. E	5. A	5. B
6. D	6. E	6. C	6. B	6. B	6. C
7. E	7. C	7. D	7. E	7. E	7. E
8. A	8. E	8. E	8. A	8. B	8. B
9. E	9. C	9. B	9. D	9. A	9. C
10. C	10. A	10. C	10. E	10. E	10. C
11. A	11. A	11. E	11. C	11. C	11. D
12. B	12. B	12. D	12. A	12. B	12. B
13. D	13. B	13. A	13. C	13. D	13. B
14. Not Scored	14. A	14. C	14. E	14. D	14. A
15. B	15. D	15. E	15. A	15. A	15. E
16. A	16. D	16. A	16. D	16. B	16. B
17. E		17. C	17. C		
18. E		18. B	18. A		
19. A		19. B	19. D		
20. B		20. E	20. B		
21. C		21. A			
22. E		22. A			
		23. C			

Explanatory Material: Sentence Correction, Section 1

1. Although early soap operas <u>were first aired on evening radio in the 1920's, they had moved to the daytime hours of the 1930's</u> when the evening schedule became crowded with comedians and variety shows.

   (A) were first aired on evening radio in the 1920's, they were moved to the daytime hours in the 1930's
   (B) were first aired on evening radio in the 1920's, they were moved to the daytime hours in the 1930's
   (C) were aired first on evening radio in the 1920's, moving to the daytime hours in the 1930's
   (D) were aired first in the evening on 1920's radio, they moved to the daytime hours of the 1930's
   (E) aired on evening radio first in the 1920's, they were moved to the 1930's in the daytime hours

Choice B is the best answer. It maintains the passive voice and the past tense (*were . . . aired*) established in the introductory clause. Choice D breaks this parallelism by shifting from passive to active voice (*moved*). Choice A also uses the active voice and inappropriately shifts to the past perfect tense (*had moved*); the past perfect should be used to indicate action completed before, not after, the action of *were aired*. In C, *moving* introduces a dangling participial phrase in place of an independent clause, thus producing a fragment. E drops *were* before *aired* and finishes the sentence with two prepositional phrases that distort the meaning.

2. In 1527 King Henry VIII sought to have his marriage to Queen Catherine annulled <u>so as to marry</u> Anne Boleyn.

   (A) so as to marry
   (B) and so could be married to
   (C) to be married to
   (D) so that he could marry
   (E) in order that he would marry

The sentence calls for an adverbial clause of purpose to explain why Henry sought the annulment. D, the best choice, does this clearly and correctly. It is introduced by an appropriate conjunction, *so that*, and contains a logically appropriate verb form, *could marry*. Awkward and imprecise, A does not specify who is *to marry* Anne. B substitutes an illogical coordinate predicate for the needed purpose clause; because the annulment had not yet been granted, Henry could not remarry. C lacks an appropriate conjunction, and the infinitive clause *to be married to . . .* makes this choice awkward and unidiomatic. Although E uses an appropriate conjunction, *in order that*, the verb form *would marry* is unidiomatic and illogical (*might marry* would be better).

3. The energy source on *Voyager 2* is not a nuclear reactor, in which atoms are actively broken <u>apart; rather</u> a kind of nuclear battery that uses natural radioactive decay to produce power.

   (A) apart; rather
   (B) apart, but rather
   (C) apart, but rather that of
   (D) apart, but that of
   (E) apart; it is that of

Choice B, the best answer, follows an idiomatic form of expression for paired coordinates — *not X, but rather Y*; here *rather* is optional but preferable because it helps establish a contrast between the two types of energy source. Choice A incorrectly uses a semicolon rather than a coordinating conjunction (*but*) to connect the coordinate parts; a semicolon should be used to join independent clauses. In choices C, D, and E, *that of* has no grammatical referent and thus produces illogical and incorrect sentences.

4. Seismologists studying the earthquake that struck northern California in October 1989 are still investigating some of its mysteries: the unexpected power of the seismic waves, <u>the upward thrust that threw one man straight into the air, and the strange electromagnetic signals detected hours before the temblor.</u>

   (A) the upward thrust that threw one man straight into the air, and the strange electromagnetic signals detected hours before the temblor
   (B) the upward thrust that threw one man straight into the air, and strange electromagnetic signals were detected hours before the temblor
   (C) the upward thrust threw one man straight into the air, and hours before the temblor strange electromagnetic signals were detected
   (D) one man was thrown straight into the air by the upward thrust, and hours before the temblor strange electromagnetic signals were detected
   (E) one man who was thrown straight into the air by the upward thrust, and strange electromagnetic signals that were detected hours before the temblor

The correct answer will maintain parallelism in a coordinate series. Three *mysteries* are mentioned, and the first establishes the form required for the other two members of the series, a noun phrase introduced by *the* (*the unexpected power . . .*). A, the best choice, correctly uses noun phrases introduced by *the* for the second and third members of the series (*the upward thrust . . .* and *the strange electromagnetic signals . . .*). Choice B substitutes a clause (*strange electromagnetic signals were detected . . .*) for the third noun phrase, and C and D use clauses instead of noun phrases for both additional members of the series. E uses two noun phrases, but they are not introduced by *the*. Furthermore, the phrase *one man who . . .* does not logically identify one of the *mysteries*.

5. A letter by Mark Twain, written in the same year as _The Adventures of Huckleberry Finn_ were published, reveals that Twain provided financial assistance to one of the first Black students at Yale Law School.

(A) A letter by Mark Twain, written in the same year as _The Adventures of Huckleberry Finn_ were published,

(B) A letter by Mark Twain, written in the same year of publication as _The Adventures of Huckleberry Finn_,

(C) A letter by Mark Twain, written in the same year that _The Adventures of Huckleberry Finn_ was published,

(D) Mark Twain wrote a letter in the same year as he published _The Adventures of Huckleberry Finn_ that

(E) Mark Twain wrote a letter in the same year of publication as _The Adventures of Huckleberry Finn_ that

In this sentence, the relative pronoun _that_ should introduce the clause _The Adventures . . . published_ to make a relative clause modifying _year_. Also, the singular title of the novel demands a singular verb: for example, one would say, "_The Adventures of Huckleberry Finn_ is (not "are") a great book." Only C, the best choice, satisfies both requirements. Choices A and D incorrectly substitute _as_ for _that_ to introduce the relative clause. Choice A also mistakes the novel title for a plural (_were published_). B confuses meaning (_written in the same year of publication as_). E creates a similar confusion of meaning, and both D and E are awkward and imprecise because _that_ is too far away from its referent (_letter_) to be clear.

6. Two new studies indicate that many people become obese more due to the fact that their bodies burn calories too slowly than overeating.

(A) due to the fact that their bodies burn calories too slowly than overeating

(B) due to their bodies burning calories too slowly than to eating too much

(C) because their bodies burn calories too slowly than that they are overeaters

(D) because their bodies burn calories too slowly than because they eat too much

(E) because of their bodies burning calories too slowly than because of their eating too much

The members of a comparison (_more X than Y_) should be expressed in parallel form. D, the best choice, correctly uses parallel clauses introduced by _because_. The clauses themselves are clear and direct. Choice E uses parallel forms, but the convoluted structures are awkward and wordy. Furthermore, the word _bodies_ would need an apostrophe (_bodies'_) since it is the logical subject of the gerund _burning_ (that is, it answers the question, "Whose burning?"). A, B, and C do not use parallel forms for the two members of the comparison. In addition, A and B use _due to_ unidiomatically to mean _because_; properly used, _due to_ is synonymous with _attributable to_.

7. As a result of the ground-breaking work of Barbara McClintock, many scientists now believe that all of the information encoded in 50,000 to 100,000 of the different genes found in a human cell are contained in merely three percent of the cell's DNA.

(A) 50,000 to 100,000 of the different genes found in a human cell are contained in merely

(B) 50,000 to 100,000 of the human cell's different genes are contained in a mere

(C) the 50,000 to 100,000 different genes found in human cells are contained in merely

(D) 50,000 to 100,000 of human cells' different genes is contained in merely

(E) the 50,000 to 100,000 different genes found in a human cell is contained in a mere

This question poses two problems: subject-verb agreement and accuracy of expression. Choice E, the best answer, states the matter clearly and grammatically. The subject, _all of the information_, must be taken as singular because the mass noun _information_ is singular. Choices A, B, and C all mistake the number of the subject and incorrectly use the plural verb _are contained_. A, B, and D do not make it clear whether _50,000 to 100,000_ represents all or a fraction of the genes in a cell. C and D, by referring to cells in the plural, do not make it clear whether the number mentioned is to be found in each individual cell or in a collection of cells.

8. So poorly educated and trained are many young recruits to the United States work force that many business executives fear this country will lose its economic preeminence.

(A) So poorly educated and trained are many young recruits to the United States work force that

(B) As poorly educated and trained as many young recruits to the United States work force are,

(C) Because of many young recruits to the United States work force who are so poorly educated and trained,

(D) That many young recruits to the United States work force are so poorly educated and trained is why

(E) Many young recruits to the United States work force who are so poorly educated and trained explains why

A, the best choice, uses the idiomatic form _So X that Y_ to establish a cause/effect relationship between clauses _X_ and _Y_. In B, the subject of the _as . . . as_ clause (_young recruits_) should be the subject of the main clause as well (e.g., _they_). Furthermore, main clauses following concessive clauses must express a contrasting notion: for example, "As ill-prepared as they are, they nevertheless find good jobs." C offers a wordy, convoluted _because_ clause. In D, the sentence form _X is why_ is unidiomatic (_X is the reason why_ would be idiomatic but needlessly wordy and awkward). E exhibits subject-verb disagreement: _young recruits . . . explains why_.

9. In the last few years, the number of convicted criminals given community service <u>sentences, which allow the criminals to remain unconfined while they perform specific jobs benefiting the public, have</u> risen dramatically.

(A) sentences, which allow the criminals to remain unconfined while they perform specific jobs benefiting the public, have

(B) sentences, performing specific jobs that benefit the public while being allowed to remain unconfined, have

(C) sentences, performing specific jobs beneficial to the public while they are allowed to remain unconfined, have

(D) sentences which allow them to remain unconfined in their performing of specific jobs beneficial to the public has

(E) sentences allowing them to remain unconfined while performing specific jobs that benefit the public has

At issue in this question is subject-verb agreement; *the number . . . has risen* must be the kernel of the main clause. Choice E, the best answer, uses a singular verb form, *has*, to agree with the singular subject, *the number*. Choices A, B, and C mistake *criminals* for the sentence subject and so incorrectly use the plural verb form *have*. In B and C the verb phrases (*performing . . .*) do not clearly modify *criminals*, because another noun (*sentences*) intrudes, nor do the verb phrases clearly establish temporal relationships among events. D is wordy and imprecise (*in their performing of specific jobs*).

10. During the early years of European settlement on a continent that was viewed as "wilderness" by the newcomers, <u>Native Americans, intimately knowing the ecology of the land, were a help in the rescuing of</u> many Pilgrims and pioneers from hardship, or even death.

(A) Native Americans, intimately knowing the ecology of the land, were a help in the rescuing of

(B) Native Americans knew the ecology and the land intimately and this enabled them to help in the rescue of

(C) Native Americans, with their intimate knowledge of the ecology of the land, helped to rescue

(D) having intimate knowledge of the ecology of the land, Native Americans helped the rescue of

(E) knowing intimately the ecology of the land, Native Americans helped to rescue

Choice A suffers from the wordy and indirect expression *were a help in the rescuing of*. B creates an awkward, redundant, fused sentence in which the first clause has to be repeated in the vague *this* of the second clause; furthermore, the comma required before *and* in larger compound sentences is omitted.

D and E are confusingly worded because they begin with present participles (*having* and *knowing*) that appear at first to refer to the immediately preceding noun, *newcomers*, rather than to *Native Americans*. D also has the wordy and unidiomatic *helped the rescue of*. Clear, direct, and economical, choice C is best.

11. Quasars are so distant that their light has taken billions of years to reach the Earth; consequently, <u>we see them as they were during</u> the formation of the universe.

(A) we see them as they were during

(B) we see them as they had been during

(C) we see them as if during

(D) they appear to us as they did in

(E) they appear to us as though in

A, the best choice, correctly employs the simple past verb tense to describe a past condition. Choice B inappropriately switches to the past perfect (*had been*); the past perfect properly describes action that is completed prior to some other event described with the simple past tense. Choice C presents a dangling adverbial modifier, *as if during . . .*, that illogically modifies *we see*. D ambiguously suggests that the quasars appeared to us *in the formation of the universe* — that is, as though we were present to view them then. In E, *as though in* distorts the meaning to suggest that we see the quasars in a hypothetical situation — that is, that they may *not* have been involved in the formation of the universe.

12. Because of the enormous research and development expenditures required <u>to survive</u> in the electronics industry, an industry marked by rapid innovation and volatile demand, such firms tend to be very large.

(A) to survive

(B) of firms to survive

(C) for surviving

(D) for survival

(E) for firms' survival

The subject of the main clause (*such firms*) presumes a prior reference to the firms in question. Furthermore, the logical subject of *to survive* and the logical complement of *required* should be made explicit. All three demands are met by B, the best choice. Choices A, C, and D, with no reference to the firms in question, meet none of these demands. In choice E, the illogical and awkward use of a prepositional phrase (*for firms' survival*) buries the needed initial reference to *firms* in a possessive modifier.

13. <u>Consumers may not think of household cleaning products to be</u> hazardous substances, but many of them can be harmful to health, especially if they are used improperly.

    (A) Consumers may not think of household cleaning products to be

    (B) Consumers may not think of household cleaning products being

    (C) A consumer may not think of their household cleaning products being

    (D) A consumer may not think of household cleaning products as

    (E) Household cleaning products may not be thought of, by consumers, as

A correct sentence will follow the idiomatic form of expression *to think of X as Y*. Only D, the best choice, uses *as* in the comparison. The infinitive *to be* in A and the participle *being* in B and C cannot grammatically and idiomatically connect those choices to the rest of the sentence. Moreover, in C the plural pronoun *their* does not agree with the singular noun referent, *consumer*. E is awkward and wordy in its use of the passive voice.

14. NOT SCORED

15. Archaeologists in Ireland believe that a recently discovered chalice, which dates from the eighth century, was probably buried <u>to keep from</u> being stolen by invaders.

    (A) to keep from
    (B) to keep it from
    (C) to avoid
    (D) in order that it would avoid
    (E) in order to keep from

noun or pronoun that specifies what it is that might be stolen. Choice B is best because it provides the pronoun *it*, which refers to *chalice*. Like choice A, choices C and E lack the pronoun. D is wordy and awkward in its use of the passive voice. Moreover, *avoid* is used imprecisely in C and D because it illogically suggests that the chalice is acting to prevent its own theft.

16. As measured by the Commerce Department, corporate profits peaked in the fourth quarter of 1988 <u>and have slipped since then, as many companies have been unable to pass on higher costs</u>.

    (A) and have slipped since then, as many companies have been unable to pass on higher costs

    (B) and have slipped since then, the reason being because many companies have been unable to pass on higher costs

    (C) and slipped since then, many companies being unable to pass on higher costs

    (D) but, many companies unable to pass on higher costs, they have slipped since then

    (E) yet are slipping since then, because many companies were unable to pass on higher costs

A, the best choice, observes an appropriate sequence of verb tenses — a single act in the past (*peaked*) followed by an extended activity reaching to the present (*have slipped*). The *as* clause states clearly the cause of the slippage. B suffers from the redundant and unidiomatic expression *the reason being because*. In C, the use of the simple past *slipped* with *since then* is unidiomatic because *since then* denotes extended time. In D, the intrusion of the awkward *many . . . costs* causes the antecedent of *they* to become unclear. Furthermore, a comma should precede the *but* since it introduces a second independent clause. In E, *yet* also requires a comma before it, *are slipping* with *since then* is illogical, and *were unable* represents an ungrammatical tense shift.

17. The recent surge in the number of airplane flights has clogged the nation's air-traffic control system, <u>to lead to 55 percent more delays at airports, and prompts</u> fears among some officials that safety is being compromised.

    (A) to lead to 55 percent more delays at airports, and prompts

    (B) leading to 55 percent more delay at airports and prompting

    (C) to lead to a 55 percent increase in delay at airports and prompt

    (D) to lead to an increase of 55 percent in delays at airports, and prompted

    (E) leading to a 55-percent increase in delays at airports and prompting

This question poses two major problems: parallel structure and precision of expression. In E, the best choice, parallel structure is maintained in the participial phrases introduced by *leading* and *prompting*, and the phrase *55-percent increase in delays* conveys the meaning more accurately than does the phrase *55 percent more delay(s)* in A and B. Also, choice A lacks parallelism. In C and D the infinitive phrase *to lead to . . .* is less idiomatic than the participial phrase *leading to . . .* Choice C uses the singular *delay* where the plural is needed to indicate an increase in the number of delays; the phrase *increase in delay* has no exact meaning.

18. Judge Bonham denied a motion to allow members of the jury to go home at the end of each day instead of to confine them to a hotel.

(A) to allow members of the jury to go home at the end of each day instead of to confine them to
(B) that would have allowed members of the jury to go home at the end of each day instead of confined to
(C) under which members of the jury are allowed to go home at the end of each day instead of confining them in
(D) that would allow members of the jury to go home at the end of each day rather than confinement in
(E) to allow members of the jury to go home at the end of each day rather than be confined to

In this sentence, *members of the jury* are presented with two options: they may (1) *go* home or (2) *be* confined to a hotel. The rejected motion would have allowed them *to do* the first rather than *[to] suffer* the second. *Members of the jury* must be the logical subject of both options, and both must be expressed in parallel form, that is, as infinitive clauses. E, the best choice, observes these requirements. In A and C, the phrase *members of the jury* is not the logical subject of the second option, *to confine them* or *confining them*, since jury members are not doing the confining. In B and D, *confined* and *confinement* are not infinitives and thus do not parallel *to go* in the first option.

19. In one of the bloodiest battles of the Civil War, fought at Sharpsburg, Maryland, on September 17, 1862, four times as many Americans were killed as would later be killed on the beaches of Normandy during D-Day.

(A) Americans were killed as
(B) Americans were killed than
(C) Americans were killed than those who
(D) more Americans were killed as there
(E) more Americans were killed as those who

Choice A, the best answer, is the only option that accurately expresses the comparison by using the idiomatic form *as many . . . as*. In B and C, *as many . . . than* is unidiomatic, and in C and E, *those who* is a wordy intrusion. In D and E, *more* is redundant because the phrase *four times as many* in the original sentence conveys the idea of *more*.

20. As a result of medical advances, many people that might at one time have died as children of such infections as diphtheria, pneumonia, or rheumatic fever now live well into old age.

(A) that might at one time have died as children
(B) who might once have died in childhood
(C) that as children might once have died
(D) who in childhood might have at one time died
(E) who, when they were children, might at one time have died

B, the best choice, uses the preferred relative pronoun, *who,* to refer to *many people.* It observes formal and logical parallelism in the wording of the relative clause and the main clause: first, adverbs (*once* and *now*); second, verbs (*might have died* and *live*); and third, adverbial prepositional phrases (*in childhood* and *into old age*). A and C use the questionable relative pronoun *that* to refer to *many people.* They also violate the parallel structure noted above. D and E, although they use the correct pronoun, *who,* offer convoluted and nonparallel structures for the relative clause.

21. Proponents of artificial intelligence say they will be able to make computers that can understand English and other human languages, recognize objects, and reason as an expert does — computers that will be used to diagnose equipment breakdowns, deciding whether to authorize a loan, or other purposes such as these.

(A) as an expert does — computers that will be used to diagnose equipment breakdowns, deciding whether to authorize a loan, or other purposes such as these
(B) as an expert does, which may be used for purposes such as diagnosing equipment breakdowns or deciding whether to authorize a loan
(C) like an expert — computers that will be used for such purposes as diagnosing equipment breakdowns or deciding whether to authorize a loan
(D) like an expert, the use of which would be for purposes like the diagnosis of equipment breakdowns or the decision whether or not a loan should be authorized
(E) like an expert, to be used to diagnose equipment breakdowns, deciding whether to authorize a loan or not, or the like

A correct sentence must maintain parallel structure. In choice A, the three-part series (*to diagnose . . . , deciding, . . . or other purposes . . .*) lacks parallelism. C, the best choice, replaces A's third element with *for such purposes as*; this phrase functions as a stem for the other two elements, which are recast as two parallel phrases — *diagnosing . . . or deciding . . . .*. Thus, choice C not only manages the parallel structure but avoids the less effective *other purposes such as these* at the end of choice A. Choice E uses faulty parallel structure (*to be used. . . , deciding . . . , or the like*). In B and D, *which* and *the use of which* introduce sentence elements that lack antecedents or reference. In addition, D is wordy.

22. Manifestations of Islamic political militancy in the first period of religious reformism were the rise of the Wahhabis in Arabia, the Sanusi in Cyrenaica, the Fulani in Nigeria, the Mahdi in the Sudan, and the victory of the Usuli "mujtahids" in Shiite Iran and Iraq.

(A) Manifestations of Islamic political militancy in the first period of religious reformism were the rise of the Wahhabis in Arabia, the Sanusi in Cyrenaica, the Fulani in Nigeria, the Mahdi in the Sudan, and

(B) Manifestations of Islamic political militancy in the first period of religious reformism were shown in the rise of the Wahhabis in Arabia, the Sanusi in Cyrenaica, the Fulani in Nigeria, the Mahdi in the Sudan, and also

(C) In the first period of religious reformism, manifestations of Islamic political militancy were the rise of the Wahhabis in Arabia, of the Sanusi in Cyrenaica, the Fulani in Nigeria, the Mahdi in the Sudan, and

(D) In the first period of religious reformism, manifestations of Islamic political militancy were shown in the rise of the Wahhabis in Arabia, the Sanusi in Cyrenaica, the Fulani in Nigeria, the Mahdi in the Sudan, and

(E) In the first period of religious reformism, Islamic political militancy was manifested in the rise of the Wahhabis in Arabia, the Sanusi in Cyrenaica, the Fulani in Nigeria, and the Mahdi in the Sudan, and in

E, the best choice, uses parallel phrases for the two major coordinate members (*in the rise of . . . and in the victory of . . .*) and also for the series listed in the first of these (*s in t, u in v, w in x, and y in z*). E's placement of the *In . . . reformism* phrase at the beginning of the sentence is direct and efficient. Choices A, B, C, and D omit *and* before *the Mahdi*, the last element in the first series; thus, they incorrectly merge the second major member (*the victory of*) into the series listed under the first member (*the rise of*). Furthermore, in A and B the *in . . . reformism* phrase has been awkwardly set between the subject and verb of the sentence.

Explanatory Material: Problem Solving, Section 2

1. As a salesperson, Phyllis can choose one of two methods of annual payment: either an annual salary of $35,000 with no commission or an annual salary of $10,000 plus a 20 percent commission on her total annual sales. What must her total annual sales be to give her the same annual pay with either method?

(A) $100,000
(B) $120,000
(C) $125,000
(D) $130,000
(E) $132,000

If s is the amount of sales needed to generate commissions so that $35,000 = 10,000 + 0.2s$, then $0.2s = 25,000$ and $s = \dfrac{\$25,000}{0.2} = \$125,000$. The best answer is C.

2. A restaurant buys fruit in cans containing $3\frac{1}{2}$ cups of fruit each. If the restaurant uses $\frac{1}{2}$ cup of the fruit in each serving of its fruit compote, what is the least number of cans needed to prepare 60 servings of the compote?

(A) 7
(B) 8
(C) 9
(D) 10
(E) 12

If the restaurant uses $\frac{1}{2}$ cup of fruit per serving, then $\frac{1}{2}(60)$ or 30 cups of fruit are needed for 60 servings. Since there are $3\frac{1}{2}$ cups in one can and 30 cups are needed, $\dfrac{30}{3\frac{1}{2}}$, or $8\frac{4}{7}$ cans are needed. Because it is not possible to purchase part of a can, 9 cans are needed. Therefore, the best answer is C.

3. If $x > 3,000$, then the value of $\dfrac{x}{2x+1}$ is closest to

(A) $\dfrac{1}{6}$
(B) $\dfrac{1}{3}$
(C) $\dfrac{10}{21}$
(D) $\dfrac{1}{2}$
(E) $\dfrac{3}{2}$

If x is greater than 3,000, the value of $\dfrac{x}{2x+1}$ is very close to the value of $\dfrac{x}{2x}$, which is equal to $\dfrac{1}{2}$. The best answer is D.

4. Machine A produces 100 parts twice as fast as machine B does. Machine B produces 100 parts in 40 minutes. If each machine produces parts at a constant rate, how many parts does machine A produce in 6 minutes?

(A) 30
(B) 25
(C) 20
(D) 15
(E) 7.5

If machine A produces the parts twice as fast as machine B does, then machine A requires half as much time as machine B does, or 20 minutes, to produce 100 parts. In 6 minutes, machine A will produce $\frac{100}{20}(6)$ or 30 parts. The best answer is A.

5. **If 18 is 15 percent of 30 percent of a certain number, what is the number?**

   (A)   9
   (B)   36
   (C)   40
   (D)   81
   (E)   400

If n represents the number, then $18 = 0.15(0.3n)$ and $n = \frac{18}{0.045} = 400$. The best answer is E.

6. **A necklace is made by stringing N individual beads together in the repeating pattern red bead, green bead, white bead, blue bead, and yellow bead. If the necklace design begins with a red bead and ends with a white bead, then N could equal**

   (A)   16
   (B)   32
   (C)   41
   (D)   54
   (E)   68

The pattern of red, green, white, blue, and yellow repeats after every 5th bead. Since the first bead is red (first in the pattern) and the last bead is white (third in the pattern), the number of beads is of the form $5n + 3$, where n is an integer. Of the options, only $68 = 5(13) + 3$ is of this form. Therefore, the best answer is E.

7. **If $x = (0.08)^2$, $y = \frac{1}{(0.08)^2}$, and $z = (1 - 0.08)^2 - 1$, which of the following is true?**

   (A) $x = y = z$
   (B) $y < z < x$
   (C) $z < x < y$
   (D) $y < x$ and $x = z$.
   (E) $x < y$ and $x = z$.

It is not necessary to compute the precise values of $x, y,$ and z. It is sufficient to see that x is between 0 and 1, y is greater than 1, and $z = (0.92)^2 - 1$ is less than 0. Therefore, $z < x < y$, and the best answer is C.

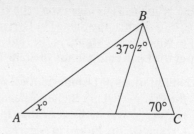

8. **In $\triangle ABC$ above, what is x in terms of z ?**

   (A) $z + 73$
   (B) $z - 73$
   (C) $70 - z$
   (D) $z - 70$
   (E) $73 - z$

The sum of the angle measures of $\triangle ABC$ is equal to $x + 37 + z + 70 = 180$. Thus, $x + z = 180 - (37 + 70) = 73$, and $x = 73 - z$. The best answer is E.

9. **In 1990 a total of x earthquakes occurred worldwide, some but not all of which occurred in Asia. If m of these earthquakes occurred in Asia, which of the following represents the ratio of the number of earthquakes that occurred in Asia to the number that did <u>not</u> occur in Asia?**

   (A) $\dfrac{x}{m}$

   (B) $\dfrac{m}{x}$

   (C) $\dfrac{m}{x - m}$

   (D) $\dfrac{x}{x - m}$

   (E) $1 - \dfrac{m}{x}$

If there was a total of x earthquakes and m of them occurred in Asia, then $x - m$ of them did not occur in Asia. Therefore, the ratio of the number that occurred in Asia to the number that did not occur in Asia is $\dfrac{m}{x - m}$. The best answer is C.

10. **If $\dfrac{x + y}{xy} = 1$, then $y =$**

   (A) $\dfrac{x}{x - 1}$

   (B) $\dfrac{x}{x + 1}$

   (C) $\dfrac{x - 1}{x}$

   (D) $\dfrac{x + 1}{x}$

   (E) x

It follows from the equation that $x + y = xy$; so $x = xy - y$ or $x = y(x - 1)$. Therefore, $y = \dfrac{x}{x - 1}$, and the best answer is A.

11. If $\dfrac{1}{2}$ of the air in a tank is removed with each stroke of a vacuum pump, what fraction of the original amount of air has been removed after 4 strokes?

(A) $\dfrac{15}{16}$

(B) $\dfrac{7}{8}$

(C) $\dfrac{1}{4}$

(D) $\dfrac{1}{8}$

(E) $\dfrac{1}{16}$

With the first stroke of the pump, $\dfrac{1}{2}$ of the air is removed; with the second stroke $\dfrac{1}{2}$ of the remaining $\dfrac{1}{2}$, or $\dfrac{1}{4}$, of the air is removed, leaving $\dfrac{1}{2} - \dfrac{1}{4} = \dfrac{1}{4}$ of the air; with the third stroke $\dfrac{1}{2}$ of $\dfrac{1}{4}$, or $\dfrac{1}{8}$, is removed, leaving $\dfrac{1}{4} - \dfrac{1}{8} = \dfrac{1}{8}$; and with the fourth stroke $\dfrac{1}{2}$ of $\dfrac{1}{8}$, or $\dfrac{1}{16}$, is removed. Therefore, $\dfrac{1}{2} + \dfrac{1}{4} + \dfrac{1}{8} + \dfrac{1}{16} = \dfrac{15}{16}$ of the air has been removed, and the best answer is A.

12. Last year Department Store X had a sales total for December that was 4 times the average (arithmetic mean) of the monthly sales totals for January through November. The sales total for December was what fraction of the sales total for the year?

(A) $\dfrac{1}{4}$

(B) $\dfrac{4}{15}$

(C) $\dfrac{1}{3}$

(D) $\dfrac{4}{11}$

(E) $\dfrac{4}{5}$

If A was the average sales total per month for the first 11 months, the December sales total was $4A$, the sales total for the first 11 months was $11A$, and the sales total for the year was $11A + 4A = 15A$. Thus, the ratio of the sales total for December to the sales total for the year was $\dfrac{4A}{15A} = \dfrac{4}{15}$. The best answer is B.

13. How many integers n are there such that $1 < 5n + 5 < 25$?

(A) Five
(B) Four
(C) Three
(D) Two
(E) One

If $1 < 5n + 5 < 25$, then subtracting 5 from each of the three parts of the inequality yields $-4 < 5n < 20$, and dividing by 5 yields $-\dfrac{4}{5} < n < 4$. The four integers that satisfy this inequality are 0, 1, 2, and 3. Therefore, the best answer is B.

14. If the two-digit integers M and N are positive and have the same digits, but in reverse order, which of the following CANNOT be the sum of M and N ?

(A) 181
(B) 165
(C) 121
(D) 99
(E) 44

If t and u are the two digits, integer M is 10 times the tens digit plus the units digit, or $10t + u$. Similarly, n is $10u + t$, and the sum of the numbers M and N is $(10t + u) + (10u + t) = 11t + 11u = 11(t + u)$. Because the sum of M and N must be a multiple of 11, you need only find which of the answer choices is *not* a multiple of 11. Since $181 = 11(16) + 5$, 181 is not a multiple of 11, and the best answer is A.

15. Working alone, printers $X, Y,$ and Z can do a certain printing job, consisting of a large number of pages, in 12, 15, and 18 hours, respectively. What is the ratio of the time it takes printer X to do the job, working alone at its rate, to the time it takes printers Y and Z to do the job, working together at their individual rates?

(A) $\dfrac{4}{11}$

(B) $\dfrac{1}{2}$

(C) $\dfrac{15}{22}$

(D) $\dfrac{22}{15}$

(E) $\dfrac{11}{4}$

If X requires 12 hours to do the job, then X can do $\frac{1}{12}$ of the job per hour. Similarly, Y can do $\frac{1}{15}$ of the job per hour and Z can do $\frac{1}{18}$ of the job per hour. Together, Y and Z can do $\left(\frac{1}{15} + \frac{1}{18}\right)$ or $\frac{11}{90}$ of the job per hour, which implies that it takes them $\frac{90}{11}$ hours to complete the job. Therefore, the ratio of the time required for X to do the job (12 hours) to the time required for Y and Z working together to do the job $\left(\frac{90}{11} \text{ hours}\right)$ is $\frac{12}{\frac{90}{11}} = \frac{12(11)}{90} = \frac{22}{15}$. The best answer is D.

16. In 1985 a company sold a brand of shoes to retailers for a fixed price per pair. In 1986 the number of pairs of the shoes that the company sold to retailers decreased by 20 percent, while the price per pair increased by 20 percent. If the company's revenue from the sales of the shoes in 1986 was $3.0 million, what was the approximate revenue from the sale of the shoes in 1985 ?

(A) $2.4 million
(B) $2.9 million
(C) $3.0 million
(D) $3.1 million
(E) $3.6 million

Let n be the number of pairs of shoes sold in 1985 and p be the price per pair in 1985. Then in 1986, the number of pairs sold was 20 percent less, or $0.8n$, and the price per pair was 20 percent more, or $1.2p$. The company's revenue in 1986 was $(0.8n)(1.2p) = 0.96np = \$3$ million. Therefore, np, the company's revenue in 1985, was $\frac{\$3 \text{ million}}{0.96}$ or approximately $3.1 million. The best answer is D.

Explanatory Material: Reading Comprehension, Section 3

1. The passage as a whole can best be characterized as which of the following?

(A) An evaluation of a scholarly study
(B) A description of an attitudinal change
(C) A discussion of an analytical defect
(D) An analysis of the causes of a phenomenon
(E) An argument in favor of revising a view

The best answer is A. This question requires you to identify the option that best describes the passage as a whole. In the first paragraph, the author of the passage compares Glatthaar's scholarly study with other "excellent" studies of its kind, noting that Glatthaar's makes more extensive use of certain types of material. The second paragraph summarizes several points of the study, noting that one point is presented "accurately" and another "appropriately." Paragraph three assesses Glatthaar's ability to "demonstrate the magnitude" of a change, asserting that he exaggerates a particular element. Thus, the passage as a whole is concerned with offering an overall "evaluation of a scholarly study"; it does not present a sustained discussion of any of the matters described by the other options.

2. According to the author, which of the following is true of Glatthaar's *Forged in Battle* compared with previous studies on the same topic?

(A) It is more reliable and presents a more complete picture of the historical events on which it concentrates than do previous studies.
(B) It uses more of a particular kind of source material and focuses more closely on a particular aspect of the topic than do previous studies.
(C) It contains some unsupported generalizations, but it rightly emphasizes a theme ignored by most previous studies.
(D) It surpasses previous studies on the same topic in that it accurately describes conditions often neglected by those studies.
(E) It makes skillful use of supporting evidence to illustrate a subtle trend that previous studies have failed to detect.

The best answer is B. Lines 3-6 state that *Forged in Battle* "uses more soldiers' letters and diaries" and "concentrates more intensely on Black-White relations in Black regiments than do any of its predecessors." Thus, the author of the passage asserts, as B states, that *Forged in Battle* "uses more of a particular kind of source material and relies more closely on a particular aspect of the topic than do previous studies." Nowhere does the passage compare the reliability of Glatthaar's work to that of earlier studies, as A and D assert. Similarly, C and E can be eliminated because the passage does not assert that previous studies neglected any particular subject, only that Glatthaar's work "concentrates more intensely on Black-White relations than do . . . its predecessors."

3. The author implies that the title of Glatthaar's book refers specifically to which of the following?

(A) The sense of pride and accomplishment that Black soldiers increasingly felt as a result of their Civil War experiences
(B) The civil equality that African Americans achieved after the Civil War, partly as a result of their use of organizational skills honed by combat
(C) The changes in discriminatory army policies that were made as a direct result of the performance of Black combat units during the Civil War
(D) The improved interracial relations that were formed by the races' facing of common dangers and their waging of a common fight during the Civil War
(E) The standards of racial egalitarianism that came to be adopted as a result of White Civil War veterans' repudiation of their previous racism

The best answer is D. In lines 6-9, the author of the passage asserts that the title of Glatthaar's work, *Forged in Battle*, "expresses his [Glatthaar's] thesis: loyalty, friendship, and respect among White officers and Black soldiers were fostered by the mutual dangers they faced in combat." That the combat dangers "fostered" such attributes suggests that they acted to improve the relations among the Black and White soldiers; thus the passage implies, as D states, that the title *Forged in Battle* refers specifically to the idea that interracial relations between Black and White soldiers fighting in the Civil War were improved by their shared experience of combat dangers. The other options describe factors that the author of the passage in no way relates to the book's title.

4. The passage mentions which of the following as an important theme that receives special emphasis in Glatthaar's book?

(A) The attitudes of abolitionist officers in Black units
(B) The struggle of Black units to get combat assignments
(C) The consequences of the poor medical care received by Black soldiers
(D) The motives of officers serving in Black units
(E) The discrimination that Black soldiers faced when trying for promotions

The best answer is B. In the second paragraph, the author of the passage describes Glatthaar's work as "appropriately emphasizing the campaign by Black soldiers and their officers to get the opportunity to fight." Thus, the "struggle of Black units to get combat assignments" (choice B) is identified as rightfully emphasized by Glatthaar — that is, as being important and receiving emphasis. None of the other options describe such themes: (choice A) is mentioned only by the author of the passage; C and E are wrong because medical care and discrimination are mentioned merely as realities that

Glatthaar "accurately describes"; and D because, although the passage mentions the motives of White officers in Black units, Glatthaar is nowhere described as giving special emphasis to the motives of all officers in such units.

5. The passage suggests that which of the following was true of Black units' disease mortality rates in the Civil War?

(A) They were almost as high as the combat mortality rates of White units.
(B) They resulted in part from the relative inexperience of these units when in combat.
(C) They were especially high because of the nature of these units' usual duty assignments.
(D) They resulted in extremely high overall casualty rates in Black combat units.
(E) They exacerbated the morale problems that were caused by the army's discriminatory policies.

The best answer is C. In lines 15-19, the passage describes "army policies that kept most Black units serving in rear-echelon assignments and working in labor battalions." The passage continues: "Thus . . . their mortality rate from disease . . . was twice as great." The use of the word "thus" here suggests that some aspect of these conditions was the cause of the high mortality rates, as C states. Nothing can be inferred from the passage about the absolute relationship between disease mortality rates of Black units and combat mortality rates of White units (choice A), or about the relative severity of overall casualty rates in Black combat units (choice D). Nor does the passage mention or suggest the role of either the inexperience (choice B) or the morale (choice E) of Black units.

6. The author of the passage quotes the White officer in lines 23-24 primarily in order to provide evidence to support the contention that

(A) virtually all White officers initially had hostile attitudes toward Black soldiers
(B) Black soldiers were often forced to defend themselves from physical attacks initiated by soldiers from White units
(C) the combat performance of Black units changed the attitudes of White soldiers toward Black soldiers
(D) White units paid especially careful attention to the performance of Black units in battle
(E) respect in the army as a whole was accorded only to those units, whether Black or White, that performed well in battle

The best answer is C. Lines 20-22 assert that the combat performance of Black units "won increasing respect from initially skeptical or hostile White soldiers." To support the assertion that the performance of the Black units changed White soldiers' attitudes toward them, the author of the passage then quotes a comment made by one of those White officers about the Black units: "they fought their way into the respect of all the army" (lines 22-24). The passage makes no assertions about whether "virtually all White officers" were hostile (choice A); or about whether White units either physically attacked Black units (choice B) or paid particular attention to the performance of Black units (choice D). Nor does it address the relationship "in the army as a whole" between a unit's performance and the respect accorded it (choice E).

7. Which of the following best describes the kind of error attributed to Glatthaar in lines 25-28 ?

   (A) Insisting on an unwarranted distinction between two groups of individuals in order to render an argument concerning them internally consistent
   (B) Supporting an argument in favor of a given interpretation of a situation with evidence that is not particularly relevant to the situation
   (C) Presenting a distorted view of the motives of certain individuals in order to provide grounds for a negative evaluation of their actions
   (D) Describing the conditions prevailing before a given event in such a way that the contrast with those prevailing after the event appears more striking than it actually is
   (E) Asserting that a given event is caused by another event merely because the other event occurred before the given event occurred

The best answer is D. To answer this question, you must determine what "kind of error" the author of the passage directly attributes to Glatthaar in lines 25-28. These lines assert that "in trying to demonstrate the magnitude of this attitudinal change" — the change in White soldiers' attitudes toward Black units — "Glatthaar seems to exaggerate the prewar racism of the White men who became officers in Black regiments." The error attributed to Glatthaar is one of exaggerating conditions before the Civil War so as to overstate the contrast between prewar and postwar conditions. Glatthaar is not specifically faulted in lines 25-28 for presenting either "an unwarranted distinction between two groups" (choice A); or irrelevant evidence (choice B); or for distorting motives in order to evaluate actions negatively (choice C); or for misattributing causality (choice E).

8. Which of the following actions can best be described as indulging in "generational chauvinism" (lines 40-41) as that practice is defined in the passage?

   (A) Condemning a present-day monarch merely because many monarchs have been tyrannical in the past
   (B) Clinging to the formal standards of politeness common in one's youth to such a degree that any relaxation of those standards is intolerable
   (C) Questioning the accuracy of a report written by an employee merely because of the employee's gender
   (D) Deriding the superstitions accepted as "science" in past eras without acknowledging the prevalence of irrational beliefs today
   (E) Labeling a nineteenth-century politician as "corrupt" for engaging in once-acceptable practices considered intolerable today

The best answer is E. This question requires you to identify a hypothetical situation that exemplifies the concept of "generational chauvinism" as it is defined in the passage. This term is defined in lines 37-41, where the author of the passage criticizes the use of "current standards of racial egalitarianism" to judge the motives of abolitionist White officers serving in Black regiments: "to call their feelings 'powerful racial prejudices' is to indulge in generational chauvinism — to judge past eras by present standards." The last phrase serves to define "generational chauvinism," a concept exemplified by the situation described in choice E, in which the "once-acceptable practices" of a nineteenth-century politician are labeled as "corrupt." None of the other options exemplify this "generational chauvinism" as it is defined in the passage.

9. The passage is primarily concerned with

   (A) detailing the evidence that has led most biologists to replace the trichotomous picture of living organisms with a dichotomous one
   (B) outlining the factors that have contributed to the current hypothesis concerning the number of basic categories of living organisms
   (C) evaluating experiments that have resulted in proof that the prokaryotes are more ancient than had been expected
   (D) summarizing the differences in structure and function found among true bacteria, archaebacteria, and eukaryotes
   (E) formulating a hypothesis about the mechanisms of evolution that resulted in the ancestors of the prokaryotes

The best answer is B. The first paragraph reviews inquiries leading to the hypothesis that two categories of organism exist; the second explains how "more recent research" (line 27) supports a three-category hypothesis. Thus, the passage is primarily concerned with outlining factors contributing to the current hypothesis about the number of such categories. Choice A is wrong because the passage describes the replacement of a dichotomous with a trichotomous model, not the reverse. C is wrong because the passage mentions no experimental proof that the prokaryotes were older than expected; D is wrong because the passage only briefly discusses the structure and function of eukaryotes and prokaryotes, never mentioning those of archaebacteria. E is wrong because the passage mentions no particular "mechanisms of evolution" that created the ancestors of the prokaryotes.

10. According to the passage, investigations of eukaryotic and prokaryotic cells at the molecular level supported the conclusion that

   (A) most eukaryotic organisms are unicellular
   (B) complex cells have well-formed nuclei
   (C) prokaryotes and eukaryotes form two funda-
        mental categories
   (D) subcellular structures are visible with a
        microscope
   (E) prokaryotic and eukaryotic cells have similar
        enzymes

The best answer is C. In lines 10-20, the passage states that, although molecular investigation revealed some similarities between prokaryotic and eukaryotic cells, "the differences between the groups and the similarities within each group made it seem certain to most biologists that the tree of life had only two stems" (lines 18-20) — that is, "two fundamental categories," as C asserts. The passage does not address what proportion of eukaryotic organisms are unicellular (choice A) or whether all complex cells have well-formed nuclei (choice B). That "subcellular structures are visible with a microscope" (choice D) is described as established "initially" — that is, before the research was "ultimately carried to the molecular level" (lines 7-10). According to the passage, molecular investigation supports the idea that "sequences of . . . enzymes tend to be typically prokaryotic or eukaryotic"— not that those enzymes are similar (lines 16-17), as E claims.

11. According to the passage, which of the following statements about the two-category hypothesis is likely to be true?

   (A) It is promising because it explains the presence of
        true bacteria-like organisms such as organelles
        in eukaryotic cells.
   (B) It is promising because it explains why eukaryotic
        cells, unlike prokaryotic cells, tend to form
        multicellular organisms.
   (C) It is flawed because it fails to account for the
        great variety among eukaryotic organisms.
   (D) It is flawed because it fails to account for the
        similarity between prokaryotes and eukaryotes.
   (E) It is flawed because it fails to recognize an
        important distinction among prokaryotes.

The best answer is E. According to the passage, the two-category hypothesis, which assumed "that all living things could be divided into two . . . categories," (lines 1-2) now "seems fundamentally wrong" (line 27) because it does not account for evidence that two kinds of prokaryotic organisms exist: true bacteria and "a distinct evolutionary branch," archaebacteria (line 40). Thus, the hypothesis is said to ignore an important distinction among prokaryotes, as E states. Choice A is wrong because the passage does not even mention bacteria-like organisms existing within eukaryotic cells. B contradicts the passage, which states that "many unicellular organisms . . . are eukaryotic." C and D are wrong because each identifies as a flaw the failure to "account for" conditions that the passage indicates the hypothesis accounted for.

12. It can be inferred from the passage that which of the following have recently been compared in order to clarify the fundamental classifications of living things?

   (A) The genetic coding in true bacteria and that in
        other prokaryotes
   (B) The organelle structures of archaebacteria, true
        bacteria, and eukaryotes
   (C) The cellular structures of multicellular organisms
        and unicellular organisms
   (D) The molecular sequences in eukaryotic RNA, true
        bacterial RNA, and archaebacterial RNA
   (E) The amino acid sequences in enzymes of various
        eukaryotic species and those of enzymes in
        archaebacterial species

This question requires you to identify information implied rather than stated in the passage. D, the best answer, can be inferred from lines 30-31, which state that it "now appears that there are three stems in the tree of life" — that is, three categories of organism — because "new techniques for determining the molecular sequence of the RNA of organisms have produced evolutionary information . . . ." From this it can be inferred, as D states, that researchers compared the molecular sequences in the RNA of each kind of organism postulated by the new view — eukaryotic, bacterial, and archaebacterial. The other choices cannot be inferred from the passage; each describes types of features discussed in the context of earlier, not later, research.

13. If the "new techniques" mentioned in line 31 were applied in studies of biological classifications other than bacteria, which of the following is most likely?

   (A) Some of those classifications will have to be reevaluated.
   (B) Many species of bacteria will be reclassified.
   (C) It will be determined that there are four main categories of living things rather than three.
   (D) It will be found that true bacteria are much older than eukaryotes.
   (E) It will be found that there is a common ancestor of the eukaryotes, archaebacteria, and true bacteria.

The best answer is A. This question requires you to select the answer that, based on information presented in the passage, describes the most likely result of applying the "new techniques" (line 31) to biological classifications other than bacteria. Lines 31-36 state that these techniques "produced . . . information about the degree to which organisms are related." Specifically, the techniques "strongly suggested" that the prokaryote category includes two distinct kinds of organisms (lines 36-37). This information, which suggests a reevaluation of the prokaryote classification, provides support for the statement that "classifications other than bacteria" are also likely to require reevaluation if the same techniques are used to study them, as A states.

14. According to the passage, researchers working under the two-category hypothesis were correct in thinking that

   (A) prokaryotes form a coherent group
   (B) the common ancestor of all living things had complex properties
   (C) eukaryotes are fundamentally different from true bacteria
   (D) true bacteria are just as complex as eukaryotes
   (E) ancestral versions of eukaryotic genes functioned differently from their modern counterparts

The best answer is C. Lines 26-28 indicate that C is an aspect of the two-category hypothesis that "has been sustained by more recent research." Thus, the passage supports the assumption, made by proponents of the two-category hypothesis, that "eukaryotes are fundamentally different from true bacteria" (choice C). The passage contradicts the idea that prokaryotes "form a coherent group" (choice A) because it states that there is "one respect" (lines 27-28) in which new evidence contradicts the hypothesis: in addition to the eukaryotes and the "true bacteria," which are prokaryotes, there exists another distinct "evolutionary branch" within the prokaryotes: the archaebacteria (38-41). The two-category hypothesis, as presented in the passage, proposes neither B nor E and asserts the opposite of D.

15. All of the following statements are supported by the passage EXCEPT:

   (A) True bacteria form a distinct evolutionary group.
   (B) Archaebacteria are prokaryotes that resemble true bacteria.
   (C) True bacteria and eukaryotes employ similar types of genetic coding.
   (D) True bacteria and eukaryotes are distinguishable at the subcellular level.
   (E) Amino acid sequences of enzymes are uniform for eukaryotic and prokaryotic organisms.

The best answer is E, the only choice NOT supported by the passage. Lines 37-38 support the idea that "true bacteria indeed form a large coherent group" of the kind postulated by the two-category hypothesis — that is, that they are a "distinct evolutionary group" (choice A). Lines 38-40 assert that "archaebacteria . . . are prokaryotes and . . . resemble true bacteria," as B states. Lines 10-13 support C: "prokaryotic and eukaryotic cells . . . translate genetic information . . . according to the same type of genetic coding." D is supported by lines 7-10 in the passage, which state that "the distinction between eukaryotes and bacteria" was "initially defined in terms of subcellular structures visible with a microscope." E, however, is contradicted by lines 25-27: "the amino acid sequences of various enzymes tend to be typically prokaryotic or eukaryotic."

16. The author's attitude toward the view that living things are divided into three categories is best described as one of

   (A) tentative acceptance
   (B) mild skepticism
   (C) limited denial
   (D) studious criticism
   (E) wholehearted endorsement

The best answer is A, which aptly describes the author's attitude toward the hypothesis that there are three categories of living things. In lines 30-31 the author states that "it now appears that there are three stems in the tree of life" because new techniques "have strongly suggested" the accuracy of the three-category view (lines 31-41). That the author accepts the three-category hypothesis is suggested by this mention of "strong" support. That this acceptance is "cautious" is conveyed by the use of the terms "seems" (line 27), "appears," and "suggested." Such caution rules out the "wholehearted endorsement" described by E; nor does the author express "denial" of (choice C), "criticism" about (choice D), or "skepticism" about (choice B) the three-category hypothesis.

17. **The author mentions each of the following as a cause of excess inventory EXCEPT**

    (A) production of too much merchandise
    (B) inaccurate forecasting of buyers' preferences
    (C) unrealistic pricing policies
    (D) products' rapid obsolescence
    (E) availability of a better product

The best answer is C. The question requires you to recognize which of the choices is NOT mentioned in the passage as a cause of excess inventory. Choice A, "production of too much merchandise," is listed as a cause in lines 2-3, where the passage states that "overstocks may accumulate through production overruns." In line 4, the assertion that "certain styles and colors prove unpopular" identifies "inaccurate forecasting of buyers' preferences" (choice B), as a cause. D, "products' rapid obsolescence," appears in lines 4-7, which indicate that "with some products . . . last year's models are difficult to move." E, "availability of a better product," is listed as a cause in lines 7-8: "Occasionally the competition introduces a better product." C, "unrealistic pricing policies," is not mentioned in the passage.

18. **The passage suggests that which of the following is a kind of product that a liquidator who sells to discount stores would be unlikely to wish to acquire?**

    (A) Furniture
    (B) Computers
    (C) Kitchen equipment
    (D) Baby-care products
    (E) Children's clothing

The best answer is B. This question requires you to identify a kind of product that information in the passage suggests a liquidator selling to discount stores is UNLIKELY to want to buy. About computers, lines 4-7 state that "last year's models are difficult to move even at a huge discount." A liquidator buying excess inventory for resale to discount stores would therefore probably avoid buying computers because demand for them would be low; thus, the passage suggests choice B. The passage does not mention choice A or choice C. Choices D and E, baby-care products and children's clothing, are mentioned as examples of products that, if dumped, might cause public relations problems; there is no information in the passage about the attractiveness of these products to liquidators.

19. **The passage provides information that supports which of the following statements?**

    (A) Excess inventory results most often from insufficient market analysis by the manufacturer.
    (B) Products with slight manufacturing defects may contribute to excess inventory.
    (C) Few manufacturers have taken advantage of the changes in the federal tax laws.
    (D) Manufacturers who dump their excess inventory are often caught and exposed by the news media.
    (E) Most products available in discount stores have come from manufacturers' excess-inventory stock.

The best answer is B. "Products with slight manufacturing defects may contribute to excess inventory," is supported by lines 2-3, which assert that "production . . . errors" can contribute to excess inventory. Lines 27-29, which describe a scenario illustrating the exposure of excess-inventory dumping, also support B: "QRS Company dumps . . . diapers because they have slight imperfections." The passage does not mention "market analysis" (choice A), nor does it include information about the relative proportion either of "manufacturers that have taken advantage of tax laws" (choice C) or of products in discount stores that come from excess-inventory stock (choice E). Far from being supported, D groundlessly asserts that the "remote possibility" described in lines 23-24 occurs "often."

20. **The author cites the examples in lines 25-29 most probably in order to illustrate**

    (A) the fiscal irresponsibility of dumping as a policy for dealing with excess inventory
    (B) the waste-management problems that dumping new products creates
    (C) the advantages to the manufacturer of dumping as a policy
    (D) alternatives to dumping explored by different companies
    (E) how the news media could portray dumping to the detriment of the manufacturer's reputation

The best answer is E. Lines 25-29 immediately follow the author's description of how manufacturers choosing excess-inventory dumping may be "caught by the news media," in which case "dumping perfectly useful products can turn into a public relations nightmare" (lines 22-25). Both scenarios described in lines 25-29 illustrate the kind of statement that, if made by the news media, would "portray dumping to the detriment of the manufacturer's reputation," as E states. Each emphasizes the reputation-damaging perception that a manufacturer has dumped useful, much-needed goods. Neither scenario illustrates A - D. Neither "fiscal responsibility" (choice A) nor "waste-management" (choice B) is mentioned in the passage. Choices C and D are mentioned elsewhere in the passage but are not organizationally or logically connected with lines 25-29.

21. By asserting that manufacturers "are simply unaware" (line 31), the author suggests which of the following?

(A) Manufacturers might donate excess inventory to charity rather than dump it if they knew about the provision in the federal tax code.

(B) The federal government has failed to provide sufficient encouragement to manufacturers to make use of advantageous tax policies.

(C) Manufacturers who choose to dump excess inventory are not aware of the possible effects on their reputation of media coverage of such dumping.

(D) The manufacturers of products disposed of by dumping are unaware of the needs of those people who would find the products useful.

(E) The manufacturers who dump their excess inventory are not familiar with the employment of liquidators to dispose of overstock.

The best answer is A. Lines 30-31 state: "The managers of these companies are not deliberately wasteful; they are simply unaware of all their alternatives." The single such "alternative" identified is one encouraged by "an above-cost federal tax deduction for companies that donate inventory to charity." By stating that the manufacturers "are simply unaware" of this more cost-saving alternative, the author suggests that, if aware of the provision, they might choose inventory-donation over inventory-dumping. Nowhere does the author suggest that the government "failed to provide sufficient encouragement" for donation (choice B), or that the manufacturers were unaware in the ways described by C, D, or E.

22. The information in the passage suggests that which of the following, if true, would make donating excess inventory to charity less attractive to manufacturers than dumping?

(A) The costs of getting the inventory to the charitable destination are greater than the above-cost tax deduction.

(B) The news media give manufacturers' charitable contributions the same amount of coverage that they give dumping.

(C) No straight-cost tax benefit can be claimed for items that are dumped.

(D) The fair-market value of an item in excess inventory is 1.5 times its cost.

(E) Items end up as excess inventory because of a change in the public's preferences.

The best answer is A. Lines 34-36 indicate that a manufacturer can save money by donating excess inventory to charity. However, if the cost of transporting inventory to a charitable destination is greater than that savings, as A indicates, the attractiveness of donating excess inventory would be lessened. Because inventory dumping involves "straight cost write-off" (line 18) and "requires little time or preparation" (line 21), dumping might seem more attractive than a donation that does not save the manufacturer money. Choices B, C, and D are consistent with the author's suggestion that inventory donation is more attractive; D is irrelevant to the comparison.

23. Information in the passage suggests that one reason manufacturers might take advantage of the tax provision mentioned in the last paragraph is that

(A) there are many kinds of products that cannot be legally dumped in a landfill

(B) liquidators often refuse to handle products with slight imperfections

(C) the law allows a deduction in excess of the cost of manufacturing the product

(D) media coverage of contributions of excess-inventory products to charity is widespread and favorable

(E) no tax deduction is available for products dumped or sold to a liquidator

The best answer is C. Lines 34-39 describe the 1976 tax provision as a financial "incentive" (line 34) that the manufacturers would take advantage of if they were not "unaware of all their alternatives" for disposing of excess inventory (line 31). This provision allows "an above-cost federal tax deduction for companies that donate inventory to charity"— specifically, deduction of up to "twice cost" for donated goods (lines 34-39). This information suggests that one reason manufacturers might take advantage of the provision is that, as C states, it allows "a deduction in excess of the cost of manufacturing the product." Choices A, B, and D each describe factors that are neither mentioned nor suggested by the passage; E contradicts lines 17-18, which state that inventory-dumping entails "a straight cost write-off on . . . taxes."

Explanatory Material: Data Sufficiency, Section 4

1. The regular price per eight-ounce can of brand X soup is $0.37, regardless of the number of cans purchased. What amount will be saved on the purchase of 3 eight-ounce cans of brand X soup if the regular price is reduced?

(1) At the reduced price, 3 eight-ounce cans of brand X soup will cost $0.99.

(2) The amount that will be saved on each eight-ounce can of brand X soup purchased at the reduced price is $0.04.

From statement (1) it can be determined that the saving on 3 cans of the soup will be 3($0.37) − $0.99 = $0.12. Thus, (1) alone is sufficient, and the answer must be A or D. From statement (2), the saving is 3($0.04) = $0.12. Since each statement alone is sufficient, the best answer is D.

2. **Does Joe weigh more than Tim?**

   (1) **Tim's weight is 80 percent of Joe's weight.**
   (2) **Joe's weight is 125 percent of Tim's weight.**

Statement (1) indicates that Tim's weight is 80 percent of Joe's weight, so Joe weighs more than Tim. Thus, (1) alone is sufficient, and the answer must be A or D. According to statement (2), Joe's weight is more than 100 percent of Tim's weight, so Joe weighs more than Tim. The best answer is therefore D.

3. **Is p^2 an odd integer?**

   (1) **p is an odd integer.**
   (2) **$\sqrt{p}$ is an odd integer.**

Statement (1) indicates that p is an odd integer, which implies that any positive integer power of p will be an odd integer since the product of two or more odd integers is odd. Statement (2) indicates $\sqrt{p}$ is an odd integer. Since $p^2 = (\sqrt{p})^4$, p^2 is a product of odd integers, which, as stated in the discussion of (1), must be odd. Because each statement alone gives sufficient information to answer the question, the best answer is D.

4. **What is the value of xy?**

   (1) **$x + y = 10$**
   (2) **$x - y = 6$**

From statement (1), $x = 10 - y$ and from statement (2), $x = 6 + y$. Neither statement alone gives sufficient information, so the answer must be C or E. The two statements can be solved simultaneously for x and y, so xy can be found. The best answer is C.

5. **Elena receives a salary plus a commission that is equal to a fixed percentage of her sales revenue. What was the total of Elena's salary and commission last month?**

   (1) **Elena's monthly salary is $1,000.**
   (2) **Elena's commission is 5 percent of her sales revenue.**

From the information in the question and statement (1), it is known that Elena's salary is $1,000 and that her commission is equal to a fixed percentage of her sales revenue, but there is no information about the percentage or sales revenue. Thus, (1) alone is not sufficient, and the answer must be B, C, or E. Statement (2) gives the percent but nothing about the sales revenue or her salary. Therefore, (2) alone is not sufficient, and the answer must be C or E. Both statements are still insufficient because they provide no information about her sales revenue. The best answer is E.

6. **Point (x, y) lies in which quadrant of the rectangular coordinate system shown above?**

   (1) **$x + y < 0$**
   (2) **$x = 4$ and $y = -7$.**

From statement (1) alone, it is not possible to determine whether x, y, or both x and y are negative; therefore, the answer must be B, C, or E. From statement (2) alone, it can be determined that the point $(4, -7)$ lies in quadrant IV. The best answer is B.

7. **What is the average (arithmetic mean) of x, y, and z?**

   (1) **$x + y = 5$**
   (2) **$y + z = 7$**

The average of x, y, and z equals $\frac{x + y + z}{3}$. Statement (1) gives no information about z, and statement (2) gives no information about x. Therefore, neither statement alone is sufficient, and the answer must be C or E. From the two statements taken together, $x + 2y + z = 12$, but the value of $x + y + z$ cannot be determined. The best answer is E.

8. **Chan and Mieko drove separate cars along the entire length of a certain route. If Chan made the trip in 15 minutes, how many minutes did it take Mieko to make the same trip?**

   (1) **Mieko's average speed for the trip was $\frac{3}{4}$ of Chan's average speed.**
   (2) **The route is 14 miles long.**

For a fixed distance, the average speed is inversely related to the amount of time required to make the trip. Therefore, from the information given in the question and statement (1), since Mieko's average speed was $\frac{3}{4}$ of Chan's, her time was $\frac{4}{3}$ as long or $\frac{4}{3}(15)$ minutes. Thus, the answer is A or D. Because statement (2) gives no information about Mieko's average speed, it is not sufficient. The best answer is A.

9. **If $xy \neq 0$, is $\frac{x}{y} < 0$?**

   (1) **$x = -y$**
   (2) **$-x = -(-y)$**

Dividing both sides of the equation given in (1) by y yields $\frac{x}{y} = -1$; thus $\frac{x}{y} < 0$, so the correct answer must be A or D. From statement (2), if each side of the equation is divided by -1, the result will be the same as statement (1), so either statement alone is sufficient to answer the question and the best answer is D.

10. What is the value of the two-digit integer x ?

   (1) The sum of the two digits is 3.
   (2) x is divisible by 3.

From statement (1), the two-digit integer must be either 12, 21, or 30. Because a single numerical value of x cannot be determined from (1), the answer must be B, C, or E. Statement (2) alone is not sufficient because there are many two-digit integers divisible by 3, for example, 15, 24, and 27. Since all three numbers from (1) are divisible by 3, statements (1) and (2) together do not provide sufficient information, and the best answer is E.

11. Is the number x between 0.2 and 0.7 ?

   (1) $560x < 280$
   (2) $700x > 280$

From statement (1) it can be determined that $x < 0.5$. Since it cannot be determined whether x is greater than 0.2, the best answer must be B, C, or E. From statement (2) it can be determined that x is greater than 0.4, but it cannot be determined whether x is less than 0.7, and the answer must be C or E. Both statements taken together imply that $0.4 < x < 0.5$, which implies that x is between 0.2 and 0.7. The best answer is C.

12. Is x an integer?

   (1) $\dfrac{x}{2}$ is an integer.
   (2) $2x$ is an integer.

Statement (1) implies that x is an even integer. Therefore, the answer must be either A or D. From statement (2), x could be an integer; but x could also be an odd number divided by 2, such as $\dfrac{1}{2}$ or $-\dfrac{1}{2}$, neither of which is an integer. Therefore, (2) alone is not sufficient, and the best answer is A.

13. A swim club that sold only individual and family memberships charged \$300 for an individual membership. If the club's total revenue from memberships was \$480,000, what was the charge for a family membership?

   (1) The revenue from individual memberships was $\dfrac{1}{4}$ of the total revenue from memberships.

   (2) The club sold 1.5 times as many family memberships as individual memberships.

Let n be the number of individual memberships at \$300 each and m be the number of family memberships at x dollars each. Then the total revenue is $300n + mx = \$480,000$.

Statement (1) yields the equation $\$300n = \dfrac{1}{4}(\$480,000)$, which can be solved for n, so $n = 40$. Substituting 40 for n in the equation $\$300n + mx = \$480,000$ and solving for mx yields $mx = \dfrac{3}{4}(\$480,000)$, but since there is no information about m or x, statement (1) is not sufficient. Statement (2) gives only the information that $m = 1.5n$, so $\$300n + 1.5n(x) = \$480,000$, which cannot be solved for x. Statement (1) yields $n = 400$, and statement (2) taken with (1) yields $\$300(400) + 1.5(400)(x) = \$480,000$, which can be solved for x. The best answer is C.

14. If x, y, and z are positive numbers, is $x > y > z$?

   (1) $xz > yz$
   (2) $yx > yz$

Dividing each side of the inequality in (1) by z yields $x > y$, but there is no information relating z to either x or y. Therefore, the answer must be B, C, or E. Similarly, (2) yields only $x > z$, and the answer must be C or E. From both statements it can be determined that x is greater than both y and z. Because it cannot be determined whether y or z is least, the correct ordering of the three numbers cannot be determined, so the best answer is E.

15. Can the positive integer p be expressed as the product of two integers, each of which is greater than 1 ?

   (1) $31 < p < 37$
   (2) p is odd.

From statement (1), p can be any of the integers 32, 33, 34, 35, or 36. Becuase each of these integers can be expressed as the product of two integers, each of which is greater than 1, the question can be answered even though the specific value of p is not known. Thus, the answer must be A or D. Statement (2) is not sufficient since some odd numbers are prime and so cannot be expressed as a product of two integers, each of which is greater than 1; other odd numbers are composite and so can be expressed as a product of two integers, each of which is greater than 1. The best answer is A.

16. Currently there are 50 picture books on each shelf in the children's section of a library. If these books were to be placed on smaller shelves with 30 picture books on each shelf, how many of the smaller shelves would be needed to hold all of these books?

   (1) The number of smaller shelves needed is 6 more than the current number of shelves.

   (2) Currently there are 9 shelves int he children's section.

The missing information in this problem is the total number of books to be distributed, 30 to a shelf, which will give the total number of smaller shelves. If s is the current number of shelves, there are $50s$ books, and statement (1) says that $30(s + 6) = 50s$, or $s = 9$. Therefore, there are $9(50)$ or 450 books to be distributed on 30 shelves. Thus, the answer must be A or D. Statement (2) also implies that there is a total of $9(50) = 450$ books. Therefore, the best answer is D.

17. Is $y = 6$?

    (1) $y^2 = 36$
    (2) $y^2 - 7y + 6 = 0$

From statement (1) it cannot be determined whether $y = 6$ or $y = -6$. Thus, the answer must be B, C, or E. Factoring the equation in (2) yields $(y - 6)(y - 1) = 0$, which implies that $y = 1$ or $y = 6$. Since a single numerical value of y cannot be determined from either equation alone, the answer must be C or E. From both equations taken together, it can be determined that $y = 6$. The best answer is C.

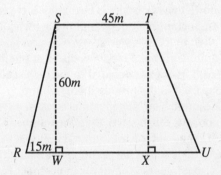

18. The figure above represents the floor plan of an art gallery that has a lobby and 18 rooms. If Lisa goes from the lobby into room A at the same time that Paul goes from the lobby into room R, and each goes through all of the rooms in succession, entering by one door and exiting by the other, which room will they be in at the same time?

    (1)   Lisa spends $2x$ minutes in each room and Paul spends $3x$ minutes in each room.
    (2)   Lisa spends 10 minutes less time in each room than Paul does.

From statement (1), if Lisa spends $\frac{2}{3}$ as much time in each room as Paul does, then Lisa will go through $\frac{3}{2}$ as many rooms as Paul does, or if r is the number of rooms Paul goes through, then $r + \frac{3r}{2} = 18$, and $r = 7.2$ and $\frac{3r}{2} = 10.5$. Thus, they will meet in room L, and the answer must be A or D. Since statement (2) does not relate Lisa's time with Paul's time in a way that is useful, the best answer is A.

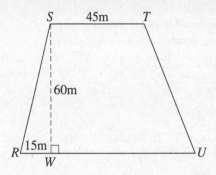

19. Quadrilateral *RSTU* shown above is a site plan for a parking lot in which side *RU* is parallel to side *ST* and *RU* is longer than *ST*. What is the area of the parking lot?

    (1) $RU = 80$ meters
    (2) $TU = 20\sqrt{10}$ meters

The area of a quadrilateral region that has parallel sides of lengths a and b and altitude h is $\frac{1}{2}(a + b)h$. Statement (1) gives the length of the base of the quadrilateral lot. Thus, the area of the lot, in square meters, is $\frac{(45 + 80)}{2}(60)$, and the answer must be A or D. If you do not know the formula, drawing the altitude from T, as shown in the figure below, can be helpful.

It can be seen that, in meters, $RU = 15 + 45 + XU$, and from (1), $80 = 15 + 45 + XU$, so $XU = 20$. The area of *RSTU* is the sum of the areas of the two triangles and the rectangle. From (2), using the Pythagorean theorem gives $60^2 + XU^2 = TU^2 = (20\sqrt{10})^2$, or $XU = 20$ meters. Then the length of RU, in square meters, is $15 + 45 + 20 = 80$, and since this is the information given in (1), it can similarly be used to find the area of *RSTU*. Therefore, the best answer is D.

20. If $xy = -6$, what is the value of $xy(x + y)$?

    (1) $x - y = 5$
    (2) $xy^2 = 18$

The question can be simplified to "What is the value of $-6(x + y)$?" From (1), $x = y + 5$, so substituting $y + 5$ for x in the equation $xy = -6$ yields $(y + 5)y = -6$, or $y^2 + 5y + 6 = 0$. Factoring the equation gives $(y + 2)(y + 3) = 0$, and $y = -2$ or $y = -3$. Since the value of y is not known, neither the value of x nor the value of $x + y$ can be determined. Thus, (1) alone is not sufficient. From statement (2), it follows that $xy^2 = (xy)y = 18$. Substituting -6 for xy in this equation yields $-6y = 18$ or $y = -3$. Since $y = -3$ and $xy = -6$, it follows that $x = -2$. Therefore, statement (2) alone is sufficient to determine the value of $x + y$ and of $-6(x + y)$. The best answer is B.

Explanatory Material:
Critical Reasoning, Section 5

1. The local board of education found that, because the current physics curriculum has little direct relevance to today's world, physics classes attracted few high school students. So to attract students to physics classes, the board proposed a curriculum that emphasizes principles of physics involved in producing and analyzing visual images.

   Which of the following, if true, provides the strongest reason to expect that the proposed curriculum will be successful in attracting students?

   (A) Several of the fundamental principles of physics are involved in producing and analyzing visual images.
   (B) Knowledge of physics is becoming increasingly important in understanding the technology used in today's world.
   (C) Equipment that a large producer of photographic equipment has donated to the high school could be used in the proposed curriculum.
   (D) The number of students interested in physics today is much lower than the number of students interested in physics 50 years ago.
   (E) In today's world the production and analysis of visual images is of major importance in communications, business, and recreation.

For the proposed curriculum change to attract students to physics classes, producing and analyzing visual images must have direct relevance to today's world. Choice E provides evidence that this is so, and thus is the best answer.

Choices A and C mention things relevant to the new curriculum: that it would indeed teach physics and that equipment facilitating its implementation is available. Choice B underscores how desirable it would be for the new curriculum to succeed, and choice D establishes that there is past precedent that more students can be attracted to physics. Not one of choices A, B, C, or D, however, indicates why the new curriculum would be thought to be attractive to students, so none of them is correct.

2. Many companies now have employee assistance programs that enable employees, free of charge, to improve their physical fitness, reduce stress, and learn ways to stop smoking. These programs increase worker productivity, reduce absenteeism, and lessen insurance costs for employee health care. Therefore, these programs benefit the company as well as the employee.

   Which of the following, if true, most significantly strengthens the conclusion above?

   (A) Physical fitness programs are often the most popular services offered to employees.
   (B) Studies have shown that training in stress management is not effective for many people.
   (C) Regular exercise reduces people's risk of heart disease and provides them with increased energy.
   (D) Physical injuries sometimes result from entering a strenuous physical fitness program too quickly.
   (E) Employee assistance programs require companies to hire people to supervise the various programs offered.

The conclusion is that the programs benefit both companies and employees. For companies, reducing employees' risk of heart disease is likely to reduce insurance costs, and increasing employee energy is likely to increase worker productivity. For employees, the benefits of having a reduced risk of heart disease and of having increased energy are self-evident. Choice C is the best answer.

Knowing which programs are popular does not bear on what benefits the programs confer, so choice A is incorrect. B and D indicate ways in which the programs can fail to provide the intended results, so neither of these is the correct answer. Having to hire additional personnel does not benefit a company, so choice E is not correct.

3. Unlike the wholesale price of raw wool, the wholesale price of raw cotton has fallen considerably in the last year. Thus, although the retail price of cotton clothing at retail clothing stores has not yet fallen, it will inevitably fall.

   Which of the following, if true, most seriously weakens the argument above?

   (A) The cost of processing raw cotton for cloth has increased during the last year.
   (B) The wholesale price of raw wool is typically higher than that of the same volume of raw cotton.
   (C) The operating costs of the average retail clothing store have remained constant during the last year.
   (D) Changes in retail prices always lag behind changes in wholesale prices.
   (E) The cost of harvesting raw cotton has increased in the last year.

The argument concludes that declining wholesale prices for raw cotton, will produce declining retail prices for cotton products. Choice A weakens the argument by pointing to higher processing costs for raw cotton, which could offset lower wholesale prices. A is therefore the best answer.

Choice B is incorrect because the argument focuses on price changes, not on relative price levels. Choice C is incorrect because it in effect denies that lower wholesale prices for cotton have been offset by rising operating costs. Choice D is incorrect because it is entirely consistent with the prediction made. Choice E is incorrect because the rising cost of harvesting raw cotton, though possibly affecting wholesale prices, cannot affect the relationship between wholesale and retail prices.

4. **Small-business groups are lobbying to defeat proposed federal legislation that would substantially raise the federal minimum wage. This opposition is surprising since the legislation they oppose would, for the first time, exempt all small businesses from paying any minimum wage.**

   Which of the following, if true, would best explain the opposition of small-business groups to the proposed legislation?

   (A) **Under the current federal minimum-wage law, most small businesses are required to pay no less than the minimum wage to their employees.**

   (B) **In order to attract workers, small companies must match the wages offered by their larger competitors, and these competitors would not be exempt under the proposed laws.**

   (C) **The exact number of companies that are currently required to pay no less than the minimum wage but that would be exempt under the proposed laws is unknown.**

   (D) **Some states have set their own minimum wages — in some cases, quite a bit above the level of the minimum wage mandated by current federal law — for certain key industries.**

   (E) **Service companies make up the majority of small businesses and they generally employ more employees per dollar of revenues than do retail or manufacturing businesses.**

The opposition of small-business groups despite an exemption apparently favoring them would be less surprising if, in fact, the exemption did not favor them. Choice B is thus the best answer because it explains that small businesses would have to match the higher wages that larger businesses are required to pay.

Choice A confirms that the new exemption constitutes a significant change but does not explain small-business opposition to that change, so choice A is incorrect. Choice C is incorrect because the exact numbers represented by the small-

business groups are surely irrelevant. Choice D suggests that in some states the proposed legislation would make no difference, and choice E suggests that most small businesses should value the exemption. Neither choice explains small-business opposition.

5. **Reviewer: The book *Art's Decline* argues that European painters today lack skills that were common among European painters of preceding centuries. In this the book must be right, since its analysis of 100 paintings, 50 old and 50 contemporary, demonstrates convincingly that none of the contemporary paintings are executed as skillfully as the older paintings.**

   Which of the following points to the most serious logical flaw in the reviewer's argument?

   (A) **The paintings chosen by the book's author for analysis could be those that most support the book's thesis.**

   (B) **There could be criteria other than the technical skill of the artist by which to evaluate a painting.**

   (C) **The title of the book could cause readers to accept the book's thesis even before they read the analysis of the paintings that supports it.**

   (D) **The particular methods currently used by European painters could require less artistic skill than do methods used by painters in other parts of the world.**

   (E) **A reader who was not familiar with the language of art criticism might not be convinced by the book's analysis of the 100 paintings.**

Because the number of old and contemporary paintings vastly exceeds the 50 of each type analyzed by *Art's Decline*, the reviewer's argument will be logically flawed if those 100 paintings do not constitute a reasonably representative sample. Choice A says that the sample might be grossly biased, so A is the best answer.

Choices B and D are both incorrect because a sharply defined focus is not a flaw in an argument; the reviewer makes clear that only artistic skill and only European painters are being considered. The reviewer's argument that the book supports its central thesis well is not weakened just because there may be readers less methodical and less competent than the reviewer. Therefore, neither C nor E is correct.

6. The pharmaceutical industry argues that because new drugs will not be developed unless heavy development costs can be recouped in later sales, the current 20 years of protection provided by patents should be extended in the case of newly developed drugs. However, in other industries new-product development continues despite high development costs, a fact that indicates that the extension is unnecessary.

Which of the following, if true, most strongly supports the pharmaceutical industry's argument against the challenge made above?

(A) No industries other than the pharmaceutical industry have asked for an extension of the 20-year limit on patent protection.

(B) Clinical trials of new drugs, which occur after the patent is granted and before the new drug can be marketed, often now take as long as 10 years to complete.

(C) There are several industries in which the ratio of research and development costs to revenues is higher than it is in the pharmaceutical industry.

(D) An existing patent for a drug does not legally prevent pharmaceutical companies from bringing to market alternative drugs, provided they are sufficiently dissimilar to the patented drug.

(E) Much recent industrial innovation has occurred in products — for example, in the computer and electronics industries — for which patent protection is often very ineffective.

The pharmaceutical industry's argument is best supported by an explanation of why the patent period sufficient for other industries to recoup their development costs is insufficient for the pharmaceutical industry. Choice B is the best answer because it provides an explanation: required clinical trials prevent new drugs from being sold for much of the time they receive patent protection.

Choice A is incorrect: the fact that the pharmaceutical industry's request is unique does nothing to justify that request. Choices C and E, if true, could undermine the pharmaceutical industry's argument, so they are incorrect. Choice D indicates that alternative drugs might render patent protection worthless, but that is clearly no reason to extend the protection.

Questions 7-8 are based on the following.

Bank depositors in the United States are all financially protected against bank failure because the government insures all individuals' bank deposits. An economist argues that this insurance is partly responsible for the high rate of bank failures, since it removes from depositors any financial incentive to find out whether the bank that holds their money is secure against failure. If depositors were more selective, then banks would need to be secure in order to compete for depositors' money.

7. The economist's argument makes which of the following assumptions?

(A) Bank failures are caused when big borrowers default on loan repayments.

(B) A significant proportion of depositors maintain accounts at several different banks.

(C) The more a depositor has to deposit, the more careful he or she tends to be in selecting a bank.

(D) The difference in the interest rates paid to depositors by different banks is not a significant factor in bank failures.

(E) Potential depositors are able to determine which banks are secure against failure.

Giving potential depositors a financial incentive to select only secure banks will not lead to increased bank security unless the potential depositors can distinguish banks that actually are secure from those that are not. Choice E is a statement of this prerequisite and is thus the best answer.

The argument is about choosing or avoiding banks likely to fail, regardless of how the failure comes about, so neither choice A nor choice D is specifically assumed. The argument is consistent with each depositor's money being held by a single bank, so B is not assumed. The argument neither asserts nor assumes that depositors currently exercise care in selecting the banks where they deposit their money. Therefore choice C, in particular, is not assumed.

8. Which of the following, if true, most seriously weakens the economist's argument?

(A) Before the government started to insure depositors against bank failure, there was a lower rate of bank failure than there is now.

(B) When the government did not insure deposits, frequent bank failures occurred as a result of depositors' fears of losing money in bank failures.

(C) Surveys show that a significant proportion of depositors are aware that their deposits are insured by the government.

(D) There is an upper limit on the amount of an individual's deposit that the government will insure, but very few individuals' deposits exceed this limit.

(E) The security of a bank against failure depends on the percentage of its assets that are loaned out and also on how much risk its loans involve.

The argument that deposit insurance, because of its impact on depositors' choice of banks, is partially responsible for the high rate of bank failures would be weakened if deposit insurance also prevented certain bank failures. Choice B suggests that deposit insurance does prevent certain bank failures, and is thus the best answer.

Choice A weakly supports the view that insuring deposits contributes to bank failures. Choice C supports the economist's position that depositors take the safety of deposits into account. Choice D supports the argument's relevance by indicating that virtually all depositors can afford to be nonselective. It follows that none of these three choices is correct. Choice E is incorrect because it fails to establish any connection between deposit insurance and the factors controlling bank failures.

9. Passengers must exit airplanes swiftly after accidents, since gases released following accidents are toxic to humans and often explode soon after being released. In order to prevent passenger deaths from gas inhalation, safety officials recommend that passengers be provided with smoke hoods that prevent inhalation of the gases.

Which of the following, if true, constitutes the strongest reason <u>not</u> to require implementation of the safety officials' recommendation?

(A) Test evacuations showed that putting on the smoke hoods added considerably to the overall time it took passengers to leave the cabin.
(B) Some airlines are unwilling to buy the smoke hoods because they consider them to be prohibitively expensive.
(C) Although the smoke hoods protect passengers from the toxic gases, they can do nothing to prevent the gases from igniting.
(D) Some experienced flyers fail to pay attention to the safety instructions given on every commercial flight before takeoff.
(E) In many airplane accidents, passengers who were able to reach emergency exits were overcome by toxic gases before they could exit the airplane.

A strong reason for rejecting the recommendation would be that the hoods endanger passengers. Passengers delayed in exiting the plane are more exposed to the risk of a gas explosion. Choice A says that the hoods would delay passengers and is thus the best answer.

If some airlines are unwilling to buy the hoods, it might be necessary to require them to, so B is incorrect. That the hoods protect from only one major risk is no reason in itself for rejection, so C is not correct. That some passengers ignore safety instructions is also no reason for rejection, so D is incorrect. Choice E is not a good answer; it supports the recommendation by indicating that the hoods might enable more passengers to exit a plane.

10. In 1960, 10 percent of every dollar paid in automobile insurance premiums went to pay costs arising from injuries incurred in car accidents. In 1990, 50 percent of every dollar paid in automobile insurance premiums went toward such costs, despite the fact that cars were much safer in 1990 than in 1960.

Which of the following, if true, best explains the discrepancy outlined above?

(A) There were fewer accidents in 1990 than in 1960.
(B) On average, people drove more slowly in 1990 than in 1960.
(C) Cars grew increasingly more expensive to repair over the period in question.
(D) The price of insurance increased more rapidly than the rate of inflation between 1960 and 1990.
(E) Health-care costs rose sharply between 1960 and 1990.

If cars were safer in 1990 than in 1960, car accidents should have resulted in fewer and in less severe injuries. Yet coverage of injuries took up a greater share of insurance premiums. One possible explanation is that the treatment cost per injury rose sharply. Choice E supports this explanation and is thus the best answer.

Choices A and B both suggest that the number of injuries decreased. Since such a decrease would not explain why injuries take up a greater share of insurance premiums, both of these choices are incorrect. Choice C is incorrect because it suggests, falsely, that costs not related to injuries rose disproportionately. Choice D is incorrect because it does not deal with shifts in the cost components that insurance premiums cover.

11. Caterpillars of all species produce an identical hormone called "juvenile hormone" that maintains feeding behavior. Only when a caterpillar has grown to the right size for pupation to take place does a special enzyme halt the production of juvenile hormone. This enzyme can be synthesized and will, on being ingested by immature caterpillars, kill them by stopping them from feeding.

Which of the following, if true, most strongly supports the view that it would <u>not</u> be advisable to try to eradicate agricultural pests that go through a caterpillar stage by spraying croplands with the enzyme mentioned above?

(A) Most species of caterpillar are subject to some natural predation.
(B) Many agricultural pests do not go through a caterpillar stage.
(C) Many agriculturally beneficial insects go through a caterpillar stage.
(D) Since caterpillars of different species emerge at different times, several sprayings would be necessary.
(E) Although the enzyme has been synthesized in the laboratory, no large-scale production facilities exist as yet.

Since the enzyme kills caterpillars of all species, spraying croplands might not be advisable if caterpillars of beneficial insect species would also be killed. According to choice C, there are many such beneficial species. Choice C thus supports the view that spraying would be inadvisable and is the best answer.

Choice A is incorrect because spraying, if effective, would make natural predation irrelevant. Choice B is incorrect because the existence of pests that the spraying is not intended to control does not make the spraying inadvisable. Choices D and E each raise a point concerning details of how and when spraying programs might be implemented, without challenging the advisability of such programs. Both choices are therefore incorrect.

12. Although aspirin has been proven to eliminate moderate fever associated with some illnesses, many doctors no longer routinely recommend its use for this purpose. A moderate fever stimulates the activity of the body's disease-fighting white blood cells and also inhibits the growth of many strains of disease-causing bacteria.

If the statements above are true, which of the following conclusions is most strongly supported by them?

(A) Aspirin, an effective painkiller, alleviates the pain and discomfort of many illnesses.
(B) Aspirin can prolong a patient's illness by eliminating moderate fever helpful in fighting some diseases.
(C) Aspirin inhibits the growth of white blood cells, which are necessary for fighting some illnesses.
(D) The more white blood cells a patient's body produces, the less severe the patient's illness will be.
(E) The focus of modern medicine is on inhibiting the growth of disease-causing bacteria within the body.

By stimulating disease-fighting white blood cells and inhibiting the growth of disease-causing bacteria, moderate fever can aid the body in fighting infection. However, aspirin can eliminate moderate fever. Thus, as choice B states, aspirin can prolong a patient's illness by eliminating moderate fever and thereby also eliminating its disease-fighting effects. B is the best answer.

Choice A is not the correct answer because no mention is made of aspirin's role as a painkiller. The passage also says nothing about aspirin's effect on the growth or production of white blood cells, mentioning only its effect on their activity, so neither C nor D is correct. Because the statements given could be true regardless of the focus of modern medicine, E is also incorrect.

13. Because postage rates are rising, *Home Decorator* magazine plans to maximize its profits by reducing by one half the number of issues it publishes each year. The quality of articles, the number of articles published per year, and the subscription price will not change. Market research shows that neither subscribers nor advertisers will be lost if the magazine's plan is instituted.

Which of the following, if true, provides the strongest evidence that the magazine's profits are likely to decline if the plan is instituted?

(A) With the new postage rates, a typical issue under the proposed plan would cost about one-third more to mail than a typical current issue would.

(B) The majority of the magazine's subscribers are less concerned about a possible reduction in the quantity of the magazine's articles than about a possible loss of the current high quality of its articles.

(C) Many of the magazine's long-time subscribers would continue their subscriptions even if the subscription price were increased.

(D) Most of the advertisers that purchase advertising space in the magazine will continue to spend the same amount on advertising per issue as they have in the past.

(E) Production costs for the magazine are expected to remain stable.

Home Decorator magazine's profits would be likely to decline if, as a result of instituting the plan, revenues were to decrease substantially. Choice D indicates that the plan would produce substantially lower revenues because most advertisers will pay the magazine the same amount per issue, but there will be only half as many issues. Therefore, D is the best answer.

Choice A notes that mailing costs per issue will rise by one third, but since there will be fewer issues, total annual mailing costs will fall. Therefore, A is incorrect. Choices B and C are incorrect because neither describes concerns that subscribers have about the plan under consideration. Choice E is incorrect because stable production costs would not lead to lower profits.

14. A study of marital relationships in which one partner's sleeping and waking cycles differ from those of the other partner reveals that such couples share fewer activities with each other and have more violent arguments than do couples in a relationship in which both partners follow the same sleeping and waking patterns. Thus, mismatched sleeping and waking cycles can seriously jeopardize a marriage.

Which of the following, if true, most seriously weakens the argument above?

(A) Married couples in which both spouses follow the same sleeping and waking patterns also occasionally have arguments that can jeopardize the couple's marriage.

(B) The sleeping and waking cycles of individuals tend to vary from season to season.

(C) The individuals who have sleeping and waking cycles that differ significantly from those of their spouses tend to argue little with colleagues at work.

(D) People in unhappy marriages have been found to express hostility by adopting a different sleeping and waking cycle from that of their spouses.

(E) According to a recent study, most people's sleeping and waking cycles can be controlled and modified easily.

The argument assumes that mismatched sleeping and waking cycles precede marital problems. Choice D weakens the argument by indicating that this assumption is false, and D is the best answer.

The argument does not depend on there being only one cause of marital problems, so choice A is incorrect. That sleeping and waking cycles can change seasonally or might not affect interactions with colleagues does not address the issue of how mismatched cycles between spouses affect their marriage, so B and C are incorrect. Choice E suggests that there is a way to test the conclusion — by bringing a couple's sleeping and waking cycles into alignment — but this by itself does not weaken the argument, so E is incorrect.

Roland: The alarming fact is that 90 percent of the people in this country now report that they know some-one who is unemployed.

Sharon: But a normal, moderate level of unemployment is 5 percent, with 1 out of 20 workers unemployed. So at any given time if a person knows approxi-mately 50 workers, 1 or more will very likely be unemployed.

15. Sharon's argument is structured to lead to which of the following as a conclusion?

   (A) The fact that 90% of the people know someone who is unemployed is not an indication that unemployment is abnormally high.
   (B) The current level of unemployment is not moderate.
   (C) If at least 5% of workers are unemployed, the result of questioning a representative group of people cannot be the percentage Roland cites.
   (D) It is unlikely that the people whose statements Roland cites are giving accurate reports.
   (E) If an unemployment figure is given as a certain percent, the actual percentage of those without jobs is even higher.

Sharon's argument is essentially that, even if the facts are as Roland presents them, they are not in and of themselves a cause for alarm. Even circumstances reassuringly normal and unremarkable — a normal, moderate unemployment rate and having 50 or more workers among one's acquaintances — imply the sort of fact Roland cites. Thus, that fact does not indicate that things are not normal (for example, that unem-ployment is alarmingly high). Choice A, therefore, is the best answer.

Sharon's argument focuses exclusively on whether Roland's alarm is logically warranted, given the fact he cites. Sharon herself takes no position whatsoever on what the actual facts concerning unemployment statistics and concerning people's self-reports are. Because choices B, C, D, and E are assertions about such matters, each is incorrect.

16. Sharon's argument relies on the assumption that

   (A) normal levels of unemployment are rarely exceeded
   (B) unemployment is not normally concentrated in geographically isolated segments of the population
   (C) the number of people who each know someone who is unemployed is always higher than 90% of the population
   (D) Roland is not consciously distorting the statistics he presents
   (E) knowledge that a personal acquaintance is unemployed generates more fear of losing one's job than does knowledge of unemployment statistics

Sharon's argument assumes that people are generally similar in how likely they are to have among their acquaintances people who are unemployed. Since heavy concentrations of unemployment in geographically isolated segments of the population would produce great differences in this respect, Sharon's argument assumes few, if any, such concentrations. Choice B is therefore the best answer.

If normal levels of unemployment were exceeded rela-tively frequently, and if Roland's figure of 90% were an exaggeration, Sharon's argument would be unaffected, so choices A and D are incorrect. At exceptionally low levels of unemployment, Sharon's argument suggests that choice C is likely to be false, so C is not assumed. The fear of losing one's job is not part of Sharon's argument, so choice E is incorrect.

Explanatory Material:
Problem Solving, Section 6

1. $\dfrac{(3)(0.072)}{0.54} =$

   (A) 0.04
   (B) 0.3
   (C) 0.4
   (D) 0.8
   (E) 4.0

To perform this computation, it is convenient to

multiply $\dfrac{(3)(0.072)}{0.54}$ by $\dfrac{100}{100}$, which gives

$\dfrac{3(7.2)}{54} = \dfrac{21.6}{54} = \dfrac{3.6}{9} = 0.4.$ The best answer is C.

2. A car dealer sold x used cars and y new cars during May. If the number of used cars sold was 10 greater than the number of new cars sold, which of the following expresses this relationship?

(A) $x > 10y$
(B) $x > y + 10$
(C) $x > y - 10$
(D) $x = y + 10$
(E) $x = y - 10$

According to the problem, if x is 10 greater than y, then $x = y + 10$, and the best answer is D.

3. What is the maximum number of $1\frac{1}{4}$-foot pieces of wire that can be cut from a wire that is 24 feet long?

(A) 11
(B) 18
(C) 19
(D) 20
(E) 30

The maximum number is the greatest integer less than or equal to the quotient when 24 feet is divided by $1\frac{1}{4}$ feet. The quotient is 19.2, and the maximum number of $1\frac{1}{4}$-foot pieces is 19. The best answer is C.

4. If each of the two lines ℓ_1 and ℓ_2 is parallel to line ℓ_3, which of the following must be true?

(A) Lines ℓ_1, ℓ_2, and ℓ_3 lie in the same plane.
(B) Lines ℓ_1, ℓ_2, and ℓ_3 lie in different planes.
(C) Line ℓ_1 is parallel to line ℓ_2.
(D) Line ℓ_1 is the same line as line ℓ_2.
(E) Line ℓ_1 is the same line as line ℓ_3.

It is a well-known fact that two lines that are parallel to the same line are parallel to each other; thus the best answer is C. To see that the other options are not necessarily true, we first recall that two lines are parallel if they lie in the same plane and are everywhere equidistant. To show A and B need not be true, consider the figure below;

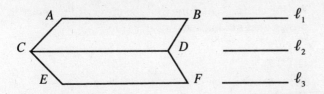

D is not necessarily true because no assumption can be made about whether or not lines ℓ_1 and ℓ_2 are coincident. That E is not necessarily true can be seen from the figures in the discussion of A and B.

$$\frac{61.24 \times (0.998)^2}{\sqrt{403}}$$

5. The expression above is approximately equal to

(A) 1
(B) 3
(C) 4
(D) 5
(E) 6

Since $\sqrt{403}$ is approximately 20 and $(0.998)^2$ is approximately 1, the value of the expression is approximately $\frac{60\,(1)}{20}$ or 3. The best answer is B.

6. Car X and car Y traveled the same 80-mile route. If car X took 2 hours and car Y traveled at an average speed that was 50 percent faster than the average speed of car X, how many hours did it take car Y to travel the route?

(A) $\frac{2}{3}$
(B) 1
(C) $1\frac{1}{3}$
(D) $1\frac{3}{5}$
(E) 3

If car X took 2 hours to drive the 80 miles, then car X drove an average speed of $\frac{80}{2}$, or 40 miles per hour, and car Y drove an average speed of $1.5(40) = 60$ miles per hour. Therefore, it took $\frac{80}{60}$ or $1\frac{1}{3}$ hours for car Y to travel the route. The best answer is C.

7. If the numbers $\frac{17}{24}$, $\frac{1}{2}$, $\frac{3}{8}$, $\frac{3}{4}$, and $\frac{9}{16}$ were ordered from greatest to least, the middle number of the resulting sequence would be

(A) $\frac{17}{24}$
(B) $\frac{1}{2}$
(C) $\frac{3}{8}$
(D) $\frac{3}{4}$
(E) $\frac{9}{16}$

The least common denominator of the five fractions is 48. When the fractions are expressed with denominator 48, they are, in the order given, $\frac{34}{48}$, $\frac{24}{48}$, $\frac{18}{48}$, $\frac{36}{48}$, and $\frac{27}{48}$. Once the fractions are expressed with the same denominator, one need only order the numerators from greatest to least. Clearly, the middle number is $\frac{27}{48}$ or $\frac{9}{16}$, and the best answer is E.

8. If a 10 percent deposit that has been paid toward the purchase of a certain product is $110, how much more remains to be paid?

   (A) $880
   (B) $990
   (C) $1,000
   (D) $1,100
   (E) $1,210

If 10 percent of the purchase is $110, the 90 percent that remains to be paid is 9($110) = $990. The best answer is B.

9. Kim purchased n items from a catalog for $8 each. Postage and handling charges consisted of $3 for the first item and $1 for each additional item. Which of the following gives the total dollar amount of Kim's purchase, including postage and handling, in terms of n ?

   (A) $8n + 2$
   (B) $8n + 4$
   (C) $9n + 2$
   (D) $9n + 3$
   (E) $9n + 4$

The purchase price of the n items at $8 each was $8n$ dollars. Postage and handling was $3 for the first item and $1(n-1)$ for the remaining $n-1$ items. The total cost was, therefore, $8n + 3 + 1(n-1) = 9n + 2$ dollars. The best answer is C.

10. $\left(\sqrt{7} + \sqrt{7}\right)^2 =$

   (A) 98
   (B) 49
   (C) 28
   (D) 21
   (E) 14

$\left(\sqrt{7} + \sqrt{7}\right)^2 = \left(2\sqrt{7}\right)^2 = 4(7) = 28$. The best answer is C.

11. If the average (arithmetic mean) of the four numbers K, $2K + 3$, $3K - 5$, and $5K + 1$ is 63, what is the value of K ?

   (A) 11
   (B) $15\frac{3}{4}$
   (C) 22
   (D) 23
   (E) $25\frac{3}{10}$

The average of the four numbers is
$$\frac{K + (2K + 3) + (3K - 5) + (5K + 1)}{4} = \frac{11K - 1}{4} = 63,$$ or
$11K - 1 = 252$; $11K = 253$ and $K = 23$. The best answer is D.

12. A rabbit on a controlled diet is fed daily 300 grams of a mixture of two foods, food X and food Y. Food X contains 10 percent protein and food Y contains 15 percent protein. If the rabbit's diet provides exactly 38 grams of protein daily, how many grams of food X are in the mixture?

   (A) 100
   (B) 140
   (C) 150
   (D) 160
   (E) 200

Let x be the number of grams of food X in the mixture. Then the number of grams of food Y in the mixture is $300 - x$. According to the problem, $0.10x + 0.15(300 - x) = 38$ grams; $0.10x - 0.15x = 38 - 45 = -7$). Thus, $x = \frac{-7}{-0.05} = 140$ grams. The best answer is B.

13. A company that ships boxes to a total of 12 distribution centers uses color coding to identify each center. If either a single color or a pair of two different colors is chosen to represent each center and if each center is uniquely represented by that choice of one or two colors, what is the minimum number of colors needed for the coding? (Assume that the order of the colors in a pair does not matter.)

   (A) 4
   (B) 5
   (C) 6
   (D) 12
   (E) 24

It is sometimes a good idea to look at the answer choices before tackling the problem. For example, if 4 colors were used, 4 centers could be identified with a single color and $_4C_2 = \dfrac{4!}{2!\,2!} = 6$ centers could be identified with two colors. Thus, only 10 centers could be identified with 4 colors. Similarly, with 5 colors, 5 centers could be identified with a single color and $_5C_2 = \dfrac{5!}{2!\,3!} = \dfrac{(5)(4)}{2} = 10$ centers could be identified with two colors for a total of 15. Therefore, a minimum of 5 colors is needed, and the best answer is B.

14. If $x + y = a$ and $x - y = b$, then $2xy =$

(A) $\dfrac{a^2 - b^2}{2}$

(B) $\dfrac{b^2 - a^2}{2}$

(C) $\dfrac{a - b}{2}$

(D) $\dfrac{ab}{2}$

(E) $\dfrac{a^2 + b^2}{2}$

$(x + y)^2 = x^2 + 2xy + y^2 = a^2$, and $(x - y)^2 = x^2 - 2xy + y^2 = b^2$. Subtracting the second equation from the first yields $4xy = a^2 - b^2$ and $2xy = \dfrac{a^2 - b^2}{2}$. The best answer is A.

15. A rectangular circuit board is designed to have width w inches, perimeter p inches, and area k square inches. Which of the following equations must be true?

(A) $w^2 + pw + k = 0$
(B) $w^2 - pw + 2k = 0$
(C) $2w^2 + pw + 2k = 0$
(D) $2w^2 - pw - 2k = 0$
(E) $2w^2 - pw + 2k = 0$

If the perimeter is p and the width is w, the length ℓ can be determined from the formula $2\ell + 2w = p$. Solving this equation for ℓ gives $\ell = \dfrac{p - 2w}{2}$. The area, k, of the rectangle is equal to ℓw. Substituting $\dfrac{p - 2w}{2}$ for ℓ gives $k = (\dfrac{p - 2w}{2})w$ or $2k = (p - 2w)w = pw - 2w^2$, which is equivalent to $2w^2 - pw + 2k = 0$. The best answer is E.

16. On a certain road, 10 percent of the motorists exceed the posted speed limit and receive speeding tickets, but 20 percent of the motorists who exceed the posted speed limit do not receive speeding tickets. What percent of the motorists on that road exceed the posted speed limit?

(A) $10\dfrac{1}{2}\%$

(B) $12\dfrac{1}{2}\%$

(C) 15%

(D) 22%

(E) 30%

Let t be the total number of motorists and let e be the number of motorists who exceed the speed limit. Then if 20 percent of the motorists who exceed the speed limit do not receive tickets, 80 percent of those who exceed the speed limit, or $0.8e$, receive tickets. Since $0.1t$ exceed the speed limit and receive tickets, $0.8e = 0.1t$ and the ratio of e to t is 1 to 8, which is equivalent to 12.5 percent. The best answer is B.

Answer Sheet: Form B

Section 1

1. Ⓐ Ⓑ Ⓒ Ⓓ Ⓔ
2. Ⓐ Ⓑ Ⓒ Ⓓ Ⓔ
3. Ⓐ Ⓑ Ⓒ Ⓓ Ⓔ
4. Ⓐ Ⓑ Ⓒ Ⓓ Ⓔ
5. Ⓐ Ⓑ Ⓒ Ⓓ Ⓔ
6. Ⓐ Ⓑ Ⓒ Ⓓ Ⓔ
7. Ⓐ Ⓑ Ⓒ Ⓓ Ⓔ
8. Ⓐ Ⓑ Ⓒ Ⓓ Ⓔ
9. Ⓐ Ⓑ Ⓒ Ⓓ Ⓔ
10. Ⓐ Ⓑ Ⓒ Ⓓ Ⓔ
11. Ⓐ Ⓑ Ⓒ Ⓓ Ⓔ
12. Ⓐ Ⓑ Ⓒ Ⓓ Ⓔ
13. Ⓐ Ⓑ Ⓒ Ⓓ Ⓔ
14. Ⓐ Ⓑ Ⓒ Ⓓ Ⓔ
15. Ⓐ Ⓑ Ⓒ Ⓓ Ⓔ
16. Ⓐ Ⓑ Ⓒ Ⓓ Ⓔ
17. Ⓐ Ⓑ Ⓒ Ⓓ Ⓔ
18. Ⓐ Ⓑ Ⓒ Ⓓ Ⓔ
19. Ⓐ Ⓑ Ⓒ Ⓓ Ⓔ
20. Ⓐ Ⓑ Ⓒ Ⓓ Ⓔ
21. Ⓐ Ⓑ Ⓒ Ⓓ Ⓔ
22. Ⓐ Ⓑ Ⓒ Ⓓ Ⓔ
23. Ⓐ Ⓑ Ⓒ Ⓓ Ⓔ

Section 2

1. Ⓐ Ⓑ Ⓒ Ⓓ Ⓔ
2. Ⓐ Ⓑ Ⓒ Ⓓ Ⓔ
3. Ⓐ Ⓑ Ⓒ Ⓓ Ⓔ
4. Ⓐ Ⓑ Ⓒ Ⓓ Ⓔ
5. Ⓐ Ⓑ Ⓒ Ⓓ Ⓔ
6. Ⓐ Ⓑ Ⓒ Ⓓ Ⓔ
7. Ⓐ Ⓑ Ⓒ Ⓓ Ⓔ
8. Ⓐ Ⓑ Ⓒ Ⓓ Ⓔ
9. Ⓐ Ⓑ Ⓒ Ⓓ Ⓔ
10. Ⓐ Ⓑ Ⓒ Ⓓ Ⓔ
11. Ⓐ Ⓑ Ⓒ Ⓓ Ⓔ
12. Ⓐ Ⓑ Ⓒ Ⓓ Ⓔ
13. Ⓐ Ⓑ Ⓒ Ⓓ Ⓔ
14. Ⓐ Ⓑ Ⓒ Ⓓ Ⓔ
15. Ⓐ Ⓑ Ⓒ Ⓓ Ⓔ
16. Ⓐ Ⓑ Ⓒ Ⓓ Ⓔ
17. Ⓐ Ⓑ Ⓒ Ⓓ Ⓔ
18. Ⓐ Ⓑ Ⓒ Ⓓ Ⓔ
19. Ⓐ Ⓑ Ⓒ Ⓓ Ⓔ
20. Ⓐ Ⓑ Ⓒ Ⓓ Ⓔ
21. Ⓐ Ⓑ Ⓒ Ⓓ Ⓔ
22. Ⓐ Ⓑ Ⓒ Ⓓ Ⓔ
23. Ⓐ Ⓑ Ⓒ Ⓓ Ⓔ

Section 3

1. Ⓐ Ⓑ Ⓒ Ⓓ Ⓔ
2. Ⓐ Ⓑ Ⓒ Ⓓ Ⓔ
3. Ⓐ Ⓑ Ⓒ Ⓓ Ⓔ
4. Ⓐ Ⓑ Ⓒ Ⓓ Ⓔ
5. Ⓐ Ⓑ Ⓒ Ⓓ Ⓔ
6. Ⓐ Ⓑ Ⓒ Ⓓ Ⓔ
7. Ⓐ Ⓑ Ⓒ Ⓓ Ⓔ
8. Ⓐ Ⓑ Ⓒ Ⓓ Ⓔ
9. Ⓐ Ⓑ Ⓒ Ⓓ Ⓔ
10. Ⓐ Ⓑ Ⓒ Ⓓ Ⓔ
11. Ⓐ Ⓑ Ⓒ Ⓓ Ⓔ
12. Ⓐ Ⓑ Ⓒ Ⓓ Ⓔ
13. Ⓐ Ⓑ Ⓒ Ⓓ Ⓔ
14. Ⓐ Ⓑ Ⓒ Ⓓ Ⓔ
15. Ⓐ Ⓑ Ⓒ Ⓓ Ⓔ
16. Ⓐ Ⓑ Ⓒ Ⓓ Ⓔ
17. Ⓐ Ⓑ Ⓒ Ⓓ Ⓔ
18. Ⓐ Ⓑ Ⓒ Ⓓ Ⓔ
19. Ⓐ Ⓑ Ⓒ Ⓓ Ⓔ
20. Ⓐ Ⓑ Ⓒ Ⓓ Ⓔ
21. Ⓐ Ⓑ Ⓒ Ⓓ Ⓔ
22. Ⓐ Ⓑ Ⓒ Ⓓ Ⓔ
23. Ⓐ Ⓑ Ⓒ Ⓓ Ⓔ

Section 4

1. Ⓐ Ⓑ Ⓒ Ⓓ Ⓔ
2. Ⓐ Ⓑ Ⓒ Ⓓ Ⓔ
3. Ⓐ Ⓑ Ⓒ Ⓓ Ⓔ
4. Ⓐ Ⓑ Ⓒ Ⓓ Ⓔ
5. Ⓐ Ⓑ Ⓒ Ⓓ Ⓔ
6. Ⓐ Ⓑ Ⓒ Ⓓ Ⓔ
7. Ⓐ Ⓑ Ⓒ Ⓓ Ⓔ
8. Ⓐ Ⓑ Ⓒ Ⓓ Ⓔ
9. Ⓐ Ⓑ Ⓒ Ⓓ Ⓔ
10. Ⓐ Ⓑ Ⓒ Ⓓ Ⓔ
11. Ⓐ Ⓑ Ⓒ Ⓓ Ⓔ
12. Ⓐ Ⓑ Ⓒ Ⓓ Ⓔ
13. Ⓐ Ⓑ Ⓒ Ⓓ Ⓔ
14. Ⓐ Ⓑ Ⓒ Ⓓ Ⓔ
15. Ⓐ Ⓑ Ⓒ Ⓓ Ⓔ
16. Ⓐ Ⓑ Ⓒ Ⓓ Ⓔ
17. Ⓐ Ⓑ Ⓒ Ⓓ Ⓔ
18. Ⓐ Ⓑ Ⓒ Ⓓ Ⓔ
19. Ⓐ Ⓑ Ⓒ Ⓓ Ⓔ
20. Ⓐ Ⓑ Ⓒ Ⓓ Ⓔ
21. Ⓐ Ⓑ Ⓒ Ⓓ Ⓔ
22. Ⓐ Ⓑ Ⓒ Ⓓ Ⓔ
23. Ⓐ Ⓑ Ⓒ Ⓓ Ⓔ

Section 5

1. Ⓐ Ⓑ Ⓒ Ⓓ Ⓔ
2. Ⓐ Ⓑ Ⓒ Ⓓ Ⓔ
3. Ⓐ Ⓑ Ⓒ Ⓓ Ⓔ
4. Ⓐ Ⓑ Ⓒ Ⓓ Ⓔ
5. Ⓐ Ⓑ Ⓒ Ⓓ Ⓔ
6. Ⓐ Ⓑ Ⓒ Ⓓ Ⓔ
7. Ⓐ Ⓑ Ⓒ Ⓓ Ⓔ
8. Ⓐ Ⓑ Ⓒ Ⓓ Ⓔ
9. Ⓐ Ⓑ Ⓒ Ⓓ Ⓔ
10. Ⓐ Ⓑ Ⓒ Ⓓ Ⓔ
11. Ⓐ Ⓑ Ⓒ Ⓓ Ⓔ
12. Ⓐ Ⓑ Ⓒ Ⓓ Ⓔ
13. Ⓐ Ⓑ Ⓒ Ⓓ Ⓔ
14. Ⓐ Ⓑ Ⓒ Ⓓ Ⓔ
15. Ⓐ Ⓑ Ⓒ Ⓓ Ⓔ
16. Ⓐ Ⓑ Ⓒ Ⓓ Ⓔ
17. Ⓐ Ⓑ Ⓒ Ⓓ Ⓔ
18. Ⓐ Ⓑ Ⓒ Ⓓ Ⓔ
19. Ⓐ Ⓑ Ⓒ Ⓓ Ⓔ
20. Ⓐ Ⓑ Ⓒ Ⓓ Ⓔ
21. Ⓐ Ⓑ Ⓒ Ⓓ Ⓔ
22. Ⓐ Ⓑ Ⓒ Ⓓ Ⓔ
23. Ⓐ Ⓑ Ⓒ Ⓓ Ⓔ

Section 6

1. Ⓐ Ⓑ Ⓒ Ⓓ Ⓔ
2. Ⓐ Ⓑ Ⓒ Ⓓ Ⓔ
3. Ⓐ Ⓑ Ⓒ Ⓓ Ⓔ
4. Ⓐ Ⓑ Ⓒ Ⓓ Ⓔ
5. Ⓐ Ⓑ Ⓒ Ⓓ Ⓔ
6. Ⓐ Ⓑ Ⓒ Ⓓ Ⓔ
7. Ⓐ Ⓑ Ⓒ Ⓓ Ⓔ
8. Ⓐ Ⓑ Ⓒ Ⓓ Ⓔ
9. Ⓐ Ⓑ Ⓒ Ⓓ Ⓔ
10. Ⓐ Ⓑ Ⓒ Ⓓ Ⓔ
11. Ⓐ Ⓑ Ⓒ Ⓓ Ⓔ
12. Ⓐ Ⓑ Ⓒ Ⓓ Ⓔ
13. Ⓐ Ⓑ Ⓒ Ⓓ Ⓔ
14. Ⓐ Ⓑ Ⓒ Ⓓ Ⓔ
15. Ⓐ Ⓑ Ⓒ Ⓓ Ⓔ
16. Ⓐ Ⓑ Ⓒ Ⓓ Ⓔ
17. Ⓐ Ⓑ Ⓒ Ⓓ Ⓔ
18. Ⓐ Ⓑ Ⓒ Ⓓ Ⓔ
19. Ⓐ Ⓑ Ⓒ Ⓓ Ⓔ
20. Ⓐ Ⓑ Ⓒ Ⓓ Ⓔ
21. Ⓐ Ⓑ Ⓒ Ⓓ Ⓔ
22. Ⓐ Ⓑ Ⓒ Ⓓ Ⓔ
23. Ⓐ Ⓑ Ⓒ Ⓓ Ⓔ

Print your full name here: _____
(last)   (first)   (middle)

Graduate
Management
Admission
Council®

**Educational
Testing Service**

Graduate Management Admission Test

NO TEST MATERIAL ON THIS PAGE.

ANALYSIS OF AN ISSUE

Time—30 minutes

<u>Directions:</u> In this section, you will need to analyze the issue presented below and explain your views on it. The question has no "correct" answer. Instead, you should consider various perspectives as you develop your own position on the issue.

Read the statement and the directions that follow it, and then make any notes in your test booklet that will help you plan your response. Begin writing your response on the separate answer document. Make sure that you use the answer document that goes with this writing task.

"Business relations are infected through and through with the disease of short-sighted motives. We are so concerned with immediate results and short-term goals that we fail to look beyond them."

Assuming that the term "business relations" can refer to the decisions and actions of any organization—for instance, a small family business, a community association, or a large international corporation—explain the extent to which you think that this criticism is valid. In your discussion of the issue, use reasons and/or examples from your own experience, your observation of others, or your reading.

NOTES

Use the space below or on the facing page to plan your response. Any writing on these pages will not be evaluated.

STOP

IF YOU FINISH BEFORE TIME IS CALLED, YOU MAY CHECK YOUR WORK ON THIS SECTION ONLY.
DO NOT TURN TO ANY OTHER SECTION IN THE TEST.

NO TEST MATERIAL ON THIS PAGE

ANALYSIS OF AN ARGUMENT

Time—30 minutes

<u>Directions:</u> In this section you will be asked to write a critique of the argument presented below. *You are NOT being asked to present your own views on the subject.*

Read the argument and the instructions that follow it, and then make any notes in your test booklet that will help you plan your response. Begin writing your response on the separate answer sheet. Make sure that you use the answer sheet that goes with this writing task.

The following appeared in the editorial section of a newspaper.

"As public concern over drug abuse has increased, authorities have become more vigilant in their efforts to prevent illegal drugs from entering the country. Many drug traffickers have consequently switched from marijuana, which is bulky, or heroin, which has a market too small to justify the risk of severe punishment, to cocaine. Thus enforcement efforts have ironically resulted in an observed increase in the illegal use of cocaine."

Discuss how well reasoned you find this argument. In your discussion be sure to analyze the line of reasoning and the use of evidence in the argument. For example, you may need to consider what questionable assumptions underlie the thinking and what alternative explanations or counterexamples might weaken the conclusion. You can also discuss what sort of evidence would strengthen or refute the argument, what changes in the argument would make it more logically sound, and what, if anything, would help you better evaluate its conclusion.

NOTES

Use the space below or on the facing page to plan your response. Any writing on these pages will not be evaluated.

STOP

IF YOU FINISH BEFORE TIME IS CALLED, YOU MAY CHECK YOUR WORK ON THIS SECTION ONLY.
DO NOT TURN TO ANY OTHER SECTION IN THE TEST.

NO TEST MATERIAL ON THIS PAGE

Section 1 starts on page 476.

SECTION 1

Time—25 minutes

16 Questions

<u>Directions:</u> For each question in this section, select the best of the answer choices given.

1. A report on acid rain concluded, "Most forests in Canada are not being damaged by acid rain." Critics of the report insist the conclusion be changed to, "Most forests in Canada do not show visible symptoms of damage by acid rain, such as abnormal loss of leaves, slower rates of growth, or higher mortality."

Which of the following, if true, provides the best logical justification for the critics' insistence that the report's conclusion be changed?

(A) Some forests in Canada are being damaged by acid rain.
(B) Acid rain could be causing damage for which symptoms have not yet become visible.
(C) The report does not compare acid rain damage to Canadian forests with acid rain damage to forests in other countries.
(D) All forests in Canada have received acid rain during the past fifteen years.
(E) The severity of damage by acid rain differs from forest to forest.

2. In the past most airline companies minimized aircraft weight to minimize fuel costs. The safest airline seats were heavy, and airlines equipped their planes with few of these seats. This year the seat that has sold best to airlines has been the safest one—a clear indication that airlines are assigning a higher priority to safe seating than to minimizing fuel costs.

Which of the following, if true, most seriously weakens the argument above?

(A) Last year's best-selling airline seat was not the safest airline seat on the market.
(B) No airline company has announced that it would be making safe seating a higher priority this year.
(C) The price of fuel was higher this year than it had been in most of the years when the safest airline seats sold poorly.
(D) Because of increases in the cost of materials, all airline seats were more expensive to manufacture this year than in any previous year.
(E) Because of technological innovations, the safest airline seat on the market this year weighed less than most other airline seats on the market.

GO ON TO THE NEXT PAGE.

3. A computer equipped with signature-recognition software, which restricts access to a computer to those people whose signatures are on file, identifies a person's signature by analyzing not only the form of the signature but also such characteristics as pen pressure and signing speed. Even the most adept forgers cannot duplicate all of the characteristics the program analyzes.

Which of the following can be logically concluded from the passage above?

(A) The time it takes to record and analyze a signature makes the software impractical for everyday use.
(B) Computers equipped with the software will soon be installed in most banks.
(C) Nobody can gain access to a computer equipped with the software solely by virtue of skill at forging signatures.
(D) Signature-recognition software has taken many years to develop and perfect.
(E) In many cases even authorized users are denied legitimate access to computers equipped with the software.

4. Division manager: I want to replace the Microton computers in my division with Vitech computers.

General manager: Why?

Division manager: It costs 28 percent less to train new staff on the Vitech.

General manager: But that is not a good enough reason. We can simply hire only people who already know how to use the Microton computer.

Which of the following, if true, most seriously undermines the general manager's objection to the replacement of Microton computers with Vitechs?

(A) Currently all employees in the company are required to attend workshops on how to use Microton computers in new applications.
(B) Once employees learn how to use a computer, they tend to change employers more readily than before.
(C) Experienced users of Microton computers command much higher salaries than do prospective employees who have no experience in the use of computers.
(D) The average productivity of employees in the general manager's company is below the average productivity of the employees of its competitors.
(E) The high costs of replacement parts make Vitech computers more expensive to maintain than Microton computers.

GO ON TO THE NEXT PAGE.

5. An airplane engine manufacturer developed a new engine model with safety features lacking in the earlier model, which was still being manufactured. During the first year that both were sold, the earlier model far outsold the new model; the manufacturer thus concluded that safety was not the customers' primary consideration.

Which of the following, if true, would most seriously weaken the manufacturer's conclusion?

(A) Both private plane owners and commercial airlines buy engines from this airplane engine manufacturer.

(B) Many customers consider earlier engine models better safety risks than new engine models, since more is usually known about the safety of the earlier models.

(C) Many customers of this airplane engine manufacturer also bought airplane engines from manufacturers who did not provide additional safety features in their newer models.

(D) The newer engine model can be used in all planes in which the earlier engine model can be used.

(E) There was no significant difference in price between the newer engine model and the earlier engine model.

6. Between 1975 and 1985, nursing-home occupancy rates averaged 87 percent of capacity, while admission rates remained constant, at an average of 95 admissions per 1,000 beds per year. Between 1985 and 1988, however, occupancy rates rose to an average of 92 percent of capacity, while admission rates declined to 81 per 1,000 beds per year.

If the statements above are true, which of the following conclusions can be most properly drawn?

(A) The average length of time nursing-home residents stayed in nursing homes increased between 1985 and 1988.

(B) The proportion of older people living in nursing homes was greater in 1988 than in 1975.

(C) Nursing home admission rates tend to decline whenever occupancy rates rise.

(D) Nursing homes built prior to 1985 generally had fewer beds than did nursing homes built between 1985 and 1988.

(E) The more beds a nursing home has, the higher its occupancy rate is likely to be.

GO ON TO THE NEXT PAGE.

7. Firms adopting "profit-related-pay" (PRP) contracts pay wages at levels that vary with the firm's profits. In the metalworking industry last year, firms with PRP contracts in place showed productivity per worker on average 13 percent higher than that of their competitors who used more traditional contracts.

If, on the basis of the evidence above, it is argued that PRP contracts increase worker productivity, which of the following, if true, would most seriously weaken that argument?

(A) Results similar to those cited for the metalworking industry have been found in other industries where PRP contracts are used.
(B) Under PRP contracts costs other than labor costs, such as plant, machinery, and energy, make up an increased proportion of the total cost of each unit of output.
(C) Because introducing PRP contracts greatly changes individual workers' relationships to the firm, negotiating the introduction of PRP contracts is complex and time consuming.
(D) Many firms in the metalworking industry have modernized production equipment in the last five years, and most of these introduced PRP contracts at the same time.
(E) In firms in the metalworking industry where PRP contracts are in place, the average take-home pay is 15 percent higher than it is in those firms where workers have more traditional contracts.

8. Crops can be traded on the futures market before they are harvested. If a poor corn harvest is predicted, prices of corn futures rise; if a bountiful corn harvest is predicted, prices of corn futures fall. This morning meteorologists are predicting much-needed rain for the corn-growing region starting tomorrow. Therefore, since adequate moisture is essential for the current crop's survival, prices of corn futures will fall sharply today.

Which of the following, if true, most weakens the argument above?

(A) Corn that does not receive adequate moisture during its critical pollination stage will not produce a bountiful harvest.
(B) Futures prices for corn have been fluctuating more dramatically this season than last season.
(C) The rain that meteorologists predicted for tomorrow is expected to extend well beyond the corn-growing region.
(D) Agriculture experts announced today that a disease that has devastated some of the corn crop will spread widely before the end of the growing season.
(E) Most people who trade in corn futures rarely take physical possession of the corn they trade.

GO ON TO THE NEXT PAGE.

9. A discount retailer of basic household necessities employs thousands of people and pays most of them at the minimum wage rate. Yet following a federally mandated increase of the minimum wage rate that increased the retailer's operating costs considerably, the retailer's profits increased markedly.

Which of the following, if true, most helps to resolve the apparent paradox?

(A) Over half of the retailer's operating costs consist of payroll expenditures; yet only a small percentage of those expenditures go to pay management salaries.

(B) The retailer's customer base is made up primarily of people who earn, or who depend on the earnings of others who earn, the minimum wage.

(C) The retailer's operating costs, other than wages, increased substantially after the increase in the minimum wage rate went into effect.

(D) When the increase in the minimum wage rate went into effect, the retailer also raised the wage rate for employees who had been earning just above minimum wage.

(E) The majority of the retailer's employees work as cashiers, and most cashiers are paid the minimum wage.

10. The cotton farms of Country Q became so productive that the market could not absorb all that they produced. Consequently, cotton prices fell. The government tried to boost cotton prices by offering farmers who took 25 percent of their cotton acreage out of production direct support payments up to a specified maximum per farm.

The government's program, if successful, will not be a net burden on the budget. Which of the following, if true, is the best basis for an explanation of how this could be so?

(A) Depressed cotton prices meant operating losses for cotton farms, and the government lost revenue from taxes on farm profits.

(B) Cotton production in several countries other than Q declined slightly the year that the support-payment program went into effect in Q.

(C) The first year that the support-payment program was in effect, cotton acreage in Q was 5% below its level in the base year for the program.

(D) The specified maximum per farm meant that for very large cotton farms the support payments were less per acre for those acres that were withdrawn from production than they were for smaller farms.

(E) Farmers who wished to qualify for support payments could not use the cotton acreage that was withdrawn from production to grow any other crop.

GO ON TO THE NEXT PAGE.

11. United States hospitals have traditionally relied primarily on revenues from paying patients to offset losses from unreimbursed care. Almost all paying patients now rely on governmental or private health insurance to pay hospital bills. Recently, insurers have been strictly limiting what they pay hospitals for the care of insured patients to amounts at or below actual costs.

Which of the following conclusions is best supported by the information above?

(A) Although the advance of technology has made expensive medical procedures available to the wealthy, such procedures are out of the reach of low-income patients.

(B) If hospitals do not find ways of raising additional income for unreimbursed care, they must either deny some of that care or suffer losses if they give it.

(C) Some patients have incomes too high for eligibility for governmental health insurance but are unable to afford private insurance for hospital care.

(D) If the hospitals reduce their costs in providing care, insurance companies will maintain the current level of reimbursement, thereby providing more funds for unreimbursed care.

(E) Even though philanthropic donations have traditionally provided some support for the hospitals, such donations are at present declining.

12. Generally scientists enter their field with the goal of doing important new research and accept as their colleagues those with similar motivation. Therefore, when any scientist wins renown as an expounder of science to general audiences, most other scientists conclude that this popularizer should no longer be regarded as a true colleague.

The explanation offered above for the low esteem in which scientific popularizers are held by research scientists assumes that

(A) serious scientific research is not a solitary activity, but relies on active cooperation among a group of colleagues

(B) research scientists tend not to regard as colleagues those scientists whose renown they envy

(C) a scientist can become a famous popularizer without having completed any important research

(D) research scientists believe that those who are well known as popularizers of science are not motivated to do important new research

(E) no important new research can be accessible to or accurately assessed by those who are not themselves scientists

13. Mouth cancer is a danger for people who rarely brush their teeth. In order to achieve early detection of mouth cancer in these individuals, a town's public health officials sent a pamphlet to all town residents, describing how to perform weekly self-examinations of the mouth for lumps.

Which of the following, if true, is the best criticism of the pamphlet as a method of achieving the public health officials' goal?

(A) Many dental diseases produce symptoms that cannot be detected in a weekly self-examination.

(B) Once mouth cancer has been detected, the effectiveness of treatment can vary from person to person.

(C) The pamphlet was sent to all town residents, including those individuals who brush their teeth regularly.

(D) Mouth cancer is much more common in adults than in children.

(E) People who rarely brush their teeth are unlikely to perform a weekly examination of their mouth.

GO ON TO THE NEXT PAGE.

14. Technological improvements and reduced equipment costs have made converting solar energy directly into electricity far more cost-efficient in the last decade. However, the threshold of economic viability for solar power (that is, the price per barrel to which oil would have to rise in order for new solar power plants to be more economical than new oil-fired power plants) is unchanged at thirty-five dollars.

Which of the following, if true, does most to help explain why the increased cost-efficiency of solar power has not decreased its threshold of economic viability?

(A) The cost of oil has fallen dramatically.

(B) The reduction in the cost of solar-power equipment has occurred despite increased raw material costs for that equipment.

(C) Technological changes have increased the efficiency of oil-fired power plants.

(D) Most electricity is generated by coal-fired or nuclear, rather than oil-fired, power plants.

(E) When the price of oil increases, reserves of oil not previously worth exploiting become economically viable.

15. Start-up companies financed by venture capitalists have a much lower failure rate than companies financed by other means. Source of financing, therefore, must be a more important causative factor in the success of a start-up company than are such factors as the personal characteristics of the entrepreneur, the quality of strategic planning, or the management structure of the company.

Which of the following, if true, most seriously weakens the argument above?

(A) Venture capitalists tend to be more responsive than other sources of financing to changes in a start-up company's financial needs.

(B) The strategic planning of a start-up company is a less important factor in the long-term success of the company than are the personal characteristics of the entrepreneur.

(C) More than half of all new companies fail within five years.

(D) The management structures of start-up companies are generally less formal than the management structures of ongoing businesses.

(E) Venture capitalists base their decisions to fund start-up companies on such factors as the characteristics of the entrepreneur and quality of strategic planning of the company.

GO ON TO THE NEXT PAGE.

16. The proportion of women among students enrolled in higher education programs has increased over the past decades. This is partly shown by the fact that in 1959, only 11 percent of the women between twenty and twenty-one were enrolled in college, while in 1981, 30 percent of the women between twenty and twenty-one were enrolled in college.

To evaluate the argument above, it would be most useful to compare 1959 and 1981 with regard to which of the following characteristics?

(A) The percentage of women between twenty and twenty-one who were not enrolled in college

(B) The percentage of women between twenty and twenty-five who graduated from college

(C) The percentage of women who, after attending college, entered highly paid professions

(D) The percentage of men between twenty and twenty-one who were enrolled in college

(E) The percentage of men who graduated from high school

STOP

IF YOU FINISH BEFORE TIME IS CALLED, YOU MAY CHECK YOUR WORK ON THIS SECTION ONLY.
DO NOT TURN TO ANY OTHER SECTION IN THE TEST.

SECTION 2

Time — 25 minutes

16 Questions

Directions: In this section solve each problem, using any available space on the page for scratchwork. Then indicate the best of the answer choices given.

Numbers: All numbers used are real numbers.

Figures: Figures that accompany problems in this section are intended to provide information useful in solving the problems. They are drawn as accurately as possible EXCEPT when it is stated in a specific problem that its figure is not drawn to scale. All figures lie in a plane unless otherwise indicated.

1. If p is an even integer and q is an odd integer, which of the following must be an odd integer?

(A) $\dfrac{p}{q}$

(B) pq

(C) $2p + q$

(D) $2(p + q)$

(E) $\dfrac{3p}{q}$

2. A certain college has a student-to-teacher ratio of 11 to 1. The average (arithmetic mean) annual salary for teachers is $26,000. If the college pays a total of $3,380,000 in annual salaries to its teachers, how many students does the college have?

(A)   130
(B)   169
(C) 1,300
(D) 1,430
(E) 1,560

3. Last year if 97 percent of the revenues of a company came from domestic sources and the remaining revenues, totaling $450,000, came from foreign sources, what was the total of the company's revenues?

(A) $1,350,000
(B) $1,500,000
(C) $4,500,000
(D) $15,000,000
(E) $150,000,000

GO ON TO THE NEXT PAGE.

-484-

4. Drum X is $\frac{1}{2}$ full of oil and drum Y, which has twice the capacity of drum X, is $\frac{2}{3}$ full of oil. If all of the oil in drum X is poured into drum Y, then drum Y will be filled to what fraction of its capacity?

(A) $\frac{3}{4}$

(B) $\frac{5}{6}$

(C) $\frac{11}{12}$

(D) $\frac{7}{6}$

(E) $\frac{11}{6}$

5. In a certain population, there are 3 times as many people aged twenty-one or under as there are people over twenty-one. The ratio of those twenty-one or under to the total population is

(A) 1 to 2
(B) 1 to 3
(C) 1 to 4
(D) 2 to 3
(E) 3 to 4

6. $\dfrac{2 + 2\sqrt{6}}{2} =$

(A) $\sqrt{6}$

(B) $2\sqrt{6}$

(C) $1 + \sqrt{6}$

(D) $1 + 2\sqrt{6}$

(E) $2 + \sqrt{6}$

7. A certain telescope increases the visual range at a particular location from 90 kilometers to 150 kilometers. By what percent is the visual range increased by using the telescope?

(A) 30%

(B) $33\frac{1}{2}\%$

(C) 40%

(D) 60%

(E) $66\frac{2}{3}\%$

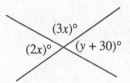

$(3x)°$
$(2x)°$ $(y + 30)°$

Note: Figure not drawn to scale.

8. In the figure above, the value of y is

(A) 6
(B) 12
(C) 24
(D) 36
(E) 42

GO ON TO THE NEXT PAGE.

9. A part-time employee whose hourly wage was increased by 25 percent decided to reduce the number of hours worked per week so that the employee's total weekly income would remain unchanged. By what percent should the number of hours worked be reduced?

(A) 12.5%
(B) 20%
(C) 25%
(D) 50%
(E) 75%

10. If $x > 0$, $\dfrac{x}{50} + \dfrac{x}{25}$ is what percent of x?

(A) 6%

(B) 25%

(C) $37\dfrac{1}{2}\%$

(D) 60%

(E) 75%

11. If the operation ⊛ is defined for all a and b by the equation $a ⊛ b = \dfrac{a^2 b}{3}$, then $2 ⊛ (3 ⊛ -1) =$

(A) 4

(B) 2

(C) $-\dfrac{4}{3}$

(D) -2

(E) -4

12. A factory that employs 1,000 assembly-line workers pays each of these workers $5 per hour for the first 40 hours worked during a week and $1\dfrac{1}{2}$ times that rate for hours worked in excess of 40. What was the total payroll for the assembly-line workers for a week in which 30 percent of them worked 20 hours, 50 percent worked 40 hours, and the rest worked 50 hours?

(A) $180,000
(B) $185,000
(C) $190,000
(D) $200,000
(E) $205,000

13. If $x \neq 2$, then $\dfrac{3x^2(x - 2) - x + 2}{x - 2} =$

(A) $3x^2 - x + 2$
(B) $3x^2 + 1$
(C) $3x^2$
(D) $3x^2 - 1$
(E) $3x^2 - 2$

GO ON TO THE NEXT PAGE.

14. In a certain school, 40 more than $\frac{1}{3}$ of all the students are taking a science course and $\frac{1}{4}$ of those taking a science course are taking physics. If $\frac{1}{8}$ of all the students in the school are taking physics, how many students are in the school?

(A) 240
(B) 300
(C) 480
(D) 720
(E) 960

16. The inside dimensions of a rectangular wooden box are 6 inches by 8 inches by 10 inches. A cylindrical cannister is to be placed inside the box so that it stands upright when the closed box rests on one of its six faces. Of all such cannisters that could be used, what is the radius, in inches, of the one that has maximum volume?

(A) 3
(B) 4
(C) 5
(D) 6
(E) 8

15. If $d > 0$ and $0 < 1 - \frac{c}{d} < 1$, which of the following must be true?

   I. $c > 0$

   II. $\frac{c}{d} < 1$

   III. $c^2 + d^2 > 1$

(A) I only
(B) II only
(C) I and II only
(D) II and III only
(E) I, II, and III

STOP

IF YOU FINISH BEFORE TIME IS CALLED, YOU MAY CHECK YOUR WORK ON THIS SECTION ONLY.
DO NOT TURN TO ANY OTHER SECTION IN THE TEST.

SECTION 3

Time — 30 minutes

23 Questions

Directions: Each passage in this group is followed by questions based on its content. After reading a passage, choose the best answer to each question and fill in the corresponding oval on the answer sheet. Answer all questions following a passage on the basis of what is stated or implied in that passage.

Historians of women's labor in the United States at first largely disregarded the story of female service workers — women earning wages in occupations such as salesclerk, domestic servant, and office secretary. These historians
(5) focused instead on factory work, primarily because it seemed so different from traditional, unpaid "women's work" in the home, and because the underlying economic forces of industrialism were presumed to be gender-blind and hence emancipatory in effect. Unfortunately, emanci-
(10) pation has been less profound than expected, for not even industrial wage labor has escaped continued sex segregation in the workplace.

To explain this unfinished revolution in the status of women, historians have recently begun to emphasize the
(15) way a prevailing definition of femininity often determines the kinds of work allocated to women, even when such allocation is inappropriate to new conditions. For instance, early textile-mill entrepreneurs, in justifying women's employment in wage labor, made much of the assumption
(20) that women were by nature skillful at detailed tasks and patient in carrying out repetitive chores; the mill owners thus imported into the new industrial order hoary stereotypes associated with the homemaking activities they presumed to have been the purview of women. Because
(25) women accepted the more unattractive new industrial tasks more readily than did men, such jobs came to be regarded as female jobs. And employers, who assumed that women's "real" aspirations were for marriage and family life, declined to pay women wages commensurate with those of
(30) men. Thus many lower-skilled, lower-paid, less secure jobs came to be perceived as "female."

More remarkable than the origin has been the persistence of such sex segregation in twentieth-century industry. Once an occupation came to be perceived as "female," employers
(35) showed surprisingly little interest in changing that

perception, even when higher profits beckoned. And despite the urgent need of the United States during the Second World War to mobilize its human resources fully, job segregation by sex characterized even the most important
(40) war industries. Moreover, once the war ended, employers quickly returned to men most of the "male" jobs that women had been permitted to master.

1. According to the passage, job segregation by sex in the United States was

(A) greatly diminished by labor mobilization during the Second World War
(B) perpetuated by those textile-mill owners who argued in favor of women's employment in wage labor
(C) one means by which women achieved greater job security
(D) reluctantly challenged by employers except when the economic advantages were obvious
(E) a constant source of labor unrest in the young textile industry

2. According to the passage, historians of women's labor focused on factory work as a more promising area of research than service-sector work because factory work

(A) involved the payment of higher wages
(B) required skill in detailed tasks
(C) was assumed to be less characterized by sex segregation
(D) was more readily accepted by women than by men
(E) fitted the economic dynamic of industrialism better

GO ON TO THE NEXT PAGE.

3. It can be inferred from the passage that early historians of women's labor in the United States paid little attention to women's employment in the service sector of the economy because

(A) the extreme variety of these occupations made it very difficult to assemble meaningful statistics about them

(B) fewer women found employment in the service sector than in factory work

(C) the wages paid to workers in the service sector were much lower than those paid in the industrial sector

(D) women's employment in the service sector tended to be much more short-term than in factory work

(E) employment in the service sector seemed to have much in common with the unpaid work associated with homemaking

4. The passage supports which of the following statements about the early mill owners mentioned in the second paragraph?

(A) They hoped that by creating relatively unattractive "female" jobs they would discourage women from losing interest in marriage and family life.

(B) They sought to increase the size of the available labor force as a means to keep men's wages low.

(C) They argued that women were inherently suited to do well in particular kinds of factory work.

(D) They thought that factory work bettered the condition of women by emancipating them from dependence on income earned by men.

(E) They felt guilty about disturbing the traditional division of labor in the family.

5. It can be inferred from the passage that the "unfinished revolution" the author mentions in line 13 refers to the

(A) entry of women into the industrial labor market

(B) recognition that work done by women as homemakers should be compensated at rates comparable to those prevailing in the service sector of the economy

(C) development of a new definition of femininity unrelated to the economic forces of industrialism

(D) introduction of equal pay for equal work in all professions

(E) emancipation of women wage earners from gender-determined job allocation

6. The passage supports which of the following statements about hiring policies in the United States?

(A) After a crisis many formerly "male" jobs are reclassified as "female" jobs.

(B) Industrial employers generally prefer to hire women with previous experience as homemakers.

(C) Post-Second World War hiring policies caused women to lose many of their wartime gains in employment opportunity.

(D) Even war industries during the Second World War were reluctant to hire women for factory work.

(E) The service sector of the economy has proved more nearly gender-blind in its hiring policies than has the manufacturing sector.

7. Which of the following words best expresses the opinion of the author of the passage concerning the notion that women are more skillful than men in carrying out detailed tasks?

(A) "patient" (line 21)

(B) "repetitive" (line 21)

(C) "hoary" (line 22)

(D) "homemaking" (line 23)

(E) "purview" (line 24)

8. Which of the following best describes the relationship of the final paragraph to the passage as a whole?

(A) The central idea is reinforced by the citation of evidence drawn from twentieth-century history.

(B) The central idea is restated in such a way as to form a transition to a new topic for discussion.

(C) The central idea is restated and juxtaposed with evidence that might appear to contradict it.

(D) A partial exception to the generalizations of the central idea is dismissed as unimportant.

(E) Recent history is cited to suggest that the central idea's validity is gradually diminishing.

GO ON TO THE NEXT PAGE.

According to a recent theory, Archean-age gold-quartz vein systems were formed over two billion years ago from magmatic fluids that originated from molten granitelike
Line bodies deep beneath the surface of the Earth. This theory is
(5) contrary to the widely held view that the systems were deposited from metamorphic fluids, that is, from fluids that formed during the dehydration of wet sedimentary rocks.

The recently developed theory has considerable practical importance. Most of the gold deposits discovered during
(10) the original gold rushes were exposed at the Earth's surface and were found because they had shed trails of alluvial gold that were easily traced by simple prospecting methods. Although these same methods still lead to an occasional discovery, most deposits not yet discovered have gone
(15) undetected because they are buried and have no surface expression.

The challenge in exploration is therefore to unravel the subsurface geology of an area and pinpoint the position of buried minerals. Methods widely used today include
(20) analysis of aerial images that yield a broad geological overview; geophysical techniques that provide data on the magnetic, electrical, and mineralogical properties of the rocks being investigated; and sensitive chemical tests that are able to detect the subtle chemical halos that often
(25) envelop mineralization. However, none of these high-technology methods are of any value if the sites to which they are applied have never mineralized, and to maximize the chances of discovery the explorer must therefore pay particular attention to selecting the ground formations most
(30) likely to be mineralized. Such ground selection relies to varying degrees on conceptual models, which take into account theoretical studies of relevant factors.

These models are constructed primarily from empirical observations of known mineral deposits and from theories
(35) of ore-forming processes. The explorer uses the models to identify those geological features that are critical to the formation of the mineralization being modeled, and then tries to select areas for exploration that exhibit as many of the critical features as possible.

9. The author is primarily concerned with

(A) advocating a return to an older methodology
(B) explaining the importance of a recent theory
(C) enumerating differences between two widely used methods
(D) describing events leading to a discovery
(E) challenging the assumptions on which a theory is based

10. According to the passage, the widely held view of Archean-age gold-quartz vein systems is that such systems

(A) were formed from metamorphic fluids
(B) originated in molten granitelike bodies
(C) were formed from alluvial deposits
(D) generally have surface expression
(E) are not discoverable through chemical tests

11. The passage implies that which of the following steps would be the first performed by explorers who wish to maximize their chances of discovering gold?

(A) Surveying several sites known to have been formed more than two billion years ago
(B) Limiting exploration to sites known to have been formed from metamorphic fluid
(C) Using an appropriate conceptual model to select a site for further exploration
(D) Using geophysical methods to analyze rocks over a broad area
(E) Limiting exploration to sites where alluvial gold has previously been found

12. Which of the following statements about discoveries of gold deposits is supported by information in the passage?

(A) The number of gold discoveries made annually has increased between the time of the original gold rushes and the present.
(B) New discoveries of gold deposits are likely to be the result of exploration techniques designed to locate buried mineralization.
(C) It is unlikely that newly discovered gold deposits will ever yield as much as did those deposits discovered during the original gold rushes.
(D) Modern explorers are divided on the question of the utility of simple prospecting methods as a source of new discoveries of gold deposits.
(E) Models based on the theory that gold originated from magmatic fluids have already led to new discoveries of gold deposits.

GO ON TO THE NEXT PAGE.

13. It can be inferred from the passage that which of the following is easiest to detect?

(A) A gold-quartz vein system originating in magmatic fluids
(B) A gold-quartz vein system originating in metamorphic fluids
(C) A gold deposit that is mixed with granite
(D) A gold deposit that has shed alluvial gold
(E) A gold deposit that exhibits chemical halos

14. The theory mentioned in line 1 relates to the conceptual models discussed in the passage in which of the following ways?

(A) It may furnish a valid account of ore-forming processes, and, hence, can support conceptual models that have great practical significance.
(B) It suggests that certain geological formations, long believed to be mineralized, are in fact mineralized, thus confirming current conceptual models.
(C) It suggests that there may not be enough similarity across Archean-age gold-quartz vein systems to warrant the formulation of conceptual models.
(D) It corrects existing theories about the chemical halos of gold deposits, and thus provides a basis for correcting current conceptual models.
(E) It suggests that simple prospecting methods still have a higher success rate in the discovery of gold deposits than do more modern methods.

15. According to the passage, methods of exploring for gold that are widely used today are based on which of the following facts?

(A) Most of the Earth's remaining gold deposits are still molten.
(B) Most of the Earth's remaining gold deposits are exposed at the surface.
(C) Most of the Earth's remaining gold deposits are buried and have no surface expression.
(D) Only one type of gold deposit warrants exploration, since the other types of gold deposits are found in regions difficult to reach.
(E) Only one type of gold deposit warrants exploration, since the other types of gold deposits are unlikely to yield concentrated quantities of gold.

16. It can be inferred from the passage that the efficiency of model-based gold exploration depends on which of the following?

I. The closeness of the match between the geological features identified by the model as critical and the actual geological features of a given area
II. The degree to which the model chosen relies on empirical observation of known mineral deposits rather than on theories of ore-forming processes
III. The degree to which the model chosen is based on an accurate description of the events leading to mineralization

(A) I only
(B) II only
(C) I and II only
(D) I and III only
(E) I, II, and III

GO ON TO THE NEXT PAGE.

While there is no blueprint for transforming a largely government-controlled economy into a free one, the experience of the United Kingdom since 1979 clearly
Line shows one approach that works: privatization, in which
(5) state-owned industries are sold to private companies. By 1979, the total borrowings and losses of state-owned industries were running at about £3 billion a year. By selling many of these industries, the government has decreased these borrowings and losses, gained over £34
(10) billion from the sales, and now receives tax revenues from the newly privatized companies. Along with a dramatically improved overall economy, the government has been able to repay 12.5 percent of the net national debt over a two-year period.
(15) In fact, privatization has not only rescued individual industries and a whole economy headed for disaster, but has also raised the level of performance in every area. At British Airways and British Gas, for example, productivity per employee has risen by 20 percent. At Associated
(20) British Ports, labor disruptions common in the 1970's and early 1980's have now virtually disappeared. At British Telecom, there is no longer a waiting list—as there always was before privatization—to have a telephone installed.
Part of this improved productivity has come about
(25) because the employees of privatized industries were given the opportunity to buy shares in their own companies. They responded enthusiastically to the offer of shares: at British Aerospace, 89 percent of the eligible work force bought shares; at Associated British Ports, 90 percent; and at
(30) British Telecom, 92 percent. When people have a personal stake in something, they think about it, care about it, work to make it prosper. At the National Freight Consortium, the new employee-owners grew so concerned about their company's profits that during wage negotiations they
(35) actually pressed their union to lower its wage demands.
Some economists have suggested that giving away free shares would provide a needed acceleration of the privatization process. Yet they miss Thomas Paine's point that "what we obtain too cheap we esteem too lightly." In
(40) order for the far-ranging benefits of individual ownership to be achieved by owners, companies, and countries, employees and other individuals must make their own decisions to buy, and they must commit some of their own resources to the choice.

17. According to the passage, all of the following were benefits of privatizing state-owned industries in the United Kingdom EXCEPT:

(A) Privatized industries paid taxes to the government.
(B) The government gained revenue from selling state-owned industries.
(C) The government repaid some of its national debt.
(D) Profits from industries that were still state-owned increased.
(E) Total borrowings and losses of state-owned industries decreased.

18. According to the passage, which of the following resulted in increased productivity in companies that have been privatized?

(A) A large number of employees chose to purchase shares in their companies.
(B) Free shares were widely distributed to individual shareholders.
(C) The government ceased to regulate major industries.
(D) Unions conducted wage negotiations for employees.
(E) Employee-owners agreed to have their wages lowered.

19. It can be inferred from the passage that the author considers labor disruptions to be

(A) an inevitable problem in a weak national economy
(B) a positive sign of employee concern about a company
(C) a predictor of employee reactions to a company's offer to sell shares to them
(D) a phenomenon found more often in state-owned industries than in private companies
(E) a deterrence to high performance levels in an industry

GO ON TO THE NEXT PAGE.

20. The passage supports which of the following statements about employees buying shares in their own companies?

(A) At three different companies, approximately nine out of ten of the workers were eligible to buy shares in their companies.

(B) Approximately 90% of the eligible workers at three different companies chose to buy shares in their companies.

(C) The opportunity to buy shares was discouraged by at least some labor unions.

(D) Companies that demonstrated the highest productivity were the first to allow their employees the opportunity to buy shares.

(E) Eligibility to buy shares was contingent on employees' agreeing to increased work loads.

21. Which of the following statements is most consistent with the principle described in lines 30-32 ?

(A) A democratic government that decides it is inappropriate to own a particular industry has in no way abdicated its responsibilities as guardian of the public interest.

(B) The ideal way for a government to protect employee interests is to force companies to maintain their share of a competitive market without government subsidies.

(C) The failure to harness the power of self-interest is an important reason that state-owned industries perform poorly.

(D) Governments that want to implement privatization programs must try to eliminate all resistance to the free-market system.

(E) The individual shareholder will reap only a minute share of the gains from whatever sacrifices he or she makes to achieve these gains.

22. Which of the following can be inferred from the passage about the privatization process in the United Kingdom?

(A) It depends to a potentially dangerous degree on individual ownership of shares.

(B) It conforms in its most general outlines to Thomas Paine's prescription for business ownership.

(C) It was originally conceived to include some giving away of free shares.

(D) It has been successful, even though privatization has failed in other countries.

(E) It is taking place more slowly than some economists suggest is necessary.

23. The quotation in line 39 is most probably used to

(A) counter a position that the author of the passage believes is incorrect

(B) state a solution to a problem described in the previous sentence

(C) show how opponents of the viewpoint of the author of the passage have supported their arguments

(D) point out a paradox contained in a controversial viewpoint

(E) present a historical maxim to challenge the principle introduced in the third paragraph

STOP

IF YOU FINISH BEFORE TIME IS CALLED, YOU MAY CHECK YOUR WORK ON THIS SECTION ONLY.
DO NOT TURN TO ANY OTHER SECTION IN THE TEST.

SECTION 4

Time — 25 minutes

16 Questions

Directions: In this section solve each problem, using any available space on the page for scratchwork. Then indicate the best of the answer choices given.

Numbers: All numbers used are real numbers.

Figures: Figures that accompany problems in this section are intended to provide information useful in solving the problems. They are drawn as accurately as possible EXCEPT when it is stated in a specific problem that its figure is not drawn to scale. All figures lie in a plane unless otherwise indicated.

1. $\dfrac{\frac{1}{2}}{\frac{1}{4} + \frac{1}{6}} =$

(A) $\dfrac{6}{5}$

(B) $\dfrac{5}{6}$

(C) $\dfrac{5}{24}$

(D) $\dfrac{1}{5}$

(E) $\dfrac{1}{12}$

2. Kelly and Chris packed several boxes with books. If Chris packed 60 percent of the total number of boxes, what was the ratio of the number of boxes Kelly packed to the number of boxes Chris packed?

(A) 1 to 6
(B) 1 to 4
(C) 2 to 5
(D) 3 to 5
(E) 2 to 3

GO ON TO THE NEXT PAGE.

3. A train travels from New York City to Chicago, a distance of approximately 840 miles, at an average rate of 60 miles per hour and arrives in Chicago at 6:00 in the evening, Chicago time. At what hour in the morning, New York City time, did the train depart for Chicago? (<u>Note:</u> Chicago time is one hour earlier than New York City time.)

(A) 4:00
(B) 5:00
(C) 6:00
(D) 7:00
(E) 8:00

4. Of the following, which is the closest approximation of $\dfrac{50.2 \times 0.49}{199.8}$?

(A) $\dfrac{1}{10}$

(B) $\dfrac{1}{8}$

(C) $\dfrac{1}{4}$

(D) $\dfrac{5}{4}$

(E) $\dfrac{25}{2}$

5. Last year Manfred received 26 paychecks. Each of his first 6 paychecks was $750; each of his remaining paychecks was $30 more than each of his first 6 paychecks. To the nearest dollar, what was the average (arithmetic mean) amount of his paychecks for the year?

(A) $752
(B) $755
(C) $765
(D) $773
(E) $775

6. A certain pair of used shoes can be repaired for $12.50 and will last for 1 year. A pair of the same kind of shoes can be purchased new for $28.00 and will last for 2 years. The average cost per year of the new shoes is what percent greater than the cost of repairing the used shoes?

(A) 3%
(B) 5%
(C) 12%
(D) 15%
(E) 24%

7. In a certain brick wall, each row of bricks above the bottom row contains one less brick than the row just below it. If there are 5 rows in all and a total of 75 bricks in the wall, how many bricks does the bottom row contain?

(A) 14
(B) 15
(C) 16
(D) 17
(E) 18

8. If 25 percent of p is equal to 10 percent of q, and $pq \neq 0$, then p is what percent of q?

(A) 2.5%
(B) 15%
(C) 20%
(D) 35%
(E) 40%

GO ON TO THE NEXT PAGE.

9. If the length of an edge of cube X is twice the length of an edge of cube Y, what is the ratio of the volume of cube Y to the volume of cube X?

(A) $\frac{1}{2}$

(B) $\frac{1}{4}$

(C) $\frac{1}{6}$

(D) $\frac{1}{8}$

(E) $\frac{1}{27}$

10. $(\sqrt{2} + 1)(\sqrt{2} - 1)(\sqrt{3} + 1)(\sqrt{3} - 1) =$

(A) 2

(B) 3

(C) $2\sqrt{6}$

(D) 5

(E) 6

11. In a certain calculus class, the ratio of the number of mathematics majors to the number of students who are not mathematics majors is 2 to 5. If 2 more mathematics majors were to enter the class, the ratio would be 1 to 2. How many students are in the class?

(A) 10
(B) 12
(C) 21
(D) 28
(E) 35

12. Machines A and B always operate independently and at their respective constant rates. When working alone, machine A can fill a production lot in 5 hours, and machine B can fill the same lot in x hours. When the two machines operate simultaneously to fill the production lot, it takes them 2 hours to complete the job. What is the value of x?

(A) $3\frac{1}{3}$

(B) 3

(C) $2\frac{1}{2}$

(D) $2\frac{1}{3}$

(E) $1\frac{1}{2}$

13. In the xy-coordinate system, if (a, b) and $(a + 3, b + k)$ are two points on the line defined by the equation $x = 3y - 7$, then $k =$

(A) 9

(B) 3

(C) $\frac{7}{3}$

(D) 1

(E) $\frac{1}{3}$

14. What is the units digit of $(13)^4 (17)^2 (29)^3$?

(A) 9
(B) 7
(C) 5
(D) 3
(E) 1

GO ON TO THE NEXT PAGE.

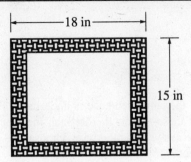

Note: Figure not drawn to scale.

15. The shaded region in the figure above represents a rectangular frame with length 18 inches and width 15 inches. The frame encloses a rectangular picture that has the same area as the frame itself. If the length and width of the picture have the same ratio as the length and width of the frame, what is the length of the picture, in inches?

(A) $9\sqrt{2}$

(B) $\dfrac{3}{2}$

(C) $\dfrac{9}{\sqrt{2}}$

(D) $15\left(1 - \dfrac{1}{\sqrt{2}}\right)$

(E) $\dfrac{9}{2}$

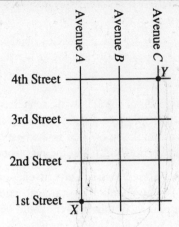

16. Pat will walk from intersection X to intersection Y along a route that is confined to the square grid of four streets and three avenues shown in the map above. How many routes from X to Y can Pat take that have the minimum possible length?

(A) Six
(B) Eight
(C) Ten
(D) Fourteen
(E) Sixteen

STOP

IF YOU FINISH BEFORE TIME IS CALLED, YOU MAY CHECK YOUR WORK ON THIS SECTION ONLY.
DO NOT TURN TO ANY OTHER SECTION IN THE TEST.

SECTION 5

Time—25 minutes

22 Questions

Directions: In each of the following sentences, some part of the sentence or the entire sentence is underlined. Beneath each sentence you will find five ways of phrasing the underlined part. The first of these repeats the original; the other four are different. If you think the original is the best of these answer choices, choose answer A; otherwise, choose one of the others. Select the best version and fill in the corresponding oval on your answer sheet.

This is a test of correctness and effectiveness of expression. In choosing answers, follow the requirements of standard written English; that is, pay attention to grammar, choice of words, and sentence construction. Choose the answer that produces the most effective sentence; this answer should be clear and exact, without awkwardness, ambiguity, redundancy, or grammatical error.

1. Lawmakers are examining measures that would require banks to disclose all fees and account requirements in writing, provide free cashing of government checks, and to create basic savings accounts to carry minimal fees and require minimal initial deposits.

   (A) provide free cashing of government checks, and to create basic savings accounts to carry
   (B) provide free cashing of government checks, and creating basic savings accounts carrying
   (C) to provide free cashing of government checks, and creating basic savings accounts that carry
   (D) to provide free cashing of government checks, creating basic savings accounts to carry
   (E) to provide free cashing of government checks, and to create basic savings accounts that carry

2. Cajuns speak a dialect brought to southern Louisiana by the four thousand Acadians who migrated there in 1755; their language is basically seventeenth-century French to which has been added English, Spanish, and Italian words.

   (A) to which has been added English, Spanish, and Italian words
   (B) added to which is English, Spanish, and Italian words
   (C) to which English, Spanish, and Italian words have been added
   (D) with English, Spanish, and Italian words having been added to it
   (E) and, in addition, English, Spanish, and Italian words are added

3.   **NOT SCORED**

4. Unlike the United States, where farmers can usually depend on rain or snow all year long, the rains in most parts of Sri Lanka are concentrated in the monsoon months, June to September, and the skies are generally clear for the rest of the year.

   (A) Unlike the United States, where farmers can usually depend on rain or snow all year long, the rains in most parts of Sri Lanka
   (B) Unlike the United States farmers who can usually depend on rain or snow all year long, the rains in most parts of Sri Lanka
   (C) Unlike those of the United States, where farmers can usually depend on rain or snow all year long, most parts of Sri Lanka's rains
   (D) In comparison with the United States, whose farmers can usually depend on rain or snow all year long, the rains in most parts of Sri Lanka
   (E) In the United States, farmers can usually depend on rain or snow all year long, but in most parts of Sri Lanka the rains

GO ON TO THE NEXT PAGE.

5. Presenters at the seminar, <u>one who</u> is blind, will demonstrate adaptive equipment that allows visually impaired people to use computers.

(A) one who
(B) one of them who
(C) and one of them who
(D) one of whom
(E) one of which

6. Dr. Tonegawa won the Nobel Prize for discovering how the body can constantly change its genes to fashion a <u>seeming unlimited number of antibodies, each specifically targeted at</u> an invading microbe or foreign substance.

(A) seeming unlimited number of antibodies, each specifically targeted at
(B) seeming unlimited number of antibodies, each targeted specifically to
(C) seeming unlimited number of antibodies, all specifically targeted at
(D) seemingly unlimited number of antibodies, all of them targeted specifically to
(E) seemingly unlimited number of antibodies, each targeted specifically at

7. It is possible that Native Americans originally <u>have migrated to the Western Hemisphere over a bridge of land that once existed</u> between Siberia and Alaska.

(A) have migrated to the Western Hemisphere over a bridge of land that once existed
(B) were migrating to the Western Hemisphere over a bridge of land that existed once
(C) migrated over a bridge of land to the Western Hemisphere that once existed
(D) migrated to the Western Hemisphere over a bridge of land that once existed
(E) were migrating to the Western Hemisphere over a bridge of land existing once

8. In the fall of 1985, only 10 percent of the women entering college planned to major in education, while 28 percent chose business, making it the most popular major for women <u>as well as for men</u>.

(A) as well as for men
(B) as well as the men
(C) and men too
(D) and men as well
(E) and also men

9. Because the Earth's crust is more solid there and thus better able to transmit shock waves, an earthquake <u>of a given magnitude typically devastates an area 100 times greater in the eastern United States than it does in the West</u>.

(A) of a given magnitude typically devastates an area 100 times greater in the eastern United States than it does in the West
(B) of a given magnitude will typically devastate 100 times the area if it occurs in the eastern United States instead of the West
(C) will typically devastate 100 times the area in the eastern United States than one of comparable magnitude occurring in the West
(D) in the eastern United States will typically devastate an area 100 times greater than will a quake of comparable magnitude occurring in the West
(E) that occurs in the eastern United States will typically devastate 100 times more area than if it occurred with comparable magnitude in the West

10. Although Napoleon's army entered Russia with far more supplies than <u>they had in their previous campaigns</u>, it had provisions for only twenty-four days.

(A) they had in their previous campaigns
(B) their previous campaigns had had
(C) they had for any previous campaign
(D) in their previous campaigns
(E) for any previous campaign

GO ON TO THE NEXT PAGE.

11. <u>Certain pesticides can become ineffective if used repeatedly in the same place; one reason is suggested by the finding that there are much larger populations of pesticide-degrading microbes in soils with a relatively long history of pesticide use than in soils that are free of such chemicals.</u>

   (A) Certain pesticides can become ineffective if used repeatedly in the same place; one reason is suggested by the finding that there are much larger populations of pesticide-degrading microbes in soils with a relatively long history of pesticide use than in soils that are free of such chemicals.

   (B) If used repeatedly in the same place, one reason that certain pesticides can become ineffective is suggested by the finding that there are much larger populations of pesticide-degrading microbes in soils with a relatively long history of pesticide use than in soils that are free of such chemicals.

   (C) If used repeatedly in the same place, one reason certain pesticides can become ineffective is suggested by the finding that much larger populations of pesticide-degrading microbes are found in soils with a relatively long history of pesticide use than those that are free of such chemicals.

   (D) The finding that there are much larger populations of pesticide-degrading microbes in soils with a relatively long history of pesticide use than in soils that are free of such chemicals is suggestive of one reason, if used repeatedly in the same place, certain pesticides can become ineffective.

   (E) The finding of much larger populations of pesticide-degrading microbes in soils with a relatively long history of pesticide use than in those that are free of such chemicals suggests one reason certain pesticides can become ineffective if used repeatedly in the same place.

12. One view of the economy contends that a large drop in oil prices should eventually lead to <u>lowering interest rates, as well as lowering fears about inflation,</u> a rally in stocks and bonds, and a weakening of the dollar.

   (A) lowering interest rates, as well as lowering fears about inflation,

   (B) a lowering of interest rates and of fears about inflation,

   (C) a lowering of interest rates, along with fears about inflation,

   (D) interest rates being lowered, along with fears about inflation,

   (E) interest rates and fears about inflation being lowered, with

13. After the Civil War, contemporaries of Harriet <u>Tubman's maintained that she has</u> all of the qualities of a great leader: coolness in the face of danger, an excellent sense of strategy, and an ability to plan in minute detail.

   (A) Tubman's maintained that she has

   (B) Tubman's maintain that she had

   (C) Tubman's have maintained that she had

   (D) Tubman maintained that she had

   (E) Tubman had maintained that she has

GO ON TO THE NEXT PAGE.

14. <u>From 1982 to 1987 sales of new small boats increased between five and ten percent annually.</u>

   (A) From 1982 to 1987 sales of new small boats increased between five and ten percent annually.
   (B) Five to ten percent is the annual increase in sales of new small boats in the years 1982 to 1987.
   (C) Sales of new small boats have increased annually five and ten percent in the years 1982 to 1987.
   (D) Annually an increase of five to ten percent has occurred between 1982 and 1987 in the sales of new small boats.
   (E) Occurring from 1982 to 1987 was an annual increase of five and ten percent in the sales of new small boats.

15. In recent years cattle breeders have increasingly used crossbreeding, <u>in part that their steers should acquire certain characteristics</u> and partly because crossbreeding is said to provide hybrid vigor.

   (A) in part that their steers should acquire certain characteristics
   (B) in part for the acquisition of certain characteristics in their steers
   (C) partly because of their steers acquiring certain characteristics
   (D) partly because certain characteristics should be acquired by their steers
   (E) partly to acquire certain characteristics in their steers

16. The peaks of a mountain range, acting like rocks in a streambed, produce ripples in the air flowing over them; the resulting flow pattern, with <u>crests and troughs that remain stationary although the air that forms them is moving rapidly, are</u> known as "standing waves."

   (A) crests and troughs that remain stationary although the air that forms them is moving rapidly, are
   (B) crests and troughs that remain stationary although they are formed by rapidly moving air, are
   (C) crests and troughs that remain stationary although the air that forms them is moving rapidly, is
   (D) stationary crests and troughs although the air that forms them is moving rapidly, are
   (E) stationary crests and troughs although they are formed by rapidly moving air, is

17. <u>Like Auden, the language of James Merrill is</u> chatty, arch, and conversational—given to complex syntactic flights as well as to prosaic free-verse strolls.

   (A) Like Auden, the language of James Merrill
   (B) Like Auden, James Merrill's language
   (C) Like Auden's, James Merrill's language
   (D) As with Auden, James Merrill's language
   (E) As is Auden's the language of James Merrill

18. In the textbook publishing business, the second quarter is historically weak, because revenues are <u>low and marketing expenses are high as companies prepare</u> for the coming school year.

   (A) low and marketing expenses are high as companies prepare
   (B) low and their marketing expenses are high as they prepare
   (C) low with higher marketing expenses in preparation
   (D) low, while marketing expenses are higher to prepare
   (E) low, while their marketing expenses are higher in preparation

19. Teratomas are unusual forms of cancer <u>because they are composed of tissues such as tooth and bone</u> not normally found in the organ in which the tumor appears.

   (A) because they are composed of tissues such as tooth and bone
   (B) because they are composed of tissues like tooth and bone that are
   (C) because they are composed of tissues, like tooth and bone, tissues
   (D) in that their composition, tissues such as tooth and bone, is
   (E) in that they are composed of tissues such as tooth and bone, tissues

GO ON TO THE NEXT PAGE.

20. The Senate approved immigration legislation that would grant permanent residency to millions of aliens currently residing here and if employers hired illegal aliens they would be penalized.

   (A) if employers hired illegal aliens they would be penalized
   (B) hiring illegal aliens would be a penalty for employers
   (C) penalize employers who hire illegal aliens
   (D) penalizing employers hiring illegal aliens
   (E) employers to be penalized for hiring illegal aliens

21. Scientists have recently discovered what could be the largest and oldest living organism on Earth, a giant fungus that is an interwoven filigree of mushrooms and rootlike tentacles spawned by a single fertilized spore some 10,000 years ago and extending for more than 30 acres in the soil of a Michigan forest.

   (A) extending
   (B) extends
   (C) extended
   (D) it extended
   (E) is extending

22. The period when the great painted caves at Lascaux and Altamira were occupied by Upper Paleolithic people has been established by carbon-14 dating, but what is much more difficult to determine are the reason for their decoration, the use to which primitive people put the caves, and the meaning of the magnificently depicted animals.

   (A) has been established by carbon-14 dating, but what is much more difficult to determine are
   (B) has been established by carbon-14 dating, but what is much more difficult to determine is
   (C) have been established by carbon-14 dating, but what is much more difficult to determine is
   (D) have been established by carbon-14 dating, but what is much more difficult to determine are
   (E) are established by carbon-14 dating, but that which is much more difficult to determine is

STOP

IF YOU FINISH BEFORE TIME IS CALLED, YOU MAY CHECK YOUR WORK ON THIS SECTION ONLY.
DO NOT TURN TO ANY OTHER SECTION IN THE TEST.

Section 6 starts on page 504.

SECTION 6

Time—25 minutes

20 Questions

Directions: Each of the data sufficiency problems below consists of a question and two statements, labeled (1) and (2), in which certain data are given. You have to decide whether the data given in the statements are <u>sufficient</u> for answering the question. Using the data given in the statements <u>plus</u> your knowledge of mathematics and everyday facts (such as the number of days in July or the meaning of *counterclockwise*), you are to fill in oval

     A if statement (1) ALONE is sufficient, but statement (2) alone is not sufficient to answer the question asked;
     B if statement (2) ALONE is sufficient, but statement (1) alone is not sufficient to answer the question asked;
     C if BOTH statements (1) and (2) TOGETHER are sufficient to answer the question asked, but NEITHER statement ALONE is sufficient;
     D if EACH statement ALONE is sufficient to answer the question asked;
     E if statements (1) and (2) TOGETHER are NOT sufficient to answer the question asked, and additional data specific to the problem are needed.

Numbers: All numbers used are real numbers.

Figures: A figure in a data sufficiency problem will conform to the information given in the question, but will not necessarily conform to the additional information given in statements (1) and (2).

     You may assume that lines shown as straight are straight and that angle measures are greater than zero.

     You may assume that the positions of points, angles, regions, etc., exist in the order shown.

     All figures lie in a plane unless otherwise indicated.

Note: In questions that ask for the value of a quantity, the data given in the statements are sufficient only when it is possible to determine exactly one numerical value for the quantity.

Example:

In $\triangle PQR$, what is the value of x ?

(1) $PQ = PR$

(2) $y = 40$

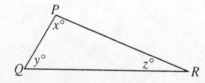

Explanation: According to statement (1), $PQ = PR$; therefore, $\triangle PQR$ is isosceles and $y = z$. Since $x + y + z = 180$, it follows that $x + 2y = 180$. Since statement (1) does not give a value for y, you cannot answer the question using statement (1) alone. According to statement (2), $y = 40$; therefore, $x + z = 140$. Since statement (2) does not give a value for z, you cannot answer the question using statement (2) alone. Using both statements together, since $x + 2y = 180$ and the value of y is given, you can find the value of x. Therefore, the answer is C.

GO ON TO THE NEXT PAGE.

A Statement (1) ALONE is sufficient, but statement (2) alone is not sufficient.
B Statement (2) ALONE is sufficient, but statement (1) alone is not sufficient.
C BOTH statements TOGETHER are sufficient, but NEITHER statement ALONE is sufficient.
D EACH statement ALONE is sufficient.
E Statements (1) and (2) TOGETHER are NOT sufficient.

1. If the list price of a new car was $12,300, what was the cost of the car to the dealer?

   (1) The cost to the dealer was equal to 80 percent of the list price.

   (2) The car was sold for $11,070, which was 12.5 percent more than the cost to the dealer.

2. If p, q, x, y, and z are different positive integers, which of the five integers is the median?

   (1) $p + x < q$

   (2) $y < z$

3. A certain employee is paid $6 per hour for an 8-hour workday. If the employee is paid $1\frac{1}{2}$ times this rate for time worked in excess of 8 hours during a single day, how many hours did the employee work today?

   (1) The employee was paid $18 more for hours worked today than for hours worked yesterday.

   (2) Yesterday the employee worked 8 hours.

4. If n is a member of the set

   $$\{33, 36, 38, 39, 41, 42\},$$

   what is the value of n?

   (1) n is even.

   (2) n is a multiple of 3.

GO ON TO THE NEXT PAGE.

A Statement (1) ALONE is sufficient, but statement (2) alone is not sufficient.
B Statement (2) ALONE is sufficient, but statement (1) alone is not sufficient.
C BOTH statements TOGETHER are sufficient, but NEITHER statement ALONE is sufficient.
D EACH statement ALONE is sufficient.
E Statements (1) and (2) TOGETHER are NOT sufficient.

5. What is the value of x?

(1) $2x + 1 = 0$

(2) $(x + 1)^2 = x^2$

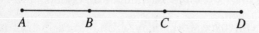

$A \qquad B \qquad C \qquad D$

6. In the figure above, what is the length of AD?

(1) $AC = 6$

(2) $BD = 6$

7. A retailer purchased a television set for x percent less than its list price, and then sold it for y percent less than its list price. What was the list price of the television set?

(1) $x = 15$

(2) $x - y = 5$

8. Is x^2 greater than x?

(1) x^2 is greater than 1.

(2) x is greater than -1.

9. What is the value of $\frac{r}{2} + \frac{s}{2}$?

(1) $\frac{r + s}{2} = 5$

(2) $r + s = 10$

10. If x, y, and z are numbers, is $z = 18$?

(1) The average (arithmetic mean) of x, y, and z is 6.

(2) $x = -y$

GO ON TO THE NEXT PAGE.

A   Statement (1) ALONE is sufficient, but statement (2) alone is not sufficient.
B   Statement (2) ALONE is sufficient, but statement (1) alone is not sufficient.
C   BOTH statements TOGETHER are sufficient, but NEITHER statement ALONE is sufficient.
D   EACH statement ALONE is sufficient.
E   Statements (1) and (2) TOGETHER are NOT sufficient.

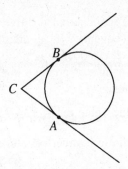

11. The circular base of an above-ground swimming pool lies in a level yard and just touches two straight sides of a fence at points A and B, as shown in the figure above. Point C is on the ground where the two sides of the fence meet. How far from the center of the pool's base is point A?

   (1) The base has area 250 square feet.

   (2) The center of the base is 20 feet from point C.

12. In 1979 Mr. Jackson bought a total of n shares of stock X and Mrs. Jackson bought a total of 300 shares of stock X. If the couple held all of their respective shares throughout 1980, and Mr. Jackson's 1980 dividends on his n shares totaled $150, what was the total amount of Mrs. Jackson's 1980 dividends on her 300 shares?

   (1) In 1980 the annual dividend on each share of stock X was $0.75.

   (2) In 1979 Mr. Jackson bought a total of 200 shares of stock X.

GO ON TO THE NEXT PAGE.

A Statement (1) ALONE is sufficient, but statement (2) alone is not sufficient.
B Statement (2) ALONE is sufficient, but statement (1) alone is not sufficient.
C BOTH statements TOGETHER are sufficient, but NEITHER statement ALONE is sufficient.
D EACH statement ALONE is sufficient.
E Statements (1) and (2) TOGETHER are NOT sufficient.

13. If Sara's age is exactly twice Bill's age, what is Sara's age?

(1) Four years ago, Sara's age was exactly 3 times Bill's age.

(2) Eight years from now, Sara's age will be exactly 1.5 times Bill's age.

14. What is the value of $\frac{x}{yz}$?

(1) $x = \frac{y}{2}$ and $z = \frac{2x}{5}$.

(2) $\frac{x}{z} = \frac{5}{2}$ and $\frac{1}{y} = \frac{1}{10}$.

15. An infinite sequence of positive integers is called an "alpha sequence" if the number of even integers in the sequence is finite. If S is an infinite sequence of positive integers, is S an alpha sequence?

(1) The first ten integers in S are even.

(2) An infinite number of integers in S are odd.

16. If $xy > 0$, does $(x - 1)(y - 1) = 1$?

(1) $x + y = xy$

(2) $x = y$

GO ON TO THE NEXT PAGE.

A   Statement (1) ALONE is sufficient, but statement (2) alone is not sufficient.
B   Statement (2) ALONE is sufficient, but statement (1) alone is not sufficient.
C   BOTH statements TOGETHER are sufficient, but NEITHER statement ALONE is sufficient.
D   EACH statement ALONE is sufficient.
E   Statements (1) and (2) TOGETHER are NOT sufficient.

17. After winning 50 percent of the first 20 games it played, Team A won all of the remaining games it played. What was the total number of games that Team A won?

(1) Team A played 25 games altogether.

(2) Team A won 60 percent of all the games it played.

$$\begin{array}{r} \square \\ + \triangle \\ \hline \bigstar \end{array}$$

18. In the addition problem above, each of the symbols $\square$, $\triangle$, and $\bigstar$ represents a positive digit. If $\square < \triangle$, what is the value of $\triangle$?

(1) $\bigstar = 4$

(2) $\square = 1$

CANCELATION FEES

Days Prior to Departure	Percent of Package Price
46 or more	10%
45-31	35%
30-16	50%
15-5	65%
4 or fewer	100%

19. The table above shows the cancelation fee schedule that a travel agency uses to determine the fee charged to a tourist who cancels a trip prior to departure. If a tourist canceled a trip with a package price of $1,700 and a departure date of September 4, on what day was the trip canceled?

(1) The cancelation fee was $595.

(2) If the trip had been canceled one day later, the cancelation fee would have been $255 more.

20. Is 5^k less than 1,000?

(1) $5^{k+1} > 3,000$

(2) $5^{k-1} = 5^k - 500$

STOP

IF YOU FINISH BEFORE TIME IS CALLED, YOU MAY CHECK YOUR WORK ON THIS SECTION ONLY.
DO NOT TURN TO ANY OTHER SECTION IN THE TEST.

Answer Key: Form B

Section 1	Section 2	Section 3	Section 4	Section 5	Section 6
1. B	1. C	1. B	1. A	1. E	1. D
2. E	2. D	2. C	2. E	2. C	2. E
3. C	3. D	3. E	3. B	3. Not Scored	3. C
4. C	4. C	4. C	4. B	4. E	4. E
5. B	5. E	5. E	5. D	5. D	5. D
6. A	6. C	6. C	6. C	6. E	6. E
7. D	7. E	7. C	7. D	7. D	7. E
8. D	8. E	8. A	8. E	8. A	8. A
9. B	9. B	9. B	9. D	9. D	9. D
10. A	10. A	10. A	10. A	10. E	10. C
11. B	11. E	11. C	11. D	11. A	11. A
12. D	12. B	12. B	12. A	12. B	12. D
13. E	13. D	13. D	13. D	13. D	13. D
14. C	14. A	14. A	14. E	14. A	14. B
15. E	15. C	15. C	15. A	15. E	15. E
16. D	16. B	16. D	16. C	16. C	16. A
		17. D		17. C	17. D
		18. A		18. A	18. A
		19. E		19. E	19. C
		20. B		20. C	20. B
		21. C		21. A	
		22. E		22. B	
		23. A			

Explanatory Material:
Critical Reasoning, Section 1

1. A report on acid rain concluded, "Most forests in Canada are not being damaged by acid rain." Critics of the report insist the conclusion be changed to, "Most forests in Canada do not show visible symptoms of damage by acid rain, such as abnormal loss of leaves, slower rates of growth, or higher mortality."

Which of the following, if true, provides the best logical justification for the critics' insistence that the report's conclusion be changed?

(A) Some forests in Canada are being damaged by acid rain.

(B) Acid rain could be causing damage for which symptoms have not yet become visible.

(C) The report does not compare acid rain damage to Canadian forests with acid rain damage to forests in other countries.

(D) All forests in Canada have received acid rain during the past fifteen years.

(E) The severity of damage by acid rain differs from forest to forest.

If, as choice B says, acid rain damage could be occurring without there yet being any visible symptoms, the absence of visible symptoms would not justify the conclusion that no damage was occurring. Thus, choice B is the best answer since it justifies the critics' insistence that the conclusion be changed.

Because the authors of the report evidently resist the change being demanded, any claim on which they and their critics are likely to be in agreement cannot provide justification for the change. Choices A, C, D, and E are all claims both parties can agree on, so none of them is correct.

2. In the past most airline companies minimized aircraft weight to minimize fuel costs. The safest airline seats were heavy, and airlines equipped their planes with few of these seats. This year the seat that has sold best to airlines has been the safest one — a clear indication that airlines are assigning a higher priority to safe seating than to minimizing fuel costs.

Which of the following, if true, most seriously weakens the argument above?

(A) Last year's best-selling airline seat was not the safest airline seat on the market.

(B) No airline company has announced that it would be making safe seating a higher priority this year.

(C) The price of fuel was higher this year than it had been in most of the years when the safest airline seats sold poorly.

(D) Because of increases in the cost of materials, all airline seats were more expensive to manufacture this year than in any previous year.

(E) Because of technological innovations, the safest airline seat on the market this year weighed less than most other airline seats on the market.

If the safest airline seats are now among the lightest, as choice E says, then buying them could be part of a strategy of minimizing fuel costs, rather than indicating a shift away from that goal. Choice E, therefore, is the best answer.

Choice A merely confirms that seat safety has improved, and thus does not weaken the argument. Many policy shifts take place without being publicly announced, so choice B does not weaken the argument. Choice C indicates that minimizing fuel costs remains a priority, but it is neutral on whether safety has become more important, so C is incorrect. Choice D does not distinguish between safe and unsafe seats, and is thus also incorrect.

3. A computer equipped with signature-recognition software, which restricts access to a computer to those people whose signatures are on file, identifies a person's signature by analyzing not only the form of the signature but also such characteristics as pen pressure and signing speed. Even the most adept forgers cannot duplicate all of the characteristics the program analyzes.

Which of the following can be logically concluded from the passage above?

(A) The time it takes to record and analyze a signature makes the software impractical for everyday use.
(B) Computers equipped with the software will soon be installed in most banks.
(C) Nobody can gain access to a computer equipped with the software solely by virtue of skill at forging signatures.
(D) Signature-recognition software has taken many years to develop and perfect.
(E) In many cases even authorized users are denied legitimate access to computers equipped with the software.

The passage asserts that skill at forging signatures is not by itself sufficient to match all of the characteristics that the software analyzes to identify signatures. Because the software gives access only after identifying a signature, access cannot be achieved by someone employing forging skill alone. Choice C is thus the best answer.

The passage gives no information about how fast the software operates or about how long the software was under development, so neither A nor D can be concluded. Choice B is incorrect since the software might have features not mentioned in the passage that make it unattractive to banks. The passages give no reason to think that errors of the sort that choice E describes, even if made, would be numerous.

4. Division manager: I want to replace the Microton computers in my division with Vitech computers.

General manager: Why?

Division manager: It costs 28 percent less to train new staff on the Vitech.

General manager: But that is not a good enough reason. We can simply hire only people who already know how to use the Microton computer.

Which of the following, if true, most seriously undermines the general manager's objection to the replacement of Microton computers with Vitechs?

(A) Currently all employees in the company are required to attend workshops on how to use Microton computers in new applications.
(B) Once employees learn how to use a computer, they tend to change employers more readily than before.
(C) Experienced users of Microton computers command much higher salaries than do prospective employees who have no experience in the use of computers.
(D) The average productivity of employees in the general manager's company is below the average productivity of the employees of its competitors.
(E) The high costs of replacement parts make Vitech computers more expensive to maintain than Microton computers.

The general manager's objection is based on avoiding training costs altogether. But if, as choice C says, hiring experienced users of Microton computers is significantly more costly than hiring otherwise qualified people who would have to be trained to use Vitech computers, the force of the objection is weakened. Choice C, therefore, is the best answer.

Choices A, B, and D are all incorrect; none of them provides information relevant to an evaluation of Microton computers as compared with Vitech computers. Choice E argues independently against replacing Microton computers with Vitechs and thus is also incorrect.

5. An airplane engine manufacturer developed a new engine model with safety features lacking in the earlier model, which was still being manufactured. During the first year that both were sold, the earlier model far outsold the new model; the manufacturer thus concluded that safety was not the customers' primary consideration.

Which of the following, if true, would most seriously weaken the manufacturer's conclusion?

(A) Both private plane owners and commercial airlines buy engines from this airplane engine manufacturer.
(B) Many customers consider earlier engine models better safety risks than new engine models, since more is usually known about the safety of the earlier models.
(C) Many customers of this airplane engine manufacturer also bought airplane engines from manufacturers who did not provide additional safety features in their newer models.
(D) The newer engine model can be used in all planes in which the earlier engine model can be used.
(E) There was no significant difference in price between the newer engine model and the earlier engine model.

The manufacturer's conclusion would be weakened if it could be argued that, in the opinion of customers, safety considerations favor the earlier model. Choice B supports such an argument and is the best answer.

The groups mentioned in choice A would both be expected to consider safety important, so their failing to buy the new model would be striking, without casting doubt on the conclusion; thus, choice A is incorrect. Choice C might support the conclusion, because customers bought other engine models that might not include the newer safety features. Choices D and E suggest that usability and price, respectively, were not the customers' primary consideration in favoring the earlier model, but neither choice weakens the conclusion that safety was not their primary consideration.

6. Between 1975 and 1985, nursing-home occupancy rates averaged 87 percent of capacity, while admission rates remained constant, at an average of 95 admissions per 1,000 beds per year. Between 1985 and 1988, however, occupancy rates rose to an average of 92 percent of capacity, while admission rates declined to 81 per 1,000 beds per year.

If the statements above are true, which of the following conclusions can be most properly drawn?

(A) The average length of time nursing-home residents stayed in nursing homes increased between 1985 and 1988.
(B) The proportion of older people living in nursing homes was greater in 1988 than in 1975.
(C) Nursing home admission rates tend to decline whenever occupancy rates rise.
(D) Nursing homes built prior to 1985 generally had fewer beds than did nursing homes built between 1985 and 1988.
(E) The more beds a nursing home has, the higher its occupancy rate is likely to be.

Between 1985 and 1988, nursing home occupancy rates rose although admission rates declined. Choice A receives support from these facts since it would be a basis for an adequate account of how they arose. Because it is the only choice that receives support, A is therefore the best answer.

Without information about the total population of older people, nothing can be concluded about percentages in nursing homes; thus, choice B is incorrect. Since there is nothing to indicate whether the development that took place between 1985 and 1988 was an unusual development or a common one, choice C receives no support. No information about numbers of beds is provided, so neither choice D nor choice E is correct.

7. Firms adopting "profit-related-pay" (PRP) contracts pay wages at levels that vary with the firm's profits. In the metalworking industry last year, firms with PRP contracts in place showed productivity per worker on average 13 percent higher than that of their competitors who used more traditional contracts.

If, on the basis of the evidence above, it is argued that PRP contracts increase worker productivity, which of the following, if true, would most seriously weaken that argument?

(A) Results similar to those cited for the metalworking industry have been found in other industries where PRP contracts are used.

(B) Under PRP contracts costs other than labor costs, such as plant, machinery, and energy, make up an increased proportion of the total cost of each unit of output.

(C) Because introducing PRP contracts greatly changes individual workers' relationships to the firm, negotiating the introduction of PRP contracts is complex and time-consuming.

(D) Many firms in the metalworking industry have modernized production equipment in the last five years, and most of these introduced PRP contracts at the same time.

(E) In firms in the metalworking industry where PRP contracts are in place, the average take-home pay is 15 percent higher than it is in those firms where workers have more traditional contracts.

According to choice D, many firms with PRP contracts also have modernized equipment. Since the cause of their improved productivity might be the modernized equipment, not the PRP contracts, this weakens the argument, so D is the best answer.

Choice A does not weaken the argument: it is merely more evidence of the sort already being used. Choice B is incorrect because it is a natural consequence of increased worker productivity if other costs remain stable. Choice C is incorrect because it explains why introducing PRP contracts is difficult, but says nothing about the results of doing so. Choice E is incorrect because it is not implausible that workers' pay should roughly correspond to their productivity.

8. Crops can be traded on the futures market before they are harvested. If a poor corn harvest is predicted, prices of corn futures rise; if a bountiful corn harvest is predicted, prices of corn futures fall. This morning meteorologists are predicting much-needed rain for the corn-growing region starting tomorrow. Therefore, since adequate moisture is essential for the current crop's survival, prices of corn futures will fall sharply today.

Which of the following, if true, most weakens the argument above?

(A) Corn that does not receive adequate moisture during its critical pollination stage will not produce a bountiful harvest.

(B) Futures prices for corn have been fluctuating more dramatically this season than last season.

(C) The rain that meteorologists predicted for tomorrow is expected to extend well beyond the corn-growing region.

(D) Agriculture experts announced today that a disease that has devastated some of the corn crop will spread widely before the end of the growing season.

(E) Most people who trade in corn futures rarely take physical possession of the corn they trade.

The argument, in predicting a drop in the price of corn futures, relies on news suggesting a good-sized corn crop. This prediction is undermined if there is, at the same time, news suggesting a small crop. Choice D presents such news and is therefore the best answer.

Choice A provides background information describing a stage at which rains are essential, and choice C makes rain over the entire corn-growing area seem more certain. Both are fully compatible with the argument and do nothing to weaken it. Past price changes (choice B) and details of who handles harvested corn (choice E) cannot affect the eventual size of this year's corn crop, so neither is relevant to the argument.

9. A discount retailer of basic household necessities employs thousands of people and pays most of them at the minimum wage rate. Yet following a federally mandated increase of the minimum wage rate that increased the retailer's operating costs considerably, the retailer's profits increased markedly.

Which of the following, if true, most helps to resolve the apparent paradox?

(A) Over half of the retailer's operating costs consist of payroll expenditures; yet only a small percentage of those expenditures go to pay management salaries.
(B) The retailer's customer base is made up primarily of people who earn, or who depend on the earnings of others who earn, the minimum wage.
(C) The retailer's operating costs, other than wages, increased substantially after the increase in the minimum wage rate went into effect.
(D) When the increase in the minimum wage rate went into effect, the retailer also raised the wage rate for employees who had been earning just above minimum wage.
(E) The majority of the retailer's employees work as cashiers, and most cashiers are paid the minimum wage.

The question to be resolved is why the mandated wage increase, which increased operating costs, was accompanied by an increase in profits. By showing how the wage increase might have led to an increase in the retailer's sales, choice B helps resolve this question, and thus is the best answer.

Choices A and E are incorrect, since they suggest that the wages that rose as a result of the mandated increase constituted a significant proportion of the retailer's expenditures, which if anything adds to the seeming paradox. Choices C and D also contribute to the paradox, since they indicate that along with increases in the minimum wage there were increases in the retailer's operating costs; so choices C and D are also incorrect.

10. The cotton farms of Country Q became so productive that the market could not absorb all that they produced. Consequently, cotton prices fell. The government tried to boost cotton prices by offering farmers who took 25 percent of their cotton acreage out of production direct support payments up to a specified maximum per farm.

The government's program, if successful, will not be a net burden on the budget. Which of the following, if true, is the best basis for an explanation of how this could be so?

(A) Depressed cotton prices meant operating losses for cotton farms, and the government lost revenue from taxes on farm profits.
(B) Cotton production in several countries other than Q declined slightly the year that the support-payment program went into effect in Q.
(C) The first year that the support-payment program was in effect, cotton acreage in Q was 5% below its level in the base year for the program.
(D) The specified maximum per farm meant that for very large cotton farms the support payments were less per acre for those acres that were withdrawn from production than they were for smaller farms.
(E) Farmers who wished to qualify for support payments could not use the cotton acreage that was withdrawn from production to grow any other crop.

If the government's program of support payments to cotton farmers succeeded in raising revenue for the government that would, in the absence of the program, not be raised, this could explain why the program will not be a net burden on the budget. Choice A suggests that the program would raise revenue: by raising the price of cotton, the direct support payments will boost cotton farmers' profits and thereby increase the tax revenues the government receives from cotton farmers. Therefore, A is the best answer.

None of the other choices provides a source of revenue to the government or suggests that savings would be realized in a governmental expense category, so choices B, C, D, and E are all incorrect.

11. United States hospitals have traditionally relied primarily on revenues from paying patients to offset losses from unreimbursed care. Almost all paying patients now rely on governmental or private health insurance to pay hospital bills. Recently, insurers have been strictly limiting what they pay hospitals for the care of insured patients to amounts at or below actual costs.

Which of the following conclusions is best supported by the information above?

(A) Although the advance of technology has made expensive medical procedures available to the wealthy, such procedures are out of the reach of low-income patients.

(B) If hospitals do not find ways of raising additional income for unreimbursed care, they must either deny some of that care or suffer losses if they give it.

(C) Some patients have incomes too high for eligibility for governmental health insurance but are unable to afford private insurance for hospital care.

(D) If the hospitals reduce their costs in providing care, insurance companies will maintain the current level of reimbursement, thereby providing more funds for unreimbursed care.

(E) Even though philanthropic donations have traditionally provided some support for the hospitals, such donations are at present declining.

The passage explains that the primary way hospitals have covered the cost of unreimbursed care in the past is no longer available to them. It follows that they have three options: finding a new way to cover that cost, reducing it by giving less unreimbursed care, or suffering a loss. This is essentially what choice B concludes, so B is the best answer.

The passage touches neither on kinds of medical procedures administered in hospitals (choice A) nor on revenue other than that received from patients or their insurers (choice E), so neither choice is correct. The passage gives no hint of who the paying patients are who do not rely on insurance, so choice C is unsupported. Concerning choice D, the passage actually suggests that it is false.

12. Generally scientists enter their field with the goal of doing important new research and accept as their colleagues those with similar motivation. Therefore, when any scientist wins renown as an expounder of science to general audiences, most other scientists conclude that this popularizer should no longer be regarded as a true colleague.

The explanation offered above for the low esteem in which scientific popularizers are held by research scientists assumes that

(A) serious scientific research is not a solitary activity, but relies on active cooperation among a group of colleagues

(B) research scientists tend not to regard as colleagues those scientists whose renown they envy

(C) a scientist can become a famous popularizer without having completed any important research

(D) research scientists believe that those who are well known as popularizers of science are not motivated to do important new research

(E) no important new research can be accessible to or accurately assessed by those who are not themselves scientists

The passage indicates that research scientists accept as colleagues only scientists with motivation to do important new research. This fact explains the tendency of scientists to reject scientists who are renowned popularizers of science only if research scientists believe popularizers lack such motivation; choice D is the best answer.

Since the passage is concerned only with whether certain scientists have the goal of doing important new research, not with how research is done, or with who understands new research, choices A and E are both incorrect. Choice B is incorrect because it suggests an alternative explanation of rejection of popularizers. Since the explanation offered remains unaffected even if unsuccessful research scientists cannot become famous popularizers, choice C is incorrect.

13. Mouth cancer is a danger for people who rarely brush their teeth. In order to achieve early detection of mouth cancer in these individuals, a town's public health officials sent a pamphlet to all town residents, describing how to perform weekly self-examinations of the mouth for lumps.

Which of the following, if true, is the best criticism of the pamphlet as a method of achieving the public health officials' goal?

(A) Many dental diseases produce symptoms that cannot be detected in a weekly self-examination.

(B) Once mouth cancer has been detected, the effectiveness of treatment can vary from person to person.

(C) The pamphlet was sent to all town residents, including those individuals who brush their teeth regularly.

(D) Mouth cancer is much more common in adults than in children.

(E) People who rarely brush their teeth are unlikely to perform a weekly examination of their mouth.

If choice E is true, the very people said to be at risk for mouth cancer are unlikely to be led by the content of the pamphlet to an early detection of this cancer. Choice E thus questions the pamphlet's utility and is the best answer.

Choice A is incorrect because it does not specifically cast doubt on self-examination as a means of detecting mouth cancer. Choice B is concerned with the situation following detection, but not with detection itself, so it is incorrect. Choice C is incorrect: although it suggests a certain inefficiency in handling the pamphlets, it does not suggest that the pamphlets will not achieve their purpose. Choice D supports the general appropriateness of sending written instructions, and is thus incorrect.

14. Technological improvements and reduced equipment costs have made converting solar energy directly into electricity far more cost-efficient in the last decade. However, the threshold of economic viability for solar power (that is, the price per barrel to which oil would have to rise in order for new solar power plants to be more economical than new oil-fired power plants) is unchanged at thirty-five dollars.

Which of the following, if true, does most to help explain why the increased cost-efficiency of solar power has not decreased its threshold of economic viability?

(A) The cost of oil has fallen dramatically.

(B) The reduction in the cost of solar-power equipment has occurred despite increased raw material costs for that equipment.

(C) Technological changes have increased the efficiency of oil-fired power plants.

(D) Most electricity is generated by coal-fired or nuclear, rather than oil-fired, power plants.

(E) When the price of oil increases, reserves of oil not previously worth exploiting become economically viable.

If gains in cost-efficiency of solar power have not improved its economical viability relative to oil-derived power, the explanation must be that oil-derived power itself has become more cost-efficient. Choice C points to this explanation and is thus the best answer.

Actual oil prices control how far, given the viability threshold, solar power is from economic viability but do not figure in the determination of the threshold, so choices A and E are incorrect. Choice B provides background on data that give rise to the puzzle but leaves the puzzle unresolved, so it is incorrect. Because the viability threshold for solar power is defined in relation to generating electricity from oil, choice D is irrelevant to determining the threshold and thus incorrect.

15. Start-up companies financed by venture capitalists have a much lower failure rate than companies financed by other means. Source of financing, therefore, must be a more important causative factor in the success of a start-up company than are such factors as the personal characteristics of the entrepreneur, the quality of strategic planning, or the management structure of the company.

Which of the following, if true, most seriously weakens the argument above?

(A) Venture capitalists tend to be more responsive than other sources of financing to changes in a start-up company's financial needs.

(B) The strategic planning of a start-up company is a less important factor in the long-term success of the company than are the personal characteristics of the entrepreneur.

(C) More than half of all new companies fail within five years.

(D) The management structures of start-up companies are generally less formal than the management structures of ongoing businesses.

(E) Venture capitalists base their decisions to fund start-up companies on such factors as the characteristics of the entrepreneur and quality of strategic planning of the company.

Given choice E, it is possible that companies with those combinations of factors that are most likely to lead to success are the very companies that venture capitalists select for financing. This weakens the argument that the financing itself must be more important for success than those factors. Thus, E is the best answer.

Choice A is incorrect because, rather than weakening the argument, it provides an explanation for how funding by venture capitalists could aid the success of a company. None of choices B, C, and D weakens because each of them makes a statement about start-up companies in general, without regard to their source of financing.

16. The proportion of women among students enrolled in higher education programs has increased over the past decades. This is partly shown by the fact that in 1959, only 11 percent of the women between twenty and twenty-one were enrolled in college, while in 1981, 30 percent of the women between twenty and twenty-one were enrolled in college.

To evaluate the argument above, it would be most useful to compare 1959 and 1981 with regard to which of the following characteristics?

(A) The percentage of women between twenty and twenty-one who were not enrolled in college

(B) The percentage of women between twenty and twenty-five who graduated from college

(C) The percentage of women who, after attending college, entered highly paid professions

(D) The percentage of men between twenty and twenty-one who were enrolled in college

(E) The percentage of men who graduated from high school

The argument presents a substantial increase in the proportion of women between twenty and twenty-one who were enrolled in college as evidence that there was an increase in the proportion of higher education students who were women. This evidence would lack force if a similar increase in college enrollment had occurred among men. Choice D is therefore the best answer.

Since percentages of men graduating from high school do not indicate the percentages enrolling in college that year, choice E is incorrect. Choices A, B, and C are incorrect because the information they refer to, being about women only, does not facilitate a comparison of women's enrollment to men's enrollment in higher education programs.

Explanatory Material: Problem Solving, Section 2

1. If p is an even integer and q is an odd integer, which of the following must be an odd integer?

   (A) $\dfrac{p}{q}$

   (B) pq

   (C) $2p + q$

   (D) $2(p + q)$

   (E) $\dfrac{3p}{q}$

The product of an even integer and any other integer is even, and the sum of an even integer and an odd integer is odd. An examination of the answer choices shows that both B, pq, and D, $2(p+q)$, must be even and that C, $2p+q$, must be an odd integer, since $2p$ is even and it is given that q is odd. With this approach, choices A and E do not have to be examined, but substitution of values for p and q, such as $p = 12$ and $q = 3$, shows that $\dfrac{p}{q}$ and $\dfrac{3p}{q}$ do not have to be odd integers. The best answer is C.

2. A certain college has a student-to-teacher ratio of 11 to 1. The average (arithmetic mean) annual salary for teachers is $26,000. If the college pays a total of $3,380,000 in annual salaries to its teachers, how many students does the college have?

   (A)   130
   (B)   169
   (C)   1,300
   (D)   1,430
   (E)   1,560

Let s be the number of students and t be the number of teachers. Then $\dfrac{s}{t} = \dfrac{11}{1}$. The number of teachers can be found by dividing total salaries by the average salary per teacher, $\dfrac{\$3,380,000}{\$26,000} = 130$. Substituting this value for t in the equation $\dfrac{s}{t} = \dfrac{11}{1}$ gives $\dfrac{s}{130} = \dfrac{11}{1}$, and $s = 1,430$. The best answer is D.

3. Last year if 97 percent of the revenues of a company came from domestic sources and the remaining revenues, totaling $450,000, came from foreign sources, what was the total of the company's revenues?

   (A) $1,350,000
   (B) $1,500,000
   (C) $4,500,000
   (D) $15,000,000
   (E) $150,000,000

If 97 percent of the revenues came from domestic sources, then the remaining 3 percent, totaling $450,000, came from foreign sources. If r represents total revenue, then $0.03r = \$450,000$ and $r = \$15,000,000$. The best answer is D.

4. Drum X is $\dfrac{1}{2}$ full of oil and drum Y, which has twice the capacity of drum X, is $\dfrac{2}{3}$ full of oil. If all of the oil in drum X is poured into drum Y, then drum Y will be filled to what fraction of its capacity?

   (A) $\dfrac{3}{4}$

   (B) $\dfrac{5}{6}$

   (C) $\dfrac{11}{12}$

   (D) $\dfrac{7}{6}$

   (E) $\dfrac{11}{6}$

Let x and y represent the capacities of drums X and Y, respectively. The amount of oil in drum X is $\dfrac{1}{2}x$ and the amount of oil in drum Y is $\dfrac{2}{3}y$. Since the capacity of drum Y is twice the capacity of drum X, it follows that $y = 2x$, or $x = \dfrac{1}{2}y$, and the oil in drum X is $\dfrac{1}{2}x = \dfrac{1}{4}y$. When the oil in drum X is poured into drum Y, Y contains $\dfrac{1}{4}y + \dfrac{2}{3}y = \dfrac{11}{12}y$, which is $\dfrac{11}{12}$ of its capacity. The best answer is C.

5. In a certain population, there are 3 times as many people aged twenty-one or under as there are people over twenty-one. The ratio of those twenty-one or under to the total population is

   (A) 1 to 2
   (B) 1 to 3
   (C) 1 to 4
   (D) 2 to 3
   (E) 3 to 4

If v represents the number of people over twenty-one, then $3v$ represents the number of people twenty-one or under, and $v + 3v$ represents the total population. Thus, the ratio of those twenty-one or under to the total population is

$\dfrac{3v}{v + 3v} = \dfrac{3v}{4v} = \dfrac{3}{4}$, or 3 to 4, and the best answer is E.

6. $\dfrac{2 + 2\sqrt{6}}{2} =$

   (A) $\sqrt{6}$
   (B) $2\sqrt{6}$
   (C) $1 + \sqrt{6}$
   (D) $1 + 2\sqrt{6}$
   (E) $2 + \sqrt{6}$

$\dfrac{2 + 2\sqrt{6}}{2} = \dfrac{2(1 + \sqrt{6})}{2} = 1 + \sqrt{6}$, and the best answer is C.

7. A certain telescope increases the visual range at a particular location from 90 kilometers to 150 kilometers. By what percent is the visual range increased by using the telescope?

   (A) 30%
   (B) $33\frac{1}{2}\%$
   (C) 40%
   (D) 60%
   (E) $66\frac{2}{3}\%$

The telescope increases the visual range by $150 - 90 = 60$ kilometers. Thus, the increase in visual range is

$\dfrac{60}{90} = \dfrac{2}{3} = 66\frac{2}{3}\%$. The best answer is E.

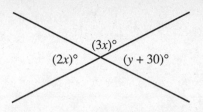

Note: Figure not drawn to scale.

8. In the figure above, the value of y is

   (A) 6
   (B) 12
   (C) 24
   (D) 36
   (E) 42

Since the indicated angles are formed by the intersection of two lines, the adjacent angles are supplementary (i.e., the sum of their measures is 180°). Thus, $2x + 3x = 180$, or $x = 36$, and $3x + y + 30 = 180$, or $3(36) + y + 30 = 180$, or $y = 42$. The best answer is E.

9. A part-time employee whose hourly wage was increased by 25 percent decided to reduce the number of hours worked per week so that the employee's total weekly income would remain unchanged. By what percent should the number of hours worked be reduced?

   (A) 12.5%
   (B) 20%
   (C) 25%
   (D) 50%
   (E) 75%

Let h be the original number of hours the employee worked per week and w be the hourly wage, for weekly income of wh. The increased wage is $1.25w$, or $\frac{5}{4}w$, and the reduced number of hours can be represented by H, for a weekly income of $\frac{5}{4}wH$. If the total weekly income is to be unchanged, then $wh = \frac{5}{4}wH$ and $h = \frac{5}{4}H$, or $H = \frac{4}{5}h$. The reduced hours are $\frac{4}{5}$ or 80% of the original hours, which is a reduction of 20%. The best answer is B.

10. If $x > 0$, $\dfrac{x}{50} + \dfrac{x}{25}$ is what percent of x?

    (A)   6%

    (B) 25%

    (C) $37\dfrac{1}{2}$%

    (D) 60%

    (E) 75%

If $x > 0$, $\dfrac{x}{50} + \dfrac{x}{25} = \dfrac{x}{50} + \dfrac{2x}{50} = \dfrac{3x}{50} = \dfrac{6x}{100}$ or 6% of x.
The best answer is A.

11. If the operation $\circledast$ is defined for all a and b by the equation $a \circledast b = \dfrac{a^2 b}{3}$, then $2 \circledast (3 \circledast -1) =$

    (A)   4

    (B)   2

    (C) $-\dfrac{4}{3}$

    (D) -2

    (E) -4

To find the value of $2 \circledast (3 \circledast -1)$, the value of $3 \circledast -1$ must be found first. By definition, $a \circledast b = \dfrac{a^2 b}{3}$; so $3 \circledast -1 = \dfrac{3^2(-1)}{3} = \dfrac{-9}{3} = -3$. Thus, $2 \circledast (3 \circledast -1) = 2 \circledast -3 = \dfrac{2^2(-3)}{3} = 4(-1) = -4$, and the best answer is E.

12. A factory that employs 1,000 assembly-line workers pays each of these workers \$5 per hour for the first 40 hours worked during a week and $1\dfrac{1}{2}$ times that rate for hours worked in excess of 40. What was the total payroll for the assembly-line workers for a week in which 30 percent of them worked 20 hours, 50 percent worked 40 hours, and the rest worked 50 hours?

    (A) \$180,000
    (B) \$185,000
    (C) \$190,000
    (D) \$200,000
    (E) \$205,000

Since there are 1,000 workers, 30 percent, or 300, worked 20 hours each; 50 percent, or 500, worked 40 hours each; and the remaining 200 worked 50 hours each. The 300 workers earned $300(20)(\$5) = \$30,000$, the 500 workers earned $500(40)(\$5) = \$100,000$, and the 200 workers earned $200[(40)(\$5) + (50 - 40)(1\dfrac{1}{2})(\$5)] = \$55,000$. Thus, the total payroll was $\$30,000 + \$100,000 + \$55,000 = \$185,000$, and the best answer is B.

13. If $x \neq 2$, then $\dfrac{3x^2(x - 2) - x + 2}{x - 2} =$

    (A) $3x^2 - x + 2$
    (B) $3x^2 + 1$
    (C) $3x^2$
    (D) $3x^2 - 1$
    (E) $3x^2 - 2$

If $x \neq 2$, then $\dfrac{3x^2(x - 2) - x + 2}{x - 2} = \dfrac{3x^2(x - 2) - (x - 2)}{x - 2} = \dfrac{(x - 2)(3x^2 - 1)}{x - 2} = 3x^2 - 1$. The best answer is D.

14. In a certain school, 40 more than $\dfrac{1}{3}$ of all the students are taking a science course and $\dfrac{1}{4}$ of those taking a science course are taking physics. If $\dfrac{1}{8}$ of all the students in the school are taking physics, how many students are in the school?

    (A) 240
    (B) 300
    (C) 480
    (D) 720
    (E) 960

If s represents the number of students in the school, then $40 + \dfrac{1}{3}s$ are taking a science course and $\dfrac{1}{4}(40 + \dfrac{1}{3}s)$ are taking physics. If $\dfrac{1}{8}$ of the students in the school are taking physics, then $\dfrac{1}{8}s = \dfrac{1}{4}(40 + \dfrac{1}{3}s)$, or $s = 2(40 + \dfrac{1}{3}s) = 80 + \dfrac{2}{3}s$, and $s - \dfrac{2}{3}s = 80$.

Thus, $s = 240$, and the best answer is A.

15. If $d > 0$ and $0 < 1 - \dfrac{c}{d} < 1$, which of the following must be true?

 I. $c > 0$

 II. $\dfrac{c}{d} < 1$

 III. $c^2 + d^2 > 1$

 (A) I only
 (B) II only
 (C) I and II only
 (D) II and III only
 (E) I, II, and III

If every value of c and d satisfying the inequalities $d > 0$ and $0 < 1 - \dfrac{c}{d} < 1$ also satisfies the inequality in statement I, II, or III, then that statement must be true.

If even one value of c and d satisfying the inequalities $d > 0$ and $0 < 1 - \dfrac{c}{d} < 1$ does not satisfy the inequality in statement I, II, or III, then that statement need not be true.

 I. Since $1 - \dfrac{c}{d} < 1$, it follows that $\dfrac{c}{d} > 0$. This together with $d > 0$ implies $c > 0$, and statement I must be true.

 II. Since $0 < 1 - \dfrac{c}{d} < 1$, it follows that $-1 < -\dfrac{c}{d} < 0$, which is equivalent to $0 < \dfrac{c}{d} < 1$, and statement II must be true.

 III. The inequalities $d > 0$ and $0 < 1 - \dfrac{c}{d} < 1$ give information about the size of $\dfrac{c}{d}$ but do not appear to give information about the size of $c^2 + d^2$; so it is reasonable to try to find positive values of c and d for which $\dfrac{c}{d}$ is less than 1. Choosing $c = \dfrac{1}{4}$ and $d = \dfrac{1}{3}$ yields $c^2 + d^2 = (\dfrac{1}{4})^2 + (\dfrac{1}{3})^2 = \dfrac{1}{16} + \dfrac{1}{9}$, which is less than 1. Therefore, statement III need not be true. The best answer is C.

16. The inside dimensions of a rectangular wooden box are 6 inches by 8 inches by 10 inches. A cylindrical cannister is to be placed inside the box so that it stands upright when the closed box rests on one of its six faces. Of all such cannisters that could be used, what is the radius, in inches, of the one that has maximum volume?

 (A) 3
 (B) 4
 (C) 5
 (D) 6
 (E) 8

The formula for the volume of a right circular cylinder is $v = \pi r^2 h$, where r is the radius and h is the height of the cylinder. The diameter of the circular top of the cannister must equal the length of the shorter dimension of the top of the box, as illustrated in the figure below.

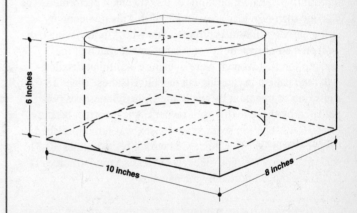

Since the box can rest on any one of its six faces, there are three possibilities to consider. These are summarized in the following table.

Dimensions of the box top	r	h	v
6 by 8	3	10	90π
6 by 10	3	8	72π
8 by 10	4	6	96π

Thus, the radius, in inches, of the cannister having the maximum volume is 4. The best answer is B.

Explanatory Material:
Reading Comprehension, Section 3

1. According to the passage, job segregation by sex in the United States was

   (A) greatly diminished by labor mobilization during the Second World War
   (B) perpetuated by those textile-mill owners who argued in favor of women's employment in wage labor
   (C) one means by which women achieved greater job security
   (D) reluctantly challenged by employers except when the economic advantages were obvious
   (E) a constant source of labor unrest in the young textile industry

The best answer is B. Lines 13-17 state that sex segregation persisted in the workplace because "a prevailing definition of femininity" dictated the kinds of tasks women performed. The passage then provides an example of this phenomenon by citing early textile-mill entrepreneurs who, "in justifying women's employment in wage labor, made much of the assumption that women were by nature skillful at detailed tasks and patient in carrying out repetitive chores" (lines 18-21). Thus, job segregation by sex in the United States was perpetuated by those textile-mill owners. A is incorrect because lines 36-40 state job segregation by sex was not diminished during World War II. Choice C is wrong because lines 30-31 state that many "female" jobs were "less secure." Choices D and E are not supported by the passage.

2. According to the passage, historians of women's labor focused on factory work as a more promising area of research than service-sector work because factory work

   (A) involved the payment of higher wages
   (B) required skill in detailed tasks
   (C) was assumed to be less characterized by sex segregation
   (D) was more readily accepted by women than by men
   (E) fitted the economic dynamic of industrialism better

The best answer is C. Lines 4-9 state that historians of women's labor focused on factory work rather than service-sector work because the "underlying economic forces of industrialism were presumed to be gender-blind and hence emancipatory in effect." Thus, the passage indicates that these historians assumed that sex segregation was less prevalent in factory work than in service-sector work. Choices A, B, D, and E can be eliminated because the passage does not state that historians focused on factory work because it involved higher wages, required skill in detailed tasks, was accepted more readily by women, or fitted the economic dynamic of industrialism better.

3. It can be inferred from the passage that early historians of women's labor in the United States paid little attention to women's employment in the service sector of the economy because

   (A) the extreme variety of these occupations made it very difficult to assemble meaningful statistics about them
   (B) fewer women found employment in the service sector than in factory work
   (C) the wages paid to workers in the service sector were much lower than those paid in the industrial sector
   (D) women's employment in the service sector tended to be much more short-term than in factory work
   (E) employment in the service sector seemed to have much in common with the unpaid work associated with homemaking

The best answer is E. In lines 4-7 the author states that historians of women's labor in the United States focused on factory work rather than the service sector because factory work "seemed so different from traditional, unpaid 'women's work' in the home." By indicating that historians preferred to study women's work in factories rather than women's work in the service sector because factory work seemed less like women's work at home, the passage suggests that historians believed that women's work in the service sector was similar to women's work at home. Choice A is incorrect because the passage does not discuss statistics. Choices B, C, and D can be eliminated because the passage does not compare women factory workers and women service workers.

4. The passage supports which of the following statements about the early mill owners mentioned in the second paragraph?

   (A) They hoped that by creating relatively unattractive "female" jobs they would discourage women from losing interest in marriage and family life.
   (B) They sought to increase the size of the available labor force as a means to keep men's wages low.
   (C) They argued that women were inherently suited to do well in particular kinds of factory work.
   (D) They thought that factory work bettered the condition of women by emancipating them from dependence on income earned by men.
   (E) They felt guilty about disturbing the traditional division of labor in the family.

The best answer is C. In lines 19-21, the author states that early textile-mill owners "made much of the assumption that women were by nature skillful at detailed tasks and patient in carrying out repetitive chores." Choice A is incorrect because the passage states that the early mill owners were interested in "justifying women's employment in wage labor" (lines 18-19). Choices B and D can be eliminated because the passage does not state that the mill owners were interested in keeping men's wages low or in bettering the condition of women. Choice E can be eliminated because the passage does not discuss mill owners' attitudes toward the traditional division of labor in the family.

5. It can be inferred from the passage that the "unfinished revolution" the author mentions in line 13 refers to the

   (A) entry of women into the industrial labor market
   (B) recognition that work done by women as homemakers should be compensated at rates comparable to those prevailing in the service sector of the economy
   (C) development of a new definition of femininity unrelated to the economic forces of industrialism
   (D) introduction of equal pay for equal work in all professions
   (E) emancipation of women wage earners from gender-determined job allocation

The best answer is E. In the last sentence of the first paragraph, the author states that emancipation for women in factory work was "less profound than expected, for not even industrial wage labor has escaped continued sex segregation in the workplace." The author goes on in the first sentence of the second paragraph to discuss "this unfinished revolution in the status of women"; the phrase "this unfinished revolution" refers back to the last sentence of the first paragraph, where the author has just mentioned the persistence of sex segregation in the industrialized work force. Choice A is incorrect because the first paragraph indicates that women have entered the industrial labor market. Choice C is wrong because the passage does not refer to any new definition of femininity unrelated to industrialism. Choices B and D are incorrect because the first paragraph discusses women's work in terms of sex segregation and not in terms of equal pay for men and women in various professions.

6. The passage supports which of the following statements about hiring policies in the United States?

   (A) After a crisis many formerly "male" jobs are reclassified as "female" jobs.
   (B) Industrial employers generally prefer to hire women with previous experience as homemakers.
   (C) Post-Second World War hiring policies caused women to lose many of their wartime gains in employment opportunity.
   (D) Even war industries during the Second World War were reluctant to hire women for factory work.
   (E) The service sector of the economy has proved more nearly gender-blind in its hiring policies than has the manufacturing sector.

The best answer is C. The last sentence of the passage states that after World War II "employers quickly returned to men most of the 'male' jobs that women had been permitted to master." Choice A is incorrect because the passage states that in the case of World War II many jobs occupied by women were returned to men. Choice D is incorrect because the last paragraph of the passage indicates that war industries did hire women, although those women were subject to job segregation by sex. The passage does not provide any information to support B or E.

7. Which of the following words best expresses the opinion of the author of the passage concerning the notion that women are more skillful than men in carrying out detailed tasks?

   (A) "patient" (line 21)
   (B) "repetitive" (line 21)
   (C) "hoary" (line 22)
   (D) "homemaking" (line 23)
   (E) "purview" (line 24)

The best answer is C. The author of the passage uses the word "hoary" in line 22 to characterize the kinds of stereotypes about women that mill owners imported into the new industrial order. Through this word, the author expresses a negative opinion about stereotypes propagating the notion that women are more skillful than men in carrying out certain tasks. Choices A and B can be eliminated because the author uses them to paraphrase the assumptions of the mill owners about the kinds of work women excelled at; the mill owners subscribed to the very stereotypes that the author describes as "hoary." Choices D and E are incorrect because the words "homemaking" and "purview" do not convey attitudes.

8. Which of the following best describes the relationship of the final paragraph to the passage as a whole?

(A) The central idea is reinforced by the citation of evidence drawn from twentieth-century history.
(B) The central idea is restated in such a way as to form a transition to a new topic for discussion.
(C) The central idea is restated and juxtaposed with evidence that might appear to contradict it.
(D) A partial exception to the generalizations of the central idea is dismissed as unimportant.
(E) Recent history is cited to suggest that the central idea's validity is gradually diminishing.

The best answer is A. To answer this question you must identify the central idea of the passage so as to determine the relationship of the content of the last paragraph to that idea. The central idea is introduced in lines 10-12 of the first paragraph: "not even industrial wage labor has escaped continued sex segregation in the workplace." The second paragraph goes on to discuss the origins of sex segregation in the industrialized workforce. The author begins the last paragraph by mentioning the persistence of sex segregation and goes on to describe such segregation in industry during and after the Second World War. Choice B is incorrect because the last paragraph focuses on the topic under discussion and does not introduce any new and different topic. Choices C, D, and E can be eliminated because the last paragraph cites evidence to support the central idea rather than to challenge it.

9. The author is primarily concerned with

(A) advocating a return to an older methodology
(B) explaining the importance of a recent theory
(C) enumerating differences between two widely used methods
(D) describing events leading to a discovery
(E) challenging the assumptions on which a theory is based

The best answer is B. In the first paragraph the author describes a recent theory concerning the formation of Archean-age gold-quartz vein systems, and in the second paragraph this theory is said to have "considerable practical importance" (lines 8-9). The remaining paragraphs explain why such theories of ore-forming processes are important for explorers seeking to locate gold deposits. The older method of prospecting for gold is mentioned, but rather than advocating this method (choice A), the author explains why prospecting is no longer viable. The author neither discusses differences between widely used methods (choice C) nor describes the events leading to a discovery (choice D). Although another, widely held view concerning ore-forming processes is mentioned, the author does not challenge the assumptions on which this view is based (choice E).

10. According to the passage, the widely held view of Archean-age gold-quartz vein systems is that such systems

(A) were formed from metamorphic fluids
(B) originated in molten granitelike bodies
(C) were formed from alluvial deposits
(D) generally have surface expression
(E) are not discoverable through chemical tests

The best answer is A. In lines 5-6 the author mentions "the widely held view that the [Archean-age gold-quartz vein] systems were deposited from metamorphic fluids." This view is said to be contrary to the recent theory that these systems originated in molten granitelike bodies, so choice B is not correct. Alluvial deposits are mentioned in the passage as having aided simple prospecting methods, but such deposits are not said to have formed the Archean-age gold-quartz vein systems (choice C). According to the author, "most deposits not yet discovered have gone undetected because they are buried and have no surface expression" (lines 14-16), so choice D is not correct. And choice E is incorrect because the author says that chemical tests can aid the discovery of gold deposits if they are conducted in areas where mineralization is likely to have taken place (lines 23-27).

11. The passage implies that which of the following steps would be the first performed by explorers who wish to maximize their chances of discovering gold?

(A) Surveying several sites known to have been formed more than two billion years ago
(B) Limiting exploration to sites known to have been formed from metamorphic fluid
(C) Using an appropriate conceptual model to select a site for further exploration
(D) Using geophysical methods to analyze rocks over a broad area
(E) Limiting exploration to sites where alluvial gold has previously been found

The best answer is C. According to the author, "to maximize the chances of discovery the explorer must . . . pay particular attention to selecting the ground formations most likely to be mineralized" (lines 27-30); the explorer begins by using conceptual models "to identify those geological features that are critical to the formation of the mineralization being modeled, and then tries to select areas for exploration" (lines 35-38). According to the author, geophysical methods are of no value if they are applied to sites that have never mineralized (lines 25-27), so choice D is not correct, and there is no indication in the passage that age of formation would narrow the explorer's choices, so choice A is not correct. Choice B is not correct because the new theory, which is said to have "considerable practical importance" (lines 8-9) for the discovery of gold, is contrary to the view that gold deposits were deposited from metamorphic fluids. And the passage says that simple prospecting methods that trace alluvial gold only occasionally lead to new discoveries, so choice E is incorrect.

12. Which of the following statements about discoveries of gold deposits is supported by information in the passage?

(A) The number of gold discoveries made annually has increased between the time of the original gold rushes and the present.

(B) New discoveries of gold deposits are likely to be the result of exploration techniques designed to locate buried mineralization.

(C) It is unlikely that newly discovered gold deposits will ever yield as much as did those deposits discovered during the original gold rushes.

(D) Modern explorers are divided on the question of the utility of simple prospecting methods as a source of new discoveries of gold deposits.

(E) Models based on the theory that gold originated from magmatic fluids have already led to new discoveries of gold deposits.

The best answer is B. According to the passage, "most [gold] deposits not yet discovered have gone undetected because they are buried and have no surface expression" (lines 14-16); as a result, an explorer uses conceptual models "to identify those geological features that are critical to the formation of the mineralization being modeled, and then tries to select areas for exploration" (lines 35-38). The passage provides no information about the number of gold discoveries or the yield of gold deposits past or present, so choices A and C are not correct. The author does not suggest that there is any disagreement concerning the utility of simple prospecting methods, which the author says only occasionally lead to new discoveries, so choice D is incorrect. And although the author indicates that the theory that gold originated from magmatic fluids has considerable practical importance, there is no information in the passage indicating that models based on this theory have already led to new discoveries of gold deposits, so choice E is incorrect.

13. It can be inferred from the passage that which of the following is easiest to detect?

(A) A gold-quartz vein system originating in magmatic fluids

(B) A gold-quartz vein system originating in metamorphic fluids

(C) A gold deposit that is mixed with granite

(D) A gold deposit that has shed alluvial gold

(E) A gold deposit that exhibits chemical halos

The best answer is D. According to the passage, "Most of the gold deposits discovered during the original gold rushes were exposed at the Earth's surface and were found because they had shed trails of alluvial gold that were easily traced by simple prospecting methods" (lines 9-12). By contrast, "most deposits not yet discovered have gone undetected because they are buried and have no surface expression" (lines 14-16), and the passage gives no indication that gold-quartz vein systems and gold deposits like those described in choices A, B, C, and E would have the kind of surface expression that would make them easy to detect.

14. The theory mentioned in line 1 relates to the conceptual models discussed in the passage in which of the following ways?

(A) It may furnish a valid account of ore-forming processes, and, hence, can support conceptual models that have great practical significance.

(B) It suggests that certain geological formations, long believed to be mineralized, are in fact mineralized, thus confirming current conceptual models.

(C) It suggests that there may not be enough similarity across Archean-age gold-quartz vein systems to warrant the formulation of conceptual models.

(D) It corrects existing theories about the chemical halos of gold deposits, and thus provides a basis for correcting current conceptual models.

(E) It suggests that simple prospecting methods still have a higher success rate in the discovery of gold deposits than do more modern methods.

The best answer is A. The passage says that the theory has "considerable practical importance" (lines 8-9), and the bulk of the passage is devoted to explaining that importance for the discovery of new gold deposits: since most remaining gold deposits are buried and have no surface expression, the passage says, conceptual models derived from theories of ore-forming processes are used to identify sites where mineralization is likely to have taken place. The theory is not said to confirm or correct current models (choices B and D), nor does it suggest that simple prospecting methods have any current value (choice E). And choice C is incorrect because it contradicts what the passage suggests about the importance of the theory for the formulation of conceptual models.

15. According to the passage, methods of exploring for gold that are widely used today are based on which of the following facts?

(A) Most of the Earth's remaining gold deposits are still molten.

(B) Most of the Earth's remaining gold deposits are exposed at the surface.

(C) Most of the Earth's remaining gold deposits are buried and have no surface expression.

(D) Only one type of gold deposit warrants exploration, since the other types of gold deposits are found in regions difficult to reach.

(E) Only one type of gold deposit warrants exploration, since the other types of gold deposits are unlikely to yield concentrated quantities of gold.

The best answer is C. According to the passage, "most deposits not yet discovered have gone undetected because they are buried and have no surface expression" (lines 14-16), and "The challenge in exploration is therefore to unravel the subsurface geology of an area and pinpoint the position of buried minerals" (lines 17-19). The "Methods widely used today" (line 19) are based on these facts, which directly contradict choice B. Choices A, D, and E are incorrect because there is no information in the passage to support these statements about methods of exploring for gold.

16. It can be inferred from the passage that the efficiency of model-based gold exploration depends on which of the following?

    I. The closeness of the match between the geological features identified by the model as critical and the actual geological features of a given area

    II. The degree to which the model chosen relies on empirical observation of known mineral deposits rather than on theories of ore-forming processes

    III. The degree to which the model chosen is based on an accurate description of the events leading to mineralization

    (A) I only
    (B) II only
    (C) I and II only
    (D) I and III only
    (E) I, II, and III

The best answer is D. According to the passage, after constructing conceptual models based on observations of known mineral deposits and theories of ore-forming processes, "The explorer uses the models to identify those geological features that are critical to the formation of the mineralization being modeled, and then tries to select areas for exploration that exhibit as many of the critical features as possible" (lines 35-39). It can be inferred from this that the efficiency of the resulting exploration will depend on how closely the features of the selected area match the features identified by the model as critical (Statement I) and on how accurately the process of mineralization has been modeled (Statement III). According to the passage, both empirical observations of known mineral deposits and theories of ore-forming processes are important in constructing the models, so Statement II cannot be part of the correct answer.

17. According to the passage, all of the following were benefits of privatizing state-owned industries in the United Kingdom EXCEPT:

    (A) Privatized industries paid taxes to the government.
    (B) The government gained revenue from selling state-owned industries.
    (C) The government repaid some of its national debt.
    (D) Profits from industries that were still state-owned increased.
    (E) Total borrowings and losses of state-owned industries decreased.

The best answer is D. The passage does not mention how industries that were still state-owned fared in terms of profits. Choice A is not the answer because lines 10-11 state that the government "now receives tax revenues from the newly privatized companies." Choice B is not the answer because lines 9-10 state that the government gained billions of pounds from selling state-owned industries. Choice C is not the answer because lines 12-14 state that "the government has been able to repay 12.5 percent of the net national debt over a two-year period." Choice E is not the answer because lines 8-9 state that the government has decreased borrowings and losses of the state-owned industries mentioned in lines 6-7.

18. According to the passage, which of the following resulted in increased productivity in companies that have been privatized?

    (A) A large number of employees chose to purchase shares in their companies.
    (B) Free shares were widely distributed to individual shareholders.
    (C) The government ceased to regulate major industries.
    (D) Unions conducted wage negotiations for employees.
    (E) Employee-owners agreed to have their wages lowered.

The best answer is A. In lines 24-26, the author attributes improved productivity partly to the opportunity given to employees of privatized industries to purchase shares in their own companies. The next sentence gives examples of how employees "responded enthusiastically to the offer of shares," thereby implying that many employees bought shares in the privatized companies. Choice B is incorrect because, although the passage mentions that some economists suggested giving away free shares, the passage does not indicate that any shares were given away. Choice C is incorrect because the subject of regulation is not addressed, and choices D and E are incorrect because the passage does not discuss the relationship between wages and productivity.

19. It can be inferred from the passage that the author considers labor disruptions to be

   (A) an inevitable problem in a weak national economy
   (B) a positive sign of employee concern about a company
   (C) a predictor of employee reactions to a company's offer to sell shares to them
   (D) a phenomenon found more often in state-owned industries than in private companies
   (E) a deterrence to high performance levels in an industry

The best answer is E. In lines 15-17, the author states that privatization has "raised the level of performance" in industry. As an example, the author mentions in lines 19-21 that at one company, "labor disruptions common in the 1970's and early 1980's have now virtually disappeared." Thus, the author is implying that an absence of labor disruptions raises the level of performance, and the converse — that labor disruptions adversely affect performance levels. Choices A, B, and C are incorrect because the passage makes no generalization about labor disruptions in a weak national economy, nor does it connect labor disruptions with employee concern or employee shareholding. Choice D is incorrect because the passage makes no generalization about the frequency of labor disruptions throughout either state-owned or private companies.

20. The passage supports which of the following statements about employees buying shares in their own companies?

   (A) At three different companies, approximately nine out of ten of the workers were eligible to buy shares in their companies.
   (B) Approximately 90% of the eligible workers at three different companies chose to buy shares in their companies.
   (C) The opportunity to buy shares was discouraged by at least some labor unions.
   (D) Companies that demonstrated the highest productivity were the first to allow their employees the opportunity to buy shares.
   (E) Eligibility to buy shares was contingent on employees' agreeing to increased work loads.

The best answer is B. In lines 27-30, the passage cites the percentage of eligible workers (rather than the percentage of total workers) who bought shares at three different companies; these percentages were respectively 89 percent, 90 percent, and 92 percent, that is, approximately 90 percent in each case. Choice A is incorrect because the passage does not state what portion of the workforce at each company was actually eligible to buy shares. Choice C is incorrect because the passage does not state labor unions' position on employee shareholding. Choices D and E are incorrect because the passage does not mention any contingency on which employees' opportunity to buy shares was based.

21. Which of the following statements is most consistent with the principle described in lines 30-32 ?

   (A) A democratic government that decides it is inappropriate to own a particular industry has in no way abdicated its responsibilities as guardian of the public interest.
   (B) The ideal way for a government to protect employee interests is to force companies to maintain their share of a competitive market without government subsidies.
   (C) The failure to harness the power of self-interest is an important reason that state-owned industries perform poorly.
   (D) Governments that want to implement privatization programs must try to eliminate all resistance to the free-market system.
   (E) The individual shareholder will reap only a minute share of the gains from whatever sacrifices he or she makes to achieve these gains.

The best answer is C. Lines 30-32 assert that people who have a personal stake in an endeavor will "work to make it prosper." In other words, self-interest is an incentive to make people perform better. Choice C makes the same assumption and uses that assumption in the context of state-owned industries to assert that the converse is also true: that when workers lack a personal stake in the fate of their industry, their performance will be poor. Thus, state-owned industries, in which employees receive no additional benefit from increased profits, perform poorly because the industries have failed to use employees' self-interest as motivation for those employees to perform well.

22. Which of the following can be inferred from the passage about the privatization process in the United Kingdom?

   (A) It depends to a potentially dangerous degree on individual ownership of shares.
   (B) It conforms in its most general outlines to Thomas Paine's prescription for business ownership.
   (C) It was originally conceived to include some giving away of free shares.
   (D) It has been successful, even though privatization has failed in other countries.
   (E) It is taking place more slowly than some economists suggest is necessary.

The best answer is E. In lines 36-38, the author notes that some economists have suggested a way to "provide a needed acceleration of the privatization process." That the acceleration is considered to be "needed" suggests that these economists see the privatization process as occurring more slowly than it should be occurring. Choice A is incorrect because the passage does not attribute any danger to individual ownership of shares. Choice B is incorrect because the sale of shares to employees was optional rather than a part of the actual privatization process. Choice C is incorrect because the passage presents no evidence that this idea was part of the original conception. Choice D is incorrect because the passage does not mention how privatization has fared elsewhere.

23. The quotation in line 39 is most probably used to

(A) counter a position that the author of the passage believes is incorrect
(B) state a solution to a problem described in the previous sentence
(C) show how opponents of the viewpoint of the author of the passage have supported their arguments
(D) point out a paradox contained in a controversial viewpoint
(E) present a historical maxim to challenge the principle introduced in the third paragraph

The best answer is A. Paine's saying asserts that people do not hold in high esteem something that comes to them too easily; in this case, the author of the passage is applying the maxim to workers in privatized industries. The author of the passage states that Paine's point is missed by those economists who believe that giving away, rather than selling, company shares to the employees of a privatized company would spur the privatization process. Thus, the author of the passage believes that the position taken by these economists is incorrect, and that the opposing position as represented by Paine's maxim is correct — that workers will value the shares more if the shares have a cost.

Explanatory Material: Problem Solving II, Section 4

1. $\dfrac{\frac{1}{2}}{\frac{1}{4} + \frac{1}{6}} =$

(A) $\dfrac{6}{5}$

(B) $\dfrac{5}{6}$

(C) $\dfrac{5}{24}$

(D) $\dfrac{1}{5}$

(E) $\dfrac{1}{12}$

One way to solve the problem is to express all fractions with the common denominator 12, that is, $\dfrac{\frac{6}{12}}{\frac{3}{12} + \frac{2}{12}} = \dfrac{\frac{6}{12}}{\frac{5}{12}} = \dfrac{6}{5}$.

The best answer is A.

2. Kelly and Chris packed several boxes with books. If Chris packed 60 percent of the total number of boxes, what was the ratio of the number of boxes Kelly packed to the number of boxes Chris packed?

(A) 1 to 6
(B) 1 to 4
(C) 2 to 5
(D) 3 to 5
(E) 2 to 3

If Chris packed 60 percent of the boxes, then Kelly packed 40 percent of the boxes. The ratio of the number of boxes Kelly packed to the number Chris packed is $\dfrac{40\%}{60\%} = \dfrac{2}{3}$. The best answer is E.

3. A train travels from New York City to Chicago, a distance of approximately 840 miles, at an average rate of 60 miles per hour and arrives in Chicago at 6:00 in the evening, Chicago time. At what hour in the morning, New York City time, did the train depart for Chicago? (Note: Chicago time is one hour earlier than New York City time.)

(A) 4:00
(B) 5:00
(C) 6:00
(D) 7:00
(E) 8:00

Because time is found by dividing distance by rate, the trip took $\frac{840}{60} = 14$ hours. The train arrived in Chicago at 6:00 in the evening Chicago time or 7:00 in the evening New York time. New York time 14 hours before 7:00 in the evening is 5:00 in the morning. The best answer is B.

4. Of the following, which is the closest approximation of $\frac{50.2 \times 0.49}{199.8}$?

(A) $\frac{1}{10}$

(B) $\frac{1}{8}$

(C) $\frac{1}{4}$

(D) $\frac{5}{4}$

(E) $\frac{25}{2}$

$\frac{50.2 \times 0.49}{199.8}$ is approximately $\frac{50 \times 0.5}{200} = \frac{25}{200} = \frac{1}{8}$. The best answer is B.

5. Last year Manfred received 26 paychecks. Each of his first 6 paychecks was $750; each of his remaining paychecks was $30 more than each of his first 6 paychecks. To the nearest dollar, what was the average (arithmetic mean) amount of his paychecks for the year?

(A) $752
(B) $755
(C) $765
(D) $773
(E) $775

The total amount in dollars of the 26 paychecks was $6(750) + (26 - 6)(750 + 30) = 6(750) + 20(780) = 4,500 + 15,600 = 20,100$. Thus, the average paycheck was $\frac{\$20,100}{26}$ or approximately $773. The best answer is D.

6. A certain pair of used shoes can be repaired for $12.50 and will last for 1 year. A pair of the same kind of shoes can be purchased new for $28.00 and will last for 2 years. The average cost per year of the new shoes is what percent greater than the cost of repairing the used shoes?

(A) 3%
(B) 5%
(C) 12%
(D) 15%
(E) 24%

Having the used shoes repaired will cost $12.50 for 1 year. The new shoes will cost $28.00 and will last for 2 years, which is an average cost of $14.00 for 1 year or $1.50 greater than the cost of repairing the used shoes. Thus, the average cost per year of the new shoes is $\frac{\$1.50}{\$12.50} = 12\%$ greater than the cost of repairing the used shoes. The best answer is C.

7. In a certain brick wall, each row of bricks above the bottom row contains one less brick than the row just below it. If there are 5 rows in all and a total of 75 bricks in the wall, how many bricks does the bottom row contain?

(A) 14
(B) 15
(C) 16
(D) 17
(E) 18

If b represents the number of bricks in the bottom row, the numbers of bricks in the next 4 rows are $b - 1$, $b - 2$, $b - 3$, and $b - 4$, respectively. The total number of bricks in the 5 rows is $b + (b - 1) + (b - 2) + (b - 3) + (b - 4) = 5b - 10 = 75$. Thus, $5b = 85$ and $b = 17$. The best answer is D.

8. If 25 percent of p is equal to 10 percent of q, and $pq \neq 0$, then p is what percent of q ?

(A) 2.5%
(B) 15%
(C) 20%
(D) 35%
(E) 40%

If $0.25p = 0.10q$, dividing both sides of the equation by 0.25 gives $p = \dfrac{0.10q}{0.25} = \dfrac{10q}{25}$. Thus, p is 40% of q, and the best answer is E.

9. **If the length of an edge of cube X is twice the length of an edge of cube Y, what is the ratio of the volume of cube Y to the volume of cube X?**

   (A) $\dfrac{1}{2}$

   (B) $\dfrac{1}{4}$

   (C) $\dfrac{1}{6}$

   (D) $\dfrac{1}{8}$

   (E) $\dfrac{1}{27}$

If y represents the length of one edge of cube Y, then the length of one edge of cube X is $2y$. The ratio of the volume of cube Y to the volume of cube X is $\dfrac{y^3}{(2y)^3} = \dfrac{y^3}{8y^3} = \dfrac{1}{8}$. The best answer is D.

10. $(\sqrt{2} + 1)(\sqrt{2} - 1)(\sqrt{3} + 1)(\sqrt{3} - 1) =$

    (A) 2
    (B) 3
    (C) $2\sqrt{6}$
    (D) 5
    (E) 6

From the relationship $(a + b)(a - b) = a^2 - b^2$,
$(\sqrt{2} + 1)(\sqrt{2} - 1) = 2 - 1 = 1$ and
$(\sqrt{3} + 1)(\sqrt{3} - 1) = 3 - 1 = 2$. Thus,
$(\sqrt{2} + 1)(\sqrt{2} - 1)(\sqrt{3} + 1)(\sqrt{3} - 1) = (1)(2) = 2$,
and the best answer is A.

11. **In a certain calculus class, the ratio of the number of mathematics majors to the number of students who are not mathematics majors is 2 to 5. If 2 more mathematics majors were to enter the class, the ratio would be 1 to 2. How many students are in the class?**

    (A) 10
    (B) 12
    (C) 21
    (D) 28
    (E) 35

Let m be the number of mathematics majors and n be the number of nonmathematics majors in the class. Thus, the ratio of $\dfrac{m}{n} = \dfrac{2}{5}$. If the number of mathematics majors is increased by 2, the ratio of $\dfrac{m + 2}{n} = \dfrac{1}{2}$. From the first equation, $m = \dfrac{2}{5}n$, and from the second equation, $m + 2 = \dfrac{1}{2}n$, or $m = \dfrac{1}{2}n - 2$. Thus, $\dfrac{1}{2}n - 2 = \dfrac{2}{5}n$ or $\dfrac{1}{2}n - \dfrac{2}{5}n = 2$, and $\dfrac{1}{10}n = 2$. Therefore, $n = 20$ and $m = \dfrac{2}{5}(20) = 8$, and the total number of students is $m + n = 20 + 8 = 28$. The best answer is D.

12. **Machines A and B always operate independently and at their respective constant rates. When working alone, machine A can fill a production lot in 5 hours, and machine B can fill the same lot in x hours. When the two machines operate simultaneously to fill the production lot, it takes them 2 hours to complete the job. What is the value of x?**

    (A) $3\dfrac{1}{3}$

    (B) 3

    (C) $2\dfrac{1}{2}$

    (D) $2\dfrac{1}{3}$

    (E) $1\dfrac{1}{2}$

Since machine A can fill a production lot in 5 hours, machine A can complete $\dfrac{1}{5}$ of the job in 1 hour. Similarly, machine B can complete $\dfrac{1}{x}$ of the job in 1 hour, and the two machines operating simultaneously can fill $\dfrac{1}{2}$ of the job in 1 hour. Therefore, $\dfrac{1}{5} + \dfrac{1}{x} = \dfrac{1}{2}$ and $\dfrac{1}{x} = \dfrac{1}{2} - \dfrac{1}{5} = \dfrac{3}{10}$ or $x = \dfrac{10}{3} = 3\dfrac{1}{3}$. The best answer is A.

13. In the *xy*-coordinate system, if (a, b) and $(a+3, b+k)$ are two points on the line defined by the equation $x = 3y - 7$, then $k =$

(A) 9

(B) 3

(C) $\dfrac{7}{3}$

(D) 1

(E) $\dfrac{1}{3}$

Since the points (a, b) and $(a+3, b+k)$ lie on the line $x = 3y - 7$, their coordinates can be substituted for x and y in the equation for the line. Thus, $a = 3b - 7$ and $a + 3 = 3(b + k) - 7$. Substituting $3b - 7$ for a in the second equation gives $(3b - 7) + 3 = 3b + 3k - 7 = (3b - 7) + 3k$. Thus, $3 = 3k$ and $k = 1$. The best answer is D.

Alternatively, the slope-intercept form of the equation of the line is $y = \dfrac{1}{3}x + \dfrac{7}{3}$; so the slope of the line is $\dfrac{1}{3}$. Since the slope is the $\dfrac{\textit{difference of y-coordinates}}{\textit{difference of x-coordinates}}$ of the two points, $\dfrac{(b + k) - b}{(a + 3) - a} = \dfrac{1}{3}$, or $\dfrac{k}{3} = \dfrac{1}{3}$ and $k = 1$.

14. What is the units digit of $(13)^4(17)^2(29)^3$?

(A) 9

(B) 7

(C) 5

(D) 3

(E) 1

The units digit of 13^4 is 1, since $3 \times 3 \times 3 \times 3 = 81$; the units digit of 17^2 is 9, since $7 \times 7 = 49$; and the units digit of 29^3 is 9, since $9 \times 9 \times 9 = 729$. Therefore, the units digit of $(13)^4(17)^2(29)^3$ is 1, since $1 \times 9 \times 9 = 81$, and the best answer is E.

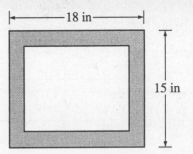

Note: Figure not drawn to scale.

15. The shaded region in the figure above represents a rectangular frame with length 18 inches and width 15 inches. The frame encloses a rectangular picture that has the same area as the frame itself. If the length and width of the picture have the same ratio as the length and width of the frame, what is the length of the picture, in inches?

(A) $9\sqrt{2}$

(B) $\dfrac{3}{2}$

(C) $\dfrac{9}{\sqrt{2}}$

(D) $15\left(1 - \dfrac{1}{\sqrt{2}}\right)$

(E) $\dfrac{9}{2}$

Let ℓ and w represent the length and width in inches, respectively, of the picture. Because the length and width of the picture have the same ratio as the length and width of the frame, $\dfrac{\ell}{w} = \dfrac{18}{15} = \dfrac{6}{5}$. The areas, in square inches, of the picture and the frame are ℓw and $(18 \times 15) - \ell w = 270 - \ell w$, respectively. Since the two areas are equal, $\ell w = 270 - \ell w$ or $\ell w = 135$. From the ratio $\dfrac{\ell}{w} = \dfrac{6}{5}$, $w = \dfrac{5}{6}\ell$. Substituting $\dfrac{5}{6}\ell$ for w in the equation $\ell w = 135$ yields $\ell(\dfrac{5}{6}\ell) = 135$ or $5\ell^2 = 6(135)$ and $\ell^2 = 6(27) = (2)(3)(3)(3)(3) = 2(9)^2$. Thus, $\sqrt{\ell^2} = \sqrt{2(9)^2}$ and $\ell = 9\sqrt{2}$. The best answer is A.

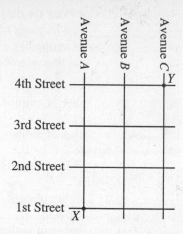

Avenue A   Avenue B   Avenue C

4th Street ———————— Y

3rd Street ————————

2nd Street ————————

1st Street ——X————————

16. Pat will walk from intersection X to intersection Y along a route that is confined to the square grid of four streets and three avenues shown in the map above. How many routes from X to Y can Pat take that have the minimum possible length?

(A) Six
(B) Eight
(C) Ten
(D) Fourteen
(E) Sixteen

In order to walk from intersection X to intersection Y by one of the routes of minimum possible length, Pat must travel upward or rightward between intersections on the map. Thus, the routes of minimum length consist of walking upwards, U, 3 times and rightward, R, twice, for a total of 5 blocks. There are 10 ways in which Pat can walk upward 3 times and rightward twice:

U U U R R	U R R U U
U U R U R	R R U U U
U U R R U	R U U U R
U R U U R	R U U R U
U R U R U	R U R U U

Thus, there are 10 routes of minimum length, and the best answer is C.

Explanatory Material: Sentence Correction, Section 5

1. Lawmakers are examining measures that would require banks to disclose all fees and account requirements in writing, provide free cashing of government checks, and to create basic savings accounts to carry minimal fees and require minimal initial deposits.

(A) provide free cashing of government checks, and to create basic savings accounts to carry
(B) provide free cashing of government checks, and creating basic savings accounts carrying
(C) to provide free cashing of government checks, and creating basic savings accounts that carry
(D) to provide free cashing of government checks, creating basic savings accounts to carry
(E) to provide free cashing of government checks, and to create basic savings accounts that carry

Choice E, the best answer, is the only choice that maintains parallelism with the infinitive phrases *to disclose . . . , [to] provide . . . ,* and *to create . . . .* In A and B, the second element lacks the infinitive marker *to*. Choice C loses parallelism by shifting to a participial phrase, *creating . . . .* Choice D loses parallelism by dropping the conjunction *and*; a modification problem results because the participial phrase *creating . . .* attaches to the noun *checks*, thus distorting the meaning of the last element of the parallel construction.

2. Cajuns speak a dialect brought to southern Louisiana by the four thousand Acadians who migrated there in 1755; their language is basically seventeenth-century French to which has been added English, Spanish, and Italian words.

(A) to which has been added English, Spanish, and Italian words
(B) added to which is English, Spanish, and Italian words
(C) to which English, Spanish, and Italian words have been added
(D) with English, Spanish, and Italian words having been added to it
(E) and, in addition, English, Spanish, and Italian words are added

The underlined section must modify the noun phrase *seventeenth-century French* by noting additions made to French subsequently from foreign vocabularies. C, the best choice, does this clearly, directly, and correctly in the form of a relative clause. Because the subject of this clause is plural (*words*), the verb must also be plural (*have been added*). A and B incorrectly use singular forms *has been added* and *is added*. B also awkwardly inverts and divides the verb phrase (*added . . . is*). D offers an awkward adverbial construction, which cannot be used to modify nouns. E offers an incoherent and incomplete new clause with the wrong verb tense and no logical complement for *are added* — that is, we are not told to what the words are added.

3. NOT SCORED

4. **Unlike the United States, where farmers can usually depend on rain or snow all year long, the rains in most parts of Sri Lanka** are concentrated in the monsoon months, June to September, and the skies are generally clear for the rest of the year.

   (A) Unlike the United States, where farmers can usually depend on rain or snow all year long, the rains in most parts of Sri Lanka
   (B) Unlike the United States farmers who can usually depend on rain or snow all year long, the rains in most parts of Sri Lanka
   (C) Unlike those of the United States, where farmers can usually depend on rain or snow all year long, most parts of Sri Lanka's rains
   (D) In comparison with the United States, whose farmers can usually depend on rain or snow all year long, the rains in most parts of Sri Lanka
   (E) In the United States, farmers can usually depend on rain or snow all year long, but in most parts of Sri Lanka the rains

In comparative structures *(unlike X, Y . . . ; in comparison with X, Y . . .) X* and *Y* must be both logically and grammatically parallel. Choices A, B, C, and D all fail to observe logical parallelism: (A) *Unlike the United States, . . . the rains . . .;* (B) *Unlike the United States farmers . . . , the rains . . . ;* (C) *Unlike those of the United States, . . . most parts of Sri Lanka's rains . . . ;* and (D) *In comparison with the United States, . . . the rains . . . .* C also suffers from the unintelligible *most parts of Sri Lanka's rains.* E, the best choice, avoids the problem by using two independent clauses linked by *but* to present a clear, direct contrast between conditions *in the United States* and those *in most parts of Sri Lanka.*

5. Presenters at the seminar, **one who** is blind, will demonstrate adaptive equipment that allows visually impaired people to use computers.

   (A) one who
   (B) one of them who
   (C) and one of them who
   (D) one of whom
   (E) one of which

The subject, *presenters*, must be followed by a limiting appositive — such as *one of whom*, that identifies an individual from among a larger group. Choice D is best: *one of whom* best serves an appositive to the subject, *presenters*, because the phrase means "one from among several or many." Choice A, *one who*, is unacceptable because *one who* cannot refer to the plural *presenters*. Choices B and C are ungrammatical because *who* competes with *one* as the subject of *is*. Choice E employs *which*, a relative pronoun that does not refer to people *(presenters)*, but only to things.

6. Dr. Tonegawa won the Nobel Prize for discovering how the body can constantly change its genes to fashion a **seeming unlimited number of antibodies, each specifically targeted at** an invading microbe or foreign substance.

   (A) seeming unlimited number of antibodies, each specifically targeted at
   (B) seeming unlimited number of antibodies, each targeted specifically to
   (C) seeming unlimited number of antibodies, all specifically targeted at
   (D) seemingly unlimited number of antibodies, all of them targeted specifically to
   (E) seemingly unlimited number of antibodies, each targeted specifically at

Choices A, B, and C incorrectly use the adjective form *seeming* to modify the participial adjective *unlimited*. B also uses the unidiomatic preposition *to* instead of the correct *at* after *targeted*, while C violates sense by having *all* the antibodies *specifically* targeted at *an*, that is, *one*, invading microbe or substance. Choice D correctly uses *seemingly*, but it repeats B's incorrect use of *targeted to* and C's illogical *all . . . specifically.* Only E, the best choice, correctly uses the form *seemingly* to modify *unlimited*, the correct preposition, *at*, with *targeted,* and the logically correct *each*, which links the specific antibodies to specific microbes or substances.

7. It is possible that Native Americans originally **have migrated to the Western Hemisphere over a bridge of land that once existed** between Siberia and Alaska.

   (A) have migrated to the Western Hemisphere over a bridge of land that once existed
   (B) were migrating to the Western Hemisphere over a bridge of land that existed once
   (C) migrated over a bridge of land to the Western Hemisphere that once existed
   (D) migrated to the Western Hemisphere over a bridge of land that once existed
   (E) were migrating to the Western Hemisphere over a bridge of land existing once

Choice D, the best answer, correctly uses the past-tense verb forms *migrated* and *existed* to refer to actions completed in the past. Choices A, B, and E present incorrect verb forms for expressing simple past action, and *existing once* in E is imprecise. Although choice C manages the correct tense, it misplaces the sentence elements so as to suggest that the Western Hemisphere *once existed between Siberia and Alaska.*

8. In the fall of 1985, only 10 percent of the women entering college planned to major in education, while 28 percent chose business, making it the most popular major for women <u>as well as for men</u>.

(A) as well as for men
(B) as well as the men
(C) and men too
(D) and men as well
(E) and also men

Two elements connected by a coordinate conjunction should be expressed in parallel form. Only A, the best choice, correctly observes this rule *(the most popular major for women as well as for men)*. B, C, D, and E omit the necessary *for* in the second element. In addition, by using the simple coordinate conjunction *and*, C, D, and E create the illogical impression that the decision of 28 percent of the women entering college in 1985 to choose business as a major *also* made the major the most popular among men. The conjunction *as well as* implies that business had already been the most popular major for men and that in 1985, for the first time, it became the most popular major for both sexes.

9. Because the Earth's crust is more solid there and thus better able to transmit shock waves, an earthquake <u>of a given magnitude typically devastates an area 100 times greater in the eastern United States than it does in the West</u>.

(A) of a given magnitude typically devastates an area 100 times greater in the eastern United States than it does in the West
(B) of a given magnitude will typically devastate 100 times the area if it occurs in the eastern United States instead of the West
(C) will typically devastate 100 times the area in the eastern United States than one of comparable magnitude occurring in the West
(D) in the eastern United States will typically devastate an area 100 times greater than will a quake of comparable magnitude occurring in the West
(E) that occurs in the eastern United States will typically devastate 100 times more area than if it occurred with comparable magnitude in the West

At issue is the accurate expression of a complex comparison. Choice D, the best answer, presents the proper form of comparison, *will typically devastate an area 100 times greater than will*; thus, choice D logically indicates that earthquakes in the eastern United States are 100 times more devastating than are western earthquakes. Choices A, B, and E use *it* incorrectly to suggest that the same quake strikes both the eastern and the western United States. In choice C, *100 times the area . . . than* is unidiomatic.

10. Although Napoleon's army entered Russia with far more supplies than <u>they had in their previous campaigns</u>, it had provisions for only twenty-four days.

(A) they had in their previous campaigns
(B) their previous campaigns had had
(C) they had for any previous campaign
(D) in their previous campaigns
(E) for any previous campaign

If *than* is followed by a clause referring to *army*, the subject of that clause must be singular (*it*). Furthermore, the verb of that clause will need to be in the past perfect form (*had had*) because it refers to a time *before* the simple past of *entered*. Finally, the preposition *for* is more precise than *in* because supplies are gathered *for* an upcoming campaign. Choices A and C incorrectly use the plural *they* and the simple past *had*. Moreover, A uses the less precise *in*. Choices D and E wisely dispense with the full clause and use a simple prepositional phrase. D, however, uses the imprecise *in* and the plural *their*. Only E, the best choice, avoids all the errors mentioned above.

11. Certain pesticides can become ineffective if used repeatedly in the same place; one reason is suggested by the finding that there are much larger populations of pesticide-degrading microbes in soils with a relatively long history of pesticide use than in soils that are free of such chemicals.

(A) Certain pesticides can become ineffective if used repeatedly in the same place; one reason is suggested by the finding that there are much larger populations of pesticide-degrading microbes in soils with a relatively long history of pesticide use than in soils that are free of such chemicals.

(B) If used repeatedly in the same place, one reason that certain pesticides can become ineffective is suggested by the finding that there are much larger populations of pesticide-degrading microbes in soils with a relatively long history of pesticide use than in soils that are free of such chemicals.

(C) If used repeatedly in the same place, one reason certain pesticides can become ineffective is suggested by the finding that much larger populations of pesticide-degrading microbes are found in soils with a relatively long history of pesticide use than those that are free of such chemicals.

(D) The finding that there are much larger populations of pesticide-degrading microbes in soils with a relatively long history of pesticide use than in soils that are free of such chemicals is suggestive of one reason, if used repeatedly in the same place, certain pesticides can become ineffective.

(E) The finding of much larger populations of pesticide-degrading microbes in soils with a relatively long history of pesticide use than in those that are free of such chemicals suggests one reason certain pesticides can become ineffective if used repeatedly in the same place.

Choice A, the best answer, is the only one that manages syntactic control of the sentence. The sentence consists of two independent clauses, beginning *Certain pesticides . . .* and *one reason*, which are connected by a semicolon. Dangling or misplaced modifiers plague choices B, C, and D: in each case, the phrase *if used repeatedly in the same place* illogically modifies *one reason* rather than *certain pesticides*. In choice E, *The finding of much larger populations . . . than in those that* is an improperly constructed comparison.

12. One view of the economy contends that a large drop in oil prices should eventually lead to lowering interest rates, as well as lowering fears about inflation, a rally in stocks and bonds, and a weakening of the dollar.

(A) lowering interest rates, as well as lowering fears about inflation,

(B) a lowering of interest rates and of fears about inflation,

(C) a lowering of interest rates, along with fears about inflation,

(D) interest rates being lowered, along with fears about inflation,

(E) interest rates and fears about inflation being lowered, with

At issue is the need for logical and formal parallelism in a coordinate series. B, the best choice, clearly and correctly uses parallel noun phrases to list three effects of a drop in oil prices: *a lowering of . . . , a rally in . . . , and a weakening of . . . .* In place of the correct *lower* before *fears*, choice A uses an incorrect participial adjective, *lowering,* that could cause confusion by seeming at first to function as a verb. A also violates parallelism. In C and D, the use of *along with* confuses meaning by making *fears about inflation* an independent effect, not an object of *lowering*. D and E violate parallelism by substituting an awkward gerund clause for the first noun phrase.

13. After the Civil War, contemporaries of Harriet Tubman's maintained that she has all of the qualities of a great leader: coolness in the face of danger, an excellent sense of strategy, and an ability to plan in minute detail.

(A) Tubman's maintained that she has
(B) Tubman's maintain that she had
(C) Tubman's have maintained that she had
(D) Tubman maintained that she had
(E) Tubman had maintained that she has

In choice D, the best answer, the phrase *contemporaries of Harriet Tubman* presents a complete possessive without adding an apostrophe (e.g., *Tubman's*). Choices A, B, and C use a redundant possessive: *contemporaries of Harriet Tubman's*. All choices other than D have errors in verb tense. Because the sentence describes essentially simultaneous actions completed in the past, the simple past tense forms *maintained* and *had* are required. Thus, the present tense forms *has* and *maintain* are incorrect in A, B, and E, as are the present perfect *have maintained* in C and the past perfect *had maintained* in E.

14. <u>From 1982 to 1987 sales of new small boats increased between five and ten percent annually.</u>

   (A) From 1982 to 1987 sales of new small boats increased between five and ten percent annually.

   (B) Five to ten percent is the annual increase in sales of new small boats in the years 1982 to 1987.

   (C) Sales of new small boats have increased annually five and ten percent in the years 1982 to 1987.

   (D) Annually an increase of five to ten percent has occurred between 1982 and 1987 in the sales of new small boats.

   (E) Occurring from 1982 to 1987 was an annual increase of five and ten percent in the sales of new small boats.

A, the best choice, conveys the relevant information clearly and directly. Because the focus of interest is the *sales of new small boats*, that should be the subject of the sentence. Since the period of time covered began and ended in the past, the verb should be in the simple past tense (*increased*). The adverb *annually* fits most logically after the amount of the increases. B, C, D, and E all distort the focus and disrupt the sensible order of ideas. In addition, B, C, and D use incorrect verb tenses to refer to the simple past (*is, have increased,* and *has occurred*). In C, the expression *five and ten percent* makes no sense without the word *between*. Finally, E is especially clumsy and confused.

15. In recent years cattle breeders have increasingly used crossbreeding, <u>in part that their steers should acquire certain characteristics</u> and partly because crossbreeding is said to provide hybrid vigor.

   (A) in part that their steers should acquire certain characteristics

   (B) in part for the acquisition of certain characteristics in their steers

   (C) partly because of their steers acquiring certain characteristics

   (D) partly because certain characteristics should be acquired by their steers

   (E) partly to acquire certain characteristics in their steers

Choice E is best; it best indicates purpose for crossbreeding — *partly to acquire*. In A, *in part that* does not grammatically connect the underlined portion to the first part of the sentence (the independent clause). In both A and B, *in part* is not parallel with *and partly* in the nonunderlined portion. Choice C causes a misreading, suggesting that the steers' acquisition has *caused* the crossbreeding. D awkwardly and illogically shifts to the passive voice: *certain characteristics should be acquired by their steers*; the steers, however, are not agents in the acquisition.

16. The peaks of a mountain range, acting like rocks in a streambed, produce ripples in the air flowing over them; the resulting flow pattern, with <u>crests and troughs that remain stationary although the air that forms them is moving rapidly, are</u> known as "standing waves."

   (A) crests and troughs that remain stationary although the air that forms them is moving rapidly, are

   (B) crests and troughs that remain stationary although they are formed by rapidly moving air, are

   (C) crests and troughs that remain stationary although the air that forms them is moving rapidly, is

   (D) stationary crests and troughs although the air that forms them is moving rapidly, are

   (E) stationary crests and troughs although they are formed by rapidly moving air, is

The main challenge in this sentence is to observe the agreement of subject and verb (*the resulting flow pattern . . . is known . . .*) despite the distraction of a complex intervening structure containing several plural elements (*with crests and troughs . . .*). Choices A, B, and D can, therefore, be eliminated because they use an incorrect plural verb form, *are*. Choice E uses the correct verb form, *is*, but it incorrectly introduces a dependent adverbial *although* clause into a prepositional phrase (*with crests . . .*). Choice D also makes this error. Such dependent clauses can only occur in the predicates of full clauses. C, the best choice, uses the correct verb form, *is*, and correctly puts the *although* clause inside the predicate of the relative clause (*that . . . rapidly*).

17. <u>Like Auden, the language of James Merrill</u> is chatty, arch, and conversational — given to complex syntactic flights as well as to prosaic free-verse strolls.

   (A) Like Auden, the language of James Merrill

   (B) Like Auden, James Merrill's language

   (C) Like Auden's, James Merrill's language

   (D) As with Auden, James Merrill's language

   (E) As is Auden's the language of James Merrill

At issue is a comparison of Auden's language with Merrill's language. Only C, the best choice, uses the elliptical *like Auden's* (*language* being understood), to compare Auden's language with Merrill's language. A, B, and D compare Auden (the person) with Merrill's language. Choice E is awkward and unidiomatic.

18. In the textbook publishing business, the second quarter is historically weak, because revenues are <u>low and marketing expenses are high as companies prepare</u> for the coming school year.

 (A) low and marketing expenses are high as companies prepare
 (B) low and their marketing expenses are high as they prepare
 (C) low with higher marketing expenses in preparation
 (D) low, while marketing expenses are higher to prepare
 (E) low, while their marketing expenses are higher in preparation

A, the best choice, correctly balances the contrasting terms *low* and *high* in parallel form (adjectives in the positive degree). It also makes clear who, exactly, is preparing for the coming school year (*companies*). B uses the plural pronouns *their* and *they* without an appropriately stated referent. C, D, and E violate the parallelism needed for the contrasting terms by making the second term an adjective in the comparative degree (*higher*). Furthermore, the use of *higher* without a stated point of comparison makes it unclear what the expenses are higher than. E also uses the pronoun *their* without an appropriate referent.

19. Teratomas are unusual forms of cancer <u>because they are composed of tissues such as tooth and bone</u> not normally found in the organ in which the tumor appears.

 (A) because they are composed of tissues such as tooth and bone
 (B) because they are composed of tissues like tooth and bone that are
 (C) because they are composed of tissues, like tooth and bone, tissues
 (D) in that their composition, tissues such as tooth and bone, is
 (E) in that they are composed of tissues such as tooth and bone, tissues

Only E, the best choice, clearly states that teratomas consist of tissues such as tooth and bone, and that such tissues are not normally found in the organ with the teratoma. Clear statement of this fact requires the repetition of *tissues* to establish the appositive — *tissues normally found* . . . . Without such repetition, A and B imprecisely state that the *tooth and bone*, as opposed to the *tissues*, are not normally found in the affected organ. Choices B and C alter the meaning with the use of *like*; that is, they suggest that the tissues are not tooth and bone, but only *like* them. The confused syntax of D states that *their composition*, not the tissues, *is found in the organ* . . . .

20. The Senate approved immigration legislation that would grant permanent residency to millions of aliens currently residing here and <u>if employers hired illegal aliens they would be penalized</u>.

 (A) if employers hired illegal aliens they would be penalized
 (B) hiring illegal aliens would be a penalty for employers
 (C) penalize employers who hire illegal aliens
 (D) penalizing employers hiring illegal aliens
 (E) employers to be penalized for hiring illegal aliens

The sentence contains a relative clause (*that* . . .) indicating, in its compound predicate, two effects of the *immigration legislation*: (it) *would grant x and (would) penalize y*. The auxiliary *would* may be omitted before *penalize*, but the main verbs must remain parallel. Only C, the best choice, observes these conditions. A and B produce incoherent, fused sentences in which the two main clauses are not parallel. Furthermore, in A the referent of *they* is unclear, and in B the statement *hiring illegal aliens would be a penalty* makes no sense. D violates parallel structure by substituting a present participle (*penalizing*) for the second main verb. E introduces an incoherent passive infinitive construction that violates sense and parallel structure.

21. Scientists have recently discovered what could be the largest and oldest living organism on Earth, a giant fungus that is an interwoven filigree of mushrooms and rootlike tentacles spawned by a single fertilized spore some 10,000 years ago and <u>extending</u> for more than 30 acres in the soil of a Michigan forest.

 (A) extending
 (B) extends
 (C) extended
 (D) it extended
 (E) is extending

Choice A, the best answer, preserves grammatical parallelism while allowing for logical expression of temporal relationships; A employs the parallel participial phrases *spawned* . . . and *extending* . . . to modify *filigree*. Other choices present different grammatical constructions that are not participial modifiers and thus not parallel to *spawned*: *extends* in B is a present-tense verb; *it extended* in D begins a new clause; and *is extending* in E ungrammatically introduces a new predicate. In C, *extended* is nonparallel if it is assumed to be a past tense verb form; if it is assumed to be a past participle, it illogically states, as does D, that the filigree extended only in the past.

22. The period when the great painted caves at Lascaux and Altamira were occupied by Upper Paleolithic people <u>has been established by carbon-14 dating, but what is much more difficult to determine are</u> the reason for their decoration, the use to which primitive people put the caves, and the meaning of the magnificently depicted animals.

(A) has been established by carbon-14 dating, but what is much more difficult to determine are

(B) has been established by carbon-14 dating, but what is much more difficult to determine is

(C) have been established by carbon-14 dating, but what is much more difficult to determine is

(D) have been established by carbon-14 dating, but what is much more difficult to determine are

(E) are established by carbon-14 dating, but that which is much more difficult to determine is

Two instances of subject-verb agreement must be observed in this sentence: *The period . . . has been established* and *what is much more difficult to determine . . . is*. Both clauses have singular subjects and must have singular verbs. Only B, the best choice, observes these requirements. A incorrectly uses the plural form *are* in the second clause. Choices C and D incorrectly use the plural form *have* in the first clause, and D incorrectly uses *are* in the second clause as well. E incorrectly uses the plural form *are* in the first clause. Furthermore, because the date of the period in question was established before the writing of the sentence, the verb of that clause must be in the present perfect form (*has been established*).

Explanatory Material: Data Sufficiency, Section 6

1. If the list price of a new car was $12,300, what was the cost of the car to the dealer?

(1) The cost to the dealer was equal to 80 percent of the list price.

(2) The car was sold for $11,070, which was 12.5 percent more than the cost to the dealer.

If C represents the cost to the dealer, then statement (1) can be written as $C = 0.80(\$12,300)$, which can be solved for C. Thus, statement (1) alone is sufficient, and the answer must be A or D. From (2) it follows that $\$11,070 = C + 0.125C$, which can be solved for C. Thus, (2) alone is also sufficient, and the best answer is D.

2. If p, q, x, y, and z are different positive integers, which of the five integers is the median?

(1) $p + x < q$

(2) $y < z$

Since there are five different integers, there are two integers greater and two integers less than the median, which is the middle number. Statement (1) gives no information about the order of y and z with respect to the other three numbers. Thus, (1) alone is not sufficient, and the answer must be B, C, or E. Similarly, statement (2) does not relate y and z to the other three integers and is also not sufficient, so the answer must be C or E. Because the two statements taken together do not relate p, x, and q to y and z, it is impossible to tell which is the median. Thus, the two statements together are not sufficient, and the best answer is E.

3. A certain employee is paid $6 per hour for an 8-hour workday. If the employee is paid $1\frac{1}{2}$ times this rate for time worked in excess of 8 hours during a single day, how many hours did the employee work today?

(1) The employee was paid $18 more for hours worked today than for hours worked yesterday.

(2) Yesterday the employee worked 8 hours.

The employee is paid $6 per hour for 8 hours and $1\frac{1}{2}$ times this rate, or $9 per hour, for time worked in excess of 8 hours. Statement (1) gives information only about the additional amount paid for hours worked today compared with hours worked yesterday. The $18 could have been for 3 hours at $6, for 2 hours at $9, or for a combination of base and overtime hours. Thus, without information about the number of hours the employee worked yesterday, (1) alone is not sufficient, and the answer must be B, C, or E. Statement (2) gives only the number of hours the employee worked yesterday. Thus, (2) alone is not sufficient, and the answer must be C or E. From (1) and (2) together, it can be determined that the employee was paid for 8 + 2, or 10 hours today. The best answer is C.

4. If n is a member of the set

$$\{33, 36, 38, 39, 41, 42\},$$

what is the value of n ?

(1) n is even.

(2) n is a multiple of 3.

Statement (1) alone implies that n is 36, or 38, or 42, and (2) alone implies that n is 33, 36, 39, or 42; so neither statement alone is sufficient. Thus, the answer must be C or E. From (1) and (2) together, it can be determined that n is either 36 or 42. Therefore, the best answer is E.

5. What is the value of x ?

(1) $2x + 1 = 0$

(2) $(x + 1)^2 = x^2$

Since $2x + 1 = 0$ can be solved for x, (1) alone is sufficient. Statement (2) can be expanded to $x^2 + 2x + 1 = x^2$, from which it follows that $2x + 1 = 0$, which was given in (1). Thus, each statement alone is sufficient, and the best answer is D.

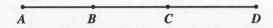

6. In the figure above, what is the length of AD ?

   (1) $AC = 6$
   (2) $BD = 6$

Since the length of AD is the sum of the lengths of AC and CD, but the length of CD is not known, (1) alone is not sufficient. Similarly, the length of AD is the sum of the lengths of AB and BD, but the length of AB is not known, and (2) alone is not sufficient. From (1) and (2) together, $AC + BD = 12$, but the two line segments overlap. Since BC, the length of the overlap, is not known, the best answer is E.

7. A retailer purchased a television set for x percent less than its list price, and then sold it for y percent less than its list price. What was the list price of the television set?

   (1) $x = 15$
   (2) $x - y = 5$

Statements (1) and (2) provide information only about the values of x and y. Since no dollar values are given, knowing the percent decreases from the list price is insufficient to determine the list price. The statements alone or together are not sufficient, and the best answer is E.

8. Is x^2 greater than x ?

   (1) x^2 is greater than 1.
   (2) x is greater than -1.

From statement (1) it follows that either $x < -1$ or $x > 1$. For all nonzero values of x, $x^2 > 0$; therefore, for $x < -1$, $x^2 > x$. If $x > 1$, multiplying both sides of the inequality gives $x^2 > x$. Thus, statement (1) alone is sufficient, and the answer must be A or D. According to (2), possible values of x are $\frac{1}{2}$, or 0, or 2, for which x^2 is less than, equal to, or greater than x, respectively; so (2) alone is not sufficient. The best answer is A.

9. What is the value of $\frac{r}{2} + \frac{s}{2}$?

   (1) $\frac{r+s}{2} = 5$
   (2) $r + s = 10$

The sum $\frac{r}{s} + \frac{s}{2} = \frac{r+s}{2}$. Thus, since the value of $r + s$ can be found from (1) and is given in (2), each statement alone is sufficient, and the best answer is D.

10. If x, y, and z are numbers, is $z = 18$?

   (1) **The average (arithmetic mean) of x, y, and z is 6.**
   (2) **$x = -y$**

From (1) it is known that $\frac{x + y + z}{3} = 6$, or $x + y + z = 18$, but nothing is known about the value of $x + y$. Therefore, (1) alone is not sufficient, and the answer must be B, C, or E. Statement (2) alone is not sufficient because it implies that $x + y = 0$ but gives no information about the values of $x, y,$ and z. Thus, the answer must be C or E. Statements (1) and (2) together are sufficient since 0 can be substituted for $x + y$ in the equation $x + y + z = 18$ to yield $z = 18$. The best answer is C.

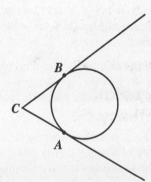

11. The circular base of an above-ground swimming pool lies in a level yard and just touches two straight sides of a fence at points A and B, as shown in the figure above. Point C is on the ground where the two sides of the fence meet. How far from the center of the pool's base is point A ?

   (1) **The base has area 250 square feet.**
   (2) **The center of the base is 20 feet from point C.**

Let Q be the center of the pool's base and r be the distance from Q to A, as shown in the figure below.

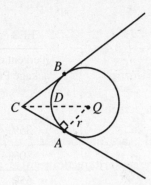

Since A is a point on the circular base, QA is a radius of the base. Thus, (1) can be written Area $= \pi r^2 = 250$ square feet, which can be solved for r. Thus, (1) alone is sufficient, and the answer must be A or D. Since CA is tangent to the base, QAC is a right triangle. From (2), $QC = 20$, but there is not enough information to determine the length of QA. Therefore, (2) alone is not sufficient, and the best answer is A.

12. In 1979 Mr. Jackson bought a total of n shares of stock X and Mrs. Jackson bought a total of 300 shares of stock X. If the couple held all of their respective shares throughout 1980, and Mr. Jackson's 1980 dividends on his n shares totaled $150, what was the total amount of Mrs. Jackson's 1980 dividends on her 300 shares?

(1) In 1980 the annual dividend on each share of stock X was $0.75.
(2) In 1979 Mr. Jackson bought a total of 200 shares of stock X.

Statement (1) alone is sufficient because the total amount of Mrs. Jackson's 1980 dividends on her 300 shares was 300 times the annual dividend per share, which is given in (1). Thus, the answer must be A or D. It is given that Mr. Jackson's 1980 dividends totaled $150, and (2) gives the number of shares of stock Mr. Jackson bought. Thus, the dividend per share was $\frac{\$150}{200} = \$0.75$, which is the information given in (1), and it follows that (2) alone is also sufficient. The best answer is D.

13. If Sara's age is exactly twice Bill's age, what is Sara's age?

(1) Four years ago, Sara's age was exactly 3 times Bill's age.
(2) Eight years from now, Sara's age will be exactly 1.5 times Bill's age.

If s and b represent Sara's and Bill's ages in years, respectively, then $s = 2b$, or $b = \frac{s}{2}$. Statement (1) can then be written algebraically as $s - 4 = 3(b - 4)$. Substituting $\frac{s}{2}$ for b in this equation gives $s - 4 = 3(\frac{s}{2} - 4)$, which can be solved for s. Similarly, (2) can be written algebraically as $s + 8 = 1.5(b + 8)$ or $s + 8 = 1.5(\frac{s}{2} + 8)$, which can be solved for s. Thus, both (1) alone and (2) alone are sufficient, and the best answer is D.

14. What is the value of $\frac{x}{yz}$?

(1) $x = \frac{y}{2}$ and $z = \frac{2x}{5}$.
(2) $\frac{x}{z} = \frac{5}{2}$ and $\frac{1}{y} = \frac{1}{10}$.

From statement (1), z can be expressed in terms of y by substituting $\frac{y}{2}$ for x in $z = \frac{2x}{5}$, which gives $z = \frac{2\left(\frac{y}{2}\right)}{5} = \frac{y}{5}$. The value of $\frac{x}{yz}$ in terms of y is then $\frac{\frac{y}{2}}{y\left(\frac{y}{5}\right)} = \frac{y}{2}\left(\frac{5}{y^2}\right) = \frac{5}{2y}$. Since no information about the value of y is given, (1) alone is not sufficient, and the answer must be B, C, or E. Statement (2) alone is sufficient because $\frac{x}{yz} = \left(\frac{1}{y}\right)\left(\frac{x}{z}\right)$ or $\left(\frac{1}{10}\right)\left(\frac{5}{2}\right)$. The best answer is B.

15. An infinite sequence of positive integers is called an "alpha sequence" if the number of even integers in the sequence is finite. If S is an infinite sequence of positive integers, is S an alpha sequence?

(1) The first ten integers in S are even.
(2) An infinite number of integers in S are odd.

Statement (1) alone is not sufficient because it gives no information about the integers in S other than the first ten; in addition to the first ten integers in S there may be any number of other even integers. Statement (2) is irrelevant because it gives information about the number of odd integers but no information about the number of even integers in S. S could have an infinite number of even integers as in the case of the set of all positive integers, or S could have a finite number of even integers. Thus, statement (2) alone is not sufficient, and since together the two statements do not give enough information about even integers, it follows that (1) and (2) together are not sufficient. The best answer is E.

16. If $xy > 0$, does $(x-1)(y-1) = 1$?

   (1) $x + y = xy$
   (2) $x = y$

The product $(x-1)(y-1)$ is equivalent to $xy - y - x + 1$. From statement (1), $x + y$ can be substituted for xy, which gives $x + y - y - x + 1 = 1$. Thus, $(x-1)(y-1) = 1$, and (1) alone is sufficient. From statement (2), substituting y for x in $(x-1)(y-1)$ gives $(y-1)(y-1)$. Since the value of y is not given, statement (2) alone is not sufficient, and the best answer is A.

17. After winning 50 percent of the first 20 games it played, Team A won all of the remaining games it played. What was the total number of games that Team A won?

   (1) Team A played 25 games altogether.
   (2) Team A won 60 percent of all the games it played.

If r is the number of remaining games, then $20 + r$ is the total number of games played. The total number of games the team won was $0.50(20) + r$ or $10 + r$. To solve the problem, the value of r is needed. According to (1), $20 + r = 25$, which can be solved for r. Thus, (1) alone is sufficient. Statement (2) implies that $0.60(20 + r) = 10 + r$, which can be solved for r. Thus, (2) alone is also sufficient, and the best answer is D.

$$\begin{array}{r} \square \\ + \triangle \\ \hline \bigstar \end{array}$$

18. In the addition problem above, each of the symbols $\square$, $\triangle$, and $\bigstar$ represents a positive digit. If $\square < \triangle$, what is the value of $\triangle$?

   (1) $\bigstar = 4$
   (2) $\square = 1$

Since each of the three symbols represents a positive digit, $\square + \triangle < 10$. Statement (1) says that $\bigstar = 4$, so $\square + \triangle = 4$, and it is given that each digit is greater than 0 and $\square < \triangle$. Thus, the only possible values of $\square$ and $\triangle$ are 1 and 3, respectively. Therefore, (1) alone is sufficient and the answer

must be A or D. Statement (2) implies that $1 + \triangle = \bigstar$, and $\triangle$ can have any value from 2 to 8, inclusive. The best answer is A.

CANCELATION FEES

Days Prior to Departure	Percent of Package Price
46 or more	10%
45-31	35%
30-16	50%
15-5	65%
4 or fewer	100%

19. The table above shows the cancelation fee schedule that a travel agency uses to determine the fee charged to a tourist who cancels a trip prior to departure. If a tourist canceled a trip with a package price of $1,700 and a departure date of September 4, on what day was the trip canceled?

   (1) The cancelation fee was $595.
   (2) If the trip had been canceled one day later, the cancelation fee would have been $255 more.

The cancelation fee given in (1) is $\frac{\$595}{\$1,700} = 35\%$ of the package price, which is the percent charged for cancelation 45-31 days prior to the departure date of September 4. Thus, (1) alone is not sufficient, and the answer must be B, C, or E. Statement (2) implies that the increase in the cancelation fee for canceling one day later would have been $\frac{\$255}{\$1,700} = 15\%$ of the package price; so the cancelation could have occurred either 31 days or 16 days prior to the departure date of September 4. Therefore, (2) alone is not sufficient, and the answer must be C or E, but (1) and (2) together imply that the trip was canceled 31 days prior to September 4. The best answer is C.

20. Is 5^k less than 1,000 ?

   (1) $5^{k+1} > 3,000$
   (2) $5^{k-1} = 5^k - 500$

Since $5^{k+1} = 5^k(5)$, or $5^k = 5\frac{5^{k+1}}{5}$, it follows from statement (1) that $\frac{5^{k+1}}{5} > \frac{3,000}{5}$, or $5^k > 600$. Thus, (1) alone is not sufficient. From statement (2), $5^k - 5^{k-1} = 500$, or $5^k - 5^k(5^{-1}) = 5^k - 5^k(\frac{1}{5}) = 500$. Factoring out 5^k gives $5^k(1 - \frac{1}{5}) = 500$, or $5^k = 500(\frac{5}{4}) = 625$, which is less than 1,000. Therefore, (2) alone is sufficient, and the best answer is B.

Answer Sheet: Form C

Section 1

1. Ⓐ Ⓑ Ⓒ Ⓓ Ⓔ
2. Ⓐ Ⓑ Ⓒ Ⓓ Ⓔ
3. Ⓐ Ⓑ Ⓒ Ⓓ Ⓔ
4. Ⓐ Ⓑ Ⓒ Ⓓ Ⓔ
5. Ⓐ Ⓑ Ⓒ Ⓓ Ⓔ
6. Ⓐ Ⓑ Ⓒ Ⓓ Ⓔ
7. Ⓐ Ⓑ Ⓒ Ⓓ Ⓔ
8. Ⓐ Ⓑ Ⓒ Ⓓ Ⓔ
9. Ⓐ Ⓑ Ⓒ Ⓓ Ⓔ
10. Ⓐ Ⓑ Ⓒ Ⓓ Ⓔ
11. Ⓐ Ⓑ Ⓒ Ⓓ Ⓔ
12. Ⓐ Ⓑ Ⓒ Ⓓ Ⓔ
13. Ⓐ Ⓑ Ⓒ Ⓓ Ⓔ
14. Ⓐ Ⓑ Ⓒ Ⓓ Ⓔ
15. Ⓐ Ⓑ Ⓒ Ⓓ Ⓔ
16. Ⓐ Ⓑ Ⓒ Ⓓ Ⓔ
17. Ⓐ Ⓑ Ⓒ Ⓓ Ⓔ
18. Ⓐ Ⓑ Ⓒ Ⓓ Ⓔ
19. Ⓐ Ⓑ Ⓒ Ⓓ Ⓔ
20. Ⓐ Ⓑ Ⓒ Ⓓ Ⓔ
21. Ⓐ Ⓑ Ⓒ Ⓓ Ⓔ
22. Ⓐ Ⓑ Ⓒ Ⓓ Ⓔ
23. Ⓐ Ⓑ Ⓒ Ⓓ Ⓔ
24. Ⓐ Ⓑ Ⓒ Ⓓ Ⓔ
25. Ⓐ Ⓑ Ⓒ Ⓓ Ⓔ
26. Ⓐ Ⓑ Ⓒ Ⓓ Ⓔ
27. Ⓐ Ⓑ Ⓒ Ⓓ Ⓔ

Section 2

1. Ⓐ Ⓑ Ⓒ Ⓓ Ⓔ
2. Ⓐ Ⓑ Ⓒ Ⓓ Ⓔ
3. Ⓐ Ⓑ Ⓒ Ⓓ Ⓔ
4. Ⓐ Ⓑ Ⓒ Ⓓ Ⓔ
5. Ⓐ Ⓑ Ⓒ Ⓓ Ⓔ
6. Ⓐ Ⓑ Ⓒ Ⓓ Ⓔ
7. Ⓐ Ⓑ Ⓒ Ⓓ Ⓔ
8. Ⓐ Ⓑ Ⓒ Ⓓ Ⓔ
9. Ⓐ Ⓑ Ⓒ Ⓓ Ⓔ
10. Ⓐ Ⓑ Ⓒ Ⓓ Ⓔ
11. Ⓐ Ⓑ Ⓒ Ⓓ Ⓔ
12. Ⓐ Ⓑ Ⓒ Ⓓ Ⓔ
13. Ⓐ Ⓑ Ⓒ Ⓓ Ⓔ
14. Ⓐ Ⓑ Ⓒ Ⓓ Ⓔ
15. Ⓐ Ⓑ Ⓒ Ⓓ Ⓔ
16. Ⓐ Ⓑ Ⓒ Ⓓ Ⓔ
17. Ⓐ Ⓑ Ⓒ Ⓓ Ⓔ
18. Ⓐ Ⓑ Ⓒ Ⓓ Ⓔ
19. Ⓐ Ⓑ Ⓒ Ⓓ Ⓔ
20. Ⓐ Ⓑ Ⓒ Ⓓ Ⓔ
21. Ⓐ Ⓑ Ⓒ Ⓓ Ⓔ
22. Ⓐ Ⓑ Ⓒ Ⓓ Ⓔ
23. Ⓐ Ⓑ Ⓒ Ⓓ Ⓔ
24. Ⓐ Ⓑ Ⓒ Ⓓ Ⓔ
25. Ⓐ Ⓑ Ⓒ Ⓓ Ⓔ
26. Ⓐ Ⓑ Ⓒ Ⓓ Ⓔ
27. Ⓐ Ⓑ Ⓒ Ⓓ Ⓔ

Section 3

1. Ⓐ Ⓑ Ⓒ Ⓓ Ⓔ
2. Ⓐ Ⓑ Ⓒ Ⓓ Ⓔ
3. Ⓐ Ⓑ Ⓒ Ⓓ Ⓔ
4. Ⓐ Ⓑ Ⓒ Ⓓ Ⓔ
5. Ⓐ Ⓑ Ⓒ Ⓓ Ⓔ
6. Ⓐ Ⓑ Ⓒ Ⓓ Ⓔ
7. Ⓐ Ⓑ Ⓒ Ⓓ Ⓔ
8. Ⓐ Ⓑ Ⓒ Ⓓ Ⓔ
9. Ⓐ Ⓑ Ⓒ Ⓓ Ⓔ
10. Ⓐ Ⓑ Ⓒ Ⓓ Ⓔ
11. Ⓐ Ⓑ Ⓒ Ⓓ Ⓔ
12. Ⓐ Ⓑ Ⓒ Ⓓ Ⓔ
13. Ⓐ Ⓑ Ⓒ Ⓓ Ⓔ
14. Ⓐ Ⓑ Ⓒ Ⓓ Ⓔ
15. Ⓐ Ⓑ Ⓒ Ⓓ Ⓔ
16. Ⓐ Ⓑ Ⓒ Ⓓ Ⓔ
17. Ⓐ Ⓑ Ⓒ Ⓓ Ⓔ
18. Ⓐ Ⓑ Ⓒ Ⓓ Ⓔ
19. Ⓐ Ⓑ Ⓒ Ⓓ Ⓔ
20. Ⓐ Ⓑ Ⓒ Ⓓ Ⓔ
21. Ⓐ Ⓑ Ⓒ Ⓓ Ⓔ
22. Ⓐ Ⓑ Ⓒ Ⓓ Ⓔ
23. Ⓐ Ⓑ Ⓒ Ⓓ Ⓔ
24. Ⓐ Ⓑ Ⓒ Ⓓ Ⓔ
25. Ⓐ Ⓑ Ⓒ Ⓓ Ⓔ
26. Ⓐ Ⓑ Ⓒ Ⓓ Ⓔ
27. Ⓐ Ⓑ Ⓒ Ⓓ Ⓔ

Section 4

1. Ⓐ Ⓑ Ⓒ Ⓓ Ⓔ
2. Ⓐ Ⓑ Ⓒ Ⓓ Ⓔ
3. Ⓐ Ⓑ Ⓒ Ⓓ Ⓔ
4. Ⓐ Ⓑ Ⓒ Ⓓ Ⓔ
5. Ⓐ Ⓑ Ⓒ Ⓓ Ⓔ
6. Ⓐ Ⓑ Ⓒ Ⓓ Ⓔ
7. Ⓐ Ⓑ Ⓒ Ⓓ Ⓔ
8. Ⓐ Ⓑ Ⓒ Ⓓ Ⓔ
9. Ⓐ Ⓑ Ⓒ Ⓓ Ⓔ
10. Ⓐ Ⓑ Ⓒ Ⓓ Ⓔ
11. Ⓐ Ⓑ Ⓒ Ⓓ Ⓔ
12. Ⓐ Ⓑ Ⓒ Ⓓ Ⓔ
13. Ⓐ Ⓑ Ⓒ Ⓓ Ⓔ
14. Ⓐ Ⓑ Ⓒ Ⓓ Ⓔ
15. Ⓐ Ⓑ Ⓒ Ⓓ Ⓔ
16. Ⓐ Ⓑ Ⓒ Ⓓ Ⓔ
17. Ⓐ Ⓑ Ⓒ Ⓓ Ⓔ
18. Ⓐ Ⓑ Ⓒ Ⓓ Ⓔ
19. Ⓐ Ⓑ Ⓒ Ⓓ Ⓔ
20. Ⓐ Ⓑ Ⓒ Ⓓ Ⓔ
21. Ⓐ Ⓑ Ⓒ Ⓓ Ⓔ
22. Ⓐ Ⓑ Ⓒ Ⓓ Ⓔ
23. Ⓐ Ⓑ Ⓒ Ⓓ Ⓔ
24. Ⓐ Ⓑ Ⓒ Ⓓ Ⓔ
25. Ⓐ Ⓑ Ⓒ Ⓓ Ⓔ
26. Ⓐ Ⓑ Ⓒ Ⓓ Ⓔ
27. Ⓐ Ⓑ Ⓒ Ⓓ Ⓔ

Section 5

1. Ⓐ Ⓑ Ⓒ Ⓓ Ⓔ
2. Ⓐ Ⓑ Ⓒ Ⓓ Ⓔ
3. Ⓐ Ⓑ Ⓒ Ⓓ Ⓔ
4. Ⓐ Ⓑ Ⓒ Ⓓ Ⓔ
5. Ⓐ Ⓑ Ⓒ Ⓓ Ⓔ
6. Ⓐ Ⓑ Ⓒ Ⓓ Ⓔ
7. Ⓐ Ⓑ Ⓒ Ⓓ Ⓔ
8. Ⓐ Ⓑ Ⓒ Ⓓ Ⓔ
9. Ⓐ Ⓑ Ⓒ Ⓓ Ⓔ
10. Ⓐ Ⓑ Ⓒ Ⓓ Ⓔ
11. Ⓐ Ⓑ Ⓒ Ⓓ Ⓔ
12. Ⓐ Ⓑ Ⓒ Ⓓ Ⓔ
13. Ⓐ Ⓑ Ⓒ Ⓓ Ⓔ
14. Ⓐ Ⓑ Ⓒ Ⓓ Ⓔ
15. Ⓐ Ⓑ Ⓒ Ⓓ Ⓔ
16. Ⓐ Ⓑ Ⓒ Ⓓ Ⓔ
17. Ⓐ Ⓑ Ⓒ Ⓓ Ⓔ
18. Ⓐ Ⓑ Ⓒ Ⓓ Ⓔ
19. Ⓐ Ⓑ Ⓒ Ⓓ Ⓔ
20. Ⓐ Ⓑ Ⓒ Ⓓ Ⓔ
21. Ⓐ Ⓑ Ⓒ Ⓓ Ⓔ
22. Ⓐ Ⓑ Ⓒ Ⓓ Ⓔ
23. Ⓐ Ⓑ Ⓒ Ⓓ Ⓔ
24. Ⓐ Ⓑ Ⓒ Ⓓ Ⓔ
25. Ⓐ Ⓑ Ⓒ Ⓓ Ⓔ
26. Ⓐ Ⓑ Ⓒ Ⓓ Ⓔ
27. Ⓐ Ⓑ Ⓒ Ⓓ Ⓔ

Section 6

1. Ⓐ Ⓑ Ⓒ Ⓓ Ⓔ
2. Ⓐ Ⓑ Ⓒ Ⓓ Ⓔ
3. Ⓐ Ⓑ Ⓒ Ⓓ Ⓔ
4. Ⓐ Ⓑ Ⓒ Ⓓ Ⓔ
5. Ⓐ Ⓑ Ⓒ Ⓓ Ⓔ
6. Ⓐ Ⓑ Ⓒ Ⓓ Ⓔ
7. Ⓐ Ⓑ Ⓒ Ⓓ Ⓔ
8. Ⓐ Ⓑ Ⓒ Ⓓ Ⓔ
9. Ⓐ Ⓑ Ⓒ Ⓓ Ⓔ
10. Ⓐ Ⓑ Ⓒ Ⓓ Ⓔ
11. Ⓐ Ⓑ Ⓒ Ⓓ Ⓔ
12. Ⓐ Ⓑ Ⓒ Ⓓ Ⓔ
13. Ⓐ Ⓑ Ⓒ Ⓓ Ⓔ
14. Ⓐ Ⓑ Ⓒ Ⓓ Ⓔ
15. Ⓐ Ⓑ Ⓒ Ⓓ Ⓔ
16. Ⓐ Ⓑ Ⓒ Ⓓ Ⓔ
17. Ⓐ Ⓑ Ⓒ Ⓓ Ⓔ
18. Ⓐ Ⓑ Ⓒ Ⓓ Ⓔ
19. Ⓐ Ⓑ Ⓒ Ⓓ Ⓔ
20. Ⓐ Ⓑ Ⓒ Ⓓ Ⓔ
21. Ⓐ Ⓑ Ⓒ Ⓓ Ⓔ
22. Ⓐ Ⓑ Ⓒ Ⓓ Ⓔ
23. Ⓐ Ⓑ Ⓒ Ⓓ Ⓔ
24. Ⓐ Ⓑ Ⓒ Ⓓ Ⓔ
25. Ⓐ Ⓑ Ⓒ Ⓓ Ⓔ
26. Ⓐ Ⓑ Ⓒ Ⓓ Ⓔ
27. Ⓐ Ⓑ Ⓒ Ⓓ Ⓔ

Print your full name here: _____
(last)   (first)   (middle)

Graduate
Management
Admission
Council®

**Educational
Testing Service**

Graduate Management Admission Test

SECTION 1

Time—30 minutes

20 Questions

Directions: In this section solve each problem, using any available space on the page for scratchwork. Then indicate the best of the answer choices given.

Numbers: All numbers used are real numbers.

Figures: Figures that accompany problems in this section are intended to provide information useful in solving the problems. They are drawn as accurately as possible EXCEPT when it is stated in a specific problem that its figure is not drawn to scale. All figures lie in a plane unless otherwise indicated.

1. A certain fishing boat is chartered by 6 people who are to contribute equally to the total charter cost of $480. If each person contributes equally to a $150 down payment, how much of the charter cost will each person still owe?

(A) $80   (B) $66   (C) $55   (D) $50   (E) $45

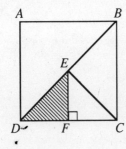

2. In square *ABCD* above, if *DE* = *EB* and *DF* = *FC*, then the area of the shaded region is what fraction of the area of square region *ABCD*?

(A) $\frac{1}{16}$ (B) $\frac{1}{8}$ (C) $\frac{1}{6}$ (D) $\frac{1}{4}$ (E) $\frac{1}{3}$

3. Craig sells major appliances. For each appliance he sells, Craig receives a commission of $50 plus 10 percent of the selling price. During one particular week Craig sold 6 appliances for selling prices totaling $3,620. What was the total of Craig's commissions for that week?

(A) $412   (B) $526   (C) $585
(D) $605   (E) $662

4. The average (arithmetic mean) of 10, 30, and 50 is 5 more than the average of 20, 40, and

(A) 15   (B) 25   (C) 35   (D) 45   (E) 55

5. What number when multiplied by $\frac{4}{7}$ yields $\frac{6}{7}$ as the result?

(A) $\frac{2}{7}$ (B) $\frac{2}{3}$ (C) $\frac{3}{2}$ (D) $\frac{24}{7}$ (E) $\frac{7}{2}$

GO ON TO THE NEXT PAGE.

6. If $y = 4 + (x - 3)^2$, then y is least when $x =$

(A) -4 (B) -3 (C) 0   (D) 3   (E) 4

7. If 3 pounds of dried apricots that cost x dollars per pound are mixed with 2 pounds of prunes that cost y dollars per pound, what is the cost, in dollars, per pound of the mixture?

(A) $\dfrac{3x + 2y}{5}$

(B) $\dfrac{3x + 2y}{x + y}$

(C) $\dfrac{3x + 2y}{xy}$

(D) $5(3x + 2y)$

(E) $3x + 2y$

8. A cashier mentally reversed the digits of one customer's correct amount of change and thus gave the customer an incorrect amount of change. If the cash register contained 45 cents more than it should have as a result of this error, which of the following could have been the correct amount of change in cents?

(A) 14   (B) 45   (C) 54   (D) 65   (E) 83

9. Which of the following is NOT equal to the square of an integer?

(A) $\sqrt{\sqrt{1}}$ (B) $\sqrt{4}$ (C) $\dfrac{18}{2}$

(D) $41 - 25$ (E) 36

GO ON TO THE NEXT PAGE.

10. An artist wishes to paint a circular region on a square poster that is 2 feet on a side. If the area of the circular region is to be $\frac{1}{2}$ the area of the poster, what must be the radius of the circular region in feet?

(A) $\frac{1}{\pi}$ (B) $\sqrt{\frac{2}{\pi}}$ (C) 1   (D) $\frac{2}{\sqrt{\pi}}$ (E) $\frac{\pi}{2}$

11. Which of the following must be equal to zero for all real numbers x ?

   I. $-\frac{1}{x}$

   II. $x + (-x)$

   III. x^0

(A) I only
(B) II only
(C) I and III only
(D) II and III only
(E) I, II, and III

12. At the rate of m meters per s seconds, how many meters does a cyclist travel in x minutes?

(A) $\frac{m}{sx}$ (B) $\frac{mx}{s}$ (C) $\frac{60m}{sx}$

(D) $\frac{60ms}{x}$ (E) $\frac{60mx}{s}$

	City A	City B	City C	City D	City E	City F
City A						
City B						
City C						
City D						
City E						
City F						

13. In the table above, what is the least number of table entries that are needed to show the mileage between each city and each of the other five cities?

(A) 15   (B) 21   (C) 25   (D) 30   (E) 36

GO ON TO THE NEXT PAGE.

14. A certain tax rate is $0.82 per $100.00. What is this rate, expressed as a percent?

    (A) 82%   (B) 8.2%   (C) 0.82%
    (D) 0.082%   (E) 0.0082%

15. Fermat primes are prime numbers that can be written in the form $2^k + 1$, where k is an integer and a power of 2. Which of the following is NOT a Fermat prime?

    (A)   3   (B)   5   (C)   17   (D)   31   (E) 257

16. A shipment of 1,500 heads of cabbage, each of which was approximately the same size, was purchased for $600. The day the shipment arrived, $\frac{2}{3}$ of the heads were sold, each at 25 percent above the cost per head. The following day the rest were sold at a price per head equal to 10 percent less than the price each head sold for on the day before. What was the gross profit on this shipment?

    (A) $100   (B) $115   (C) $125
    (D) $130   (E) $135

17. If $(t - 8)$ is a factor of $t^2 - kt - 48$, then $k =$

    (A) −6   (B) −2   (C)   2   (D)   6   (E)   14

GO ON TO THE NEXT PAGE.

18. If a is a positive integer, and if the units' digit of a^2 is 9 and the units' digit of $(a + 1)^2$ is 4, what is the units' digit of $(a + 2)^2$?

    (A) 1   (B) 3   (C) 5   (D) 7   (E) 9

19. The ratio, by volume, of soap to alcohol to water in a certain solution is 2 : 50 : 100. The solution will be altered so that the ratio of soap to alcohol is doubled while the ratio of soap to water is halved. If the altered solution will contain 100 cubic centimeters of alcohol, how many cubic centimeters of water will it contain?

    (A) 50   (B) 200   (C) 400   (D) 625   (E) 800

20. If 75 percent of a class answered the first question on a certain test correctly, 55 percent answered the second question on the test correctly, and 20 percent answered neither of the questions correctly, what percent answered both correctly?

    (A) 10%   (B) 20%   (C) 30%
    (D) 50%   (E) 65%

STOP

**IF YOU FINISH BEFORE TIME IS CALLED, YOU MAY CHECK YOUR WORK ON THIS SECTION ONLY.
DO NOT TURN TO ANY OTHER SECTION IN THE TEST.**

SECTION 2

Time – 30 minutes

27 Questions

Directions: In each of the following sentences, some part of the sentence or the entire sentence is underlined. Beneath each sentence you will find five ways of phrasing the underlined part. The first part of these repeats the original; the other four are different. If you think the original is the best of these answer choices, choose answer A; otherwise, choose one of the others. Select the best version and fill in the corresponding oval on your answer sheet.

This is a test of correctness and effectiveness of expression. In choosing answers, follow the requirements of standard written English; that is, pay attention to grammar, choice of words, and sentence construction. Choose the answer that produces the most effective sentence; this answer should be clear and exact, without awkwardness, ambiguity, redundancy, or grammatical error.

1. The Baldrick Manufacturing Company has for several years followed a policy aimed at decreasing operating costs and improving the efficiency of its distribution system.

   (A) aimed at decreasing operating costs and improving
   (B) aimed at the decreasing of operating costs and to improve
   (C) aiming at the decreasing of operating costs and improving
   (D) the aim of which is the decreasing of operating costs and improving
   (E) with the aim to decrease operating costs and to improve

2. *The Federalist* papers, a strong defense of the United States Constitution and important as a body of work in political science as well, represents the handiwork of three different authors.

   (A) and important as a body of work in political science as well, represents
   (B) as well as an important body of work in political science, represent
   (C) and also a body of work of importance in political science is representing
   (D) an important body of work in political science and has been representative of
   (E) and as political science an important body of work too, represent

3. Although the term "psychopath" is popularly applied to an especially brutal criminal, in psychology it is someone who is apparently incapable of feeling compassion or the pangs of conscience.

   (A) it is someone who is
   (B) it is a person
   (C) they are people who are
   (D) it refers to someone who is
   (E) it is in reference to people

GO ON TO THE NEXT PAGE.

4. A representative of the Women's Bureau of the United States Department of Labor contends that employers who offer benefits which permit that employees can balance home and work responsibilities better, realizing gains in attendance, recruiting, and retention.

(A) which permit that employees can balance home and work responsibilities better, realizing

(B) which permit employees balancing home and work responsibilities better will realize

(C) that permit employees to balance the responsibilities of home and work better will realize

(D) that permit employees a better balance between the responsibilities of home and work, thus realizing

(E) such that employees are permitted a balance between home and work responsibilities, and they will realize

5. Parliament did not accord full refugee benefits to twelve of the recent immigrants because it believed that to do it rewards them for entering the country illegally.

(A) to do it rewards

(B) doing it rewards

(C) to do this would reward

(D) doing so would reward

(E) to do it would reward

6. Many policy experts say that shifting a portion of health-benefit costs back to the workers helps to control the employer's costs, but also helps to limit medical spending by making patients more careful consumers.

(A) helps to control the employer's costs, but also helps

(B) helps the control of the employer's costs, and also

(C) not only helps to control the employer's costs, but also helps

(D) helps to control not only the employer's costs, but

(E) not only helps to control the employer's costs, and also helps

7. The plot of *The Bostonians* centers on the rivalry between Olive Chancellor, an active feminist, with her charming and cynical cousin, Basil Ransom, when they find themselves drawn to the same radiant young woman whose talent for public speaking has won her an ardent following.

(A) rivalry between Olive Chancellor, an active feminist, with her charming and cynical cousin, Basil Ransom

(B) rivals Olive Chancellor, an active feminist, against her charming and cynical cousin, Basil Ransom

(C) rivalry that develops between Olive Chancellor, an active feminist, and Basil Ransom, her charming and cynical cousin

(D) developing rivalry between Olive Chancellor, an active feminist, with Basil Ransom, her charming and cynical cousin

(E) active feminist, Olive Chancellor, and the rivalry with her charming and cynical cousin Basil Ransom

8. Despite protests from some waste-disposal companies, state health officials have ordered the levels of bacteria in seawater at popular beaches to be measured and that the results be published.

(A) the levels of bacteria in seawater at popular beaches to be measured and that the results be

(B) that seawater at popular beaches should be measured for their levels of bacteria, with the results being

(C) the measure of levels of bacteria in seawater at popular beaches and the results to be

(D) seawater measured at popular beaches for levels of bacteria, with their results

(E) that the levels of bacteria in seawater at popular beaches be measured and the results

GO ON TO THE NEXT PAGE.

9. While larger banks can afford to maintain their own data-processing operations, many smaller regional and community banks are finding that the cost associated with upgrading data-processing equipment and with the development and maintenance of new products and technical staff are prohibitive.

(A) cost associated with
(B) costs associated with
(C) costs arising from
(D) cost of
(E) costs of

10. For almost a hundred years after having its beginning in 1788, England exiled some 160,000 criminals to Australia.

(A) For almost a hundred years after having its beginning in 1788,
(B) Beginning in 1788 for a period of a hundred years,
(C) Beginning a period of almost a hundred years, in 1788
(D) During a hundred years, a period beginning in 1788,
(E) Over a period of a hundred years beginning in 1788,

11. Eating saltwater fish may significantly reduce the risk of heart attacks and also aid for sufferers of rheumatoid arthritis and asthma, according to three research studies published in the *New England Journal of Medicine*.

(A) significantly reduce the risk of heart attacks and also aid for
(B) be significant in reducing the risk of heart attacks and aid for
(C) significantly reduce the risk of heart attacks and aid
(D) cause a significant reduction in the risk of heart attacks and aid to
(E) significantly reduce the risk of heart attacks as well as aiding

12. By a vote of 9 to 0, the Supreme Court awarded the Central Intelligence Agency broad discretionary powers enabling it to withhold from the public the identities of its sources of intelligence information.

(A) enabling it to withhold from the public
(B) for it to withhold from the public
(C) for withholding disclosure to the public of
(D) that enable them to withhold from public disclosure
(E) that they can withhold public disclosure of

13. As business grows more complex, students majoring in specialized areas like those of finance and marketing have been becoming increasingly successful in the job market.

(A) majoring in specialized areas like those of finance and marketing have been becoming increasingly
(B) who major in such specialized areas as finance and marketing are becoming more and more
(C) who majored in specialized areas such as those of finance and marketing are being increasingly
(D) who major in specialized areas like those of finance and marketing have been becoming more and more
(E) having majored in such specialized areas as finance and marketing are being increasingly

14. Inuits of the Bering Sea were in isolation from contact with Europeans longer than Aleuts or Inuits of the North Pacific and northern Alaska.

(A) in isolation from contact with Europeans longer than
(B) isolated from contact with Europeans longer than
(C) in isolation from contact with Europeans longer than were
(D) isolated from contact with Europeans longer than were
(E) in isolation and without contacts with Europeans longer than

GO ON TO THE NEXT PAGE.

15. Once the economic and social usefulness of the motor car was demonstrated <u>and with its superiority to the horse being</u> proved, much of the early hostility to it in rural regions disappeared.

    (A) and with its superiority to the horse being
    (B) and its superiority over the horse had been
    (C) and its superiority to the horse
    (D) its superiority over the horse
    (E) with its superiority to the horse having been

16. Minnesota is the only one of the contiguous forty-eight states <u>that still has a sizable wolf population, and where</u> this predator remains the archenemy of cattle and sheep.

    (A) that still has a sizable wolf population, and where
    (B) that still has a sizable wolf population, where
    (C) that still has a sizable population of wolves, and where
    (D) where the population of wolves is still sizable;
    (E) where there is still a sizable population of wolves and where

17. Pablo Picasso, the late Spanish painter, credited African art <u>with having had</u> a strong influence on his work.

    (A) with having had
    (B) for its having
    (C) to have had
    (D) for having
    (E) in that it had

18. Judicial rules in many states require <u>that the identities of all prosecution witnesses are made known to defendants so they can attempt to rebut</u> the testimony, but the Constitution explicitly requires only that the defendant have the opportunity to confront an accuser in court.

    (A) that the identities of all prosecution witnesses are made known to defendants so they can attempt to rebut
    (B) that the identities of all prosecution witnesses be made known to defendants so that they can attempt to rebut
    (C) that the defendants should know the identities of all prosecution witnesses so they can attempt a rebuttal of
    (D) the identities of all prosecution witnesses should be made known to defendants so they can attempt rebutting
    (E) making known to defendants the identities of all prosecution witnesses so that they can attempt to rebut

19. Quasars, at billions of light-years from Earth the most distant observable objects in the universe, <u>believed to be</u> the cores of galaxies in an early stage of development.

    (A) believed to be
    (B) are believed to be
    (C) some believe them to be
    (D) some believe they are
    (E) it is believed that they are

GO ON TO THE NEXT PAGE.

20. The colorization of black-and-white films by computers is defended by those who own the film rights, for the process can mean increased revenues for them; many others in the film industry, however, contend that the technique degrades major works of art, which they liken to putting lipstick on a Greek statue.

(A) which they liken to putting lipstick on a Greek statue
(B) which they liken to a Greek statue with lipstick put on it
(C) which they liken to lipstick put on a Greek statue
(D) likening it to a Greek statue with lipstick put on it
(E) likening it to putting lipstick on a Greek statue

21. In reference to the current hostility toward smoking, smokers frequently expressed anxiety that their prospects for being hired and promoted are being stunted by their habit.

(A) In reference to the current hostility toward smoking, smokers frequently expressed anxiety that
(B) Referring to the current hostility toward smoking, smokers frequently expressed anxiety about
(C) When referring to the current hostility toward smoking, smokers frequently express anxiety about
(D) With reference to the current hostility toward smoking, smokers frequently expressed anxiety about
(E) Referring to the current hostility toward smoking, smokers frequently express anxiety that

22. Ms. Chambers is among the forecasters who predict that the rate of addition to arable lands will drop while those of loss rise.

(A) those of loss rise
(B) it rises for loss
(C) those of losses rise
(D) the rate of loss rises
(E) there are rises for the rate of loss

23. Unlike auto insurance, the frequency of claims does not affect the premiums for personal property coverage, but if the insurance company is able to prove excessive loss due to owner negligence, it may decline to renew the policy.

(A) Unlike auto insurance, the frequency of claims does not affect the premiums for personal property coverage
(B) Unlike with auto insurance, the frequency of claims do not affect the premiums for personal property coverage
(C) Unlike the frequency of claims for auto insurance, the premiums for personal property coverage are not affected by the frequency of claims
(D) Unlike the premiums for auto insurance, the premiums for personal property coverage are not affected by the frequency of claims
(E) Unlike with the premiums for auto insurance, the premiums for personal property coverage is not affected by the frequency of claims

GO ON TO THE NEXT PAGE.

24. Recently implemented "shift-work equations" based on studies of the human sleep cycle have reduced sickness, sleeping on the job, <u>fatigue among shift workers, and have raised</u> production efficiency in various industries.

   (A) fatigue among shift workers, and have raised
   (B) fatigue among shift workers, and raised
   (C) and fatigue among shift workers while raising
   (D) lowered fatigue among shift workers, and raised
   (E) and fatigue among shift workers was lowered while raising

25. The physical structure of the human eye enables it to sense light of wavelengths up to 0.0005 millimeters; <u>infrared radiation, however, is invisible because its wavelength—0.1 millimeters—is too long to be registered by the eye.</u>

   (A) infrared radiation, however, is invisible because its wavelength—0.1 millimeters—is too long to be registered by the eye
   (B) however, the wavelength of infrared radiation—0.1 millimeters—is too long to be registered by the eye making it invisible
   (C) infrared radiation, however, is invisible because its wavelength—0.1 millimeters—is too long for the eye to register it
   (D) however, because the wavelength of infrared radiation is 0.1 millimeters, it is too long for the eye to register and thus invisible
   (E) however, infrared radiation has a wavelength of 0.1 millimeters that is too long for the eye to register, thus making it invisible

26. Spanning more than fifty years, Friedrich <u>Müller began his career in an unpromising apprenticeship as</u> a Sanskrit scholar and culminated in virtually every honor that European governments and learned societies could bestow.

   (A) Müller began his career in an unpromising apprenticeship as
   (B) Müller's career began in an unpromising apprenticeship as
   (C) Müller's career began with the unpromising apprenticeship of being
   (D) Müller had begun his career with the unpromising apprenticeship of being
   (E) the career of Müller has begun with an unpromising apprenticeship of

27. The Coast Guard is conducting tests <u>to see whether pigeons can be trained to help find</u> survivors of wrecks at sea.

   (A) to see whether pigeons can be trained to help find
   (B) to see whether pigeons can be trained as help to find
   (C) to see if pigeons can be trained for helping to find
   (D) that see if pigeons are able to be trained in helping to find
   (E) that see whether pigeons are able to be trained for help in finding

STOP

IF YOU FINISH BEFORE TIME IS CALLED, YOU MAY CHECK YOUR WORK ON THIS SECTION ONLY.
DO NOT TURN TO ANY OTHER SECTION IN THE TEST.

SECTION 3

Time – 30 minutes

25 Questions

Directions: Each of the data sufficiency problems below consists of a question and two statements, labeled (1) and (2), in which certain data are given. You have to decide whether the data given in the statements are <u>sufficient</u> for answering the question. Using the data given in the statements <u>plus</u> your knowledge of mathematics and everyday facts (such as the number of days in July or the meaning of *counterclockwise*), you are to fill in oval

A if statement (1) ALONE is sufficient, but statement (2) alone is not sufficient to answer the question asked;

B if statement (2) ALONE is sufficient, but statement (1) alone is not sufficient to answer the question asked;

C if BOTH statements (1) and (2) TOGETHER are sufficient to answer the question asked, but NEITHER statement ALONE is sufficient;

D if EACH statement ALONE is sufficient to answer the question asked;

E if statements (1) and (2) TOGETHER are NOT sufficient to answer the question asked, and additional data specific to the problem are needed.

Numbers: All numbers used are real numbers.

Figures: A figure in a data sufficiency problem will conform to the information given in the question, but will not necessarily conform to the additional information given in statements (1) and (2).

You may assume that lines shown as straight are straight and that angle measures are greater than zero.

You may assume that the positions of points, angles, regions, etc., exist in the order shown.

All figures lie in a plane unless otherwise indicated.

Note: In questions that ask for the value of a quantity, the data given in the statements are sufficient only when it is possible to determine exactly one numerical value for the quantity.

Example:

In $\triangle PQR$, what is the value of x ?

(1) $PQ = PR$

(2) $y = 40$

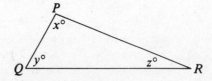

Explanation: According to statement (1), $PQ = PR$; therefore, $\triangle PQR$ is isosceles and $y = z$. Since $x + y + z = 180$, it follows that $x + 2y = 180$. Since statement (1) does not give a value for y, you cannot answer the question using statement (1) alone. According to statement (2), $y = 40$; therefore, $x + z = 140$. Since statement (2) does not give a value for z, you cannot answer the question using statement (2) alone. Using both statements together, since $x + 2y = 180$ and the value of y is given, you can find the value of x. Therefore, the answer is C.

GO ON TO THE NEXT PAGE.

A Statement (1) ALONE is sufficient, but statement (2) alone is not sufficient.
B Statement (2) ALONE is sufficient, but statement (1) alone is not sufficient.
C BOTH statements TOGETHER are sufficient, but NEITHER statement ALONE is sufficient.
D EACH statement ALONE is sufficient.
E Statements (1) and (2) TOGETHER are NOT sufficient.

1. If Hans purchased a pair of skis and a ski jacket, what was the cost of the skis?

   (1) The ratio of the cost of the skis to the cost of the jacket was 5 to 1.

   (2) The total cost of the skis and the jacket was $360.

2. Is $x < y$?

   (1) $z < y$

   (2) $z < x$

3. If a certain city is losing 12 percent of its daily water supply each day because of water-main breaks, what is the dollar cost to the city per day for this loss?

   (1) The city's daily water supply is 350 million gallons.

   (2) The cost to the city for each 12,000 gallons of water lost is $2.

4. Machine X runs at a constant rate and produces a lot consisting of 100 cans in 2 hours. How much less time would it take to produce the lot of cans if both machines X and Y were run simultaneously?

   (1) Both machines X and Y produce the same number of cans per hour.

   (2) It takes machine X twice as long to produce the lot of cans as it takes machines X and Y running simultaneously to produce the lot.

5. If x and y are positive, what is the value of x?

   (1) 200 percent of x equals 400 percent of y.

   (2) xy is the square of a positive integer.

GO ON TO THE NEXT PAGE.

A Statement (1) ALONE is sufficient, but statement (2) alone is not sufficient.
B Statement (2) ALONE is sufficient, but statement (1) alone is not sufficient.
C BOTH statements TOGETHER are sufficient, but NEITHER statement ALONE is sufficient.
D EACH statement ALONE is sufficient.
E Statements (1) and (2) TOGETHER are NOT sufficient.

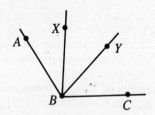

6. In the figure above, what is the measure of $\angle ABC$?

(1) BX bisects $\angle ABY$ and BY bisects $\angle XBC$.

(2) The measure of $\angle ABX$ is 40°.

7. If $-10 < k < 10$, is $k > 0$?

(1) $\frac{1}{k} > 0$

(2) $k^2 > 0$

	R	S	T	U
R	0	y	x	62
S	y	0	56	75
T	x	56	0	69
U	62	75	69	0

8. The table above shows the distance, in kilometers, by the most direct route, between any two of the four cities, R, S, T, and U. For example, the distance between City R and City U is 62 kilometers. What is the value of x?

(1) By the most direct route, the distance between S and T is twice the distance between S and R.

(2) By the most direct route, the distance between T and U is 1.5 times the distance between R and T.

9. Buckets X and Y contained only water and bucket Y was $\frac{1}{2}$ full. If all of the water in bucket X was then poured into bucket Y, what fraction of the capacity of Y was then filled with water?

(1) Before the water from X was poured, X was $\frac{1}{3}$ full.

(2) X and Y have the same capacity.

10. If n is an integer, is $n + 2$ a prime number?

(1) n is a prime number.

(2) $n + 1$ is not a prime number.

GO ON TO THE NEXT PAGE.

A   Statement (1) ALONE is sufficient, but statement (2) alone is not sufficient.
B   Statement (2) ALONE is sufficient, but statement (1) alone is not sufficient.
C   BOTH statements TOGETHER are sufficient, but NEITHER statement ALONE is sufficient.
D   EACH statement ALONE is sufficient.
E   Statements (1) and (2) TOGETHER are NOT sufficient.

11. Is x between 0 and 1 ?

    (1) x^2 is less than x.

    (2) x^3 is positive.

12. Did Sally pay less than x dollars, including sales tax, for her bicycle?

    (1)   The price Sally paid for the bicycle was $(0.9)x$ dollars, excluding the 10 percent sales tax.

    (2)   The price Sally paid for the bicycle was $170, excluding sales tax.

13. Is the positive square root of x an integer?

    (1) $x = n^4$ and n is an integer.

    (2) $x = 16$

14. If the successive tick marks shown on the number line above are equally spaced and if x and y are the numbers designating the end points of intervals as shown, what is the value of y ?

    (1) $x = \dfrac{1}{2}$

    (2) $y - x = \dfrac{2}{3}$

15. In a certain senior citizens' club, are more than $\dfrac{1}{4}$ of the members over 75 years of age?

    (1)   Exactly 60 percent of the female members are over 60 years of age, and, of these, $\dfrac{1}{3}$ are over 75 years of age.

    (2)   Exactly 10 male members are over 75 years of age.

GO ON TO THE NEXT PAGE.

A Statement (1) ALONE is sufficient, but statement (2) alone is not sufficient.
B Statement (2) ALONE is sufficient, but statement (1) alone is not sufficient.
C BOTH statements TOGETHER are sufficient, but NEITHER statement ALONE is sufficient.
D EACH statement ALONE is sufficient.
E Statements (1) and (2) TOGETHER are NOT sufficient.

16. If $t \neq 0$, is r greater than zero?

(1) $rt = 12$
(2) $r + t = 7$

17. If x is an integer, is y an integer?

(1) The average (arithmetic mean) of x, y, and $y - 2$ is x.
(2) The average (arithmetic mean) of x and y is not an integer.

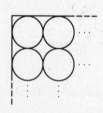

18. The inside of a rectangular carton is 48 centimeters long, 32 centimeters wide, and 15 centimeters high. The carton is filled to capacity with k identical cylindrical cans of fruit that stand upright in rows and columns, as indicated in the figure above. If the cans are 15 centimeters high, what is the value of k?

(1) Each of the cans has a radius of 4 centimeters.
(2) 6 of the cans fit exactly along the length of the carton.

19. If $R = \dfrac{8x}{3y}$ and $y \neq 0$, what is the value of R?

(1) $x = \dfrac{2}{3}$
(2) $x = 2y$

20. Is the positive integer n a multiple of 24?

(1) n is a multiple of 4.
(2) n is a multiple of 6.

GO ON TO THE NEXT PAGE.

A   Statement (1) ALONE is sufficient, but statement (2) alone is not sufficient.
B   Statement (2) ALONE is sufficient, but statement (1) alone is not sufficient.
C   BOTH statements TOGETHER are sufficient, but NEITHER statement ALONE is sufficient.
D   EACH statement ALONE is sufficient.
E   Statements (1) and (2) TOGETHER are NOT sufficient.

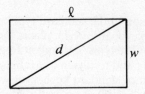

21. What is the area of the rectangular region above?

(1) $\ell + w = 6$
(2) $d^2 = 20$

22. If Aaron, Lee, and Tony have a total of \$36, how much money does Tony have?

(1) Tony has twice as much money as Lee and $\frac{1}{3}$ as much as Aaron.
(2) The sum of the amounts of money that Tony and Lee have is half the amount that Aaron has.

23. If n is a positive integer, is the value of $b - a$ at least twice the value of $3^n - 2^n$?

(1) $a = 2^{n+1}$ and $b = 3^{n+1}$
(2) $n = 3$

24. The price per share of stock X increased by 10 percent over the same time period that the price per share of stock Y decreased by 10 percent. The reduced price per share of stock Y was what percent of the original price per share of stock X?

(1) The increased price per share of stock X was equal to the original price per share of stock Y.
(2) The increase in the price per share of stock X was $\frac{10}{11}$ the decrease in the price per share of stock Y.

25. Any decimal that has only a finite number of non-zero digits is a terminating decimal. For example, 24, 0.82, and 5.096 are three terminating decimals. If r and s are positive integers and the ratio $\frac{r}{s}$ is expressed as a decimal, is $\frac{r}{s}$ a terminating decimal?

(1) $90 < r < 100$
(2) $s = 4$

STOP

**IF YOU FINISH BEFORE TIME IS CALLED, YOU MAY CHECK YOUR WORK ON THIS SECTION ONLY.
DO NOT TURN TO ANY OTHER SECTION IN THE TEST.**

SECTION 4

Time—30 minutes

20 Questions

Directions: For each question in this section, select the best of the answer choices given.

Questions 1-2 are based on the following.

Companies O and P each have the same number of employees who work the same number of hours per week. According to records maintained by each company, the employees of Company O had fewer job-related accidents last year than did the employees of Company P. Therefore, employees of Company O are less likely to have job-related accidents than are employees of Company P.

1. Which of the following, if true, would most strengthen the conclusion above?

(A) Company P manufactures products that are more hazardous for workers to produce than does Company O.

(B) Company P holds more safety inspections than does Company O.

(C) Company P maintains a more modern infirmary than does Company O.

(D) Company O paid more for new job-related medical claims than did Company P.

(E) Company P provides more types of health-care benefits than does Company O.

2. Which of the following, if true, would most weaken the conclusion above?

(A) The employees of Company P lost more time at work due to job-related accidents than did the employees of Company O.

(B) Company P considered more types of accidents to be job-related than did Company O.

(C) The employees of Company P were sick more often than were the employees of Company O.

(D) Several employees of Company O each had more than one job-related accident.

(E) The majority of job-related accidents at Company O involved a single machine.

3. In comparison to the standard typewriter keyboard, the EFCO keyboard, which places the most-used keys nearest the typist's strongest fingers, allows faster typing and results in less fatigue. Therefore, replacement of standard keyboards with the EFCO keyboard will result in an immediate reduction of typing costs.

Which of the following, if true, would most weaken the conclusion drawn above?

(A) People who use both standard and EFCO keyboards report greater difficulty in the transition from the EFCO keyboard to the standard keyboard than in the transition from the standard keyboard to the EFCO keyboard.

(B) EFCO keyboards are no more expensive to manufacture than are standard keyboards and require less frequent repair than do standard keyboards.

(C) The number of businesses and government agencies that use EFCO keyboards is increasing each year.

(D) The more training and experience an employee has had with the standard keyboard, the more costly it is to train that employee to use the EFCO keyboard.

(E) Novice typists can learn to use the EFCO keyboard in about the same amount of time it takes them to learn to use the standard keyboard.

GO ON TO THE NEXT PAGE.

Questions 4-5 are based on the following.

Half of the subjects in an experiment—the experimental group—consumed large quantities of a popular artificial sweetener. Afterward, this group showed lower cognitive abilities than did the other half of the subjects—the control group—who did not consume the sweetener. The detrimental effects were attributed to an amino acid that is one of the sweetener's principal constituents.

4. Which of the following, if true, would best support the conclusion that some ingredient of the sweetener was responsible for the experimental results?

(A) Most consumers of the sweetener do not consume as much of it as the experimental group members did.

(B) The amino acid referred to in the conclusion is a component of all proteins, some of which must be consumed for adequate nutrition.

(C) The quantity of the sweetener consumed by individuals in the experimental group is considered safe by federal food regulators.

(D) The two groups of subjects were evenly matched with regard to cognitive abilities prior to the experiment.

(E) A second experiment in which subjects consumed large quantities of the sweetener lacked a control group of subjects who were not given the sweetener.

5. Which of the following, if true, would best help explain how the sweetener might produce the observed effect?

(A) The government's analysis of the artificial sweetener determined that it was sold in relatively pure form.

(B) A high level of the amino acid in the blood inhibits the synthesis of a substance required for normal brain functioning.

(C) Because the sweetener is used primarily as a food additive, adverse reactions to it are rarely noticed by consumers.

(D) The amino acid that is a constituent of the sweetener is also sold separately as a dietary supplement.

(E) Subjects in the experiment did not know whether they were consuming the sweetener or a second, harmless substance.

6. Adult female rats who have never before encountered rat pups will start to show maternal behaviors after being confined with a pup for about seven days. This period can be considerably shortened by disabling the female's sense of smell or by removing the scent-producing glands of the pup.

Which of the following hypotheses best explains the contrast described above?

(A) The sense of smell in adult female rats is more acute than that in rat pups.

(B) The amount of scent produced by rat pups increases when they are in the presence of a female rat that did not bear them.

(C) Female rats that have given birth are more affected by olfactory cues than are female rats that have never given birth.

(D) A female rat that has given birth shows maternal behavior toward rat pups that she did not bear more quickly than does a female rat that has never given birth.

(E) The development of a female rat's maternal interest in a rat pup that she did not bear is inhibited by the odor of the pup.

7. The interview is an essential part of a successful hiring program because, with it, job applicants who have personalities that are unsuited to the requirements of the job will be eliminated from consideration.

The argument above logically depends on which of the following assumptions?

(A) A hiring program will be successful if it includes interviews.

(B) The interview is a more important part of a successful hiring program than is the development of a job description.

(C) Interviewers can accurately identify applicants whose personalities are unsuited to the requirements of the job.

(D) The only purpose of an interview is to evaluate whether job applicants' personalities are suited to the requirements of the job.

(E) The fit of job applicants' personalities to the requirements of the job was once the most important factor in making hiring decisions.

GO ON TO THE NEXT PAGE.

8. An overly centralized economy, not the changes in the climate, is responsible for the poor agricultural production in Country X since its new government came to power. Neighboring Country Y has experienced the same climatic conditions, but while agricultural production has been falling in Country X, it has been rising in Country Y.

Which of the following, if true, would most weaken the argument above?

(A) Industrial production also is declining in Country X.
(B) Whereas Country Y is landlocked, Country X has a major seaport.
(C) Both Country X and Country Y have been experiencing drought conditions.
(D) The crops that have always been grown in Country X are different from those that have always been grown in Country Y.
(E) Country X's new government instituted a centralized economy with the intention of ensuring an equitable distribution of goods.

9. Useful protein drugs, such as insulin, must still be administered by the cumbersome procedure of injection under the skin. If proteins are taken orally, they are digested and cannot reach their target cells. Certain nonprotein drugs, however, contain chemical bonds that are not broken down by the digestive system. They can, thus, be taken orally.

The statements above most strongly support a claim that a research procedure that successfully accomplishes which of the following would be beneficial to users of protein drugs?

(A) Coating insulin with compounds that are broken down by target cells, but whose chemical bonds are resistant to digestion
(B) Converting into protein compounds, by procedures that work in the laboratory, the nonprotein drugs that resist digestion
(C) Removing permanently from the digestive system any substances that digest proteins
(D) Determining, in a systematic way, what enzymes and bacteria are present in the normal digestive system and whether they tend to be broken down within the body
(E) Determining the amount of time each nonprotein drug takes to reach its target cells

10. Country Y uses its scarce foreign-exchange reserves to buy scrap iron for recycling into steel. Although the steel thus produced earns more foreign exchange than it costs, that policy is foolish. Country Y's own territory has vast deposits of iron ore, which can be mined with minimal expenditure of foreign exchange.

Which of the following, if true, provides the strongest support for Country Y's policy of buying scrap iron abroad?

(A) The price of scrap iron on international markets rose significantly in 1987.
(B) Country Y's foreign-exchange reserves dropped significantly in 1987.
(C) There is virtually no difference in quality between steel produced from scrap iron and that produced from iron ore.
(D) Scrap iron is now used in the production of roughly half the steel used in the world today, and experts predict that scrap iron will be used even more extensively in the future.
(E) Furnaces that process scrap iron can be built and operated in Country Y with substantially less foreign exchange than can furnaces that process iron ore.

11. Last year the rate of inflation was 1.2 percent, but for the current year it has been 4 percent. We can conclude that inflation is on an upward trend and the rate will be still higher next year.

Which of the following, if true, most seriously weakens the conclusion above?

(A) The inflation figures were computed on the basis of a representative sample of economic data rather than all of the available data.
(B) Last year a dip in oil prices brought inflation temporarily below its recent stable annual level of 4 percent.
(C) Increases in the pay of some workers are tied to the level of inflation, and at an inflation rate of 4 percent or above, these pay raises constitute a force causing further inflation.
(D) The 1.2 percent rate of inflation last year represented a ten-year low.
(E) Government intervention cannot affect the rate of inflation to any significant degree.

GO ON TO THE NEXT PAGE.

12. Because no employee wants to be associated with bad news in the eyes of a superior, information about serious problems at lower levels is progressively softened and distorted as it goes up each step in the management hierarchy. The chief executive is, therefore, less well informed about problems at lower levels than are his or her subordinates at those levels.

The conclusion drawn above is based on the assumption that

(A) problems should be solved at the level in the management hierarchy at which they occur
(B) employees should be rewarded for accurately reporting problems to their superiors
(C) problem-solving ability is more important at higher levels than it is at lower levels of the management hierarchy
(D) chief executives obtain information about problems at lower levels from no source other than their subordinates
(E) some employees are more concerned about truth than about the way they are perceived by their superiors

13. In the United States in 1986, the average rate of violent crime in states with strict gun-control laws was 645 crimes per 100,000 persons—about 50 percent higher than the average rate in the eleven states where strict gun-control laws have never been passed. Thus one way to reduce violent crime is to repeal strict gun control laws.

Which of the following, if true, would most weaken the argument above?

(A) The annual rate of violent crime in states with strict gun-control laws has decreased since the passage of those laws.
(B) In states with strict gun-control laws, few individuals are prosecuted for violating such laws.
(C) In states without strict gun-control laws, many individuals have had no formal training in the use of firearms.
(D) The annual rate of nonviolent crime is lower in states with strict gun-control laws than in states without such laws.
(E) Less than half of the individuals who reside in states without strict gun-control laws own a gun.

14. Corporate officers and directors commonly buy and sell, for their own portfolios, stock in their own corporations. Generally, when the ratio of such inside sales to inside purchases falls below 2 to 1 for a given stock, a rise in stock prices is imminent. In recent days, while the price of MEGA Corporation stock has been falling, the corporation's officers and directors have bought up to nine times as much of it as they have sold.

The facts above best support which of the following predictions?

(A) The imbalance between inside purchases and inside sales of MEGA stock will grow even further.
(B) Inside purchases of MEGA stock are about to cease abruptly.
(C) The price of MEGA stock will soon begin to go up.
(D) The price of MEGA stock will continue to drop, but less rapidly.
(E) The majority of MEGA stock will soon be owned by MEGA's own officers and directors.

15. The proposal to hire ten new police officers in Middletown is quite foolish. There is sufficient funding to pay the salaries of the new officers, but not the salaries of additional court and prison employees to process the increased caseload of arrests and convictions that new officers usually generate.

Which of the following, if true, will most seriously weaken the conclusion drawn above?

(A) Studies have shown that an increase in a city's police force does not necessarily reduce crime.
(B) When one major city increased its police force by 19 percent last year, there were 40 percent more arrests and 13 percent more convictions.
(C) If funding for the new police officers' salaries is approved, support for other city services will have to be reduced during the next fiscal year.
(D) In most United States cities, not all arrests result in convictions, and not all convictions result in prison terms.
(E) Middletown's ratio of police officers to citizens has reached a level at which an increase in the number of officers will have a deterrent effect on crime.

GO ON TO THE NEXT PAGE.

16. A recent report determined that although only three percent of drivers on Maryland highways equipped their vehicles with radar detectors, thirty-three percent of all vehicles ticketed for exceeding the speed limit were equipped with them. Clearly, drivers who equip their vehicles with radar detectors are more likely to exceed the speed limit regularly than are drivers who do not.

The conclusion drawn above depends on which of the following assumptions?

(A) Drivers who equip their vehicles with radar detectors are less likely to be ticketed for exceeding the speed limit than are drivers who do not.

(B) Drivers who are ticketed for exceeding the speed limit are more likely to exceed the speed limit regularly than are drivers who are not ticketed.

(C) The number of vehicles that were ticketed for exceeding the speed limit was greater than the number of vehicles that were equipped with radar detectors.

(D) Many of the vehicles that were ticketed for exceeding the speed limit were ticketed more than once in the time period covered by the report.

(E) Drivers on Maryland highways exceeded the speed limit more often than did drivers on other state highways not covered in the report.

17. There is a great deal of geographical variation in the frequency of many surgical procedures—up to tenfold variation per hundred thousand between different areas in the numbers of hysterectomies, prostatectomies, and tonsillectomies.

To support a conclusion that much of the variation is due to unnecessary surgical procedures, it would be most important to establish which of the following?

(A) A local board of review at each hospital examines the records of every operation to determine whether the surgical procedure was necessary.

(B) The variation is unrelated to factors (other than the surgical procedures themselves) that influence the incidence of diseases for which surgery might be considered.

(C) There are several categories of surgical procedure (other than hysterectomies, prostatectomies, and tonsillectomies) that are often performed unnecessarily.

(D) For certain surgical procedures, it is difficult to determine after the operation whether the procedures were necessary or whether alternative treatment would have succeeded.

(E) With respect to how often they are performed unnecessarily, hysterectomies, prostatectomies, and tonsillectomies are representative of surgical procedures in general.

GO ON TO THE NEXT PAGE.

18. Researchers have found that when very overweight people, who tend to have relatively low metabolic rates, lose weight primarily through dieting, their metabolisms generally remain unchanged. They will thus burn significantly fewer calories at the new weight than do people whose weight is normally at that level. Such newly thin persons will, therefore, ultimately regain weight until their body size again matches their metabolic rate.

The conclusion of the argument above depends on which of the following assumptions?

(A) Relatively few very overweight people who have dieted down to a new weight tend to continue to consume substantially fewer calories than do people whose normal weight is at that level.

(B) The metabolisms of people who are usually not overweight are much more able to vary than the metabolisms of people who have been very overweight.

(C) The amount of calories that a person usually burns in a day is determined more by the amount that is consumed that day than by the current weight of the individual.

(D) Researchers have not yet determined whether the metabolic rates of formerly very overweight individuals can be accelerated by means of chemical agents.

(E) Because of the constancy of their metabolic rates, people who are at their usual weight normally have as much difficulty gaining weight as they do losing it.

19. In 1987 sinusitis was the most common chronic medical condition in the United States, followed by arthritis and high blood pressure, in that order.

The incidence rates for both arthritis and high blood pressure increase with age, but the incidence rate for sinusitis is the same for people of all ages.

The average age of the United States population will increase between 1987 and 2000.

Which of the following conclusions can be most properly drawn about chronic medical conditions in the United States from the information given above?

(A) Sinusitis will be more common than either arthritis or high blood pressure in 2000.

(B) Arthritis will be the most common chronic medical condition in 2000.

(C) The average age of people suffering from sinusitis will increase between 1987 and 2000.

(D) Fewer people will suffer from sinusitis in 2000 than suffered from it in 1987.

(E) A majority of the population will suffer from at least one of the medical conditions mentioned above by the year 2000.

20. Parasitic wasps lay their eggs directly into the eggs of various host insects in exactly the right numbers for any suitable size of host egg. If they laid too many eggs in a host egg, the developing wasp larvae would compete with each other to the death for nutrients and space. If too few eggs were laid, portions of the host egg would decay, killing the wasp larvae.

Which of the following conclusions can properly be drawn from the information above?

(A) The size of the smallest host egg that a wasp could theoretically parasitize can be determined from the wasp's egg-laying behavior.

(B) Host insects lack any effective defenses against the form of predation practiced by parasitic wasps.

(C) Parasitic wasps learn from experience how many eggs to lay into the eggs of different host species.

(D) Failure to lay enough eggs would lead to the death of the developing wasp larvae more quickly than would laying too many eggs.

(E) Parasitic wasps use visual clues to calculate the size of a host egg.

STOP

IF YOU FINISH BEFORE TIME IS CALLED, YOU MAY CHECK YOUR WORK ON THIS SECTION ONLY.
DO NOT TURN TO ANY OTHER SECTION IN THE TEST.

SECTION 5

Time—30 minutes

20 Questions

Directions: In this section solve each problem, using any available space on the page for scratchwork. Then indicate the best of the answer choices given.

Numbers: All numbers used are real numbers.

Figures: Figures that accompany problems in this section are intended to provide information useful in solving the problems. They are drawn as accurately as possible EXCEPT when it is stated in a specific problem that its figure is not drawn to scale. All figures lie in a plane unless otherwise indicated.

1. $\dfrac{31}{125} =$

(A) 0.248
(B) 0.252
(C) 0.284
(D) 0.312
(E) 0.320

2. Members of a social club met to address 280 news-letters. If they addressed $\frac{1}{4}$ of the newsletters during the first hour and $\frac{2}{5}$ of the remaining newsletters during the second hour, how many newsletters did they address during the second hour?

(A) 28   (B) 42   (C) 63   (D) 84   (E) 112

3. If $x^2 = 2y^3$ and $2y = 4$, what is the value of $x^2 + y$?

(A) -14
(B) -2
(C) 3
(D) 6
(E) 18

4. If the cost of 12 eggs varies between \$0.90 and \$1.20, then the cost per egg varies between

(A) \$0.06 and \$0.08
(B) \$0.065 and \$0.085
(C) \$0.07 and \$0.09
(D) \$0.075 and \$0.10
(E) \$0.08 and \$0.105

GO ON TO THE NEXT PAGE.

5. $(\sqrt{3} + 2)(\sqrt{3} - 2) =$

(A) $\sqrt{3} - 4$ (B) $\sqrt{6} - 4$ (C) -1

(D) 1 (E) 2

6. A glucose solution contains 15 grams of glucose per 100 cubic centimeters of solution. If 45 cubic centimeters of the solution were poured into an empty container, how many grams of glucose would be in the container?

(A) 3.00
(B) 5.00
(C) 5.50
(D) 6.50
(E) 6.75

7. If Sam were twice as old as he is, he would be 40 years older than Jim. If Jim is 10 years younger than Sam, how old is Sam?

(A) 20
(B) 30
(C) 40
(D) 50
(E) 60

8. If $\frac{1}{2} + \frac{1}{3} + \frac{1}{4} = \frac{13}{x}$, which of the following must be an integer?

I. $\frac{x}{8}$

II. $\frac{x}{12}$

III. $\frac{x}{24}$

(A) I only (B) II only (C) I and III only
(D) II and III only (E) I, II, and III

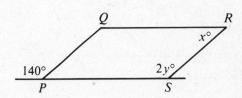

9. In the figure above, if $PQRS$ is a parallelogram, then $y - x =$

(A) 30 (B) 35 (C) 40 (D) 70 (E) 100

GO ON TO THE NEXT PAGE.

10. The temperature in degrees Celsius (C) can be converted to temperature in degrees Fahrenheit (F) by the formula $F = \frac{9}{5}C + 32$. What is the temperature at which $F = C$?

(A) $20°$　(B) $\left(\frac{32}{5}\right)°$　(C) $0°$

(D) $-20°$　(E) $-40°$

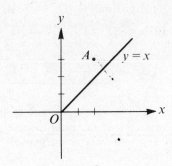

11. In the rectangular coordinate system above, the line $y = x$ is the perpendicular bisector of segment AB (not shown), and the x-axis is the perpendicular bisector of segment BC (not shown). If the coordinates of point A are $(2,3)$, what are the coordinates of point C?

(A) $(-3,-2)$
(B) $(-3, 2)$
(C) $(2,-3)$
(D) $(3,-2)$
(E) $(2, 3)$

12. If 1 kilometer is approximately 0.6 mile, which of the following best approximates the number of kilometers in 2 miles?

(A) $\frac{10}{3}$　(B) 3　(C) $\frac{6}{5}$　(D) $\frac{1}{3}$　(E) $\frac{3}{10}$

13. A \$500 investment and a \$1,500 investment have a combined yearly return of 8.5 percent of the total of the two investments. If the \$500 investment has a yearly return of 7 percent, what percent yearly return does the \$1,500 investment have?

(A)　9%

(B)　10%

(C)　$10\frac{5}{8}$%

(D)　11%

(E)　12%

GO ON TO THE NEXT PAGE.

-574-

14. A store currently charges the same price for each towel that it sells. If the current price of each towel were to be increased by $1, 10 fewer of the towels could be bought for $120, excluding sales tax. What is the current price of each towel?

(A) $1
(B) $2
(C) $3
(D) $4
(E) $12

15. If the sum of n consecutive integers is 0, which of the following must be true?

   I. n is an even number.
   II. n is an odd number.
   III. The average (arithmetic mean) of the n integers is 0.

(A) I only   (B) II only   (C) III only

(D) I and III   (E) II and III

16. In the formula $V = \dfrac{1}{(2r)^3}$, if r is halved, then V is multiplied by

(A) 64

(B) 8

(C) 1

(D) $\dfrac{1}{8}$

(E) $\dfrac{1}{64}$

17. For any integer n greater than 1, $\lfloor n$ denotes the product of all the integers from 1 to n, inclusive. How many prime numbers are there between $\lfloor 6 + 2$ and $\lfloor 6 + 6$, inclusive?

(A) None   (B) One   (C) Two
(D) Three   (E) Four

GO ON TO THE NEXT PAGE.

18. In how many arrangements can a teacher seat 3 girls and 3 boys in a row of 6 seats if the boys are to have the first, third, and fifth seats?

(A) 6   (B) 9   (C) 12   (D) 36   (E) 720

19. A circular rim 28 inches in diameter rotates the same number of inches per second as a circular rim 35 inches in diameter. If the smaller rim makes x revolutions per second, how many revolutions per minute does the larger rim make in terms of x?

(A) $\dfrac{48\pi}{x}$

(B) $75x$

(C) $48x$

(D) $24x$

(E) $\dfrac{x}{75}$

20. The cost C of manufacturing a certain product can be estimated by the formula $C = 0.03rst^2$, where r and s are the amounts, in pounds, of the two major ingredients and t is the production time, in hours. If r is increased by 50 percent, s is increased by 20 percent, and t is decreased by 30 percent, by approximately what percent will the estimated cost of manufacturing the product change?

(A) 40% increase
(B) 12% increase
(C) 4% increase
(D) 12% decrease
(E) 24% decrease

STOP

IF YOU FINISH BEFORE TIME IS CALLED, YOU MAY CHECK YOUR WORK ON THIS SECTION ONLY.
DO NOT TURN TO ANY OTHER SECTION IN THE TEST.

NO TEST MATERIAL ON THIS PAGE

SECTION 6

Time—30 minutes

23 Questions

Directions: Each passage in this group is followed by questions based on its content. After reading a passage, choose the best answer to each question and fill in the corresponding oval on the answer sheet. Answer all questions following a passage on the basis of what is stated or implied in that passage.

In 1977 the prestigious Ewha Women's University in Seoul, Korea, announced the opening of the first women's studies program in Asia. Few academic
Line programs have ever received such public attention. In
(5) broadcast debates, critics dismissed the program as a betrayal of national identity, an imitation of Western ideas, and a distraction from the real task of national unification and economic development. Even supporters underestimated the program; they thought it would be
(10) merely another of the many Western ideas that had already proved useful in Asian culture, akin to airlines, electricity, and the assembly line. The founders of the program, however, realized that neither view was correct. They had some reservations about the appli-
(15) cability of Western feminist theories to the role of women in Asia and felt that such theories should be closely examined. Their approach has thus far yielded important critiques of Western theory, informed by the special experience of Asian women.
(20)   For instance, like the Western feminist critique of the Freudian model of the human psyche, the Korean critique finds Freudian theory culture-bound, but in ways different from those cited by Western theorists. The Korean theorists claim that Freudian theory
(25) assumes the universality of the Western nuclear, male-headed family and focuses on the personality formation of the individual, independent of society. An analysis based on such assumptions could be valid for a highly competitive, individualistic society. In the Freudian
(30) family drama, family members are assumed to be engaged in a Darwinian struggle against each other—father against son and sibling against sibling. Such a concept projects the competitive model of Western society onto human personalities. But in the Asian
(35) concept of personality there is no ideal attached to indi-vidualism or to the independent self. The Western model of personality development does not explain major char-acteristics of the Korean personality, which is social and group-centered. The "self" is a social being defined by
(40) and acting in a group, and the well-being of both men and women is determined by the equilibrium of the group, not by individual self-assertion. The ideal is one of interdependency.
    In such a context, what is recognized as "depen-
(45) dency" in Western psychiatric terms is not, in Korean terms, an admission of weakness or failure. All this bears directly on the Asian perception of men's and women's psychology because men are also "dependent." In

Korean culture, men cry and otherwise easily show their
(50) emotions, something that might be considered a betrayal of masculinity in Western culture. In the kinship-based society of Korea, four generations may live in the same house, which means that people can be sons and daugh-ters all their lives, whereas in Western culture, the roles of husband and son, wife and daughter, are often incom-patible.

1. Which of the following best summarizes the content of the passage?

(A) A critique of a particular women's studies program
(B) A report of work in social theory done by a particular women's studies program
(C) An assessment of the strengths and weaknesses of a particular women's studies program
(D) An analysis of the philosophy underlying women's studies programs
(E) An abbreviated history of Korean women's studies programs

2. It can be inferred from the passage that Korean scholars in the field of women's studies undertook an analysis of Freudian theory as a response to which of the following?

(A) Attacks by critics of the Ewha women's studies program
(B) The superficiality of earlier critiques of Freudian theory
(C) The popularity of Freud in Korean psychiatric circles
(D) Their desire to encourage Korean scholars to adopt the Freudian model
(E) Their assessment of the relevance and limita-tions of Western feminist theory with respect to Korean culture

GO ON TO THE NEXT PAGE.

3. Which of the following conclusions about the introduction of Western ideas to Korean society can be
supported by information contained in the passage?

(A) Except for technological innovations, few
Western ideas have been successfully transplanted into Korean society.
(B) The introduction of Western ideas to Korean
society is viewed by some Koreans as a challenge to Korean identity.
(C) The development of the Korean economy
depends heavily on the development of new
academic programs modeled after Western
programs.
(D) The extent to which Western ideas must be
adapted for acceptance by Korean society is
minimal.
(E) The introduction of Western ideas to Korean
society accelerated after 1977.

4. It can be inferred from the passage that the broadcast media in Korea considered the establishment of
the Ewha women's studies program

(A) praiseworthy
(B) insignificant
(C) newsworthy
(D) imitative
(E) incomprehensible

5. It can be inferred from the passage that the position
taken by some of the supporters of the Ewha
women's studies program was problematic to the
founders of the program because those supporters

(A) assumed that the program would be based on
the uncritical adoption of Western theory
(B) failed to show concern for the issues of national
unification and economic development
(C) were unfamiliar with Western feminist theory
(D) were not themselves scholars in the field of
women's studies
(E) accepted the universality of Freudian theory

6. Which of the following statements is most consistent
with the view of personality development held by the
Ewha women's studies group?

(A) Personality development occurs in identifiable
stages, beginning with dependency in childhood and ending with independence in adulthood.
(B) Any theory of personality development, in
order to be valid, must be universal.
(C) Personality development is influenced by the
characteristics of the society in which a
person lives.
(D) Personality development is hindered if a person
is not permitted to be independent.
(E) No theory of personality development can
account for the differences between Korean
and Western culture.

7. Which of the following statements about the
Western feminist critique of Freudian theory can be
supported by information contained in the passage?

(A) It recognizes the influence of Western culture
on Freudian theory.
(B) It was written after 1977.
(C) It acknowledges the universality of the nuclear,
male-headed family.
(D) It challenges Freud's analysis of the role of
daughters in Western society.
(E) It fails to address the issue of competitiveness in
Western society.

8. According to the passage, critics of the Ewha
women's studies program cited the program as a
threat to which of the following?

I. National identity
II. National unification
III. Economic development
IV. Family integrity

(A) I only
(B) I and II only
(C) I, II, and III only
(D) II, III, and IV only
(E) I, II, III, and IV

GO ON TO THE NEXT PAGE.

In choosing a method for determining climatic conditions that existed in the past, paleoclimatologists invoke four principal criteria. First, the material—rocks, lakes, vegetation, etc.—on which the method relies must be
(5) widespread enough to provide plenty of information, since analysis of material that is rarely encountered will not permit correlation with other regions or with other periods of geological history. Second, in the process of formation, the material must have received an environ-
(10) mental signal that reflects a change in climate and that can be deciphered by modern physical or chemical means. Third, at least some of the material must have retained the signal unaffected by subsequent changes in the environment. Fourth, it must be possible to deter-
(15) mine the time at which the inferred climatic conditions held. This last criterion is more easily met in dating marine sediments, because dating of only a small number of layers in a marine sequence allows the age of other layers to be estimated fairly reliably by extrapola-
(20) tion and interpolation. By contrast, because sedimentation is much less continuous in continental regions, estimating the age of a continental bed from the known ages of beds above and below is more risky.

One very old method used in the investigation of past
(25) climatic conditions involves the measurement of water levels in ancient lakes. In temperate regions, there are enough lakes for correlations between them to give us a reliable picture. In arid and semiarid regions, on the other hand, the small number of lakes and the great
(30) distances between them reduce the possibilities for correlation. Moreover, since lake levels are controlled by rates of evaporation as well as by precipitation, the interpretation of such levels is ambiguous. For instance, the fact that lake levels in the semiarid southwestern United
(35) States appear to have been higher during the last ice age than they are now was at one time attributed to increased precipitation. On the basis of snow-line elevations, however, it has been concluded that the climate then was not necessarily wetter than it is now, but rather
(40) that both summers and winters were cooler, resulting in reduced evaporation.

Another problematic method is to reconstruct former climates on the basis of pollen profiles. The type of vegetation in a specific region is determined by identifying
(45) and counting the various pollen grains found there. Although the relationship between vegetation and climate is not as direct as the relationship between climate and lake levels, the method often works well in the temperate zones. In arid and semiarid regions in
(50) which there is not much vegetation, however, small changes in one or a few plant types can change the picture dramatically, making accurate correlations between neighboring areas difficult to obtain.

9. Which of the following statements about the difference between marine and continental sedimentation is supported by information in the passage?

(A) Data provided by dating marine sedimentation is more consistent with researchers' findings in other disciplines than is data provided by dating continental sedimentation.
(B) It is easier to estimate the age of a layer in a sequence of continental sedimentation than it is to estimate the age of a layer in a sequence of marine sedimentation.
(C) Marine sedimentation is much less widespread than continental sedimentation.
(D) Researchers are more often forced to rely on extrapolation when dating a layer of marine sedimentation than when dating a layer of continental sedimentation.
(E) Marine sedimentation is much more continuous than is continental sedimentation.

10. Which of the following statements best describes the organization of the passage as a whole?

(A) The author describes a method for determining past climatic conditions and then offers specific examples of situations in which it has been used.
(B) The author discusses the method of dating marine and continental sequences and then explains how dating is more difficult with lake levels than with pollen profiles.
(C) The author describes the common requirements of methods for determining past climatic conditions and then discusses examples of such methods.
(D) The author describes various ways of choosing a material for determining past climatic conditions and then discusses how two such methods have yielded contradictory data.
(E) The author describes how methods for determining past climatic conditions were first developed and then describes two of the earliest known methods.

GO ON TO THE NEXT PAGE.

11. It can be inferred from the passage that paleoclimatologists have concluded which of the following on
the basis of their study of snow-line elevations in the
southwestern United States?

(A) There is usually more precipitation during an
ice age because of increased amounts of evaporation.
(B) There was less precipitation during the last ice
age than there is today.
(C) Lake levels in the semiarid southwestern United
States were lower during the last ice age than
they are today.
(D) During the last ice age, cooler weather led to
lower lake levels than paleoclimatologists had
previously assumed.
(E) The high lake levels during the last ice age may
have been a result of less evaporation rather
than more precipitation.

12. Which of the following would be the most likely
topic for a paragraph that logically continues the
passage?

(A) The kinds of plants normally found in arid
regions
(B) The effect of variation in lake levels on pollen
distribution
(C) The material best suited to preserving signals of
climatic changes
(D) Other criteria invoked by paleoclimatologists
when choosing a method to determine past
climatic conditions
(E) A third method for investigating past climatic
conditions

13. The author discusses lake levels in the southwestern
United States in order to

(A) illustrate the mechanics of the relationship
between lake level, evaporation, and precipitation
(B) provide an example of the uncertainty involved
in interpreting lake levels
(C) prove that there are not enough ancient lakes
with which to make accurate correlations
(D) explain the effects of increased rates of evaporation on levels of precipitation
(E) suggest that snow-line elevations are invariably
more accurate than lake levels in determining
rates of precipitation at various points in the
past

14. It can be inferred from the passage that an environmental signal found in geological material would not
be useful to paleoclimatologists if it

(A) had to be interpreted by modern chemical
means
(B) reflected a change in climate rather than a long-
term climatic condition
(C) was incorporated into a material as the material
was forming
(D) also reflected subsequent environmental
changes
(E) was contained in a continental rather than a
marine sequence

15. According to the passage, the material used to determine past climatic conditions must be widespread
for which of the following reasons?

I. Paleoclimatologists need to make comparisons
between periods of geological history.
II. Paleoclimatologists need to compare materials
that have supported a wide variety of vegetation.
III. Paleoclimatologists need to make comparisons
with data collected in other regions.

(A) I only
(B) II only
(C) I and II only
(D) I and III only
(E) II and III only

16. Which of the following can be inferred from the
passage about the study of past climates in arid and
semiarid regions?

(A) It is sometimes more difficult to determine past
climatic conditions in arid and semiarid
regions than in temperate regions.
(B) Although in the past more research has been
done on temperate regions, paleoclimatologists have recently turned their attention to
arid and semiarid regions.
(C) Although more information about past climates
can be gathered in arid and semiarid than in
temperate regions, dating this information is
more difficult.
(D) It is difficult to study the climatic history of
arid and semiarid regions because their
climates have tended to vary more than those
of temperate regions.
(E) The study of past climates in arid and semiarid
regions has been neglected because temperate
regions support a greater variety of plant and
animal life.

GO ON TO THE NEXT PAGE.

Since the late 1970's, in the face of a severe loss of market share in dozens of industries, manufacturers in the United States have been trying to improve produc-
Line tivity—and therefore enhance their international
(5) competitiveness—through cost-cutting programs. (Cost-cutting here is defined as raising labor output while holding the amount of labor constant.) However, from 1978 through 1982, productivity—the value of goods manufactured divided by the amount of labor input—
(10) did not improve; and while the results were better in the business upturn of the three years following, they ran 25 percent lower than productivity improvements during earlier, post-1945 upturns. At the same time, it became clear that the harder manufacturers worked to imple-
(15) ment cost-cutting, the more they lost their competitive edge.

With this paradox in mind, I recently visited 25 companies; it became clear to me that the cost-cutting approach to increasing productivity is fundamentally
(20) flawed. Manufacturing regularly observes a "40, 40, 20" rule. Roughly 40 percent of any manufacturing-based competitive advantage derives from long-term changes in manufacturing structure (decisions about the number, size, location, and capacity of facilities) and in approaches
(25) to materials. Another 40 percent comes from major changes in equipment and process technology. The final 20 percent rests on implementing conventional cost-cutting. This rule does not imply that cost-cutting should not be tried. The well-known tools of this approach—
(30) including simplifying jobs and retraining employees to work smarter, not harder—do produce results. But the tools quickly reach the limits of what they can contribute.

Another problem is that the cost-cutting approach
(35) hinders innovation and discourages creative people. As Abernathy's study of automobile manufacturers has shown, an industry can easily become prisoner of its own investments in cost-cutting techniques, reducing its ability to develop new products. And managers under
(40) pressure to maximize cost-cutting will resist innovation because they know that more fundamental changes in processes or systems will wreak havoc with the results on which they are measured. Production managers have always seen their job as one of minimizing costs and
(45) maximizing output. This dimension of performance has until recently sufficed as a basis of evaluation, but it has created a penny-pinching, mechanistic culture in most factories that has kept away creative managers.

Every company I know that has freed itself from the
(50) paradox has done so, in part, by developing and imple-menting a manufacturing strategy. Such a strategy focuses on the manufacturing structure and on equip-ment and process technology. In one company a manu-facturing strategy that allowed different areas of the
(55) factory to specialize in different markets replaced the conventional cost-cutting approach; within three years

the company regained its competitive advantage. Together with such strategies, successful companies are also encouraging managers to focus on a wider set of
(60) objectives besides cutting costs. There is hope for manu-facturing, but it clearly rests on a different way of managing.

17. The author of the passage is primarily concerned with

(A) summarizing a thesis
(B) recommending a different approach
(C) comparing points of view
(D) making a series of predictions
(E) describing a number of paradoxes

18. It can be inferred from the passage that the manu-facturers mentioned in line 2 expected that the measures they implemented would

(A) encourage innovation
(B) keep labor output constant
(C) increase their competitive advantage
(D) permit business upturns to be more easily predicted
(E) cause managers to focus on a wider set of objectives

19. The primary function of the first paragraph of the passage is to

(A) outline in brief the author's argument
(B) anticipate challenges to the prescriptions that follow
(C) clarify some disputed definitions of economic terms
(D) summarize a number of long-accepted explana-tions
(E) present a historical context for the author's observations

20. The author refers to Abernathy's study (line 36) most probably in order to

(A) qualify an observation about one rule governing manufacturing
(B) address possible objections to a recommenda-tion about improving manufacturing compet-itiveness
(C) support an earlier assertion about one method of increasing productivity
(D) suggest the centrality in the United States economy of a particular manufacturing industry
(E) give an example of research that has questioned the wisdom of revising a manufacturing strategy

GO ON TO THE NEXT PAGE.

21. The author's attitude toward the culture in most factories is best described as

    (A) cautious
    (B) critical
    (C) disinterested
    (D) respectful
    (E) adulatory

22. In the passage, the author includes all of the following EXCEPT

    (A) personal observation
    (B) a business principle
    (C) a definition of productivity
    (D) an example of a successful company
    (E) an illustration of a process technology

23. The author suggests that implementing conventional cost-cutting as a way of increasing manufacturing competitiveness is a strategy that is

    (A) flawed and ruinous
    (B) shortsighted and difficult to sustain
    (C) popular and easily accomplished
    (D) useful but inadequate
    (E) misunderstood but promising

STOP

IF YOU FINISH BEFORE TIME IS CALLED, YOU MAY CHECK YOUR WORK ON THIS SECTION ONLY.
DO NOT TURN TO ANY OTHER SECTION IN THE TEST.

Answer Key: Form C

Section 1	Section 2	Section 3	Section 4	Section 5	Section 6
1. C	1. A	1. C	1. A	1. A	1. B
2. B	2. B	2. E	2. B	2. D	2. E
3. E	3. D	3. C	3. D	3. E	3. B
4. A	4. C	4. D	4. D	4. D	4. C
5. C	5. D	5. E	5. B	5. C	5. A
6. D	6. C	6. C	6. E	6. E	6. C
7. A	7. C	7. A	7. C	7. B	7. A
8. E	8. E	8. B	8. D	8. B	8. C
9. B	9. B	9. C	9. A	9. A	9. E
10. B	10. E	10. E	10. E	10. E	10. C
11. B	11. C	11. A	11. B	11. D	11. E
12. E	12. A	12. A	12. D	12. A	12. E
13. A	13. B	13. D	13. A	13. A	13. B
14. C	14. D	14. D	14. C	14. C	14. D
15. D	15. C	15. E	15. E	15. E	15. D
16. C	16. E	16. C	16. B	16. B	16. A
17. C	17. A	17. A	17. B	17. A	17. B
18. A	18. B	18. D	18. A	18. D	18. C
19. E	19. B	19. B	19. C	19. C	19. E
20. D	20. E	20. E	20. A	20. D	20. C
	21. E	21. C			21. B
	22. D	22. A			22. E
	23. D	23. A			23. D
	24. C	24. D			
	25. A	25. B			
	26. B				
	27. A				

Explanatory Material:
Problem Solving 1, Section 1

1. A certain fishing boat is chartered by 6 people who are to contribute equally to the total charter cost of $480. If each person contributes equally to a $150 down payment, how much of the charter cost will each person still owe?

   (A) $80 (B) $66 (C) $55 (D) $50 (E) $45

Since each person contributed equally to the $150 down payment and the total cost of the chartered boat is $480, each person still owes $\frac{\$480-\$150}{6} = \$55$. Thus, the best answer is C.

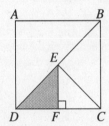

2. In square ABCD above, if DE = EB and DF = FC, then the area of the shaded region is what fraction of the area of square region ABCD ?

   (A) $\frac{1}{16}$ (B) $\frac{1}{8}$ (C) $\frac{1}{6}$ (D) $\frac{1}{4}$ (E) $\frac{1}{3}$

Since DE = EB and DF = FC, the area of the shaded region is one-fourth the area of triangular region BCD. Since BD divides square ABCD into two equal triangular regions, the shaded region is $\left(\frac{1}{2}\right)\left(\frac{1}{4}\right)$, or $\frac{1}{8}$, of the area of square region ABCD. Hence, the best answer is B.

3. Craig sells major appliances. For each appliance he sells, Craig receives a commission of $50 plus 10 percent of the selling price. During one particular week Craig sold 6 appliances for selling prices totaling $3,620. What was the total of Craig's commissions for that week?

   (A) $412 (B) $526 (C) $585
   (D) $605 (E) $662

Since Craig receives a commission of $50 on each appliance plus a 10 percent commission on total sales, his commission for that week was 6($50) + (0.1)($3,620) = $662. Thus, the best answer is E.

4. The average (arithmetic mean) of 10, 30, and 50 is 5 more than the average of 20, 40, and

   (A) 15 (B) 25 (C) 35 (D) 45 (E) 55

Since the average of 10, 30, and 50 is 30, the average of 20, 40, and some number x is 30 − 5, or 25. If the average of 20, 40, and x is 25, then the sum of the three numbers is 75, and x = 15. The best answer is A.

5. What number when multiplied by $\frac{4}{7}$ yields $\frac{6}{7}$ as the result?

   (A) $\frac{2}{7}$ (B) $\frac{2}{3}$ (C) $\frac{3}{2}$ (D) $\frac{24}{7}$ (E) $\frac{7}{2}$

If n represents the number, $\frac{4}{7}n = \frac{6}{7}$, which yields $n = \frac{3}{2}$. Thus, the best answer is C.

6. If $y = 4 + (x - 3)^2$, then y is least when x =

   (A) −4 (B) −3 (C) 0 (D) 3 (E) 4

Since the expression $(x - 3)^2$ must be greater than or equal to zero, y will be least when $(x - 3) = 0$. Therefore, the least value for y occurs when x is 3, and the best answer is D.

7. If 3 pounds of dried apricots that cost x dollars per pound are mixed with 2 pounds of prunes that cost y dollars per pound, what is the cost, in dollars, per pound of the mixture?

   (A) $\frac{3x+2y}{5}$

   (B) $\frac{3x+2y}{x+y}$

   (C) $\frac{3x+2y}{xy}$

   (D) $5(3x + 2y)$

   (E) $3x + 2y$

The total number of pounds in the mixture is 3 + 2 = 5 pounds, and the total cost of the mixture is 3x + 2y dollars. Therefore, the cost per pound of the mixture is $\frac{3x+2y}{5}$ dollars, and the best answer is A.

8. A cashier mentally reversed the digits of one customer's correct amount of change and thus gave the customer an incorrect amount of change. If the cash register contained 45 cents more than it should have as a result of this error, which of the following could have been the correct amount of change in cents?

   (A) 14 (B) 45 (C) 54 (D) 65 (E) 83

Let x represent the units' digit and y represent the tens' digit in the correct amount of change before the digits were reversed. Since the cash register contained 45 cents more than it should have, it follows that $(10x + y) - (10y + x) = 45$. Simplifying yields $9x - 9y = 45$, or $x - y = 5$, which implies that the difference in the two digits is 5. Since 83 is the only number given whose digits have a difference of 5, the best answer is E.

9. Which of the following is NOT equal to the square of an integer?

 (A) $\sqrt{\sqrt{1}}$ (B) $\sqrt{4}$ (C) $\dfrac{18}{2}$

 (D) $41 - 25$ (E) 36

In choice B, $\sqrt{4} = 2$, which is not the square of an integer. Thus, the best answer is B. It can be verified that the remaining answer choices represent the squares of 1, 3, 4, and 6, respectively.

10. An artist wishes to paint a circular region on a square poster that is 2 feet on a side. If the area of the circular region is to be $\dfrac{1}{2}$ the area of the poster, what must be the radius of the circular region in feet?

 (A) $\dfrac{1}{\pi}$ (B) $\sqrt{\dfrac{2}{\pi}}$ (C) 1 (D) $\dfrac{2}{\sqrt{\pi}}$ (E) $\dfrac{\pi}{2}$

The area of the square poster is $2^2 = 4$ square feet. Since the area of the circular region is to be $\dfrac{1}{2}$ the area of the poster, $\pi r^2 = \dfrac{1}{2}(4)$, where r is the radius of the circle. Solving the equation yields $r = \sqrt{\dfrac{2}{\pi}}$. Thus, the best answer is B.

11. Which of the following must be equal to zero for all real numbers x ?

 I. $-\dfrac{1}{x}$
 II. $x + (-x)$
 III. x^0

 (A) I only
 (B) II only
 (C) I and III only
 (D) II and III only
 (E) I, II, and III

With respect to I, $-\dfrac{1}{x}$ cannot be zero since 1 divided by any number can never be zero. With respect to II, $x + (-x)$ equals zero for all real numbers x. With respect to III, x^0 equals 1 for all nonzero real numbers x. Therefore, the best answer is B.

12. At the rate of m meters per s seconds, how many meters does a cyclist travel in x minutes?

 (A) $\dfrac{m}{sx}$ (B) $\dfrac{mx}{s}$ (C) $\dfrac{60\,m}{sx}$

 (D) $\dfrac{60\,ms}{x}$ (E) $\dfrac{60\,mx}{s}$

Since the cyclist travels $\dfrac{m}{s}$ meters per second, he travels $\dfrac{60\,m}{s}$ meters per minute. Thus, in x minutes he will travel $\dfrac{60\,mx}{s}$ meters, and the best answer is E.

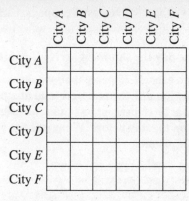

13. In the table above, what is the least number of table entries that are needed to show the mileage between each city and each of the other five cities?

 (A) 15 (B) 21 (C) 25 (D) 30 (E) 36

In the table, draw a diagonal from the upper left to the lower right corner. The entries along this diagonal should not be counted since a cell on the diagonal represents the distance from the city to itself. Because the diagonal divides the remaining cells into two equal halves, each of which would contain the same set of distances, count only the cells in one of the halves, $5 + 4 + 3 + 2 + 1 = 15$. Hence, the best answer is A.

14. A certain tax rate is $0.82 per $100.00. What is this rate, expressed as a percent?

 (A) 82% (B) 8.2% (C) 0.82%
 (D) 0.082% (E) 0.0082%

The tax rate $0.82 per $100.00 can be written as the fraction $\dfrac{\$\,0.82}{\$100.00} = 0.82\%$. The best answer is C.

15. Fermat primes are prime numbers that can be written in the form $2^k + 1$, where k is an integer and a power of 2. Which of the following is NOT a Fermat prime?

 (A) 3 (B) 5 (C) 17 (D) 31 (E) 257

Since Fermat primes can be written in the form $2^k + 1$, where k is an integer and a power of 2, check each answer choice to find the number that cannot be so expressed.

$$3 = 2^1 + 1, \text{ where } k = 1 = 2^0$$
$$5 = 2^2 + 1, \text{ where } k = 2 = 2^1$$
$$17 = 2^4 + 1, \text{ where } k = 4 = 2^2$$
$$31 = 30 + 1, \text{ but } 30 \text{ cannot be expressed as an integer}$$
$$\text{power of 2}$$
$$257 = 2^8 + 1, \text{ where } k = 8 = 2^3$$

Thus, the best answer is D.

16. A shipment of 1,500 heads of cabbage, each of which was approximately the same size, was purchased for $600. The day the shipment arrived, $\frac{2}{3}$ of the heads were sold, each at 25 percent above the cost per head. The following day the rest were sold at a price per head equal to 10 percent less than the price each head sold for on the day before. What was the gross profit on this shipment?

(A) $100 (B) $115 (C) $125
(D) $130 (E) $135

The cost of a head of cabbage was $\frac{\$600.00}{1,500} = \$0.40$. Since the selling price of a head of cabbage on the day the shipment arrived was $(1.25)(\$0.40) = \$0.50$, the revenue for the first day was $\frac{2}{3}(1,500)(\$0.50) = \$500.00$. On the second day the remaining cabbage heads were sold at a selling price of $(0.9)(\$0.50) = \$0.45$ per head, which yields $\frac{1}{3}(1,500)(\$0.45) = \$225.00$ in revenue. The gross profit for the shipment was $\$500.00 + \$225.00 - \$600.00 = \$125.00$. Thus, the best answer is C.

17. If $(t - 8)$ is a factor of $t^2 - kt - 48$, then $k =$

(A) -6 (B) -2 (C) 2 (D) 6 (E) 14

If $(t - 8)$ is a factor of the expression $t^2 - kt - 48$, then the expression can be written as the product $(t - 8)(t + a)$. When multiplying this product, $(-8)(a) = -48$, or $a = 6$. Thus, the product becomes $(t - 8)(t + 6)$, which has the middle term $6t - 8t = -2t$. Therefore, $k = 2$, and the best answer is C.

18. If a is a positive integer, and if the units' digit of a^2 is 9 and the units' digit of $(a + 1)^2$ is 4, what is the units' digit of $(a + 2)^2$?

(A) 1 (B) 3 (C) 5 (D) 7 (E) 9

If 9 is the units' digit of a^2, then either 3 or 7 must be the units' digit of a, since only numbers ending in 3 or 7 would yield a units' digit of 9 when squared. Then $a + 1$ must have a units' digit of either $3 + 1$ or $7 + 1$. But if 4 were the units' digit of $a + 1$, then $(a + 1)^2$ would have units' digit 6 instead of 4 as given. Therefore, the units' digit of $a + 1$ must be 8, which implies that the units' digit of $a + 2$ would have to be $8 + 1 = 9$. Since the units' digit of 9^2 is 1, the units digit of $(a + 2)^2$ must be 1. Thus, the best answer is A.

19. The ratio, by volume, of soap to alcohol to water in a certain solution is 2 : 50 : 100. The solution will be altered so that the ratio of soap to alcohol is doubled while the ratio of soap to water is halved. If the altered solution will contain 100 cubic centimeters of alcohol, how many cubic centimeters of water will it contain?

(A) 50 (B) 200 (C) 400 (D) 625 (E) 800

Originally the ratio of soap to alcohol to water was 2:50:100. When the ratio 2:50 is doubled, the new ratio will be 4:50; when the ratio 2:100 is halved, the new ratio will be 1:100 or 4:400. Thus, the ratio of soap to alcohol to water will be 4:50:400. Since 100 cubic centimeters represents the 50 parts of alcohol in the new solution, 800 cubic centimeters will represent the 400 parts of water in the solution. Thus, the best answer is E.

20. If 75 percent of a class answered the first question on a certain test correctly, 55 percent answered the second question on the test correctly, and 20 percent answered neither of the questions correctly, what percent answered **both** correctly?

(A) 10% (B) 20% (C) 30%
(D) 50% (E) 65%

For questions of this type, it is convenient to draw a Venn diagram to represent the conditions in the problem. For example:

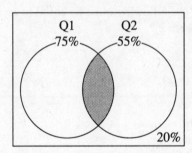

Now it is clear that the two circles represent 80 percent of the students. If x is the percent corresponding to the shaded region (the percent who answered both questions correctly), then $75\% + 55\% - x = 80\%$, and $x = 50\%$. Thus, the best answer is D.

Alternatively, if 75 percent of the class answered the first question correctly and 20 percent of the class answered both questions incorrectly, then 5 percent of the class answered the second question correctly but the first incorrectly. Since 55 percent of the class answered the second question correctly, the percent who answered both questions correctly is $55\% - 5\% = 50\%$.

Explanatory Material: Sentence Correction, Section 2

1. The Baldrick Manufacturing Company has for several years followed a policy aimed at decreasing operating costs and improving the efficiency of its distribution system.

   (A) aimed at decreasing operating costs and improving
   (B) aimed at the decreasing of operating costs and to improve
   (C) aiming at the decreasing of operating costs and improving
   (D) the aim of which is the decreasing of operating costs and improving
   (E) with the aim to decrease operating costs and to improve

The best choice, A, offers an adjective phrase unequivocally modifying *policy* and exhibiting grammatical parallelism (*decreasing . . .* and *improving*). In choice B, the gerund *the decreasing* is not grammatically parallel with the infinitive *to improve*. Likewise, in C and D, *the decreasing of . . . costs* is not parallel with *improving the efficiency*. In E, the infinitives *to decrease* and *to improve*, while parallel, are less idiomatic than the prepositional phrase *of decreasing . . . and improving* in modifying the noun *aim*. Also, *with the aim . . . improve* can easily be construed as referring to the Baldrick Manufacturing Company and so does not refer unequivocally to *policy*.

2. *The Federalist* papers, a strong defense of the United States Constitution and important as a body of work in political science as well, represents the handiwork of three different authors.

   (A) and important as a body of work in political science as well, represents
   (B) as well as an important body of work in political science, represent
   (C) and also a body of work of importance in political science is representing
   (D) an important body of work in political science and has been representative of
   (E) and as political science an important body of work too, represent

Choices A, C, and D contain singular verbs that do not agree in number with the plural subject, *papers*. Furthermore, A violates parallelism by aligning the adjective *important* with the noun *defense*; C, employing the present progressive tense, wrongly suggests that the triple authorship of *The Federalist* papers is a developing situation rather than an accomplished fact; and D, employing the present perfect tense, suggests that the situation of triple authorship is no longer the case. D is also garbled syntactically because the conjunction *and* has been misplaced. In E, the wording is awkward. Choice B is best.

3. Although the term "psychopath" is popularly applied to an especially brutal criminal, in psychology it is someone who is apparently incapable of feeling compassion or the pangs of conscience.

   (A) it is someone who is
   (B) it is a person
   (C) they are people who are
   (D) it refers to someone who is
   (E) it is in reference to people

In choices A and B, the pronoun *it* simultaneously refers forward to *someone* (or a *person*) and backward to the term "*psychopath*." As a result, the sentence asserts illogically that the term is actually a kind of person rather than a word referring to a kind of person. Choice C repeats this fault and adds an error in agreement: *they* (plural) does not agree in number with *the term* (singular). E omits a main verb, such as *applied*, that, in grammatical context here, is required after *is*. Also, the word *people* incorrectly shifts number from singular to plural. In choice D, the best answer, the verb *refers* is correctly used after *it*, and the alignment of pronouns and antecedents is both logical and grammatical.

4. A representative of the Women's Bureau of the United States Department of Labor contends that employers who offer benefits which permit that employees can balance home and work responsibilities better, realizing gains in attendance, recruiting, and retention.

   (A) which permit that employees can balance home and work responsibilities better, realizing
   (B) which permit employees balancing home and work responsibilities better will realize
   (C) that permit employees to balance the responsibilities of home and work better will realize
   (D) that permit employees a better balance between the responsibilities of home and work, thus realizing
   (E) such that employees are permitted a balance between home and work responsibilities, and they will realize

Choices A and D ungrammatically substitute the participle *realizing* for *will realize* in the sequence *employers* (subject) *will realize* (verb) *gains* (object). The resulting statement, illogical as well as ungrammatical, suggests that employees, not their employers, stand to realize gains. Choice E ungrammatically makes *they*, a pronoun of ambiguous reference, subject of *will realize*: *employers* now has no verb. Another group of errors involves the restrictive clause modifying *benefits*. In A, the use of *that employees . . . better* as object of *permit* is unidiomatic; in B, the participial phrase *balancing . . . better* unintentionally and inappropriately modifies *employees*; in E, *such that* is clumsy; and finally, usage experts generally prefer *that* (C and D) over *which* (A and B) for introducing restrictive clauses. Choice C, the best answer, is idiomatic, grammatical, and clear.

5. Parliament did not accord full refugee benefits to twelve of the recent immigrants because it believed that to do it rewards them for entering the country illegally.

   (A) to do it rewards
   (B) doing it rewards
   (C) to do this would reward
   (D) doing so would reward
   (E) to do it would reward

Choice D, the best answer, appropriately uses the adverb *so* to refer back to the verb *accord*. The other choices inappropriately use pronouns (*it* or *this*) to refer back to the verb. Also, A and B use the indicative verb *rewards*, whereas the logic of the sentence demands the conditional *would reward* (what Parliament believes to be the undue rewarding of illegal immigrants has not actually taken place but is considered only as an outcome of a hypothetical action).

6. Many policy experts say that shifting a portion of health-benefit costs back to the workers helps to control the employer's costs, but also helps to limit medical spending by making patients more careful consumers.

   (A) helps to control the employer's costs, but also helps
   (B) helps the control of the employer's costs, and also
   (C) not only helps to control the employer's costs, but also helps
   (D) helps to control not only the employer's costs, but
   (E) not only helps to control the employer's costs, and also helps

To convey the idea that shifting a portion of health-benefit costs back to workers has two complementary effects, the correct sentence must link grammatically parallel statements of these effects with *and also* or with *not only . . . but also*. In choice A, *helps . . . but also* undermines the *and also* paradigm, wrongly suggesting a contrast in the effects. In choice E, the unidiomatic *not only . . . and* violates the *not only . . . but also* paradigm. Choices B and D are not parallel. Also, the phrase *helps the control* in B is vague and unidiomatic. Choice C, the best answer, develops the parallel *not only helps to . . . but also helps to*.

7. The plot of *The Bostonians* centers on the rivalry between Olive Chancellor, an active feminist, with her charming and cynical cousin, Basil Ransom, when they find themselves drawn to the same radiant young woman whose talent for public speaking has won her an ardent following.

   (A) rivalry between Olive Chancellor, an active feminist, with her charming and cynical cousin, Basil Ransom
   (B) rivals Olive Chancellor, an active feminist, against her charming and cynical cousin, Basil Ransom
   (C) rivalry that develops between Olive Chancellor, an active feminist, and Basil Ransom, her charming and cynical cousin
   (D) developing rivalry between Olive Chancellor, an active feminist, with Basil Ransom, her charming and cynical cousin
   (E) active feminist, Olive Chancellor, and the rivalry with her charming and cynical cousin Basil Ransom

The enumeration of the rivals requires the conjunction *and*: either *the rivalry between x and y* or *the rivals x and y*. Choices A and D wrongly substitute *with* for *and* in the first paradigm; choice B wrongly substitutes *against* for *and* in the second. Choice E does not clearly state that Chancellor is party to the rivalry. E also awkwardly pairs *Chancellor* and *rivalry*, not *Chancellor* and *Ransom*, as antecedents of *they*. Choice C, the best answer, correctly uses the *between x and y* paradigm and clearly and unequivocally identifies both parties in the rivalry.

8. Despite protests from some waste-disposal companies, state health officials have ordered the levels of bacteria in seawater at popular beaches to be measured and that the results be published.

   (A) the levels of bacteria in seawater at popular beaches to be measured and that the results be
   (B) that seawater at popular beaches should be measured for their levels of bacteria, with the results being
   (C) the measure of levels of bacteria in seawater at popular beaches and the results to be
   (D) seawater measured at popular beaches for levels of bacteria, with their results
   (E) that the levels of bacteria in seawater at popular beaches be measured and the results

In this sentence, English idiom requires one of two paradigms: *x ordered y to be z'ed* or *x ordered that y be z'ed*. Choice E, the best answer, employs the second of these paradigms. Choice A mixes the two paradigms (*levels . . . to be measured* and *that the results be published*), producing a sentence that lacks parallelism. C and D use neither paradigm and are thus unidiomatic. Also, in D, the pronoun *their* has no logical and grammatical antecedent. Choice B unidiomatically employs the verb *should* (not in either paradigm); also, the pronoun *their* does not agree in number with *seawater*, its most logical antecedent.

9. **While larger banks can afford to maintain their own data-processing operations, many smaller regional and community banks are finding that the cost associated with upgrading data-processing equipment and with the development and maintenance of new products and technical staff are prohibitive.**

   (A) cost associated with
   (B) costs associated with
   (C) costs arising from
   (D) cost of
   (E) costs of

The correct option must offer a noun that agrees in number with the plural verb *are*, the second-to-last word in the sentence, to produce the grammatical sequence *costs . . . are prohibitive*. Also, the best answer will use the preposition *with* to complete the parallel construction *costs associated with upgrading . . . and with the development . . . .* Choice B, the best answer, is the only option that meets both requirements.

10. **For almost a hundred years after having its beginning in 1788, England exiled some 160,000 criminals to Australia.**

    (A) For almost a hundred years after having its beginning in 1788,
    (B) Beginning in 1788 for a period of a hundred years,
    (C) Beginning a period of almost a hundred years in 1788,
    (D) During a hundred years, a period beginning in 1788,
    (E) Over a period of a hundred years beginning in 1788,

Aside from being wordy and awkward, choice A is illogical: because *its* refers grammatically to *England*, A states nonsensically that England had *its beginning in 1788*. Choice B is similarly illogical, because the initial verb phrase *Beginning in 1788 . . .* modifies *England*, the subject of the main clause. Choice C is imprecise, saying that England in 1788 was *Beginning a period . . .* but not conveying the sense that anything happened within that period. Choice D is awkward and unidiomatic, and nonsensically suggests that *a hundred years* is defined as *a period beginning in 1788*. Precise and idiomatically phrased, choice E is best.

11. **Eating saltwater fish may significantly reduce the risk of heart attacks and also aid for sufferers of rheumatoid arthritis and asthma, according to three research studies published in the *New England Journal of Medicine*.**

    (A) significantly reduce the risk of heart attacks and also aid for
    (B) be significant in reducing the risk of heart attacks and aid for
    (C) significantly reduce the risk of heart attacks and aid
    (D) cause a significant reduction in the risk of heart attacks and aid to
    (E) significantly reduce the risk of heart attacks as well as aiding

Choices A, B, and D each produce a clearly unintended meaning: by using *aid* as a noun rather than a verb, each creates a misleading parallel with the noun *risk* so that the sentences nonsensically state that eating saltwater fish may reduce *aid* as well as *risk*. In addition, B and D are wordy and awkward. Choice C, the best answer, avoids the prepositions *for* (from A and B) and *to* (from D), instead using *aid* as a verb that is parallel with *reduce*. Choice E lacks the grammatical parallelism of *may reduce . . . and aid*, the compound verb in C.

12. **By a vote of 9 to 0, the Supreme Court awarded the Central Intelligence Agency broad discretionary powers enabling it to withhold from the public the identities of its sources of intelligence information.**

    (A) enabling it to withhold from the public
    (B) for it to withhold from the public
    (C) for withholding disclosure to the public of
    (D) that enable them to withhold from public disclosure
    (E) that they can withhold public disclosure of

Choice A is best: *enabling . . .* clearly modifies *powers*, *it* refers logically and grammatically to *the Central Intelligence Agency*, and *to withhold from the public* is concisely and idiomatically phrased. In choices B and C, the preposition *for* is used unidiomatically in place of the "-ing" modifier to introduce the phrase describing *powers*. In choices C, D, and E, *withhold(ing) . . . disclosure* is wordy and imprecise, since it is really *the identities* that are to be withheld. The plural pronouns *them* in D and *they* in E do not agree with the singular *Agency*, and *that* in E mistakenly introduces a new independent clause rather than a modifying phrase for *powers*.

13. As business grows more complex, students <u>majoring in specialized areas like those of finance and marketing have been becoming increasingly</u> successful in the job market.

   (A) majoring in specialized areas like those of finance and marketing have been becoming increasingly
   (B) who major in such specialized areas as finance and marketing are becoming more and more
   (C) who majored in specialized areas such as those of finance and marketing are being increasingly
   (D) who major in specialized areas like those of finance and marketing have been becoming more and more
   (E) having majored in such specialized areas as finance and marketing are being increasingly

The phrase *As business grows more complex* introduces an ongoing condition that is leading to consequences described in the rest of the sentence. Those consequences should, like the causal condition, be expressed with simple present-tense or present progressive verb forms. Only choice B, the best answer, consistently employs these forms: *who major . . . and . . . are becoming*. In A and D, the use of *like* rather than *such as* is incorrect: *like* makes a comparison; *such as* introduces examples. In A, C, and D, *those of* is unnecessary verbiage, and *being* in C and E is less precise than *becoming* for describing a pattern of events that is unfolding.

14. Inuits of the Bering Sea were <u>in isolation from contact with Europeans longer than</u> Aleuts or Inuits of the North Pacific and northern Alaska.

   (A) in isolation from contact with Europeans longer than
   (B) isolated from contact with Europeans longer than
   (C) in isolation from contact with Europeans longer than were
   (D) isolated from contact with Europeans longer than were
   (E) in isolation and without contacts with Europeans longer than

The phrasing of the comparisons in choices A, B, and E is incomplete, so the comparisons are ambiguous: because *longer than* could be followed by either *from* or *were*, it is unclear whether Inuits of the Bering Sea were isolated from Europeans longer than from the other Native American groups, or whether they were isolated from Europeans longer than the other groups were. In A and C, *in isolation from contact* is wordy and unidiomatic. The awkward phrasing of E further distorts the sense of the sentence: because *with* cannot idiomatically serve as the preposition for *in isolation*, the sentence suggests that the Bering Sea Inuits were totally isolated. Choice D is best: it employs concise, idiomatic phrasing to express a logically complete comparison.

15. Once the economic and social usefulness of the motor car was demonstrated <u>and with its superiority to the horse being</u> proved, much of the early hostility to it in rural regions disappeared.

   (A) and with its superiority to the horse being
   (B) and its superiority over the horse had been
   (C) and its superiority to the horse
   (D) its superiority over the horse
   (E) with its superiority to the horse having been

In choice C, the best answer, the main predication *usefulness . . . was demonstrated* is paralleled by *superiority* [*was*] *proved*, with [*was*] omitted as understood. In choices A and E, the prepositional phrase beginning *with . . .* violates this parallelism; in A, B, and E, the verb forms *being*, *had been*, and *having been* are not consistent with the simple past tense in *was demonstrated*. The phrase *superiority over* is unidiomatic in B and D: *x* is superior *to y*, not *over y*. D is also faulty because no function word, such as the conjunction *and*, grammatically connects *its superiority . . .* to the rest of the sentence.

16. Minnesota is the only one of the contiguous forty-eight states <u>that still has a sizable wolf population, and where</u> this predator remains the archenemy of cattle and sheep.

   (A) that still has a sizable wolf population, and where
   (B) that still has a sizable wolf population, where
   (C) that still has a sizable population of wolves, and where
   (D) where the population of wolves is still sizable;
   (E) where there is still a sizable population of wolves and where

In choices A and C, the construction *that still has . . . , and where* modifies *Minnesota* with clauses that are not grammatically parallel. In choice B, the omission of *and* illogically makes the *where . . .* clause modify *wolf population* rather than *Minnesota* — that is, choice B says in effect that the wolf population is where the wolf remains the archenemy of cattle and sheep. Choice D is grammatically constructed, but it lacks a conjunction that establishes a logical relation between the clauses; since *Minnesota* as a grammatical subject is separated from the clause following the semicolon, the statement there need not even pertain to Minnesota. In E, the best choice, the parallel construction of *where . . . and where . . .* allows both clauses to modify *Minnesota*.

17. Pablo Picasso, the late Spanish painter, credited African art <u>with having had</u> a strong influence on his work.

   (A) with having had
   (B) for its having
   (C) to have had
   (D) for having
   (E) in that it had

Choice A is the best. In this sentence, where *credit(ed)* is used as a verb, the idiom in English is to *credit* something *with* having had some effect. Thus only choice A is idiomatic. Both *for* (in B and D) and *to* (in C) can be used idiomatically when *credit* is a noun, as in "Picasso gave credit <u>to</u> African art <u>for</u> having had a strong influence on his work." The verb form *having had* is used appropriately in choice A to indicate action that occurred prior to action expressed in the simple past tense — that is, to indicate that African art had influenced Picasso before he credited it with having done so.

18. Judicial rules in many states require <u>that the identities of all prosecution witnesses are made known to defendents so they can attempt to rebut</u> the testimony, but the Constitution explicitly requires only that the defendant have the opportunity to confront an accuser in court.

    (A) that the identities of all prosecution witnesses are made known to defendants so they can attempt to rebut
    (B) that the identities of all prosecution witnesses be made known to defendants so that they can attempt to rebut
    (C) that the defendants should know the identities of all prosecution witnesses so they can attempt a rebuttal of
    (D) the identities of all prosecution witnesses should be made known to defendants so they can attempt rebutting
    (E) making known to defendants the identities of all prosecution witnesses so that they can attempt to rebut

In English the subjunctive mood is used to express a wish or requirement that a certain course of action be taken. Such phrasing takes the form *to wish* [or] *require that x be y*, not *that x should be y* or *that x is y*. Choice B, therefore, is best. In place of the subjunctive, A uses the indicative *are* and E uses an awkward gerund, *making*, while C and D contain the unnecessary *should*. A and C also omit *that* after *so*, and D omits *that* after *require*. The phrase *attempt to rebut* is more idiomatic than the phrases that replace it in C and D. Choices C and E awkwardly place the plural noun *witnesses* between the plural pronoun *they* and its referent, *defendants*.

19. Quasars, at billions of light-years from Earth the most distant observable objects in the universe, <u>believed to be</u> the cores of galaxies in an early stage of development.

    (A) believed to be
    (B) are believed to be
    (C) some believe them to be
    (D) some believe they are
    (E) it is believed that they are

Only B, the best answer, supplies a verb that grammatically connects *Quasars* and *cores*: *Quasars . . . are believed to be the cores . . . .* Choice A produces a sentence fragment because

it omits the verb *are* and supplies only an adjectival phrase, *believed to be . . . .* Choices C, D, and E all introduce new clauses (*some believe . . . , it is believed . . . .*) that cannot grammatically complete the construction begun with *Quasars*.

20. The colorization of black-and-white films by computers is defended by those who own the film rights, for the process can mean increased revenues for them; many others in the film industry, however, contend that the technique degrades major works of art, <u>which they liken to putting lipstick on a Greek statue.</u>

    (A) which they liken to putting lipstick on a Greek statue
    (B) which they liken to a Greek statue with lipstick put on it
    (C) which they liken to lipstick put on a Greek statue
    (D) likening it to a Greek statue with lipstick put on it
    (E) likening it to putting lipstick on a Greek statue

Choice E, the best answer, correctly and logically compares *the technique* of colorization to the act of *putting lipstick on a Greek statue*. In A, B, and C, the relative pronoun *which* refers not to *the technique* but to the noun phrase immediately preceding it, *major works of art*. As a result, these works are compared to *putting lipstick on . . .* in A, to *a Greek statue* in B, and to *lipstick* in C. Choice D corrects this problem by eliminating the *which* construction and supplying the pronoun *it*, thus referring clearly to *the technique*, but it illogically compares *the technique* to *a Greek statue*.

21. <u>In reference to the current hostility toward smoking, smokers frequently expressed anxiety that</u> their prospects for being hired and promoted are being stunted by their habit.

    (A) In reference to the current hostility toward smoking, smokers frequently expressed anxiety that
    (B) Referring to the current hostility toward smoking, smokers frequently expressed anxiety about
    (C) When referring to the current hostility toward smoking, smokers frequently express anxiety about
    (D) With reference to the current hostility toward smoking, smokers frequently expressed anxiety about
    (E) Referring to the current hostility toward smoking, smokers frequently express anxiety that

Choices A, B, and D inappropriately use the past tense verb *expressed*; only the present tense is logical here, since both the *current hostility* to which the *smokers* refer and the anxiety described in the clause *their prospects . . . are being stunted* clearly apply to the present. Furthermore, B, C, and D produce ungrammatical sentences by introducing this clause with the preposition *about*; the conjunction *that* is required to link *anxiety* with the clause that modifies it. Choice E, the best answer, correctly uses both the conjunction *that* and the present-tense verb *express*.

22. **Ms. Chambers is among the forecasters who predict that the rate of addition to arable lands will drop while those of loss rise.**

   (A) those of loss rise
   (B) it rises for loss
   (C) those of losses rise
   (D) the rate of loss rises
   (E) there are rises for the rate of loss

Choice D, the best answer, uses the idiomatic and clear construction *the rate of addition . . . will drop while the rate of loss rises*. All of the other choices use incorrect, illogical, or imprecise constructions in place of *the rate of loss rises*. In A and C, the plural pronoun *those* has no plural noun to which it can logically refer. In B, *it* refers to *the rate of addition*; consequently, B makes the nonsensical statement that *the rate of addition . . . rises for loss*. Choice E supplies the idiomatic *the rate of loss* but introduces it with the unidiomatic and wordy *there are rises for*.

23. **Unlike auto insurance, the frequency of claims does not affect the premiums for personal property coverage, but if the insurance company is able to prove excessive loss due to owner negligence, it may decline to renew the policy.**

   (A) Unlike auto insurance, the frequency of claims does not affect the premiums for personal property coverage
   (B) Unlike with auto insurance, the frequency of claims do not affect the premiums for personal property coverage
   (C) Unlike the frequency of claims for auto insurance, the premiums for personal property coverage are not affected by the frequency of claims
   (D) Unlike the premiums for auto insurance, the premiums for personal property coverage are not affected by the frequency of claims
   (E) Unlike with the premiums for auto insurance, the premiums for personal property coverage is not affected by the frequency of claims

Choice D, the best answer, correctly and clearly compares *the premiums for auto insurance* and *the premiums for personal property coverage*. Choices A and C fail to express this comparison: A illogically compares *auto insurance* and *the frequency of claims*, and C illogically compares *the frequency of claims* and *premiums*. *Unlike with* in choices B and E is an unidiomatic form of comparison. In B, the plural *do not affect* fails to agree with *frequency*; in E, the singular *is* does not agree with *premiums*.

24. **Recently implemented "shift-work equations" based on studies of the human sleep cycle have reduced sickness, sleeping on the job, fatigue among shift workers, and have raised production efficiency in various industries.**

   (A) fatigue among shift workers, and have raised
   (B) fatigue among shift workers, and raised
   (C) and fatigue among shift workers while raising
   (D) lowered fatigue among shift workers, and raised
   (E) and fatigue among shift workers was lowered while raising

The best answer, C, grammatically states that the *equations . . . have reduced x, y, and z* and have raised *efficiency*. Choices A and B fail to use *and* to signal that *fatigue among shift workers* completes the series begun by *have reduced*, and so produce awkward and unclear sentences. Both D and E fail to use *and* to introduce the last item in the list, which is *sleeping* in these constructions. In E, *while raising* has no logical referent, producing only the absurd statement that *fatigue* has raised efficiency.

25. **The physical structure of the human eye enables it to sense light of wavelengths up to 0.0005 millimeters; infrared radiation, however, is invisible because its wavelength — 0.1 millimeters — is too long to be registered by the eye.**

   (A) infrared radiation, however, is invisible because its wavelength — 0.1 millimeters — is too long to be registered by the eye
   (B) however, the wavelength of infrared radiation — 0.1 millimeters — is too long to be registered by the eye making it invisible
   (C) infrared radiation, however, is invisible because its wavelength — 0.1 millimeters — is too long for the eye to register it
   (D) however, because the wavelength of infrared radiation is 0.1 millimeters, it is too long for the eye to register and thus invisible
   (E) however, infrared radiation has a wavelength of 0.1 millimeters that is too long for the eye to register, thus making it invisible

Choice A, the best answer, is clear, idiomatic, and grammatically correct. In B, the misplaced participial phrase *making it invisible* modifies *eye* rather than *wavelength*, thus producing a confusing statement that distorts the meaning. In C, D, and E the use of the second *it* is so imprecise as to be confusing. Furthermore, in D, *and thus invisible* incorrectly modifies wavelength rather than *infrared radiation*. Choice E produces an illogical statement by using a restrictive clause introduced by *that* where a comma followed by the nonrestrictive "which" is required: *a wavelength of 0.1 millimeters that is too long* nonsensically suggests that not all wavelengths *of 0.1 millimeters* are *too long for the eye to register*.

26. Spanning more than fifty years, Friedrich <u>Müller</u> <u>began his career in an unpromising apprenticeship as</u> a Sanskrit scholar and culminated in virtually every honor that European governments and learned societies could bestow.

(A) Müller began his career in an unpromising apprenticeship as
(B) Müller's career began in an unpromising apprenticeship as
(C) Müller's career began with the unpromising apprenticeship of being
(D) Müller had begun his career with the unpromising apprenticeship of being
(E) the career of Müller has begun with an unpromising apprenticeship of

The best answer, B, uses the logical and grammatically correct construction, *Spanning more than fifty years, Friedrich Müller's career began . . . and culminated.* Note that the noun phrase appearing after the comma is modified by *Spanning* and serves as the subject of *began* and *culminated.* Choice A produces an illogical statement by placing *Friedrich Müller* in this subject position. Choice C corrects this error but produces an unidiomatic construction by using *apprenticeship of being* instead of *apprenticeship as.* Choice D repeats both this error and the subject error of A. D and E needlessly change the simple past tense *began* to the past perfect *had begun* and the present perfect *has begun*, respectively, and E uses *apprenticeship of*, which is unidiomatic in this context.

27. The Coast Guard is conducting tests <u>to see whether pigeons can be trained to help find</u> survivors of wrecks at sea.

(A) to see whether pigeons can be trained to help find
(B) to see whether pigeons can be trained as help to find
(C) to see if pigeons can be trained for helping to find
(D) that see if pigeons are able to be trained in helping to find
(E) that see whether pigeons are able to be trained for help in finding

Choice A, the best answer, idiomatically expresses the idea of purpose by using the infinitives *to see* and *to help*: the purpose of the tests is *to see whether pigeons can be trained*, and the purpose of training them is *to help find survivors.* The other choices all produce constructions that are used unidiomatically with *trained*: *as help to find* in B, *for helping to find* in C, *in helping to find* in D, and *for help in finding* in E. In C and D, *whether* would be preferable to *if* in presenting the situation as possible rather than conditional or hypothetical. In D and E, *tests that see* is imprecise, because it is the Coast Guard that will see whether pigeons can be trained.

Explanatory Material: Data Sufficiency, Section 3

1. If Hans purchased a pair of skis and a ski jacket, what was the cost of the skis?

(A) The ratio of the cost of the skis to the cost of the jacket was 5 to 1.
(2) The total cost of the skis and the jacket was $360.

Statement (1) alone is not sufficient because only the relative cost of the skis and jacket is given; there is no information about dollar costs. Thus, the answer must be B, C, or E. Statement (2) alone is not sufficient since it does not give information about the relative cost of the jacket and the skis. Hence, the answer must be C or E. From (1) and (2) together, if x is the cost of the jacket, then $5x$ is the cost of the skis and $5x + x = 360$. Because this equation can be solved for x, the best answer is C.

2. Is $x < y$?

(1) $z < y$
(2) $z < x$

Since statement (1) gives no information about x and statement (2) gives no information about y, neither statement alone is sufficient, and the answer must be C or E. From (1) and (2) together, it can be determined only that z is less than either x or y. Since x can be greater than, equal to, or less than y, the best answer is E.

3. If a certain city is losing 12 percent of its daily water supply each day because of water-main breaks, what is the dollar cost to the city per day for this loss?

(1) The city's daily water supply is 350 million gallons.
(2) The cost to the city for each 12,000 gallons of water lost is $2.

In order to solve this problem, the cost of the water and the number of gallons in the daily water supply must be known. Statement (1) gives the daily water supply, which is not sufficient by itself, and statement (2) gives the cost of water, which also is not sufficient by itself. Thus, the answer must be C or E. From both statements together, it can be concluded that the dollar cost for the water lost is $\dfrac{0.12\,(350{,}000{,}000)\times \$2}{12{,}000}$. The best answer is C.

4. Machine X runs at a constant rate and produces a lot consisting of 100 cans in 2 hours. How much less time would it take to produce the lot of cans if both machines X and Y were run simultaneously?

(1) Both machines X and Y produce the same number of cans per hour.
(2) It takes machine X twice as long to produce the lot of cans as it takes machines X and Y running simultaneously to produce the lot.

-595-

Since the problem states that the job is to produce 100 cans and machine X can do it in 2 hours, the only information needed to answer the question is either the rate for machine Y or the time for X and Y together. Statement (1) says that the rate for Y is the same as that for X, which is given; so the answer must be A or D. From statement (2) alone, it can be determined that X and Y together take 1 hour, since the rate for X is twice that for X and Y running simultaneously. Thus each statement alone is sufficient, and the best answer is D.

5. If x and y are positive, what is the value of x ?

   (1) 200 percent of x equals 400 percent of y.
   (2) xy is the square of a positive integer.

From statement (1) alone, it can only be determined that $x = 2y$. Since this equation has an infinite number of solutions, the answer must be B, C, or E. From statement (2) alone, it can only be determined that $xy = k^2$, where k is a positive integer. This equation has an infinite number of solutions. If (1) and (2) are taken together, the two equations in three unknowns cannot be solved for a unique value of x. The best answer is E.

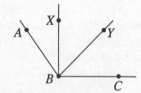

6. In the figure above, what is the measure of $\angle ABC$?

   (1) BX bisects $\angle ABY$ and BY bisects $\angle XBC$.
   (2) The measure of $\angle ABX$ is 40°.

From statement (1) alone it can be determined that $\angle ABX$, $\angle XBY$, and $\angle YBC$ are equal in measure, but the measure of $\angle ABC$ cannot be determined. Therefore, the answer must be B, C, or E. Statement (2) alone is also not sufficient since it gives no information about the measure of $\angle XBC$. Therefore, the answer must be C or E. From (1) and (2) together, it can be determined that the measure of $\angle ABX =$ the measure of $\angle XBY =$ the measure of $\angle YBC = 40°$, so $\angle ABC$ measures $3(40) = 120$ degrees. Thus, the best answer is C.

7. If $-10 < k < 10$, is $k > 0$?

   (1) $\dfrac{1}{k} > 0$
   (2) $k^2 > 0$

Statement (1) alone is sufficient since k must be a positive number if its reciprocal $\dfrac{1}{k}$ is positive; so the answer must be A or D. Statement (2) alone is not sufficient since it permits k to be either positive or negative. The best answer is A.

	R	S	T	U
R	0	y	x	62
S	y	0	56	75
T	x	56	0	69
U	62	75	69	0

8. The table above shows the distance, in kilometers, by the most direct route, between any two of the four cities, R, S, T, and U. For example, the distance between City R and City U is 62 kilometers. What is the value of x ?

   (1) By the most direct route, the distance between S and T is twice the distance between S and R.
   (2) By the most direct route, the distance between T and U is 1.5 times the distance between R and T.

The value of x is the distance between City R and City T; the value of y is the distance between City R and City S. From statement (1) alone, it can be determined only that $56 = 2y$. Since no information is given about x, the answer must be B, C, or E. Statement (2) alone yields the equation $1.5x = 69$, which can be solved for x. Hence, the best answer is B.

9. Buckets X and Y contained only water and bucket Y was $\dfrac{1}{2}$ full. If all of the water in bucket X was then poured into bucket Y, what fraction of the capacity of Y was then filled with water?

   (1) Before the water from X was poured, X was $\dfrac{1}{3}$ full.
   (2) X and Y have the same capacity.

Statement (1) alone is not sufficient since it gives no information about the relative capacities of the two buckets. Thus, the answer must be B, C, or E. Statement (2) alone is not sufficient since it gives no information about the amount of water in bucket X. Thus, the answer must be C or E. If (1) and (2) are considered together, it can be determined that bucket Y is filled to $\left(\dfrac{1}{2} + \dfrac{1}{3} \right)$ of its capacity. Therefore, the best answer is C.

10. If n is an integer, is $n + 2$ a prime number?

    (1) n is a prime number
    (2) $n + 1$ is not a prime number.

For problems such as this, trying out two or three values of n can be very helpful. In statement (1), consider the prime numbers 2, 3, or 7, for example. Statement (1) alone is not sufficient since for these values $n + 2 = 4, 5$, or 9, respectively, and only 5 is prime. Thus, the answer must be B, C, or E. Similarly, for statement (2), if $n = 3$ or 7, then $n + 1 = 4$ or 8, and $n + 2 = 5$ or 9. Thus, the answer must be C or E. Since neither of the statements gives any definitive information about $n + 2$, the two statements taken together are still not sufficient to determine whether $n + 2$ is a prime number, and the best answer is E.

11. Is x between 0 and 1 ?

    (1) x^2 is less than x.
    (2) x^3 is positive.

Since x^2 is always nonnegative, it follows from statement (1) that x must be positive. For $x = 0$ or 1, $x^2 = x$; for $x > 1$, $x^2 > x$. Therefore, x must be between 0 and 1. Thus, statement (1) alone is sufficient, and the answer must be A or D. Statement (2) alone is not sufficient since x can be any positive number. Thus, the best answer is A.

12. Did Sally pay less than x dollars, including sales tax, for her bicycle?

    (1) The price Sally paid for the bicycle was $(0.9)x$ dollars, excluding the 10 percent sales tax.
    (2) The price Sally paid for the bicycle was \$170, excluding sales tax.

Statement (1) alone is sufficient since the price, including sales tax, was $(0.9)x + (0.1)(0.9)x = 0.99x$, which is less than x. Thus, the answer must be A or D. Statement (2) alone is not sufficient since there is no information given relating the \$170 Sally paid and the value of x. Thus, the best answer is A.

13. Is the positive square root of x an integer?

    (1) $x = n^4$ and n is an integer.
    (2) $x = 16$

Statement (1) alone is sufficient since the positive square root of x is n^2, which must be an integer since n is an integer. Thus, the answer must be A or D. Statement (2) alone is also sufficient since the positive square root of 16 is the integer 4. The best answer is D.

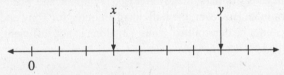

14. If the successive tick marks shown on the number line above are equally spaced and if x and y are the numbers designating the end points of intervals as shown, what is the value of y ?

    (1) $x = \dfrac{1}{2}$
    (2) $y - x = \dfrac{2}{3}$

From statement (1) it can be established that each subdivision of the line represents $\dfrac{1}{3}\left(\dfrac{1}{2}\right) = \dfrac{1}{6}$, so the value of y is $\dfrac{7}{6}$. Thus, (1) alone is sufficient, and the answer must be A or D. From statement (2) alone, the four equal subdivisions represent a total distance of $\dfrac{2}{3}$ which implies that each subdivision of the number line has length $\dfrac{1}{4}\left(\dfrac{2}{3}\right) = \dfrac{1}{6}$. Therefore, the best answer is D.

15. In a certain senior citizens' club, are more than $\dfrac{1}{4}$ of the members over 75 years of age?

    (1) Exactly 60 percent of the female members are over 60 years of age, and, of these, $\dfrac{1}{3}$ are over 75 years of age.
    (2) Exactly 10 male members are over 75 years of age.

From statement (1) it can be determined only that $\dfrac{1}{3}\left(\dfrac{3}{5}\right) = \dfrac{1}{5}$ of the female members are over 75. Thus, (1) alone is not sufficient, and the answer must be B, C, or E. Statement (2) gives only the number of male members over 75. Thus, (2) alone is not sufficient, and the answer must be C or E. Both statements together are still insufficient since they provide no information about the number of female members and the total number of members. The best answer is E.

16. If $t \neq 0$, is r greater than zero?

    (1) $rt = 12$
    (2) $r + t = 7$

Statement (1) alone is not sufficient since r and t could be either both positive or both negative. Statement (2) alone is not sufficient since both r and t can be positive or t can be positive and r negative (e.g., $r = 3$ and $t = 4$, or $r = -3$ and $t = 10$). If (1) and (2) are considered together, the system of equations can be solved to show that r must be either 3 or 4. Thus, the best answer is C.

17. If x is an integer, is y an integer?

    (1) The average (arithmetic mean) of x, y, and $y - 2$ is x.
    (2) The average (arithmetic mean) of x and y is <u>not</u> an integer.

From statement (1), $\dfrac{x + y + (y - 2)}{3} = x$ simplifies to $y = x + 1$. Since x is an integer, x and y are consecutive integers. Thus, (1) alone is sufficient, and the answer must be A or D. From statement (2) alone, y might be an integer (e.g., $x = 5$ and $y = 6$) or y might not be an integer (e.g., $x = 5$ and $y = 6.2$). In both examples the average is <u>not</u> an integer. Therefore, (2) alone is not sufficient, and the best answer is A.

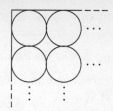

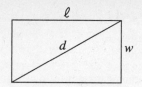

18. The inside of a rectangular carton is 48 centimeters long, 32 centimeters wide, and 15 centimeters high. The carton is filled to capacity with k identical cylindrical cans of fruit that stand upright in rows and columns, as indicated in the figure above. If the cans are 15 centimeters high, what is the value of k ?

   (1)   Each of the cans has a radius of 4 centimeters.
   (2)   6 of the cans fit exactly along the length of the carton.

Statement (1) alone establishes that the diameter of each can is 8 centimeters. Along the length of the carton 6 cans ($48 \div 8$) can be placed; along the width of the carton 4 cans ($32 \div 8$) can be placed. Hence, $k = 24$, and (1) alone is sufficient. Thus, the answer must be A or D. Statement (2) also implies that the diameter of each can is 8 centimeters since 6 cans fit along the length of the carton ($48 \div 6$). Thus, (2) alone is also sufficient, and the best answer is D.

19. If $R = \dfrac{8x}{3y}$ and $y \neq 0$, what is the value of R ?

   (1) $x = \dfrac{2}{3}$
   (2) $x = 2y$

Statement (1) alone is not sufficient to determine the value of R since the value of y is not known. Thus, the answer must be B, C, or E. Statement (2) alone is sufficient since $R = \dfrac{8x}{3y} = \dfrac{8(2y)}{3y} = \dfrac{16}{3}$. The best answer is B.

20. Is the positive integer n a multiple of 24 ?

   (1) n is a multiple of 4.
   (2) n is a multiple of 6.

Statement (1) alone is not sufficient because it says only that n is a multiple of 4 (e.g., n could be 8 or 24), and statement 2 alone is not sufficient because it says only that n is a multiple of 6 (e.g., n could be 12 or 48). Since both statements together imply only that n is a multiple of the least common multiple of 4 and 6, namely, 12, the best answer is E.

21. What is the area of the rectangular region above?

   (1) $\ell + w = 6$
   (2) $d^2 = 20$

The area of the rectangular region is ℓw. Statement (1) alone is not sufficient since the dimensions ℓ and w cannot be determined. Thus, the answer must be B, C, or E. Statement (2) alone is not sufficient because the length of the diagonal will not uniquely determine the length and width of the rectangle. Thus, the answer must be C or E. The Pythagorean theorem together with both (1) and (2) yield the equations $\ell^2 + w^2 = d^2 = 20$ and $(\ell + w)^2 = \ell^2 + 2\ell w + w^2 = 36$. Combining these equations gives $\ell w = 8$. Hence, the best answer is C.

22. If Aaron, Lee, and Tony have a total of $36, how much money does Tony have?

   (1)   Tony has twice as much money as Lee and $\dfrac{1}{3}$ as much as Aaron.
   (2)   The sum of the amounts of money that Tony and Lee have is half the amount that Aaron has.

From statement (1) alone it can be determined that if Lee has x dollars, then Tony has $2x$ dollars, Aaron has $6x$ dollars, and together they have $9x = 36$ dollars. Thus, the amount that Tony has can be determined, and the answer must be A or D. From statement (2), if the sum of the amounts that Tony and Lee have is y dollars, then Aaron has $2y$ dollars, and y can be determined. However, the individual amounts for Tony and Lee cannot be determined. Thus, (2) alone is not sufficient, and the best answer is A.

23. If n is a positive integer, is the value of $b - a$ at least twice the value of $3^n - 2^n$?

   (1) $a = 2^{n+1}$ and $b = 3^{n+1}$
   (2) $n = 3$

From statement (1) alone it can be determined that $b - a$ is more than twice $3^n - 2^n$, since

$$b - a = 3^{n+1} - 2^{n+1} = 3(3^n) - 2(2^n), \text{ and}$$
$$3(3^n) - 2(2^n) > 2(3^n) - 2(2^n), \text{ or } 2(3^n - 2^n).$$

Therefore, the answer must be either A or D. Since statement (2) alone gives no information about $b - a$, it is not sufficient. Thus, the best answer is A.

24. The price per share of stock X increased by 10 percent over the same time period that the price per share of stock Y decreased by 10 percent. The reduced price per share of stock Y was what percent of the original price per share of stock X ?

(1) The increased price per share of stock X was equal to the original price per share of stock Y.

(2) The increase in the price per share of stock X was $\frac{10}{11}$ the decrease in the price per share of stock Y.

The amount that stock X increased per share can be represented by $0.1x$, where x represents the original price per share of stock X. The amount that stock Y decreased per share can be represented by $0.1y$, where y represents the original price per share of stock Y. The reduced price per share of stock Y as a percent of the original price per share of stock X can be determined if a relationship between x and y is known. Statement (1) establishes that $1.1x = y$, and statement (2) establishes that $0.1x = \frac{10}{11}(0.1y)$. Since each statement alone is sufficient, the best answer is D.

25. Any decimal that has only a finite number of nonzero digits is a terminating decimal. For example, 24, 0.82, and 5.096 are three terminating decimals. If r and s are positive integers and the ratio $\frac{r}{s}$ is expressed as a decimal, is $\frac{r}{s}$ a terminating decimal?

(1) $90 < r < 100$

(2) $s = 4$

Statement (1) alone is not sufficient to determine that $\frac{r}{s}$ is a terminating decimal since there is no information about the value of s. For example, $\frac{92}{5} = 18.4$ terminates, but $\frac{92}{3} = 30.666\ldots$ does not terminate. Therefore, the answer must be B, C, or E. Statement (2) alone is sufficient since division by the number 4 must terminate: the remainder when dividing by 4 must be 0, 1, 2, or 3, so the quotient must end with .0, .25, .5, or .75, respectively. Thus, the best answer is B.

Explanatory Material: Critical Reasoning, Section 4

Questions 1-2 are based on the following.

Companies O and P each have the same number of employees who work the same number of hours per week. According to records maintained by each company, the employees of Company O had fewer job-related accidents last year than did the employees of Company P. Therefore, employees of Company O are less likely to have job-related accidents than are employees of Company P.

1. Which of the following, if true, would most strengthen the conclusion above?

(A) Company P manufactures products that are more hazardous for workers to produce than does Company O.

(B) Company P holds more safety inspections than does Company O.

(C) Company P maintains a more modern infirmary than does Company O.

(D) Company O paid more for new job-related medical claims than did Company P.

(E) Company P provides more types of health-care benefits than does Company O.

The passage's statistical data support the conclusion, but give information about one year only and identify no factor that would cause a higher accident rate at Company P. By describing such a factor, choice A, the best answer, suggests that these data can support a generalization like the conclusion.

Company P's greater number of safety inspections (choice B) may simply indicate greater attention to workers' safety. The infirmary (choice C) and health benefits (choice E) perhaps indicate that Company P makes better provisions for accident victims, but do not mean that accidents are more frequent there. That Company O paid more in job-related medical claims (choice D) says something about the consequences of accidents at the two companies, but not about causes of accidents.

2. Which of the following, if true, would most weaken the conclusion above?

(A) The employees of Company P lost more time at work due to job-related accidents than did the employees of Company O.

(B) Company P considered more types of accidents to be job-related than did Company O.

(C) The employees of Company P were sick more often than were the employees of Company O.

(D) Several employees of Company O each had more than one job-related accident.

(E) The majority of job-related accidents at Company O involved a single machine.

The data used to support the conclusion come from the companies' own records. Since, however, choice B indicates that, as compared with Company O, Company P tends to overstate the number of job-related accidents, choice B weakens the conclusion drawn and is the best answer. Choice A does not weaken the conclusion, but is simply a consequence that would be expected given the data. The relevance of employees' sicknesses (choice C) cannot be assessed without information about the links, if any, between sickness and job-related accidents. Choices D and E both give reasons for predicting a smaller likelihood that any arbitrary employee of Company O will have a job-related accident, and thus support the conclusion.

3. In comparison to the standard typewriter keyboard, the EFCO keyboard, which places the most-used keys nearest the typist's strongest fingers, allows faster typing and results in less fatigue. Therefore, replacement of standard keyboards with the EFCO keyboard will result in an immediate reduction of typing costs.

Which of the following, if true, would most weaken the conclusion drawn above?

(A) People who use both standard and EFCO keyboards report greater difficulty in the transition from the EFCO keyboard to the standard keyboard than in the transition from the standard keyboard to the EFCO keyboard.

(B) EFCO keyboards are no more expensive to manufacture than are standard keyboards and require less frequent repair than do standard keyboards.

(C) The number of businesses and government agencies that use EFCO keyboards is increasing each year.

(D) The more training and experience an employee has had with the standard keyboard, the more costly it is to train that employee to use the EFCO keyboard.

(E) Novice typists can learn to use the EFCO keyboard in about the same amount of time it takes them to learn to use the standard keyboard.

Choice D, the best answer, undermines the conclusion by pointing to a serious short-term cost of replacing standard keyboards with EFCO keyboards. The employees who are probably the most productive currently, those with the most training and experience, will cause the greatest retraining costs, according to choice D.

Choice A, by contrast, suggests that the transition to the EFCO keyboard is comparatively easy, at least for typists already experienced with both types of keyboards. Choices B and E both eliminate possible sources of increased expense associated with the EFCO keyboard, namely equipment expenses (choice B) and training of new typists (choice E). Choice C, which suggests that some offices have found the switch advantageous, is consistent with there being an immediate reduction of typing costs.

Questions 4-5 are based on the following.

Half of the subjects in an experiment — the experimental group — consumed large quantities of a popular artificial sweetener. Afterward, this group showed lower cognitive abilities than did the other half of the subjects — the control group — who did not consume the sweetener. The detrimental effects were attributed to an amino acid that is one of the sweetener's principal constituents.

4. Which of the following, if true, would best support the conclusion that some ingredient of the sweetener was responsible for the experimental results?

(A) Most consumers of the sweetener do not consume as much of it as the experimental group members did.

(B) The amino acid referred to in the conclusion is a component of all proteins, some of which must be consumed for adequate nutrition.

(C) The quantity of the sweetener consumed by individuals in the experimental group is considered safe by federal food regulators.

(D) The two groups of subjects were evenly matched with regard to cognitive abilities prior to the experiment.

(E) A second experiment in which subjects consumed large quantities of the sweetener lacked a control group of subjects who were not given the sweetener.

If, as choice D indicates, the two groups were evenly matched with regard to cognitive abilities prior to the experiment, the conclusion that some ingredient of the sweetener was detrimental to cognitive functioning is strongly supported. Thus, D is the best answer.

Neither choice A nor choice C provides additional reason to believe that some ingredient in the sweetener was responsible for the experimental results, because neither is relevant to interpreting the experimental results. Choice B indicates that, outside of the experiment, both groups consume the amino acid. If relatively small quantities are involved, the conclusion is unaffected; otherwise it is weakened. Choice E claims that a second experiment lacked a control group; yet this failing has no bearing on the experiment at issue.

5. Which of the following, if true, would best help explain how the sweetener might produce the observed effect?

(A) The government's analysis of the artificial sweetener determined that it was sold in relatively pure form.

(B) A high level of the amino acid in the blood inhibits the synthesis of a substance required for normal brain functioning.

(C) Because the sweetener is used primarily as a food additive, adverse reactions to it are rarely noticed by consumers.

(D) The amino acid that is a constituent of the sweetener is also sold separately as a dietary supplement.

(E) Subjects in the experiment did not know whether they were consuming the sweetener or a second, harmless substance.

Choice B entails that a principal constituent of the sweetener can impede normal brain functioning if high levels of it occur in the blood. Since diminished brain functioning would account for a decline in cognitive abilities, choice B helps explain the results and is the best answer.

Choice A suggests that the effect was not due to an impurity in the sweetener, and choice D suggests that further testing could be done using the amino acid alone, but neither helps explain how the sweetener might produce the effect. Neither does choice C: what it helps explain is how the sweetener could be thought harmless even if the sweetener is responsible for diminished cognitive functioning. Choice E gives a reason to trust the experimental results, but it does not explain them.

6. Adult female rats who have never before encountered rat pups will start to show maternal behaviors after being confined with a pup for about seven days. This period can be considerably shortened by disabling the female's sense of smell or by removing the scent-producing glands of the pup.

Which of the following hypotheses best explains the contrast described above?

(A) The sense of smell in adult female rats is more acute than that in rat pups.
(B) The amount of scent produced by rat pups increases when they are in the presence of a female rat that did not bear them.
(C) Female rats that have given birth are more affected by olfactory cues than are female rats that have never given birth.
(D) A female rat that has given birth shows maternal behavior toward rat pups that she did not bear more quickly than does a female rat that has never given birth.
(E) The development of a female rat's maternal interest in a rat pup that she did not bear is inhibited by the odor of the pup.

The contrast to be explained is that female rats develop maternal behaviors toward pups that are not their own faster when they cannot smell the pups than when they can. If the odor of a strange pup inhibits the development of maternal interest, the contrast is explained, so E is the best answer.

The other choices can only explain different contrasts. Choice A explains contrasts between pups and adult females. Choice B explains contrasts between pups that are in different circumstances. Choices C and D explain contrasts between two different groups of females, those that have given birth and those that have not.

7. The interview is an essential part of a successful hiring program because, with it, job applicants who have personalities that are unsuited to the requirements of the job will be eliminated from consideration.

The argument above logically depends on which of the following assumptions?

(A) A hiring program will be successful if it includes interviews.
(B) The interview is a more important part of a successful hiring program than is the development of a job description.
(C) Interviewers can accurately identify applicants whose personalities are unsuited to the requirements of the job.
(D) The only purpose of an interview is to evaluate whether job applicants' personalities are suited to the requirements of the job.
(E) The fit of job applicants' personalities to the requirements of the job was once the most important factor in making hiring decisions.

If interviewers cannot accurately identify unsuitable applicants, then interviews cannot play the role that is claimed to make them an essential part of a successful hiring program. Thus the argument depends on choice C being true, making C the best answer.

Although the argument claims that the interview is an essential part of a successful hiring program, the interview need not ensure success (contrary to choice A), nor need it be more important than another part (contrary to choice B). The interview can also have other purposes, such as checking on technical qualifications, so D is not depended upon. Nothing is implied about how past hiring decisions were made, so there is no dependence on choice E either.

8. An overly centralized economy, not the changes in the climate, is responsible for the poor agricultural production in Country X since its new government came to power. Neighboring Country Y has experienced the same climatic conditions, but while agricultural production has been falling in Country X, it has been rising in Country Y.

Which of the following, if true, would most weaken the argument above?

(A) Industrial production also is declining in Country X.
(B) Whereas Country Y is landlocked, Country X has a major seaport.
(C) Both Country X and Country Y have been experiencing drought conditions.
(D) The crops that have always been grown in Country X are different from those that have always been grown in Country Y.
(E) Country X's new government instituted a centralized economy with the intention of ensuring an equitable distribution of goods.

The argument assumes that agricultural production in Countries X and Y would be affected in the same way by given climatic changes. By pointing out that the crops grown in the two countries differ, choice D undermines this assumption and is the best answer.

The dissimilarity between Country X and Country Y that choice B describes is unlikely to explain why their trends in agricultural production have diverged. The information in Choice A cannot be evaluated without more information about industries in Country X, whereas Choice C merely supplies a detail about climate, which has already been explicitly considered in the argument. Choice E explains why Country X's government chose a centralized economy, but it does not address the effects of that choice.

9. **Useful protein drugs, such as insulin, must still be administered by the cumbersome procedure of injection under the skin. If proteins are taken orally, they are digested and cannot reach their target cells. Certain nonprotein drugs, however, contain chemical bonds that are not broken down by the digestive system. They can, thus, be taken orally.**

   The statements above most strongly support a claim that a research procedure that successfully accomplishes which of the following would be beneficial to users of protein drugs?

   (A) **Coating insulin with compounds that are broken down by target cells, but whose chemical bonds are resistant to digestion**
   (B) **Converting into protein compounds, by procedures that work in the laboratory, the nonprotein drugs that resist digestion**
   (C) **Removing permanently from the digestive system any substances that digest proteins**
   (D) **Determining, in a systematic way, what enzymes and bacteria are present in the normal digestive system and whether they tend to be broken down within the body**
   (E) **Determining the amount of time each nonprotein drug takes to reach its target cells**

Coating insulin as described in choice A, the best answer, would benefit protein-drug users by removing the obstacle identified in the passage that prevents protein drugs, such as insulin, from being taken orally. The insulin would become available to the target cells, since these cells would break down the coating.

Converting nonprotein drugs into protein compounds (choice B) would necessitate administration by injection, benefiting neither their users nor users of protein drugs. If removing substances that digest proteins (choice C) enabled protein drugs to be taken orally, it would be at the expense of normal digestive function. The breakdown of normally occurring bacteria and enzymes (choice D) and the activity of nonprotein drugs (choice E) are irrelevant to the problems associated with protein drugs.

10. **Country Y uses its scarce foreign-exchange reserves to buy scrap iron for recycling into steel. Although the steel thus produced earns more foreign exchange than it costs, that policy is foolish. Country Y's own territory has vast deposits of iron ore, which can be mined with minimal expenditure of foreign exchange.**

    Which of the following, if true, provides the strongest support for Country Y's policy of buying scrap iron abroad?

    (A) **The price of scrap iron on international markets rose significantly in 1987.**
    (B) **Country Y's foreign-exchange reserves dropped significantly in 1987.**
    (C) **There is virtually no difference in quality between steel produced from scrap iron and that produced from iron ore.**
    (D) **Scrap iron is now used in the production of roughly half the steel used in the world today, and experts predict that scrap iron will be used even more extensively in the future.**
    (E) **Furnaces that process scrap iron can be built and operated in Country Y with substantially less foreign exchange than can furnaces that process iron ore.**

Choice E, the best answer, furnishes two pieces of information that together support the policy. First, furnaces that process scrap iron may be unable to process iron ore. Second, obtaining and operating furnaces that can process iron ore would require substantially more foreign exchange, thus possibly offsetting any advantage from processing domestic iron ore.

The possibility of increases in scrap iron's price (choice A) speaks against the policy. The vulnerability of Country Y's foreign-exchange reserves (choice B) emphasizes the need to conserve foreign exchange, but does not indicate which mode of steel production best accomplishes this. Choice C is neutral between the modes of production. Choice D would support the policy only with assumptions about the reasons for the experts' prediction.

11. Last year the rate of inflation was 1.2 percent, but for the current year it has been 4 percent. We can conclude that inflation is on an upward trend and the rate will be still higher next year.

Which of the following, if true, most seriously weakens the conclusion above?

(A) The inflation figures were computed on the basis of a representative sample of economic data rather than all of the available data.
(B) Last year a dip in oil prices brought inflation temporarily below its recent stable annual level of 4 percent.
(C) Increases in the pay of some workers are tied to the level of inflation, and at an inflation rate of 4 percent or above, these pay raises constitute a force causing further inflation.
(D) The 1.2 percent rate of inflation last year represented a ten-year low.
(E) Government intervention cannot affect the rate of inflation to any significant degree.

According to choice B, last year's inflation figure was an anomaly, and inflation has returned to its recent stable level. There is thus less reason to conclude that inflation will rise any further, making B the best answer.

So long as the sample on which the figures are based is representative, there is no reason to doubt that they are essentially accurate, so choice A does not affect the argument. Choice C supports the conclusion by suggesting that there are forces in place to push inflation higher, and choice E supports it indirectly by suggesting that the government is powerless to prevent further increases. Finally, choice D by itself has no clearly defined consequences one way or the other with respect to the conclusion.

12. Because no employee wants to be associated with bad news in the eyes of a superior, information about serious problems at lower levels is progressively softened and distorted as it goes up each step in the management hierarchy. The chief executive is, therefore, less well informed about problems at lower levels than are his or her subordinates at those levels.

The conclusion drawn above is based on the assumption that

(A) problems should be solved at the level in the management hierarchy at which they occur
(B) employees should be rewarded for accurately reporting problems to their superiors
(C) problem-solving ability is more important at higher levels than it is at lower levels of the management hierarchy
(D) chief executives obtain information about problems at lower levels from no source other than their subordinates
(E) some employees are more concerned about truth than about the way they are perceived by their superiors

Unless chief executives rely solely on their subordinates for information about problems at lower levels, the progressive softening and distorting of information described in the passage need not bar the chief executive from obtaining accurate information. Thus, the conclusion that the chief executive is comparatively poorly informed about such problems is based on assuming choice D, which is therefore the best answer.

None of the other choices is assumed. Choices A and B are recommendations that the facts in the passage might support. The issue of where problem-solving ability is best deployed (choice C) may be affected by the conclusion's truth or falsity, but need not be decided in order to draw the conclusion. Choice E, if true, would tend to counteract the phenomenon the passage describes.

13. In the United States in 1986, the average rate of violent crime in states with strict gun-control laws was 645 crimes per 100,000 persons — about 50 percent higher than the average rate in the eleven states where strict gun-control laws have never been passed. Thus one way to reduce violent crime is to repeal strict gun control laws.

Which of the following, if true, would most weaken the argument above?

(A) The annual rate of violent crime in states with strict gun-control laws has decreased since the passage of those laws.
(B) In states with strict gun-control laws, few individuals are prosecuted for violating such laws.
(C) In states without strict gun-control laws, many individuals have had no formal training in the use of firearms.
(D) The annual rate of nonviolent crime is lower in states with strict gun-control laws than in states without such laws.
(E) Less than half of the individuals who reside in states without strict gun-control laws own a gun.

The argument assumes that it is because of their strict gun-control laws that states with such laws have a high rate of violent crime. If that were so, passage of these laws should be associated with increased violent crime. Choice A, the best answer, indicates that the opposite is true and so weakens the argument.

No other choice undermines the argument. The infrequency of prosecutions under strict gun-control laws (choice B) does not indicate that these laws have no effect on violent crime. For choices C and E to be relevant more information is needed, such as comparative data about states with strict gun-control laws. Similarly, without more information the relevance of the nonviolent crime rate (choice D) cannot be assessed.

14. Corporate officers and directors commonly buy and sell, for their own portfolios, stock in their own corporations. Generally, when the ratio of such inside sales to inside purchases falls below 2 to 1 for a given stock, a rise in stock prices is imminent. In recent days, while the price of MEGA Corporation stock has been falling, the corporation's officers and directors have bought up to nine times as much of it as they have sold.

The facts above best support which of the following predictions?

(A) The imbalance between inside purchases and inside sales of MEGA stock will grow even further.
(B) Inside purchases of MEGA stock are about to cease abruptly.
(C) The price of MEGA stock will soon begin to go up.
(D) The price of MEGA stock will continue to drop, but less rapidly.
(E) The majority of MEGA stock will soon be owned by MEGA's own officers and directors.

Since MEGA's officers and directors have bought almost nine times as much of MEGA's stock as they have sold, the ratio of inside sales to inside purchases is roughly 1 to 9, well below 2 to 1. Hence, by the generalization stated in the passage, a rise in MEGA's stock price is imminent and choice C is the best answer.

Since the prediction in choice D runs counter to the stated generalization, choice D is not supported. The passage does not suggest there will be an increase in the imbalance between such purchases and sales. Thus, choice A is not supported. Similarly, the passage suggests neither that inside purchases are about to cease nor that the majority of MEGA stocks will soon be owned by MEGA officers and directors. Thus, neither choice B nor choice E is supported.

15 The proposal to hire ten new police officers in Middletown is quite foolish. There is sufficient funding to pay the salaries of the new officers, but not the salaries of additional court and prison employees to process the increased caseload of arrests and convictions that new officers usually generate.

Which of the following, if true, will most seriously weaken the conclusion drawn above?

(A) Studies have shown that an increase in a city's police force does not necessarily reduce crime.
(B) When one major city increased its police force by 19 percent last year, there were 40 percent more arrests and 13 percent more convictions.
(C) If funding for the new police officers' salaries is approved, support for other city services will have to be reduced during the next fiscal year.
(D) In most United States cities, not all arrests result in convictions, and not all convictions result in prison terms.
(E) Middletown's ratio of police officers to citizens has reached a level at which an increase in the number of officers will have a deterrent effect on crime.

The passage says that hiring new officers usually brings new court expenses, but according to choice E hiring new officers in Middletown will lead to a reduction in crime and thus, perhaps, a reduction in court and prison expenses. Therefore, choice E weakens the conclusion drawn and is the best answer.

Three of the other choices tend to support claims made in the passage; choice A suggests that arrests will increase, choice B says that in one city arrests did increase, and choice C confirms the scarcity of funds. Choice D is irrelevant; it merely states the obvious about rates of arrest, conviction, and imprisonment.

16. A recent report determined that although only three percent of drivers on Maryland highways equipped their vehicles with radar detectors, thirty-three percent of all vehicles ticketed for exceeding the speed limit were equipped with them. Clearly, drivers who equip their vehicles with radar detectors are more likely to exceed the speed limit regularly than are drivers who do not.

The conclusion drawn above depends on which of the following assumptions?

(A) Drivers who equip their vehicles with radar detectors are less likely to be ticketed for exceeding the speed limit than are drivers who do not.

(B) Drivers who are ticketed for exceeding the speed limit are more likely to exceed the speed limit regularly than are drivers who are not ticketed.

(C) The number of vehicles that were ticketed for exceeding the speed limit was greater than the number of vehicles that were equipped with radar detectors.

(D) Many of the vehicles that were ticketed for exceeding the speed limit were ticketed more than once in the time period covered by the report.

(E) Drivers on Maryland highways exceeded the speed limit more often than did drivers on other state highways not covered in the report.

The conclusion concerns regularly exceeding the speed limit, but the data derive from isolated occasions when drivers exceed the speed limit and are ticketed. The conclusion thus assumes that these instances provide evidence of regular behavior — that drivers ticketed for exceeding the speed limit are likely to be drivers who regularly exceed it. Choice B states this assumption and is the best answer.

Choices A, C, and D provide additional data that might be relevant to the conclusion, but if choice B is assumed, the additional data are unnecessary for drawing the conclusion. The difference that choice E describes between Maryland and other states would simply suggest that the report's findings cannot be extrapolated to other states. It does not help in drawing the conclusion.

17. There is a great deal of geographical variation in the frequency of many surgical procedures — up to tenfold variation per hundred thousand people between different areas in the numbers of hysterectomies, prostatectomies, and tonsillectomies.

To support a conclusion that much of the variation is due to unnecessary surgical procedures, it would be most important to establish which of the following?

(A) A local board of review at each hospital examines the records of every operation to determine whether the surgical procedure was necessary.

(B) The variation is unrelated to factors (other than the surgical procedures themselves) that influence the incidence of diseases for which surgery might be considered.

(C) There are several categories of surgical procedure (other than hysterectomies, prostatectomies, and tonsillectomies) that are often performed unnecessarily.

(D) For certain surgical procedures, it is difficult to determine after the operation whether the procedures were necessary or whether alternative treatment would have succeeded.

(E) With respect to how often they are performed unnecessarily, hysterectomies, prostatectomies, and tonsillectomies are representative of surgical procedures in general.

To establish that much of the variation is due to unnecessary surgical procedures, it is necessary to eliminate the possibility that the geographical variation reflects variation in the incidence of diseases treated with these procedures. Choice B, if established, would eliminate this possibility and is thus the best answer.

Review boards (choice A) would provide some control against unnecessary procedures, so choice A would, if anything, tell against the suggested conclusion. Neither choice C nor choice E bears on the conclusion, since neither the conclusion nor the cited geographical variation involves procedures other than the three specified. Even if these procedures are of the kind choice D describes, the difficulty of determining an individual operation's necessity would merely increase the difficulty of verifying the suggested conclusion.

18. Researchers have found that when very overweight people, who tend to have relatively low metabolic rates, lose weight primarily through dieting, their metabolisms generally remain unchanged. They will thus burn significantly fewer calories at the new weight than do people whose weight is normally at that level. Such newly thin persons will, therefore, ultimately regain weight until their body size again matches their metabolic rate.

The conclusion of the argument above depends on which of the following assumptions?

(A) Relatively few very overweight people who have dieted down to a new weight tend to continue to consume substantially fewer calories than do people whose normal weight is at that level.
(B) The metabolisms of people who are usually not overweight are much more able to vary than the metabolisms of people who have been very overweight.
(C) The amount of calories that a person usually burns in a day is determined more by the amount that is consumed that day than by the current weight of the individual.
(D) Researchers have not yet determined whether the metabolic rates of formerly very overweight individuals can be accelerated by means of chemical agents.
(E) Because of the constancy of their metabolic rates, people who are at their usual weight normally have as much difficulty gaining weight as they do losing it.

If, compared with people who have not been overweight, newly thin people burned fewer calories but also generally consumed fewer calories, one could not reliably conclude that the newly thin people would regain weight. Therefore, the conclusion assumes that the newly thin do not generally consume fewer calories, making choice A the best answer.

The conclusion does not rely on differences in the variability of the metabolism (choice B), just on differences in the rate of metabolism, nor does it rely on the relative significance of different factors in determining how many calories a person burns in a day (choice C). Neither does the conclusion assume anything about whether accelerators for the metabolism have been discovered (choice D), or about why some people have difficulty gaining weight (choice E).

19. In 1987 sinusitis was the most common chronic medical condition in the United States, followed by arthritis and high blood pressure, in that order.

The incidence rates for both arthritis and high blood pressure increase with age, but the incidence rate for sinusitis is the same for people of all ages.

The average age of the United States population will increase between 1987 and 2000.

Which of the following conclusions can be most properly drawn about chronic medical conditions in the United States from the information given above?

(A) Sinusitis will be more common than either arthritis or high blood pressure in 2000.
(B) Arthritis will be the most common chronic medical condition in 2000.
(C) The average age of people suffering from sinusitis will increase between 1987 and 2000.
(D) Fewer people will suffer from sinusitis in 2000 than suffered from it in 1987.
(E) A majority of the population will suffer from at least one of the medical conditions mentioned above by the year 2000.

Given that the incidence rate for sinusitis is the same for people of all ages, and that the average age of the population will increase, it follows that the average age of people suffering from sinusitis will increase. Therefore, C is the best answer.

Although it follows that sinusitis will become less common relative to arthritis and high blood pressure, nothing can be concluded about the exact ranking of the three diseases, so choices A and B are ruled out. Just because sinusitis will become relatively less common, one cannot conclude that it will become absolutely less common (choice D). Lacking information about levels of incidence of the diseases, one cannot conclude what proportion of the population has at least one of them (choice E).

20. Parasitic wasps lay their eggs directly into the eggs of various host insects in exactly the right numbers for any suitable size of host egg. If they laid too many eggs in a host egg, the developing wasp larvae would compete with each other to the death for nutrients and space. If too few eggs were laid, portions of the host egg would decay, killing the wasp larvae.

Which of the following conclusions can properly be drawn from the information above?

(A) The size of the smallest host egg that a wasp could theoretically parasitize can be determined from the wasp's egg-laying behavior.

(B) Host insects lack any effective defenses against the form of predation practiced by parasitic wasps.

(C) Parasitic wasps learn from experience how many eggs to lay into the eggs of different host species.

(D) Failure to lay enough eggs would lead to the death of the developing wasp larvae more quickly than would laying too many eggs.

(E) Parasitic wasps use visual clues to calculate the size of a host egg.

Comparing two host eggs in which parasitic wasps have laid different numbers of eggs, it is theoretically possible to determine what size of host egg would be required for a single wasp egg. This would be the smallest egg the wasp could parasitize, so A is the best answer.

None of the other choices follows from the information given. Host insects could conceal their eggs from the wasps (choice B), and the wasps could have inborn abilities to lay appropriate numbers of eggs (choice C). Laying too many eggs could lead to the death of the larvae faster than laying too few (choice D), and the wasps could use tactile clues to calculate the size of a host egg (choice E).

Explanatory Material:
Problem Solving II, Section 5

1. $\dfrac{31}{125} =$

(A) 0.248
(B) 0.252
(C) 0.284
(D) 0.312
(E) 0.320

The fraction $\dfrac{31}{125}$ can be converted to decimal form by dividing 31 by 125, which yields 0.248. Thus, the best answer is A.

Alternatively, since $8(125) = 1,000$, $\dfrac{31}{125} \times \dfrac{8}{8} = \dfrac{248}{1,000} = 0.248$.

2. Members of a social club met to address 280 newsletters. If they addressed $\dfrac{1}{4}$ of the newsletters during the first hour and $\dfrac{2}{5}$ of the remaining newsletters during the second hour, how many newsletters did they address during the second hour?

(A) 28 (B) 42 (C) 63 (D) 84 (E) 112

Three-fourths of 280, or 210, newsletters were not addressed during the first hour. Therefore, $\dfrac{2}{5}(210) = 84$ newsletters were addressed during the second hour, and the best answer is D.

3. If $x^2 = 2y^3$ and $2y = 4$, what is the value of $x^2 + y$?

(A) -14
(B) -2
(C)   3
(D)   6
(E) 18

If $2y = 4$, then $y = 2$ and $x^2 = 2y^3 = 2(2)^3 = 16$. Therefore, $x^2 + y = 16 + 2 = 18$, and the best answer is E.

4. If the cost of 12 eggs varies between \$0.90 and \$1.20, then the cost per egg varies between

(A) \$0.06 and \$0.08
(B) \$0.065 and \$0.085
(C) \$0.07 and \$0.09
(D) \$0.075 and \$0.10
(E) \$0.08 and \$0.105

If the cost of 12 eggs varies between \$0.90 and \$1.20, the cost per egg varies between $\dfrac{\$0.90}{12}$ and $\dfrac{\$1.20}{12}$, or between \$0.075 and \$0.10. Thus, the best answer is D.

5. $(\sqrt{3} + 2)(\sqrt{3} - 2) =$

(A) $\sqrt{3} - 4$ (B) $\sqrt{6} - 4$ (C) -1
(D) 1 (E) 2

$(\sqrt{3} + 2)(\sqrt{3} - 2) = (\sqrt{3})^2 + 2\sqrt{3} - 2\sqrt{3} + 2(-2)$
$$= 3 - 4 = -1$$

Thus, the best answer is C.

6. A glucose solution contains 15 grams of glucose per 100 cubic centimeters of solution. If 45 cubic centimeters of the solution were poured into an empty container, how many grams of glucose would be in the container?

(A) 3.00
(B) 5.00
(C) 5.50
(D) 6.50
(E) 6.75

If x is the number of grams of glucose in the 45 cubic centimeters of solution, then $\frac{x}{45} = \frac{15}{100}$, and $x = 6.75$. Thus, the best answer is E.

7. If Sam were twice as old as he is, he would be 40 years older than Jim. If Jim is 10 years younger than Sam, how old is Sam?

   (A) 20
   (B) 30
   (C) 40
   (D) 50
   (E) 60

Let S be Sam's current age and let J be Jim's current age. The statement "if Sam were twice as old as he is, he would be 40 years older than Jim" can be represented by the equation $2S = J + 40$, and the statement "Jim is 10 years younger than Sam" can be represented by the equation $S - 10 = J$. Substituting $S - 10$ for J in the equation $2S = J + 40$ yields $2S = S + 30$. Thus, $S = 30$, and the best answer is B.

8. If $\frac{1}{2} + \frac{1}{3} + \frac{1}{4} = \frac{13}{x}$, which of the following must be an integer?

   I. $\frac{x}{8}$

   II. $\frac{x}{12}$

   III. $\frac{x}{24}$

   (A) I only
   (B) II only
   (C) I and III only
   (D) II and III only
   (E) I, II, and III

The fractions can be added using the least common denominator 12:

$\frac{13}{x} = \frac{1}{2} + \frac{1}{3} + \frac{1}{4} = \frac{6}{12} + \frac{4}{12} + \frac{3}{12} = \frac{13}{12}$, so $x = 12$.

I. $\frac{x}{8} = \frac{12}{8}$, which is not an integer.

II. $\frac{x}{12} = \frac{12}{12} = 1$, which is an integer.

III. $\frac{x}{24} = \frac{12}{24} = \frac{1}{2}$, which is not an integer.

Thus, only II is an integer, and the best answer is B.

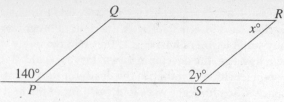

9. In the figure above, if $PQRS$ is a parallelogram, then $y - x =$

   (A) 30 (B) 35 (C) 40 (D) 70 (E) 100

Since PQ and SR are parallel, $2y = 140$ and $y = 70$. Since QR and PS are parallel, $x + 2y = 180$; so $x + 2(70) = 180$, or $x = 40$. Thus, $y - x = 30$, and the best answer is A.

10. The temperature in degrees Celsius (C) can be converted to temperature in degrees Fahrenheit (F) by the formula $F = \frac{9}{5}C + 32$. What is the temperature at which $F = C$?

   (A) $20°$ (B) $\left(\frac{32}{5}\right)°$ (C) $0°$
   (D) $-20°$ (E) $-40°$

Substituting F for C in the equation $F = \frac{9}{5}C + 32$ yields $F = \frac{9}{5}F + 32$. Thus, $-\frac{4}{5}F = 32$, or $F = 32(-\frac{5}{4}) = -40$, and the best answer is E.

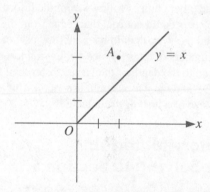

11. In the rectangular coordinate system above, the line $y = x$ is the perpendicular bisector of segment AB (not shown), and the x-axis is the perpendicular bisector of segment BC (not shown). If the coordinates of point A are (2, 3), what are the coordinates of point C?

   (A) $(-3, -2)$
   (B) $(-3, 2)$
   (C) $(2, -3)$
   (D) $(3, -2)$
   (E) $(2, 3)$

Since the line $y = x$ is the perpendicular bisector of AB, B is the reflection of A through this line. In any reflection through the line $y = x$, the x-coordinate and y-coordinate of a point become interchanged. Thus, the coordinates of B are (3,2).

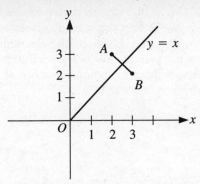

Since the x-axis is the perpendicular bisector of *BC*, *C* is the reflection of *B* through the x-axis. Thus, the x-coordinates of *C* and *B* are the same, and the y-coordinate of *C* is the negative of the y-coordinate of *B*.

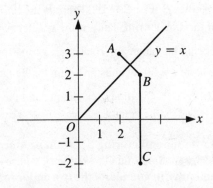

The coordinates of *C* are therefore $(3, -2)$, and the best answer is D.

12. If 1 kilometer is approximately 0.6 mile, which of the following best approximates the number of kilometers in 2 miles?

(A) $\frac{10}{3}$ (B) 3 (C) $\frac{6}{5}$ (D) $\frac{1}{3}$ (E) $\frac{3}{10}$

If x is the number of kilometers in 2 miles, then $\frac{1}{0.6} = \frac{x}{2}$.
So $x = \frac{2}{0.6} = \frac{20}{6} = \frac{10}{3}$, and the best answer is A.

13. A $500 investment and a $1,500 investment have a combined yearly return of 8.5 percent of the total of the two investments. If the $500 investment has a yearly return of 7 percent, what percent yearly return does the $1,500 investment have?

(A) 9%
(B) 10%
(C) $10\frac{5}{8}$%
(D) 11%
(E) 12%

The total of the two investments, or $2,000, has a yearly return of 8.5 percent, or $170. The $500 investment has a yearly return of 7 percent, or $35. Thus, the $1,500 investment has a yearly return of $170 − $35, or $135. The $135 yearly return is $\frac{135}{1,500}$, or 9 percent, of $1,500. The best answer is A.

14. A store currently charges the same price for each towel that it sells. If the current price of each towel were to be increased by $1, 10 fewer of the towels could be bought for $120, excluding sales tax. What is the current price of each towel?

(A) $1
(B) $2
(C) $3
(D) $4
(E) $12

Let *p* be the price per towel and let *n* be the number of towels that can be sold for $120. Thus, $np = 120$ and $(p + 1)(n - 10) = 120$. Solving the first equation for *n* yields $n = \frac{120}{p}$. Substituting $\frac{120}{p}$ for *n* in the second equation yields $(p + 1)(\frac{120}{p} - 10) = 120$, which can be solved as follows:

$$(p + 1)(120 - 10p) = 120p$$
$$10(p + 1)(12 - p) = 120p$$
$$(p + 1)(12 - p) = 12p$$
$$-p^2 + 11p + 12 = 12p$$
$$p^2 + p - 12 = 0$$
$$(p - 3)(p + 4) = 0$$
$$p = 3 \text{ or } -4$$

Since *p* is the price per towel, *p* cannot be −4. Thus, $p = 3$, and the best answer is C.

15. If the sum of *n* consecutive integers is 0, which of the following must be true?

  I. *n* is an even number.
  II. *n* is an odd number.
  III. The average (arithmetic mean) of the *n* integers is 0.

(A) I only (B) II only (C) III only
(D) I and III (E) II and III

Recall that for every integer *a*, $a + (-a) = 0$. Therefore, by pairing 1 with −1, 2 with −2, and so on, one can see that in order to sum to zero, a list of consecutive integers must contain the same number of positive integers as negative integers, in addition to containing the integer 0. Therefore, the list has an odd number of integers. Thus, I is false and II is true. The average of a list of *n* numbers is equal to their sum divided by *n*. Thus, III is true, and the best answer is E.

-609-

16. In the formula $V = \dfrac{1}{(2r)^3}$, if r is halved, then V is multiplied by

(A) 64
(B) 8
(C) 1
(D) $\dfrac{1}{8}$
(E) $\dfrac{1}{64}$

If $V = \dfrac{1}{(2r)^3} = \dfrac{1}{8r^3}$, then substituting $\dfrac{1}{2}r$ for r yields

$\dfrac{1}{8\left(\frac{r}{2}\right)^3} = \dfrac{1}{r^3} = 8 \times \dfrac{1}{8r^3} = 8\,V$. Thus, if r is halved, V is

multiplied by 8, and the best answer is B.

17. For any integer n greater than 1, $\lfloor n$ denotes the product of all the integers from 1 to n, inclusive. How many prime numbers are there between $\lfloor 6 + 2$ and $\lfloor 6 + 6$, inclusive?

(A) None (B) One (C) Two
(D) Three (E) Four

$\lfloor 6 = (6)(5)(4)(3)(2)(1) = 720$
Thus, the question is asking how many prime numbers are between 722 and 726, inclusive. The numbers 722, 724, and 726 are divisible by 2, and 725 is divisible by 5. The only remaining number is 723, which is divisible by 3. Thus, there are no prime numbers between $\lfloor 6 + 2$ and $\lfloor 6 + 6$, inclusive, and the best answer is A.

18. In how many arrangements can a teacher seat 3 girls and 3 boys in a row of 6 seats if the boys are to have the first, third, and fifth seats?

(A) 6 (B) 9 (C) 12 (D) 36 (E) 720

Any one of the 3 boys could be seated in the first seat, either of the remaining 2 boys in the third seat, and the remaining boy in the fifth seat. Thus there are $3(2)(1) = 6$ ways the boys could be arranged. There are also 3 girls to be arranged in 3 seats; thus, by the same reasoning, there are 6 ways in which the girls can be arranged. Since for each arrangement of the boys, there are 6 arrangements of the girls, there are $6(6) = 36$ ways in which the 3 boys and the 3 girls can be arranged. Thus, the best answer is D.

19. A circular rim 28 inches in diameter rotates the same number of inches per second as a circular rim 35 inches in diameter. If the smaller rim makes x revolutions per second, how many revolutions per __minute__ does the larger rim make in terms of x ?

(A) $\dfrac{48\pi}{x}$
(B) $75x$
(C) $48x$
(D) $24x$
(E) $\dfrac{x}{75}$

One rotation of circular rims of diameters 28 and 35 inches is 28π and 35π inches, respectively. Since the two circular rims rotate the same number of inches per second, the number of rotations per second of the larger rim is $\dfrac{28}{35}$ times the number of rotations of the smaller rim. Thus, if the smaller rim rotates x times per second, the larger rim rotates $\dfrac{28}{35}x$ times per second. Since there are 60 seconds in 1 minute, the larger rim rotates $(60)\dfrac{28}{35}x = 48x$ times per minute, and the best answer is C.

20. The cost C of manufacturing a certain product can be estimated by the formula $C = 0.03rst^2$, where r and s are the amounts, in pounds, of the two major ingredients and t is the production time, in hours. If r is increased by 50 percent, s is increased by 20 percent, and t is decreased by 30 percent, by approximately what percent will the estimated cost of manufacturing the product change?

(A) 40% increase
(B) 12% increase
(C) 4% increase
(D) 12% decrease
(E) 24% decrease

If r is increased by 50 percent, s is increased by 20 percent, and t is decreased by 30 percent, then, according to the formula, the new estimated cost of manufacturing the product will be

$$0.03(1.5r)(1.2s)(0.7t)^2 = [0.03(1.5)(1.2)(0.7)^2]rst^2$$
$$= 0.882(0.03rst^2).$$

This is a decrease of approximately 12 percent, and the best answer is D.

Explanatory Material:
Reading Comprehension, Section 6

1. **Which of the following best summarizes the content of the passage?**

   (A) A critique of a particular women's studies program
   (B) A report of work in social theory done by a particular women's studies program
   (C) An assessment of the strengths and weaknesses of a particular women's studies program
   (D) An analysis of the philosophy underlying women's studies programs
   (E) An abbreviated history of Korean women's studies programs

The best answer is B. In stating that the founders of the Ewha women's studies program "had some reservations about the applicability of Western feminist theories to the role of women in Asia" (lines 14-16), the first paragraph introduces the idea that the program was concerned with social theory. The second and third paragraphs report on the Ewha theorists' analysis of Freudian theory in terms of Korean society. Thus, the passage can be described as a report of the Ewha program's work in social theory. Because the passage does not provide a broad description of the program's work, A and C are incorrect. Choices D and E are incorrect because only the Ewha women's studies program is discussed in the passage.

2. **It can be inferred from the passage that Korean scholars in the field of women's studies undertook an analysis of Freudian theory as a response to which of the following?**

   (A) Attacks by critics of the Ewha women's studies program
   (B) The superficiality of earlier critiques of Freudian theory
   (C) The popularity of Freud in Korean psychiatric circles
   (D) Their desire to encourage Korean scholars to adopt the Freudian model
   (E) Their assessment of the relevance and limitations of Western feminist theory with respect to Korean culture

The best answer is E. The passage cites the Freudian model as an example of a theory chosen to be studied because of the Ewha group's "reservations about the applicability of Western feminist theories to the role of women in Asia" (lines 14-16). In the second and third paragraphs, some of the group's concerns about the relevance and limitations of the model with respect to Korean culture are explained. Since group members criticized the assumptions of the Freudian model, they would

not encourage Korean scholars to adopt it (choice D). There is no indication that the Ewha scholars were responding to the criticisms of the program (choice A), to the superficiality of earlier critiques (choice B), or to the popularity of Freudian theory (choice C).

3. **Which of the following conclusions about the introduction of Western ideas to Korean society can be supported by information contained in the passage?**

   (A) Except for technological innovations, few Western ideas have been successfully transplanted into Korean society.
   (B) The introduction of Western ideas to Korean society is viewed by some Koreans as a challenge to Korean identity.
   (C) The development of the Korean economy depends heavily on the development of new academic programs modeled after Western programs.
   (D) The extent to which Western ideas must be adapted for acceptance by Korean society is minimal.
   (E) The introduction of Western ideas to Korean society accelerated after 1977.

The best answer is B. Lines 5-7 state that "critics dismissed the program as a betrayal of national identity" and "an imitation of Western ideas." Thus, it can be concluded from the passage that some Koreans view Western ideas as a challenge to Korean society. Choice A can be eliminated because, although the information in the passage does suggest that Freud's ideas could not be transplanted into Korean society, no information is given about the transplantation of other nontechnical Western ideas. There is no information in the passage to suggest that either C or E could be correct. Choice D is contradicted by the information in the passage.

4. **It can be inferred from the passage that the broadcast media in Korea considered the establishment of the Ewha women's studies program**

   (A) praiseworthy
   (B) insignificant
   (C) newsworthy
   (D) imitative
   (E) incomprehensible

The best answer is C. The fact that the Ewha women's studies program was the subject of "broadcast debates" (line 5) suggests that the broadcast media considered the establishment of the program to be "newsworthy" (choice C), not "insignificant" (choice B). There is no indication in the passage that the media considered the program to be either "imitative" (choice D) or "incomprehensible" (choice E), nor is there an indication of the opinion of the media concerning the program's praiseworthiness (choice A).

5. It can be inferred from the passage that the position taken by some of the supporters of the Ewha women's studies program was problematic to the founders of the program because those supporters

   (A) assumed that the program would be based on the uncritical adoption of Western theory
   (B) failed to show concern for the issues of national unification and economic development
   (C) were unfamiliar with Western feminist theory
   (D) were not themselves scholars in the field of women's studies
   (E) accepted the universality of Freudian theory

The best answer is A. According to lines 8-12 in the passage, supporters thought that the program was simply another Western idea that would be useful in Asian culture. That is, they made the general assumption that Western ideas would be adopted uncritically (choice A). This is the only direct reference in the passage to supporters of the program. Therefore, there is no information in the passage to suggest that B, C, D, or E could be true of the program's supporters.

6. Which of the following statements is most consistent with the view of personality development held by the Ewha women's studies group?

   (A) Personality development occurs in identifiable stages, beginning with dependency in childhood and ending with independence in adulthood.
   (B) Any theory of personality development, in order to be valid, must be universal.
   (C) Personality development is influenced by the characteristics of the society in which a person lives.
   (D) Personality development is hindered if a person is not permitted to be independent.
   (E) No theory of personality development can account for the differences between Korean and Western culture.

The best answer is C. The second paragraph of the passage discusses the Ewha group's analysis of the Freudian theory of personality formation. In the group's comparison of the Asian concept of personality with the Western, or Freudian, model, the effects on personality of Western competitive, individualistic society are contrasted with the effects of Korean society, which is social and group centered. The Ewha group's assessment of the effects of culture on personality are further discussed in the last paragraph. The generalizations stated in A, B, and D are contradicted by the information in the second and third paragraphs. The issue presented in E is not discussed in the passage.

7. Which of the following statements about the Western feminist critique of Freudian theory can be supported by information contained in the passage?

   (A) It recognizes the influence of Western culture on Freudian theory.
   (B) It was written after 1977.
   (C) It acknowledges the universality of the nuclear, male-headed family.
   (D) It challenges Freud's analysis of the role of daughters in Western society.
   (E) It fails to address the issue of competitiveness in Western society.

The best answer is A. According to lines 21-23 in the passage, ". . . the Korean critique finds Freudian theory culture-bound, but in ways different from those cited by Western theorists." Therefore, one can conclude that Western theorists also find Freudian theory to be culture-bound, and thus that they recognize that Western culture has some influence on Freudian theory. Though the statements made in choices B, C, D, and E might be true, there is no information in the passage to support the conclusion that any of them is correct.

8. According to the passage, critics of the Ewha women's studies program cited the program as a threat to which of the following?

   I. National identity
   II. National unification
   III. Economic development
   IV. Family integrity

   (A) I only
   (B) I and II only
   (C) I, II, and III only
   (D) II, III, and IV only
   (E) I, II, III, and IV

The best answer is C. The views of critics of the Ewha women's studies program are discussed in lines 5-8 of the passage. According to the passage, critics believed the program to be "a betrayal of national identity" (I) and "a distraction from the real task of national unification and economic development" (II and III). Thus, "national identity," "national unification," and "economic development" were seen as threatened. No mention is made of the effect of the program on family integrity (IV). Therefore choice C, "I, II, and III," is the best answer.

9. Which of the following statements about the difference between marine and continental sedimentation is supported by information in the passage?

(A) Data provided by dating marine sedimentation is more consistent with researchers' findings in other disciplines than is data provided by dating continental sedimentation.

(B) It is easier to estimate the age of a layer in a sequence of continental sedimentation than it is to estimate the age of a layer in a sequence of marine sedimentation.

(C) Marine sedimentation is much less widespread than continental sedimentation.

(D) Researchers are more often forced to rely on extrapolation when dating a layer of marine sedimentation than when dating a layer of continental sedimentation.

(E) Marine sedimentation is much more continuous than is continental sedimentation.

The best answer is E. Lines 16-23 state that it is easier to date marine sediments than it is to date continental sediments because "sedimentation is much less continuous in continental regions." Thus, the passage supports the statement in E that marine sedimentation is more continuous than continental sedimentation. Choice B can be eliminated because it contradicts the information provided in the passage about the relative easiness of dating marine sedimentation in comparison to continental sedimentation. Choice D is incorrect because the passage does not contrast how often extrapolation is required for each of the two types of sediments. The passage does not provide information to support either A or C.

10. Which of the following statements best describes the organization of the passage as a whole?

(A) The author describes a method for determining past climatic conditions and then offers specific examples of situations in which it has been used.

(B) The author discusses the method of dating marine and continental sequences and then explains how dating is more difficult with lake levels than with pollen profiles.

(C) The author describes the common requirements of methods for determining past climatic conditions and then discusses examples of such methods.

(D) The author describes various ways of choosing a material for determining past climatic conditions and then discusses how two such methods have yielded contradictory data.

(E) The author describes how methods for determining past climatic conditions were first developed and then describes two of the earliest known methods.

The best answer is C. In the first paragraph, the author describes the criteria for choosing a method to determine past climatic conditions and then in the following two paragraphs the author discusses examples of such methods. Choice C, therefore, is the best description of the organization of the passage as a whole. Choice A can be eliminated because the author does not focus on only one method for determining past climatic conditions. Choice B is incorrect because the passage does not compare the relative difficulty of the lake level versus the pollen profile method. Choices D and E are incorrect because the passage does not mention contradictory data yielded by both of the methods discussed, nor does it mention the initial development of methods for determining past climates.

11. It can be inferred from the passage that paleoclimatologists have concluded which of the following on the basis of their study of snow-line elevations in the southwestern United States?

(A) There is usually more precipitation during an ice age because of increased amounts of evaporation.

(B) There was less precipitation during the last ice age than there is today.

(C) Lake levels in the semiarid southwestern United States were lower during the last ice age than they are today.

(D) During the last ice age, cooler weather led to lower lake levels than paleoclimatologists had previously assumed.

(E) The high lake levels during the last ice age may have been a result of less evaporation rather than more precipitation.

The best answer is E. In lines 33-41, the author implies that scientists, after studying snow-line elevations, concluded that the high lake levels in the southwestern United States were the result of reduced evaporation rather than increased precipitation. Choices C and D are incorrect because they contradict information in the passage, and A and B are incorrect because they are not supported by information in the passage.

12. Which of the following would be the most likely topic for a paragraph that logically continues the passage?

(A) The kinds of plants normally found in arid regions

(B) The effect of variation in lake levels on pollen distribution

(C) The material best suited to preserving signals of climatic changes

(D) Other criteria invoked by paleoclimatologists when choosing a method to determine past climatic conditions

(E) A third method for investigating past climatic conditions

Only E, the best answer, suggests a likely topic for a paragraph that logically continues the passage. Since the last two paragraphs of the passage discuss methods of investigating past climatic conditions, it follows logically that a subsequent paragraph might continue this discussion by introducing a third method of investigation. Choices A and B introduce topics that diverge from the primary focus of the passage (the various methods that can be used to determine past climatic conditions). The topic suggested in C does not logically continue the passage because the focus of the preceding paragraphs is methods for determining climatic conditions, not the best material for preserving signals of climatic change. And, since the four criteria for choosing a method to determine past climatic conditions are discussed in the first paragraph, it does not follow logically that a subsequent paragraph, as suggested in D, would introduce other criteria for choosing such methods.

13. **The author discusses lake levels in the southwestern United States in order to**

   (A) **illustrate the mechanics of the relationship between lake level, evaporation, and precipitation**
   (B) **provide an example of the uncertainty involved in interpreting lake levels**
   (C) **prove that there are not enough ancient lakes with which to make accurate correlations**
   (D) **explain the effects of increased rates of evaporation on levels of precipitation**
   (E) **suggest that snow-line elevations are invariably more accurate than lake levels in determining rates of precipitation at various points in the past**

The best answer is B. In lines 31-33, the author states that it is difficult to interpret lake levels because such levels are controlled by "rates of evaporation as well as by precipitation." The author then mentions lake levels in the southwestern United States to provide a specific example of the difficulty involved in interpreting lake levels. In this case, scientists attributed higher lake levels to increased precipitation rather than to the actual cause, which was reduced evaporation. The passage does not provide information to support any of the other answer choices as a plausible reason why the author discusses lake levels in the southwestern United States.

14. **It can be inferred from the passage that an environmental signal found in geological material would not be useful to paleoclimatologists if it**

   (A) **had to be interpreted by modern chemical means**
   (B) **reflected a change in climate rather than a long-term climatic condition**
   (C) **was incorporated into a material as the material was forming**
   (D) **also reflected subsequent environmental changes**
   (E) **was contained in a continental rather than a marine sequence**

The best answer is D. In lines 12-14, the author states that one criterion for choosing a method to determine past climatic conditions is that geological material must have retained an

environmental signal "unaffected by subsequent changes in the environment." Thus, it can be inferred that material containing an environmental signal that reflects subsequent environmental changes would not be useful to paleoclimatologists. Choices A and C can be eliminated because the passage states that environmental signals are interpreted by modern chemical means and that an environmental signal should have been incorporated into a material while the material was forming. Choice B is incorrect because the passage suggests that an environmental signal reflecting a change in climate would be useful to paleoclimatologists. Choice E can be eliminated because, although the passage does indicate that continental sequences are more difficult to date than marine sequences, it does not dismiss continental sediment as a material for determining past climates.

15. **According to the passage, the material used to determine past climatic conditions must be widespread for which of the following reasons?**

   I. **Paleoclimatologists need to make comparisons between periods of geological history.**
   II. **Paleoclimatologists need to compare materials that have supported a wide variety of vegetation.**
   III. **Paleoclimatologists need to make comparisons with data collected in other regions.**

   (A) **I only**
   (B) **II only**
   (C) **I and II only**
   (D) **I and III only**
   (E) **II and III only**

The best answer is D. In lines 3-8, the author states that geological material used to determine past climatic conditions must be widespread or it "will not permit correlation with other regions or with other periods of geological history." Thus, only statements I and III give reasons why geological material must be widespread. Although the author mentions that vegetation or geological materials must be widespread in order to provide sufficient information for determining climatic conditions (lines 3-5), the author does not state that any particular geological material must have supported a wide variety of vegetation. Statement II, therefore, is incorrect.

16. Which of the following can be inferred from the passage about the study of past climates in arid and semiarid regions?

   (A) It is sometimes more difficult to determine past climatic conditions in arid and semiarid regions than in temperate regions.
   (B) Although in the past more research has been done on temperate regions, paleoclimatologists have recently turned their attention to arid and semiarid regions.
   (C) Although more information about past climates can be gathered in arid and semiarid than in temperate regions, dating this information is more difficult.
   (D) It is difficult to study the climatic history of arid and semiarid regions because their climates have tended to vary more than those of temperate regions.
   (E) The study of past climates in arid and semiarid regions has been neglected because temperate regions support a greater variety of plant and animal life.

The best answer is A. In lines 28-31, the author states that the small number of and great distance between lakes in arid and semiarid regions reduces the possibilities for correlations in these regions on the basis of water levels in lakes. On the other hand, the author notes that there are enough lakes in temperate regions to allow for correlations and to provide a reliable picture of past climatic conditions (lines 26-28). In addition, the smaller amount of vegetation in arid and semiarid regions than in temperate zones makes it more difficult for scientists to use pollen profiles to reconstruct former climates (lines 46-53). Thus, it can be inferred that it is sometimes more difficult to determine past climatic conditions in arid and semiarid regions than it is in temperate zones. There is no information in the passage to support the statements contained in the other choices.

17. The author of the passage is primarily concerned with

   (A) summarizing a thesis
   (B) recommending a different approach
   (C) comparing points of view
   (D) making a series of predictions
   (E) describing a number of paradoxes

The best answer is B. In the first paragraph, the author describes cost-cutting, an approach often used by manufacturers who are trying to enhance their competitive edge. In the second and third paragraphs, the author discusses the limitations of cost-cutting. In the last paragraph, the author describes an alternative approach — developing and implementing a manufacturing strategy — that has been more effective than cost-cutting in helping companies regain their competitive edge. Thus, the author is primarily concerned with recommending an approach other than cost-cutting.

18. It can be inferred from the passage that the manufacturers mentioned in line 2 expected that the measures they implemented would

   (A) encourage innovation
   (B) keep labor output constant
   (C) increase their competitive advantage
   (D) permit business upturns to be more easily predicted
   (E) cause managers to focus on a wider set of objectives

The best answer is C. Lines 2-5 state that "manufacturers in the United States have been trying to improve productivity — and therefore enhance their international competitiveness — through cost-cutting programs." The author goes on to state that cost-cutting did not significantly improve productivity and concludes that the "harder manufacturers worked to implement cost-cutting, the more they lost their competitive edge" (lines 14-16). Thus, it can be inferred that the manufacturers mentioned in line 2 implemented cost-cutting measures to increase their competitive advantage. Choice B can be eliminated because the passage suggests that manufacturers expected cost-cutting to raise labor output. Choices A, D, and E are not discussed in relation to the manufacturers mentioned in line 2.

19. The primary function of the first paragraph of the passage is to

   (A) outline in brief the author's argument
   (B) anticipate challenges to the prescriptions that follow
   (C) clarify some disputed definitions of economic terms
   (D) summarize a number of long-accepted explanations
   (E) present a historical context for the author's observations

The best answer is E. The author begins the first paragraph by stating that manufacturers used cost-cutting as a manufacturing strategy in the late 1970's and 1980's. The author goes on to point out that the use of such a strategy did not immediately improve productivity and that when productivity was finally improved it was at rates lower than those achieved in the past. The author provides this background information about the effectiveness of cost-cutting in order to indicate that an alternative approach to improving productivity is necessary. Thus, the author uses the first paragraph to present a historical context for the ensuing discussion of implementing strategies other than cost-cutting. Choice A can be eliminated because the first paragraph does not outline the author's entire argument. Choices B, C, and D are incorrect because they do not accurately describe the content of the first paragraph.

20. The author refers to Abernathy's study (line 36) most probably in order to

(A) qualify an observation about one rule governing manufacturing

(B) address possible objections to a recommendation about improving manufacturing competitiveness

(C) support an earlier assertion about one method of increasing productivity

(D) suggest the centrality in the United States economy of a particular manufacturing industry

(E) give an example of research that has questioned the wisdom of revising a manufacturing strategy

The best answer is C. In lines 18-20, the author asserts that cost-cutting, one method of improving productivity, is "fundamentally flawed." In lines 34-35, the author elaborates on this assertion by stating that cost-cutting "hinders innovation and discourages creative people." The author supports these observations by mentioning in lines 35-39 that Abernathy's study indicates that automobile manufacturers' commitment to cost-cutting reduces the ability to develop new products. Thus, the author is supporting an assertion about the inability of cost-cutting to ultimately improve productivity. Choice A is incorrect because Abernathy's study is not mentioned in the context of the second paragraph's discussion of the rules governing manufacturing. Choice B can be eliminated because the author is raising objections to a widely-used manufacturing strategy. Choice D can be eliminated because the author does not discuss types of manufacturing industries. Choice E is incorrect because Abernathy's study suggests that it would be wise to alter a manufacturing strategy.

21. The author's attitude toward the culture in most factories is best described as

(A) cautious
(B) critical
(C) disinterested
(D) respectful
(E) adulatory

The best answer is B. In lines 43-45, the author states that managers have seen their job as "one of minimizing costs and maximizing output." The author goes on to state that this approach "has created a penny-pinching, mechanistic culture in most factories" (lines 47-48). Thus, the author's attitude toward the culture in most factories can best be described as critical. Choice D can be eliminated because, although the passage suggests that the author may respect the culture of specific companies (lines 53-57), there is no information to suggest that the author respects the culture in most factories. Choice A can be eliminated because the only caution expressed by the author is toward the general future of manufacturing (lines 60-62), rather than toward the cultures of manufacturing companies.

22. In the passage, the author includes all of the following EXCEPT

(A) personal observation
(B) a business principle
(C) a definition of productivity
(D) an example of a successful company
(E) an illustration of a process technology

The best answer is E. This question requires you to recognize which of the choices is an element that is NOT included in the passage. Choice A can be eliminated because the author in lines 49-51 provides a personal observation about companies that have successfully improved productivity. Choice B can be eliminated because in the second paragraph the author describes a business principle — the "40, 40, 20" rule observed by most manufacturers. Choices C and D are incorrect because lines 8-9 provide a definition of productivity and lines 53-57 provide an example of a successful company. Choice E, therefore, is the best answer because it is the only element that is NOT included in the passage.

23. The author suggests that implementing conventional cost-cutting as a way of increasing manufacturing competitiveness is a strategy that is

(A) flawed and ruinous
(B) shortsighted and difficult to sustain
(C) popular and easily accomplished
(D) useful but inadequate
(E) misunderstood but promising

The best answer is D. In lines 29-33, the author states that although the well-known tools of the cost-cutting approach can "produce results," the tools "quickly reach the limits of what they can accomplish." Thus, the author suggests that cost-cutting can be useful but is inadequate as the only strategy implemented to improve productivity. Choices A and B can be eliminated because, although the author does indicate that cost-cutting can be flawed and shortsighted, the author does not indicate that it is ruinous or difficult to implement for a long period of time. Choices C and E are not supported by information in the passage.

Scoring Information

NOTE ABOUT THE SCORING OF THE ANALYTICAL WRITING ASSESSMENT

The detailed scoring information on the following pages describes how to calculate your scores on the multiple-choice sections of the tests in Chapter 9 and, just as importantly, how to interpret those scores. This note is intended to provide information about the scoring of the Analytical Writing Assessment.

The Analytical Writing Assessment, described in Chapter 8 of this book, consists of two writing tasks: Analysis of an Issue and Analysis of an Argument. The responses to each of these tasks are scored on a 6-point scale, with 6 the highest score and 1 the lowest. A score of zero (0) is given to responses that are illegible or not written on the assigned topic. The readers who evaluate the responses are college and university faculty members from various subject matter areas, including management education. These readers read holistically — that is, they respond to the overall quality of your critical thinking and writing. To ensure the greatest possible accuracy and consistency in scoring, the readers are rigorously trained, using actual candidates' responses, by a "chief reader" chosen for his or her expertise in the holistic reading process. In addition, each candidate's response is read independently by two different readers. If the readers disagree about the score by more than a point, a third reader adjudicates. Readers are retrained periodically throughout the scoring session.

Your final score is the average (rounded to the nearest half point) of the four scores independently awarded to your responses — two scores for the Analysis of an Issue and two for the Analysis of an Argument. For example, if you earned scores of 6 and 5 on the Analysis of an Issue and 4 and 4 on the Analysis of an Argument, your final score would be 5: $(6 + 5 + 4 + 4) \div 4 = 4.75$, which rounds up to 5.

Your score on the Analytical Writing Assessment will be reported as a separate score. That is, you will receive four scores: your verbal score, your quantitative score, your total (multiple-choice) score, and your writing score. The schools that you have designated to receive your scores will also receive a copy of your responses to the two writing tasks that comprise the Analytical Writing Assessment. Your own copy of your score report will not include copies of your responses.

Failure to write essays or work on the multiple-choice sections will result in no reportable scores.

How to Calculate Your Scores: Form A

Your Verbal Raw Score

Step 1:	Using the answer key, mark your answer sheet as follows: put a C next to each question that you answered correctly; put an I next to each question that you answered incorrectly. Cross out any questions that you did not answer or for which you marked more than one answer; these will not be counted in the scoring.	
Step 2:	Sections 1, 3, and 5 are used to determine your verbal score. In these sections only, count the number of correct answers (marked C) and enter this number here	_____
Step 3:	In these same sections (1, 3, and 5), count the number of questions that you answered incorrectly (marked I). Enter the number here	_____
Step 4:	Count the number of questions in sections 1, 3, and 5 that you crossed out because you did not answer them or marked more than one answer. Enter this number here	_____
Step 5:	Add the numbers in Steps 2, 3, and 4. Enter the number here . . . . (This number should be 60, the total number of verbal questions. If it is not, check your work for Steps 2, 3, and 4.)	_____
Step 6:	Enter the number from Step 2 here	_____
Step 7:	Enter the number from Step 3 here $\dfrac{_____}{4}$; divide it by 4. (This is the correction for guessing.) Write the resulting number here	− _____
Step 8:	Subtract the number in Step 7 from the number in Step 6; enter the result here	_____
Step 9:	Add .5 to the number in Step 8. Enter the result here	+ _____.5_____ _____
Step 10:	Drop all the digits to the right of the decimal point and write the result here	_____
This is your verbal raw score corrected for guessing. Instructions for converting this score to a scaled score are on page 629.		

Your Quantitative Raw Score

Step 1:	Sections 2, 4, and 6 are used to determine your quantitative score. In these sections only, count the number of correct answers (marked C) and enter this number here	_____
Step 2:	In these same sections (2, 4, and 6), count the number of questions that you answered incorrectly (marked I). Enter the number here	_____
Step 3:	Count the number of questions in sections 2, 4, and 6 that you crossed out because you did not answer them or marked more than one answer. Enter this number here	_____
Step 4:	Add the numbers in Steps 1, 2, and 3. Enter the total here . . . . (This number should be 52, the total number of quantitative questions. If it is not, check your work for Steps 1, 2, and 3.)	_____
Step 5:	Enter the number from Step 1 here	_____
Step 6:	Enter the number from Step 2 here $\dfrac{_____}{4}$; divide it by 4. (This is the correction for guessing.) Write the resulting number here	$-$ _____
Step 7:	Subtract the number in Step 6 from the number in Step 5; enter the result here	_____
Step 8:	Add .5 to the number in Step 7. Enter the result here	$+$ ____.5____ _____
Step 9:	Drop all the digits to the right of the decimal point and write the result here	_____

This is your quantitative raw score corrected for guessing. Instructions for converting this score to a scaled score are on page 629.

Your Total Raw Score

Step 1:	Using all the sections of the test, count the number of correct answers (marked C) and enter this number here	_____
Step 2:	Count the number of questions in all the sections that you answered incorrectly (marked I). Enter the number here	_____
Step 3:	Count the number of questions in all sections that you crossed out because you did not answer them or marked more than one answer. Enter this number here	_____
Step 4:	Add the numbers in Steps 1, 2, and 3. Enter the total here . . . . (This number should be 112, the total number of questions in the test. If it is not, check your work for Steps 1, 2, and 3.)	_____
Step 5:	Enter the number from Step 1 here	_____
Step 6:	Enter the number from Step 2 here $\dfrac{_____}{4}$; divide it by 4. (This is the correction for guessing.) Write the resulting number here	$-$ _____
Step 7:	Subtract the number in Step 6 from the number in Step 5; enter the result here	_____
Step 8:	Add .5 to the number in Step 7. Enter the result here	$+$ _____.5_____ _____
Step 9:	Drop all the digits to the right of the decimal point and write the result here	_____

This is your total raw score corrected for guessing. It is possible that the sum of your verbal and quantitative raw scores may be one point higher or lower than the total raw score due to the rounding procedures for each score. Instructions for converting this score — and your verbal and quantitative raw scores corrected for guessing — to scaled scores are on page 629.

How to Calculate Your Scores: Form B

Your Verbal Raw Score

Step 1:	Using the answer key, mark your answer sheet as follows: put a C next to each question that you answered correctly; put an I next to each question that you answered incorrectly. Cross out any questions that you did not answer or for which you marked more than one answer; these will not be counted in the scoring.
Step 2:	Sections 1, 3, and 5 are used to determine your verbal score. In these sections only, count the number of correct answers (marked C) and enter this number here . . . . _____
Step 3:	In these same sections (1, 3, and 5), count the number of questions that you answered incorrectly (marked I). Enter the number here . . . . _____
Step 4:	Count the number of questions in sections 1, 3, and 5 that you crossed out because you did not answer them or marked more than one answer. Enter this number here . . . . _____
Step 5:	Add the numbers in Steps 2, 3, and 4. Enter the number here . . . . _____ (This number should be 60, the total number of verbal questions. If it is not, check your work for Steps 2, 3, and 4.)
Step 6:	Enter the number from Step 2 here . . . . _____
Step 7:	Enter the number from Step 3 here $\dfrac{_____}{4}$; divide it by 4. (This is the correction for guessing.) Write the resulting number here . . . . − _____
Step 8:	Subtract the number in Step 7 from the number in Step 6; enter the result here . . . . _____
Step 9:	Add .5 to the number in Step 8. Enter the result here . . . . + ____.5____ _____
Step 10:	Drop all the digits to the right of the decimal point and write the result here . . . . _____
This is your verbal raw score corrected for guessing. Instructions for converting this score to a scaled score are on page 629.	

Your Quantitative Raw Score

Step 1:	Sections 2, 4, and 6 are used to determine your quantitative score. In these sections only, count the number of correct answers (marked C) and enter this number here	_____
Step 2:	In these same sections (2, 4, and 6), count the number of questions that you answered incorrectly (marked I). Enter the number here	_____
Step 3:	Count the number of questions in sections 2, 4, and 6 that you crossed out because you did not answer them or marked more than one answer. Enter this number here	_____
Step 4:	Add the numbers in Steps 1, 2, and 3. Enter the total here . . . . (This number should be 52, the total number of quantitative questions. If it is not, check your work for Steps 1, 2, and 3.)	_____
Step 5:	Enter the number from Step 1 here	_____
Step 6:	Enter the number from Step 2 here _____; divide it by 4. (This is the correction for guessing.) Write the resulting number here	− _____
Step 7:	Subtract the number in Step 6 from the number in Step 5; enter the result here	_____
Step 8:	Add .5 to the number in Step 7. Enter the result here	+ _____.5_____ _____
Step 9:	Drop all the digits to the right of the decimal point and write the result here	_____
This is your quantitative raw score corrected for guessing. Instructions for converting this score to a scaled score are on page 629.		

Your Total Raw Score

Step 1:	Using all the sections of the test, count the number of correct answers (marked C) and enter this number here	_____
Step 2:	Count the number of questions in all the sections that you answered incorrectly (marked I). Enter the number here	_____
Step 3:	Count the number of questions in all sections that you crossed out because you did not answer them or marked more than one answer. Enter this number here	_____
Step 4:	Add the numbers in Steps 1, 2, and 3. Enter the total here . . . . (This number should be 112, the total number of questions in the test. If it is not, check your work for Steps 1, 2, and 3.)	_____
Step 5:	Enter the number from Step 1 here	_____
Step 6:	Enter the number from Step 2 here $\dfrac{_____}{4}$; divide it by 4. (This is the correction for guessing.) Write the resulting number here	− _____
Step 7:	Subtract the number in Step 6 from the number in Step 5; enter the result here	_____
Step 8:	Add .5 to the number in Step 7. Enter the result here	+ _____.5_____ _____
Step 9:	Drop all the digits to the right of the decimal point and write the result here	_____

This is your total raw score corrected for guessing. It is possible that the sum of your verbal and quantitative raw scores may be one point higher or lower than the total raw score due to the rounding procedures for each score. Instructions for converting this score — and your verbal and quantitative raw scores corrected for guessing — to scaled scores are on page 629.

How to Calculate Your Scores: Form C

Your Verbal Raw Score

Step 1:	Using the answer key, mark your answer sheet as follows: put a C next to each question that you answered correctly; put an I next to each question that you answered incorrectly. Cross out any questions that you did not answer or for which you marked more than one answer; these will not be counted in the scoring.
Step 2:	Sections 2, 4, and 6 are used to determine your verbal score. In these sections only, count the number of correct answers (marked C) and enter this number here .... _____
Step 3:	In these same sections (2, 4, and 6), count the number of questions that you answered incorrectly (marked I). Enter the number here .... _____
Step 4:	Count the number of questions in sections 2, 4, and 6 that you crossed out because you did not answer them or marked more than one answer. Enter this number here .... _____
Step 5:	Add the numbers in Steps 2, 3, and 4. Enter the number here .... _____ (This number should be 70, the total number of verbal questions. If it is not, check your work for Steps 2, 3, and 4.)
Step 6:	Enter the number from Step 2 here .... _____
Step 7:	Enter the number from Step 3 here $\dfrac{\text{_____}}{4}$; divide it by 4. (This is the correction for guessing.) Write the resulting number here .... − _____
Step 8:	Subtract the number in Step 7 from the number in Step 6; enter the result here .... _____
Step 9:	Add .5 to the number in Step 8. Enter the result here .... _____ $+$ ___.5___
Step 10:	Drop all the digits to the right of the decimal point and write the result here .... _____
This is your verbal raw score corrected for guessing. Instructions for converting this score to a scaled score are on page 629.	

Your Quantitative Raw Score

Step 1:	Sections 1, 3, and 5 are used to determine your quantitative score. In these sections only, count the number of correct answers (marked C) and enter this number here	_____
Step 2:	In these same sections (1, 3, and 5), count the number of questions that you answered incorrectly (marked I). Enter the number here	_____
Step 3:	Count the number of questions in sections 1, 3, and 5 that you crossed out because you did not answer them or marked more than one answer. Enter this number here	_____
Step 4:	Add the numbers in Steps 1, 2, and 3. Enter the total here .... (This number should be 65, the total number of quantitative questions. If it is not, check your work for Steps 1, 2, and 3.)	_____
Step 5:	Enter the number from Step 1 here	_____
Step 6:	Enter the number from Step 2 here _____; divide $\overline{4}$ it by 4. (This is the correction for guessing.) Write the resulting number here	– _____
Step 7:	Subtract the number in Step 6 from the number in Step 5; enter the result here	_____
Step 8:	Add .5 to the number in Step 7. Enter the result here	+ _____.5_____ _____
Step 9:	Drop all the digits to the right of the decimal point and write the result here	_____
This is your quantitative raw score corrected for guessing. Instructions for converting this score to a scaled score are on page 629.		

Your Total Raw Score

Step 1:	Using all the sections of the test, count the number of correct answers (marked C) and enter this number here	_____
Step 2:	Count the number of questions in all the sections that you answered incorrectly (marked I). Enter the number here	_____
Step 3:	Count the number of questions in all sections that you crossed out because you did not answer them or marked more than one answer. Enter this number here	_____
Step 4:	Add the numbers in Steps 1, 2, and 3. Enter the total here . . . . (This number should be 135, the total number of questions in the test. If it is not, check your work for Steps 1, 2, and 3.)	_____
Step 5:	Enter the number from Step 1 here	_____
Step 6:	Enter the number from Step 2 here $\dfrac{\text{_____}}{4}$; divide it by 4. (This is the correction for guessing.) Write the resulting number here	− _____
Step 7:	Subtract the number in Step 6 from the number in Step 5; enter the result here	_____
Step 8:	Add .5 to the number in Step 7. Enter the result here	+ ___.5___ _____
Step 9:	Drop all the digits to the right of the decimal point and write the result here	_____
This is your total raw score corrected for guessing. It is possible that the sum of your verbal and quantitative raw scores may be one point higher or lower than the total raw score due to the rounding procedures for each score. Instructions for converting this score — and your verbal and quantitative raw scores corrected for guessing — to scaled scores are on page 629.		

Converting Your Raw Scores to Scaled Scores

The raw scores corrected for guessing that you have obtained (last step in each worksheet) may be converted to scaled scores using the conversion tables on the following pages. Raw scores are converted to scaled scores to ensure that a score earned on any one form of the GMAT is directly comparable to the same scaled score earned (within a five-year period) on any other form of the test. The scaling process also ensures comparability between tests with different numbers of questions, so that a test with 112 questions (Forms A and B) is directly comparable to a test with 135 questions (Form C). Scaled scores are "standard scores" with understood and accepted meanings. The scores reported to schools when you take the actual GMAT will be scaled scores.

Using the conversion tables, for each form of the test that you took (A,B,C), find the GMAT scaled scores that correspond to your three raw scores (verbal, quantitative, total), corrected for guessing. For example, a verbal raw score of 44 on Form A would correspond to a scaled score of 39; a quantitative raw score of 44 on Form A would correspond to a scaled score of 45. A total raw score of 88 on Form A would correspond to a scaled score of 680.

When you take the GMAT at an actual administration, one or more of your scores will probably differ from the scaled scores you obtained on these representative GMAT tests. Even the same student performs at different levels at different times—for a variety of reasons unrelated to the test itself. In addition, your test scores may differ because the conditions under which you took these tests could not be exactly the same as those at an actual test administration.

After you have scored your tests, analyze the results with a view to improving your performance when you take the actual GMAT.

■ Did the time you spent reading directions make serious inroads on the time you had available for answering questions? If you become thoroughly familiar with the directions given in this book (in Chapter 1, Chapters 3-8, and the representative tests), you may need to spend less time reading directions in the actual test.

■ Did you run out of time before you reached the end of a section? If so, could you pace yourself better in the actual test? Remember, not everyone finishes all sections; accuracy is also important.

■ Look at the specific questions you missed. In which ones did you suffer from lack of knowledge? Faulty reasoning? Faulty reading of the questions? Being aware of the causes of your errors may enable you to avoid some errors when you actually take the GMAT.

What Your Scaled Scores Mean

The tables on page 633 contain information that will be of help in understanding your scaled scores. Each table consists of a column marked "Scaled Score" and a column indicating the percentage of test takers in the time period specified who scored below the scores listed. For example, if you earned a total scaled score of about 600 on a representative test and you are able to achieve the same score on an actual GMAT, the 81 opposite 600 tells you that 81 percent of the 623,190 people taking the test in the 1992-1995 period earned scores lower than that; the remainder earned the same or a higher score. Also given in each table is the average score of the group tested in the 1992-1995 time period.

Graduate school admissions officers understand the statistical meaning of GMAT scores, but each institution uses and interprets the scores according to the needs of its own programs. You should, therefore, consult the schools to which you are applying to learn how they will interpret and use your scores.

Some Cautions about Score Interpretation

1. The multiple-choice portion of the GMAT is designed to yield only the reported verbal, quantitative, and total scaled scores. One should not calculate raw scores for individual test sections and infer specific strengths or weaknesses from a comparison of the raw score results by section. There are two reasons for this.

   First, different sections have different numbers of questions and, even if the numbers were the same or if percentages were used to make the numbers comparable, the sections might not be equally difficult. For illustrative purposes only, suppose that one section had 20 items and another had 25. Furthermore, suppose you received a corrected raw score of 10 on the first and 10 on the second. It would be inappropriate to conclude that you had equal ability in the two sections because the corrected raw scores were equal, as you really obtained 50 percent on the first section and only 40 percent on the second. It could be equally inappropriate, however, to conclude from the percentages that you were better on the first section than on the second. Suppose the first section was relatively easy for most test takers (say, an average corrected raw score percentage across examinees of 55 percent) and the second was relatively difficult (an average corrected raw score percentage of 35 percent). Now you might conclude that you were worse than average on the first section and better than average on the second.

   Differences in difficulty level between editions are accounted for in the procedure for converting the verbal, quantitative, and total corrected raw scores to scaled scores. Since the raw scores for individual sections are not converted to produce scaled scores by section, performance on individual sections of the test cannot be compared.

   Second, corrected raw scores by section are not converted to scaled scores by section because the GMAT is not designed to reliably measure specific strengths and weaknesses beyond the general verbal and quantitative abilities for which separate scaled scores are reported. Reliability is dependent, in part, on the number of questions in the test — the more questions, the higher the reliability. The relatively few questions in each section, taken alone, are not sufficient to produce a reliable result for each section. On the multiple-choice portion of the GMAT, only the reported verbal, quantitative, and total scaled scores (which include questions across several sections) have sufficient reliability to permit their use in counseling and predicting graduate school performance.

2. It is possible, if you repeat the test, that your second raw scores corrected for guessing could be higher than on the first test, but your scaled scores could be lower and vice versa. This is a result of the slight differences in difficulty level between editions of the test, which are taken into account when corrected raw scores are converted to the GMAT scaled scores. That is, for a given scaled score, a more difficult edition requires a lower corrected raw score and an easier edition requires a higher corrected raw score.

Verbal Converted (Scaled) Scores Corresponding to Corrected Raw Scores for Three Forms of the GMAT

Corrected Raw Scores	Scaled Scores			Corrected Raw Scores	Scaled Scores			Corrected Raw Scores	Scaled Scores		
	Form A	Form B	Form C		Form A	Form B	Form C		Form A	Form B	Form C
70			51	45	39	39	35	20	22	21	19
69			50	44	39	38	34	19	21	20	18
68			50	43	38	37	34	18	21	20	17
67			49	42	37	36	33	17	20	19	17
66			48	41	37	36	32	16	19	18	16
65			48	40	36	35	32	15	19	18	15
64			47	39	35	34	31	14	18	17	15
63			46	38	35	34	30	13	17	16	14
62			46	37	34	33	30	12	17	16	14
61			45	36	33	32	29	11	16	15	13
60	51	51	44	35	33	32	28	10	15	14	12
59	50	50	44	34	32	31	28	9	15	13	12
58	49	49	43	33	31	30	27	8	14	13	11
57	48	48	43	32	30	29	26	7	13	12	10
56	47	47	42	31	30	29	26	6	12	11	10
55	46	46	41	30	29	28	25	5	12	11	9
54	46	45	41	29	28	27	25	4	11	10	8
53	45	44	40	28	28	27	24	3	10	9	8
52	44	43	39	27	27	26	23	2	10	9	7
51	44	43	39	26	26	25	23	1	9	8	6
50	43	42	38	25	26	25	22	0	8	7	6
49	42	41	37	24	25	24	21				
48	42	41	37	23	24	23	21				
47	41	40	36	22	24	22	20				
46	40	39	35	21	23	22	19				

Quantitative Converted (Scaled) Scores Corresponding to Corrected Raw Scores
for Three Forms of the GMAT

Corrected Raw Scores	Scaled Scores			Corrected Raw Scores	Scaled Scores			Corrected Raw Scores	Scaled Scores		
	Form A	Form B	Form C		Form A	Form B	Form C		Form A	Form B	Form C
				45	46	47	39	20	28	28	23
				44	45	47	38	19	27	28	23
				43	45	46	38	18	26	27	22
				42	44	45	37	17	26	26	21
				41	43	44	36	16	25	25	21
65			51	40	43	44	36	15	24	25	20
64			51	39	42	43	35	14	23	24	20
63			50	38	41	42	34	13	23	23	19
62			50	37	40	41	34	12	22	22	18
61			49	36	40	40	33	11	21	21	18
60			49	35	39	40	33	10	20	21	17
59			48	34	38	39	32	9	20	20	16
58			47	33	37	38	31	8	19	19	16
57			46	32	37	37	31	7	18	18	15
56			46	31	36	37	30	6	17	17	15
55			45	30	35	36	29	5	17	16	14
54			44	29	34	35	29	4	16	15	13
53			44	28	34	34	28	3	15	14	13
52	51	51	43	27	33	34	28	2	14	13	12
51	50	51	43	26	32	33	27	1	13	12	11
50	50	51	42	25	31	32	26	0	12	11	10
49	49	50	41	24	31	31	26				
48	49	50	41	23	30	31	25				
47	48	49	40	22	29	30	24				
46	47	48	39	21	29	29	24				

Total Converted (Scaled) Scores Corresponding to Corrected Raw Scores
for Three Forms of the GMAT

Corrected Raw Scores	Scaled Scores			Corrected Raw Scores	Scaled Scores			Corrected Raw Scores	Scaled Scores		
	Form A	Form B	Form C		Form A	Form B	Form C		Form A	Form B	Form C
135			800	85	670	670	580	35	410	410	360
134			800	84	660	660	580	34	410	400	360
133			790	83	660	660	570	33	400	400	350
132			790	82	650	650	570	32	400	390	350
131			790	81	650	650	560	31	390	390	350
130			780	80	640	640	560	30	390	380	340
129			780	79	640	640	560	29	380	380	340
128			770	78	630	630	550	28	380	370	330
127			770	77	630	630	550	27	370	370	330
126			760	76	620	620	540	26	370	360	320
125			760	75	620	620	540	25	360	360	320
124			750	74	610	610	530	24	360	350	320
123			750	73	610	610	530	23	350	340	310
122			740	72	600	600	530	22	350	340	310
121			740	71	600	590	520	21	340	330	300
120			740	70	590	590	520	20	340	330	300
119			730	69	590	580	510	19	330	320	290
118			730	68	580	580	510	18	330	320	290
117			720	67	580	570	500	17	320	310	280
116			720	66	570	570	500	16	320	310	280
115			710	65	570	560	490	15	310	300	280
114			710	64	560	560	490	14	310	300	270
113			710	63	560	550	490	13	300	290	270
112	800	800	700	62	550	550	480	12	300	290	260
111	800	800	700	61	550	540	480	11	290	280	260
110	800	800	690	60	540	540	470	10	290	280	250
109	800	790	690	59	530	530	470	9	280	270	250
108	790	790	680	58	530	530	460	8	280	270	250
107	780	790	680	57	520	520	460	7	270	260	240
106	780	780	670	56	520	520	460	6	270	260	240
105	770	770	670	55	510	510	450	5	260	250	230
104	760	770	670	54	510	510	450	4	250	250	230
103	760	760	660	53	500	500	440	3	240	240	220
102	750	760	660	52	500	500	440	2	230	220	220
101	750	750	650	51	490	490	430	1	220	210	210
100	740	750	650	50	490	490	430	0	210	200	200
99	740	740	640	49	480	480	420				
98	730	740	640	48	480	480	420				
97	730	730	630	47	470	470	420				
96	720	730	630	46	470	460	410				
95	720	720	630	45	460	460	410				
94	710	710	620	44	460	450	400				
93	710	710	620	43	450	450	400				
92	700	700	610	42	450	440	390				
91	700	700	610	41	440	440	390				
90	690	690	600	40	440	430	390				
89	690	690	600	39	430	430	380				
88	680	680	600	38	430	420	380				
87	680	680	590	37	420	420	370				
86	670	670	590	36	420	410	370				

Test Content

If you have questions about specific items in the representative tests, about any of the sample tests included in Chapters 3-7, or about any of the sample writing tasks included in Chapter 8, please write to School and Higher Education Test Development, Educational Testing Service, P.O. Box 6656, Princeton, NJ 08541-6656. Please include in your letter the page number on which the item appears and the number of the question,

along with specifics on your inquiry or comment. If you have a question about particular items or writing tasks in an actual GMAT, please write to the same address and include in your letter your name, address, sex, date of birth, the date on which you took the test, the test center name, the section number(s) and number(s) of the questions involved. This information is necessary for ETS to retrieve your answer sheet and determine the particular form of the GMAT you took.

Table 1
Percentages of Candidates Tested from June 1992 through March 1995 (including repeaters) Who Scored below Selected Verbal and Quantitative Scores

Scaled Score	Percentages Below	
	Verbal	Quantitative
50-60	>99	>99
48	>99	99
46	99	99
44	98	97
42	96	94
40	92	90
38	87	85
36	82	80
34	75	74
32	67	66
30	59	59
28	51	52
26	43	44
24	35	36
22	27	28
20	21	22
18	16	16
16	11	11
14	7	7
12	4	4
10	2	2
0-8	<1	<1
Number of Candidates	623,190	623,190
Mean	27	31
Standard Deviation	9	9

Table 2
Percentages of Candidates Tested from June 1992 through March 1995 (including repeaters) Who Scored below Selected Total Scores

Scaled Score	Percentages Below
750-800	>99
720-740	99
700	97
680	96
660	93
640	90
620	86
600	81
580	76
560	70
540	63
520	56
500	49
480	42
460	35
440	29
420	23
400	18
380	13
360	10
340	7
320	4
300	3
280	1
200-260	<1
Number of Candidates	623,190
Mean	497
Standard Deviation	105

Table 3
Percentages of Candidates Tested from October 1994 through June 1995 (including repeaters) Scoring below AWA Scores

AWA Score	Percentage Below
6.0	99
5.5	95
5.0	84
4.5	65
4.0	43
3.5	25
3.0	13
2.5	6
2.0	2
0.0 - 1.5	0
Number of Candidates	146,993
Mean	3.8
Standard Deviation	1.0

Guidelines for Use of Graduate Management Admission Test Scores

Introduction

These guidelines have been prepared to provide information about appropriate score use for those who interpret scores and set criteria for admission and to protect students from unfair decisions based on inappropriate use of scores.

The guidelines are based on several policy and psychometric considerations.

■ The Graduate Management Admission Council has an obligation to inform users of the scores' strengths and limitations and the users have a concomitant obligation to use the scores in an appropriate, rather than the most convenient, manner.

■ The purpose of any testing instrument, including the Graduate Management Admission Test, is to provide information to *assist* in making decisions; the test alone should not be presumed to be a decision maker.

■ GMAT test scores are but one of a number of sources of information and should be used, whenever possible, in combination with other information and, in every case, with full recognition of what the test can and cannot do.

The primary asset of the GMAT is that it provides a common measure, administered under standard conditions, with known reliability, validity, and other psychometric qualities, for evaluating the academic skills of many individuals. The GMAT has two primary limitations: (1) it cannot and does not measure all the qualities important for graduate study in management and other pursuits; (2) there are psychometric limitations to the test — for example, only score differences of certain magnitudes are reliable indicators of real differences in performance. Such limits should be taken into consideration as GMAT scores are used.

Specific Guidelines

1. **In recognition of the test's limitations, use multiple criteria.** The GMAT itself does not measure every discipline-related skill necessary for academic work, nor does it measure subjective factors important to academic and career success, such as motivation, creativity, and interpersonal skills. Therefore, all available pertinent information about an applicant must be considered before a selection decision is made, with GMAT scores being *only one* of these several criteria. The test's limitations are discussed clearly in the GMAT *Bulletin of Information* and in the *GMAT Technical Report*.

2. **Interpret the analytical writing score on the basis of the criteria and standards established in the GMAT scoring guides.** These criteria and standards are the best source for interpreting the analytical writing score. Recognize that the score is based on two 30-minute written responses that represent first-draft writing samples. Each response is evaluated according to the scoring guides although the average score can result from different combinations of ratings. For example, a test taker whose individual ratings are 5 and 6 on the first topic and 3 and 3 on the second topic for an average score of 4.5 (rounded to the nearest half-point interval) receives the same score as a student whose individual ratings are 5 and 5 on the first topic and 4 and 4 on the second topic.

3. **Establish the relationship between GMAT scores and performance in your graduate management school.** It is incumbent on any institution using GMAT scores in the admissions process that it demonstrate empirically the relationship between test scores and measures of performance in its academic program. Data should be collected and analyzed to provide information about the predictive validity of GMAT scores and their appropriateness for the particular use and in the particular circumstances at the score-using school. In addition, any formula used in the admissions process that combines test scores with other criteria should be validated and reviewed regularly to determine whether the weights attached to the particular measures are appropriate for optimizing the prediction of performance in the program.

4. **Avoid the use of cutoff scores.** The use of arbitrary cutoff scores (below which no applicant will be considered for admission) is strongly discouraged, primarily for the reasons cited in the introduction to these guidelines. Distinctions based on score differences not substantial enough to be reliable should be avoided. (For information about reliability, see the GMAT *Examinee Score Interpretation Guide*.) Cutoff scores should be used only if there is clear empirical evidence that a large proportion of the applicants scoring below the cutoff scores have substantial difficulty doing satisfactory graduate work. In addition, it is incumbent on the school to demonstrate that the use of cutoff scores does not result in the systematic exclusion of members of either sex, of any age or ethnic groups, or of any other relevant groups in the face of other evidence that would indicate their competence or predict their success.

5. **Do not compare GMAT scores with those on other tests.** GMAT scores cannot be derived from scores on other tests. While minor differences among different editions of the GMAT that have been constructed to be parallel can be compensated for by the statistical process of score equating, the GMAT is not intended to be parallel to graduate admission tests offered by other testing programs.

6. **Interpret the scores of persons with disabilities cautiously.** The GMAT is offered with special arrangements to accommodate the needs of candidates with visual, physical, hearing, and learning disabilities. Test scores earned under nonstandard conditions are reported with a special notice that disabled persons may be at a disadvantage when taking standardized tests such as the GMAT, even when the test is administered in a manner chosen by the candidate to minimize any adverse effect of his or her disability on test performance. In using these scores, admissions officers should note the usual caution that GMAT scores be considered as only one part of an applicant's record.

Normally Appropriate Uses of GMAT Scores

1. **For selection of applicants for graduate study in management.** A person's GMAT scores tell how the person performed on a test designed to measure general verbal and quantitative abilities that are associated with success in the first year of study at graduate schools of management and that have been developed over a long period of time. The scores can be used in conjunction with other information to help estimate performance in a graduate management program.

2. **For selection of applicants for financial aid based on academic potential.**

3. **For counseling and guidance.** Undergraduate counselors, if they maintain appropriate records, such as the test scores and undergraduate grade-point averages of their students accepted by various graduate management programs, may be able to help students estimate their chances of acceptance at given graduate management schools.

Normally Inappropriate Uses of GMAT Scores

1. **As a requisite for awarding a degree.** The GMAT is designed to measure broadly defined verbal and quantitative skills and is primarily useful for predicting success in graduate management schools. The use of the test for anything other than selection for graduate management study, financial aid awards, or counseling and guidance is to be avoided.

2. **As a requirement for employment, for licensing or certification to perform a job, or for job-related rewards (raises, promotions, etc.).** For the reasons listed in number 1 above, the use of the GMAT for these purposes is inappropriate. Further, approved score-receiving institutions are not permitted to make score reports available for any of these purposes.

3. **As an achievement test.** The GMAT is not designed to assess an applicant's achievement or knowledge in specific subject areas.

Order Form for Official GMAC Publications

For fastest service (credit card orders only):

- call **800-982-6740, Dept. G36,**
  M-F, 8 a.m. - 8 p.m. Eastern time
  (outside the U.S. or Canada, call **609-771-7243**)

- visit our website: **http://www.gmat.org**
- fax **609-771-7385**

Or mail this order form with your payment to the address at right.

Prices are effective through August 31, 1997. The telephone numbers above are for publications credit card orders only; for other GMAT services or information, call 609-771-7330.

Payment Method: ☐ VISA   ☐ MasterCard   ☐ American Express   ☐ Check/Money Order (in U.S. dollars, payable to ETS/GMAT)

Credit Card Number _ _ _ _ _ _ _ _ _ _ _ _ _ _ _ _   Expiration Date _____/_____

Cardholder's or Authorized User's Signature _____

Daytime Telephone Number _____

		U.S. Delivery*	Foreign Delivery*	Price
The Official Guide for GMAT Review	238415	☐ $15.95	☐ $24.95	$_____
*GMAT POWERPREP Software***	238350	☐ $59.95	☐ $74.95	_____
Special Value! GMAT Review Set**	238351	☐ $65.00	☐ $85.00	_____
(GMAT book and software)				

SUBTOTAL _____

In CA, DC, and GA, add sales tax _____

In Canada, add GST 13141 4468 RT _____

TOTAL ORDER $_____

* See shipping information on reverse side.
** See hardware requirements on reverse side.

GRADUATE MANAGEMENT ADMISSION TEST   696-01
EDUCATIONAL TESTING SERVICE   GMAC
P.O. BOX 6108   GUIDES
PRINCETON, NJ 08541-6108   G-96

TO

This is your mailing label. Type or print clearly.

Order Form for Official GMAC Publications

For fastest service (credit card orders only):

- call **800-982-6740, Dept. G36,**
  M-F, 8 a.m. - 8 p.m. Eastern time
  (outside the U.S. or Canada, call **609-771-7243**)

- visit our website: **http://www.gmat.org**
- fax **609-771-7385**

Or mail this order form with your payment to the address at right.

Prices are effective through August 31, 1997. The telephone numbers above are for publications credit card orders only; for other GMAT services or information, call 609-771-7330.

Payment Method: ☐ VISA   ☐ MasterCard   ☐ American Express   ☐ Check/Money Order (in U.S. dollars, payable to ETS/GMAT)

Credit Card Number _ _ _ _ _ _ _ _ _ _ _ _ _ _ _ _   Expiration Date _____/_____

Cardholder's or Authorized User's Signature _____

Daytime Telephone Number _____

The Official Guide for GMAT Review   238415   ☐ $15.95   ☐ $24.95 $_____
GMAT POWERPREP Software**   238350   ☐ $59.95   ☐ $74.95   _____
Special Value! GMAT Review Set**   238351   ☐ $65.00   ☐ $85.00   _____
(GMAT book and software)

SUBTOTAL _____
In CA, DC, and GA, add sales tax _____
In Canada, add GST 13141 4468 RT _____
TOTAL ORDER $_____

* See shipping information on reverse side.
** See hardware requirements on reverse side.

GRADUATE MANAGEMENT ADMISSION TEST   696-01
EDUCATIONAL TESTING SERVICE   GMAC
P.O. BOX 6108   GUIDES
PRINCETON, NJ 08541-6108   G-96

TO

This is your mailing label. Type or print clearly.

Order Form for Official GMAC Publications

For fastest service (credit card orders only):

- call **800-982-6740, Dept. G36,**
  M-F, 8 a.m. - 8 p.m. Eastern time
  (outside the U.S. or Canada, call **609-771-7243**)

- visit our website: **http://www.gmat.org**
- fax **609-771-7385**

Or mail this order form with your payment to the address at right.

Prices are effective through August 31, 1997. The telephone numbers above are for publications credit card orders only; for other GMAT services or information, call 609-771-7330.

Payment Method: ☐ VISA   ☐ MasterCard   ☐ American Express   ☐ Check/Money Order (in U.S. dollars, payable to ETS/GMAT)

Credit Card Number _ _ _ _ _ _ _ _ _ _ _ _ _ _ _ _   Expiration Date _____/_____

Cardholder's or Authorized User's Signature _____

Daytime Telephone Number _____

The Official Guide for GMAT Review   238415   ☐ $15.95   ☐ $24.95 $_____
GMAT POWERPREP Software**   238350   ☐ $59.95   ☐ $74.95   _____
Special Value! GMAT Review Set**   238351   ☐ $65.00   ☐ $85.00   _____
(GMAT book and software)

SUBTOTAL _____
In CA, DC, and GA, add sales tax _____
In Canada, add GST 13141 4468 RT _____
TOTAL ORDER $_____

* See shipping information on reverse side.
** See hardware requirements on reverse side.

GMAC PUBLICATIONS:
The only source for real GMAT questions.

The Official Guide for GMAT Review,
8th Edition

- contains three *actual* tests plus samples of each question type — more than 900 questions in all!
- gives answers and explanations by GMAT test authors
- provides helpful strategies, sample questions, and actual responses for the Analytical Writing Assessment
- includes comprehensive math review

Test Preparation for the GMAT: POWERPREP Software, **Release 1.0**

- includes two *actual* tests (different from those in the *GMAT Review* book) with on-screen timer and automatic scoring

- provides helpful strategies, sample questions, and actual responses for the Analytical Writing Assessment
- **Hardware requirements:** IBM compatible computer with 386 or better processor; 4 megabytes of RAM; 15 megabytes of hard disk space; 3.5˝, 1.44 megabyte high density floppy disk drive; Microsoft Windows version 3.1 or higher; VGA monitor; mouse; printer optional.

Ordering Information: To order, see reverse side. The publications are also sold in many bookstores.

Shipping Information: Orders sent to the U.S., Guam, Puerto Rico, U.S. Virgin Islands, and U.S. territories are shipped by first class mail or UPS (*street address required*). Allow two to three weeks from time of order receipt for delivery. Orders shipped outside the U.S. are sent airmail; allow four to six weeks from time of order receipt for delivery.
In a hurry? Call for faster delivery options.

GMAC PUBLICATIONS:
The only source for real GMAT questions.

The Official Guide for GMAT Review,
8th Edition

- contains three *actual* tests plus samples of each question type — more than 900 questions in all!
- gives answers and explanations by GMAT test authors
- provides helpful strategies, sample questions, and actual responses for the Analytical Writing Assessment
- includes comprehensive math review

Test Preparation for the GMAT: POWERPREP Software, **Release 1.0**

- includes two *actual* tests (different from those in the *GMAT Review* book) with on-screen timer and automatic scoring

- provides helpful strategies, sample questions, and actual responses for the Analytical Writing Assessment
- **Hardware requirements:** IBM compatible computer with 386 or better processor; 4 megabytes of RAM; 15 megabytes of hard disk space; 3.5˝, 1.44 megabyte high density floppy disk drive; Microsoft Windows version 3.1 or higher; VGA monitor; mouse; printer optional.

Ordering Information: To order, see reverse side. The publications are also sold in many bookstores.

Shipping Information: Orders sent to the U.S., Guam, Puerto Rico, U.S. Virgin Islands, and U.S. territories are shipped by first class mail or UPS (*street address required*). Allow two to three weeks from time of order receipt for delivery. Orders shipped outside the U.S. are sent airmail; allow four to six weeks from time of order receipt for delivery.
In a hurry? Call for faster delivery options.

GMAC PUBLICATIONS:
The only source for real GMAT questions.

The Official Guide for GMAT Review,
8th Edition

- contains three *actual* tests plus samples of each question type — more than 900 questions in all!
- gives answers and explanations by GMAT test authors
- provides helpful strategies, sample questions, and actual responses for the Analytical Writing Assessment
- includes comprehensive math review

Test Preparation for the GMAT: POWERPREP Software, **Release 1.0**

- includes two *actual* tests (different from those in the *GMAT Review* book) with on-screen timer and automatic scoring

- provides helpful strategies, sample questions, and actual responses for the Analytical Writing Assessment
- **Hardware requirements:** IBM compatible computer with 386 or better processor; 4 megabytes of RAM; 15 megabytes of hard disk space; 3.5˝, 1.44 megabyte high density floppy disk drive; Microsoft Windows version 3.1 or higher; VGA monitor; mouse; printer optional.

Ordering Information: To order, see reverse side. The publications are also sold in many bookstores.

Shipping Information: Orders sent to the U.S., Guam, Puerto Rico, U.S. Virgin Islands, and U.S. territories are shipped by first class mail or UPS (*street address required*). Allow two to three weeks from time of order receipt for delivery. Orders shipped outside the U.S. are sent airmail; allow four to six weeks from time of order receipt for delivery.
In a hurry? Call for faster delivery options.

Order Form for 1996-97 GMAT® Bulletin and Registration Form

The *Graduate Management Admission Test®* *(GMAT) Bulletin and Registration Form* contains:

- a registration form, return envelope, and instructions for taking the test
- sample multiple-choice questions and writing topics
- test-taking directions and suggestions
- general information concerning the test administration including accommodations for persons with disabilities, Sabbath-observers, and international applicants
- a form for requesting previous GMAT scores to be sent to schools
- information about ordering GMAT review publications

See reverse side for test dates and registration deadlines.

For a free copy of the *GMAT Bulletin:*

- **Mail or Fax** the completed address label at the right to

  GMAT
  Educational Testing Service
  P.O. Box 6101
  Princeton, NJ 08541-6101

  Fax: 609-883-4349

- **Telephone**
  (24-hour voice mail):   609-771-7330

- **TTY device for deaf and hard-of-hearing people**:   609-734-9362

- **E-mail**:   gmat@ets.org

Or visit our website at **http://www.gmat.org** to register for the GMAT, order GMAC publications, search for a school, or learn about opportunities and resources available to prospective MBAs.

This is your mailing label. Type or print clearly.

➤

TO _____

_____

GRADUATE MANAGEMENT ADMISSION TEST   666-17
EDUCATIONAL TESTING SERVICE   GMAT
P.O. BOX 6101   BULLETIN
PRINCETON, NJ 08541-6101   G-99

Order Form for 1996-97 GMAT® Bulletin and Registration Form

The *Graduate Management Admission Test®* *(GMAT) Bulletin and Registration Form* contains:

- a registration form, return envelope, and instructions for taking the test
- sample multiple-choice questions and writing topics
- test-taking directions and suggestions
- general information concerning the test administration including accommodations for persons with disabilities, Sabbath-observers, and international applicants
- a form for requesting previous GMAT scores to be sent to schools
- information about ordering GMAT review publications

See reverse side for test dates and registration deadlines.

For a free copy of the *GMAT Bulletin:*

- **Mail or Fax** the completed address label at the right to

  GMAT
  Educational Testing Service
  P.O. Box 6101
  Princeton, NJ 08541-6101

  Fax: 609-883-4349

- **Telephone**
  (24-hour voice mail):   609-771-7330

- **TTY device for deaf and hard-of-hearing people**:   609-734-9362

- **E-mail**:   gmat@ets.org

Or visit our website at **http://www.gmat.org** to register for the GMAT, order GMAC publications, search for a school, or learn about opportunities and resources available to prospective MBAs.

This is your mailing label. Type or print clearly.

➤

TO _____

_____

GRADUATE MANAGEMENT ADMISSION TEST   666-17
EDUCATIONAL TESTING SERVICE   GMAT
P.O. BOX 6101   BULLETIN
PRINCETON, NJ 08541-6101   G-99

Order Form for 1996-97 GMAT® Bulletin and Registration Form

The *Graduate Management Admission Test®* *(GMAT) Bulletin and Registration Form* contains:

- a registration form, return envelope, and instructions for taking the test
- sample multiple-choice questions and writing topics
- test-taking directions and suggestions
- general information concerning the test administration including accommodations for persons with disabilities, Sabbath-observers, and international applicants
- a form for requesting previous GMAT scores to be sent to schools
- information about ordering GMAT review publications

See reverse side for test dates and registration deadlines.

For a free copy of the *GMAT Bulletin:*

- **Mail or Fax** the completed address label at the right to

  GMAT
  Educational Testing Service
  P.O. Box 6101
  Princeton, NJ 08541-6101

  Fax: 609-883-4349

- **Telephone**
  (24-hour voice mail):   609-771-7330

- **TTY device for deaf and hard-of-hearing people**:   609-734-9362

- **E-mail**:   gmat@ets.org

Or visit our website at **http://www.gmat.org** to register for the GMAT, order GMAC publications, search for a school, or learn about opportunities and resources available to prospective MBAs.

This is your mailing label. Type or print clearly.

➤

TO _____

_____

GRADUATE MANAGEMENT ADMISSION TEST   666-17
EDUCATIONAL TESTING SERVICE   GMAT
P.O. BOX 6101   BULLETIN
PRINCETON, NJ 08541-6101   G-99

1996-97 GMAT® Registration Calendar

Test Dates	DOMESTIC REGISTRATION GMAT administrations in the U.S., Guam, Puerto Rico, U.S. Virgin Islands, and U.S. Territories			INTERNATIONAL REGISTRATION GMAT administrations in all other countries	
	SPECIAL REQUESTS	**REGULAR REGISTRATION**	**LATE REGISTRATION & CENTER CHANGE**	**SPECIAL REQUESTS**	**FINAL REGISTRATION & CENTER CHANGE**
	Last **receipt** date for supplementary centers and Saturday-Sabbath observer administrations*	Registration forms **received** after this date must be accompanied by the late registration fee.	Add the late registration fee. Registration forms **received** after this period will be returned.	Last date for **receipt** of requests for supplementary centers† and Saturday-Sabbath observer administrations*	Registration forms **received** after this date will be returned.
	Deadline Dates				
Oct. 19, 1996*†	Aug. 27	Sept. 13	Sept. 14-20	Aug. 16	Aug. 30
Jan. 18, 1997*	Dec. 3	Dec. 20	Dec. 21-27	Nov. 22	Dec. 6
Mar. 15, 1997*	Jan. 28	Feb. 14	Feb. 15-21	Jan. 17	Jan. 31
June 21, 1997*	May 6	May 23	May 24-30	April 25	May 9

*Administration dates for observers of the Saturday Sabbath are Monday, October 21, 1996; Tuesday, January 21, 1997; Monday, March 17, 1997; and Monday, June 23, 1997.

†No supplementary centers will be established for international registration for the October 1996 test date.

1996-97 GMAT® Registration Calendar

Test Dates	DOMESTIC REGISTRATION GMAT administrations in the U.S., Guam, Puerto Rico, U.S. Virgin Islands, and U.S. Territories			INTERNATIONAL REGISTRATION GMAT administrations in all other countries	
	SPECIAL REQUESTS	**REGULAR REGISTRATION**	**LATE REGISTRATION & CENTER CHANGE**	**SPECIAL REQUESTS**	**FINAL REGISTRATION & CENTER CHANGE**
	Last **receipt** date for supplementary centers and Saturday-Sabbath observer administrations*	Registration forms **received** after this date must be accompanied by the late registration fee.	Add the late registration fee. Registration forms **received** after this period will be returned.	Last date for **receipt** of requests for supplementary centers† and Saturday-Sabbath observer administrations*	Registration forms **received** after this date will be returned.
	Deadline Dates				
Oct. 19, 1996*†	Aug. 27	Sept. 13	Sept. 14-20	Aug. 16	Aug. 30
Jan. 18, 1997*	Dec. 3	Dec. 20	Dec. 21-27	Nov. 22	Dec. 6
Mar. 15, 1997*	Jan. 28	Feb. 14	Feb. 15-21	Jan. 17	Jan. 31
June 21, 1997*	May 6	May 23	May 24-30	April 25	May 9

*Administration dates for observers of the Saturday Sabbath are Monday, October 21, 1996; Tuesday, January 21, 1997; Monday, March 17, 1997; and Monday, June 23, 1997.

†No supplementary centers will be established for international registration for the October 1996 test date.

1996-97 GMAT® Registration Calendar

Test Dates	DOMESTIC REGISTRATION GMAT administrations in the U.S., Guam, Puerto Rico, U.S. Virgin Islands, and U.S. Territories			INTERNATIONAL REGISTRATION GMAT administrations in all other countries	
	SPECIAL REQUESTS	**REGULAR REGISTRATION**	**LATE REGISTRATION & CENTER CHANGE**	**SPECIAL REQUESTS**	**FINAL REGISTRATION & CENTER CHANGE**
	Last **receipt** date for supplementary centers and Saturday-Sabbath observer administrations*	Registration forms **received** after this date must be accompanied by the late registration fee.	Add the late registration fee. Registration forms **received** after this period will be returned.	Last date for **receipt** of requests for supplementary centers† and Saturday-Sabbath observer administrations*	Registration forms **received** after this date will be returned.
	Deadline Dates				
Oct. 19, 1996*†	Aug. 27	Sept. 13	Sept. 14-20	Aug. 16	Aug. 30
Jan. 18, 1997*	Dec. 3	Dec. 20	Dec. 21-27	Nov. 22	Dec. 6
Mar. 15, 1997*	Jan. 28	Feb. 14	Feb. 15-21	Jan. 17	Jan. 31
June 21, 1997*	May 6	May 23	May 24-30	April 25	May 9

*Administration dates for observers of the Saturday Sabbath are Monday, October 21, 1996; Tuesday, January 21, 1997; Monday, March 17, 1997; and Monday, June 23, 1997.

†No supplementary centers will be established for international registration for the October 1996 test date.

Schools are searching for you. GMASS℠ puts you in touch!

Don't miss this free, one-time opportunity to find out about graduate management schools and programs you may not have considered. One of them might be just right for you.

Sign up for the Graduate Management Admission Search Service (GMASS) and become one of the GMAT test takers to whom schools and institutions send information about their graduate management programs. Test takers are chosen to receive a particular school's mailings because their background characteristics match those the school looks for in applicants for admission. You'll become aware of

- full- and part-time graduate programs,
- admission procedures, and
- financial aid opportunities.

For this free service, fill in "yes" in item 9 on the GMAT registration form.

MBA LOANS℠

A Program of the Graduate Management Admission Council

Is It Too Early To Think About Financing Your MBA?

It's NEVER too early to think about financing your education. MBA LOANS is designed by business schools especially for graduate business students – with a complete portfolio of federal and private loan options. And choosing MBA LOANS can save you time and money.

Why MBA LOANS? Here are a few good reasons:

Comprehensive!

Loan programs to meet every aspect of your financing needs.

Low Cost!

Competitive rates, lower life-of-loan costs, interest rate reductions for on-time payments.

Flexible Repayment Options!

Repayment benefits, graduated repayment options, deferments, forbearances, personal repayment counseling, loan consolidation.

Application A Phone Call Away!

Call **1-800-FON-MBAS** *(1-800-366-6227). Press 3 to talk with a customer service representative.*

The MBA LOANS program is available to U.S. citizens, and also to international students and permanent residents if they obtain a U.S.-citizen cosigner.

For more information on financing your MBA, call 1-800-366-6227, see your school's financial aid office, or visit our Web site, MBA Explorer, at http://www.gmat.org.

Graduate
Management
Admission
Council®

A diverse work force needs diverse management.

Multiculturalism, new technologies, and globalization are transforming American business. A degree in management gives you access to the careers that are leading this transformation.

Destination MBA^{SM}

Destination MBA, sponsored by the Graduate Management Admission Council, the National Black MBA Association, and the National Society of Hispanic MBAs, is a free seminar designed especially for people from groups that are underrepresented in the profession of business administration. The three-hour event will introduce you to management careers and the MBA degree. African-American and Latino MBA students will share their school and work experiences; business school admission and financial aid officers will give expert advice on entry requirements and ways to pay for your MBA education.

Destination MBA participants are eligible for special scholarships and membership benefits offered by the National Black MBA Association and the National Society of Hispanic MBAs.

✳ **Admission to Destination MBA is free**

✳ **Registration begins at 8:30 am**

✳ **For further information and program specifics, please call 800 446-0807**

	1996-97 Schedule		Hours	Followed by	Hours
San Juan, PR	September 14	Caribe Hilton, San Geronimo Grounds	9 AM–12	School Fair	1–4 PM
Pittsburgh, PA	September 21	Westin William Penn, 530 William Penn Place	9 AM–12	School Fair	1–4 PM
Cleveland, OH	September 28	Sheraton City Centre Hotel, 777 St. Clair Avenue	9 AM–12	MBA Forum	12–4 PM
Boston, MA	October 5	57 Park Plaza (Howard Johnson), 200 Stuart Street	9 AM–12	MBA Forum	12–4 PM
Houston, TX	October 12	Doubletree Hotel at Post Oak, 2001 Post Oak Blvd.	9 AM–12	MBA Forum	12–4 PM
Atlanta, GA	October 19	Radisson Hotel, 165 Courtland & International Blvd.	9 AM–12	School Fair	1–4 PM
Washington, DC	October 26	Capital Hilton, 16th & K Streets, NW	9 AM–12	MBA Forum	12–4 PM
Chicago, IL	November 2	Palmer House Hilton, 17 East Monroe Street	9 AM–12	MBA Forum	12–4 PM
New York, NY	November 9	Marriott Financial Center, 85 West Street	9 AM–12	MBA Forum	12–4 PM
Los Angeles, CA	November 16	Doubletree Hotel, L.A. Airport, 5400 W. Century Blvd.	9 AM–12	MBA Forum	12–4 PM
San Francisco, CA	November 23	Sheraton Palace Hotel, 2 New Montgomery Street	9 AM–12	MBA Forum	12–4 PM
St. Louis, MO	January 25	Marriott Pavilion Hotel, One South Broadway	9 AM–12	School Fair	1–4 PM
Durham, NC	February 1	Omni Durham Hotel, 201 Foster Street	9 AM–12	School Fair	1–4 PM

National Conferences:

NBMBAA
September 25–29
Marriott Hotel
555 Canal Street
New Orleans

NSHMBA
October 31–November 2
Westin Rio Mar Beach Resort
Palmer, Puerto Rico

Graduate
Management
Admission
Council